THE HISTORY OF ICSID

SECOND EDITION

The History of ICSID

Second Edition

ANTONIO R. PARRA

OXFORD
UNIVERSITY PRESS

OXFORD
UNIVERSITY PRESS

Great Clarendon Street, Oxford, OX2 6DP,
United Kingdom

Oxford University Press is a department of the University of Oxford.
It furthers the University's objective of excellence in research, scholarship,
and education by publishing worldwide. Oxford is a registered trade mark of
Oxford University Press in the UK and in certain other countries

First Edition published in 2012
Second Edition published in 2017

Published in the United States of America by Oxford University Press
198 Madison Avenue, New York, NY 10016, United States of America

British Library Cataloguing in Publication Data
Data available

Library of Congress Control Number: 2016953197

ISBN 978–0–19–876746–6

This book is dedicated to the memory of
Aron Broches
1914–1997
and
Ibrahim F.I. Shihata
1937–2001

Foreword to the First Edition

The launch of the International Centre for Settlement of Investment Disputes (ICSID) in 1966 opened a whole new chapter in international dispute settlement. While a lot has been written on ICSID, no comprehensive history of ICSID existed so far. This book, arising from a PhD thesis presented at the University of Geneva, fills this gap remarkably. The book is noteworthy for many reasons. I highlight three of them, leaving the reader to discover the others.

First, there is no doubt in my mind that detailed analysis of the negotiating history of the ICSID Convention will regularly be quoted by parties and tribunals when seeking to interpret the Convention. Among other things, this analysis dispels some common misconceptions about ICSID arbitration. ICSID arbitration procedure was not based on commercial arbitration. The drafters relied on public international law instruments such as the Statute and Rules of the International Court of Justice (ICJ) or the Model Rules on Arbitral Procedure of the International Law Commission (ILC), to name a few. Further, ICSID arbitration was not designed primarily for resolution of contract disputes. From the start, the development of ICSID arbitration was closely linked to investment treaties. The 1959 Abs–Shawcross Draft Convention on Investment Abroad or the Organisation for Economic Co-operation and Development (OECD) Draft Convention on the Protection of Property of 1962 both provided arbitral procedures which were very much in the minds of those spearheading the efforts towards the ICSID Convention. A better understanding of the origins of the Convention may help overcome the challenges which ICSID arbitration faces today and to which I will return.

Second, this book provides a most interesting piece of institutional history. It is illuminating to see how much a few men (no women yet!), animated by strong convictions and benefiting from the support of the institution, can achieve. It also shows the links of ICSID with the World Bank evolving from a close relationship —"exceedingly close," says the author—to increasing autonomy. What makes this book especially valuable is that the history is written by one of its principal actors. People close to the Centre say that Antonio Parra embodies the institutional memory of ICSID. Albeit this can have its drawbacks: we all know of actors who have rewritten history, placing their own role in a better light. This actor has avoided this pitfall. While one feels that his profound knowledge and understanding of the institution draws on personal experience, he has been overly modest about his own contribution to ICSID's success.

Finally, it is one of the merits of this book to bring to light the challenges ahead. The description of ICSID's success, starting from the origins and negotiation of the Convention, through the quieter early years of the Centre to the more recent arbitration boom, the discussion of cases divided into several periods, the analysis of the procedural rules and their application, besides being tremendously enriching, also reveal the weaknesses of the system and the challenges it faces. In his conclusion, the author usefully addresses possible remedies.

There are several weaknesses and challenges. For instance, in respect of arbitrators, the statistics on appointments established by the author document an alarming lack of diversity. Additionally, there is a real need for States to nominate more people with expertise on their lists, whether or not they are nationals of the country in question.

Another weakness concerns the control of arbitral awards. There is a question of quality of the bodies exercising control which refers back to the previous weakness. There is also the well-known issue of consistency, or, rather, lack of consistency, of case law. Inconsistencies are probably unavoidable in a decentralized system with a control mechanism providing very limited power of review on the merits. The early evolutionary stage of international investment law may well be another reason for the present inconsistencies. The absence of a mechanism to redress inconsistency tempts annulment committees to overstep the boundaries of their strict mandate. While this should not be condoned, it raises a legitimate question: should ICSID take measures to ensure compliance with the restricted mission of the control body as it now exists or should it work towards a mechanism promoting consistency? The question is not new. The idea of an appeal mechanism was mooted a few years ago, but the question has remained.

Yet another weakness is insufficient transparency of ICSID arbitrations. Considering that ICSID was a pioneer in the area of transparency in international arbitration, this may come as a surprise. However, in light of the recent evolution in the thinking on transparency recognizing the strong public interest involved, ICSID's rules remain relatively timid. A situation which is "positively anomalous"—to use the author's words—for an institution linked to the World Bank which itself allows access to all information in its possession, subject to limited exceptions. The rules should thus be amended, the revision providing a sound balance between two competing objectives: public access to information, on one hand, and the efficacy of arbitration, on the other. The current work on transparency by the UNCITRAL Working Group may provide some inspiration.

These are just a few thoughts that come to mind when reading this rich and enlightening work. No doubt the reader will have many more.

Gabrielle Kaufmann-Kohler
Geneva, April 2012

Foreword to the Second Edition

Nobody is better qualified to write a history of ICSID than its long-term Deputy Secretary-General Antonio Parra, who is rightly described as its institutional memory.

From modest beginnings in 1966, ICSID has truly developed into the "Premier International Investment Arbitration Facility in the World," as described in Chapter 11 of this second edition. The rise of investment arbitration in the course of the last half century is difficult to imagine without ICSID and its leadership in this field. Its success should be measured not just by looking at the number of cases it has dealt with, but also by appreciating its contribution to the development of international investment law and international law in general.

This success has also raised a number of problems. The interpretation of the ICSID Convention has led to controversies on issues of corporate and individual nationality, on the concept of investment, on the scope of annulment and on the appointment and disqualification of arbitrators, to name just a few. Not surprisingly, the practice under the Convention has also led to some inconsistencies. This may be irritating to practitioners and scholarly observers, but is probably inevitable in a system that depends on individual tribunals with changing composition.

There have been recurrent calls for reform of the system. So far, these reforms have been modest and are reflected only in amendments to the rules and regulations accompanying the Convention. An important obstacle in the way of major reform is the high threshold for amendments to the Convention, which would require affirmative acceptance by all Contracting States. Some may see this as an impediment to progress. Others may welcome it as a safeguard against precipitate adjustment to fashionable sentiments.

A recurrent theme in the debates about ICSID reform is the introduction of an appeal system. A basic difficulty lies in the fact the Convention specifically excludes appeal as a remedy against an award. Curiously, in the discussion about the introduction of an appeal, there is little debate about the purpose of such an innovation. An appeals facility may have two potential benefits. One would be a better decision than the one rendered by the original tribunal. That would require a higher degree of wisdom on the part of the appellate body and not merely another decision by the same number of people with the same qualifications.

The other potential benefit of an appeals system might be a higher degree of consistency of decision-making. That would require a central institution that gives guidance to future tribunals. A number of scattered appeals bodies created by several bilateral treaties will hardly achieve consistency. Moreover, there are better and simpler ways to achieve consistency, such as the introduction of a system of preliminary rulings that gives guidance to tribunals before they make decisions.

Reform is to be welcomed if it leads to an improvement of the *status quo*. However, not every change deserves to be called a reform. Alterations that serve the sole purpose of placating the whims of public opinion are not reform but opportunism.

More recently, investment arbitration has come under general attack in the media. The underlying assumption of these attacks is invariably that investment arbitration, including at ICSID, is in the exclusive interest of big business. This assumption is as erroneous as it is illogical.

Private foreign investment is by far the most important element in economic development. Legal security is an indispensable precondition for foreign investment. A key element of legal security is an effective system for the settlement of disputes between host states and foreign investors. The drafters of the ICSID Convention clearly understood the importance of investment arbitration for economic development. The Preamble to the ICSID Convention in its first paragraph refers to "economic development, and the role of private international investment therein."

Another important function of investment arbitration is to depoliticize disputes and avoid international conflicts between states. There was a period when disputes about the treatment of foreign investments would lead to bitter international confrontations between host States and the home States of investors. It was not unusual that these confrontations would lead to armed interventions. For instance, the long-running conflict between Cuba and the United States, which at one point led to the brink of nuclear war, had its origin in an investment dispute. Quarrels, political and sometimes military, have been the frequent result of an inability to settle investment disputes in an orderly fashion by judicial means.

States have recognized for a long time that the settlement of investment disputes through arbitration is in their interest. Treaties providing for investment arbitration have been concluded for over 50 years not just between countries in the North and South but also between East and West. In addition, and most notably, there are now several hundred such treaties between developing countries. Anyone who has read the first edition of this important book knows that developing countries have embraced the ICSID Convention from its earliest beginnings.

Large-scale international migration is another, more recent, context for the public discourse about international investment. A common answer to the phenomenon of international mass migration is that the problem must be tackled at its source, i.e. in the countries of origin. Only if economic conditions in these countries improve will the tide of migrants abate. We are told that the recipe for improved economic conditions is more investments.

Without offering investors a credible framework of legal protection, it will be impossible to achieve more investments in the countries that need them most. It is entirely unrealistic to expect that foreign investment will resolve the problems of mass migration unless we offer investors reasonable guarantees, including access to credible judicial remedies.

ICSID's importance reaches far beyond the immediate context of the settlement of certain economic disputes. It plays an important role in tackling some of the most pressing international problems of our time.

Christoph Schreuer
Vienna, September 2016

Preface

The first edition of this book recounted the history of ICSID up until the end of its 2010 fiscal year on June 30, 2010. This second edition continues the history to June 30, 2015. The new cut-off date required a number of changes in Chapters 1 to 9. Updating gave me the opportunity to remedy some faults in those chapters. Chapter 10, on the period 2000 to 2010, was extensively revised, not only to cover the full decade, but also to discuss selected aspects of cases registered at ICSID between 2000 and 2010, the subject of a separate chapter in the first edition. An entirely new chapter, Chapter 11, was added on the activities of ICSID from the beginning of 2011 to mid-2015, a time in which the Centre registered another almost 200 cases. The conclusion, Chapter 12, was largely rewritten. It was possible, in that last chapter, to take into account developments to the end of June 2016.

My heartfelt thanks go to Christoph Schreuer for his foreword to this edition. I have the pleasure of renewing my gratitude to Gabrielle Kaufmann-Kohler for her foreword to the first edition, also included in the present volume.

Frank Berman, Andrés Rigo and Christoph Schreuer kindly read and gave me comments on drafts of Chapters 11 and 12 of this second edition. At ICSID, Meg Kinnear, Gonzalo Flores, Milanka Kostadinova and Martina Polasek were good enough to go through those drafts and provide me with suggestions on them. My longtime colleague at the World Bank and ICSID, Margrete Stevens, applied her welcome sharp scrutiny to drafts of Chapters 10 to 12. Chuck Ziegler, coordinator of the World Bank History Thematic Group of the 1818 Society, graciously accepted to review Chapter 2. To all of them: Thank you very much for helping me to improve the texts. Needless to say, remaining shortcomings are mine alone.

At Oxford University Press, I was fortunate to have the support and guidance of the superb editorial team of Faye Mousley and Katie Hooper. I was pleased to work again with Ela Kotkowska, a very skillful copyeditor. Penny Dickman prepared the index, Nicola Lennon compiled the tables and Raji Siva managed the production process. I much appreciate each of their contributions.

In Easton, my wife Lisa took the time from her own busy schedule to transform my scrawl into flawless initial typescripts. Judi Loscomb at Laser Letters, Inc. carried forward to perfection the preparation of the entire manuscript for submission to the Press.

Like the first edition of the book, this second edition is dedicated to the memory of Aron Broches and Ibrahim Shihata. My admiration for their achievements has only grown over the years.

Antonio R. Parra
Easton, Maryland, October 2016

Contents

Table of Cases xvii
Table of Treaties xxv
List of Abbreviations xxxiii

1. Introduction 1
I. The International Bank for Reconstruction and Development 2
II. The International Finance Corporation, International Development Association and Multilateral Investment Guarantee Agency 5
III. The International Centre for Settlement of Investment Disputes 7

2. Origins of the Convention 11
I. Proposed multilateral approaches to the promotion of private foreign investment 12
A. Investment insurance 12
B. A code of conduct 13
C. An arbitral body for investment disputes 15
II. The World Bank considers the proposals 17
A. The Bank's work on an IIIA 17
B. The proposed code of conduct 18
C. The dispute settlement approach 19
III. The role of "Black's Bank" in the settlement of investment disputes 20
IV. The Bank begins to work on the initiative 23

3. Broches's "Working Paper" 25
I. The Working Paper 27
A. Provisions on the establishment and organization of the Center 28
B. Provisions on the jurisdiction of the Center 31
C. Provisions on conciliation and arbitration 32
II. The initial meetings of the Committee of the Whole 34

4. The Preliminary Draft of the Convention 39
I. The Preliminary Draft 40
A. Provisions on the establishment and organization of the Center 40
B. Provisions on the jurisdiction of the Center 41
C. Provisions on conciliation and arbitration 42
D. Other provisions 44
II. Sources for the Preliminary Draft 45
III. The regional consultative meetings 48
A. Discussions regarding the establishment and organization of the Center 49
B. Discussions regarding the jurisdiction of the Center 51
C. Discussions regarding conciliation and arbitration 53
D. Discussions regarding inter-State proceedings, amendments and participation in the Convention 56

5. Finalizing the Text of the Convention 59
I. The First Draft 61
A. Provisions on the establishment and organization of the Center 62
B. Provisions on the jurisdiction of the Center 63
C. Provisions on conciliation and arbitration 64
D. Other provisions 67
II. The Legal Committee meetings 67
A. Discussions regarding the establishment and organization of the Centre 69
B. Discussions regarding the jurisdiction of the Centre 71
C. Discussions regarding conciliation and arbitration 75
D. Discussions of other provisions 79
III. Concluding steps 80
A. The final meetings of the Committee of the Whole 81
B. Approval of the final text 85

6. Establishment and Launch of the Centre 87
I. The inaugural meeting of the Administrative Council 89
A. Election of the first Secretary-General of ICSID 90
B. Adoption of the Provisional Regulations and Rules 91
C. Approval of administrative and budgetary arrangements 92
II. The Provisional Regulations and Rules of the Centre 94
A. The Provisional Administrative and Financial Regulations 94
B. The Provisional Institution Rules 98
C. The Provisional Conciliation Rules and Provisional Arbitration Rules 98
III. The Memorandum of Administrative Arrangements 102
IV. The first annual meeting of the Administrative Council 103
A. The definitive Regulations and Rules 105
B. The arrangements with the Permanent Court of Arbitration 106

7. ICSID's First Two Decades 109
I. Institutional developments 111
A. Ratifications of the Convention 111
B. The Administrative Council 112
C. The Secretariat 114
D. Designations to the Panels of Conciliators and of Arbitrators 117
E. Other measures by Contracting States pursuant to the Convention 118
II. Promoting consents to the jurisdiction of ICSID 120
III. An overview of the early cases 123
IV. The 1984 amendments of the ICSID Regulations and Rules 126
V. The Additional Facility 128
A. The initial proposal for an Additional Facility 129
B. The draft Additional Facility Rules 132
C. Adoption of the Additional Facility Rules 134
D. Continuation of the Additional Facility 135
VI. The appointing authority role 137
VII. The investment law publishing activities 139

8. Aspects of the Early Cases 143
I. Registration of requests to institute proceedings 143

II. The constitution of commissions and tribunals 146
III. Approaches to jurisdiction 150
IV. Provisional measures 157
V. Applicable law 162
VI. Annulment decisions of the 1980s 167
VII. Enforcement of awards 172

9. ICSID from 1989 to 1999 177

I. The growing network of investment treaties 180
II. Institutional developments 185
A. Ratifications of the Convention 185
B. The Secretariat 186
C. The Panels of Conciliators and of Arbitrators 187
D. Agreements with other arbitration institutions 188
III. An overview of cases submitted to ICSID between 1989 and 1999 189
IV. The first Additional Facility Proceedings 193
V. Some leading BIT cases of the 1990s 202
A. *Fedax v. Venezuela* 203
B. *Vivendi v. Argentina* 205
C. *Maffezini v. Spain* 207
D. *Wena v. Egypt* 209

10. ICSID from 2000 to 2010 211

I. Institutional developments 216
A. Ratifications of the Convention 216
B. The Secretariat 217
C. The Panels of Conciliators and of Arbitrators 220
II. The 2003 amendments of the Regulations and Rules 221
III. The 2006 amendments of the Regulations and Rules 224
IV. Aspects of cases submitted to ICSID from 2000 to 2010 230
A. Registration of requests to institute proceedings 232
B. The constitution of commissions and tribunals 236
C. Approaches to jurisdiction 240
D. Provisional measures 254
E. Applicable law 256
F. Annulment decisions 259
G. Enforcement of awards 262

11. "The Premier International Investment Arbitration Facility in the World" 267

I. Institutional developments 269
A. Participation in the Convention 269
B. The Administrative Council 269
C. The Secretariat 270
D. The Panels of Conciliators and of Arbitrators 272
E. Agreements with other arbitration institutions 273
II. The appointment and disqualification of arbitrators 274
A. Trends in appointments 274
B. Disqualification proposals 276

III. The first awards in the cases registered from 2011 to 2015 277
A. Awards upholding claims 278
B. Awards dismissing claims 278
C. An interim assessment 282
IV. New challenges 282

12. Conclusion 287
I. General observations 287
II. Meeting new challenges 289
A. Promoting conciliation 289
B. Enhancing transparency 290
C. Preparing for a possible appellate mechanism and permanent investment tribunal 291
III. Possible changes in other areas 294

Appendices
I. Working Paper in the Form of a Draft Convention for the Resolution of Disputes between States and Nationals of Other States, June 5, 1962 297
II. Preliminary Draft of a Convention on the Settlement of Investment Disputes between States and Nationals of Other States, October 15, 1963 311
III. Draft Convention on the Settlement of Investment Disputes between States and Nationals of Other States (First Draft), September 11, 1964 332
IV. Convention on the Settlement of Investment Disputes between States and Nationals of Other States and Accompanying Report of the Executive Directors, March 18, 1965 351

Select Bibliography 373
Index 381

Table of Cases

ICSID CONVENTION CASES

Asian Agricultural Products Limited v Democratic Socialist Republic of Sri Lanka, ARB/87/3, *short title* AAPL v Sri Lanka 124–6, 128, 153, 155, 166–7, 200, 202, 257

Abaclat and Others v Argentine Republic, ARB/07/5, *short title* Abaclat v Argentina 231, 277

Accession Mezzanine Capital L.P. and Danubius Kereskedöház Vagyonkezelö Zrt. v Hungary, ARB/12/3, *short title* Accession Mezzanine v Hungary 277, 282

ADC Affiliate Ltd. and ADC & ADMC Management Ltd. v Republic of Hungary, ARB/03/16, *short title* ADC v Hungary 232, 257–8, 281

AGIP S.p.A. v People's Republic of the Congo, ARB/77/1, *short title* AGIP v Congo 116, 124–6, 147, 160–2, 165

Aguas del Tunari S.A. v Republic of Bolivia, ARB/02/3, *short title* Aguas del Tunari v Bolivia 212–14, 229, 295

AHS Niger and Menzies Middle East and Africa S.A. v Republic of Niger, ARB/11/11, *short title* AHS v Niger 277n, 278, 282

Alcoa Minerals of Jamaica, Inc. v Jamaica, ARB/74/2, *short title* Alcoa v Jamaica 120, 124, 147

Giovanni Alemanni and others v Argentine Republic, ARB/07/8, *short title* Alemanni v Argentina 231

Alimenta S.A. v Republic of The Gambia, ARB/99/5, *short title* Alimenta v Gambia 189–90

Swiss Aluminium Limited and Icelandic Aluminium Company Limited v Iceland, ARB/83/1, *short title* ALUSUISSE v Iceland 124–5, 146

Ambiente Ufficio S.p.A. and others v Argentine Republic, ARB/08/9, *short title* Ambiente v Argentina 231

Amco Asia Corp. and others v Republic of Indonesia, ARB/81/1, *short title* Amco v Indonesia 124–5, 146, 149, 151, 153, 162, 164–5, 167–8, 170, 172–3, 239, 258, 262

American Manufacturing & Trading, Inc. v Democratic Republic of the Congo, ARB/93/1, *short title* AMT v DRC 189–90, 193

Mr. Franck Charles Arif v Republic of Moldova, ARB/11/23, *short title* Arif v Moldova 277, 278n, 282

Astaldi S.p.A. & Columbus Latinoamericana de Contrucciones S.A. v Republic of Honduras, ARB/99/8, *short title* Astaldi v Honduras 190, 192

Astaldi S.p.A. v Republic of Honduras, ARB/07/32, *short title* Astaldi v Honduras 236

Atlantic Triton Company Limited v People's Revolutionary Republic of Guinea, ARB/84/1, *short title* Atlantic Triton v Guinea 124–7, 158

Banro American Resources, Inc. and Société Aurifère du Kivu et du Maniema S.A.R.L. v Democratic Republic of the Congo, ARB/98/7, *short title* Banro v DRC 189, 194

Bayindir Insaat Turizm Ticaret Ve Sanayi A.S. v Islamic Republic of Pakistan, ARB/03/29, *short title* Bayindir v Pakistan 243

S.A.R.L. Benvenuti & Bonfant v People's Republic of the Congo, ARB/77/2, *short title* Benvenuti & Bonfant v Congo 124–6, 144, 147, 173–5

Biwater Gauff (Tanzania) Ltd. v United Republic of Tanzania, ARB/05/22, *short title* Biwater Gauff v Tanzania 245

Blue Bank International & Trust (Barbados) Ltd. v Bolivarian Republic of Venezuela, ARB 12/20, *short title* Blue Bank v Venezuela 276–7

Booker plc v Co-operative Republic of Guyana, ARB/01/9, *short title* Booker v Guyana 236

Burimi SRL and Eagle Games SH.A. v Republic of Albania, ARB/11/18, *short title* Burimi v Albania 277, 280, 282

Burlington Resources Inc. v Republic of Ecuador, ARB/08/5, *short title* Burlington Resources v Ecuador 213, 277n

Cable Television of Nevis, Ltd. and Cable Television of Nevis Holdings, Ltd. v Federation of St. Kitts and Nevis, ARB/95/2, *short title* Cable TV v St. Kitts and Nevis 189–90, 193

Caratube International Oil Company LLP v The Republic of Kazakhstan, ARB/13/13, *short title* Caratube v Kazakhstan 277
Caravelí Cotaruse Transmisora de Energía S.A.C. v Republic of Peru, ARB/11/9, *short title* Caravelí v Peru 267, 277, 278, 279, 282
CDC Group plc v Republic of Seychelles, ARB/02/14, *short title* CDC v Seychelles 236, 262
Compañía del Desarrollo de Santa Elena S.A. v Republic of Costa Rica, ARB/96/1, *short title* CDSE v Costa Rica 189, 193
Compagnie Française pour le Développement des Fibres Textiles v Côte d'Ivoire, ARB/97/8, *short title* CFDT v Côte d'Ivoire 189, 192
City Oriente Ltd. v Republic of Ecuador and Empresa Estatal Petróleos del Ecuador (Petroecuador), ARB/06/21, *short title* City Oriente v Ecuador 255
Compagnie Minière Internationale Or S.A. v Republic of Peru, ARB/98/6, *short title* CMIO v Peru 189
CMS Gas Transmission Co. v Argentine Republic, ARB/01/8, *short title* CMS v Argentina 258–63
Colt Industries Operating Corporation v Republic of Korea, ARB/4/2, *short title* Colt v Korea 124–5
ConocoPhillips Co. and others v Bolivarian Republic of Venezuela, ARB/07/30, *short title* ConocoPhillips v Venezuela 231
Československá obchodni banka, a.s. v Slovak Republic, ARB/97/4, *short title* CSOB v Slovak Republic 189, 193
Deutsche Bank AG v Democratic Socialist Republic of Sri Lanka, ARB/09/02, *short title* Deutsche Bank v Sri Lanka 246
Duke Energy International Peru Investments No. 1 Ltd. v Republic of Peru, ARB/03/28, *short title* Duke Energy v Peru 265
Government of the Province of East Kalimantan v PT Kaltim Prima Coal and others, ARB/07/3, *short title* East Kalimantan v PT Kaltim 231
Elsamex, A.S. v Republic of Honduras, ARB/09/4, *short title* Elsamex v Honduras 236
Emmis International Holding, B.V., Emmis Radio Operating, B.V., MEM Magyar Electronic Media Kereskedelmi és Szolgáltató Kft. v The Republic of Hungary, ARB/12/2, *short title* Emmis v Hungary 277, 282, 294
Empresa Nacional de Electricidad S.A. v Argentine Republic, ARB/99/4, *short title* ENDESA v Argentina 189, 191, 212
Enron Creditors Recovery Corp. (formerly Enron Corp.) and Ponderosa Assets, L.P. v Argentine Republic, ARB/01/3, *short title* Enron v Argentina 241, 259–64
Saba Fakes v Republic of Turkey, ARB/07/20, *short title* Fakes v Turkey 246
Fedax N.V. v Republic of Venezuela, ARB/96/3, *short title* Fedax v Venezuela 189, 191, 193, 202–5, 240–2
Fraport AG Frankfurt Airport Services Worldwide v Republic of the Philippines, ARB/03/25, *short title* Fraport v Philippines 260, 269–70, 277, 281–2
Gabon v Société Serete S.A., ARB/76/1, *short title* Gabon v Serete 124–5
Gambrinus, Corp. v Bolivarian Republic of Venezuela, ARB/11/31, *short title* Gambrinus v Venezuela 277, 281
Adriano Gardella S.p.A. v Côte d'Ivoire, ARB/74/1, *short title* Gardella v Côte d'Ivoire 124–5
Generation Ukraine Inc. v Ukraine, ARB/00/9, *short title* Generation Ukraine v Ukraine 238
Alex Genin and others v Republic of Estonia, ARB/99/2, *short title* Genin v Estonia 189, 193
Global Trading Resource Corp. and Globex International, Inc. v Ukraine, ARB/09/11, *short title* Globex v Ukraine 236
Antoine Goetz and others v Republic of Burundi, ARB/95/3, *short title* Goetz v Burundi 189, 192
Philippe Gruslin v Malaysia, ARB/94/1, *short title* Gruslin v Malaysia 189–91, 193
Philippe Gruslin v Malaysia, ARB/99/3, *short title* Gruslin v Malaysia 189–91, 193
Rachel S. Grynberg, Stephen M. Grynberg, Miriam Z. Grynberg and RSM Production Company v Grenada, ARB/10/6, *short title* Grynberg v Grenada 236
Guadalupe Gas Products Corp. v Nigeria, ARB/78/1, *short title* Guadalupe v Nigeria 124–5
Helnan International Hotels A/S v Arab Republic of Egypt, ARB/05/19, *short title* Helnan v Egypt 243, 260

Highbury International AVV and Ramstein Trading Inc. v Bolivarian Republic of Venezuela, ARB/11/1, *short title* Highbury v Venezuela 277, 280, 282
Holiday Inns S.A. and others v Morocco, ARB/72/1, *short title* Holiday Inns v Morocco 123–5, 145–6, 148, 150–3, 160, 378
Houston Industries Energy, Inc. and others v Argentine Republic, ARB/98/1, *short title* Houston Industries v Argentina 189
Inversión y Gestión de Bienes, IGB v Kingdom of Spain, ARB/12/17, *short title* IGB v Spain 274
Isolux Corsán Concesiones S.A. v Republic of Peru, ARB/12/5, *short title* Isolux v Peru 268
International Trust Company of Liberia v Republic of Liberia, ARB/98/3, *short title* ITC v Liberia 189, 192
Jan de Nul N.V. and Dredging International N.V. v Arab Republic of Egypt, ARB/04/13, *short title* Jan de Nul v Egypt 243
Joy Mining Machinery Ltd. v Arab Republic of Egypt, ARB/03/11, *short title* Joy Mining v Egypt 242
Kaiser Bauxite Company v Jamaica, ARB/74/3, *short title* Kaiser v Jamaica 120, 124, 147
Klöckner Industrie-Anlagen GmbH and others v United Republic of Cameroon and Société Camerounaise des Engrais, ARB/81/2, *short title* Klöckner v Cameroon 124–6, 146, 148, 163–4, 167–8, 172, 222, 258
Société Kufpec (Congo) Limited v Republic of Congo, ARB/97/2, *short title* Kufpec v Congo 189–91
Lanco International, Inc. v Argentine Republic, ARB/97/6, *short title* Lanco v Argentina . . . 189–91
Leaf Tobacco A. Michaelides S.A. and Greek-Albanian Leaf Tobacco & Co. S.A. v Republic of Albania, ARB/95/1, *short title* Leaf Tobacco v Albania 189, 191
Consortium Groupement L.E.S.I.-DIPENTA v People's Democratic Republic of Algeria, ARB/03/8, *short title* LESI v Algeria 245
Liberian Eastern Timber Corporation v Republic of Liberia, ARB/83/2, *short title* LETCO v Liberia 124–6, 152, 165, 174
Renée Rose Levy de Levi v Republic of Peru, ARB/10/17, *short title* Levy v Peru 277, 281, 282
Libananco Holdings Co. Ltd. v Republic of Turkey, ARB/06/8, *short title* Libananco v Turkey 256
Emilio Agustin Maffezini v Kingdom of Spain, ARB/97/7, *short title* Maffezini v Spain 189–91, 193, 202, 207–8, 240, 251–6
Mamidoil Jetoil Greek Petroleum Products Societe S.A. v Republic of Albania, ARB/11/24, *short title* Mamidoil v Albania 277, 279
Metalpar S.A. and Buen Aire S.A. v Argentine Republic, ARB/03/5, *short title* Metalpar v Argentina 233–4
Malaysian Historical Salvors, SDN, BHD v Malaysia, ARB/05/10, *short title* MHS v Malaysia 236, 243–4, 246, 260
Manufacturers Hanover Trust Company v Arab Republic of Egypt and General Authority for Investment and Free Zones, ARB/89/1, *short title* MHT v Egypt 121, 189
Middle East Cement Shipping and Handling Co. S.A. v Arab Republic of Egypt, ARB/99/6, *short title* Middle East Cement v Egypt 189, 193
Maritime International Nominees Establishment v Republic of Guinea, ARB/84/4, *short title* MINE v Guinea 124–5, 127, 145, 157–8, 160–2, 171–2
Misima Mines Pty. Ltd. v Independent State of Papua New Guinea, ARB 96/2, *short title* Misima Mines v Papua New Guinea 189–91
Patrick Mitchell v Democratic Republic of the Congo, ARB/99/7, *short title* Mitchell v DRC 189, 193, 243
Mobil Argentina S.A. v Argentine Republic, ARB/99/1, *short title* Mobil v Argentina 189, 191
Mobil Oil Corporation and others v New Zealand, ARB/87/2, *short title* Mobil v New Zealand 124–5, 128, 148, 162
National Gas S.A.E. v Arab Republic of Egypt, ARB/11/7, *short title* National Gas v Egypt 277, 279, 282
Occidental Petroleum Corp. and Occidental Exploration and Production Co. v Republic of Ecuador, ARB/06/11, *short title* Occidental v Ecuador 232, 256

Occidental of Pakistan, Inc. v Islamic Republic of Pakistan, ARB/87/4, *short title* Occidental v Pakistan 124–5
OI European Group B.V. v Bolivarian Republic of Venezuela, ARB/11/25, *short title* OI v Venezuela 277, 278
Eudoro A. Olguín v Republic of Paraguay, ARB/98/5, *short title* Olguín v Paraguay 189, 191–3
Pac Rim Cayman LLC v Republic of El Salvador, ARB/09/12, *short title* Pacific Rim v El Salvador 229
Pantechniki S.A. Contractors & Engineers v Republic of Albania, ARB/07/21, *short title* Pantechniki v Albania 236
Perenco Ecuador Ltd. v Republic of Ecuador and Empresa Estatal Petróleos del Ecuador (Petroecuador), ARB/08/6, *short title* Perenco v Ecuador 255–6
Ping An Life Insurance Company, Limited and Ping An Insurance (Group) Company, Limited v The Government of Belgium, ARB/12/29, *short title* Ping An v Belgium 277, 282
Victor Pey Casado and President Allende Foundation v Republic of Chile, ARB/98/2, *short title* Pey Casado v Chile 189, 238, 245–6, 254–6
Ghaith R. Pharaon v Republic of Tunisia, ARB/86/1, *short title* Pharaon v Tunisia 124–5, 153
Phoenix Action Ltd. v Czech Republic, ARB/06/5, *short title* Phoenix Action v Czech Republic 232
Plama Consortium Ltd. v Republic of Bulgaria, ARB/03/24, *short title* Plama v Bulgaria 252–4
Planet Mining Pty Ltd. v Republic of Indonesia, ARB/12/14 and 12/40, *short title* Planet Mining v Indonesia 122
Pluspetrol Perú Corporation and others v Perupetro S.A., ARB/12/28, *short title* Pluspetrol v Perupetro 277, 278, 279
PNG Sustainable Development Program Ltd. v Independent State of Papua New Guinea, ARB/13/33, *short title* PNG Sustainable Development v Papua New Guinea 277, 278, 282
Poštová Banka, a.s. and ISTROKAPITAL SE v Hellenic Republic, ARB/13/8, *short title* Poštová Banka v Greece 277, 280, 281
Repsol, S.A. and Repsol Butano, S.A. v Argentine Republic, ARB/12/38, *short title* Repsol v Argentina 277n
Repsol YPF Ecuador, S.A. and others v Republic of Ecuador and Empresa Estatal Petróleos del Ecuador (PetroEcuador), ARB/01/10 and ARB/08/10, *short title* Repsol v Ecuador 262
Reynolds Jamaica Mines Limited and Reynolds Metals Company v Jamaica, ARB/74/4, *short title* Reynolds v Jamaica 120, 124, 147
Rafat Ali Rizvi v Republic of Indonesia, ARB/11/13, *short title* Rizvi v Indonesia 277, 281, 282
RSM Production Corporation v Republic of Cameroon, CONC/11/1, *short title* RSM v Cameroon 268
RSM Production Corporation v Saint Lucia, ARB/12/10, *short title* RSM v St. Lucia 294
Rumeli Telekom A.S. and Telsim Mobil Telekomunikasyon Hizmetleri A.S. v Republic of Kazakhstan, ARB/05/16, *short title* Rumeli Telekom v Kazakhstan 265
Salini Costruttori S.p.A. and Italstrade S.p.A. v Hashemite Kingdom of Jordan, ARB/02/13, *short title* Salini v Jordan 251
Salini Costruttori S.p.A. and Italstrade S.p.A. v Kingdom of Morocco, ARB/00/4, *short title* Salini v Morocco 242–5
Scimitar Exploration Limited v Bangladesh and Bangladesh Oil, Gas and Mineral Corporation, ARB/92/2, *short title* Scimitar v Bangladesh 189–90, 193, 222
SEDITEX Engineering Beratungsgesellschaft für die Textilindustrie m.b.H. v Democratic Republic of Madagascar, CONC/82/1, *short title* SEDITEX v Madagascar 123–4
SEDITEX Engineering Beratungsgesellschaft für die Textilindustrie m.b.H. v Magagascar, CONC/94/1, *short title* SEDITEX v Madagascar 189
Sempra Energy International v Argentine Republic, ARB/02/16, *short title* Sempra v Argentina 259–62
Shareholders of SESAM v Central African Republic, CONC/07/1, *short title* SESAM v CAR 230

Société d'Etudes de Travaux et de Gestion SETIMEG S.A. v Republic of Gabon, ARB/87/1, *short title* SETIMEG v Gabon 124–5, 148
SGS Société Générale de Surveillance S.A. v Islamic Republic of Pakistan, ARB/01/13, *short title* SGS v Pakistan 247–50, 258
SGS Société Générale de Surveillance S.A. v Republic of the Philippines, ARB/02/6, *short title* SGS v Philippines 249–251
Société Industrielle des Boissons de Guinée v Republic of Guinea, ARB/12/8, *short title* SIBG v Guinea 277, 278, 280, 282
Siemens A.G. v Argentine Republic, ARB/02/8, *short title* Siemens v Argentina 251–2, 257, 263
Société d'Investigation de Recherche et d'Exploitation Minière v Burkina Faso, ARB/97/1, *short title* SIREM v Burkina Faso 189–90, 193
Slovak Gas Holding BV, GDF International SAS and E.ON Ruhrgas International GmbH v Slovak Republic, ARB/12/7, *short title* Slovak Gas v Slovak Republic 268
Société Ouest Africaine des Bétons Industriels v Senegal, ARB/82/1, *short title* SOABI v Senegal 124–5, 148, 173–5
Southern Pacific Properties (Middle East) Limited v Arab Republic of Egypt, ARB/84/3, *short title* SPP v Egypt 121, 124–5, 145–6, 148, 153–6, 165, 172–3, 175, 242
Suez, Sociedad General de Aguas de Barcelona S.A. and Interaguas Servicios Integrales de Agua S.A. v Argentine Republic, ARB/03/17, *short title* Suez, AGBAR and Interaguas v Argentina 239–40
Suez, Sociedad General de Aguas de Barcelona S.A. and Vivendi Universal S.A. v Argentine Republic, ARB/03/19, *short title* Suez, AGBAR and Vivendi v Argentina 229, 239–40
Tanzania Electric Supply Co. Ltd. v Independent Power Tanzania Ltd., ARB/98/8, *short title* Tanesco v IPTL 189–90, 193
Tesoro Petroleum Corporation v Trinidad and Tobago, CONC/83/1, *short title* Tesoro v Trinidad and Tobago 123–5, 146
TG World Petroleum Ltd. v Republic of Niger, CONC/03/1, *short title* TGW v Niger 230
Togo Electricité v Republic of Togo, CONC/05/1, *short title* Togo Electricité v Togo 230
Togo Electricité and GDF-Suez Energie Services v Republic of Togo, ARB/06/7, *short title* Togo Electricité v Togo 230
Tokios Tokelés v Ukraine, ARB/02/18, *short title* Tokios Tokelés v Ukraine 254–5
Tradex Hellas S.A. v Republic of Albania, ARB/94/2, *short title* Tradex Hellas v Albania 189–90, 193
Tulip Real Estate and Development Netherlands B.V. v Republic of Turkey, ARB/11/28, *short title* Tulip Real Estate v Turkey 277, 278–9, 282
Türkiye Petrolleri Anonim Ortaklığı v Republic of Kazakhstan, ARB/11/2, *short title* Türkiye Petrolleri v Kazakhstan 268
Vacuum Salt Products Ltd. v Republic of Ghana, ARB/92/1, *short title* Vacuum Salt v Ghana 189, 193, 222
Vattenfall AB, Vattenfall Europe AG, Vattenfall Europe Generation AG v Federal Republic of Germany, ARB/09/6, *short title* Vattenfall v Germany 231
Venezuela Holdings, B.V., et al. v Bolivarian Republic of Venezuela, ARB/07/27, *short title* Venezuela Holdings v Venezuela 265
Venoklim Holding B.V. v Bolivarian Republic of Venezuela, ARB/12/22, *short title* Venoklim v Venezuela 277, 278, 280
Vigotop Limited v Hungary, ARB/11/22, *short title* Vigotop v Hungary 277, 281, 282
Compañia de Aguas del Aconquija S.A. and Vivendi Universal S.A. v Argentine Republic, ARB/97/3, *short title* Vivendi v Argentina 189–90, 192, 202, 205–6, 229, 239–40, 246–8, 258, 269, 277
Wena Hotels Limited v Arab Republic of Egypt, ARB/98/4, *short title* Wena v Egypt 193, 202, 209–10, 240, 257–9
WRB Enterprises and Grenada Private Power Limited v Grenada, ARB/97/5, *short title* WRB v Grenada 189–90, 192

ADDITIONAL FACILITY CASES

ADF Group Inc. v United States of America, ARB(AF)/00/1, *short title* ADF v U.S. 231
Archer Daniels Midland Co. and Tate & Lyle Ingredients Americas Inc. v United Mexican States, ARB(AF)/04/5, *short title* ADM v Mexico 238
Alasdair Ross Anderson and others v Republic of Costa Rica, ARB(AF)/07/3, *short title* Anderson v Costa Rica 256
Apotex Holdings Inc. and Apotex Inc. v United States of America, ARB(AF)/12/1, *short title* Apotex v U.S. 277, 278, 279, 282
Robert Azinian and others v United Mexican States, ARB(AF)/97/2, *short title* Azinian v Mexico 189, 193, 195–6
Cargill, Inc. v United Mexican States, ARB(AF)/05/2, *short title* Cargill v Mexico 259
Corn Products International Inc. v United Mexican States, ARB(AF)/04/1, *short title* Corn Products v Mexico 238
Republic of Equatorial Guinea v CMS Energy Corporation and others, CONC(AF)/12, *short title* Equatorial Guinea v CMS 268
Marvin Roy Feldman Karpa v United Mexican States, ARB(AF)/99/1, *short title* Feldman v Mexico 189, 193, 195–6, 201
Piero Foresti, Laura de Carli & Others v The Republic of South Africa, ARB(AF)/07/01, *short title* Foresti v South Africa 284
Gold Reserve Inc. v Bolivarian Republic of Venezuela, ARB(AF)/09/1, *short title* Gold Reserve v Venezuela 259
Hess Corporation v Republic of Equatorial Guinea, CONC(AF)/12/1, *short title* Hess v Equatorial Guinea 268n
Joseph C. Lemire v Ukraine, ARB(AF)/98/1, *short title* Lemire v Ukraine 189–90, 192, 195
The Loewen Group, Inc. and Raymond L. Loewen v United States of America, ARB/(AF)/98/3, *short title* Loewen v U.S. 189, 193, 195–6, 201
Metalclad Corp. v United Mexican States, ARB(AF)/97/1, *short title* Metalclad v Mexico 189, 193, 195–6, 198–200, 223
Mobil Investments Canada Inc. and Murphy Oil Corporation v Canada, ARB(AF)/07/04, *short title* Mobil v Canada 231, 259
Mondev International Ltd. v United States of America, ARB(AF)/99/2, *short title* Mondev v U.S. 189, 193, 195, 197
Nova Scotia Power Incorporated v Bolivarian Republic of Venezuela, ARB(AF)/11/1, *short title* NSP v Venezuela 277, 278, 281, 282
Waste Management, Inc. v United Mexican States, ARB(AF)/98/2, *short title* Waste Management v Mexico 189–90, 193–5

NON-ICSID CASES

Biloune and Marine Drive Complex Ltd. v Ghana Investments Centre and the Government of Ghana, UNCITRAL Arbitration Rules Proceeding, *short title* Biloune v Ghana 139
Canfor Corporation v United States of America, NAFTA/UNCITRAL Arbitration Rules Proceeding, *short title* Canfor v U.S. 229, 238
Ethyl Corporation v Government of Canada, NAFTA/UNCITRAL Arbitration Rules Proceeding, *short title* Ethyl v Canada 184, 191, 196, 202
Glamis Gold Ltd. v United States of America, NAFTA/UNCITRAL Arbitration Rules Proceeding, *short title* Glamis Gold v U.S. 229
Grand River Enterprises Six Nations, Ltd., et al. v United States of America, NAFTA/UNCITRAL Arbitration Rules Proceeding, *short title* Grand River Enterprises v U.S. 229
Himpurna California Energy Ltd. v PT (Persero) Perusahaan Listruik Negara, UNCITRAL Arbitration Rules Proceeding, *short title* Himpurna v PLN 139
International Thunderbird Gaming Corporation v Mexico, NAFTA/UNCITRAL Arbitration Rules Proceeding, *short title* Thunderbird v Mexico 237
Karaha Bodas Company L.L.C. v Perusahaan Pertambangan Minyak Dan Gas Bumi Negara, UNCITRAL Arbitration Rules Proceeding, *short title* Karaha Bodas v Pertamina and PLN 138

Merrill & Ring Forestry L.P. v Government of Canada, NAFTA/UNCITRAL Arbitration Rules Proceeding, *short title* Merrill & Ring v Canada 229, 237
Methanex v United States of America NAFTA/UNCITRAL Arbitration Rules Proceeding, *short title* Methanex v U.S. 215, 229
Pope & Talbot Inc. v Canada, NAFTA/UNCITRAL Arbitration Rules Proceeding, *short title* Pope & Talbot v Canada 196
S.D. Myers, Inc. v Government of Canada, NAFTA/UNCITRAL Arbitration Rules Proceeding, *short title* S.D. Myers v Canada 192, 196
Southern Bluefin Tuna case, Australia and New Zealand v Japan, Proceeding before Arbitral Tribunal constituted under Annex VII of the UN Convention on the Law of the Sea, *short title* Southern Bluefin Tuna 218, 229
Tembec Forest Products Ltd. v United States of America, NAFTA/UNCITRAL Arbitration Rules Proceeding, *short title* Tembec et al. v U.S. 238
United Parcel Service of America v Government of Canada, NAFTA/UNCITRAL Arbitration Rules Proceeding, *short title* UPS v Canada 215, 229, 237
Vito G. Gallo v Canada, NAFTA/UNCITRAL Arbitration Rules Proceeding, *short title* Vito Gallo v Canada 237, 238n

Table of Treaties

MULTILATERAL TREATIES

Agreement Establishing the African Development Bank, 1963
Art. 50 62
Agreement Establishing the World Trade Organization, 1994 177
American Treaty on Pacific Settlement, 1948 47
Articles of Agreement of the International Bank for Reconstruction and Development (IBRD), 1945
Art. I(i) 2
Art. I(ii) 5
Art. II(1) 2
Art. III(4) 2
Art. III(4)(i) 5
Art. IV(10) 21
Art. V(2)(a) 3
Art. V(2)(b) 3, 28
Art. V(2)(c) 3, 46
Art. V(2)(d) 46
Art. V(2)(e) 46
Art. V(3)(a) 3
Art. V(4)(a) 4
Art. V(4)(g) 4
Art. V(4)(i) 27
Art. V(4)(b)(i) 3
Art. V(4)(c) 4
Art. V(4)(e) 4
Art. V(5)(a) 4, 28
Art. V(5)(b) 4, 46
Art. V(5)(c) 5
Art. V(5)(d) 4
Art. V(9)(a) 5
Art. VII(1) 5
Art. VII(2) 5
Art. VII(3) 8
Art. VII(5) 5
Art. VII(8)(i) 5
Art. VII(8)(ii) 5
Art. VII(9) 5
Art. VII(9)(c) 30
Art. VIII 3–4, 48
Articles of Agreement of the International Development Association (IDA), 1960
Art. II(1) 6
Art. VI(1) 6
Art. VI(2)(b) 6, 103
Art. VI(2)(e) 103
Art. VI(3) 6
Art. VI(4)(b) 6
Art. VI(5)(a) 7, 28
Art. VI(5)(b) 6
Art. VI(8) 6
Art. VIII 6
Art. VIII(3) 8
Art. IX 48
Art. XI(3) 48
Art. XI(5) 48
Articles of Agreement of the International Finance Corporation (IFC), 1955
Art. II(1) 6
Art. IV(1) 6
Art. IV(2)(b) 6, 103
Art. IV(2)(e) 103
Art. IV(3)(a) 6
Art. IV(4)(b) 6
Art. IV(5)(a) 28
Art. IV(5)(b) 6
Art. IV(8) 6
Art. VI 6
Art. VI(3) 8
Art. VII 48
Articles of Agreement of the International Monetary Fund (IMF), 1945 30
Canada-EU Comprehensive Economic and Trade Agreement (CETA) 283
Art 8.27(16) 293
Charter of the United Nations, 1945
Art. 57 9
Art. 63 4
Art. 93(1) 83
Art. 93(2) 83
Art. 96 47
Art. 102 . . . . 45, 89
Art. 104 30
Art. 105 30
Convention Establishing the Multilateral Investment Guarantee Agency (MIGA), 1985
Ch. VII 6
Art. 4(a) 6
Art. 30 6
Art. 31(b) 6
Art. 32(b) 6
Art. 33(b) 6
Art. 36(a) 6
Art. 39(a) 6
Art. 44 8
Convention for the Conservation of Southern Bluefin Tuna, 1993 218
Convention for the Pacific Settlement of International Disputes, 1899
Ch. II 46

Convention for the Pacific Settlement of International Disputes, 1907
Ch. II . . . 46
Art. 26 . . . 46
Art. 47 . . . 46
Convention on the Privileges and Immunities of the Specialized Agencies, 1948 . . . 4
Convention on the Privileges and Immunities of the United Nations, 1946
Art. I . . . 63
Convention on the Settlement of Investment Disputes between States and Nationals of Other States, 1965
Art. 1(1) . . . 81
Art. 1(2) . . . 128
Art. 2 . . . 8
Art. 4 . . . 8
Art. 4(2) . . . 8, 103
Art. 5 . . . 8
Art. 6(1) . . . 91, 112, 131
Art. 6(1)(d) . . . 92
Art. 6(1)(f) . . . 8, 92
Art. 6(1)(g) . . . 8, 104
Art. 6(2) . . . 292
Art. 6(3) . . . 296
Art. 7(1) . . . 8, 89
Art. 7(4) . . . 94
Art. 10(1) . . . 8, 90
Art. 10(2) . . . 90
Art. 11 . . . 95
Art. 12 . . . 95, 106
Art. 13(2) . . . 118
Art. 14(1) . . . 149, 221, 238–9, 276
Art. 14(2) . . . 118
Art. 15(3) . . . 221, 273
Art. 17 . . . 96, 219
Art. 18 . . . 8
Art. 19 . . . 8
Art. 20 . . . 8, 97
Art. 21 . . . 8, 97, 271
Art. 21(a) . . . 97
Art. 22 . . . 8, 97
Art. 23 . . . 8
Art. 23(2) . . . 69
Art. 24 . . . 8
Art. 25 . . . 129–31, 236, 241
Art. 25(1) . . . 7, 118–20, 151, 155, 203–4, 240, 244, 260
Art. 25(2)(b) . . . 152–3, 279
Art. 25(3) . . . 119
Art. 25(4) . . . 119–20, 213
Art. 26 . . . 127, 157–61, 226
Art. 28 . . . 97–8
Art. 28(3) . . . 98, 143–4, 368
Art. 29 . . . 290
Art. 29(2)(b) . . . 99
Art. 34(1) . . . 69
Art. 36 . . . 97–8
Art. 36(1) . . . 144, 235
Art. 36(3) . . . 98, 143–4, 235, 268, 294, 368
Art. 37 . . . 275
Art. 37(2)(a) . . . 293
Art. 37(2)(b) . . . 99, 147
Art. 38 . . . 147, 188, 191, 221, 273, 275–6, 295
Art. 39 . . . 99, 148, 197
Art. 40 . . . 147
Art. 40(1) . . . 221, 288
Art. 41(5) . . . 235n, 236
Art. 42(1) . . . 143, 162–6, 209–10, 257–9
Art. 44 . . . 128, 223, 234
Art. 47 . . . 143, 157–8, 160–1, 208, 254, 255
Art. 48(2) . . . 127
Art. 48(3) . . . 101, 146
Art. 48(5) . . . 95, 291
Art. 49 . . . 97, 101
Art. 49(1) . . . 101
Art. 49(2) . . . 145
Art. 50 . . . 97, 101
Art. 51 . . . 97, 101
Art. 51(2) . . . 145
Art. 52 . . . 97, 101, 125, 143, 162, 167–9, 171, 193, 206, 209, 226–7, 232, 295
Art. 52(1) . . . 168
Art. 52(1)(b) . . . 168
Art. 52(1)(e) . . . 168
Art. 52(2) . . . 145
Art. 52(3) . . . 170, 221
Art. 52(5) . . . 169, 206, 262
Art. 53 . . . 171, 174, 263–4
Art. 53(1) . . . 226, 263
Art. 54 . . . 167, 173–4, 262–4
Art. 54(1) . . . 264
Art. 54(2) . . . 120, 221, 273
Art. 55 . . . 173
Art. 56 . . . 148
Art. 57 . . . 149–50, 239–40, 276–7
Art. 58 . . . 149, 238, 277, 295
Art. 59 . . . 97
Art. 60(1) . . . 96, 113
Art. 61(2) . . . 96, 101, 126
Art. 63 . . . 188, 273–4
Art. 63(a) . . . 106, 271
Art. 64 . . . 291
Art. 66(1) . . . 129
Art. 67 . . . 8, 93
Art. 68 . . . 84
Art. 70 . . . 155
Art. 71 . . . 213, 269
Art. 72 . . . 234

Art. 74 84
Art. 75 84
Dominican Republic–Central America–United States Free Trade Agreement, 2004 . . . . . 211, 224, 226–9, 267
Energy Charter Treaty, 1994 . . . . . 182, 211, 253, 267
Pts III and V 182
Art. 26(4)(a) 182
Art. 26(4)(c) 182
Art. 26(24)(b) 182
European Convention on Human Rights and Fundamental Freedoms, 1950
Art. 46(2) 55
New York Convention on the Recognition and Enforcement of Foreign Arbitral Awards, 1958
Art. III 134
Art. IV 134
Art. V 47, 55, 134
Art. VI 47
Art. VIII(1) 67
North American Agreement on Environmental Cooperation, 1994 179
North American Agreement on Labor Cooperation, 1993 179
North American Free Trade Agreement (NAFTA), 1992 . . . . . 230, 267
Ch. 11 . . . . . 182, 184
Art. 102(1) 198
Art. 1101 200
Art. 1102 . . . . . 196, 200
Art. 1105 . . . . . 196, 198–9, 200–2
Art. 1106 200
Art. 1107 200
Art. 1108 200
Art. 1109 200
Art. 1110 . . . . . 196, 198–9, 200–1
Art. 1111 200
Art. 1112 200
Art. 1113 200
Art. 1114 200
Art. 1115 200
Art. 1116 200
Art. 1117 200
Art. 1131 202
Art. 1125 197
Art. 1126 237
Art. 1130(a) 200
Art. 1502(3)(a) 200
Art. 1503(2) 200
Art. 1801 201
Art. 1802 201
Art. 1803 201
Art. 1804 201
Art. 1805 201
Art. 1806 201
Art. 2001 201
Art. 2001(2)(c) 202
OECD Convention on Combating Bribery of Foreign Public Officials in International Business Transactions, 1997
Art. 1 178
Statute of the International Atomic Energy Agency (IAEA), 1956
Art. XVII 47
Statute of the International Court of Justice (ICJ)
Art. 2 46
Art. 6 46
Art. 9 46
Art. 36 44
Art. 38 66
Art. 41 47
Art. 43 100
Art. 43(2) 100
Art. 49 66
Art. 53 47
Art. 54(3) 101
Art. 59 66
Art. 60 47
Art. 61 47
Trans-Pacific Partnership (TPP) Agreement 282–3
Treaty Establishing the European Community, 1957
Art. 192 47
United Nations Convention on the Law of the Sea (UNCLOS), 1982
Art. 287 219
Annex VII 219
Annex VIII 219
United Nations Convention on Transparency in Treaty-based Investor–State Arbitration, March 17, 2015 284
Art. 2 . . . . . 284n
Art. 3 . . . . . 284n
United States–Colombia Trade Promotion Agreement, November 22, 2006
Art. 10.4(2) 254n
United States–Peru Trade Promotion Agreement, April 12, 2006
Art. 10.4(2) 254n
Vienna Convention on Diplomatic Relations, 1961 174
Vienna Convention on the Law of Treaties, 1969
Art. 31 244
Art. 31(2) 244
Art. 32 244
Art. 41 226

BILATERAL TREATIES

Bilateral investment treaties (BITs)

Albania–Greece BIT, 1993 279
Algeria–Italy BIT, 1991 245
Art. 8 245
Argentina–Chile BIT, 1991 251–2
Art. 10 251
Art. 10(2) 252
Argentina–Ecuador BIT, 1994 214
Argentina–France BIT, 1991 205
Art. 8(1) 203
Argentina–Germany, 1991 ...... 251–2, 257
Art. 3 251–2
Art. 10 251
Art. 10(2) 251
Art. 10(4) 251
Art. 10(5) 257
Argentina–Spain BIT, 1991 .... 203, 207
Argentina–United States BIT,
1991 .... 182, 260–1
Art. II(2)(a) 260
Art. II(2)(c) 260
Art. IV(1) 260
Art. XI 260, 261
Bahrain–United Kingdom BIT, 1991 181
Belgium–Indonesia BIT, 1970 122
Belgium–Luxembourg Economic
Union–China BIT, 2005
Art. 8 282
Belize–United Kingdom BIT, 1982 136
Bolivia–Netherlands BIT, 1992 234
Art. 9(6) 234
Bulgaria–Cyprus BIT, 1987 253
Bulgaria–Finland BIT, 1997 253
Art. 8(2) 253
Canada–Ecuador BIT, 1996 213
Chad–Italy BIT, 1969 121
Chile–Ecuador BIT, 1993 213
Chile–Spain BIT, 1991 207
China–Ecuador BIT, 1994 213
Côte d'Ivoire–Italy BIT, 1969 121
Cuba–Ecuador BIT, 1997 213
Cyprus–Bulgaria BIT, 1987
Art. 3 253
Art. 4 253
Art. 4(1) 253
Art. 4(3) 253
Cyprus–Greece BIT, 1992
Art. 9.......................... 280
Cyprus–Hungary BIT, 1989 ..... 257–8, 281
Art. 4(1) 258
Art. 7 257
Art. 7(1) 257, 281
Czech Republic–United States BIT,
1991 182
Czech and Slovak Republic–Greece
BIT, 1991
Art. 1 280
Art. 1(a) 280
Art. 1(c) 280
Art. 10 280
Dominican Republic–Ecuador BIT,
1998 213
Ecuador–El Salvador BIT, 1994......... 213
Ecuador–Finland BIT, 2001 213
Ecuador–France BIT, 1994 213
Ecuador–Germany BIT, 1996 213
Ecuador–Honduras BIT, 2000 213
Ecuador–Netherlands BIT, 1999 213
Ecuador–Nicaragua BIT, 2000 213
Ecuador–Paraguay BIT, 1994 213
Ecuador–Romania BIT, 1996 213
Ecuador–Sweden BIT, 2001 213
Ecuador–Switzerland BIT, 1968 213
Ecuador–United Kingdom BIT, 1994 213
Ecuador–United States BIT, 1993 213
Ecuador–Uruguay BIT, 1985 213
Egypt–United Arab Emirates BIT,
1999 279
Egypt–United Kingdom BIT, 1975 122,
155, 203, 209
Egypt–United States BIT, 1982 ..... 122, 180
El Salvador–United States BIT, 1999 251
Art. VIII(4)(a) 251
Art. VIII(4)(b) 251
France–Jordan BIT, 1978 122
France–Mauritius BIT, 1973 122
France–Moldova BIT, 1997
Art. 3 278
France–Mongolia BIT, 1991 181
Germany–India BIT, 1995 138
Germany–Pakistan BIT, 1959 19
Germany–South Africa BIT, 1995 182
Germany–St Lucia (BIT), 1985 122
Germany–Thailand BIT, 1961 19
Haiti–United Kingdom BIT, 1995 181
Hungary–Netherlands BIT, 1987
Art. 10 281
Hungary–Switzerland BIT, 1988
Art. 10 .... 281, 282
Hungary–United Kingdom BIT, 1987
Art. 8 281
Indonesia–Netherlands BIT, 1968 122
Art. 11 122
Italy–Jordan BIT, 1996 251
Art. 9(2) 251
Italy–Morocco BIT, 1990 242
Lithuania–Ukraine BIT, 1994 254
Malawi–Netherlands BIT, 2003 211
Malaysia–United Arab Emirates BIT, 1991 .. 181
Malaysia–United Kingdom BIT, 1981 243

Netherlands–Turkey BIT, 1986 279
Netherlands–Venezuela BIT, 1991 . . . . 203–5, 278
Norway–Russia BIT, 1995 182
Pakistan–Switzerland BIT, 1995 247–50
Art. 9 . . . . 247, 248
Art. 11 . . . . 248, 250
Art. VIII 249–50
Panama–United States BIT, 1982 136
Philippines–Switzerland BIT, 1997 249
Art. X(2) 249n
Poland–United States BIT, 1990 182
Senegal–United States BIT, 1983 136
Sri Lanka–United Kingdom BIT, 1980 . . . . 156, 166–7
St. Lucia–United Kingdom BIT, 1983 136
Switzerland–Congo BIT, 1962 19
Switzerland–Turkey BIT, 1988 122
Ukraine–Lithuania BIT, 1994 254
Ukraine–United States BIT, 1994 195
U.S. Model BIT, 1992 182
U.S. Model BIT, 2004 . . . . 216, 224
Art. 28(10) 285
U.S. Model BIT, 2012 282
Art. 24 283
Art. 25 283
Art. 28(10) 285

Bilateral free trade agreements (FTAs)

Australia–United States FTA, 2004 . . . . 211, 231
Bahrain–United States FTA, 2004 211
Chile–United States FTA, 2003 . . . . . 211, 224
Colombia–United States FTA, 2006 . . . . 211, 254
Jordan–United States FTA, 2000 211
Korea–United States FTA, 2007 211
Morocco–United States FTA, 2004 211
Oman–United States FTA, 2006 211
Panama–United States FTA, 2007 211
Art 11.20 . . . . 285n
Peru–United States FTA, 2006 . . . . . 211, 254
Singapore–United States FTA, 2003 . . . . 211, 224

Other

Bahrain–United States Investment Incentive Agreement, 1987 138
Canada–United States Treaty Relating to the Skagit River and Ross Lake, and the Seven Mile Reservoir on the Pend d'Oreille River (High Ross Treaty), 1984 138
India–Pakistan Indus Waters Treaty, 1960 . . . . 22, 218

DRAFT CONVENTIONS

Abs–Shawcross Draft Convention on Investments Abroad, 1959
Art. I 13
Art. II 13
Art. III 13
Art. VII(1) 14
Art. VII(2) 14
Annex, para. 1 14
Annex, para. 6 14
Multilateral Agreement on Investment (MAI), 1998 . . . . 179, 183–4, 283
OECD Draft Convention on the Protection of Foreign Property, 1962 . . . . 15, 18–19, 180, 287
Art. 1(b) 15
Art. 3 18
Art. 7(a) 15
Art. 7(b)(ii) 15
Annex, para. 6(b) 15
Annex, para. 6(c) 15
OECD Draft Convention on the Protection of Foreign Property, 1967 . . . . 18–19, 180, 287
Art. 3 18
Preliminary Draft of a Convention on the Settlement of Investment Disputes between States and Nationals of Other States, 1963
Preamble 40
Art. I(1) 41
Art. I(2) 41
Art. I(2)(2) 41
Art. I(2)(3) 41
Art. I(3) 41
Art. I(4) 41
Art. I(4)(2) 41
Art. I(5) 40–1
Art. I(6) 41
Art. I(6)(i) 41
Art. I(6)(ii) 41
Art. I(6)(iii) 41
Art. I(6)(iv) 41
Art. I(6)(v) 41
Art. I(6)(vi) 41
Art. I(7) 46
Art. I(8) 40
Art. I(9) 40
Art. I(10)(1) 40, 46
Art. I(15) 46
Art. I(17) 46
Art. II(1) 42, 46
Art. II(2) 46
Art. II(3)(1) 43, 46
Art. II(3)(2) 43
Art. II(3)(3) 43

Preliminary Draft of a Convention on the Settlement of Investment Disputes between States and Nationals of Other States, 1963 (*cont.*)
Art. III(1) 42
Art. III(2)(1) 42
Art. III(5)(1) 43, 47
Art. IV(1) 42
Art. IV(2)(1) 42
Art. IV(3) 42, 47
Art. IV(7)(1) 43
Art. IV(8) 43, 47
Art. IV(10) 47
Art. IV(11) 47
Art. IV(12) 47
Art. IV(13) 47
Art. IV(13)(1) 43
Art. IV(13)(2) 44
Art. IV(13)(4) 44
Art. IV(13)(5) 44
Art. IV(13)(6) 44
Art. IV(15) 44
Art. IV(16) 53
Art. IV(17) 46
Art. IV(17)(2) 44
Art. V 43
Art. V(2) 42
Art. V(2)(a) 43
Art. V(2)(b) 43
Art. VII(1) 41
Art. VIII 44, 47
Art. IX 45
Art. X(1) 42
Art. X(2) 42
Art. X(4) 45
Art. XI(1) 45
Art. XI(2) 45
Art. XI(3) 45
Art. XI(4) 48
Art. XI(5) 45
Art. XI(6) 45
Art. XI(7) 45, 48
Draft Convention on the Settlement of Investment Disputes between States and Nationals of Other States (First Draft), 1964
preambular para. 5 62
Art. 1(1) 62
Art. 1(2) 62
Art. 5 62
Art. 6(ii) 65
Art. 6(vi) 62
Art. 10(1) 62
Art. 10(2) 62
Art. 13 62
Art. 14(1) 62
Art. 15(1) 62
Art. 18 62
Art. 19 62
Art. 21(i) 62
Art. 26(1) 63–4
Art. 26(2) 64
Art. 27(2) 64
Art. 29 64
Art. 30(i) 63
Art. 30(ii) 64
Art. 30(iii)(a) 64
Art. 31(2) 64
Art. 31(3) 65
Art. 32(2)(a) 65
Art. 34(2) 65
Art. 35(2) 65
Art. 36 65
Art. 40(2) 64
Art. 40(3) 65
Art. 41(2)(a) 65
Art. 43(1) 65
Art. 43(3) 65
Art. 44(2) 65
Art. 45(1) 65
Art. 46 66
Art. 47 65
Art. 48 66
Art. 49 66
Art. 50(1) 66
Art. 50(2) 66
Art. 53 66
Art. 55(1)(a) 66
Art. 55(1)(b) 66
Art. 55(1)(d) 66
Art. 55(1)(e) 66
Art. 56 66
Art. 57 66
Art. 58 66
Art. 60 65
Art. 64(1) 65
Art. 65 65
Art. 67 .... 67, 82
Art. 68 64
Art. 69 83
Art. 69(1) 67
Art. 69(2) 67
Art. 70 67
Art. 73 89
Art. 74 84
Art. 75 84
Working Paper in the Form of a Draft Convention for the Resolution of Disputes between States and Nationals of Other States, 1962
Art. I 28
Art. II 31
Art. II(1) 31
Art. II(2) 31

Art. II(3) 31
Art. II(4) 31
Art. II(5) 32
Art. III(1) 28, 30, 33
Art. III(2)(1) 30
Art. III(2)(2) 30
Art. III(2)(3) 31
Art. III(4) 28
Art. III(7) 29
Art. III(8) 28
Art. III(9) 29
Art. III(9)(2) 30
Art. III(9)(4) 29
Art. III(10) 29
Art. III(11) 29
Art. III(11)(2) 29
Art. III(12) 29
Art. III(13) 29
Art. III(13)(3) 28
Art. III(14) 29
Art. III(14)(2) 29
Art. III(14)(3) 28
Art. III(15) 29
Art. III(17)(1) 29–30
Art. III(17)(2) 30
Art. III(18) 31
Art. III(19) 30
Art. III(19)(1) 30
Art. III(20)(2) 30
Art. III(21) 30
Art. III(22) 30
Art. III(22)(2) 30
Art. III(22)(3) 30
Art. IV(1)(i) 31
Art. IV(2) 31, 33
Art. IV(3) 33
Art. IV(4) 29
Art. IV(4)(1) 33
Art. IV(4)(3) 33
Art. IV(5) 33
Art. IV(b) 33
Art. V(1) 32
Art. V(2) 32
Art. V(3) 29
Art. V(3)(1) 28
Art. V(3)(2) 32
Art. V(4)(2) 33
Art. V(6) 33
Art. VI(1) 32
Art. VI(2) 32
Art. VI(3) 29
Art. VI(3)(1) 28
Art. VI(3)(2) 32
Art. VI(5)(1) 33
Art. VI(6) 33
Art. VI(7) 33
Art. VI(9) 33
Art. VI(10) 33
Art. VI(11) 34
Art. VI(12) 34
Art. VII(2) 33
Art. VII(3) 33
Art. VII(4) 29, 32
Art. VII(5) 32
Art. VII(6)(1) 32
Art. VII(6)(2) 32

List of Abbreviations

General

AAA	American Arbitration Association
AALCO	Asian-African Legal Consultative Organization
AMI	Accord multilatéral sur l'investissement
AMS	World Bank Administrative Manual Statement
ASEAN	Association of Southeast Asian Nations
BIT	bilateral investment treaty
CAFTA-DR	Dominican Republic–Central America–United States Free Trade Agreement
CETA	Canada–EU Comprehensive Economic and Trade Agreement
CIDS	Center for International Dispute Settlement
CIEL	Center for International Environmental Law
CRCICA	Cairo Regional Centre for International Commercial Arbitration
DAC	Development Assistance Committee of the OECD
ECOSOC	Economic and Social Council (U.N.)
ECT	Energy Charter Treaty
FCN	friendship, commerce and navigation treaty
FDI	foreign direct investment(s)
FSIA	1976 Foreign Sovereign Immunities Act (U.S.)
FTA	free trade agreement
IAEA	International Atomic Energy Agency
IBA	International Bar Association
IBRD	International Bank for Reconstruction and Development
ICC	International Chamber of Commerce
ICJ	International Court of Justice
ICSID	International Centre for Settlement of Investment Disputes
IDA	International Development Association
IFC	International Finance Corporation
IIIA	International Investment Insurance Agency
IISD	International Institute for Sustainable Development
ILC	International Law Commission
IMF	International Monetary Fund
LCIA	London Court of International Arbitration
MAI	Multilateral Agreement on Investment
MFN	most-favored-nation
MIGA	Multilateral Investment Guarantee Agency
MMCW	Memorandum of the Meeting of the Committee of the Whole (of the Executive Directors of the World Bank)
NAFTA	North American Free Trade Agreement
NGO	non-governmental organization
NIEO	New International Economic Order
OECD	Organisation for Economic Co-operation and Development
OEEC	Organisation for European Economic Co-operation (since 1960, the OECD)
OPEC	Organization of the Petroleum Exporting Countries
OPIC	Overseas Private Investment Corporation
PCA	Permanent Court of Arbitration
PPI	Producer Price Index
SCC	Stockholm Chamber of Commerce

SIAC	Singapore International Arbitration Centre
SOE	State-owned enterprise
SPLCM	Summary Proceedings of the Legal Committee Meeting
SRSG	Special Representative of the U.N. Secretary-General on Business and Human Rights
TNC	transnational corporation
TPP	Trans-Pacific Partnership
TTIP	EU–United States Transatlantic Trade and Partnership
UNCITRAL	United Nations Commission on International Trade Law
UNCTAD	United Nations Conference on Trade and Development
WTO	World Trade Organization

Publications

AJIL	American Journal of International Law
Broches *Selected Essays*	Aron Broches, *Selected Essays: World Bank, ICSID, and Other Subjects of Public and Private Investment Law* (1995)
BYBIL	British Yearbook of International Law
History of the ICSID Convention	ICSID, *History of the ICSID Convention: Documents Concerning the Origin and Formulation of the Convention on the Settlement of Investment Disputes between States and Nationals of Other States* (1970) (a collection of documents comprising the *travaux préparatoires* of the Convention)
ICLQ	International and Comparative Law Quarterly
ICSID Rep.	ICSID Reports
ICSID Rev.—FILJ	ICSID Review—Foreign Investment Law Journal
IIC	International Investment Claims (included with a unique identifying number on all cases at <http://www.investmentclaims.com>)
ILM	International Legal Materials
TDM	Transnational Dispute Management
UNTS	United Nations Treaty Series
YBCA	Yearbook of Commercial Arbitration
YBILC	Yearbook of the International Law Commission

1

Introduction

On March 18, 1965, the Executive Directors of the International Bank for Reconstruction and Development approved the submission, to member governments of the Bank, of the text of a Convention on the Settlement of Investment Disputes between States and Nationals of Other States. The text of the Convention was "submitted to member governments for consideration with a view to signature and ratification."[1] The Convention was to provide procedures for the settlement by conciliation or arbitration of investment disputes between States and foreign investors. Also to be established by the Convention was "an autonomous international institution"[2] to administer those procedures, the International Centre for Settlement of Investment Disputes (ICSID or the Centre). By September 14, 1966, 20 countries had signed and ratified the Convention; in accordance with its terms, the Convention entered into force 30 days later, on October 14, 1966.

Much has since been written about ICSID and the Convention.[3] The published literature does not, however, include an overall history of the institution and its constituent treaty. With the Centre and Convention marking their fiftieth anniversaries, this book aims to provide such a history.

Chapter 2 of the book looks at the immediate origins of the ICSID Convention, in the years 1955 to 1962. Chapters 3, 4 and 5 give a detailed, stage-by-stage narrative of the drawing up of the text of the Convention between 1962 and 1965. Recounted in Chapter 6 are details of bringing the Convention into force in 1966 and the launch of the Centre in 1967. A focus of Chapter 6 is on the elaboration of the initial versions of the Regulations and Rules of the Centre.

The periods 1968 to 1988 and 1989 to 1999 are covered in Chapters 7 and 9, while Chapters 10 and 11 deal with the periods 2000 to 2010 and 2011 to 2015. These chapters discuss institutional developments and give overviews of the conciliation and arbitration cases submitted to the Centre in the respective periods. They examine expansions of the Centre's activities and changes made to the Regulations and Rules over the years.

Selected aspects of the conciliation and arbitration cases submitted to the Centre in the 1970s and 1980s are the subject of Chapter 8. Four leading Convention cases of the 1990s are examined in Chapter 9, as are the first proceedings brought under the Additional Facility Rules mentioned in section III below. The same aspects of the cases discussed in Chapter 8 are addressed in Chapter 10 in relation to cases brought to ICSID in the period 2000 to 2010. The first awards in cases registered from 2011 to 2015 are discussed in Chapter 11.

[1] Report of the Executive Directors on the Convention on the Settlement of Investment Disputes between States and Nationals of Other States, March 18, 1965, reprinted at App. IV of this book, para. 3.

[2] Ibid. para. 15.

[3] *See especially* C.H. Schreuer and others, *The ICSID Convention: A Commentary* (2d ed. 2009) and its consolidated bibliography.

Some of the broad themes emerging from the history are discussed in the concluding Chapter 12, as are a number of suggestions for further changes at ICSID to help ensure its continued success.

An effort is made throughout to place events in their broader political, economic and, above all, institutional context. The broader institutional setting is, of course, that of the World Bank Group of intergovernmental organizations. The following sections of this introductory chapter furnish brief descriptions of these organizations, including the Centre itself, as of June 30, 2015 (the end of the organizations' 2015 fiscal year).

I. The International Bank for Reconstruction and Development

The largest of the organizations, and the progenitor of the others, is the International Bank for Reconstruction and Development (the IBRD or Bank). Its constituent treaty was drawn up at the United Nations Monetary and Financial Conference held in July 1944 at Bretton Woods, New Hampshire.[4] The treaty, the Articles of Agreement of the IBRD, came into force at the end of 1945.[5] The Bank began operating the following year. Already then, it was being referred to informally as the "World Bank," a sobriquet that the institution eventually adopted officially.[6] In this book, the IBRD is often also referred to as the World Bank.[7]

The purposes of the Bank, as set forth in its Articles of Agreement, include assisting in the reconstruction of the economies of members destroyed or disrupted by war and in the development of productive facilities and resources in less developed countries.[8] Early in its history, the Bank moved out of the reconstruction field, focusing instead on its other purpose of helping in the development of its developing member countries.[9] It serves the purpose by providing financing, mainly loans, for investment projects and economic reform. The loans are made to, or with the guarantee of, creditworthy developing member countries.[10] The Bank also provides technical assistance and other advisory services to its member countries, undertakes research and training and administers, on behalf of donors, funds for specific uses.[11]

Membership in the Bank is open to countries that are members of the International Monetary Fund (IMF).[12] There are now 188 members of the IBRD. Their

[4] *See* Final Act of the Bretton Woods Conference, July 22, 1944, in *United Nations Monetary and Financial Conference: Bretton Woods, Final Act and Related Documents* 11–27 (U.S. Government Printing Office, 1944).

[5] Articles of Agreement of the International Bank for Reconstruction and Development, December 27, 1945, 2 UNTS 134 (Articles of Agreement of the IBRD).

[6] *See* IBRD, *A Guide to the World Bank* 11 (3d ed. 2011).

[7] In keeping with common usage and the practice of the Bank itself during much of its history. It should be noted, however, that "World Bank" is now officially employed to mean both the IBRD and its affiliate the International Development Association (IDA) described in section II of this chapter. *See* IBRD (n. 6) 11.

[8] *See* Articles of Agreement of the IBRD (n. 5) Art. I(i).

[9] R. Gardner, *Sterling-Dollar Diplomacy: The Origins and Prospects of Our International Economic Order* 303–304 (1969) as quoted in D. Kapur and others, 1 *The World Bank: Its First Half Century* 74 (1997) (explaining that as the European Recovery Program, commonly known as the Marshall Plan, gained momentum when the IBRD turned from its initial emphasis on assisting with the reconstruction of the war-damaged European countries to the task of helping developing countries).

[10] *See* Articles of Agreement of the IBRD (n. 5) Art. III(4).

[11] *See* IBRD, Information Statement 26–27 (September 2015) (Information Statement). The funds mentioned in the text, held in trust by the IBRD, amounted to US$23.2 billion in fiscal year 2015.

[12] *See* Articles of Agreement of the IBRD (n. 5) Art. II(1).

subscriptions to the capital stock of the Bank are determined on the basis of their IMF quotas (which in turn broadly reflect members' relative economic strength). A small proportion of the subscribed capital is paid in; the rest is subject to call to meet obligations of the Bank. The callable capital supports borrowing by the IBRD in the capital markets to fund its lending operations. At June 30, 2015, the subscribed capital was US$252.8 billion, of which US$15.2 billion was paid in, leaving US$237.6 billion subject to call.[13]

The Articles of Agreement give the Bank a tripartite organizational structure, comprising a Board of Governors; Executive Directors; and President and staff. The Board of Governors consists of a Governor and an Alternate Governor appointed by each member for a renewable five-year term.[14] Members typically appoint as Governors their minister for finance or economy. The Articles of Agreement provide that "[a]ll powers of the Bank shall be vested in the Board of Governors."[15] In the By-Laws of the Bank, the Board of Governors has delegated to the Executive Directors all the powers of the Bank except those specifically reserved to the Board of Governors in the Articles of Agreement.[16] The reserved powers of the Board of Governors include admitting new members and determining the conditions of their admission, increasing the capital stock and raising the number of Executive Directors.[17] Governors exercise the voting power of the members that appointed them, each member having an equal number of basic votes plus one vote for each share subscribed.[18] The Board of Governors meets once annually.[19]

There are 25 Executive Directors. The members with the five largest shareholdings each appoint an Executive Director. These members are the United States, Japan, China, Germany and France and the United Kingdom (tied for fifth).[20] The other Executive Directors are elected by the Governors of the remaining members, grouped for the purpose in different voting constituencies. Under the Articles of Agreement, the Executive Directors are "responsible for the conduct of the general operations of the Bank," exercising the powers delegated to them by the Board of Governors, and provide "direction" to the President in the latter's conduct of the ordinary business of the Bank.[21] Each Executive Director casts the number of votes of the member or members by which the Director is appointed or elected.[22] The Executive Directors function as a resident board at the principal office of the IBRD, meeting as often as may be required.[23] Alternates appointed by the Executive Directors act for them in their absence.[24] In the discharge of their duties, Executive Directors have a dual character, as

[13] *See* Information Statement (n. 11) 2.

[14] *See* Articles of Agreement of the IBRD (n. 5) Art. V(2)(a).

[15] Ibid.

[16] *See* By-Laws of the IBRD, as amended, September 26, 1980, sec. 14.

[17] *See* Articles of Agreement of the IBRD (n. 5) Arts. V(2)(b), V(4)(b) and VIII.

[18] *See* ibid. Art. V(3)(a). The number of basic votes of members represent 5.55% of the total voting power in the aggregate.

[19] *See* Articles of Agreement of the IBRD (n. 5) Art. V(2)(c).

[20] *Cf.* ibid. Art. V(4)(b)(i) and Information Statement (n. 11) 60.

[21] Articles of Agreement of the IBRD (n. 5) Art. V(4)(a) and V(5)(b).

[22] Ibid. Art. V(4)(g). Under the weighted voting system of the IBRD, the five largest shareholders (*see* n. 20 and accompanying text) have about 40% of the total voting power; the largest single shareholder, the U.S., has about 16% of the voting power. As the acceptance of three-fifths of the members having 85% of the total voting power is required for amendments of the Articles of Agreement of the IBRD (Articles of Agreement of the IBRD (n. 5) Art. VIII), the acceptance of the U.S. is needed for any such amendment.

[23] Articles of Agreement of the IBRD (n. 5) Art. V(4)(e).

[24] Ibid. Art. V(4)(c).

officials of the Bank and as representatives of the member or members that appointed or elected them.[25]

The Articles of Agreement refer to the President as the "chief of the operating staff of the Bank."[26] As indicated above, the President conducts "the ordinary business of the Bank."[27] "Subject to the general control of the Executive Directors," the President is "responsible for the organization, appointment and dismissal of the officers and staff."[28] The President is selected by the Executive Directors of the Bank for a renewable five-year term.[29] He or she serves as Chairman of the Executive Directors without, however, a vote other than a deciding vote in case of an equal division.[30] In appointing officers and staff, the President is urged by the Articles of Agreement to seek geographic diversity without sacrificing "the highest standards of efficiency and technical competence."[31] There are now about 12,000 Bank staff members from 172 countries.[32] The Articles of Agreement emphasize that in their work the President, officers and staff "owe their duty entirely to the Bank and to no other authority."[33] All members are to "respect the international character of this duty."[34]

The principal office of the Bank is in Washington, D.C.[35] The Bank maintains another 127 offices around the world. The Articles of Agreement provide that the Bank will, in the territories of members, have full juridical personality and certain immunities and privileges.[36] The immunities of the Bank include archival immunity and immunity from taxation.[37] Governors, Executive Directors, Alternates, officers and staff of the Bank have immunity from legal process with respect to acts performed in their official capacity.[38] With some exceptions, they are also exempt from taxation on their remuneration by the Bank.[39] The IBRD is a specialized agency brought into relationship with the United Nations[40] and also benefits from provisions of the Convention on the Privileges and Immunities of the Specialized Agencies.[41]

[25] *See* I.F.I. Shihata, *The World Bank Legal Papers* 657 (2000).

[26] Articles of Agreement of the IBRD (n. 5) Art. V(5)(b). [27] Ibid. [28] Ibid.

[29] "All of the Bank's presidents have been U.S. citizens. According to an unwritten convention, it is the prerogative of the United States to nominate the president [for selection by the Executive Directors]. The custom was based less on the position of the United States as the Bank's largest shareholder than on the critical importance of the Bank's access to the U.S. capital markets." *See* J. Kraske and others, *Bankers with a Mission: The Presidents of the World Bank, 1946–91* at 5 (1996).

[30] *See* Articles of Agreement of the IBRD (n. 5) Art. V(5)(a). [31] Ibid. Art. V(5)(d).

[32] Staff numbers in this chapter are of full-time staff.

[33] Articles of Agreement of the IBRD (n. 5) Art. V(5)(c). [34] Ibid.

[35] The Articles of Agreement of the IBRD (ibid. Art. V(9)(a)) require that the Bank's principal office be "in the territory of the member holding the largest number of shares," which is the U.S. The By-Laws of the IBRD ((n. 16) sec. 1(a)) fix the location as Washington, D.C. It was chosen as the site of the Bank over New York City at the inaugural meeting of the Board of Governors of the IBRD in 1946 despite the objection of some delegations that "the Bank as an international institution should not be too closely associated with the capital of any nation." Inaugural Meeting of the Board of Governors of the International Bank for Reconstruction and Development, Selected Documents 61–62 (May 1946) as quoted in E.S. Mason and R.E. Asher, *The World Bank Since Bretton Woods* 37 (1973).

[36] *See* Articles of Agreement of the IBRD (n. 5) Art. VII(1) and VII(2).

[37] *See* ibid. Art. VII(5) and VII(9). [38] *See* ibid. Art. VII(8)(i).

[39] *See* ibid. Art. VII(8)(ii).

[40] Under Art. 63 of the U.N. Charter. *See* Agreement between the United Nations and the International Bank for Reconstruction and Development, approved by the Board of Governors of the IBRD on September 16, 1947 and by the General Assembly of the U.N. on November 15, 1947.

[41] December 2, 1948, 33 UNTS 261.

II. The International Finance Corporation, International Development Association and Multilateral Investment Guarantee Agency

The objectives of the IBRD include promoting private investment and in particular private foreign investment in member countries.[42] The Articles of Agreement of the Bank, however, require that loans to private enterprises be guaranteed by the government, central bank or comparable agency of the member country in which the project to be financed is located.[43] The Bank soon realized that private enterprises would for this reason often be reluctant to seek Bank financing, and that governments could be equally hesitant to provide the necessary guarantees.[44] In light of this, the Bank sponsored the establishment in 1956 of the International Finance Corporation (IFC) as an affiliate of the Bank. The IFC lends to private enterprises in developing member countries without a government guarantee and makes equity investments in such enterprises. It has some US$2.6 billion in authorized capital[45] and, like the IBRD, raises funds by borrowing in the capital markets.

Both the IBRD and the IFC lend to creditworthy borrowers at nonconcessional rates. The International Development Association (IDA) was established as another affiliate of the Bank in 1960 to provide concessional finance for poorer member countries. IDA makes long-term, interest-free loans to such countries for development projects and programs. It does not have a share capital, depending instead on voluntary contributions of high-income member countries. They meet every three years to replenish IDA funds. The 2013 replenishment totaled US$52.1 billion.[46]

In pursuance of its objective of promoting private foreign investment, the Bank sponsored the establishment in 1988 of a third financial affiliate, the Multilateral Investment Guarantee Agency (MIGA). It encourages foreign investment in developing member countries by providing investors in such countries with guarantees against such noncommercial risks as war, civil disturbance and expropriation.[47] MIGA's subscribed and paid-in capital are some US$1.9 billion and US$366 million, respectively.[48]

Although the term is applied to them above, with some historical justification,[49] the IFC, IDA and MIGA are not "affiliates" or subsidiaries of the Bank in the sense of being owned by the parent organization. Each is a distinct international organization with its own constituent treaty, membership and assets.[50] At June 30, 2015, the IFC

[42] *See* Articles of Agreement of the IBRD (n. 5) Art. I(ii).

[43] *See* ibid. Art. III(4)(i).

[44] *See, e.g.*, IBRD 1951/1952 Ann. Rep. 12.

[45] *See* IFC, Management's Discussion and Analysis and Consolidated Financial Statements June 30, 2015 at 16.

[46] *See* World Bank Press Release, December 17, 2013.

[47] As a further activity, MIGA "actively pursues the resolution of [investment] disputes affecting MIGA-supported projects." MIGA, Management's Discussion and Analysis and Consolidated Financial Statements June 30, 2015 at 3.

[48] *See* ibid. 8.

[49] At their inception, the IFC and IDA were each referred to as being set up as "an affiliate of the Bank." *See* Explanatory Memorandum [of the World Bank Executive Directors] on the Proposed Articles of Agreement of the International Finance Corporation (Approved April 11, 1955) sec. 8; Report of the Executive Directors on the Articles of Agreement of the International Development Associations (Approved January 26, 1960), para. 20.

[50] *See* Articles of Agreement of the International Finance Corporation, May 25, 1955, 264 UNTS 117 (Articles of Agreement of the IFC); Articles of Agreement of the International Development Association, January 26, 1960, 439 UNTS 249 (Articles of Agreement of IDA); Convention Establishing the Multilateral Investment Guarantee Agency, October 11, 1985, 1508 UNTS 99 (Convention Establishing MIGA).

had 184 member countries, IDA had 170 and MIGA 181. Members are the shareholders of the IFC and MIGA; and although the IBRD contributes to the resources of IDA, the main contributors are, as indicated above, member countries. The IFC, IDA and MIGA have the same tripartite organizational structure as the IBRD, consisting of a plenary Board of Governors (Council of Governors, in the case of MIGA), a smaller Board of Directors and President and staff.[51] As in the IBRD, voting power of the members of the IFC, IDA and MIGA is weighted according to their financial participation in the respective organization.[52] Under their constituent treaties, the IFC, IDA and MIGA have privileges and immunities fashioned after those of the Bank.[53] The IFC and IDA (but not MIGA) are specialized agencies with their own relationship agreements with the United Nations.[54]

The IFC, IDA and MIGA are nevertheless closely connected with the IBRD. The texts of their constituent treaties—the IFC and IDA Articles of Agreement and MIGA Convention—were formulated by the IBRD, more precisely by its Executive Directors, acting in each instance at the request of the Board of Governors of the IBRD. Membership in the IBRD is a prerequisite for IFC, IDA and MIGA membership.[55] The principal offices of the IFC, IDA and MIGA are required to be at, or in the same place as, the principal office of the IBRD.[56] Governors of the IBRD for IFC and IDA members are ex officio Governors of the IFC and IDA. Executive Directors of the Bank similarly serve ex officio as Directors of the IFC and IDA (so long as the country that appointed them or any country that elected them is an IFC and IDA member).[57] The Governors of MIGA are appointed separately; and MIGA's Directors are likewise separately elected.[58] But the persons chosen to be Governors and Directors of MIGA are for the most part Governors and Executive Directors of the IBRD. The President of the IBRD is also President of the IFC, IDA and MIGA and Chairman of the Boards of Directors of the IFC, IDA and MIGA.[59] IDA does not have separate staff; IBRD

[51] *See* Articles of Agreement of the IFC (n. 50) Art. IV(1); Articles of Agreement of IDA (n. 50) Art. VI(1); Convention Establishing MIGA (n. 50) Art. 30.

[52] *See* Articles of Agreement of the IFC (n. 50) Art. IV(3)(a); Articles of Agreement of IDA (n. 50) Art. VI(3); Convention Establishing MIGA (n. 50) Art. 39(a).

[53] *See* Articles of Agreement of the IFC (n. 50) Art. VI; Articles of Agreement of IDA (n. 50) Art. VIII; Convention Establishing MIGA (n. 50) Ch. VII.

[54] *See* Agreement between the United Nations and the International Bank for Reconstruction and Development (Acting for and on Behalf of the International Finance Corporation) on Relationship between the United Nations and the International Finance Corporation, approved by the Boards of Governors of the IBRD and the IFC on January 31, 1957 and the U.N. General Assembly on February 20, 1957; Agreement between the United Nations and the International Development Association, approved by the Board of Governors of IDA on February 24, 1961 and the U.N. General Assembly on March 27, 1961.

[55] *See* Articles of Agreement of the IFC (n. 50) Art. II(1); Articles of Agreement of IDA (n. 50) Art. II(1); Convention Establishing MIGA (n. 50) Art. 4(a). In the latter provision, membership in MIGA was also made open to Switzerland, which joined the Bank only in 1992, four years after the establishment of MIGA.

[56] *See* Articles of Agreement of the IFC (n. 50) Art. IV(8); Articles of Agreement of IDA (n. 50) Art. VI(8); Convention Establishing MIGA (n. 50) Art. 36(a). Of these, only the provision of the Convention Establishing MIGA specifically refers to the principal office being located "in Washington, D.C." while also providing for the possibility of the principal office of the Agency being moved by decision of the Council of Governors.

[57] *See* Articles of Agreement of the IFC (n. 50) Art. IV(2)(b) and IV(4)(b); Articles of Agreement of IDA (n. 50) Art. VI(2)(b) and VI(4)(b).

[58] *See* Convention Establishing MIGA (n. 50) Arts. 31(b) and 32(b).

[59] The Articles of Agreement of IDA ((n. 50) Art. VI(5)(a)) provide that the President of the IBRD shall be ex officio the President of IDA. The Articles of Agreement of the IFC ((n. 50) Art. IV(5)(b)) and the Convention Establishing MIGA ((n. 50) Art. 33(b)) allow for the selection of separate Presidents of those organizations. The IFC initially had a separate President (in the period 1956–1961),

staff are instead appointed to serve concurrently as staff of IDA.[60] The IFC and MIGA have distinct staff and administrative budgets; IFC staff comprise some 3,600 persons and MIGA staff about 120. IBRD and IDA, IFC and MIGA personnel are nevertheless all subject to the same staff rules, procedures for staff grievances and staff pension arrangements. The IFC and MIGA also benefit from certain services, for example corporate secretariat services, of the IBRD and IDA.

III. The International Centre for Settlement of Investment Disputes

As explained in detail in Chapter 2, the IBRD from its earliest days asserted an interest in the resolution of disputes between members and foreign investors. On a number of occasions, the Bank or its President took an active role in promoting the settlement of such disputes. The experience helped to convince the Bank that there was a need for international conciliation and arbitration facilities and procedures to address this kind of case. In 1964, the Board of Governors of the IBRD took the step of requesting the Executive Directors to formulate a convention establishing the needed facilities and procedures, and to submit the text of the convention to member governments with such recommendations as the Executive Directors deemed appropriate.[61] As mentioned at the outset of this chapter, the Executive Directors completed this work in March of 1965, submitting the text of the Convention on the Settlement of Investment Disputes between States and Nationals of Other States (the Convention or ICSID Convention)[62] to member governments for consideration with a view to signature and notification. With the entry into force of the Convention the following year, ICSID was established; but in its first ten years, the Centre received only a handful of cases, all arbitrations.

The type of dispute covered by the Convention is limited in several respects.[63] It must be a legal dispute arising directly out of an investment. The dispute must be between a Contracting State—a country that has become a party to the Convention by signing and ratifying it—or a designated constituent subdivision or agency of the State on the one hand and a national of another Contracting State on the other hand. Lastly, the Convention procedures being available on a voluntary basis, the parties must have consented in writing to submit the dispute to the Centre. The dearth of cases in ICSID's initial years prompted the creation of the Additional Facility in 1978. It is governed by Additional Facility Rules authorizing the Secretariat of the Centre to administer certain categories of proceedings between States and foreign nationals that fall outside the scope of the ICSID Convention. These include conciliation and arbitration proceedings for the settlement of legal disputes that would not be covered by the Convention because either the State party to the dispute or the foreign national's home State is not a Contracting State, or because the dispute does not arise directly

but the President of the IBRD has since been selected to serve as President of the IFC as well. The President of the IBRD has always been selected to serve as President of MIGA.

[60] *See* Articles of Agreement of IDA (n. 50) Art. VI(5)(b).

[61] *See* Resolution No. 214 of the Board of Governors of the IBRD, September 10, 1964, reprinted in 2 *History of the ICSID Convention* 608 (2006).

[62] Convention on the Settlement of Investment Disputes between States and Nationals of Other States, March 18, 1965, 575 UNTS 159 (ICSID Convention), reprinted at App. IV.

[63] The limitations described in the next three sentences of the text are set out in Art. 25(1) of the ICSID Convention.

out of an investment, provided that at least one of the parties is a Contracting State or a national of such a State.[64]

With the introduction of the Additional Facility, a wider spectrum of proceedings could be handled by the Centre. But the caseload of ICSID remained light for the next two decades. The situation changed in the second half of the 1990s, with a large influx of new cases brought to the Centre under the dispute settlement provisions of a rapidly expanding network of investment promotion and protection treaties. There has since continued to be strong growth in the caseload.

Like the IFC, IDA and MIGA, ICSID is a distinct international organization. Its constituent Convention endows it with "full international legal personality" and privileges and immunities comparable to those of the other organizations.[65] The Convention gives ICSID a simpler organizational structure, however, consisting only of an Administrative Council and a Secretariat. The Administrative Council is composed of one Representative of each Convention Contracting State.[66] The Council meets annually.[67] It approves the administrative budget and annual report of the Centre.[68] The Council also elects the Secretary-General and any Deputy Secretary-General, each of whom serves for renewable terms of up to six years.[69] The Secretary-General heads the Secretariat; at present, it has some 55 staff. They carry out the day-to-day work of the Centre on the proceedings, which includes the provision of administrative support services to the conciliation commissions and arbitral tribunals that are constituted for each dispute.

But ICSID is with good reason counted as one of the "affiliated institutions" that are referred to collectively as the World Bank Group. Membership in the IBRD entitles a country to become an ICSID Convention Contracting State.[70] The seat of the Centre is at the principal office of the Bank.[71] The Representatives of ICSID Convention Contracting States on the Administrative Council of ICSID are generally their Governors of the IBRD.[72] The President of the Bank is ex officio the Chairman of the Administrative Council.[73] Under arrangements concluded in 1967, the administrative budget of ICSID is supported by the Bank and the Secretary-General and staff of ICSID are World Bank staff provided to the Centre.[74]

ICSID nevertheless stands apart from the other institutions of the World Bank Group. It is the only non-financial institution among them. ICSID departs in several respects from the organizational pattern of the other institutions. It lacks a share capital and a weighted voting system. There are no intermediate Executive Directors between the plenary organ, the Administrative Council and the Secretariat. The President of the Bank does not also serve as the chief executive of the Centre, a role given to a separate

[64] *See* Doc. ICSID/11, ICSID Additional Facility Rules (April 2006), Art. 2.

[65] *See* ICSID Convention (n. 62) Arts. 18–24. It may be noted, however, that under the ICSID Convention (Art. 20), the Centre enjoys immunity from all legal process whereas there is a waiver of immunity from legal process in the constituent agreements of the other World Bank Group institutions. *See* Articles of Agreement of the IBRD (n. 5) Art. VII(3); Articles of Agreement of the IFC (n. 50) Art. VI(3); Articles of Agreement of IDA (n. 50) Art. VIII(3); Convention Establishing MIGA (n. 50) Art. 44. The waiver is needed to enable the institutions to borrow in capital markets. *See* I.F.I. Shihata, *MIGA and Foreign Investment* 280 (1988).

[66] *See* ICSID Convention (n. 62) Art. 4. [67] *See* ibid. Art. 7(1).

[68] *See* ibid. Art. 6(1)(f) and 6(1)(g). [69] *See* ibid. Art. 10(1).

[70] *See* ibid. Art. 67. [71] *See* ibid. Art. 2. [72] *See* ibid. Art. 4(2).

[73] *See* ibid. Art. 5.

[74] *See* Memorandum of Administrative Arrangements Agreed between the International Bank for Reconstruction and Development and the International Centre for Settlement of Investment Disputes, February 13, 1967, reprinted in ICSID First Ann. Rep. 1966/1967, 16.

Secretary-General. Like MIGA, but unlike the IBRD, the IFC and IDA, ICSID is not a specialized agency of the United Nations.[75] Moreover, important links between ICSID and the Bank have lately been loosened. The position of the Secretary-General of the Centre is no longer combined, as it was for many years, with the position of General Counsel of the Bank. Increased revenues from the cases have also enabled ICSID, once wholly dependent on the Bank for its administrative budget, to achieve a large measure of financial self-sufficiency. With its ever-increasing caseload and associated responsibilities, further organizational changes at ICSID may be inevitable.

[75] Article 57 of the Charter of the United Nations describes specialized agencies eligible to be brought into relationship with the U.N. as those "having wide international responsibilities, as defined in their basic instruments, in economic, social, cultural, educational, health, and related fields." According to Aron Broches, it was decided after the entry into force of the ICSID Convention that the Centre would not propose a relationship agreement with the U.N. as ICSID "clearly did not meet the description" of a specialized agency in Art. 57 of the U.N. Charter. A. Broches, On the Finality of Awards: A Reply to Michael Reisman, 8 ICSID Rev.—FILJ 92, 99–100 (1993).

2

Origins of the Convention

The history of the ICSID Convention has many strands, some extending back over a century. Important influences include, for example, the Conventions for the Pacific Settlement of International Disputes of 1899 and 1907.[1] This chapter is, however, concerned with the immediate origins of the ICSID Convention. The focus is on the period 1955 to 1962.

During those years, poorer developing countries were coalescing into what had just been baptized "the Third World."[2] The retreat of colonialism, condemned by the Bandung Conference of 1955 as "an evil which should speedily be brought to an end,"[3] quickly increased the number of these countries. Decolonization was hastened by the debacle for Britain and France of their failed invasion of the Suez area in 1956.[4] Between 1957 and 1962, 30 newly independent countries joined the United Nations. By the early 1960s, almost all of them had joined the IBRD too, increasing by about 50 percent the number of its developing country members. The period also saw an intensification of the Cold War rivalry between the East and West, culminating in the Cuban missile crisis of 1962. Economic development of the developing countries became an important objective in this rivalry.[5]

Against this background, many new bilateral and multilateral programs and organizations were established in the second half of the 1950s and early 1960s to provide development assistance to developing countries. Thus, in this period, the United States strengthened its assistance program; Canada's aid agency was established; Japan created an overseas cooperation fund; and, in Europe, bilateral organizations were set up by Belgium, Denmark, France, Germany, Norway and Switzerland.[6]

At the multilateral level, the European Investment Bank, and its developing country facility the European Investment Fund, were established in 1958.[7] The Inter-American Development Bank came into being the following year.[8] And, as mentioned in Chapter 1, the World Bank Group's private sector financing facility, the IFC, was established in 1956 and its concessional assistance agency, IDA, in 1960.[9] Also in 1960, the Organisation for European Economic Co-operation (OEEC) was transformed into

[1] Reprinted in Permanent Court of Arbitration, Basic Documents 1 and 17 (2005).

[2] D. Kapur and others, *The World Bank: Its First Half Century* 97 (1997). The expression was said to have been coined in a 1952 article by French economist and demographer Alfred Sauvy. *See* ibid. (note 41).

[3] Asian-African Conference, Bandung, April 18–24, 1955, Final Communiqué, sec. D(1)(a). For first-hand impressions of the historic event, *see* Richard Wright's *The Color Curtain: A Report on the Bandung Conference* (1956).

[4] The Suez affair is outlined at n. 88.

[5] This was vividly expressed by the statement of U.S. Secretary of State John Foster Dulles in 1956 that "East and West are in a contest in the field of development of the undeveloped countries.... Defeat ... could be as disastrous as defeat in the arms race." Kapur and others (n. 2) 136 (quoting a citation in W. LaFeber, *America, Russia, and the Cold War, 1945–1992* at 177 (1993)).

[6] For details, *see* Kapur and others (n. 2) 151–152.

[7] Ibid. 152.

[8] The two other main regional development banks, the African Development Bank and the Asian Development Bank, were established soon thereafter, in 1964 and 1966, respectively.

[9] *See* Ch. 1, section II.

the Organisation for Economic Co-operation and Development (OECD) with what became, in 1961, the OECD's aid-coordinating Development Assistance Committee.[10]

Heeding a call of U.S. President John F. Kennedy, the U.N. General Assembly resolved, at the end of 1961, to designate the 1960s as the United Nations Development Decade, in which States would intensify their support for attaining substantial increases in growth rates of developing countries.[11] By then, levels of official development assistance, after rising substantially in the late 1950s, had begun to stagnate and remained inadequate to meet the needs of developing countries for external finance. It was hoped that private foreign investment would become an increasingly important source of funds. Developing countries, however, still attracted only a relatively small proportion of world investment flows.[12] Then as now, factors limiting investment in these countries were "of diverse character, economic, legal, social, and psychological ... follow[ing] no fixed hierarchy of importance and ... largely cumulative in their effects."[13] Perceptions of political or non-commercial risks were, however, identified as a major deterrent to increased investments in developing countries.[14] While the expropriation risk was frequently highlighted in this context, apprehensions extended in a broader sense to all government measures that might tend to impair the rights or assets of foreign investors.[15] Several multilateral approaches to this problem were proposed in the late 1950s.

I. Proposed multilateral approaches to the promotion of private foreign investment

A. Investment insurance

One proposed approach to the promotion of private foreign investment involved offering foreign investors insurance against non-commercial risks. By the late 1950s, three industrial countries—the Federal Republic of Germany, Japan and the United States—had programs making such insurance available to their foreign investors.[16] It seemed doubtful, however, that many more countries would have the resources to introduce similar national investment insurance or guarantee schemes in the near future. Suggestions were therefore made for the establishment of multilateral investment guarantee schemes. In 1957, a study group of the Council of Europe's Consultative Assembly proposed the creation of such a scheme to cover European investments in Africa.[17] The following year, the Inter-Parliamentary Union suggested that an international guarantee fund for private foreign investment be set up under the auspices of the United Nations.[18] Other similar proposals included one put forward in 1960 by the Association for the Promotion and Protection of Private Foreign Investment.[19]

[10] Kapur and others (n. 2) 152.

[11] *See* G.A. Resolution 1710 (XVI), United Nations Development Decade, December 19, 1961.

[12] Less than 40% of world flows, according to Argyrios Fatouros, writing in 1962. A.A. Fatouros, *Government Guarantees to Foreign Investors* 26 (1962).

[13] Ibid. 30.

[14] *See, e.g.*, The Promotion of the International Flow of Private Capital: Progress Report by the Secretary-General, United Nations Economic and Social Council, E/3325, 8 (February 26, 1960) (U.N. 1960 Report).

[15] Ibid. 63 (citing as examples "discriminatory tax demands, denial of import licenses or foreign exchange" as well as direct measures such as expropriations).

[16] Ibid. 66. [17] I.F.I. Shihata, *MIGA and Foreign Investment* 31 (1988).

[18] U.N. 1960 Report (n. 14) 69.

[19] For details on this association, *see* section I(B) of this chapter.

B. A code of conduct

A second proposed approach was to elaborate an international "code of conduct" for host governments in their treatment of foreign investments. Supporting the idea was the private German Society for the Protection of Foreign Investments, founded and led by Hermann J. Abs, the Spokesman of the Board of Managing Directors of Deutsche Bank. In 1957, this society called for the adoption of a convention that would be an "International Magna Carta" for the protection of private investment abroad.[20] Early in 1958, another proposal for a convention on the protection of foreign investment was made by a group of European lawyers working under the chairmanship of former British Attorney-General Hartley Shawcross.[21] Also in 1958, the idea was taken up by Tunku Abdul Rahman, Prime Minister of Malaya. In a speech before the United Nations Commission for Asia and the Far East, he suggested that it would be a "powerful incentive" to the investment of private capital in Asia if countries in the region were to draw up an "international charter to regulate the treatment of that capital."[22]

Shawcross praised Abdul Rahman's speech as "most significant" and as "giv[ing] added impetus" to the earlier initiative of "the celebrated German banker Herman [*sic*] Abs."[23] It was, Shawcross wrote, "shortly after this speech that I met Herman Abs, for the first time and we became good friends."[24] The two combined forces to produce a joint draft convention on investments abroad. Abs and Shawcross presented the draft to the Association for the Promotion and Protection of Private Foreign Investment, an international study group they helped to establish at the end of 1958. The Association adopted the draft in 1959 "as a basis on which to attract discussion of what it might be practicable to achieve."[25]

The Abs–Shawcross Draft Convention, as it came to be known, envisaged that each party would accord fair and equitable treatment to the property of nationals of the other parties; that the property would be given the most constant protection and security and that its management, use and enjoyment would not be impaired by unreasonable or discriminatory measures; that each party would ensure the observance of any undertakings it had given in relation to investments made by nationals of any other party; and that no party would take any measures against nationals of another party to deprive them directly or indirectly of their property except under due process of law, and provided that such measures were not discriminatory or contrary to undertakings given by that party and were accompanied by the payment of just and effective compensation.[26] The draft presented itself as a "restatement" of such "principles of conduct," meaning that it was intended to reflect rules of customary international law regarding the treatment of aliens.[27] The drafters also acknowledged their debt to

[20] The interest of Abs in the topic was related to his experience as head of the delegation of Germany in negotiations between 1951 and 1953 to settle the country's post-war debts, which Abs had sought to have offset by expropriated German foreign assets. *See* M. Pohl, *Hermann J. Abs: A Biography in Text and Pictures* 76–92 (1983). *See also* R. Dolzer and C. Scheuer, *Principles of International Investment Law* 18 (2008).

[21] Fatouros (n. 12) 81. In his memoirs, Shawcross explained that he developed an interest in the position of industrial country investments in developing countries as a result of his involvement from 1956 to 1965, first as a legal adviser and then as director, with Royal Dutch Shell. H. Shawcross, *Life Sentence: The Memoirs of Lord Shawcross* 306 (1995).

[22] U.N. 1960 Report (n. 14) 72. Abdul Rahman was the first Prime Minister of independent Malaya from 1957 to 1963 and of the federation of Malaysia from 1963 to 1970.

[23] Shawcross (n. 21) 307. [24] Ibid. [25] Ibid. 308.

[26] Draft Convention on Investments Abroad, April 1959, 9 J. Public Law 115 (1960) Arts. I–III (Abs–Shawcross Draft Convention).

[27] Ibid. second preambular para. and Comment on the Draft Convention by its Authors, 9 J. Public Law 119 (1960) sec. I.

provisions of the friendship, commerce and navigation treaties concluded by some industrial countries, notably the United States.[28]

Procedures for the arbitral settlement of disputes were set out in an annex to the Abs–Shawcross Draft Convention. In accordance with these procedures, there would be constituted for each dispute an arbitral tribunal consisting of three arbitrators, one appointed by each party, and the third, referred to in the draft as the umpire, appointed by agreement of the parties.[29] The award of the tribunal, which could be rendered by default, would be final and binding on the parties, each of which would be obligated to abide by and comply with the award.[30] The procedures were to be available for the resolution of disputes between the States parties as to the interpretation or application of the convention.[31] The draft provided that the prior consent of the disputing States, whether in "the form of specific agreements or unilateral declarations," would be necessary for any recourse by them to the arbitration procedures.[32] In the absence of such consent or any other agreement between the parties on the means of settlement, the dispute could be submitted by either party to the International Court of Justice (ICJ).[33]

Importantly, the draft provided that a national of a party claiming that it had been injured by measures in breach of the convention might also have access to the arbitration procedures of the annex to bring a claim against the party responsible for the measures concerned.[34] The draft contemplated that parties willing to permit such claims to be brought directly against them by nationals of other parties would make a general declaration to that effect.[35] This was not presented by the drafters as greatly innovative. It was not, they explained, a new idea that an individual might have a right of access directly to an international tribunal:

> Procedural capacity of this character was enjoyed by individuals in relation to the Central American Court of Justice and certain mixed arbitral tribunals, and is enjoyed by them today in relation to such diverse bodies as the Court of the European Community, the European Commission of Human Rights, and the administrative tribunals of the international organizations. It is, therefore, no real departure from legal tradition to suggest that similar rights be conferred on individuals in connection with investment matters.[36]

Following the issuance of the Abs–Shawcross Draft Convention, Germany took the initiative of introducing it into the Organisation for European Economic Co-operation as a proposal for a multilateral treaty that might be adhered to by members

[28] Comment on the Draft Convention by its Authors (n. 27) secs. II and IV. *See also* text accompanying n. 69.

[29] The draft further provided that if the parties could not agree on the umpire, the President of the ICJ, or failing appointment by him, the Secretary-General of the U.N., could be called upon to appoint the umpire. If either party failed to appoint an arbitrator, the umpire would have the responsibility of making the appointment. Abs–Shawcross Draft Convention (n. 26) Annex, para. 1.

[30] Ibid. Annex, para. 6. Most of the arbitration procedures set out in the Annex to the Abs–Shawcross Draft Convention (including the appointing authority arrangements described in n. 29) were drawn from the arbitration provisions of the Loan Regulations (now the General Conditions for Loan and Guarantee Agreements) of the IBRD. *See* Comment on the Draft Convention by its Authors (n. 27) sec. VI. An obvious advantage of those provisions was that they had proven in the context of IBRD Loan and Guarantee Agreements to be acceptable to developing countries.

[31] Abs–Shawcross Draft Convention (n. 26) Art. VII(1). [32] Ibid. [33] Ibid.

[34] Ibid. Art. VII(2). [35] Ibid.

[36] Comment on the Draft Convention by its Authors (n. 27) sec. VI. By "certain mixed arbitral tribunals," the drafters appear to have been referring to the Mixed Arbitral Tribunals set up after the First World War. *See* H. Lauterpacht, 1 *Oppenheim's International Law* 638, note 3 (1955).

and non-members alike. The OEEC, it will be recalled, was transformed in 1960 into the Organisation for Economic Co-operation and Development.

In 1962, the OECD published a revised, and renamed, Draft Convention on the Protection of Foreign Property. This 1962 OECD Draft Convention was published with a statement that the OECD Council had not yet taken a decision on the principle and content of the draft, but was merely making it available to non-member governments "or other interested circles in order to obtain any comments they might make."[37] The substantive provisions of the 1962 OECD Draft Convention were broadly similar to the Abs–Shawcross Draft Convention, though more tightly and elaborately drawn in certain respects.[38] For example, the 1962 OECD Draft Convention, unlike the Abs–Shawcross Draft Convention, specifically provided that the general treatment obligations would not extend to the admission of investments.[39]

There were conspicuous differences in regard to the settlement of disputes. The 1962 OECD Convention omitted any reference to the ICJ, providing only the annexed arbitration procedures for the settlement of disputes between States parties.[40] Controls were also added to the use of those procedures by nationals of a party. Thus, the 1962 OECD Draft Convention would have precluded a national of a party from instituting proceedings against another party if the claimant's home country had itself instituted such proceedings over the same matter, or would do so within a certain time limit.[41] In addition, the 1962 OECD Draft Convention provided that, in the case of proceedings instituted by a national of a party, the tribunal could, on the application of the respondent, order the claimant to give security for costs or dismiss the claim if it appeared to be frivolous or vexatious.[42] In provisions applicable both to proceedings instituted by a party and proceedings instituted by nationals of a party, the 1962 OECD Draft Convention also provided that an arbitral tribunal could permit the intervention in the proceeding by an interested non-disputing party to the convention; consolidate pending proceedings with the agreement of any other tribunal established under the convention; and, provided no party objected, stay the proceedings if other proceedings arising out of the same facts and raising substantially the same issues were pending before any other international tribunal or commission.[43]

C. An arbitral body for investment disputes

Hersch Lauterpacht explained in 1955 that:

> By a universally recognized customary rule of International Law every State holds a right of protection over its citizens abroad … [and] every State is entitled to exercise this right when one of its subjects is wronged in his person or property, either by the State itself on whose territory such person or property is for the time being, or by the officials or the citizens of such State, if it does not interfere for the purpose of making good the wrong done. This right can be exercised in several ways. Thus, a State whose subjects are wronged can insist, through diplomatic channels, upon the wrongdoers being punished according to the law of the land and upon damages, if necessary, being paid to its injured subjects.[44]

[37] Organisation for Economic Co-operation and Development, Draft Convention on the Protection of Foreign Property, 2 ILM 241 (1963) (1962 OECD Draft Convention).

[38] Georg Schwarzenberger, Professor of International Law at University College London, called the 1962 OECD Draft Convention a "toned-down" version of the Abs–Shawcross Draft Convention. *See* G. Schwarzenberger, *Foreign Investments and International Law* 153 (1969).

[39] *See* 1962 OECD Draft Convention (n. 37) Art. 1(b).

[40] Ibid. Art. 7(a).

[41] Ibid. Art. 7(b)(ii).

[42] Ibid. Annex, para. 6(c).

[43] Ibid. Annex, para. 6(b).

[44] Lauterpacht (n. 36) 686–687 (footnotes omitted).

Lauterpacht made it clear, however, that "[a]s far as International Law is concerned, there is no duty incumbent upon a State to exercise its protection over its citizens abroad."[45] Exercise of this right of diplomatic protection could be subject to political or other considerations not directly related to the matter at hand.

A third approach to the problem of the perceived insecurity of private foreign investments was proposed in the late 1950s in light of such drawbacks of the institution of diplomatic protection. This was to set up an international arbitral body to which foreign investors might have access for resolving disputes with their host governments, without having to enlist the support of their home governments to present claims on their behalf.

At the United Nations, steps were being taken to promote arbitration. Foremost among these was the opening for signature, in 1958, of the Convention on the Recognition and Enforcement of Foreign Arbitral Awards.[46] Another development in 1958 was the adoption by the U.N.'s International Law Commission of its Model Rules on Arbitral Procedure.[47] Passed by the General Assembly a few years later, the United Nations Declaration on Permanent Sovereignty Over Natural Resources referred to arbitration as a method that States and other parties concerned could appropriately agree upon for the resolution of expropriation disputes.[48]

There also already existed international commercial arbitration institutions, notably the Court of Arbitration of the International Chamber of Commerce. It was judged, however, that "a separate arbitral body not identified with a commercial approach might be more readily acceptable to the governments of some capital-receiving countries in matters involving the rights and assets of foreign investors."[49] In 1960, the International Bar Association and the International Law Association put forward plans for the creation of a special arbitral body for investment disputes.[50] Also in 1960, the International Bureau of the Permanent Court of Arbitration (PCA) raised the possibility of its offering procedures for the arbitration and conciliation of disputes between States and non-State parties. Two years later, the possibility was realized with the issuance by the PCA of Rules of Arbitration and Conciliation for Settlement of Investment Disputes between Two Parties of Which Only One is a State.[51]

Although the PCA was established by treaty, its above-mentioned rules were not themselves treaty rules, and an undertaking on the part of a State to submit to arbitration under them could only with difficulty be characterized as an international law obligation.[52] A comprehensive treaty framework for the arbitral mechanism could help to ensure that the undertaking to arbitrate would have that irrevocable quality.[53] As

[45] Ibid. 686.

[46] 10 June 1958, 330 UNTS 3. The following year, the United Nations Economic and Social Council adopted a resolution suggesting measures to increase the effective use of arbitration for "international trade and other private law transactions." United Nations ECOSOC Resolution 708 (XXVII), April 17, 1959, E/3262.

[47] Reprinted in 1958 (II) YBILC 82.

[48] *See* G.A. Resolution 1803 (XVII), December 14, 1962, para. 4.

[49] U.N. 1960 Report (n. 14) 80–81.

[50] The Promotion of the International Flow of Private Capital: Further Report by the Secretary-General, United Nations Economic and Social Council, E/3492, 101 (May 18, 1961).

[51] Reprinted in G. Wetter, 5 *The International Arbitral Process: Public and Private* 53 (1979).

[52] The PCA was established by the 1899 and 1907 Conventions for the Pacific Settlement of International Disputes (n. 1) to provide facilities for the arbitration of disputes between States. The rules referred to in the text accompanying n. 51 were adopted under Art. 47 of the 1907 Convention authorizing the PCA Bureau "to place its offices and staff at the disposal of the Contracting Powers for the use of any special Board of Arbitration."

[53] The importance of this consideration was illustrated for many at the time by Iran's argument that it was not obligated to submit to arbitration under the arbitration provisions of its concession

explained above, the Abs–Shawcross and OECD Draft Conventions included provisions for such an arbitral mechanism. Some considered that an independent investment arbitration treaty would, however, be a better alternative, "at least as an intermediary solution,"[54] given the difficulty of reaching agreement on a broader "code of conduct." Shawcross himself repeatedly highlighted the need in this field for "some international arbitral tribunal ... to which private nationals might have recourse in direct proceedings against states."[55]

A report issued by the United Nations in early 1960 pointed out that an independent arbitration treaty might in fact provide broader protection than an investment charter; the arbitration treaty might be made to cover all investment disputes, while the protection of the investment charter would normally be limited to the rules that the parties had agreed to include in the charter.[56] The report foresaw that if an arbitration agency set up under such treaty "were able to achieve a wide practice and prestige, it might in time become the natural fulcrum for the conclusion of bilateral, and possibly multilateral, agreements between governments on private foreign investment."[57] Another possibility was that a "code of conduct" might in effect eventually be created by the accumulation of decisions issued by tribunals constituted under the auspices of such an agency.[58]

II. The World Bank considers the proposals

A. The Bank's work on an IIIA

In 1961, the Development Assistance Committee (DAC) of the OECD asked the World Bank to undertake a study of possible multilateral investment guarantee schemes.[59] Approaching the task with careful neutrality,[60] the Bank completed its study in early 1962 and transmitted it to the DAC. The report reviewed the schemes proposed to date without expressing a position of the Bank, or recommending the creation of a scheme or discussing what role, if any, the Bank would play in that regard.[61]

agreement with the Anglo-Iranian Oil Company following the repudiation of that agreement by Iran in 1951. *See, e.g.*, S.M. Schwebel and J.G. Wetter, Arbitration and the Exhaustion of Local Remedies, 60 AJIL 484, 490–493 (1966).

54 U.N. 1960 Report (n. 14) 79.

55 Shawcross (n. 21) 308. *See also* H. Shawcross, The Problems of Foreign Investment in International Law, 102 Recueil des Cours 339 (1961).

56 U.N. 1960 Report (n. 14) 79.

57 Ibid. 81.

58 *Cf.* The Promotion of the International Flow of Private Capital: Third Report by the Secretary-General, United Nations Economic and Social Council, 3/3665/Rev.1, 44 (July 23, 1962). This report recalled (at 44, note 1) that the possibility had been raised of setting up the arbitration agency within the framework of the U.N. In a presentation at the American Society of International Law annual meeting in 1965, Aron Broches explained that, in the U.N. context, such initiatives "never reached the take-off point because of political opposition ... [especially from] countries of the Eastern bloc." Broches *Selected Essays* 79, 81.

59 Shihata (n. 17) 33.

60 In announcing at the 1961 Annual Meeting of the IBRD Board of Governors that the Bank would be carrying out the study, the President of the Bank made it clear that the Bank was doing so without any "preconceived ideas about ... [the] usefulness or feasibility" of the various multilateral investment guarantee proposals. World Bank, 1961 Board of Governors Annual Meetings IBRD–IDA–IFC Proceedings, 8.

61 Shihata (n. 17) 33. Some in the Bank had reservations as to a possible role for the institution in this area, arguing that it should not be put in a position where it was both an insurer of investments by others in a country and a lender to that country. World Bank Oral History Program, Transcript of Interview of Aron Broches, May 23, 1984, 29 (Broches Interview). For biographical information regarding Broches, *see* n. 94.

The matter was, however, brought back to the IBRD in 1964 by the first United Nations Conference on Trade and Development (UNCTAD), which recommended that the Bank "expedite its studies on investment insurance in consultation with governments in both developing and developed countries."[62] There followed in 1965 a proposal of the OECD that the Bank work toward the establishment of an investment guarantee organization along the lines indicated in a report prepared at the OECD.[63] In response, the Bank commenced work on a charter of an International Investment Insurance Agency (IIIA). Successive drafts were prepared and discussed with the Executive Directors of the Bank and member countries. Disagreements surfaced over such important issues as loss-sharing and subrogation. Eventually, with broad support for the IIIA seemingly gone, the Bank ceased work on it in 1973. A multilateral investment guarantee scheme was established the following year, but only on a regional basis, for inter-Arab investments.[64] The creation under World Bank auspices of a globally operating scheme had to await the establishment of MIGA in 1988.[65]

B. The proposed code of conduct

After its 1962 Draft Convention on the Protection of Foreign Property had been published, the OECD also asked the IBRD if it would take over the project for developing such a code of conduct. The Bank declined to do so, believing that it could not bridge the divide between industrial and developing countries in this contentious area and still produce a meaningful document.[66] The OECD worked further on the draft in the following years, finally reissuing it in 1967, with a few more modifications and the endorsement of the OECD Council.[67] Although this 1967 OECD Draft Convention was approved for publication, it lacked enough support among members to progress beyond the draft stage. In its resolution on the draft, the OECD Council reaffirmed that members nonetheless adhered "to the principles of international law embodied in the Draft Convention" and commended it "as a basis for further extending and rendering more effective the application of these principles."[68]

[62] Shihata (n. 17) 35. [63] Ibid. 34.

[64] For a discussion of the constituent convention of the agency Inter-Arab Investment Guarantee Corporation, *see* I.F.I. Shihata, Arab Investment Guarantee Corporation—A Regional Investment Guarantee Corporation, 6 J. World Trade Law 185 (1972).

[65] Resumption of World Bank efforts to set up a multilateral investment insurance agency was suggested in 1981 to the then new President of the Bank, A.W. Clausen, by the Bank's Vice President and General Counsel at the time, Heribert Golsong. Later that year, Clausen commended the idea to members in his first address to the Board of Governors of the Bank. From 1983, the work on what became MIGA was led by Golsong's successor, Ibrahim F.I. Shihata, who was also closely involved with the creation of the Inter-Arab Investment Guarantee Corporation (n. 64 and accompanying text). Shihata was Vice President and General Counsel of the World Bank from 1983 to 1998 (with the rank of Senior Vice President from 1994) and Secretary-General of ICSID from 1983 to 2000. His work on the establishment of the Inter-Arab Investment Guarantee Corporation was undertaken when he was serving, from 1972 to 1976, as Legal Adviser at the Kuwait Fund for Arab Economic Development.

[66] *Cf.* Broches Interview (n. 61) 30. As Schwarzenberger tartly put it, the IBRD was "not prepared to touch" the project. Schwarzenberger (n. 38) 153.

[67] Draft Convention on the Protection of Foreign Property and Resolution of the Council of the OECD on the Draft Convention, October 12, 1967 (OECD Publication 1967) (1967 OECD Draft Convention and OECD Council Resolution). The modifications of the 1967 draft included the omission of a requirement in the 1962 draft article on expropriation (Art. 3 in both drafts) that the expropriating measure not be "contrary to any undertaking" of the expropriating party.

[68] OECD Council Resolution (n. 67) paras. I and II.

During the 1950s, the United States entered into 17 friendship, commerce and navigation treaties (FCNs). These more recent FCNs dealt chiefly with investment problems—so much so that they were also called bilateral investment treaties by some contemporary observers.[69] Bilateral investment treaties (BITs) proper then started to be made, principally by Germany, which entered into a dozen such treaties between 1959 and 1962.[70] These treaties typically set out undertakings of each party to guarantee, in respect of investments of nationals of the other party, non-discriminatory treatment, protection and security; just compensation in the event of expropriation, such compensation to be actually realizable, freely transferable and paid without undue delay; and freedom from restrictions on the transfer of capital and returns.[71] Developed in tandem with the Abs–Shawcross Draft Convention and its forerunners, the BITs thus addressed many of the same substantive concerns. The BITs also provided for the arbitral settlement of disputes between the parties as to the interpretation or application of the treaties.[72] They did not, however, separately address the resolution of disputes between a party and nationals of the other party. In the continued absence of a multilateral convention embodying a code of conduct, more industrial countries began to enter into BITs with developing countries after 1962, drawing for their provisions on the earlier FCNs and BITs, on the OECD Draft Conventions and, through them, on the Abs–Shawcross Draft Convention.[73]

C. The dispute settlement approach

Under "general pressure to do something in the field of encouragement of foreign investment"[74] in the late 1950s and early 1960s, the management of the IBRD considered that, of the proposals circulating at the time, the Bank might most productively tackle the dispute settlement approach. It appeared to be the least controversial approach and would not require a large organization or much money.[75] The IBRD also had a longstanding interest in the settlement of disputes between member countries and foreign investors. As far back as 1947, the Bank had identified a need for some sort of international machinery to address such disputes.[76] Moreover, during the 1950s

[69] *See* Fatouros (n. 12) 93–97.

[70] The first of these treaties was concluded by Germany with Pakistan, Treaty for the Promotion and Protection of Investments, Germany–Pakistan, November 25, 1959, reproduced in ICSID, Investment Treaties, Release 92-3 (October 1992) (Germany–Pakistan BIT). In 1961, Switzerland launched a program of bilateral treaties addressing investment protection; most of these treaties, however, dealt only briefly with the matter and also covered trade issues and technical cooperation. *See, e.g.*, Accord de commerce, de protection des investissements et de coopération technique, Switzerland–Congo (Brazzaville), October 18, 1962, reproduced in ICSID, Investment Treaties, Release 92-3 (October 1992).

[71] *See, e.g.*, Germany–Pakistan BIT (n. 70) Arts. 2–4; Treaty Concerning the Promotion and Reciprocal Protection of Investments, Germany–Thailand, December 13, 1961, reproduced in ICSID, Investment Treaties, Release 92-3 (October 1992) (Germany–Thailand BIT). The BITs were closely linked to Germany's investment insurance program, launched in 1959 in parallel with the inauguration of the BIT program. The insurance was only available in respect of investments in countries with which there was such a BIT. In addition to helping to minimize the risks assumed by the insuring party, the BITs also had provisions under which, in the event such a risk nevertheless materialized and the insuring party paid a claim, its resulting subrogation rights would be recognized by the host country party to the BIT. *See, e.g.*, Germany–Pakistan BIT (n. 70) Art. 5; Germany–Thailand BIT, Art. 5.

[72] *See, e.g.*, Germany–Pakistan BIT (n. 70) Art. 11; Germany–Thailand BIT (n. 71) Art. 11.

[73] Proposals for a multilateral code of conduct were again made in the 1990s. These more recent proposals are discussed in Ch. 9, section I.

[74] Broches interview (n. 61) 35. [75] Ibid.

[76] *See* IBRD 1946/1947 Ann. Rep. 13 (raising the possibility of setting up an "impartial body of technical experts" to recommend settlements of investment disputes).

and early 1960s, the Bank had itself become involved in assisting in the settlement of investment disputes. Its role at the time in this area is examined in the next section of this chapter.

III. The role of "Black's Bank" in the settlement of investment disputes

As mentioned in section II, the World Bank had long taken an interest in the settlement of disputes between its member countries and foreign investors. There were several reasons for this. A basic one stemmed from the mandate that the Articles of Agreement of the IBRD gave the Bank to promote private foreign investment in member countries.[77] An unresolved investment dispute could discourage further flows of investment into a country. Moreover, the IBRD had to rely, for the major part of its lendable funds, on borrowings in the capital markets. The Bank soon concluded that its own standing in the markets would be undermined if it were to lend to countries that did not make reasonable efforts to settle debt defaults or expropriation disputes.[78] In addition, it will be remembered that IDA, the Bank's concessional lending affiliate, depended from the start on voluntary contributions of capital-exporting countries; and their willingness to make such contributions could be affected by the record of countries seeking credits from IDA in settling disputes with nationals of donor countries over defaults and expropriations.[79]

The Bank not only had an interest in the settlement of investment disputes; it soon also came to be seen as being well qualified to assist in the resolution of such disputes. The multilateral character of the Bank and its position as a financial intermediary between capital-exporting and capital-importing countries helped to inspire confidence in its impartiality on the part of both foreign investors and their host governments. During the long tenure of Eugene R. Black as President of the Bank, from 1949 to 1962,[80] the Bank embraced a focus on project lending, above all on loans for infrastructure projects. The focus on concrete projects was seen as strengthening the Bank's credit with private lenders and keeping it out of politics to a degree that seemed

[77] *See* Ch. 1, n. 42 and accompanying text.

[78] E.S. Mason and R.E. Asher, *The World Bank Since Bretton Woods* 336–337 (1973). Approval of the very first development loan of the Bank, to Chile, in 1948 was delayed until after the country had agreed to negotiate outstanding foreign debt obligations. Then IBRD Vice President, Robert Garner, explained to Chilean government representatives that the Bank did not see how it could "make loans in the face of widespread dissatisfaction in financial and investment circles to whom the Bank must sell its own bonds" (ibid. 156–157). The present policy of the IBRD in this respect is set out in its Operational Policy 7.40 (Disputes Over Defaults on External Debt, Expropriation and Breach of Contract), July 2001, revised March 2012. It makes clear the importance, to the Bank's response, of the impact that the situation involved has on the creditworthiness of the borrower. The policy provides that the Bank may refrain from extending new loans to a country that is not making reasonable efforts to settle expropriation disputes that are substantially harming the country's international credit standing or external debt disputes that have a significant effect on the country's creditworthiness or on its ability to implement Bank-financed projects or service Bank loans.

[79] This possibility was made explicit in the 1986 version of the World Bank policy on the subject, Operational Manual Statement No. 128 (Disputes Over Defaults on External Debt, Expropriation and Breach of Contract), May 1986.

[80] Black was Executive Director of the Bank for the U.S. from 1947 until he succeeded John J. McCloy as President in 1949. Before joining the IBRD, he was Senior Vice President of Chase National Bank.

more difficult to achieve in the case of balance of payments support lending.[81] In order to be a project specialist, the Bank also had to acquire technical expertise, and did so with extensive recruitment of technical specialists.[82] A "technocrat standing above the political fray,"[83] the Bank was all the more credible as a dispute resolver. Added to this was the fact that the prospect of financing from the Bank might in suitable cases assist with the settlement of a dispute. A further indispensable element was support from the Bank's senior management for this activity. President Black regarded helping in the resolution of economic and financial disputes as an important part of the Bank's service to its membership.[84] Black himself also brought to the role a "knack for bargaining," as well as a reputation for wise judgment and absolute integrity.[85]

During the 1950s and early 1960s, there were several instances of "Black's Bank," as many called it, or the President himself promoting the settlement of a dispute by good offices, mediation or conciliation. One of the first instances began in 1951, after the nationalization by Iran of its oil industry and termination of the concession there of the largely British-owned Anglo-Iranian Oil Company. The Bank suggested to Iranian and British authorities that it might act as trustee for resumed oil operations in Iran during an interim period in which the parties could negotiate a permanent settlement.[86] Consultations of the Bank with the parties continued until early 1952. The discussions with the parties at a stalemate, the Bank then called a halt to its efforts to foster a settlement. One observer considered that those efforts were nevertheless useful, in maintaining contacts "at a time when the chief parties were no longer on speaking terms with each other" and in obtaining and checking information "which proved invaluable to all concerned in the subsequent phase of the dispute," leading to a settlement after the overthrow of Iranian Prime Minister Mohammad Mosaddeq in 1953.[87]

In 1956, after the withdrawal of American and British offers to assist in financing the Aswan High Dam project, Egypt nationalized the Suez Canal Company.[88] The Bank and its President were prominently involved in helping to settle the claims for compensation of the mainly French and British shareholders of the company. President Black accepted an invitation to lend the good offices of the IBRD to negotiations between the Egyptian government and the shareholders, which took place in the first half of 1958 and resulted in a settlement.[89] As part of the settlement, the Bank undertook to

[81] Kapur and others (n. 2) 8. The apolitical character of the IBRD was mandated by its Articles of Agreement, which prohibited the Bank and its officers from interfering in the political affairs of any member or from being influenced in their decisions by the political character of the member or members concerned. Articles of Agreement of the IBRD, December 27, 1945, 2 UNTS 134, Art. IV(10).

[82] Kapur and others (n. 2) 8. [83] Ibid.

[84] J. Kraske and others, *Bankers With a Mission: The Presidents of the World Bank, 1946–91* at 96 (1996).

[85] Ibid. 94.

[86] Mason and Asher (n. 78) 598. The IBRD further proposed that it would designate a person or organization to operate the company's nationalized oil fields and refinery; find the funds necessary to bring those properties back into operation; and put into escrow part of the proceeds of oil sales pending their distribution under the terms of a final settlement (ibid.).

[87] Schwarzenberger (n. 38) 82.

[88] The nationalization was announced by Egyptian President Gamal Abdel Nasser in July 1956. In October, after a series of border incidents, Israeli forces crossed into Egypt. British and French troops invaded the Suez area in November, ostensibly to protect the canal, only to have to leave the next month under U.S. pressure. Israel pulled its own troops out of Egypt in March 1957. The failure of the Suez expedition demonstrated that Britain could no longer maintain a global colonial presence; within a decade, it had lost 18 colonies. Mason and Asher (n. 78) 641; T. Judt, *Postwar: A History of Europe Since 1945* at 296–298 (2006).

[89] Black was represented in the negotiations by William A.B. Iliff, Vice President of the Bank. Helping Iliff in the negotiations was George D. Woods, then Chairman of First Boston Corporation, who succeeded Black as President of the Bank. Black and Iliff also led the Bank's mediation of

Eugene R. Black, President of the World Bank from 1949 to 1962.
World Bank Group Archives

act as fiscal agent for the transfer of the periodic compensation payments to be made by the government.[90] The Bank subsequently agreed to provide financing for improvements of the canal.[91]

Also in 1958, the City of Tokyo and French holders of bonds issued by the city asked the President of the Bank to conciliate their longstanding difference over the payment of principal and interest on the bonds. The President, who was requested by the parties "to draft a concrete and workable plan for settling in a fair and feasible manner the controversy," delivered his plan to them in 1960.[92] While there were other instances of providing good offices, mediation or conciliation in the period, neither the Bank nor its President ever agreed to act as arbitrator, viewing it as inappropriate for them to assume the role of making a binding decision on a dispute. On a number

the dispute between India and Pakistan over the division of the waters of the Indus River system, which resulted in the conclusion in 1960 by India and Pakistan of the Indus Waters Treaty, a success described soon thereafter as a demonstration of the Bank's "unforeseen powers as a peacemaker." J. Morris, *The Road to Huddersfield: A Journey to Five Continents* 219 (1963). Many years later, ICSID was to administer an expert determination proceeding under the dispute-settlement provisions of the treaty. *See* S. Salman and E. Obadia, The Indus Waters Treaty, the Baglihar Difference and ICSID Administration of the Proceedings, 23(2) News from ICSID 1 (2006).

[90] IBRD 1957/1958 Ann. Rep. 6.

[91] Reflecting on the settlement of the compensation claims, Black observed that "the Bank was able to act as a successful channel of negotiations, not because of any feats of personal diplomacy, not because the basic causes of tension were removed, but because the Bank was in working contact with all parties and able to use that position to resolve arguments. While a development institution alone cannot solve fundamental disputes between nations, it can often turn the edge of such disputes by directing the attention and efforts of the nations toward absorption in their own development." E. Black, *The Diplomacy of Economic Development* 48–49 (1960).

[92] World Bank Press Release, City of Tokyo Bonds of 1912, April 4, 1960. The conciliation was undertaken by the President of the Bank "in his personal capacity." Referring to another such case, James (now Jan) Morris quipped that this meant the President was helped "only by one vice-president of the Bank and two heads of departments." Morris (n. 89) 213.

of occasions, however, the Bank or its President agreed to help with the conclusion of arbitration agreements or to act as the appointing authority of arbitrators for differences between governments and foreign private parties.[93]

IV. The Bank begins to work on the initiative

This experience of the Bank helped to convince its management to pursue the dispute settlement approach to the encouragement of foreign investment. Leading the way under the President of the Bank was its General Counsel, Aron Broches.[94] He raised the topic with the Executive Directors of the Bank in a note he sent to them at the end of August 1961.[95] Further elaboration was provided in additional notes to the Executive Directors, one sent by the Bank's President Black in December 1961, and another by Broches in January 1962.[96] The notes together sketched out the rationale for main features of an international agreement that the Bank might help draw up on the settlement of investment disputes. The agreement would establish a center not only for the arbitration of such disputes, but also for their conciliation, given the value that conciliation had been shown to have in the Bank's own experience. The chief justification lay, of course, in the contribution that specific international machinery for the settlement of investment disputes could make to increasing the flow of private capital, "an objective of special concern to the Bank." The prior experience of the Bank in this area had demonstrated both the need and the potentialities of such machinery. The machinery could also relieve the Bank of some of the "extra-curricular burdens" it occasionally assumed to help settle investment disputes and to shift those burdens to the suggested center. The center would, however, retain some continuing link with the Bank to inspire confidence in the institution while taking care not to impair its independence. The center could have a small secretariat, a panel of arbitrators or conciliators and a governing council composed of representatives of governments participating in the center. The Bank might meet the administrative costs of the center, which would in any event be slight, while the disputing parties involved would cover the costs of the proceedings.

Under the projected international agreement, the center would only have jurisdiction over disputes that the parties had agreed to submit to the institution. A State might give its agreement in advance by way of a general declaration or by agreement with a particular investor. The international agreement establishing the center would provide that, once a State had agreed to submit a specific

[93] One such case concerned a dispute between Colombia and the paper mill company Parsons & Whittemore. *See* 2 *History of the ICSID Convention* 7.

[94] Broches was Secretary of the Netherlands delegation both at the Bretton Woods Conference in 1944 that led to the establishment of the IBRD and the IMF and at the inaugural meetings of the Boards of Governors of the IBRD and the IMF at Savannah in 1946. He joined the Legal Department of the IBRD in 1946, becoming its Director 10 years later. Broches was appointed General Counsel of the Bank in 1959 and served in that position (with the rank of Vice President from 1972) until his retirement in 1979. He also was the first Secretary-General of ICSID, holding that position from 1967 to 1980. Following the conclusion of the ICSID Convention in 1965, Broches led the efforts of the Bank on formulating articles of agreement of an International Investment Insurance Agency, from 1966 to 1973 (*see* section II(A) of this chapter). He also represented the Bank in discussions with the OECD in the early 1960s regarding a proposed multilateral code of conduct for the treatment of foreign investment (*see* n. 66 and accompanying text).

[95] The note is reprinted in 2 *History of the ICSID Convention* 1.

[96] These further notes are reproduced in ibid. 4, 6.

dispute or disputes to the center, that agreement would be a binding international obligation. The international agreement would also provide that after jurisdiction had thus been established, the private party might proceed against a State directly before the center, without having to get its home government to espouse the case. Further provisions would prevent frustration of an undertaking to arbitrate by failure of a party to appoint arbitrators or otherwise to cooperate in the proceedings. Substantive rules regarding the treatment of foreign investment would not, however, be included in the international agreement. It would, in the view of the Bank's management, have been unrealistic to try for a more far-reaching agreement. Sticking to the procedural angle as proposed seemed to be relatively uncontroversial and much more likely to succeed.

President Black had informed the Board of Governors of the Bank in September 1961 that he would be exploring, with other institutions and with members, the possibility of promoting the establishment of a special forum for the conciliation and arbitration of disputes between governments and private investors.[97] With the benefit of the notes from Black and Broches, the Executive Directors of the Bank discussed the possibility informally in meetings that took place early in 1962. There were generally favorable reactions to the proposal as outlined in the notes, although many members had yet to give instructions to their Executive Directors. Two speakers emphasized the importance of keeping the proposed center independent of the Bank, one cautioning that "it might in practice have a great deal of business, because many foreign investors would insert a clause in their agreements providing that disputes should be referred to the Center; and many governments might insert similar clauses in their commercial treaties."[98]

The Executive Directors agreed that "the General Counsel should formulate more concrete suggestions, possibly in the form of a draft convention, in order to facilitate further discussion of the question."[99] Thus in June 1962, Broches transmitted to them a Working Paper in the Form of a Draft Convention for the Resolution of Disputes between States and Nationals of Other States.[100] The Working Paper was then sent to member governments for their views. Pending the receipt of comments from members, the Executive Directors requested and received from the Board of Governors of the Bank in September 1962 a formal mandate "to consider the desirability and practicability of establishing institutional facilities, sponsored by the Bank, for the settlement through conciliation and arbitration of investment disputes between governments and private parties."[101]

[97] *See* extract from Black's address to the Annual Meeting of the Board of Governors of the IBRD, Vienna, September 19, 1962, reprinted in 2 *History of the ICSID Convention* 3.

[98] Memorandum of Meeting of Executive Directors, April 10, 1965, reprinted in 2 *History of the ICSID Convention* 13, 2–3 (pages cited are of original document). The quoted remarks were those of Ali Akbar Khosropur, Alternative Executive Director of the Bank for Pakistan, United Arab Republic, Iran, Saudi Arabia, Sudan, Iraq, Jordan, Ethiopia and Sudan. He served as Alternate Director from 1953 to 1966, having previously been Vice Governor of Bank Melli Iran.

[99] Working Paper in the form of a Draft Convention, June 5, 1962, reprinted in 2 *History of the ICSID Convention* 19, introductory note.

[100] The Working Paper is discussed in detail in Ch. 3.

[101] IBRD Board of Governors Resolution No. 174, September 18, 1962, reprinted in 2 *History of the ICSID Convention* 51.

3

Broches's "Working Paper"

This chapter and Chapters 4 and 5 are devoted to the fashioning of the text of the ICSID Convention in the period 1962 to 1965. The organization undertaking the task, the World Bank, differed in some obvious ways from the Bank today. Its membership had increased to 102 countries by 1965. But none of the Soviet bloc countries belonged to the Bank. China was represented in the IBRD by the Taiwan government. Reflecting the smaller membership, there were just 20 Executive Directors of the Bank.[1] At about 40 annually, the number of IBRD lending operations was approximately one-third of the corresponding total for 2015.[2] Lending was mainly for capital infrastructure projects, contrasting with the broader array of loans today for economic reform and social investment purposes as well. With such differences in the scale and variety of activities, it is not surprising that there were far fewer staff: just 1,000 in 1965 as compared with about 12,000 in 2015.

Work on what became the ICSID Convention had hardly begun when Eugene Black was succeeded by George D. Woods as President of the Bank.[3] Woods quickly familiarized himself with the proposal and was soon one of its most ardent proponents. A few months after assuming the presidency of the Bank, he assured the Executive Directors of his support for the "sponsorship by the Bank of machinery for the settlement of investment disputes" created "within the framework of an intergovernmental agreement."[4] In his first address to the Board of Governors of the Bank at its Annual Meeting in September 1963, Woods proclaimed his "enthusiasm for the proposal to establish a conciliation and arbitration center" for international investment disputes; this reflected, he said, his "interest in exploring all possible ways in which the Bank can help to widen and deepen the flow of private capital to the developing countries."[5]

Reference was made at the end of Chapter 2 to the September 1962 resolution of the Board of Governors of the IBRD directing the Executive Directors of the Bank to consider the desirability of the establishment of institutional facilities for the conciliation and arbitration of investment disputes. The same resolution asked the Executive Directors, if they concluded that such action would be advisable, to "draft an agreement providing for such facilities for submission to governments."[6] A resolution adopted by the Board of Governors two years later made it clear that the Executive Directors were

[1] As mentioned in Ch. 1, at June 30, 2015 the near-universal membership of the Bank comprised 188 countries and there were 25 Executive Directors of the IBRD.

[2] The dollar volume of IBRD lending in 1965 was roughly 30% of the level of 2015 in real terms.

[3] Woods served as President of the Bank from the beginning of 1963 to 1968. He was previously Chairman of First Boston Corporation. As mentioned in Ch. 2, n. 89, Woods had in 1958 helped the Bank in the negotiations of the Suez Canal expropriation claims.

[4] Statement by President Regarding Settlement of Investment Disputes, May 6, 1963, reprinted in 2 *History of the ICSID Convention* 85.

[5] Address by the President to the Annual Meeting of the Board of Governors, September 30, 1963, excerpted in 2 *History of the ICSID Convention* 183.

[6] IBRD Board of Governors Resolution No. 174, September 18, 1962, reprinted in 2 *History of the ICSID Convention* 51.

George D. Woods, President of the World Bank from 1963 to 1968.
World Bank Group Archives

to formulate a convention and submit its text to governments as a final step, rather than for further discussion.[7]

The Executive Directors had similarly been entrusted with the formulation of the Articles of Agreement of the IFC and IDA. The Bank might instead have taken the more usual approach of having the texts of such treaties drawn up at international conferences convened for the purpose, the method that was followed for the IBRD's own constituent treaty. At best, however, this would have entailed long delays in completion of the work.[8]

It need hardly be said that formulating such treaties was not among the functions specifically enumerated for the Bank in its Articles of Agreement. But on the advice of Broches, as of other General Counsel of the Bank, the IBRD had long held the position that its powers were not limited to the specific transactions mentioned in the Articles of Agreement; it also had implied powers to undertake any other actions to further its objectives (provided, of course, that the exercise of such powers did not run counter to any provisions of the Articles of Agreement).[9] Drawing up the IFC and IDA Articles of

[7] This second resolution is discussed in the introductory part of Ch. 5.

[8] As in the cases of the constituent treaties of the IFC, IDA and ICSID, the text of the MIGA Convention was finalized, in 1985, by the Executive Directors of the IBRD. The General Counsel of the Bank at the time, Ibrahim Shihata, who led the staff work on the MIGA Convention, took the following unfavorable view of the alternative of an international conference in this context:

> In my experience, [treaty-negotiating conferences] take years to prepare. They group together delegates who rarely know, let alone trust, each other and who are accustomed to lengthy procedures and a confrontational atmosphere. Quite often, participants in such conferences are more concerned with broader, and at times irrelevant, issues of a political character and in some cases pay greater attention to pleasing their respective national audiences rather than to reaching agreement on the subject matter at hand.

I.F.I. Shihata, *MIGA and Foreign Investment* 77 (1988).

[9] The position was expressed as follows by Broches in his 1959 lectures at the Hague Academy of International Law on The International Legal Aspects of the Operations of the World Bank:

> ... the Bank's powers are not limited to those that are granted in express terms. The fact that an operation or transaction is not expressly authorized or contemplated by a specific

Agreement and ICSID Convention and offering them to members was clearly meant to further the Bank's objectives of promoting investment and development.

It might nonetheless have been unacceptable for the Executive Directors to be given responsibility for drawing up a multilateral treaty if in doing so they were to apply the Bank's weighted voting system under which a small number of countries could control decision-making. The Executive Directors had, however, developed the practice of seeking a consensus or balance of views on issues before them.[10] This could be and was done in meetings of committees of the Executive Directors, which took no formal votes and were limited to making recommendations for decisions by the Executive Directors as such.[11] The committee device was used for the Bank's first foray into multilateral treaty drafting, when preliminary discussions on the Articles of Agreement of the IFC were held in the then existing Financial Policy Committee of the Executive Directors.[12]

For their work on what became the ICSID Convention, the Executive Directors convened a committee of the whole comprising all of the Executive Directors. Called the Committee of the Whole on the Settlement of Investment Disputes, it held six initial meetings during the period from December 1962 to June 1963. In these meetings, the Executive Directors discussed the Working Paper in the form of a Draft Convention for the Resolution of Disputes between States and Nationals of Other States. As mentioned at the end of Chapter 2, Broches had submitted this Working Paper to the Executive Directors in June 1962. The following sections of this chapter examine the Working Paper and the discussions of it in the Committee of the Whole.

I. The Working Paper

The Working Paper in the Form of a Draft Convention for the Resolution of Disputes between States and Nationals of Other States (the Working Paper) was dated June 5, 1962.[13] It contained seven draft articles, with explanatory comments, on the proposed

> provision of the Articles, does not mean that the Bank has no power to undertake it. Whether it has or does not have a particular power must be determined in the light of the Bank's purposes, by which all the Bank's decisions must be guided. For a finding that the Bank has such power, the power need not be shown to be necessarily or even reasonably implicit in any power given expressly by the Articles. It is enough that its exercise may further the achievement of the Bank's purposes, and that it is not prohibited by or inconsistent with the Bank's Articles of Agreement.

Broches *Selected Essays* 28. For the similar views of a successor of Broches as IBRD General Counsel, *see* I.F.I. Shihata, *The World Bank Legal Papers* 852–854 (2000). Their stance reflected a broad conception of the doctrine of implied powers of international organizations, under which powers may be implied if they can be hooked up to the purposes of the organization. J. Klabbers, *An Introduction to International Organizations Law* 60 (3d. ed. 2015) (citing the rule formulated by the ICJ in Certain Expenses of the United Nations, 1949 ICJ Rep. 151, 168 that "when the Organization takes action which warrants the assertion that it was appropriate for the fulfillment of one of the stated purposes of the United Nations, the presumption is that action is not *ultra vires* the Organization").

[10] A. Broches, Development of International Law by the International Bank for Reconstruction and Development, reprinted in Broches *Selected Essays* 79, 80.

[11] *See* Articles of Agreement of the IBRD, December 27, 1945, 2 UNTS 134, Art. V(4)(i), authorizing the Executive Directors "to appoint such committees as they deem desirable," and adding that "[m]embership of such committees need not be limited to governors or directors or their alternates."

[12] Shihata (n. 8) 78.

[13] The Working Paper is reprinted in 2 *History of the ICSID Convention* 19 and as App. I of this book.

center and system of conciliation and arbitration.[14] An introductory article defined the purpose of the Convention as being "to promote the resolution of disputes arising between Contracting States and nationals of other Contracting States by encouraging and facilitating recourse to international conciliation and arbitration."[15]

A. Provisions on the establishment and organization of the Center

The Working Paper envisaged the establishment of an "International Conciliation and Arbitration Center" with "full juridical personality."[16] It would have a President, an Administrative Council, a Secretariat, a Panel of Conciliators and a Panel of Arbitrators.

As in the case of IDA, the President of the IBRD would be ex officio President of the Center.[17] He would also be Chairman of the Administrative Council, just as he was Chairman of the Executive Directors of the IBRD, the IFC and IDA, with no vote except a deciding vote in case of an equal division.[18] The Administrative Council could delegate any of its powers to the President except the power to appoint the Secretary-General and Deputy Secretaries-General of the Center.[19] Under the Working Paper, the President could be called upon by a party to complete the constitution of a conciliation commission or arbitral tribunal that was not established by the otherwise applicable method within a certain time limit.[20] He would also have the right to designate persons to serve on the Panels of Conciliators and of Arbitrators.[21]

The Administrative Council was to be the "principal organ"[22] of the Center. In addition to being responsible for the adoption of rules and regulations for the Center and for the appointment of its Secretary-General and Deputy Secretary-General, the Administrative Council would exercise "such other powers as may be necessary or useful for the operation of the Center and the achievement of the purposes of this Convention."[23] The Administrative Council would consist of one Representative and one Alternate Representative of each Contracting State of the Convention. The explanatory comments in the Working Paper suggested that consideration be given to allowing non-IBRD members to become parties to the Convention, but that if

[14] The Working Paper noted that four further articles remained to be added on recognition of awards rendered pursuant to the Convention, disputes between States parties to it, definitions of such terms as "national" and such matters as signature and ratification of the Convention. The Working Paper was not as brief as the relatively small number of articles might suggest. The articles, divided into sections, corresponded to the chapters, divided into sections and articles, of the final text of the ICSID Convention. The Working Paper was in this respect modeled after the Articles of Agreement of the IBRD, the IFC and IDA.

[15] Working Paper, Art. I.

[16] Ibid. Art. III(1). The reference to its juridical personality underscored that it would be distinct from the Bank.

[17] Ibid. Art. III(4).

[18] Ibid. As Chairman of the Executive Directors of the IBRD, the IFC and IDA, the President of the IBRD also had a casting vote in case of an equal division. *See* Articles of Agreement of the IBRD (n. 11) Art. V(5)(a); Articles of Agreement of the IFC, May 25, 1955, 264 UNTS 117, Art. IV(5)(a); Articles of Agreement of IDA, January 26, 1960, 439 UNTS 249, Art. VI(5)(a).

[19] Working Paper, Art. III(8). As the Center was to lack an intermediate executive board, between the plenary Administrative Council and the Secretariat, the President was in this regard to have a role comparable to that of Executive Directors of the IBRD, to whom the Board of Governors of the IBRD likewise could (and had) delegated most of its powers. *See* Articles of Agreement of the IBRD (n. 11) Art. V(2)(b) and By-Laws of the IBRD, as amended, September 26, 1980, sec. 14.

[20] Working Paper, Arts. V(3)(1) and VI(3)(1).

[21] Ibid. Art. III(13)(3) and III(14)(3). The number of such designees was left blank in the Working Paper.

[22] Ibid. Art. III(8). [23] Ibid.

it were decided otherwise the Convention could provide that the IBRD Governors and Alternate Governors of parties would ex officio be their Representatives and Alternate Representatives on the Council of the Center.[24] The comments also pointed out that the Panels of Conciliators and of Arbitrators would consist mainly of persons designated by the respective Contracting States, rather than being elected by the Administrative Council, and that the Secretary-General was to be an administrative official with no judicial or quasi-judicial powers.[25] It thus seemed unlikely that there could be matters within the competence of the Administrative Council that would lead to major controversies.[26] Instead of carrying over into the Council the weighted voting system of the IBRD, the Working Paper therefore simply provided that each member of the Council would cast one vote and that all matters before the Council would be decided by majority vote.[27]

The Secretariat was to consist of a Secretary-General, one or more Deputy Secretaries-General and staff.[28] The Secretary-General would be "the principal administrative officer of the Center … responsible for its administration, including the appointment of staff."[29] In the context of proceedings under the Convention, specific functions envisaged for the Secretary-General included receiving certain notices from parties, consulting with them in regard to a requested appointment by the President of a conciliator or arbitrator and fixing the place of the proceeding in the absence of agreement thereon of the parties.[30] The commentary in the Working Paper foresaw that, in addition to such functions, the Secretary-General "could in practice perform a valuable task in promoting use of the Center's facilities and by giving informal assistance and advice to the parties in connection with proceedings under the Center's auspices."[31] As it would be necessary for the Secretary-General to be able to inspire confidence, the Working Paper provided that the office (and that of Deputy Secretary-General) would be incompatible with the exercise of any political function and, in principle, with any other employment or occupation.[32] The Working Paper, however, excluded from incompatibility employment by the IBRD or by the PCA, with which it was anticipated the Center might develop a working relationship.[33] This was done as there could be no certainty that activities under the Convention would be such as to provide full-time occupation for a Secretary-General and Deputy Secretary-General.[34]

The Working Paper provided that the Panels of Conciliators and of Arbitrators would consist of qualified persons designated to serve thereon for four years.[35] Each Contracting State would be required to designate a certain number of persons to each Panel; the President of the Center would be entitled to make designations to the Panels as well.[36] Designees of Contracting States, who could be of any nationality, were expected to be persons of "high moral character and recognized competence in the fields of law, commerce, industry or finance."[37] To help ensure that would be the case, Contracting States would be required, before making their designations, to "seek such advice as they may deem appropriate from their highest courts of justice, schools of law, bar associations and such commercial, industrial and financial organizations and

[24] Ibid. comment on Art. III(7). [25] Ibid. comment on Art. III(9). [26] Ibid.
[27] Ibid. Art. III(9)(4). [28] Ibid. Art. III(10). [29] Ibid. Art. III(12).
[30] Ibid. Art. IV(4), V(3), VI(3) and VII(4). [31] Ibid. comment on Art. III(11).
[32] Ibid. Art. III(11)(2). [33] Ibid. *See also* text accompanying nn. 49 and 76.
[34] Working Paper, comment on Art. III(11).
[35] Ibid. Art. III(13), III(14) and III(15).
[36] Ibid. Art. III(13) and III(14). The numbers of designations of a Contracting State were left blank, as were those of the President.
[37] Ibid. Art. III(13)(2), III(14)(2) and III(17)(1).

shall be considered representative of the professions they embrace."[38] In designating Panel members, the President for his part would be required to "pay due regard to the importance of assuring representation on the Panels of the principal legal systems of the world and the main forms of economic activity."[39]

The Working Paper set forth the privileges and immunities that the Center would enjoy in the territories of Contracting States.[40] These included absolute immunity from legal process, inviolability of archives and immunity from taxation.[41] In addition, the President, the members of the Administrative Council, and the officers and employees of the Secretariat would have qualified immunity from legal process with respect to acts performed by them in their official capacity.[42] Except for local nationals, they were also to be immune from immigration restrictions and national service obligations and exempt from taxation in respect of salaries or emoluments paid to them by the Center.[43] Participants in proceedings under the Convention, including conciliators, arbitrators, parties and their counsel, were to have immunity from immigration restrictions and the like in connection with their travel to and from, and stay at, the place where the proceedings were held.[44] The Working Paper further provided that no tax was to be levied on the fees received by conciliators or arbitrators for their services in proceedings if the sole jurisdictional basis for the tax was the location of the Center or the place where the proceedings were conducted or the place where the fees were paid.[45]

As already mentioned, the Working Paper provided that the President of the World Bank would be ex officio President of the Center, and that the Secretary-General and Deputy Secretaries-General could be employees of the Bank. In expectation of the possibility that the Representatives of Contracting States on the Administrative Council would be their Governors of the Bank, the Working Paper also provided that the annual meetings of the Council would be held in conjunction with those of the Board of Governors of the IBRD.[46] Further provisions of the Working Paper linking the Center to the Bank included one specifying that the seat of the Center would be at the headquarters of the IBRD.[47] In addition, the Center could "make arrangements with the Bank for the use of the Bank's offices and other services and facilities."[48] The Center might similarly make arrangements with the PCA for the use of its organization and

38 Ibid. Art. III(17)(1). 39 Ibid. Art. III(17)(2).

40 This approach of defining the privileges and immunities of the organization in its constituent treaty, rather than in another treaty, was taken in the Articles of Agreement of the IMF and IBRD and followed in the charters of the IFC and IDA (and later MIGA). Jean-Flavien Lalive called their provisions on privileges and immunities "véritables petits codes" on the subject. J.-F. Lalive, L'immunité des Etats et des organizations internationales, 84 Recueil des Cours 205, 365 (1953). The constituent treaties of other international organizations commonly contained only general provisions on their privileges and immunities which were defined in detail in other international agreements. For example, the privileges and immunities of the U.N. were defined primarily by the Convention on the Privileges and Immunities of the United Nations approved by the General Assembly in 1946 pursuant to Arts. 104 and 105 of the U.N. Charter.

41 Working Paper, Art. III(19), III(21) and III(22). 42 Ibid. Art. III(19)(1).

43 Ibid. Art. III(1) and III(22)(2).

44 Ibid. Art. III(20)(2). A mistaken cross-reference in this provision of the Working Paper made it appear that such participants in proceedings were to be accorded qualified immunity from legal process; while this was not the intention in the Working Paper, the conclusion was eventually reached that they should indeed be given such immunity. *See* Ch. 4, text accompanying n. 119.

45 Working Paper, Art. III(22)(3). This at first sight curious provision was based on Art. VII(9)(c) of the Articles of Agreement of the IBRD (n. 11), according to which no tax was to be levied on securities issued by the Bank if the sole jurisdictional basis for the tax was the place or currency in which they were issued, made payable or paid, or the location of any office of the Bank.

46 Working Paper, Art. III(9)(2). 47 Ibid. Art. III(2)(1). 48 Ibid. Art. III(2)(2).

facilities.[49] In regard to financing the cost of the Center, the Working Paper provided that it would be borne by Contracting States to the extent that it would not be met out of charges for the use of the facilities of the Center or "out of other receipts."[50] The last-quoted words were included in anticipation of the possibility that the Bank would finance the cost of the Center.[51]

B. Provisions on the jurisdiction of the Center

The Working Paper set out an extraordinarily flexible and open framework for conciliation and arbitration of disputes between Contracting States and nationals of other Contracting States. The jurisdiction of the Center was to be based on consent.[52] The consent could be evidenced by an undertaking of the parties to have recourse to conciliation or arbitration under the Convention for the resolution of an existing or future dispute between them.[53] The only formal requirement for the undertaking was that it be in writing.[54] There were to be no limitations as to the nature of the dispute, even though the Convention and Center would be meant primarily for investment disputes.[55] A main reason for this was simply that it should be left to the parties to decide whether they wished to bring their undertaking within the scope of the Convention.[56] Indeed, the primacy that the Working Paper accorded to the undertaking of the parties was taken so far as to provide that any of the provisions of the Convention would yield to other arrangements in the undertaking.[57] The commentary in the Working Paper offered, as another reason for not limiting the scope of covered disputes, that it was difficult to define "investment dispute" with precision. The resulting room for uncertainty could undermine confidence that the undertakings to resort to conciliation or arbitration would be carried out.[58] In addition to such undertakings in writing, the necessary consent to the jurisdiction of the Center could, the Working Paper envisaged, be evidenced by the acceptance by a party of such jurisdiction in respect of a dispute submitted to the Center by the other party.[59] The Working Paper thus adopted the doctrine of *forum prorogatum* as applied in the practice of the Permanent International Court of Justice and the ICJ as a flexible way to establish the jurisdiction of the Court.[60]

The Working Paper emphasized that an undertaking to have recourse to conciliation or arbitration constituted a legal obligation and had to be carried out in good faith.[61] An undertaking to have recourse to arbitration also carried an obligation to comply with the arbitral award and perform it in good faith.[62] The Working Paper furthermore made it explicit that such an undertaking would, unless otherwise stated, be deemed to be an undertaking to have recourse to arbitration in lieu of any other remedy.[63] A principal purpose of the Convention would be to enable a private party to

[49] Ibid. Art. III(2)(3). [50] Ibid. Art. III(18). [51] Ibid. comment on Art. III(18).
[52] Ibid. Art. IV(1)(i). [53] Ibid. Arts. II(1) and IV(2). [54] Ibid. Art. II(1).
[55] Although there were to be no limitations as to the nature of the dispute, the Working Paper provided that the Center would not exercise jurisdiction in respect of claims below US$100,000 equivalent (roughly US$780,000 in current dollars) determined as of the time of the submission of the dispute (ibid. Art. IV(3)). This provision did not survive in subsequent drafts of the Convention as it was realized that the pecuniary value of a claim might not always reflect its importance or even be readily ascertainable.
[56] Ibid. comment on Art. II. [57] Ibid. Art. II(6)(c).
[58] Ibid. comment on Art. II. [59] Ibid. Art. IV(2).
[60] *See* A. Zimmermann and others, *The Statute of the International Court of Justice: A Commentary* 898–902 (2006).
[61] Working Paper, Art. II(2) and II(3). [62] Ibid. Art. II(3). [63] Ibid. Art. II(4).

bring a claim against a foreign State before an international arbitral tribunal, instead of seeking diplomatic protection of its State or having the home State bring an international claim. A natural concomitant of the recognition of a party's right to direct access to an international jurisdiction would, according to the commentary in the Working Paper, be to exclude action by the home State where such access was available under the Convention.[64] The Working Paper therefore included a provision by which each Contracting State would be prohibited from giving diplomatic protection or bringing an international claim in respect of a dispute that one of its nationals and another Contracting State had undertaken to submit, or had submitted, to arbitration under the Convention.[65] The right of the home State to give diplomatic protection or bring an international claim would, however, revive in the event of an alleged violation by the first State of any of its obligations under the Convention in respect of the dispute.[66]

C. Provisions on conciliation and arbitration

According to the Working Paper, any dispute within the jurisdiction of the Center could be the subject of a request for conciliation by a conciliation commission or a request for arbitration by an arbitral tribunal.[67] Beyond this, the Working Paper did not address the initiation of proceedings or elaborate on what role the Secretariat might have in this respect. The conciliation commission or arbitral tribunal would consist of one or several conciliators or arbitrators appointed as the parties might have agreed.[68] In the absence of agreement, the commission or tribunal would consist of three conciliators or arbitrators, one appointed by each party and the third appointed by agreement of the parties, all appointees to be selected from the respective Panels.[69] Conciliators and arbitrators appointed by the President of the Center in his appointing authority role would likewise have to be chosen from the Panels.[70] Once a commission or tribunal was constituted and the proceeding began, its composition would remain unchanged barring the death, incapacity or resignation of one of its members.[71] In those cases, the resulting vacancy would normally be filled by the same method as that used for the original appointment. To discourage collusive resignations, however, a party-appointed conciliator or arbitrator who resigned without the consent of the commission or tribunal concerned would instead be replaced by the President of the Center.[72] The Working Paper also had provisions on the disqualification of conciliators and arbitrators: a party could propose such a disqualification on the ground that the conciliator or arbitrator concerned had an interest in the subject matter of the dispute or had, prior to being appointed, dealt with the dispute in some capacity.[73] The proposal would be decided upon by the other members of the commission or tribunal, unless they were evenly divided or the proposal related to a sole conciliator or arbitrator, in which cases the President of the Center would decide.[74]

Conciliation and arbitration proceedings were to be conducted in accordance with rules of procedure to be adopted under the Convention, but the parties could agree otherwise.[75] The proceedings would be held at the seat of the Center or of the PCA, as the parties might agree, or at any other place agreed by the parties with the approval of the commission or tribunal, after consultation with the Secretary-General.[76] In

[64] Ibid. comment on Art. II(5). [65] Ibid. Art. II(5). [66] Ibid.
[67] Ibid. Arts. V(1) and VI(1). [68] Ibid. Arts. V(2) and VI(2). [69] Ibid.
[70] Ibid. Arts. V(3)(2) and VI(3)(2). [71] Ibid. Art. VII(5). [72] Ibid.
[73] Ibid. Art. VII(6)(1). [74] Ibid. Art. VII(6)(2). [75] Ibid.
[76] Ibid. Art. VII(4).

principle, each party was to bear its own expenses and share equally with the other party the fees and expenses of the commission or tribunal and of the Center.[77] The fees and expenses of the Center to be charged to the parties would be fixed by the Secretary-General within limits approved by the Administrative Council; in the absence of agreement with the parties, the commission or tribunal would fix its fees and expenses after consultation with the Secretary-General.[78]

A conciliation commission might recommend terms of settlement to the parties, who were to give their most serious consideration to such recommendations.[79] An arbitral tribunal was, by contrast, to decide the dispute. In the absence of agreement of the parties on the law to be applied, and unless they had given the tribunal *ex aequo et bono* decision-making power, the tribunal would decide "in accordance with such rules of law, whether national or international, as it shall determine to be applicable."[80] The tribunal was also to have the power to prescribe provisional measures necessary for the protection of the rights of the parties and to hear and determine counter-claims arising directly out of the subject matter of the dispute.[81]

The Working Paper drew somewhat unwieldy distinctions in regard to objections to jurisdiction. In an arbitration proceeding, a party raising an objection based on the alleged inexistence of a dispute or of a valid undertaking to arbitrate would be entitled to have it decided by the tribunal as a preliminary question.[82] In the context of a conciliation proceeding, a similar objection would be referred to arbitration, the reasoning being that it seemed best not to ask conciliators to settle a difference concerning the legal obligation to resort to conciliation.[83] Another ground on which jurisdiction could be contested, in either a conciliation or arbitration, was that the non-State party to the dispute lacked the nationality of a Contracting State. In such a case, the State party to the dispute would send a notice of its objection to the Secretary-General.[84] Because the drafters saw this as a matter primarily concerning the respective States, the procedure would then be taken to the inter-State level. The Secretary-General would forward the notice to the purported home State of the non-State party.[85] If neither that State nor any third Contracting State claimed the non-State party as its national within a certain time limit, then the Secretary-General would declare the Center to be without jurisdiction.[86] On the other hand, if a Contracting State claimed the non-State party as its national within that limit, the Secretary-General would so notify the State party, which could then decide not to pursue its objection.[87] If the State party instead maintained its objection, then the resulting difference of views between the States concerned would be referred to the State-State dispute settlement procedures of the Convention.[88]

The award of an arbitral tribunal, which could be rendered by default, was to be final and binding on the parties.[89] Each party was to abide by and comply with the award immediately, unless the arbitral tribunal had allowed a time limit for its performance.[90]

[77] Ibid. Art. III(1). This provision, however, would have allowed a commission or tribunal to assess costs against a party that had instituted the proceeding frivolously or in bad faith.

[78] Ibid. Art. VII(2) and VII(3). In subsequent drafts of the Convention, as in the final text (Art. 59), the words "fees and expenses" in relation to the Center (as opposed to the conciliation commission or arbitral tribunal) were replaced with "charges ... for the use of the facilities" of the institution with a view to their covering out-of-pocket costs or other costs attributable to a particular proceeding. This language was, however, broad enough to accommodate the eventual introduction of charges or fees aimed at recovering overhead expenditures as well. *Cf.* Ch. 10, nn. 45–50 and accompanying text.

[79] Working Paper, Art. V(4)(2) and V(6).

[80] Ibid. Art. VI(5)(1).

[81] Ibid. Art. VI(6) and VI(7).

[82] Ibid. Art. IV(3).

[83] Ibid. Art. IV(2).

[84] Ibid. Art. IV(4)(1).

[85] Ibid.

[86] Ibid. Art. IV(4)(3).

[87] Ibid. Art. IV(b).

[88] Ibid. Art. IV(5).

[89] Ibid. Art. VI(9) and VI(10).

[90] Ibid. Art. VI(10).

Only two post-award remedies were provided for in the Working Paper. The first was interpretation of the award, which either of the parties could request if a dispute arose between them as to the meaning or scope of the award.[91] The second remedy was revision of the award. It could be sought on the ground of the discovery of a new fact that would have decisively affected the award.[92] The tribunal would have to have been ignorant, and the party seeking revision non-negligently ignorant, of the fact when the award was rendered.[93] An interpretation request would have to be made within a certain number of months after the rendition of the award.[94] Revision could only be requested within six months of the discovery of the new fact, and in any event within ten years of the rendering of the award.[95] Both types of request would, if possible, be submitted to the tribunal that rendered the award, failing which a new tribunal would be constituted.[96]

II. The initial meetings of the Committee of the Whole

As mentioned earlier, the Committee of the Whole on the Settlement of Investment Disputes of the World Bank's Executive Directors had six initial meetings between late 1962 and mid-1963. They were convened to discuss the Working Paper. A basic question raised in the meetings was whether a convention was needed at all to establish the Center. The question was raised by the three Executive Directors representing Latin American countries.[97] They suggested that the Center could more readily be established administratively or by simple resolution of the Board of Governors or of the Executive Directors of the Bank.[98] Most of the Executive Directors, however, thought otherwise, having been persuaded by arguments made by Broches in this respect.[99] A convention, he explained, would be needed to establish that the agreements to resort to conciliation or arbitration would be valid international obligations. Governments, he added, might be reluctant to accept international procedures for the settlement of investment disputes if they would still be subject to diplomatic representations or claims by the home State of the foreign investor. A convention would eliminate that problem by, in effect, excluding such representations or claims when an arbitration agreement was in effect and being carried out by the host State. A convention would

[91] Ibid. Art. VI(11). [92] Ibid. Art. VI(12). [93] Ibid.

[94] Ibid. Art. VI(11). The number of months was left blank in the Working Paper.

[95] Ibid. Art. VI(12). [96] Ibid. Art. VI(11) and VI(12).

[97] The Executive Directors concerned were Luis Machado (Executive Director for Mexico, Venezuela, Peru, Haiti, Costa Rica, Guatemala, El Salvador, Honduras, Nicaragua and Panama), Jorge Mejia-Palacio (Executive Director for Brazil, the Philippines, Colombia, Ecuador and the Dominican Republic) and Fernando Illanes (Executive Director for Argentina, Chile, Bolivia, Uruguay and Paraguay). A Cuban lawyer, Machado took part in the Bretton Woods Conference that led to the establishment of the IBRD and the IMF. He served as an Executive Director of the Bank from 1946 to 1948 and from 1952 to 1970. Mejia-Palacio, briefly Minister of Finance of Colombia, was Executive Director of the Bank from 1952 to 1968. Illanes served as Executive Director from 1962 to 1964, having previously been Vice President of the Central Bank of Chile.

[98] See Memorandum of the Meeting of the Committee of the Whole (MMCW), May 28, 1963, reprinted in 2 *History of the ICSID Convention* 86, paras. 6, 21 and 22; MMCW, June 4, 1963, reprinted in 2 *History of the ICSID Convention* 99, paras. 11 and 37; MMCW, June 6, 1963, reprinted in 2 *History of the ICSID Convention* 106, para. 19.

[99] These arguments, summarized in the next four sentences of the text, were set out in para. 19 of a February 18, 1963 paper prepared by Broches for the Executive Directors entitled Settlement of Investment Disputes: An Analysis of the Bank's Tentative Proposals and of the Principal Issues Raised Thereby. The paper is reprinted in 2 *History of the ICSID Convention* 71.

The World Bank's Executive Directors in 1962, the year in which their Committee of the Whole on the Settlement of Investment Disputes held its first meetings.
World Bank Group Archives

also provide rules to assure that a conciliation or arbitration agreement could not be unilaterally frustrated by a party and that, in the case of arbitration, the award would be complied with.

Another Executive Director[100] wondered whether the Center could be set up as suggested by his Latin American colleagues, with a convention to follow in due course. The Center might be in place earlier, accumulating experience and creating confidence that could help in achieving the eventual convention.[101] There was, however, little support for this alternative. One Executive Director[102] thought that, if set up this way, the Center could undermine the prospects for a convention by making it seem superfluous.[103]

In the initial meetings of the Committee of the Whole, Executive Directors were concerned to ensure that, if there were to be a center created by a convention, its role and organizational structure be kept as modest as possible. Thus, referring to the provision of the Working Paper on the purpose of the Convention,[104] one Executive Director said that it should simply be "providing for" recourse to international conciliation and arbitration rather than "encouraging and facilitating" it.[105] The same Executive Director objected to the broad powers, envisaged for the Administrative

[100] This was Pieter Lieftinck (Executive Director for Cyprus, Israel, the Netherlands and Yugoslavia). Lieftinck had been Professor of Political Economy at the Netherlands School of Economics in Rotterdam before the Second World War, and Minister of Finance of the Netherlands (and Governor of the IBRD) in the immediate post-war years. He served as Executive Director from 1955 to 1971.

[101] *See* MMCW, May 28, 1963 (n. 98) para. 60.

[102] John C. Bullitt (Executive Director for the United States), Assistant Secretary for International Affairs at the U.S. Treasury before serving as Executive Director of the Bank from 1962 to 1965.

[103] MMCW, May 28, 1963 (n. 98) para. 62.

[104] *See* n. 15 and accompanying text.

[105] *See* MMCW, December 18, 1962, reprinted in 2 *History of the ICSID Convention* 53, para. 27. This was said by C.S. Krishna Moorthi (Executive Director for India). He was an Executive Director from 1962 to 1963, having previously served as Alternate Executive Director and in various senior positions in the Ministry of Finance of India.

Council of the Center, to do whatever might be "necessary or useful for the operation of the Center and the achievement of the purposes of the Convention."[106] It should, he argued, be made clear that the Council would have no more than merely administrative powers.[107] Other Executive Directors cautioned against the erection of a needlessly large or duplicative bureaucracy. One even suggested that the word "center" had an undesirable connotation of size and importance, given that the entity would have only procedural functions, and might be replaced with "secretariat" or "registry."[108] Suggestions to avoid duplication and overlapping included "dovetailing" activities of the proposed center with those of the PCA at The Hague or, more concretely, having a joint secretariat with the PCA.[109] One Executive Director asked that provision be made for cooperation with other organizations, besides the PCA.[110]

The relationship between the proposed center and the World Bank was another fundamental issue discussed in the initial meetings of the Committee of the Whole. Some Executive Directors emphasized the importance of a close link with the Bank, seeing it as essential to the success of the Center, allowing it to share in the Bank's prestige and credibility with investors and governments alike.[111] Others stressed the need for the Center to be independent in view of its role in settling disputes.[112] A particular danger to be guarded against was that the Bank might somehow influence the substance of proceedings before the Center.[113] Two of the Executive Directors[114] saw that the relationship might have to evolve as the Center began to receive cases. Since access to the Center would be unrestricted once the prescribed conditions were satisfied, it might, they predicted, have to deal with cases that could have political repercussions for the Bank or involve its interests, such as where a case concerned a project financed by the Bank.[115] While it might therefore be useful to start with a close relationship, it would, they urged, be wise to provide for the possibility of a later loosening of the connection.[116]

Specific suggestions made by the Executive Directors in that regard included not insisting on an identification of the Administrative Council of the Center with the Board of the Governors of the Bank; ensuring that it would not be mandatory for the Secretary-General of the Center to be a staff member of the Bank; and making it possible for the headquarters of the Center eventually to be moved away from those of the Bank.[117] One Executive Director also forcefully argued that the President of the

[106] *See* n. 23 and accompanying text.

[107] MMCW, June 6, 1963 (n. 98) paras. 13 and 16.

[108] MMCW, December 18, 1962 (n. 105) para. 10 (intervention of Lieftinck).

[109] *See* MMCW, June 6, 1963 (n. 98) paras. 36 and 52. The suggestions came from Lieftinck, naturally enough given his Dutch nationality, joined by J.M. Garland (Executive Director for Australia, South Africa and Vietnam). Garland, a former Lecturer in Economics at the Universities of Adelaide and Melbourne, was Executive Director of the Bank from 1959 to 1966.

[110] MMCW, June 6, 1963 (n. 98) para. 29. This request was made by Otto Donner (Executive Director for Germany), past Professor of Economics at Hamburg and Georgetown Universities, and Executive Director of the Bank from 1954 to 1968.

[111] *See, e.g.*, MMCW, June 4, 1963 (n. 98) paras. 19 and 23–26.

[112] *See, e.g.*, MMCW, May 28, 1963 (n. 98) paras. 21 and 24.

[113] *See, e.g.*, ibid. para. 14; MMCW, June 4, 1963 (n. 98) para. 37.

[114] Garland and Leftinck.

[115] *See* MMCW, June 6, 1963 (n. 98) paras. 38, 39, 49 and 50.

[116] Ibid. paras. 38 and 50.

[117] Ibid. paras. 39, 51 and 66–68. Garland and Lieftinck were joined in these suggestions by Andre van Campenhout (Executive Director for Belgium, Austria, Turkey and Luxembourg), who had been the first General Counsel of the IMF before becoming Executive Director of the IMF in 1954 and Executive Director of the Bank in 1960. He remained Executive Director of the Bank until 1973.

Bank should not be made President of the Center as such, with full executive authority over the Secretary-General, but only Chairman of the Administrative Council, with the Secretary-General remaining independent even of the Bank's President.[118] Another Executive Director asked that it be made clear that any "services"[119] the Bank might provide to the Center would be confined to administrative services.[120] As shown later in this book, all of these suggestions were reflected in the subsequent drafts of the Convention.

The discussions in the initial meetings of the Committee of the Whole also influenced the development of the conciliation and arbitration provisions of the Convention in important ways. Thus, it was objected early on in the discussions that the Working Paper went too far in apparently subordinating all of the provisions to any contrary dispositions in the conciliation or arbitration agreement of the parties.[121] Several Executive Directors faulted the Working Paper for being overly broad in scope in that it provided no limitation or definition of the type of dispute that might be submitted to the Center.[122] Two Executive Directors detected an imbalance in the provisions of the Working Paper regarding the enforcement of arbitral awards.[123] A State party to the Convention would have an international obligation thereunder to comply with an award made against it; and in the event of non-compliance, the investor might seek the diplomatic protection of its home State.[124] The Convention should, the Executive Directors said, have provisions committing States to the enforcement of awards against investors as well.[125]

As explained in Chapter 2, Germany was in the early 1960s a pioneer with BITs and investment insurance. In the initial meetings of the Committee of the Whole, the Executive Director for Germany[126] made proposals reflecting his country's preoccupation with its investment treaty and insurance programs. A first such proposal concerned the situation when a State had provided investment insurance to a national and then indemnified the latter under the insurance policy and became subrogated to claims of the insured against the host State. It was proposed that in such a case the home State should, as subrogee, be able to bring the claims against the host State before the Center.[127] A second suggestion was that the Convention make clear that it would not preclude a State from submitting to arbitration questions concerning the interpretation of a BIT, where the BIT itself made provision for arbitration of such questions.[128] Also brought up by the German Executive Director was a more general concern about the possibility of contradictory decisions relating to the same subject

[118] Ibid. paras. 50 and 51 (intervention of Lieftinck).

[119] *Cf.* n. 48 and accompanying text.

[120] MMCW, June 4, 1963 (n. 98) para. 30 (intervention of Krishna Moorthi).

[121] MMCW, December 18, 1962 (n. 105) para. 9. *Cf.* n. 57 and accompanying text.

[122] *See, e.g.*, MMCW, December 18, 1962 (n. 105) paras. 24 and 28; MMCW, December 27, 1962, reprinted in 2 *History of the ICSID Convention* 61, paras. 25 and 44. *Cf.* n. 55 and accompanying text. Executive Directors making this point included van Campenhout, Krishna Moorthi and Gengo Suzuki (Executive Director for Japan, Thailand, Burma and Ceylon (as it was then called)), a former Financial Commissioner in the Ministry of Finance of Japan and Executive Director of the Bank from 1960 to 1966.

[123] The two Executive Directors were Krishna Moorthi and Alice A. Brun (Executive Director for Denmark, Iceland, Norway and Sweden), who had been a senior official in the Danish Ministry of Finance before serving as the first woman Executive Director of the Bank from 1962 to 1964.

[124] *Cf.* nn. 61 and 66 and accompanying text.

[125] MMCW, December 18, 1962 (n. 105) para. 31; MMCW, December 27, 1962 (n. 122) para. 19.

[126] *See* n. 110.

[127] MMCW, December 27, 1962 (n. 122) para. 8.

[128] Ibid. para. 10.

matter rendered by different tribunals operating in the field under discussion; these might include tribunals set up under BITs or the projected OECD Convention, or by the Bank's proposed center or the PCA.[129] In response to the last point, Broches explained that the risk of contradictory decisions in cases arising between different parties, but based on similar facts, was inherent in any system of ad hoc arbitration; the risk might be averted by having a standing tribunal instead but "that was clearly impractical in the present context."[130]

[129] MMCW, June 6, 1963 (n. 98) para. 34. [130] Ibid. para. 47.

4

The Preliminary Draft of the Convention

Following the initial meetings of the Committee of the Whole, Aron Broches prepared a First Preliminary Draft of a Convention on the Settlement of Investment Disputes between States and Nationals of Other States.[1] This draft, dated August 9, 1963, was discussed at a meeting of the Executive Directors of the Bank in September 1963. At that meeting, the Executive Directors agreed to the circulation to member governments of a slightly revised Preliminary Draft of a Convention on the Settlement of Investment Disputes between States and Nationals of Other States (the Preliminary Draft).[2] This would be done making it clear that, while the Preliminary Draft reflected discussions of the proposals by the Executive Directors, it had not been approved by them. At their September 1963 meeting, the Executive Directors also agreed that the Bank should convene four regional consultative meetings of legal experts designated by governments. The meetings would be convened by the Bank in Addis Ababa, Santiago, Geneva and Bangkok.[3] The meetings would be conducted by Broches with the assistance of some of his staff.[4] The meetings would provide occasions to explain the proposals and benefit from the comments of participating experts.[5] Member countries would be reimbursed by the Bank for the travel and subsistence expenses of up to two experts. The Preliminary Draft would be the working paper for the meetings.[6]

This chapter describes the Preliminary Draft, focusing on the main differences between it and the Working Paper. It also reviews the sources or antecedents for the Preliminary Draft (and the Working Paper before it). The chapter then turns to the discussions at the regional consultative meetings.

[1] Reprinted in 2 *History of the ICSID Convention* 133.

[2] The Preliminary Draft is reprinted in 2 *History of the ICSID Convention* 184 and as App. II of this book.

[3] The venues were the headquarters cities respectively of the United Nations Economic Commissions for Africa, Latin America and the Caribbean, Europe and Asia and the Pacific.

[4] The staff included Piero Sella, who was Assistant General Counsel of the Bank; Leopoldo Cancio, eventually a Chief Counsel in the Legal Department of the Bank; and Christopher W. Pinto, in later years Secretary-General of the Iran–U.S. Claims Tribunal.

[5] Many years later, Broches elaborated on the rationale for holding the regional consultative meetings. The Executive Directors of the Bank had been discussing a draft convention but:

> ... they didn't have proper feedback from home. Executive Directors report to Ministries of Finance, and while the purpose of the exercise was developmental, the technique was not only legal, but procedural. It was particularly difficult for people who are not lawyers, or who are lawyers but not interested in procedural matters. Then we hit on the idea of taking the show on the road to get comments from member countries, because we didn't get them through the Directors, and also to relieve the Directors of the tedium of having to go over this thing all the time.

World Bank Oral History Program, Transcript of Interview with Aron Broches, May 23, 1984, 37.

[6] *See* Memorandum of Discussion by Executive Directors, September 10, 1963, reprinted in 2 *History of the ICSID Convention* 174, paras. 2–7.

I. The Preliminary Draft

The Preliminary Draft, dated October 15, 1963, was complete in that it included a preamble and articles deferred by the Working Paper.[7] Altogether, the Preliminary Draft had 11 articles, divided into 65 sections; as in the Working Paper, the text was accompanied by explanatory comments. The provisions of the Preliminary Draft were more polished and logically arranged than those of the Working Paper. Much of the substance of the Working Paper was, however, retained in the Preliminary Draft. The following paragraphs therefore concentrate on the differences between the two.

Carrying the title that was to be kept through to the final text, the Preliminary Draft was of a Convention on the Settlement of Investment Disputes between States and Nationals of Other States.[8] The preamble consisted of six paragraphs. The first recalled the objective of promoting international investment to advance economic development. The second paragraph acknowledged the need to respect "the principle of equal rights of States in the exercise of their sovereignty in accordance with international law." It was made clear in the third paragraph that the procedures of the Convention would not be meant as a general substitute for national legal processes. The fourth and sixth paragraphs emphasized that recourse to conciliation or arbitration under the Convention would be voluntary. The fifth recognized that undertakings to resort to such conciliation or arbitration would be legal obligations to be carried out in good faith. As the preamble would provide a general statement of the aims of the Convention, the Preliminary Draft omitted the article on the purposes of the treaty that had been included in the Working Paper.[9]

A. Provisions on the establishment and organization of the Center

The provisions of the Preliminary Draft on the establishment and organization of the "International Conciliation and Arbitration Center" differed from those of the Working Paper in regard to the link with the World Bank and the role of the Administrative Council. Reflecting the discussions in the Committee of the Whole, the link with the Bank was looser in the Preliminary Draft. Most significantly, under the Preliminary Draft, the President of the Bank would not also be President of the Center but instead only the Chairman of its Administrative Council.[10] In the Preliminary Draft, the Secretary-General therefore became "the principal officer of the Center."[11] Also dropped in the Preliminary Draft was the possibility of the President receiving delegated powers from the Council.[12] The Preliminary Draft provided that the Governor of the Bank of a Contracting State would be ex officio its Representative on the Administrative Council but made this subject to any contrary designation by the

[7] *See* Ch. 3, n. 14 and accompanying text.

[8] The new title thus substituted "settlement" for the Working Paper's "resolution" and added "investment," immediately signaling a limitation on the subject matter of the disputes absent from the Working Paper. *Cf.* Ch. 3, text accompanying n. 55.

[9] Preliminary Draft, comment on preamble. *Cf.* Ch. 3, n. 15 and accompanying text.

[10] *See* Preliminary Draft, Art. I(5).

[11] Ibid. Art. I(10)(1). In the Working Paper, the Secretary-General was just the principal "administrative" officer. *See* Ch. 3, n. 29 and accompanying text. The commentary in the Preliminary Draft continued, however, to characterize the role of the Secretary-General as "administrative" having "no influence whatever on the outcome of proceedings under the auspices of the Center." Preliminary Draft, comment on Art. I(8)–I(10).

[12] *Cf.* Ch. 3, n. 19 and accompanying text.

Contracting State concerned.[13] There would thus be flexibility for Bank members and allowance made for other States as the Preliminary Draft envisaged that Bank membership would not be a prerequisite for participation in the Convention.[14] Flexibility was also provided in regard to the location of the seat of the Center in that it could, under the Preliminary Draft, be moved from the headquarters of the Bank with the approval of a qualified majority of the Administrative Council.[15] The Preliminary Draft made it clear that the Center might make arrangements with the Bank for the use of the latter's offices and "administrative" services and facilities only, adding that the Center might make similar arrangements not only with the PCA but also with "other public international institutions" designated by the Administrative Council.[16] Summing up the relationship between the Center and the Bank, the commentary in the Preliminary Draft observed that the Center would be sponsored by the Bank, which might also give it "housekeeping" facilities and staff. The link would impart to the Center the Bank's image, prestige and reputation for impartiality. "On the other hand," the commentary insisted, "the Bank would have no role to play, and could not exercise any influence whatsoever on the proceedings under the auspices of the Center."[17]

Again reflecting the discussions in the Committee of the Whole, the Preliminary Draft defined the role of the Administrative Council more narrowly than the Working Paper. Thus, the Preliminary Draft specified which rules and regulations the Council might adopt: "administrative rules and regulations, including financial regulations, ... Conciliation Rules and Arbitration Rules not inconsistent with any provision of this Convention."[18] Apart from its other powers under the Convention, the Council would also have responsibility for approving the terms of service of the Secretary-General and of any Deputy Secretary-General and for approving the annual budget and annual report of the Center.[19] Gone from the Preliminary Draft were the Working Paper's ambitions for the Administrative Council to be the "principal organ" of the Center with broad powers to advance the operation of the Center and purposes of the Convention.[20] Additional reassurance was offered in the commentary in the Preliminary Draft, which explained that the Administrative Council, as its name implied, would just "have purely administrative functions."[21]

B. Provisions on the jurisdiction of the Center

In keeping with the wishes expressed by Executive Directors in the initial meetings of the Committee of the Whole, the Preliminary Draft provided a generally more restrictive framework for conciliation and arbitration than that of the Working Paper. Thus, the Preliminary Draft lacked the provision of the Working Paper under which parties would be entirely free to substitute their own arrangements for those of the Convention.[22] Moreover, the Preliminary Draft explicitly limited the nature of covered

[13] Preliminary Draft, Art. I(4)(2).

[14] *See* further n. 62 and accompanying text.

[15] *See* Preliminary Draft, Art. I(6)(vi).

[16] Ibid. Art. I(2)(2) and I(2)(3). Under the Preliminary Draft (Art. VII(1)), proceedings could, if the parties agreed, be held not only at the seat of the Center or of the PCA but also at the seat of any "other public international institution" with which such arrangements had been made.

[17] Ibid. comment on Art. I(1)–I(3).

[18] Ibid. Art. I(6)(i) and I(6)(v).

[19] *See* ibid. Art. I(6)(vi). Under the Preliminary Draft (Art. VII(1)), proceedings could, if the parties agreed, be held not only at the seat of the Center or of the PCA but also at the seat of any "other public international institution" with which such arrangements had been made. Art. I(6)(ii)–I(6)(iv).

[20] *Cf.* Ch. 3, nn. 22 and 23 and accompanying text.

[21] Preliminary Draft, comment on Art. I(4)–I(6).

[22] *Cf.* Ch. 3, n. 57 and accompanying text.

disputes to "investment dispute[s] of a legal character."[23] On the other hand, the Preliminary Draft envisaged that the jurisdiction of the Center would extend to disputes between Contracting States, when one of them was "subrogated in the rights of its national," as well as to disputes between Contracting States and nationals of other Contracting States.[24]

The Preliminary Draft broadly defined "nationals" as including natural or juridical persons as well as associations of such persons.[25] Under the definition, a company might be a national of a Contracting State because it had that nationality under the State's law or because it was controlled by nationals of that State.[26] According to the Preliminary Draft, any national of a Contracting State other than the State party to the dispute would qualify as an eligible "national of another Contracting State" even if the person concerned were at the same time a national of the State party to the dispute or of a non-Contracting State.[27] In all cases, nationality would be determined as of the date on which the person's consent to the jurisdiction of the Center became effective.[28]

C. Provisions on conciliation and arbitration

Unlike the Working Paper, the Preliminary Draft provided expressly for requests for conciliation or arbitration to be addressed to the Secretary-General.[29] While a party would have to state in its request that the other party had consented to jurisdiction of the Center,[30] the Preliminary Draft remained silent as to what role, if any, the Secretary-General might have in verifying that statement or in otherwise scrutinizing the request.

The Preliminary Draft, like the Working Paper, envisaged that the parties would be essentially free to agree on the number of conciliators or arbitrators and the method of their appointment.[31] The provisions made in the drafts for cases where the parties had no agreement on the matter were also similar except for one important difference in regard to the appointment of arbitrators. This was the "new principle"[32] introduced in the Preliminary Draft, that none of the arbitrators appointed in such cases could be nationals of the State party to the dispute or of the home State of the other party.[33] The comments in the Preliminary Draft explained that the purpose of this was "to minimize as far as possible the danger, inherent in conventional systems, of appointment of partisan arbitrators."[34] It was envisaged by the Preliminary Draft that the principle would also apply to appointments of arbitrators by the Chairman of the Administrative Council, who retained in the Preliminary Draft the appointing authority role he had had as President in the Working Paper.[35]

There were also differences between the Preliminary Draft and Working Paper in regard to the disqualification of conciliators and arbitrators. The Preliminary Draft provided more broadly that such a disqualification could be proposed by a party "on account of any fact."[36] The Preliminary Draft distinguished between proposals to disqualify party-appointed conciliators or arbitrators and proposals to disqualify conciliators or arbitrators appointed by the Chairman of the Administrative Council. The

[23] Preliminary Draft, Art. II(1). [24] Ibid. *Cf.* Ch. 3, text accompanying n. 127.
[25] Preliminary Draft, Art. X(1) and comment thereon. [26] Ibid.
[27] Ibid. Art. X(2). [28] Ibid. Art. X(1). [29] Ibid. Arts. III(1) and IV(1).
[30] Ibid. [31] *See* ibid. Arts. III(2)(1) and IV(2)(1).
[32] The phrase used in ibid. comment on Art. IV(1)–IV(3). [33] *See* ibid. Art. IV(2)(2).
[34] Ibid. comment on Art. IV(1)–IV(3). [35] *See* ibid. Art. IV(3).
[36] Ibid. Art. V(2). The Working paper provided only for disqualification proposals based on interest in the subject matter or prior involvement with the dispute. *See* Ch. 3, n. 73 and accompanying text.

disqualification of a party-appointed conciliator or arbitrator might be proposed on account of a fact arising before or after the constitution of the commission or tribunal.[37] In contrast, the proposal in respect of a conciliator or arbitrator appointed by the Chairman could as a rule be founded only on a fact arising after the constitution of the commission or tribunal.[38] The commentary in the Preliminary Draft explained that this distinction was made because the Chairman had to "be deemed to have passed conclusively on the qualifications of his nominees."[39] The Preliminary Draft did, however, allow for proposals to disqualify such nominees based on a fact existing prior to the constitution of the commission or tribunal if it could be shown that the Chairman had made the appointment without knowledge of the fact or as a result of fraud.[40]

There were several differences between the Working Paper and the Preliminary Draft in regard to the powers and functions of conciliation commissions and arbitral tribunals. The Preliminary Draft specified that it would be the duty of a conciliation commission to "clarify the points in dispute between the parties and to endeavor to bring about agreement between them upon mutually acceptable terms."[41] The provisions of the Preliminary Draft regarding objections to jurisdiction were simpler than those of the Working Paper.[42] The Preliminary Draft provided that any conciliation commission or arbitral tribunal constituted under the Convention would be the judge of its own competence.[43] Any claim by a party that the commission or tribunal lacked competence, including a claim that the non-State party to the dispute lacked the nationality of a Contracting State, would be dealt with by the commission or tribunal as a preliminary question.[44] The Preliminary Draft did, however, retain something of the previous approach of referring an objection based on nationality to the purported home State. It provided that, in the event of such an objection, a written affirmation of nationality signed by or on behalf of the minister of foreign affairs of the State whose nationality was claimed, and issued for the purpose of the particular proceeding, would be conclusive proof of the facts stated therein.[45]

The Preliminary Draft also made it clear that an arbitral award would have to state the reasons on which it was based.[46] In addition, in contrast to the Working Paper's fleeting reference to the possibility of an award being rendered by default,[47] the Preliminary Draft explicitly provided that if a party failed to appear or present its case, the other party could call on the tribunal to rule in its favor; the tribunal could in turn render an award if it were satisfied that it had jurisdiction and that the claim appeared to be well-founded in fact and law.[48]

Importantly, the Preliminary Draft provided that, in addition to the post-award remedies of interpretation and revision, a party might seek the annulment of an award rendered pursuant to the Convention. According to the Preliminary Draft, either party could challenge "[t]he validity of an award" on one or more of three grounds. These were that the tribunal had exceeded its powers, that one of its members was corrupt, and that there had been a serious departure from a fundamental rule of procedure, including failure to state reasons for the award.[49] Such a challenge would be made

[37] Preliminary Draft, Art. V(2)(a). [38] Ibid. Art. V(2)(b).
[39] Ibid. comment on Art. V. [40] Ibid. Art. V(2)(b). [41] Ibid. Art. III(5)(1).
[42] The Working Paper provisions on this subject are discussed in Ch. 3, nn. 82–88 and accompanying text.
[43] Preliminary Draft, Art. II(3)(1).
[44] Ibid. Art. II(3)(2). In such a case, there therefore would have been a mandatory bifurcation of the proceeding between jurisdictional and merits phases.
[45] Ibid. Art. II(3)(3). [46] Ibid. Art. IV(7)(1).
[47] *See* Ch. 3, n. 89 and accompanying text. [48] Preliminary Draft, Art. IV(8).
[49] Ibid. Art. IV(13)(1).

by application to the Chairman of the Administrative Council within 60 days of the rendering of the award unless it were based on corruption, in which case the application could be submitted within six months.[50] On receipt of such an application, the Chairman of the Administrative Council would appoint from the Panel of Arbitrators an ad hoc committee "competent to declare the nullity of the award or any part thereof" on any of the specified grounds.[51] None of the committee members could have served on the tribunal that rendered the award, or be a national of the State party to the dispute or of the home State of the other party, or have acted as a conciliator in the same dispute.[52] The committee would have the power to stay enforcement of the award pending its decision and could recommend provisional measures necessary for the protection of the rights of the parties.[53] If the committee declared the award invalid, the dispute would, at the request of either party, be submitted to a new tribunal.[54]

It will be recalled that, in the initial meetings of the Committee of the Whole, it was urged that the obligation of each Contracting State to comply with an award made against it be balanced by a commitment of every Contracting State to enforce an award made against an investor as well.[55] The Preliminary Draft therefore included a provision under which each Contracting State would recognize an award rendered pursuant to the Convention as binding and enforce it within its territories as if it were a final judgment of the State's courts.[56] In the course of the regional consultative meetings, Broches proposed that there should be added a provision spelling out that, to obtain this result, the award should be presented to the authority that each Contracting State would designate for the purpose; the designated authority would then issue the enforcement order after doing no more than verifying the authenticity of the award. The additional provision would also make it clear that forced execution of the award would be governed by the rules of civil procedure of the State in whose territory it took place.[57]

D. Other provisions

Inter-State proceedings were the subject of two new provisions in the Preliminary Draft. Under the first, an addition to the article precluding the exercise of diplomatic protection, the investor's home State might nevertheless bring a claim against the host State if the facts of a dispute between the investor and host State also gave rise to a dispute concerning the interpretation or application of a treaty between the two States.[58] The second provision was a compromissory clause according to which "[a]ny question or dispute" arising between Contracting States over the interpretation or application of the Convention which was not settled by negotiation would be referred to the ICJ unless the States concerned agreed to another mode of settlement.[59] It was, however, realized that issues regarding the interpretation or application of the Convention could

[50] Ibid. Art. IV(13)(2) and IV(13)(4). [51] Ibid. Art. IV(13)(2). [52] Ibid.

[53] Ibid. Art. IV(13)(5). [54] Ibid. Art. IV(13)(6).

[55] *See* Ch. 3, nn. 124 and 125 and accompanying text.

[56] Preliminary Draft, Art. IV(15).

[57] *See* Summary Record of Proceedings, Bangkok Consultative Meeting, April 27–May 1, 1964 (Bangkok Record), reprinted in 2 *History of the ICSID Convention* 458, 60–61 (for this and other regional consultative meetings summary records, page numbers cited are of the original document).

[58] Preliminary Draft, Art. IV(17)(2). *Cf.* Ch. 3, text accompanying n. 128.

[59] Preliminary Draft, Art. VIII. The draft was infelicitous in that under the Statute of the ICJ (Art. 36) its jurisdiction in inter-State relationships extends only to disputes. A. Zimmermann and others, *The Statute of the International Court of Justice: A Commentary* 597 (2006). *See also* n. 95 and accompanying text.

well also arise in the context of investor–State arbitration proceedings pursuant to the Convention. During the regional consultative meetings, Broches and his staff team tentatively suggested supplementing the clause with a further provision to address that situation. The further provision would have permitted an arbitral tribunal, if a question of interpretation or application of the Convention arose during the arbitral proceeding, to suspend the proceeding to allow interested Contracting States to bring the matter before the ICJ if they so wished.[60]

Lastly, the Preliminary Draft dealt with the amendment, entry into force, territorial application and denunciation of the Convention, as well as the inauguration of the Center and the registration of the Convention with the United Nations Secretariat. It was envisaged that the Administrative Council of the Center would be competent to amend the Convention by a qualified majority of its members.[61] The Convention would be open for signature on behalf of all members of the World Bank "and all other sovereign States."[62] It would be subject to ratification by signatory States in accordance with their respective constitutional procedures and would enter into force when ratified by a certain number of States.[63] A colonial clause (obviously not called that in the draft) provided that by signing the Convention a State would agree to its application in respect of all territories for whose international relations it was responsible, except those excluded by the State on signature or subsequently.[64] A Contracting State could denounce the Convention by notice to the World Bank; the denunciation would take effect a specified number of months after the Bank received the notice, provided that obligations of the State concerned arising out of undertakings given prior to the date of the notice would "remain in full force and effect."[65] The World Bank would be designated the depositary of the Convention.[66] Its President would convene the inaugural meeting of the Administrative Council on entry into force of the Convention.[67] The Bank also would be authorized to register the Convention with the United Nations Secretariat under Article 102 of the U.N. Charter.[68]

II. Sources for the Preliminary Draft

For the preparation of the Articles of Agreement of the IFC and IDA, the drafters could rely extensively on the precedent afforded by the Articles of Agreement of the World Bank itself. There was no similar parallel for the comprehensive Convention on the Settlement of Investment Disputes foreseen by Broches and colleagues. Parts of their Preliminary Draft (and of the preceding Working Paper) were wholly original creations; many portions were based on or inspired by a variety of different instruments and seamlessly joined together by the drafters.

[60] For the text of the further provision, *see* Summary Record of Proceedings, Addis Ababa Consultative Meeting, December 16–20, 1963 (Addis Ababa Record), reprinted in 2 *History of the ICSID Convention* 236, 51–52.

[61] Preliminary Draft, Art. IX. The Preliminary Draft tentatively suggested that a four-fifths majority of Council members be required for the adoption of amendments of the Convention.

[62] Ibid. Art. XI(1).

[63] Ibid. Art. XI(2) and XI(3). The number of ratifications required for entry into force was left blank in the draft.

[64] Ibid. Art. X(4).

[65] Ibid. Art. XI(5). The number of months for the notice to take effect was tentatively suggested as 12 in the draft.

[66] Ibid. concluding formula. [67] Ibid. Art. XI(6). [68] Ibid. Art. XI(7).

An example of an article that seems to have been entirely their own invention is the one precluding the exercise of diplomatic protection.[69] Examples of articles of the Preliminary Draft that were conspicuously influenced by other instruments were those concerning the organization, privileges and immunities of the Center. The organizational structure envisaged for the Center broadly followed the example of the structure given to the PCA by the Conventions for the Pacific Settlement of International Disputes—Administrative Council, International Bureau and List of Arbitrators designated by the Contracting Powers.[70] Many of the details of the Preliminary Draft regarding the Administrative Council and Secretariat of the Center were suggested by provisions of the Articles of Agreement of the IBRD. For example, a section of the Preliminary Draft regarding meetings of the Administrative Council[71] echoed provisions in the Articles of Agreement on meetings of the Board of Governors of the Bank.[72] Another section of the Preliminary Draft, stating in general terms the role the Secretary-General,[73] included elements from a provision of the Articles of Agreement on the role of the Bank's President.[74] As acknowledged in the commentary in the Preliminary Draft, the provisions on the privileges and immunities of the Center were also "in general patterned after the privileges and immunities of the Bank."[75] The Statute of the ICJ was consulted for the section of the Preliminary Draft regarding the desired qualities of designees to the Panels of Conciliators and of Arbitrators. Provisions of the Statute on the personal characteristics of members of the ICJ, the consultations that should precede their nomination, and the need to ensure diversity of the body as a whole[76] were all adapted for this section of the Preliminary Draft.[77]

In using the term "jurisdiction" in its section delineating the scope of the facilities to be made available by the Center, the Preliminary Draft[78] followed the precedents of the Conventions for the Pacific Settlement of International Disputes, which spoke of the "jurisdiction" of the PCA even though it, like the proposed Center, did not itself exercise judicial functions.[79] The drafting of the provisions of the Preliminary Draft on undertakings to have recourse to conciliation or arbitration under the Convention[80] was influenced by provisions of the Model Rules on Arbitral Procedure of the International Law Commission (ILC Model Rules).[81] The formulation of the *Kompetenz–Kompetenz* principle in the Preliminary Draft[82] also appears to have been taken from the ILC Model Rules.[83]

[69] *See* ibid. Art. IV(17) and Ch. 3, text accompanying n. 65.

[70] *See* Chapter II of both the 1899 and 1907 Conventions on the Pacific Settlement of International Disputes, reprinted in PCA, Basic Documents: Conventions, Rules, Model Clauses and Guidelines 3 and 19.

[71] Preliminary Draft, Art. I(7).

[72] *See* Articles of Agreement of the IBRD, December 27, 1945, 2 UNTS 134, Art. V(2)(c)–V(2)(e).

[73] Preliminary Draft, Art. I(10)(1).

[74] *See* Articles of Agreement of the IBRD (n. 72) Art. V(5)(b).

[75] Preliminary Draft, comment on Art. I(17). The commentary pointed out that the Center had, however, "been given full immunity from legal process, whereas the Bank in view of the nature of its dealings with capital markets, enjoys only limited immunity in that respect." *See also* on this Ch. 1, n. 65. The privileges and immunities of the Bank were set out in Art. VII of its Articles of Agreement (n. 72).

[76] *See* Statute of the ICJ, reprinted in Zimmermann and others (n. 59) 1491, Arts. 2, 6 and 9 (ICJ Statute).

[77] Preliminary Draft, Art. I(15).

[78] Ibid. Art. II(1).

[79] Ibid. comment on Art. II. *See also* 1899 and 1907 Conventions for the Pacific Settlement of International Disputes (n. 70) Arts. 26 and 47, respectively.

[80] Preliminary Draft, Art. II(2).

[81] Reprinted in 1958 (II) YBILC 82, preamble, Arts. 1 and 2 (ILC Model Rules).

[82] Preliminary Draft, Art. II(3)(1).

[83] ILC Model Rules (n. 81) Art. 9.

The key conciliation provision of the Preliminary Draft, describing the duties of conciliators,[84] was based on corresponding provisions of the American Treaty on Pacific Settlement[85] and of the Revised General Act for the Pacific Settlement of International Disputes.[86] The ILC Model Rules influenced the drafting of the provisions on the constitution, powers and functions of arbitral tribunals, as did the Statute of the ICJ.[87] The provisions on the interpretation and revision of arbitral awards were partly derived from the same sources.[88] The section of the Preliminary Draft on the annulment of awards was based on the ILC Model Rules articles on the subject.[89]

It was mentioned earlier that during the regional consultative meetings, Broches proposed adding a provision on steps to be taken for the issuance of award enforcement orders by designated authorities of Contracting States and making it clear that forced execution of awards would be governed by the relevant local procedural rules.[90] The proposed new provision was modeled after an article of the Treaty Establishing the European Community on the enforcement of decisions of the EC Council or Commission imposing a pecuniary obligation on non-State parties.[91] As eventually drafted, the provision also borrowed terminology from the New York Convention on the Recognition and Enforcement of Foreign Arbitral Awards.[92] Following the regional consultative meetings, it was decided to add a further article clarifying that the enforcement provisions should not be construed as derogating from the law of any Contracting State regarding sovereign immunity from execution.[93] This further article incorporated the substance of provisions of the then Loan Regulations (now General Conditions Applicable to Loan and Guarantee Agreements) of the IBRD.[94]

A comment in the Preliminary Draft explained that the clause providing for the reference to the ICJ of questions or disputes concerning the interpretation or application of the Convention followed "the pattern of similar clauses in the constituent instruments of international organizations within the United Nations family."[95] In providing for amendments of the Convention to be adopted by the Administrative Council,

[84] To clarify the points in dispute between the parties and to endeavor to bring about agreement between them on mutually acceptable terms. Preliminary Draft, Art. III(5)(1).

[85] April 30, 1948, 30 UNTS 55, Art. 22.

[86] Adopted by the U.N. General Assembly April 28, 1949, 71 UNTS 101, Art. 15(1).

[87] For example, the Preliminary Draft provision on the appointment of arbitrators by the Chairman of the Administrative Council, Art. IV(3), was patterned after the provisions of the ILC Model Rules (n. 81) Art. 3(2) and 3(3), on the appointment of arbitrators by the President of the ICJ; the provisions of the Preliminary Draft on default procedures and provisional measures, Art. IV(8) and IV(10), were based on the corresponding provisions of the ICJ Statute (n. 76) Arts. 53 and 41, and ILC Model Rules, Arts. 25 and 1(2).

[88] *See* Preliminary Draft, Art. IV(11) and IV(12); ILC Model Rules (n. 81) Arts. 33 and 38; ICJ Statute (n. 76) Arts. 60 and 61.

[89] *See* Preliminary Draft, Art. IV(13); ILC Model Rules (n. 81) Arts. 35–37.

[90] *See* text accompanying n. 57.

[91] Treaty Establishing the European Community, March 25, 1957, 298 UNTS 11, Art. 192.

[92] June 10, 1958, 330 UNTS 3 (New York Convention). The borrowed terminology was "competent authority," taken from Arts. V and VI of the New York Convention, to refer to the designated authority for award enforcement.

[93] *See* Ch. 5, text accompanying n. 58.

[94] IBRD, Loan Regulations Nos. 3 and 4, February 15, 1961, Art. VII(7.03)(k) and VII(7.04)(k) respectively.

[95] Preliminary Draft, comment on Art. VIII. Examples included the Statute of the International Atomic Energy Agency (IAEA), October 26, 1956, 276 UNTS 3, Art. XVII. Unlike the Preliminary Draft clause, however, this clause of the IAEA Statute was not confined to questions or disputes "arising between Contracting States" and also provided for the possibility of the IAEA being authorized under Art. 96 of the U.N. Charter to seek from the ICJ an advisory opinion on any legal "question" arising within the scope of the Agency's activities. *Cf.* n. 59.

the Preliminary Draft followed the example of the Articles of Agreement of the IFC, which designated the Board of Governors of the Corporation as competent to amend the Articles.[96] The Preliminary Draft was prepared only a few years after the conclusion of the Articles of Agreement of the World Bank's affiliate IDA. This latest example was relied upon for the sections of the Preliminary Draft on the territorial application and registration of the Convention.[97]

III. The regional consultative meetings

The regional consultative meetings, each lasting a week, took place between December 1963 and May 1964. At the Addis Ababa meeting, there were experts from 29 African countries. Participants in the Santiago meeting included experts nominated by 20 Western Hemisphere countries. At the Geneva meeting, there were experts named by 17 European countries and South Africa. Experts designated by 19 countries in the Asia and Pacific region participated in the Bangkok meeting. Some of the designated participants were diplomats or economists, but most were government lawyers. Several of them had or were earning high international reputations.[98]

The meetings were all chaired by Broches. He began each with the same statement outlining the background and main features of the proposed Convention. The World Bank, Broches explained, had taken the initiative of promoting such an agreement as a way of helping to foster increased international investment, which was "universally recognized as a factor of crucial importance in the economic development of the less developed parts of the world." The institutional facilities and procedures that would be provided might, Broches pointed out, be made available without an intergovernmental agreement. These were, however, secondary to other parts of the proposal, which it was necessary to embody in a Convention. A Convention could impart to the conciliation and arbitration agreements the internationally binding character that they would otherwise lack. As a corollary of allowing an investor direct and effective access to a foreign State in an international forum without the intervention of the home State, the latter would under the Convention no longer be able to espouse the claim of its national. Awards rendered pursuant to the Convention would be enforceable in all Contracting States as if they were final judgments of their national courts. The Convention would not lay down standards of conduct by States or by investors; it would not be concerned with the merits of investment disputes but with the procedure for settling them. Broches concluded his statement by emphasizing that the Convention would leave States and investors free to establish their mutual relations on whatever basis they deemed proper:

[96] *See* Articles of Agreement of the IFC, May 25, 1955, 264 UNTS 117, Art. VII. By contrast, the Articles of Agreement of the IBRD and IDA required acceptance of amendments by members as well as by the respective Boards of Governors. *See* Articles of Agreement of the IBRD (n. 72) Art. VIII; Articles of Agreement of IDA, December 16, 1960, 439 UNTS 249, Art. IX.

[97] Preliminary Draft, Art. XI(4) and XI(7). *Cf.* Articles of Agreement of IDA (n. 96) Art. XI(3) and XI(5).

[98] A participant in the Addis Ababa meeting specially praised by Broches in a report to the Executive Directors of the Bank was T.O. Elias, Attorney General and Minister of Justice of Nigeria and member of the ILC, who later became a member and eventually President of the ICJ. *See* Statement by Mr. Broches Regarding the Regional Meeting Held in Addis Ababa, Ethiopia, December 16–21, 1963, reprinted in 2 *History of the ICSID Convention* 295, 2.

Its true significance lay in the fact that it ensured that if the parties agreed to have recourse to an international forum, their agreement would be given full effect. This would create an element of confidence which would, in turn, contribute to a healthier investment climate.[99]

At each of the meetings, Broches's introductory statement was followed by general comments on the initiative from participating experts. Most of these were supportive, some enthusiastically so.[100] Several of the Latin American participants in the Santiago meeting, however, expressed fundamental opposition to the proposals. This was perhaps to be expected given the wide acceptance in Latin America of the Calvo Doctrine. Named for the nineteenth-century Argentine publicist Carlos Calvo, the doctrine aimed at restricting diplomatic protection. Based on rules of national sovereignty, equality of States and territorial jurisdiction, it advocated nonintervention and the absolute equality of foreigners with nationals, who could seek redress for grievances only from the local authorities.[101] Thus, it was objected at the Santiago meeting that the Convention would grant foreign investors "a legally privileged position, in violation of the principle of full equality before the law" and unacceptably delegate to an international organization "powers belonging to national institutions."[102] Fears for the impact of the Convention on national sovereignty also surfaced at the Bangkok meeting. One participant there doubted the appropriateness of its seemingly always placing "the foreign investor and the State on a par," while another thought the Convention might "enable pressure to be brought to bear on the developing countries thereby impairing their national dignity and self-respect."[103] Despite such fears, the ensuing discussions at all of the meetings were remarkably productive. These were section-by-section discussions of the Preliminary Draft.

A. Discussions regarding the establishment and organization of the Center

In the discussions of the sections on the establishment and organization of the proposed Center, it was suggested that the words "for investment disputes" should be added to the end of the name of the institution.[104] It was also suggested that the Convention should specifically bestow international legal personality on the Center and spell out the legal capacities it would have in Contracting States.[105] One participant in the

[99] For the full summaries of Broches's introductory statement, *see* Addis Ababa Record (n. 60) 1–5; Summary Record of Proceedings, Santiago Consultative Meeting, February 3–7, 1964 (Santiago Record), reprinted in 2 *History of the ICSID Convention* 298, 2–6; Summary Record of Proceedings, Geneva Consultative Meeting, February 17–22, 1964 (Geneva Record), reprinted in 2 *History of the ICSID Convention* 367, 1–5; Bangkok Record (n. 57) 3–6.

[100] *See, e.g.*, Addis Ababa Record (n. 60) 6 (intervention of Mr. Elias (Nigeria)); Santiago Record (n. 99) 8 (intervention of Mr. Summers (Canada)); Geneva Record (n. 99) 8 (intervention of Mr. Allott (United Kingdom)); Bangkok Record (n. 57) 13 (intervention of Mr. Himadeh (Lebanon)).

[101] D.R. Shea, *The Calvo Clause: A Problem of Inter-American and International Law and Diplomacy* 19 (1955).

[102] Santiago Record (n. 99) 7 and 8–9 (interventions of Mr. Ribeiro (Brazil) and Mr. Barboza (Argentina)).

[103] Bangkok Record (n. 57) 11 and 89 (interventions of Mr. Adarkar (India) and Mr. Gooneratne (Ceylon)).

[104] *See* Geneva Record (n. 99) 13 (intervention of Mr. van Santen (Netherlands)). *See also* Addis Ababa Record (n. 60) 9 (intervention of Mr. Elias (Nigeria) similarly suggesting that it be called the International "Investment" Conciliation and Arbitration Center).

[105] *See* Santiago Record (n. 99) 14 (intervention of Mr. Rattray (Jamaica)); Geneva Record (n. 99) 12 (interventions of Mr. Broches (Chairman) and reference to proposal at Addis Ababa consultative meeting).

Aron Broches, General Counsel of the World Bank from 1959 to 1979 (with the rank of Vice President from 1972) and Secretary-General of ICSID from 1967 to 1980.
World Bank Group Archives

meetings proposed that, in addition to its role in the settlement of investment disputes, the Center have a "preventive" function of advising on new investment agreements to assure their clarity and fairness.[106] Some participants wanted the Center to have a close link with the World Bank; others desired a more distant relationship, or none at all. Reflecting this diversity of views, specific suggestions in this regard ranged from highlighting the link with the Bank in the preamble to the Convention[107] to loosening the link by making it possible for annual meetings of the Administrative Council to be held separately from those of the Board of Governors of the Bank.[108] The trend that had begun in the initial meetings of the Committee of the Whole, of reducing the role of the Chairman of the Administrative Council and enlarging that of the Secretary-General of the Center, continued in the regional consultative meetings. It was thus argued at the meetings that the Chairman should not even have a tie-breaking vote in the Council,[109] while the functions of the Secretary-General should be more amply defined in the Convention.[110] The Convention should not, it was also urged, refer to the office of Secretary-General as possibly being combined with employment by the World Bank, or by the PCA.[111] Several participants felt that the Administrative Council should have a greater say in choosing a Secretary-General, rather than simply appointing the person nominated by the Chairman, and that the length of tenure of

106 Bangkok Record (n. 57) 14 (intervention of Mr. Himadeh (Lebanon)).

107 *See* Geneva Record (n. 99) 85 (intervention of Mr. van Santen (Netherlands)) and 88 (intervention of Mr. Deguen (France)).

108 *See* Bangkok Record (n. 57) 21 (intervention of Mr. O'Donovan (Australia)).

109 Addis Ababa Record (n. 60) 12 (intervention of Mr. Bigay (Central African Republic)); Santiago Record (n. 99) 16 (intervention of Mr. Arroyo (Panama)).

110 *See* Addis Ababa Record (n. 60) 11 (intervention of Mr. Mpanjo (Cameroon)); Bangkok Record (n. 57) 25 (intervention of Mr. Mansouri (Iran)).

111 *See* Addis Ababa Record (n. 60) 13 (intervention of Mr. Elias (Nigeria)); Geneva Record (n. 99) 16 (intervention of Mr. Bertram (F.R. Germany)); Bangkok Record (n. 57) 24 (intervention of Mr. Gooneratne (Ceylon)).

the post should be specified in the Convention.[112] Greater autonomy was likewise sought for Contracting States in designating persons to the Panels of Conciliators and of Arbitrators: they should, it was said, be entirely free as to whom to consult for their designations.[113] As for the number of designees of Contracting States, some of the experts thought there should be three, others four (as with the list of the PCA) and yet others, up to six.[114] Opinions were equally diverse as to whether and if so how many designations might be made by the Administrative Council Chairman.[115] One participant thought that the designees of the Chairman should each have a different nationality.[116] Two of the experts suggested that the term of Panel members, tentatively suggested as four years in the Preliminary Draft, should instead be six years (again as for the members of the PCA list).[117] Another expert made the important proposal that mention be made of the need to designate to the Panels persons capable of exercising independent judgment.[118] Other proposals included extending the provision on immunity from legal process to cover conciliators, arbitrators, parties and their representatives and adding a reference to the possibility of waivers of immunity.[119]

B. Discussions regarding the jurisdiction of the Center

The jurisdiction of the proposed center received much attention at the regional consultative meetings. Simply restricting the subject matter to an "investment dispute of a legal character" was unsatisfactory to many of the developing country experts in particular. They felt that both "investment" and "dispute of a legal character" should be defined.[120] For these experts, relying on the voluntary nature of the mechanism to obviate the need for such definition placed too heavy a burden on States, exposing them to the possible embarrassment of having to withhold consents to an overly broad jurisdiction.[121] Further restrictions proposed to be embodied in the Convention included limiting its scope to disputes arising out of contractual transactions.[122] Participants from some of the newly independent countries argued that the Convention should not apply to old investments made before the host State was the "master of its own destiny."[123] At the meetings, Broches explained that the scope of the jurisdiction of the

[112] *See* Santiago Record (n. 99) 18 and 19 (interventions of Mr. Rattray (Jamaica) and Mr. Arroyo (Panama); Bangkok Record (n. 57) 26 (interventions of Mr. Adarkar (India) and Mr. Himadeh (Lebanon)).

[113] *See* Addis Ababa Record (n. 60) 15 (intervention of Mr. Elias (Nigeria)); Bangkok Record (n. 57) 28 (intervention of Mr. Gae (India)). *Cf.* Ch. 3, n. 38 and accompanying text.

[114] *See* Addis Ababa Record (n. 60) 15 (intervention of Mr. Elias (Nigeria)); Geneva Record (n. 99) 19 (intervention of Mrs. Pilz (Austria)); Santiago Record (n. 99) 19 (intervention of Mr. Salazar (Ecuador)).

[115] *See, e.g.*, Santiago Record (n. 99) 20 (intervention of Mr. Palomo (Guatemala)); Geneva Record (n. 99) 18 (intervention of Mr. Rodocanachi (France)).

[116] *See* Santiago Record (n. 99) 19 (intervention of Mr. Arroyo (Panama)).

[117] *See* Geneva Record (n. 99) 17 and 18 (interventions of Mr. Bilgen (Turkey) and Mr. Bertram (F.R. Germany)).

[118] *See* ibid. 18 (intervention of Mr. van Santen (Netherlands)).

[119] *See* ibid. 21–23 (interventions of Mr. Allott (United Kingdom) and Mr. Amlie (Norway)).

[120] *See, e.g.*, Addis Ababa Record (n. 60) 20 and 23 (interventions of Mr. Brown (Tanganyika) and Mr. Gachem (Tunisia)); Bangkok Record (n. 57) 33, 37 and 38 (interventions of Mr. Ghanem (Lebanon), Mr. Tsai (China) and Mr. Heth (Israel)).

[121] *See* Addis Ababa Record (n. 60) 21 (intervention of Mr. Gachem (Tunisia)); Bangkok Record (n. 57) 34, 39 and 42 (interventions of Mr. Adarkar (India), Mr. Heth (Israel) and Mr. Wanasundera (Ceylon)).

[122] *See* Santiago Record (n. 99) 22 (intervention of Mr. Espinosa (Venezuela)).

[123] *See* Bangkok Record (n. 57) 77, 89 and 91 (interventions of Mr. Ghanem (Lebanon), Mr. Gooneratne (Ceylon) and Mr. Abas (Malaysia)).

Center should be stated in broad terms to accommodate the different ways in which States dealt with foreign investors in different parts of the world. The concern that signing a Convention of this scope could raise false expectations in the minds of investors, and engender criticism if consent were then refused, might, Broches, suggested, be addressed by allowing each State to declare in advance which types of disputes it would or would not consider submitting to the Center.[124]

There was considerable debate at the consultative meetings over the definition of a "national of another Contracting State" capable of bringing a Contracting State before the Center. The debate largely focused on whether a national of the State party to the dispute might nevertheless qualify as a "national of another Contracting State." Since it recognized a "controlling interest" by foreigners in a company as conferring foreign nationality, the Preliminary Draft would have allowed this in the case of a locally incorporated but foreign-controlled company.[125] While it was acknowledged that foreign investments often had to be channeled through such a company, several participants in the meetings expressed unease at the vagueness of the criterion of a "controlling interest."[126] The Preliminary Draft would also have permitted proceedings between a State and a natural person with its nationality if the individual concurrently possessed the nationality of another Contracting State.[127] This possibility aroused strong opposition at the consultative meetings.[128] Further criticism was directed at the provision of the Preliminary Draft, according to which a written affirmation of nationality by the minister of foreign affairs of the State whose nationality was claimed would be "conclusive proof of nationality."[129] This was seen by some experts as going too far in the direction of "making things easier for the investor"[130] or allowing the assumption of a "fictitious nationality."[131] An additional proposal regarding nationality was that the qualifying nationality of a natural person should have to be maintained throughout the proceeding.[132]

A proposal made at the outset of the consultative meetings that quickly won general acceptance was to include political subdivisions and agencies of a Contracting State as potential parties to proceedings if they had obtained the approval of the State.[133] It will be remembered from Chapter 2 that, at the time of the consultative meetings, investment promotion initiatives under consideration at the World Bank and in other international fora included the eventual establishment of a multilateral investment guarantee agency.[134] The question was thus raised at the consultative meetings whether

[124] Ibid. 40. *See also* Santiago Record (n. 99) 64.

[125] *Cf.* n. 26 and accompanying text.

[126] *See* Santiago Record (n. 99) 62 (intervention of Mr. Rattray (Jamaica)); Geneva Record (n. 99) 80 (interventions of Mr. Monaco (Italy) and Mr. Arnold (F.R. Germany)); Bangkok Record (n. 57) 79 (intervention of Mr. Tsai (China)).

[127] *Cf.* n. 27 and accompanying text.

[128] *See* Addis Ababa Record (n. 60) 22 and 47 (interventions of Mr. Ogbagzy (Ethiopia) and Mr. Ratsirahonana (Malagasy Republic)); Santiago Record (n. 99) 26 (intervention of Mr. Meneses (Nicaragua)).

[129] *See* n. 45 and accompanying text.

[130] Addis Ababa Record (n. 60) 18 (intervention of Mr. Elias (Nigeria)).

[131] Santiago Record (n. 99) 24 (intervention of Mr. Pinto (Guatemala), referring to States that "conferred their nationalities ... in return for payment").

[132] *See* Geneva Record (n. 99) 27 (intervention of Mr. Gould (South Africa)). The particular concern was that the individual might otherwise voluntarily acquire the nationality of the State party to the dispute after the proceeding was under way.

[133] *See* Addis Ababa Record (n. 60) 20 (interventions of Mr. Brown (Tanganyika) and Mr. Broches (Chairman)).

[134] *See* Ch. 2, sections I(A) and II(A).

the Convention should enable such an agency, as well as a State, to be a party when subrogated in the rights of an investor.[135]

As regards consent to the jurisdiction of the Center, the most significant change proposed at the consultative meetings was to omit from the Convention the possibility of applying the doctrine of *forum prorogatum* to establish jurisdiction, that is, of one party eliciting the consent of the other by submitting the dispute to the Center.[136] One participant in the consultative meetings saw in this the danger that an investor could bring a case to the Center before obtaining the State's consent and then "try to use the good offices of the Secretary-General to secure the consent."[137] The idea emerged that a party requesting conciliation or arbitration should instead always submit to the Secretary-General evidence of the consent of the other party. This would enable the Secretary-General to ensure that proceedings were not initiated without at least some prima facie indication that there was mutual consent.[138] The prior consent of the State party, it was acknowledged at the consultative meetings, could among other possibilities take the form of an advance consent in investment legislation of the State.[139] Another issue regarding consent that came up at the consultative meetings concerned the provision according to which consent to have recourse to arbitration pursuant to the Convention would, unless otherwise stated, be deemed consent to have recourse to such proceedings to the exclusion of any other remedy.[140] To some experts, the provision appeared to reverse the international law rule requiring the exhaustion of local remedies before the bringing of an international claim.[141] Broches sought to reassure them with the explanation that the provision merely made it clear that an unqualified consent should not be interpreted as tacitly requiring the prior exhaustion of local remedies but that parties would be free to incorporate this requirement in their consent agreements if they so wished.[142]

C. Discussions regarding conciliation and arbitration

Participants at the consultative meetings pointed out that the provisions of the Preliminary Draft allowing conciliation commissions and arbitral tribunals to have "several" members should be corrected to refer to "any uneven" number of members.[143] If appointed from outside the Panels of Conciliators and of Arbitrators they should, one expert urged, have the qualities required for designation to the Panels.[144] Another expert doubted that the procedure for the disqualification of conciliators and arbitrators should distinguish between appointees of the parties and appointees of the Chairman of the Administrative Council.[145] Two experts considered that the grounds

[135] *See* Addis Ababa Record (n. 60) 19 (interventions of Mr. Foalem (Organisation Africaine et Malagache de Coopération Economique) and Mr. Broches (Chairman)).

[136] *Cf.* Ch. 3, text accompanying n. 60.

[137] Bangkok Record (n. 57) 11 (intervention of Mr. Adarkar (India)).

[138] *See* Santiago Record (n. 99) 28 (intervention of Mr. Ucros (Panama)); Geneva Record (n. 99) 83 (intervention of Mr. van Santen (Netherlands)).

[139] *See* Geneva Record (n. 99) 37 (interventions of Mr. Gould (South Africa) and Mr. Broches (Chairman)).

[140] Preliminary Draft (n. 2) Art. IV(16). *Cf.* Ch. 3, n. 63 and accompanying text.

[141] *See* Geneva Record (n. 99) 63 (intervention of Mr. Bilgen (Turkey)); Bangkok Record (n. 57) 67 (intervention of Mr. Heth (Israel)).

[142] *See* ibid. (interventions of Mr. Broches (Chairman)).

[143] *See* Addis Ababa Record (n. 60) 25 (intervention of Mr. Elias (Nigeria)); Santiago Record (n. 99) 30 (intervention of Mr. Espinosa (Venezuela)).

[144] *See* Addis Ababa Record (n. 60) 27 (intervention of Mr. Elias (Nigeria)).

[145] *See* ibid. 38 (intervention of Mr. Bouiti (Congo, Brazzaville)).

for disqualification proposals should be specifically enumerated in the Convention.[146] Conciliators and arbitrators should, it was argued, be expected to set their fees and expenses within a predetermined "tariff," rather than being left "to sit down and haggle" with the parties in each case.[147] One expert added that the Convention should provide for conciliation and arbitration proceedings to be held at the Center when the parties had not agreed otherwise, rather than having the place determined by the Secretary-General in the absence of party agreement on the matter.[148]

In regard to the powers and functions of arbitral tribunals, it was proposed that the Convention permit a tribunal to raise jurisdictional issues of its own motion and to join objections to jurisdiction to the merits.[149] Comments were made by several experts on the provision of the Preliminary Draft authorizing tribunals to apply the rules of national or international law they deemed applicable in the absence of party agreement on the matter.[150] These included comments to the effect that national law should be applied in the first instance, that the applicable national law should always be that of the host State, that the reference to international law should be clarified and that national and international law should be applicable cumulatively, rather than as alternatives.[151] Suggestions for the default procedure included adding a provision to ensure that the non-appearing party received due notice and the opportunity to present its case.[152] It was pointed out that the provision on incidental and counter-claims should make it clear that these could be presented to a tribunal only if they fell within the scope of the parties' consent to arbitration.[153] Several of the participants asked how, if a tribunal could prescribe provisional measures, such measures would be enforced; one of them proposed that the Convention authorize a tribunal to "recommend" rather than prescribe provisional measures, particularly against the governmental party whose actions might be dictated by "reasons of necessity on national policy."[154] A further comment was that the Convention should include a statement of the powers of tribunals to make inquiries and site visits.[155]

Among the suggestions of experts for the provisions on post-award remedies was one to the effect that no time limit should be fixed in the Convention for interpretation requests. The reason given was that an award in an investment dispute might impose a continuing obligation over a long period so that questions as to its meaning could arise even after a considerable delay.[156] With respect to the annulment remedy, it was proposed that the first of the grounds for annulment should be narrowed to refer to a

[146] *See* Geneva Record (n. 99) 68 (intervention of Mr. Bilgen (Turkey)); Bangkok Record (n. 57) 70 (intervention of Mr. Ghanem (Lebanon)).

[147] *See* Addis Ababa Record (n. 60) 39 (interventions of Mr. Elias (Nigeria) and Mr. Ogbagzy (Ethiopia)).

[148] *See* ibid. 40 (intervention of Mr. Macaulay (Sierra Leone)).

[149] *See* Geneva Record (n. 99) 39 (intervention of Mr. Allott (United Kingdom)); Santiago Record (n. 99) 26 (intervention of Mr. Rattray (Jamaica)).

[150] *Cf.* Ch. 3, n. 80 and accompanying text.

[151] *See* Geneva Record (n. 99) 50, 51 and 53 (interventions of Mr. Bilgen (Turkey), Mr. Melchor (Spain) and Mr. Deguen (France)); Bangkok Record (n. 57) 55 (intervention of Mr. Tsai (China)).

[152] *See* Addis Ababa Record (n. 60) 31 (invervention of Mr. Moustafa (United Arab Republic)); Santiago Record (n. 99) 37 (intervention of Mr. Cherrie (Trinidad and Tobago)); Geneva Record (n. 99) 54 (intervention of Mr. Allott (United Kingdom)).

[153] *See* Addis Ababa Record (n. 60) 32 (intervention of Mr. Moustafa (United Arab Republic)); Santiago Record (n. 99) 38 (intervention of Mr. Belin (United States)).

[154] *See* Santiago Record (n. 99) 39 (interventions of Mr. Salazar (Ecuador) and Mr. Palomo (Guatemala)); Bangkok Record (n. 57) 56 (intervention of Mr. Tsai (China)).

[155] *See* Addis Ababa Record (n. 60) 6 (intervention of Mr. Bigay (Central African Republic)).

[156] *See* Santiago Record (n. 99) 40 (intervention of Mr. Rattray (Jamaica)).

"manifest" excess of powers.[157] One of the experts thought that the Convention should specify that an excess of powers could include a failure on the part of the tribunal to apply the applicable law.[158] Another put forward the idea of expanding the grounds for annulment to include the case where an arbitrator had been a national of either the home or host State of the investor and hence ineligible for appointment to the tribunal.[159]

As explained earlier, the Preliminary Draft sought to balance the obligation of each Contracting State to comply with an award made against it with a commitment of every Contracting State to enforce a Convention award as if it were a final judgment of the State's courts, that commitment being particularly directed at awards against investors.[160] Enforcement would be obtained on simple presentation of the award to the competent authority that each Contracting State would designate for the purpose.[161] A participant in the Geneva consultative meeting asked if those arrangements might, on the one hand, not go far enough in assuring compliance by States with awards made against them and, on the other hand, go too far in the direction of depriving national authorities of control over the enforcement of awards.[162] He raised the possibility of creating a surveillance committee for compliance with awards by States and, for the second aspect, following the system of the New York Convention on the Recognition and Enforcement of Foreign Arbitral Awards, under which national courts could refuse enforcement of an award on certain specified grounds.[163] Broches vigorously replied that this would fail to:

> ... establish the full mutuality or equivalence between the treatment of States and individuals which it was desired to achieve. The developing countries had pointed out that a State coming before a tribunal automatically surrendered part of its sovereignty, because it put the decision in the hands of an arbitral tribunal, agreed without qualification to abide by the award, waived any right of appeal and submitted to an autonomous system in which immediate sanctions would be incurred if an award against it were not complied with. Apart from legal sanctions based on the revival of the right of diplomatic protection of the investor's State there would be even more serious indirect sanctions because a State which did not comply would fail to meet its obligations not only to the investor but also to the community of Contracting States which would presumably include capital-exporting countries from which the losing State could expect assistance. On the other hand no such sanction would exist against an investor who lost a case.... The present Convention ought to contain a clear statement of the position of a State which had won an award against a private investor brought before the Center.... [I]t was essential in order to obtain the widest possible acceptance of this Convention, particularly by the developing countries, to ensure that a winning State could obtain satisfaction of the rights conferred by the award wherever the investor's property was located without being subject to undue delays and being met by defenses based on local laws.[164]

[157] *See* Geneva Record (n. 99) 55 (intervention of Mr. Bertram (Germany)).

[158] *See* Bangkok Record (n. 57) 58 (intervention of Mr. Tsai (China)). The proposal was also made that the annulment remedy should be available for serious misapplication of the applicable law. As pointed out at the time, this would have been tantamount to providing for an appeal. *See* Santiago Record (n. 99) 41 (interventions of Mr. Ramirez (Honduras) and Mr. Broches (Chairman)).

[159] *See* Geneva Record (n. 99) 55 (intervention of Mr. Bilgen (Turkey)).

[160] *See* n. 56 and accompanying text.

[161] *See* n. 57 and accompanying text.

[162] *See* Geneva Record (n. 99) 56 (intervention of Mr. Arnold (F.R. Germany)).

[163] *See* ibid. The surveillance committee idea, never pursued, was reminiscent of the role given to the Committee of Ministers of the Council of Europe to supervise the execution of judgments of the European Court of Human Rights under the European Convention on Human Rights and Fundamental Freedoms, November 5, 1950, as amended November 1, 1998, reprinted in I. Brownlie and G. Goodwin-Gill, *Basic Documents on Human Rights* (2002) Art. 46(2). With regard to the award enforcement point described in the text, *see* New York Convention (n. 92) Art. V.

[164] Geneva Record (n. 99) 57.

Another participant at the Geneva meeting counseled against excessive concern over the provisions on the enforcement of awards. Investors, he observed, were more likely to be suing States before the Center than vice versa; the need for the provisions was therefore "almost wholly political."[165]

D. Discussions regarding inter-State proceedings, amendments and participation in the Convention

In his remarks on the enforcement of awards at the Geneva meeting, Broches referred to the article of the Preliminary Draft withdrawing the right of the home State of the investor to exercise diplomatic protection in respect of the dispute. Paradoxically perhaps, at the Santiago consultative meeting, some of the Latin American experts objected to this article of the Preliminary Draft. They saw it as implicitly recognizing the right of diplomatic protection, a right denied by the Calvo Doctrine.[166] It will be recalled that there had been added to the article a provision intended to make it clear that the rule against the exercise of diplomatic protection would not prevent recourse by the investor's home State to the inter-State dispute settlement machinery of an investment treaty between it and the host State.[167] In the consultative meetings, it was observed that the additional provision was not necessary.[168] The provision, however, prompted one expert to stress the need to avoid conflicts between decisions of arbitral tribunals set up under bilateral treaties and those constituted under the Convention.[169] He made the observation, interesting in light of later developments, that "[i]t would be desirable, with a view to avoiding any contradictory situations, for future bilateral agreements, possibly multilateral agreements of the type envisaged [by the OECD] …, to provide for compulsory arbitration through the Center."[170]

To ensure some uniformity of decisions on questions of interpretation of the Convention itself, Broches and his colleagues had, as explained earlier, tentatively proposed permitting an arbitral tribunal faced with such a question to suspend its proceeding to give interested Contracting States the opportunity to submit the matter to the ICJ under the compromissory clause referring to it in the Convention.[171] The proposal was criticized by several of the experts at the consultative meetings; the procedure could, they suspected, lead to unnecessary delay and confusion, compromise the authority of arbitral tribunals and possibly provide an occasion for a State to espouse its national's case.[172] Broches gave a negative answer to the inquiry of two experts whether, as an alternative, the Center might become a specialized agency able to seek advisory opinions from the ICJ.[173] In response to the suggestion of another expert,

[165] Ibid. 58 (intervention of Mr. Trolle (Denmark)).

[166] *See* Santiago Record (n. 99) 49–51 (interventions of Mr. Espinonsa (Venezuela), Mr. Meneses (El Salvador) and Mr. Canal (Colombia)).

[167] *See* n. 58 and accompanying text.

[168] *See* Geneva Record (n. 99) 65 and 67 (interventions of Mr. Melchor (Spain) and Mr. Broches (Chairman)).

[169] The same concern had of course been raised in the initial meetings of the Committee of the Whole of the Executive Directors of the World Bank. *See* Ch. 3, text accompanying n. 129.

[170] Geneva Record (n. 99) 67 (intervention of Mr. Rodocanachi (France)).

[171] *See* text accompanying n. 60.

[172] *See* Santiago Record (n. 99) 55 (intervention of Mr. Belin (United States)); Geneva Record (n. 99) 71 (intervention of Mr. Melchor (Spain)).

[173] *See* Santiago Record (n. 99) 57 (interventions of Mr. Rattray (Jamaica) and Mr. Broches (Chairman)); Bangkok Record (n. 57) 74 (interventions of Mr. Ghanem (Lebanon) and Mr. Broches (Chairman)). *Cf.* Ch. 1, n. 75 and accompanying text.

Broches expressed doubt as to the feasibility of establishing a procedure for the arbitral tribunals to seek advisory opinions of the ICJ through the U.N. General Assembly.[174]

As mentioned earlier, the Preliminary Draft envisaged that the Convention could be amended by a qualified majority decision of the Administrative Council of the Center.[175] At the consultative meetings, several participants indicated that their countries would be unable to accept such an "open-ended" Convention that might be amended without their own ratification.[176] Broches pointed out that the Articles of Agreement of the IBRD, the IFC and IDA could be amended by majority vote (of the Board of Governors in the case of the IFC Articles and of the Boards of Governors and members in the cases of the IBRD and IDA Articles).[177] One expert replied that unlike those instruments, to be implemented, the Convention would require changes in domestic legislation.[178]

Most of the opponents of the amendment provision were representatives of industrial countries. They must also have been influenced in their view by the fact that the Convention would not incorporate the weighted voting system of the IBRD, the IFC and IDA under which their countries wielded large shares of the voting power in those institutions.[179] A possible solution put forward at the consultative meetings was to stipulate that amendments passed by majority vote would not bind dissenting States.[180] It was, however, pointed out that having an amendment apply to some but not all parties to the Convention could create "insoluble problems regarding the legal relationships among Contracting States."[181]

A final issue discussed at the consultative meetings was whether participation in the Convention should be open to all States. This was the approach taken by the Preliminary Draft. As already indicated, it envisaged that participation would be open to "all … sovereign States."[182] A participant in the Bangkok meeting, echoed by another, suggested that participation should instead be restricted to members of the IBRD.[183] An alternative proposed at the Santiago meeting, and strongly supported at the Geneva meeting, was to limit participation in the Convention to members of the IBRD, the United Nations or any of its specialized agencies.[184]

[174] *See* Geneva Record (n. 99) 52 (interventions of Mr. Gould (South Africa) and Mr. Broches (Chairman)). Broches pointed out that the proposal, "linked as it was with the entire question of foreign investment, was unlikely to gain unanimous support in the forum of the United Nations" (ibid.), whose members then included Soviet bloc Communist countries.

[175] *See* nn. 61 and 96 and accompanying text.

[176] *See* Santiago Record (n. 99) 58 (intervention of Mr. Lowenfeld (United States)); Geneva Record (n. 99) 73 (interventions of Mr. Karelle (Belgium), Mr. Koinzer (F.R. Germany), Mr. Trolle (Denmark) and Mr. Van Santen (Netherlands)).

[177] *See* Santiago Record (n. 99) 59. *See also* n. 96.

[178] *See* Santiago Record (n. 99) 59 (intervention of Mr. Espinosa (Venezuela)).

[179] *See* Ch. 1, nn. 22 and 52 and accompanying text.

[180] *See* Santiago Record (n. 99) 58 (intervention of Mr. Lowenfeld (United States)).

[181] Geneva Record (n. 99) 74 (intervention of Mr. Rodocanachi (France)).

[182] *See* n. 62 and accompanying text.

[183] Bangkok Record (n. 57) 88, 89 and 92 (interventions of Mr. Hoan (Vietnam) and Mr. Park (Korea)). It need hardly be pointed out that this would have excluded the northern Communist halves of the speakers' divided nations.

[184] Santiago Record (n. 99) 63 (intervention of Mr. Lowenfeld (United States)); Geneva Record (n. 99) 74 (interventions of Mr. Allott (United Kingdom) and Mr. Koinzer (F.R. Germany)). Nonmembers of both the IBRD and the U.N. at the time included the Communist States of East Germany, North Korea and North Vietnam. Though the question had been the subject of annual credentials disputes since 1950, the Communist government of China had still not been accepted as representing the country in the U.N. The Taiwan government represented China in the U.N. until 1971 and at the IBRD until 1980. *See further* Ch. 7, n. 24 and accompanying text.

5

Finalizing the Text of the Convention

The Executive Directors of the World Bank received briefings from Aron Broches and his staff team on the regional consultative meetings as they took place. Also provided to the Executive Directors were the summary records of the meetings and a report by Broches summarizing the main points raised at them.[1] Follow-up steps were recommended in a memorandum that Bank President George Woods sent to the Executive Directors' Committee of the Whole in June 1964, the month after the last of the consultative meetings.[2] In his memorandum, Woods acknowledged the fundamental objections that some experts, notably those from Latin American countries, had expressed at the meetings. But a large majority of the experts, the memorandum pointed out, had found the idea of such a convention on the settlement of investment disputes to be basically acceptable. It seemed that their disagreements on specific issues could be worked out in further negotiations. In view of this, Woods proposed that the Executive Directors now seek from the Bank's Board of Governors the authority to prepare a convention in final form to be transmitted to governments for signature and ratification.

Less than two years earlier, it will be recalled, the Board of Governors had adopted a resolution giving the Executive Directors a mandate to draft a convention on the conciliation and arbitration of investment disputes for submission to governments.[3] The intention surely was for the Executive Directors to draw up and present the convention to governments in final form, rather than for further discussion, just as the Executive Directors had done with the Articles of Agreement of the IFC and IDA. As adopted, however, the resolution left open the possibility that the Executive Directors should instead merely prepare a draft for consideration at a diplomatic conference convened for the purpose. Several of the experts at the consultative meetings had advocated this approach. Apart from the fact that the subject matter of the projected convention was outside the expertise of the Executive Directors as a body, such a conference would, it was felt by these experts, allow for a more "frank exchange of views between capital-exporting and capital-importing countries on all the issues involved."[4]

In his memorandum to the Committee of the Whole, Woods dismissed these arguments as unpersuasive, pointing to the danger that a diplomatic conference might "unnecessarily delay and impede progress toward an objective which has broad support in the Bank's membership." The Executive Directors could, he proposed, obtain the technical guidance needed to finalize a convention by establishing a committee composed of legal experts named by the countries in their respective constituencies. To the extent desired by the nominating governments, the experts would act on their instructions, in contrast to the experts at the regional consultative meetings, who did

[1] The report, dated July 9, 1964, is reprinted in 2 *History of the ICSID Convention* 557.

[2] The memorandum, dated June 10, 1964, is reprinted in 2 *History of the ICSID Convention* 554.

[3] *See* Ch. 3, n. 6 and accompanying text.

[4] Summary Record of Proceedings, Bangkok Consultative Meeting, April 27–May 1, 1964, reprinted in 2 *History of the ICSID Convention* 458, 89 (intervention of Mr. Gooneratne (Ceylon)).

not act as official representatives. Through the committee of legal experts, all member countries would have an opportunity to participate directly in the final process of formulating the text of the treaty. Woods suggested that, if the Executive Directors agreed, they should ask the Board of Governors to instruct them to proceed on this basis.

The Executive Directors convened twice again as the Committee of the Whole in July 1964. Reflecting the sentiments of their constituents, two of the Executive Directors representing Latin American countries expressed disagreement with the entire approach outlined in Woods's memorandum. They repeated their opposition to establishing a center for the settlement of investment disputes by treaty; they also questioned the authority of the Bank to draw up such a treaty and the appropriateness of possibly applying its weighted voting system to related decisions.[5] Most of the Executive Directors, however, endorsed Woods's recommendations. Some of the speakers[6] argued that the issues involved were too complex to be dealt with effectively in a diplomatic conference; others[7] cautioned that the Bank could with such a conference fall into "the trap of perfectionism ... lead[ing] to complete frustration of all further action."[8] Broches advised that formulating the contemplated treaty would clearly come within the Bank's implied powers; that it would be difficult to imagine a small number of members taking advantage of their superior voting power in this context; and that, at any rate, no vote was ever taken by the Executive Directors in this or other committees.[9] One Executive Director[10] more bluntly added that it was not the practice of the Executive Directors "to ram decisions through by a majority of the voting power but on the contrary to try to achieve consensus."[11] Chairing the second of these two further meetings of the Committee of the Whole, Woods sought to provide further reassurance by emphasizing the voluntary nature of the facilities and procedures to be provided under the proposed convention. All it would do, he said in terms reflecting his remarkable engagement with the initiative, "was to create a house; the door of the house would be open and governments would be free to enter ... with respect to a given controversy."[12]

Shortly after the July 1964 meetings of the Committee of the Whole, the Executive Directors approved a report recommending that the Board of Governors of the Bank adopt, at its Annual Meeting in Tokyo in September 1964, a resolution asking the Executive Directors to formulate the envisaged convention on the settlement of investment disputes and to submit its text to member governments with such recommendations as they deemed appropriate. The report explained that the Executive Directors would be assisted in this task by a committee of legal experts representing member countries wishing to participate in the preparation of the text.[13] In addition

[5] The Executive Directors concerned were Mejia-Palacio and Illanes (Ch. 3, n. 97). *See* Memorandum of the Meeting of the Committee of the Whole (MMCW), July 14, 1964, reprinted in 2 *History of the ICSID Convention* 585, para. 19; MMCW, July 23, 1964, reprinted in 2 *History of the ICSID Convention* 589, paras. 6–9 and 13.

[6] Lieftinck (Ch. 3, n. 100) and G. d'Andelot Belin (Temporary Alternate Executive Director for the United States). Belin was General Counsel of the U.S. Treasury in the administrations of Presidents John F. Kennedy and Lyndon B. Johnson. *See* MMCW, July 23, 1964 (n. 5) paras. 3 and 5.

[7] Donner (Ch. 3, n. 110) and Eric Roll (Executive Director for the United Kingdom). Roll, who had been Professor of Economics and Commerce at University College of Hull and held various senior positions in the U.K. Ministry of Agriculture, was Executive Director from 1963 to 1965. *See* MMCW, July 14, 1964 (n. 5) paras. 14 and 15; MMCW, July 23, 1964, paras. 17 and 18.

[8] MMCW, July 14, 1964 (n. 5) para. 15.

[9] Ibid. paras. 21, 22 and 24. *Cf.* Ch. 3, nn. 11 and 12 and accompanying text.

[10] Donner.

[11] MMCW, July 23, 1964 (n. 5) para. 18. *Cf.* Ch. 3, n. 10 and accompanying text.

[12] MMCW, July 23, 1964 (n. 5) para. 41.

[13] The report, dated August 6, 1964, is reprinted in 2 *History of the ICSID Convention* 606.

to approving the report, the Executive Directors agreed that, following the decision of the Board of Governors, the Bank would invite member governments to designate experts to take part in the work of the committee of legal experts that would convene at the Bank for three weeks starting in late November 1964. The Bank would defray the transportation and subsistence expenses of the participating experts.[14]

At the Annual Meeting in Tokyo, the Board of Governors adopted the recommended resolution, thus clearing the way for the Executive Directors to proceed to finalize the proposed convention with the help of the committee of legal experts.[15] This was, however, done despite negative votes cast by Governors representing 21 countries, including all 19 of the Latin American members of the Bank.[16] Speaking on behalf of the Latin American members, the Governor for Chile explained their vote against the resolution in the following terms:

> The legal and constitutional systems of all the Latin American countries that are members of the Bank offer the foreign investor at the present time the same rights and protection as their own nationals; they prohibit confiscation and discrimination and require that any expropriation on justifiable grounds of public interest shall be accompanied by fair compensation fixed, in the final resort, by the law courts.
>
> The new system that has been suggested would give the foreign investor, by virtue of the fact that he is a foreigner, the right to sue a sovereign state outside its national territory, dispensing with the courts of law. This provision is contrary to the accepted legal principles of our countries and, de facto, would confer a privilege on the foreign investor, placing the nationals of the country concerned in a position of inferiority.[17]

In short, their negative vote, afterwards dubbed *El No de Tokio*, reflected tenets of the Calvo Doctrine underlying similar opposition to the initiative among Latin American experts at the consultative meeting held seven months earlier in Santiago.[18]

The day after the adoption of the resolution, the President of the Bank addressed a letter to all member countries notifying them, as planned, that they could each designate a representative to serve on the committee of legal experts which would commence its work the next month. Enclosed with the President's letter was a first Draft Convention on the Settlement of Investment Disputes between States and Nationals of Other States (the First Draft). It was to serve as a working paper for the meetings of the committee. The following sections of this chapter describe the First Draft, the meetings of the committee of legal experts and the concluding steps in the formulation of the Convention.

I. The First Draft

Dated September 11, 1964, the First Draft was a revision of the Preliminary Draft prepared by Broches and his staff in light of the discussions at the regional consultative meetings.[19] The First Draft had a preamble and 78 continuously numbered articles

[14] *See* Note from the President to the Executive Directors Concerning the Legal Committee, August 5, 1964, reprinted in 2 *History of the ICSID Convention* 604.

[15] IBRD Board of Governors Resolution No. 214, September 10, 1964, reprinted in 2 *History of the ICSID Convention* 608.

[16] The two other countries voting against the resolution were Iraq and the Philippines.

[17] Excerpt from statement of Felix Ruiz, Governor for Chile, September 9, 1964, Tokyo, in 2 *History of the ICSID Convention* 606.

[18] *See* Ch. 4, nn. 101 and 102 and accompanying text.

[19] The First Draft is reprinted in 2 *History of the ICSID Convention* 610 and as App. III of this book.

across ten main chapters.[20] The elaborate explanatory comments included with the Preliminary Draft were replaced in the First Draft with notes merely indicating, with telegraph-style brevity, which provisions had been retained and which changed in the new draft. As Broches later explained to the committee of legal experts, substantive commentary would be included in an explanatory memorandum or report that the Executive Directors of the World Bank would append to the text of the Convention when they transmitted it to governments.[21]

A. Provisions on the establishment and organization of the Center

As suggested at the consultative meetings, the First Draft gave the Center a name more reflective of its special role: "the International Center for the Settlement of Investment Disputes."[22] It also provided for the possibility that, with the approval of the Administrative Council, the Center might undertake "ancillary activities, including research and the collection and dissemination of information in the field of international investment."[23] In regard to the link with the World Bank, the First Draft continued the search for the right balance by introducing a new preambular paragraph that acknowledged the Bank's sponsorship of the initiative while, on the other hand, modifying the main provision on the Secretary-General so that it no longer specifically allowed that official to be concurrently employed by the Bank (or the PCA).[24] Reflecting the discussions in the consultative meetings, the First Draft deprived the Chairman of even a casting vote in the Administrative Council and provided for the Secretary-General to be elected by the Council from among possibly several candidates, rather than just being appointed by the Council on the nomination of the Chairman.[25] The First Draft also restored to the text a clause providing for the Administrative Council, in addition to its previously listed powers and functions, to "exercise such other powers and perform such other functions as it shall determine to be necessary or useful for the implementation of the provisions of this Convention or for the achievement of its purposes."[26] In regard to the Panels of Conciliators and of Arbitrators, the First Draft added reliability for independent judgment to the qualities required of Panel members, left Contracting States free as to whom to consult about their Panel designations, specified that the States could each designate four Panel members and the Chairman ten, and set the term of all Panel members at four years.[27] As proposed at the consultative meetings, the First Draft attributed international legal personality to the Center, specified the legal capacities (to contract, acquire and dispose of property and institute legal proceedings) that it would have in Contracting States and extended immunity from legal process to conciliators and arbitrators.[28]

[20] The First Draft thus abandoned the arrangement of earlier drafts, in which the main individual provisions were sections of articles, as in the Articles of Agreement of the IBRD, the IFC and IDA.

[21] *See* Summary Proceedings of the Legal Committee Meeting (SPLCM), November 23, 1964 (morning), reprinted in 2 *History of the ICSID Convention* 672, 3 (page numbers cited are of original documents). The Executive Directors had attached such explanatory memoranda to the texts of the Articles of Agreement of the IFC and IDA in submitting them to members.

[22] First Draft, Art. 1(1). [23] Ibid. Art. 1(2).

[24] Ibid. preambular para. 5 and Art. 10(2). [25] Ibid. Arts. 5 and 10(1).

[26] Ibid. Art. 6(vi). [27] Ibid. Arts. 13, 14(1) and 15(1).

[28] Ibid. Arts. 18, 19 and 21(i). The constituent treaties of most international organizations, including the IBRD, the IFC and IDA, did not expressly grant them international legal personality, as opposed to legal personality at the national level. *Cf.* C.F. Amerasinghe, *Principles of the Institutional Law of International Organizations* 84 (2d ed. 2005). An exception was the Agreement Establishing the African Development Bank (August 4, 1963, 510 UNTS 3). Its provision (Art. 50) attributing international personality to the African Development Bank was a model for the new provision,

Hayato Ikeda, Prime Minister of Japan, addressing the opening session of the 1964 annual meetings in Tokyo of the Boards of Governors of the IMF, the IBRD, the IFC and IDA. Adopted at the meetings was Resolution No. 214 of the Board of Governors of the IBRD asking the Executive Directors to formulate what became the ICSID Convention and to submit its text to member governments with such recommendations as they deemed appropriate.

World Bank Group Archives

B. Provisions on the jurisdiction of the Center

The First Draft differed significantly from the Preliminary Draft with respect to the jurisdiction of the Center. Responding to the wishes of experts at the consultative meetings for greater delineation of the subject matter of covered disputes, the First Draft provided that they would comprise "all legal disputes ... arising out of or in connection with any investment" and added definitions for this purpose of "legal dispute" and "investment."[29] The latter term was defined as meaning "any contribution of money or other asset of economic value for an indefinite period or, if the period be defined, for not less than five years."[30] The definition of "legal dispute" was "any

suggested at the Addis Ababa consultative meeting, on the international personality of the Center. The new provision on legal capacities was based on the Convention on the Privileges and Immunities of the United Nations, 1 UNTS 15, February 13, 1946, Art. I. While the First Draft gave immunity from legal process to conciliators and arbitrators, it was not until the subsequent draft that the immunity was also extended to parties to proceedings, their counsel and witnesses and experts. The reluctance of States to accept a proliferation of categories of persons covered by the immunity explains the caution with which it was extended over successive drafts of the Convention.

[29] First Draft, Art. 26(1).

[30] Ibid. Art. 30(i).

dispute concerning a legal right or obligation or concerning a fact relevant to the determination of a legal right or obligation."[31]

The First Draft also introduced changes to the definition of a "national of another Contracting State" eligible to initiate proceedings against a Contracting State under the Convention. In the First Draft, the definition was no longer expressly extended to cover persons concurrently possessing the nationality of the State party to the dispute. It provided that, in the case of a natural person, qualifying foreign nationality should be held continuously, from the date of consent through to the date of the institution of proceedings.[32] For juridical persons, the definition in the First Draft discarded the vague "controlling interest" criterion that had been criticized at the consultative meetings. To ensure that investments made through local companies could be covered if the parties so desired, the definition instead simply provided that eligible juridical persons would comprise, in addition to those having the nationality of another Contracting State on the date of consent, any juridical person that the parties had agreed should be treated as a "national of another Contracting State." Deleted in the First Draft was the Preliminary Draft's provision under which a certificate of nationality issued by the foreign minister of the country concerned would conclusively prove the foreign nationality of the "national of another Contracting State." Other new provisions of the First Draft on potential parties to proceedings made it clear that a political subdivision or agency of a State could consent to the jurisdiction of the Center with the State's approval and that a "public international institution" (such as the multilateral investment guarantee agency that was then being contemplated), as well as a State insurer, could after having compensated an investor and being subrogated to its rights, substitute for the investor in proceedings under the Convention.[33]

It will be recalled that at the consultative meetings, experts from developing countries had expressed concern that the Convention would expose States to pressures to consent to the jurisdiction of the Center in respect of disputes that they would prefer to have solved by other means. This concern was addressed by the First Draft's tighter definition of the jurisdiction of the Center. Additional protection was offered by a new article according to which a Contracting State could at any time send the Secretary-General, for purposes of information, a statement indicating the class or classes of disputes within the jurisdiction of the Center that it would in principle consider submitting to conciliation or arbitration pursuant to the Convention.[34] The First Draft also dropped the reference of previous drafts to the possibility of applying the doctrine of *forum prorogatum*, which a participant at the consultative meetings had thought could draw the Secretary-General of the Center into efforts to obtain the missing consent of a prospective respondent.[35]

C. Provisions on conciliation and arbitration

Elaborating on the idea put forward at the consultative meetings, the First Draft provided that a party requesting conciliation or arbitration should instead always include with its request addressed to the Secretary-General "information concerning the subject-matter of the dispute, the identity of the parties and their consent" to conciliation or arbitration "sufficient to establish *prima facie* that the dispute is within the jurisdiction of the Center."[36] The Secretary-General would notify the other party of

[31] Ibid. Art. 30(ii). [32] Ibid. Art. 30(iii)(a).
[33] Ibid. Arts. 26(1), 26(2) and 27(2). [34] Ibid. Art. 29.
[35] *See* Ch. 4, nn. 136 and 137 and accompanying text.
[36] First Draft, Arts. 31(2) and 40(2).

the request only if it met that test.[37] Anticipating the need for further details on this new procedure, the First Draft added to the list of regulations and rules to be adopted by the Administrative Council "rules governing the procedure for the institution of proceedings pursuant to this Convention."[38]

On the composition of conciliation commissions and arbitral tribunals, the First Draft made it clear that they could not have an even number of members and that any conciliators or arbitrators appointed from outside the respective Panels should have the qualities required of designees to the Panels.[39] Like the Preliminary Draft, the First Draft contained a provision excluding from appointment to an arbitral tribunal any national of the State party to the dispute or of the home State of the foreign national concerned. In the First Draft, however, the provision was made more stringent by also excluding from appointment any person designated to the Panel of Arbitrators by either State.[40] As explained in Chapter 4, under the Preliminary Draft, a proposal to disqualify a conciliator or arbitrator could be made "on account of any fact"; but if the proposal related to an appointee of the Chairman of the Administrative Council, the fact would, as a rule, have to have arisen after the appointment. The First Draft eliminated the special rule for appointees of the Chairman and provided that the "fact" invoked in a disqualification proposal had to be one indicating "a manifest lack" of the qualities of integrity, competence and reliability for independent judgment needed for designation to the Panel of Conciliators or the Panel of Arbitrators.[41] Also provided for in the First Draft was the possibility of a disqualification proposal based on an arbitrator's ineligibility for appointment under the above-mentioned provision excluding "national arbitrators."[42] Another notable difference between the Preliminary Draft and the First Draft concerned the determination of the fees and expenses of conciliators and arbitrators in cases where there was no agreement on the matter between the commission or tribunal and the parties. Instead of leaving this entirely to the discretion of the commission or tribunal after consultation with the Secretary-General, the First Draft provided that in such cases the determination would be made "within limits established from time to time by the Administrative Council."[43] In regard to the place of conciliation and arbitration proceedings, the First Draft, following the proposal made in this regard at the consultative meetings, designated the seat of the Center as the default venue of proceedings, rather than having the place fixed by the Secretary-General for each case where the parties failed to agree on the matter.[44]

As proposed at the consultative meetings, the First Draft allowed conciliators and arbitrators to join jurisdictional objections to the merits of the dispute (instead of requiring that such objections always be dealt with as preliminary questions).[45] In the absence of agreement between the parties on the law to be applied, a tribunal was, under the First Draft, to decide the dispute in accordance with the applicable rules of national and international law, rather than being confined either to national or to international law rules.[46] The First Draft added that "international law" was in

[37] *See* ibid. Arts. 31(3) and 40(3).

[38] Ibid. Art. 6(ii). These were to be a separate set of rules that could not, in contrast to the conciliation and arbitration rules, be modified by agreement of the parties. *Cf.* ibid. Arts. 36 and 47 (referring to the conciliation and arbitration rules governing the conduct of proceedings "[e]xcept as the parties otherwise agree").

[39] *See* ibid. Arts. 32(2)(a), 34(2), 41(2)(a) and 43(3).

[40] *See* ibid. Art. 43(1). As in the Preliminary Draft, any person who had been a conciliator in the same dispute was excluded from appointment as well.

[41] Ibid. Art. 60. [42] Ibid. [43] Ibid. Art. 64(1). [44] *See* ibid. Art. 65.

[45] *See* ibid. Arts. 35(2) and 44(2). [46] Ibid. Art. 45(1).

this context to be understood "in the sense given to it by Article 38 of the Statute of the International Court of Justice."[47] A new article included in the First Draft made it clear that an arbitral tribunal could call on the parties to produce documents or other information and visit the scene connected with the dispute.[48] Taking account of observations made at the consultative meetings, the First Draft provided for a period of grace to be accorded to a defaulting party before the tribunal rendered its award and made it clear that a tribunal could entertain a counter-claim only if it were within the jurisdiction of the Center.[49] Like the Preliminary Draft, the First Draft provided that a tribunal could "prescribe" provisional measures.[50] The First Draft addressed the enforcement difficulties that had been highlighted at the consultative meetings by adding that the tribunal could "fix a penalty for failure to comply with such ... measures."[51]

The First Draft elaborated on the idea of the basic finality of the award by adding that it would be "without appeal."[52] Reflecting the point made at the consultative meetings, that an award might have to be implemented over a long period, with disputes as to its meaning possibly arising after a considerable delay, the First Draft omitted any time limit for requests for the interpretation of an award.[53] The First Draft also introduced changes to the grounds for the annulment of an award. It added the ground of improper constitution of the tribunal and narrowed the ground of excess of powers by specifying that it should be manifest.[54] Another change was to make failure to state reasons for the award a distinct ground for annulment, rather than including it in the ground of serious departure from a fundamental rule of procedure.[55] In making this change, however, the First Draft provided that the newly distinct ground would not apply if "the parties have agreed that reasons need not be stated."[56]

The First Draft had the article, proposed by Broches during the consultative meetings, providing for the issuance of award enforcement orders by designated authorities of Contracting States and specifying that forced execution of awards would be governed by the rules of civil procedure of the enforcement forum.[57] That article was followed in the First Draft with another making it clear that nothing in the preceding article should be construed as derogating from the law of any Contracting State regarding sovereign immunity from execution.[58]

[47] Ibid. Article 38 of the ICJ Statute (reprinted in A. Zimmermann and others, *The Statute of the International Court of Justice: A Commentary* 1491 (2006)) provided that:

> The Court, whose function is to decide in accordance with international law such disputes as are submitted to it, shall apply:
> (a) international conventions, whether general or particular, establishing rules expressly recognized by the contesting States;
> (b) international custom, as evidence of a general practice accepted as law;
> (c) the general principles of law recognized by civilized nations;
> (d) subject to the provisions of Article 59, judicial decisions and the teachings of the most highly qualified publicists of the various nations, as subsidiary means for the determination of rules of law.

[48] First Draft, Art. 46. This new article appears to have been based on provisions of the ICJ Statute (n. 47) Art. 49, and of the Model Rules on Arbitral Procedure of the International Law Commission, 1958 (II) YBILC 82, Art. 18.

[49] *See* First Draft, Arts. 48 and 49. [50] *See* ibid. Art. 50(1). [51] Ibid. Art. 50(2).

[52] *See* ibid. Art. 56. [53] *See* ibid. Art. 53.

[54] *See* ibid. Art. 55(1)(a) and 55(1)(b). [55] *See* ibid. Art. 55(1)(d) and 55(1)(e).

[56] Ibid. Art. 55(1)(e). [57] Ibid. Art. 57. [58] Ibid. Art. 58.

D. Other provisions

In the First Draft, the compromissory clause referring to the ICJ was corrected to cover only disputes (and not also "questions") between Contracting States over the interpretation or application of the Convention.[59] Not pursued in the First Draft was the idea, put forward at the consultative meetings, of supplementing the clause with a provision permitting an arbitral tribunal, if an issue of interpretation or application arose during the arbitral proceeding, to suspend the proceeding to give interested Contracting States the opportunity to bring the matter to the ICJ. Also omitted from the First Draft was the stipulation of the Preliminary Draft that the home State of an investor could bring an international claim without infringing on the Convention's provision regarding diplomatic protection if the underlying facts also gave rise to a breach of a treaty with the host State.

As explained in Chapter 4, several of the experts at the regional consultative meetings, referring to the Preliminary Draft's provision allowing amendments of the Convention by a two-thirds majority vote of the Administrative Council, had doubted that their countries could adhere to a convention that might then be altered without their own ratification. The First Draft sought to meet the concern with an article providing that amendments "involving new obligations for Contracting States or any fundamental alteration in the nature or scope of this Convention" would require for their adoption the approval of all members of the Administrative Council and that only the other, less important amendments could be adopted by the two-thirds majority vote of the Council.[60] It had also been suggested at the consultative meetings that the Convention should only be open for signature by countries belonging to the World Bank, the United Nations or any of the U.N. specialized agencies. Incorporating this suggestion, the First Draft added that the Convention would also be open to States parties to the ICJ Statute.[61]

II. The Legal Committee meetings

The Legal Committee on the Settlement of Investment Disputes (the Legal Committee), as the World Bank named it, had 14 days of meetings, between November 23 and December 11, 1964. Experts from 61 countries took part in the meetings. The majority of the Latin American members of the Bank were represented at the meetings, despite their opposition to the initiative. Some of the participating experts were diplomats and others economists; most were lawyers at ministries of justice, finance or foreign affairs.[62]

The Executive Directors of the Bank had approved a set of Rules of Procedure for the Conduct of Proceedings of the Legal Committee.[63] The Rules of Procedure

[59] Ibid. Art. 67.

[60] Ibid. Art. 69(1) and 69(2). This article was inspired by the amendment provision of the UNESCO Constitution. *See* Constitution of the United Nations Educational, Scientific and Cultural Organization, November 16, 1945, 4 UNTS 276, Art. XIII(1).

[61] *See* First Draft, Art. 70. An example cited by the drafters for this was the New York Convention on the Recognition and Enforcement of Foreign Arbitral Awards, June 10, 1958, 330 UNTS 3, which provided (Art. VIII(1)) that it would be open for signature on behalf of members of the U.N. or any of its specialized agencies or parties to the ICJ Statute.

[62] Prominent experts at the meetings included Fuad Rouhani, who had served until earlier in 1964 as the first Secretary General of the Organization of the Petroleum Exporting Countries, and Shabtai Rosenne, later Permanent Representative of Israel to the United Nations in Geneva.

[63] Reprinted in 2 *History of the ICSID Convention* 647.

designated the General Counsel of the Bank, who of course was Broches, Chairman of the Committee.[64] The Chairman would direct the discussion of the First Draft of the Convention at all meetings of the Committee.[65] The First Draft, like the Preliminary Draft, had been distributed to governments in English, French and Spanish versions.[66] Under the Rules of Procedure of the Legal Committee, the Chairman would appoint nine Committee members to serve on a Drafting Sub-Committee responsible for reviewing and revising the English, French and Spanish texts as the discussions progressed.[67] The Bank would provide the Secretariat of the Legal Committee and Drafting Sub-Committee.[68]

As explained in Chapter 3, the Executive Directors had developed the practice of seeking consensus or a balance of views, rather than relying for their decisions on formal votes, which in the Bank would have meant applying its weighted voting system. The Rules of Procedure of the Legal Committee provided that it would operate in similar fashion. Consensus would be sought on each provision, if necessary after consideration by a working group appointed by the Chairman from among Committee members who had expressed diverging or conflicting views on a provision.[69] Once consensus was reached on a provision, it would be referred to the Drafting Sub-Committee.[70] A consensus would be deemed to have been reached if, at the end of the discussions, no Committee member present raised an objection.[71] Any provision on which it proved impossible to reach consensus would be reported to the Executive Directors for their directions.[72] Though there would be no formal votes, the Chairman had the right to "poll the members and announce the results."[73] This "voting-non-voting system" was to work well. As Broches later remembered, "[i]n practice, it was hands up hands down all the time, and ... it was immediately accepted that if there appeared to be a majority for a particular proposition, and opponents did not consider it to be of essential interest, then that would be regarded as decided."[74]

The first meeting of the Legal Committee was opened by a welcome from World Bank President Woods and by introductory remarks of Broches.[75] As Chairman of the Committee, Broches reminded participants that the meetings would no longer be concerned with the question of the desirability of creating machinery for facilitating the settlement of investment disputes since that question had been answered in the affirmative.[76] The major task of the Committee would be to assist the Executive

[64] The Rules of Procedure (n. 63) para. 2(a), stated that he would be Chairman "as representative of the President of the Bank," presumably in order to link his chairmanship of this committee of the Executive Directors with the role of the President of the Bank as Chairman of the Executive Directors of the Bank under its Articles of Agreement (Articles of Agreement of the IBRD, December 27, 1949, 2 UNTS 134, Art. V(5)(a)).

[65] Rules of Procedure (n. 63) para. 2(b).

[66] In contrast to the Articles of Agreement of the IBRD, the IFC and IDA, which were done in English only, the Convention was to have authentic texts in English, French and Spanish.

[67] Rules of Procedure (n. 63) para. 4(a).

[68] Ibid. para. 6(a). Piero Sella was named Secretary of the Legal Committee and Christopher Pinto Deputy Secretary. On these two members of Broches's staff, *see* Ch. 4, n. 4.

[69] *See* Rules of Procedure (n. 63) para. 4(c). [70] *See* ibid. paras. 4(b) and 4(d).

[71] Ibid. para. 4(f). [72] *See* ibid. para. 4(e). [73] Ibid. para. 2(b).

[74] World Bank Oral History Program, Transcript of Interview of Aron Broches, May 23, 1984, 38.

[75] *See* SPLCM, November 23, 1964 (morning) (n. 21) 1–3.

[76] This admonition was in general heeded by participants, though in the course of the meetings two of the Latin American experts took the floor to make statements reiterating their countries' general opposition to the initiative. *See* SPLCM, November 25, 1964 (afternoon), reprinted in 2 *History of the ICSID Convention* 699, 1 (intervention of Mr. Espinosa (Venezuela)); SPLCM, December 11, 1964, reprinted in 2 *History of the ICSID Convention* 899, 1 (intervention of Mr. Guido (Uruguay)).

Directors of the Bank in formulating a detailed text of a convention that would then be submitted by the Executive Directors to governments. The role of the Committee was advisory, but the Executive Directors would rely heavily on its work.

Explaining the Rules of Procedure, Broches pointed out that, as it would be working simultaneously on the three language versions of the Convention, the nine-member Drafting Sub-Committee should have three each of English-, French- and Spanish-speaking experts. He later announced that the members would be the experts from India, the United Kingdom, the United States, Dahomey (now Benin), France, Greece, Ecuador, Guatemala and Spain, with the U.K. member to serve as Chairman of the Drafting Sub-Committee.[77]

Some governments had provided written comments on the First Draft. These were circulated by the Secretariat as the Legal Committee commenced its discussions.[78] As at the regional consultative meetings, these were article-by-article discussions of the draft text. They are described below.

A. Discussions regarding the establishment and organization of the Centre

In its first report to the Legal Committee, the Drafting Sub-Committee tersely announced that it had "decided to use English rather than American spelling" for the English text of the draft Convention.[79] The "Center" was thenceforth the "Centre."[80]

In the Legal Committee discussions, several experts questioned the provision of the First Draft on possible ancillary activities of the Centre, such as the collection and dissemination of information on investment law. They saw the provision as lacking precision and as suggesting unnecessary and possibly expensive new functions for the Centre.[81] Another expert defended the provision, arguing that the ancillary activities could, if they extended to giving advice on the clarity and fairness of investment agreements, help to avoid disputes.[82] After further consideration of the issue by a working group, it was decided to delete the provision. In supporting this decision, one expert observed that even if the Convention did not confer on the Centre a specific power to engage in ancillary activities, it might well give advice and supply information just as was done by the Registry of the ICJ.[83] Providing in the Convention for the creation of regional seats of the Centre was another possibility that the Legal Committee

[77] *See* SPLCM, November 24, 1964 (morning), reprinted in 2 *History of the ICSID Convention* 680, 1; SPLCM, November 25, 1964 (morning), reprinted in 2 *History of the ICSID Convention* 691, 1. The U.K. member and Chairman of the Drafting Sub-Committee was Fred Burrows, then Assistant Legal Adviser at the Foreign Office.

[78] On several of the written comments, *see* nn. 85, 100, 103 and 114 and accompanying text.

[79] *See* Drafting Sub-Committee Interim Report, December 3, 1964, reprinted in 2 *History of the ICSID Convention* 749. The decision was presumably taken by the Drafting Sub-Committee at the prompting of its British Chairman. *See* n. 77 and accompanying text.

[80] Two other words in the final text of the Convention reflected the switch to British spelling: "favourable" in Art. 23(2) and "endeavour" in Art. 34(1).

[81] *See* SPLCM, November 23, 1964 (morning) (n. 21) 6 (interventions of Mr. Sapateiro (Portugal) and Mr. Lokur (India)).

[82] Ibid. (intervention of Mr. Himadeh (Lebanon)). This argument had been made by the same expert at the regional consultative meetings. *See* Ch. 4, n. 106 and accompanying text.

[83] *See* Report of Working Group I, November 24, 1964 reprinted in 2 *History of the ICSID Convention* 687 (the expert referred to in the text was Victor Salomon Pinto of the Guatemalan Ministry of Economy).

considered but rejected primarily because of its potential cost implications.[84] In regard to finances, the written comments of one government included the proposal that the Convention reflect an undertaking by the World Bank, rather than the Contracting States, to meet the excess of expenditure over income of the Centre.[85] The proposal was squelched by a note to the Legal Committee from Broches explaining that it would be unsound for one institution to assume in perpetuity an obligation to defray the expenditure of another, particularly when their respective budgets would, as here, be approved by bodies with different compositions following different voting systems.[86] Broches's note added that the President of the Bank was, however, prepared to recommend to the Executive Directors of the Bank that it underwrite the basic overhead expenditure of the Centre for an initial period and make some contribution to the expenditure as long as the Centre had its headquarters at the Bank. If this were approved by the Executive Directors it could, the note concluded, be mentioned in the Report of the Executive Directors submitting the Convention to governments. As will be seen, in the course of the deliberations of the Legal Committee, agreement was facilitated on a number of other points by the suggestion that understandings unsuitable for inclusion in the text of the Convention could instead be reflected in the accompanying Report of the Executive Directors (or in the eventual regulations and rules of the Centre).

One delegate at the Legal Committee meetings proposed that the organizational structure of the Centre include an intermediate organ between the plenary Administrative Council and the Secretariat. This would be an executive committee exercising "general control and supervision over the activities of the Centre" and having responsibility, in particular, for reviewing conciliation and arbitration requests and electing any Deputy Secretaries-General.[87] Envisaging, therefore, a role for the executive committee comparable to that of the Executive Directors of the IBRD, the proposal unsurprisingly suggested that they should be ex officio members of the committee.[88] Other experts at the meetings thought that the limited activities of the Centre would not warrant a multiplication of organs; there was also concern that the proposed executive committee would link the Centre too closely with the Bank.[89] Nevertheless, to allow for the creation of an executive committee if the need arose, it was agreed that the Convention should authorize the Administrative Council to appoint such committees as it might deem necessary.[90] Another change agreed for the Administrative Council was to confine its previous more sweeping general powers to those necessary for the implementation

[84] *See* SPLCM, November 24, 1964 (morning) (n. 77) 1 and 4 (interventions of Mr. Bigay (Central African Republic), Mr. Bernard (Liberia), Mr. Kpognon (Dahomey), Mr. van Santen (Netherlands) and Mr. Ghachem (Lebanon)).

[85] *See* Comments and Observations of Member Governments on the Draft Convention for the Settlement of Investment Disputes between States and Nationals of Other States, November 23, 1964, reprinted in 2 *History of the ICSID Convention* 651, comments of Belgium.

[86] *See* Note from the Chairman to the Legal Committee, November 30, 1964, reprinted in 2 *History of the ICSID Convention* 735, 2.

[87] *See* Proposals of Mr. Lokur (India) to the Legal Committee, November 27, 1964, reprinted in 2 *History of the ICSID Convention* 688.

[88] *See* ibid.

[89] *See* SPLCM, November 30, 1964 (morning) reprinted in 2 *History of the ICSID Convention* 711, 6–7 (interventions of Mr. O'Donovan (Australia), Mr. Pinto (Guatemala), Mr. Kpognon (Dahomey), Mr. Bohani (Tanzania) and Mr. Manirakiza (Burundi)).

[90] *See* ibid. (interventions of Mr. O'Donovan (Australia) and Mr. Lokur (India)); SPLCM, November 30, 1964 (afternoon), reprinted in 2 *History of the ICSID Convention* 725, 7 (intervention of Mr. Broches (Chairman)).

of the provisions of the Convention.[91] The Legal Committee also decided to delete the provision requiring the annual meetings of the Administrative Council to be held in conjunction with those of the Board of Governors of the World Bank, on the understanding that such a provision could be included in the regulations of the Centre.[92]

In regard to the Secretary-General and any Deputy Secretaries-General of the Centre, the Legal Committee agreed that the Chairman of the Administrative Council should have to consult with the members of the Council before making nominations for those offices.[93] The Convention should, an expert urged, set a limit to the number of Deputy Secretaries-General, to avoid an unnecessary proliferation of high officials of the Centre.[94] The consensus in the Legal Committee was against such proliferation but in favor of this being reflected in the Report of the Executive Directors rather than in a numerical limit in the Convention.[95] On the Panels of Conciliators and of Arbitrators, the Committee agreed that the Convention should emphasize the importance of legal competence for membership in the Panel of Arbitrators.[96] As had been suggested at the regional consultative meetings, the Committee also voted in favor of increasing the term of members of the Panels to six years.[97]

A number of other ideas put forward at the regional consultative meetings but not incorporated in the First Draft were again pursued at the Legal Committee meetings. Thus, for example, in the Legal Committee meetings, the proposal was successfully renewed to make it clear in the Convention that the Centre might in appropriate cases waive its immunity from legal process.[98] In addition, as redrafted by the Legal Committee, the text extended this immunity to the full range of participants in proceedings under the Convention, including in particular parties, their counsel, witnesses and experts.[99]

B. Discussions regarding the jurisdiction of the Centre

As at the regional consultative meetings, the jurisdiction of the Centre was the subject of much debate at Legal Committee meetings. Opinion was again divided between experts, mainly from developing countries, who thought that the jurisdiction of the Centre should be more strictly circumscribed and experts who favored a more flexible, open approach. Even with the definitions of "legal dispute" and "investment" that had been added in the First Draft, experts in the first group saw that delineation of the

[91] *See* SPLCM, November 25, 1964 (morning), reprinted in 2 *History of the ICSID Convention* 691, 7 (interventions of Mr. van Santen (Netherlands), Mr. Pinto (Guatemala), Mr. Dodoo (Ghana) and Mr. Bernard (Liberia)).

[92] *See* SPLCM, November 30, 1964 (morning) (n. 89) 3–4 (interventions of Mr. Burrows (United Kingdom), Mr. Melchor (Spain) and Mr. Broches (Chairman)).

[93] *See* ibid. 9–10 (interventions of Mr. Pinto (Guatemala) and Mr. Broches (Chairman)).

[94] *See* ibid. 8 (intervention of Mr. Manirakiza (Burundi)).

[95] *See* ibid. 9 (intervention of Mr. Broches (Chairman)).

[96] *See* SPLCM, November 25, 1964 (afternoon), reprinted in 2 *History of the ICSID Convention* 725, 5 (intervention of Mr. Broches (Chairman)).

[97] *See* ibid. 725, 7 (intervention of Mr. Broches (Chairman)).

[98] *See* SPLCM, December 1, 1964 (morning), reprinted in 2 *History of the ICSID Convention* 737, 5.

[99] *See* Drafting Sub-Committee Interim Report (n. 79) 6 (in the First Draft, only conciliators and arbitrators shared the immunity with the Chairman and members of the Administrative Council and the officers and employees of the Secretariat).

nature of the dispute as insufficiently "accurate and specific."[100] Several of these experts argued that the Convention might undermine a State's sovereignty if disputes over the interpretation of local laws or concerning economic or fiscal policies of the State could be submitted to the Centre. They urged that the jurisdiction of the Centre should therefore be limited to disputes arising out of investment contracts concluded with the host State or guarantee obligations assumed by it in respect of specific investments.[101] One of the Francophone experts added that the jurisdiction of the Centre should be confined to disputes arising directly out of covered investments rather than also extending to disputes arising "in connection with" investments, which in the French version of the First Draft had been translated as "indirectement."[102] For this first group of experts, relying on the "consent power" seemed too weak a way to limit jurisdiction.[103] Nor were all of them reassured by the possibility of notifications indicating in advance the types of dispute a State might be willing to submit to the jurisdiction of the Centre; one of the delegates thought that a notifying State would risk being compared unfavorably with other States hoping to attract investments.[104]

Experts in the second group saw various defects in the First Draft's definition of "investment," such as that it would exclude large investments that could be made for fewer than five years. They argued that it would be best to omit a definition of the term from the Convention.[105] Some of them also doubted that it would be necessary to include a definition of "legal dispute" in the Convention.[106] These experts stressed that the jurisdiction of the Centre would be based on the consent of the parties, who could always exclude undesirable matters by refusing their consent, rather than being constrained by "complicated definitions" in the Convention.[107]

For his part, Broches pleaded with delegates to remember the difference between the scope of the Convention or jurisdiction of the Centre on the one hand, and the scope of the consent of the parties on the other hand.[108] To help allay fears of his developing country colleagues, an industrial country expert suggested that the Convention allow States to give notice not only of the classes of disputes they would be willing in principle to submit to the Centre, but also of the class of disputes they would not consider suitable for submission to the Centre.[109] After a working group failed to find

[100] SPLCM, November 25, 1964 (afternoon) (n. 76) 6 (intervention of Mr. Melchor (Spain)). *See also* ibid. 5 (intervention of Mr. Pinto (Guatemala)); Comments and Observations of Member Governments (n. 85) comments of China, Thailand and Vietnam.

[101] SPLCM, November 27, 1964 (morning), reprinted in 2 *History of the ICSID Convention* 705, 2 and 4 (interventions of Mr. Lokur (India) and Mr. Sapateiro (Portugal)). *See also* Working Group IV Summary Report on Views Expressed on Jurisdiction of the Centre, reprinted in 2 *History of the ICSID Convention* 829, 1 and 2 (summaries of comments of Mr. Brinas (Philippines), Mr. Ortiz (Peru) and Mr. Ouma (Uganda)).

[102] *See* SPLCM, November 27, 1964 (morning) (n. 101) 3 (intervention of Mr. Bigay (Central African Republic)).

[103] *Cf.* Comments and Observations of Member Governments (n. 85) comments of China.

[104] *See* SPLCM, December 8, 1964 (afternoon), reprinted in 2 *History of the ICSID Convention* 821, 3–4 (intervention of Mr. Bigay (Central African Republic)).

[105] *See* SPLCM, November 25, 1964 (afternoon) (n. 76) 4 and 5 (interventions of Mr. Burrows (United Kingdom) and Mr. Quill (New Zealand)); SPLCM, November 27, 1964 (morning) (n. 101) 2 and 3 (intervention of Mr. Hellners (Sweden)).

[106] *See* SPLCM, November 27, 1964 (morning) (n. 101) 3 (intervention of Mr. Ukawa (Japan)).

[107] *See* SPLCM, November 25, 1964 (afternoon) (n. 76) 4 (intervention of Mr. Burrows (United Kingdom)); SPLCM, November 27, 1964 (morning) (n. 101) 2 (intervention of Mr. Hellners (Sweden)).

[108] *See* SPLCM, November 27, 1964 (morning) (n. 101) 3 (intervention of Mr. Broches (Chairman)).

[109] *See* Working Group IV Summary Report (n. 101) 2 (summary of comments of Mr. van Santen (Netherlands)).

consensus on the matter, successive shows of hands in the Legal Committee indicated that a majority was in favor of the flexible, open approach towards the nature of the dispute.[110] The text later circulated by the Drafting Sub-Committee was thus similar in this respect to that of the First Draft but omitted to define "investment," or "legal dispute," while confining covered disputes to those arising "directly" out of investments and also providing that a State might give advance notice of the types of disputes that it would or would not consider submitting to the Centre.[111]

In regard to possible parties to proceedings under the Convention, one of the delegates made the practical point that investors should have the possibility of easily ascertaining which political subdivisions or agencies could appear before the Centre. It was then agreed that the Convention should provide for such subdivisions and agencies to be designated to the Centre by the State concerned.[112] The Legal Committee also agreed to maintain the requirement of approval by the State of the consent to jurisdiction on the part of its subdivision or agency, except where the State concerned had indicated that the approval was not required.[113]

As for the "national of another Contracting State," the Legal Committee decided to redraft the relevant provision so that it would absolutely exclude natural persons who simultaneously possessed the nationality of the host State.[114] In respect of locally established but foreign-controlled juridical persons, one delegate suggested reintroducing into the text their control as an element qualifying them to engage in proceedings with the host State rather than relying entirely on the consent of the parties.[115] With this change, the provision was put to a vote, but only a narrow majority was in favor of retaining the possibility of such local entities bringing disputes with the host State to the Centre. Despite efforts to reach consensus in a working group, many of the experts remained unconvinced of the need for any such exception to the exclusion of proceedings between a State and its own nationals.[116] Broches announced that the issue would therefore be reported to the Executive Directors of the Bank for their decision.[117]

The Legal Committee similarly deadlocked on the provision of the First Draft allowing a governmental or intergovernmental insurer to participate in proceedings against another Contracting State as subrogee of an indemnified investor. Some experts objected that the provision would "destroy the principle established in the Convention"

[110] *See* Report of the Chairman of the Legal Committee on Settlement of Investment Disputes, December 23, 1964, reprinted in 2 *History of the ICSID Convention* 934, 3. In words reminiscent of Justice Potter Stewart's famous observation in *Jacobellis v. Ohio*, 378 U.S. 184, 197 (1964) (that perhaps he could never succeed in intelligibly defining hard-core pornography but knew it when he saw it), Broches later said that the majority had agreed that "while it might be difficult to define 'investment,' an investment was in fact readily recognizable." MMCW, February 16, 1965, reprinted in 2 *History of the ICSID Convention* 965, 8.

[111] *See* Drafting Sub-Committee Fourth Interim Report, December 11, 1964, reprinted in 2 *History of the ICSID Convention* 879, 1.

[112] *See* SPLCM, December 9, 1964 (afternoon), reprinted in 2 *History of the ICSID Convention* 853, 5 (interventions of Mr. Burrows (United Kingdom) and Mr. Broches (Chairman)).

[113] *See* ibid. 6 and 8 (interventions of Mrs. Villgratner (Austria) and Mr. Broches (Chairman)).

[114] *See* SPLCM, December 10, 1964 (morning), reprinted in 2 *History of the ICSID Convention* 868, 2 (intervention of Mr. Broches (Chairman)). *Cf.* Comments and Observations of Member Governments (n. 85) comments of Malagasy Republic, South Africa and Austria.

[115] *See* SPLCM, November 25, 1964 (afternoon) (n. 76) 5 (intervention of Mr. Belin (United States)).

[116] *See* SPLCM, December 10, 1964 (morning) (n. 114) 3 (interventions of Mr. Ratsirahonana (Malagasy Republic), Mr. Ortiz (Peru) and Mr. Lokur (India)).

[117] *See* ibid. 4.

that it should not cover disputes between States.[118] Others defended the provision, arguing that for the insurer "to inherit a legal claim was a commendable thing because otherwise the settlement of the dispute would be confined to the political plane."[119] One expert indicated that he could agree to the provision if it made it clear that, in order to appear before the Centre as subrogee of the investor, the State insurer would have to waive its other remedies, such as might exist under a treaty between it and the host State.[120] After debate in a working group, the provision, redrafted to provide for such a waiver, received the support of only a small majority of the Legal Committee. It too, Broches said, would have to be considered further by the Executive Directors.[121]

Changes agreed in the Legal Committee regarding consent to the jurisdiction of the Centre included adding to the text a sentence specifying that once all parties to a dispute had given such consent, no party could thereafter withdraw its consent unilaterally.[122] As at the regional consultative meetings, there was much discussion in the Legal Committee meetings of the provision according to which consent to arbitration under the Convention would, unless otherwise stated, be deemed consent to such arbitration to the exclusion of any other remedy. Broches again explained that the provision was intended as interpretative, that a consent to refer a dispute to an international tribunal should be understood as implying a waiver of the competence of local courts.[123] Several of the Legal Committee members suggested in reply that the provision should be recast to reverse the presumption, so that in the absence of a statement to the contrary disputes could be taken to the Centre only after the exhaustion of local remedies.[124] Other participants argued in favor of retaining the original provision.[125] To help meet the objections that had been made to the provision, one of the experts suggested adding text to make it clear that it did not affect the right of States to insist on the exhaustion of local remedies.[126] Although some of the experts objected that this very same idea was already expressed by the phrase "unless otherwise stated" in the original provision, the Legal Committee agreed in the end to tack onto the provision the reassuring sentence that a State could make its consent conditional on prior recourse to local remedies.[127] Another change agreed upon by the Legal Committee was to clarify that, while consent to the jurisdiction of the Centre would

[118] SPLCM, November 27, 1964 (morning) (n. 101) 1 (intervention of Mr. Melchor (Spain)). *See also* ibid. 6 (intervention of Mr. Rouhani (Iran)); SPLCM, December 2, 1964 (morning), reprinted in 2 *History of the ICSID Convention* 756, 6 (interventions of Mr. Lopez (Panama), Mr. Lokur (India), Mr. Ouma (Uganda) and Mr. Malaplate (France)).

[119] SPLCM, December 2, 1964 (morning) (n. 118) 7 (intervention of Mr. Bertram (Germany)). *See also* ibid. 5 (interventions of Mr. Gourevitch (United States) and Mr. O'Donovan (Australia)).

[120] *See* ibid. 4 (intervention of Mr. Tsai (China)).

[121] *See* Report of the Chairman of the Legal Committee (n. 110) 4.

[122] The addition was proposed by the U.K., possibly in view of its experience with the refusal of Iran to submit to arbitration under its concession agreement with the Anglo-Iranian Oil Company following Iran's repudiation of that agreement in 1951. *See* Ch. 2, n. 53 and accompanying text. For the U.K. proposal, *see* Comments and Observations of Member Governments (n. 85) comments of the United Kingdom; SPLCM, December 2, 1964 (morning) (n. 118) 2 (intervention of Mr. Burrows (United Kingdom)).

[123] *See* SPLCM, December 2, 1964 (morning) (n. 118) 1 (intervention of Mr. Broches (Chairman)).

[124] *See* ibid. 1 and 2 (interventions of Mr. Bilgen (Turkey), Mr. Brinas (Philippines), Mr. Lopez (Panama) and Mr. Heth (Israel)).

[125] *See* ibid. 3 and 4 (interventions of Mr. Bertram (Germany), Mr. Gourevitch (United States), Mr. Burrows (United Kingdom) and Mr. Melchor (Spain)).

[126] *See* ibid. 3 (intervention of Mr. Ouma (Uganda)).

[127] *See* ibid. (intervention of Mr. Burrows (United Kingdom)); SPLCM, December 4, 1964 (morning), reprinted in 2 *History of the ICSID Convention* 782, 2 and 3 (interventions of Mr. Hellners (Sweden) and intervention of Mr. Broches (Chairman)).

exclude exercises of the right of diplomatic protection, this would not rule out informal diplomatic exchanges solely intended to facilitate a settlement of the dispute.[128]

C. Discussions regarding conciliation and arbitration

The Legal Committee made several refinements to the provisions on the institution of conciliation and arbitration proceedings. Some of the experts had misgivings about the extent of the power envisaged for the Secretary-General by the First Draft, to ascertain whether the information provided in a request for conciliation or arbitration sufficed to establish prima facie that the dispute was within the jurisdiction of the Centre. The Legal Committee rejected proposals to subject exercises of this power to review or appeal.[129] It instead voted to reformulate the power in negative terms which would "better convey the intention of giving the Secretary-General power only for a formal screening."[130] The wording that the Legal Committee settled upon was that the Secretary-General would permit the conciliation or arbitration to proceed "unless he finds that the dispute is manifestly outside of the jurisdiction of the Centre."[131] Text approved by the Legal Committee also introduced the idea of the registration (or refusal of registration) of the requests by the Secretary-General at this stage.[132] Another change agreed upon by the Committee was that the Secretary-General would on receipt of a request send a copy of it to the other party, rather than providing the other party with the copy only after scrutiny and registration of the request.[133]

Several of the Legal Committee members thought that the First Draft went too far in totally excluding from service on tribunals nationals of the home or host State of the investor concerned. Such "national arbitrators," one expert said, could be needed because of their knowledge of local conditions and might be allowed if the parties so agreed.[134] On Broches's motion, the Legal Committee voted in favor of allowing a majority of national arbitrators where the parties specifically agreed to the appointment of the individual arbitrators.[135] Experts also saw as excessive the provision of the First Draft restricting parties in their choice of arbitrators to members of the Panel of Arbitrators in cases where the parties had not agreed on the number of arbitrators and the method of their appointment. The Legal Committee adopted a proposal to leave the parties entirely free to select arbitrators from outside the Panel.[136] As changed by the Legal Committee, the text left only the Chairman of the Administrative Council,

128 *See* SPLCM, December 2, 1964 (afternoon), reprinted in 2 *History of the ICSID Convention* 762, 2–3 (interventions of Mr. Burrows (United Kingdom), Mr. Ukawa (Japan) and Mr. Broches (Chairman)).

129 *See* SPLCM, December 3, 1964 (morning), reprinted in 2 *History of the ICSID Convention* 768, 3–6 (interventions of Mr. Heth (Israel), Mr. Lokur (India), Mr. Hellners (Sweden), Mr. Agoro (Nigeria) and Mr. Broches (Chairman)).

130 Ibid. 7 (intervention of Mr. Ghachem (Tunisia)). *See also* ibid. 4 (intervention of Mr. Bertram (Germany)).

131 *See* ibid. 7 (intervention of Mr. Broches (Chairman)).

132 *See* SPLCM, December 4, 1964 (morning) (n. 127) 6 (note to intervention of Mr. Broches (Chairman)).

133 *See* SPLCM, December 3, 1964 (morning) (n. 129) 2, 4 and 6 (interventions of Mr. Awooner-Renner (Sierra Leone), Mr. Funes (El Salvador) and Mr. Broches (Chairman)). This change was proposed in order to "give the parties a last opportunity for settling their dispute before conciliation or arbitration proceedings actually start" (ibid. 2) (intervention of Mr. Awooner-Renner (Sierra Leone)).

134 *See* SPLCM, December 4, 1964 (morning) (n. 127) 8 (intervention of Mr. Bilgen (Turkey)).

135 *See* ibid. (interventions of Mr. Broches (Chairman)).

136 *See* SPLCM, December 4, 1964 (afternoon), reprinted in 2 *History of the ICSID Convention* 792, 7 (interventions of Mr. Lokur (India) and Mr. Broches (Chairman)).

One of 22 meetings of the Legal Committee on the Settlement of Investment Disputes held in Washington, D.C., between November 23 and December 11, 1964.
World Bank Group Archives

when acting as appointing authority of arbitrators, restricted in his choice to members of the Panel. In addition to maintaining this restriction, the Legal Committee voted to require the Chairman to consult with both parties as far as possible before acting on the request of one of them to appoint an arbitrator.[137]

In respect of the place of conciliation and arbitration proceedings, the First Draft, like the Preliminary Draft, allowed the parties to agree to hold proceedings at the seat of the PCA or such other public international institutions with which the Centre might have the necessary arrangements, or at any other place approved by the conciliation commission or arbitral tribunal. The Legal Committee decided to broaden the range of possible host institutions to include private ones as well.[138] At the suggestion of one expert, it was agreed that the Report of the World Bank Executive Directors on the Convention should record that institutions hosting the proceedings might be also asked to provide secretariat functions.[139]

At Broches's suggestion, the provision on applicable law was divided into two sentences, the first dealing with agreement of the parties on applicable law and the second on the law to be applied by the arbitrators in the absence of such agreement. The Legal Committee agreed that the freedom of the parties in this respect would be better conveyed by a first sentence stating that the tribunal should decide the dispute in accordance with such rules of law as had been agreed upon by the

[137] *See* ibid. 6 and 7 (interventions of Mr. Lokur (India), Mr. O'Donovan (Australia) and Mr. Broches (Chairman)).

[138] *See* SPLCM, November 24, 1964 (morning) (n. 77) 4–5 (intervention of Mr. Broches (Chairman)).

[139] *See* ibid. 5 (intervention of Mr. van Santen (Netherlands)).

parties.[140] Several of the experts from developing countries were unhappy with the provision of the First Draft leaving it entirely to the arbitrators, in the absence of a choice of law by the parties, to determine which "rules of national and international law" would be applicable. They urged that the reference to national law should be limited to that of the host State.[141] Some of them also thought that the reference to international law should be omitted from the provision.[142] Other experts, however, saw a role for the application of international law rules in this context, at least on a supplementary basis.[143] The Legal Committee then voted in favor of a redraft by Broches under which the tribunal, failing agreement of the parties on the rules of law to be applied, would apply the law of the State party to the dispute, including its rules on the conflict of laws, and such international law principles as might be applicable.[144] The First Draft's definition of "international law" was dropped from the new text (but eventually included in the Report of the Executive Directors of the Bank on the Convention). At the request of one expert, a vote was taken on a suggestion to limit the application of international law to cases where the law of the host State was silent; this motion was defeated by a substantial majority.[145]

The Legal Committee redrafted the provision on the default procedure to dispel any impression that the tribunal might automatically make "an award in favor" of the appearing party.[146] With respect to provisional measures, several experts felt that it would be too much to have a tribunal "prescribing" measures which, for example, might lead to unacceptable attempts "to prevent legislative or administrative acts" of the State party to the dispute.[147] It was also observed that the clause in the First Draft allowing a penalty to be imposed for non-compliance with a provisional measure was "too vague" and in any event superfluous.[148] By a large majority, the Legal Committee voted to delete that clause and to provide that the power of the tribunal would be limited to recommending, as opposed to prescribing, provisional measures.[149] It was agreed that, while that Convention would not specifically mention the point, a tribunal could take into account in its award the effect of any non-compliance with a recommended provisional measure.[150]

At the proposal of Broches, the Legal Committee decided that the Convention should require a tribunal to rule on every issue submitted to it. After rejecting the suggestion that a failure to comply with this duty should be made a ground for annulment, the Legal Committee voted in favor of providing for a supplemental procedure

[140] *See* SPLCM, December 7, 1964 (morning), reprinted in 2 *History of the ICSID Convention* 799, 5 and 6 (interventions of Mr. Broches (Chairman)).

[141] *See* ibid. 3 and 4 (interventions of Mr. Tsai (China), Mr. Bilgen (Turkey) and Mr. da Cunha (Brazil)).

[142] *See* ibid. (interventions of Mr. Wanasundera (Ceylon) and Mr. Ortiz (Peru)).

[143] *See* ibid. 4 and 5 (interventions of Mr. Kpognon (Dahomey), Mr. Lokur (India), Mr. Gourevitch (United States), Mrs. Villgrattner (Austria), Mr. Lara (Costa Rica) and Mr. Florenzano (Ivory Coast)).

[144] *See* ibid. 6 (intervention of Mr. Broches (Chairman)).

[145] *See* ibid. (intervention of Mr. Lokur (India)).

[146] *See* SPLCM, December 10, 1964 (afternoon), reprinted in 2 *History of the ICSID Convention* 861, 3 (intervention of Mr. Lokur (India)).

[147] *See* SPLCM, December 8, 1964 (morning), reprinted in 2 *History of the ICSID Convention* 812, 3 (intervention of Mr. Guarino (Italy)). *See also* ibid. 2–3 (interventions of Mr. Tsai (China), Mr. Gonzalez (Spain) and Mr. Mantzoulinos (Greece)).

[148] *See* ibid. 2–3 (interventions of Mr. Tsai (China) and Mr. Heth (Israel)).

[149] *See* ibid. 3 (intervention of Mr. Broches (Chairman)).

[150] *See* ibid. 4 (intervention of Mr. Broches (Chairman)).

through which a tribunal could repair its omissions.[151] An eventual text prepared by the Drafting Sub-Committee provided also for the possibility of a tribunal rectifying clerical, arithmetical or similar errors in its award.[152] With regard to the allocation of the costs of an arbitration proceeding, the Legal Committee agreed to allow tribunals to decide the matter as they saw fit unless the parties agreed otherwise.[153] As to the publication of the award, one delegate suggested a new provision stating that, unless the parties otherwise agreed, the Centre could publish the awards.[154] Another expert countered that the provision should instead provide that the Centre could not publish the awards without the consent of the parties.[155] This counter-proposal was approved by a large majority.[156]

In the discussions of post-award remedies, several proposals were made to broaden the scope of the annulment remedy. These included proposals to make the remedy available for all excesses of jurisdiction, rather than just manifest ones; to extend the remedy to cover manifestly incorrect applications of the proper law; to make it sanction misconduct generally on the part of an arbitrator, as well as corruption; and to give parties an immediate right of redress after a tribunal had decided it was properly constituted, without having to wait for the award to invoke the remedy.[157] The proposals were defeated after delegates had argued that they might unduly detract from the finality of the awards.[158] At the same time, the Legal Committee voted to delete the proviso in the First Draft permitting the parties to waive the requirement that an award state the reasons on which it was based.[159]

The provisions on the recognition and enforcement of Convention awards were redrafted by the Legal Committee. To make them more readily applicable across different national legal systems, terms such as "writ of execution" were dropped from the text.[160] It was made clear that the Secretary-General of the Centre would have the responsibility of certifying the copies of awards to be presented for enforcement.[161] On the proposal of one expert, a clause was added to permit a federal State to enforce the awards in or through its federal courts and to provide that the awards would be so enforced as if they were final judgments of the courts of a constituent State.[162]

[151] *See* SPLCM, December 9, 1964 (morning), reprinted in 2 *History of the ICSID Convention* 845, 5.

[152] *See* Drafting Sub-Committee Sixth Interim Report, December 11, 1964, reprinted in 2 *History of the ICSID Convention* 861, Art. 52(2).

[153] *See* SPLCM, December 10, 1964 (morning), reprinted in 2 *History of the ICSID Convention* 868, 6 (interventions of Mrs. Villgrattner (Austria) and Mr. Broches (Chairman)). The Legal Committee thus changed the provision that had stood from the Working Paper according to which each party would ordinarily bear its own expenses and share equally with the other party the fees and expenses of the tribunal and of the Centre. *See* Ch. 3, note 77 and accompanying text.

[154] SPLCM, December 8, 1964 (morning) (n. 147) 6 (intervention of Mr. Gourevitch (United States)).

[155] Ibid. (intervention of Mr. Lokur (India)).

[156] Ibid. (intervention of Mr. Broches (Chairman)).

[157] SPLCM, December 9, 1964 (morning) (n. 151) 7 (interventions of Mr. Tsai (China) and Mr. Lokur (India)).

[158] *See* ibid. 8 (interventions of Mr. van Santen (Netherlands) and Mr. Burrows (United Kingdom)); SPLCM, December 9, 1964 (afternoon), reprinted in 2 *History of the ICSID Convention* 853, 1 and 2 (interventions of Mr. Broches (Chairman)).

[159] *See* SPLCM, December 9, 1964 (afternoon) (n. 158) 2 (intervention of Mr. Broches (Chairman)).

[160] *Cf.* Report of Chairman of the Legal Committee (n. 110) 6.

[161] *See* SPLCM, December 11, 1964 (morning), reprinted in 2 *History of the ICSID Convention* 899, 4 (intervention of Mr. Broches (Chairman)).

[162] *See* Working Group VI Report on Article 57, December 8, 1964, reprinted in 2 *History of the ICSID Convention* 892, 2 (referring to proposal of Mr. Gourevitch (United States)).

The Legal Committee also considered, but rejected, the possibility of allowing a Contracting State not party to the dispute to refuse to enforce an award if it were contrary to the public policy of that State.[163]

D. Discussions of other provisions

Provisions addressed by the Legal Committee at its last day of meetings included the clause providing for the submission to the ICJ of disputes between Contracting States over the interpretation or application of the Convention. Concerned that it might be used to frustrate conciliation or arbitration proceedings, a participant had proposed that the clause specifically exclude disputes involved in such proceedings.[164] Broches said that he thought the point was already implicitly covered by the provisions regarding diplomatic protection and the power of arbitral tribunals to determine their own jurisdiction; the clause referring to the ICJ would, he thought, relate to such matters as questions on privileges and immunities and disputes arising from failures to comply with awards.[165] The proposal was then withdrawn on the understanding that the Report of the Executive Directors accompanying the Convention would make it clear that the clause would not enable a State to frustrate Convention arbitration proceedings by a referral of the matter to the ICJ.[166]

In its final session, the Legal Committee also considered a working group report on the amendment provision of the Convention. In the First Draft, the provision envisaged that the Convention could be amended by decision of the Administrative Council, with certain important amendments requiring the unanimous approval of Council members and others a two-thirds majority.[167] The report of the working group gave short shrift to this approach, saying that most Contracting States would reject a procedure that did not provide for approval by their legislatures at some stage. The working group had examined the possibility of providing for amendments to come into force after ratification by a qualified majority of Contracting States, with no State being bound by an amendment unless it had itself ratified the amendment. It was realized, however, that this could result in the formation of two groups of States: one bound by the original provisions of the Convention, and the other by the Convention as amended. The report of the working group therefore recommended that the provision should require ratification by all Contracting States before an amendment entered into force.[168] At its last session, the Legal Committee approved this recommendation.

The Legal Committee also agreed at this session to add to the text a provision to remind Contracting States that they should take such legislative or other measures as might be necessary to make the Convention effective in their territories.[169] Broches announced that the remaining final provisions, dealing with such matters as signature, ratification and entry into force of the Convention, as well as the preamble of

[163] *See* SPLCM, December 11, 1964 (morning) (n. 161) 5 (intervention of Mr. Broches (Chairman)). Experts in favor of such a public policy exception included Wilhelm Bertram at the German Federal Ministry of Justice. *See* ibid. The idea was subsequently pursued by the World Bank Executive Director representing Germany. See nn. 178 and 179 and accompanying text.

[164] *See* Amendment to Article 67 submitted by Mr. Gourevitch (United States), December 10, 1964, reprinted in 2 *History of the ICSID Convention* 910.

[165] *See* SPLCM, December 11, 1964 (morning) (n. 161) 8.

[166] *See* ibid. (intervention of Mr. Belin (United States)).

[167] *See* n. 60 and accompanying text.

[168] *See* Working Group VII Report on Chapter IX—Amendment, December 8, 1964, reprinted in 2 *History of the ICSID Convention* 909.

[169] *See* SPLCM, December 11, 1964 (morning) (n. 161) 9 (intervention of Mr. Lokur (India)).

the Convention, would be dealt with by the Executive Directors of the Bank. This, Broches explained, was because those parts of the Convention "were largely lacking in specific juridical complexity and were more in the nature of matters to be decided by the Executive Directors in the light of governmental instructions."[170]

III. Concluding steps

Following the meetings of the Legal Committee, the Executive Directors of the Bank received a Revised Draft of the Convention (the Revised Draft). Dated December 11, 1964, the Revised Draft incorporated the changes to the First Draft decided upon by the Legal Committee.[171] The changes were summarized in a report by Broches that was also provided to the Executive Directors.[172] Broches and his staff undertook a tidying of the text of the Revised Draft. It resulted in a number of "minor technical changes" that Broches communicated to the Executive Directors in early January 1965.[173] These notably included changes to make it clear that the findings, by the Secretary-General of the Centre, regarding the registrability or otherwise of a request for conciliation or arbitration should be based solely on the information contained in the request.[174]

Later in January 1965, Broches submitted to the Executive Directors a draft of their report to accompany the Convention when it would be submitted to governments (the Draft Report).[175] The Draft Report had 49 paragraphs divided into nine sections. The first section recited the 1964 resolution of the Board of Governors; explained that the Executive Directors had, pursuant to that resolution, formulated the Convention and approved its text, as attached to the Report, for submission to member governments of the Bank; and thereby submitted it to them for consideration with a view to signature and ratification. The second section of the Draft Report described the steps in the preparation of the Convention, including the holding of the regional consultative meetings and the work of the Legal Committee. The overall objective of the Convention, of encouraging a larger flow of foreign investment, and its balance of interests between those of investors and host States, were outlined in the third section of the Draft Report. The organizational structure of the Centre and its jurisdiction were described in the fourth and fifth sections. Proceedings under the Convention were discussed in the fifth section, which highlighted the consensual character of the system and pointed

[170] Ibid. 8.

[171] The Revised Draft is reprinted in 2 *History of the ICSID Convention* 911.

[172] *See* n. 110.

[173] *See* Memorandum from the General Counsel and List of Proposed Changes to the Revised Draft Convention, January 8, 1965, reprinted in 2 *History of the ICSID Convention* 943.

[174] This change took account of the decision of the Legal Committee that the request should be communicated immediately to the prospective respondent but not with a view to reintroducing the possibility of applying the doctrine of *forum prorogatum*. *See* n. 133 and accompanying text. It was also at this time that the definite article between "for" and "Settlement" was dropped from the name of the Centre in the English version of Art. 1(1) of the Convention.

[175] *See* Memorandum from the General Counsel and Draft Report of the Executive Directors to accompany the Convention, January 19, 1965, reprinted in 2 *History of the ICSID Convention* 952. On the importance of the Report of the Executive Directors in the interpretation of the Convention, *see* Ch. 10, n. 236.

The description in the above text of the first section of the Draft Report assumes that that section was basically the same as the corresponding part of the final Report (since there appear to have been no comments on the first section of the Draft Report by the Executive Directors). However, the first section was omitted from the above-cited reprint of the Draft Report in the *History of the ICSID Convention*, for reasons unknown to the present author.

out its limitations as regards the forced execution of awards. The provisions on the place of proceedings were touched upon in the seventh section. The two remaining sections of the Draft Report described the provisions on disputes between Contracting States and on signature, ratification and entry into force of the Convention.

The Draft Report proclaimed the consent of the parties to be "the cornerstone of the jurisdiction of the Centre." The Working Paper and the Preliminary Draft of the Convention had specified that such consent might be given in respect of an existing dispute or in respect of future disputes arising between the parties. The provision was omitted as unnecessary in subsequent drafts of the Convention but included in the Draft Report, along with a reference to the possibility of States providing their consent unilaterally and in general terms in investment legislation. The definitions of "legal dispute" and "international law" that were dropped in the Revised Draft of the Convention similarly found a home in the Draft Report. Also included in the Draft Report were the various understandings that the Legal Committee had agreed should be recorded in the Report. Thus, it anticipated a decision by the Executive Directors that the Bank would house the Centre at no charge and underwrite its basic overhead for an initial period. The Draft Report likewise set out the understandings that the Centre would be unlikely to need "more than one or two full time high officials" and that it might make arrangements with other institutions not merely to host proceedings but even to provide "complete secretariat services." In addition, as had been requested by one of the Legal Committee members, the Draft Report made it clear that the provision conferring jurisdiction on the ICJ over disputes between Contracting States concerning the interpretation or application of the Convention would not allow the ICJ to review jurisdictional decisions of conciliation commissions or arbitral tribunals.

A. The final meetings of the Committee of the Whole

The Revised Draft, with the changes proposed by Broches, and the Draft Report were discussed by the Executive Directors, sitting again as the Committee of the Whole on the Settlement of Investment Disputes, in meetings held from mid-February to early March 1965. At these meetings, the Executive Directors agreed with almost all of the conclusions of the Legal Committee, although not without debate on some points. For example, one Executive Director argued, unsuccessfully, for greater flexibility in regard to amendments of the Convention. Requiring unanimity for all amendments could result in a needed change being "frustrated by a single dissident country."[176]

In some other respects, the Executive Directors departed from the recommendations of the Legal Committee. Thus, it was decided, in these final meetings of the Committee of the Whole, that the Convention should specify the terms of office and eligibility for re-election of the Secretary-General and of any Deputy Secretary-General of the Centre.[177] A more important question was raised by the Executive Director representing Germany[178] in regard to the provision requiring every Contracting State

[176] MMCW, February 25, 1965 (morning), reprinted in 2 *History of the ICSID Convention* 998, 5. The Executive Director concerned, Luis Machado (*see* Ch. 3, n. 97), illustrated the sort of change that might eventually be needed by suggesting that "it might be desirable for the Centre to become completely separate from and independent of the Bank. The President of the Bank might well be too busy with his other functions to perform those given to him under the Convention." MMCW, February 25, 1965 (morning) 5.

[177] *See* MMCW, February 16, 1965 (n. 110) 5. The agreement was that they would be elected for terms of up to six years and could be re-elected.

[178] Donner (*see* Ch. 3, n. 110).

to enforce a Convention award as if it were a final judgment of the State's courts. He explained that the German authorities would find it impossible not to permit their courts to check, before enforcement, whether the award violated the public policy of the country.[179] Other Executive Directors opposed weakening the enforcement provision with a public policy exception.[180] Broches suggested that the enforcement obligation might be narrowed to apply to the pecuniary obligations imposed by the award as opposed to the award as a whole; this would not detract from the obligation to comply with the award but might, he hoped, help to overcome the difficulties that the German authorities had with the provision.[181] The suggestion was accepted after it proved to be attractive to several of the Executive Directors (though not the German).[182]

As explained earlier, the Legal Committee voted only narrowly in favor of two exceptions to the general rule that proceedings under the Convention could only be between a State and a national of another State. The first exception related to locally established but foreign-controlled juridical persons, while the second was for a State or international organization that had compensated an investor under an investment insurance scheme and had been subrogated to the latter's claim against the host State. In the final meetings of the Committee of the Whole, the Executive Directors chose to maintain the first exception, apparently without discussion. The second exception was, however, examined at length by the Executive Directors. Some Executive Directors, principally from industrial countries, favored retaining the exception; strong opposition to it was voiced by other Executive Directors, who objected to allowing the transformation of "a dispute between an individual and a government into a dispute between States or between a State and a still unknown international organization."[183] In the end, it was decided to drop the exception, the point having been made that the entire problem could be avoided by the insurer requiring the investor to have recourse to the Centre before being indemnified.[184]

In the final meetings of the Committee of the Whole, the Executive Directors also considered the parts of the Convention that the Legal Committee had not dealt with, namely the preamble and the final provisions. At the suggestion of two Latin American Executive Directors,[185] it was agreed to remove the references, in the second and sixth preambular paragraphs, to the sovereign equality of States and the need to observe conciliation and arbitration agreements in good faith (the concern about the latter reference being that it might be taken to imply occasional bad faith on the part of States).[186]

As in the First Draft, the first of the final provisions of the Revised Draft provided that the Convention would be open for signature on behalf of States members of the World Bank, the United Nations or any of its specialized agencies or parties to the ICJ Statute.[187] One Executive Director[188] was apprehensive that, as there had recently been efforts to bring it into the specialized agencies, "Mainland China" might become

179 *See* MMCW, February 23, 1965 (afternoon), reprinted in 2 *History of the ICSID Convention* 989, 1.

180 *See* ibid. 3.

181 *See* ibid. 2–3.

182 *See* MMCW, March 4, 1965, reprinted in 2 *History of the ICSID Convention* 1017, 2–3.

183 MMCW, February 18, 1965, reprinted in 2 *History of the ICSID Convention* 976, 1–6. The statement quoted in the text was by Joaquin Gutierrez Cano, Executive Director for Spain, Italy, Greece and Portugal, who had been a member of Spain's diplomatic service and was Executive Director of the Bank from 1963 to 1968.

184 *See* ibid. 5–6; MMCW, March 4, 1965 (n. 182) 1–2.

185 Mejia-Palacio and Machado. *See* Ch. 3, n. 97.

186 *See* MMCW, March 4, 1965 (n. 182) 4–5.

187 Revised Draft (n. 171) Art. 67.

188 Mejia-Palacio.

eligible to participate in the Convention. Another Executive Director[189] suggested that non-members of the Bank might be permitted to accede to the Convention on acceptance of their candidatures by a two-thirds majority vote of the members of the Administrative Council.[190] This suggestion was incorporated into the agreed solution, which was to provide for the Convention to be open for signature on behalf of Bank members and on behalf of other countries which were parties to the ICJ Statute and invited to sign the Convention by such a vote in the Administrative Council.[191]

Like the First Draft, the Revised Draft provided that the Executive Directors of the Bank would bring the Convention into force by issuing a declaration to that effect at any time after the Convention had been ratified by 12 States.[192] This procedure was mainly intended to ensure that the Convention would not come into force until it had been ratified by a reasonable number of both capital-importing and capital-exporting States.[193] At the Committee of the Whole meetings, however, the Executive Directors objected to the procedure, which one of them saw as placing them in the position of determining what combination of States should bring the Convention into effect.[194] The Executive Directors favored simply providing that the Convention would come into force following its ratification by a specified number of States. At the suggestion of Bank President Woods, it was agreed that this number should be 20.[195]

During the final meetings of the Committee of the Whole, the Executive Directors received from Broches re-drafts of the provisions according to which any Contracting State could denounce the Convention by notice to the World Bank, the denunciation to take effect six months after the Bank's receipt of the notice without, however, affecting the denouncing State's rights or obligations under the Convention arising from consents to the jurisdiction of the Centre given before receipt of the notice by the Bank.[196] The Executive Directors approved the provisions, though one of them[197] first asked what the situation would be where there was no bilateral consent agreement between a State and investor "but only a general declaration on the part of the State in favor of submission of claims to the Centre and a subsequent withdrawal from the Convention by that State before any claim had in fact been submitted to the Centre."[198] Would, he asked, the State still be obligated to accept the jurisdiction of the Centre? Broches replied that, if a State withdrew a unilateral statement of the kind mentioned before it had been accepted by the investor, no investor could later bring a

189 Machado.

190 *See* MMCW, February 23, 1965 (morning), reprinted in 2 *History of the ICSID Convention* 989, 8.

191 *See* MMCW, February 25, 1965 (morning) (n. 176) 2. The reference to U.N. membership was presumably deleted as unnecessary since, under Art. 93(1) of the U.N. Charter, all members of the U.N. were ipso facto parties to the ICJ Statute. On the other hand, a non-U.N. member could, in accordance with Art. 93(2) of the Charter, become a party to the ICJ Statute on conditions determined by the General Assembly upon the recommendation of the Security Council. Although it did not then belong to the U.N. or the World Bank, Switzerland had become a party to the ICJ Statute by this route. The World Bank would welcome participation in the Convention by Switzerland, which despite its lack of Bank membership had long cooperated with the Bank, providing an important market for its bond issues.

192 Revised Draft (n. 171) Art. 69.

193 MMCW, February 25, 1965 (afternoon), reprinted in 2 *History of the ICSID Convention* 1003, 1 (intervention of Mr. Broches (Chairman)).

194 Ibid. (intervention of Mr. Machado).

195 *See* ibid. 3. On Broches's proposal, the Executive Directors agreed to the further refinement that there should be a 30-day interval between the twentieth ratification and entry into force. *See* ibid. 4.

196 *See* ibid. 5. 197 Gutierrez Cano. *See* n. 183.

198 MMCW, February 25, 1965 (afternoon) (n. 193) 8.

Aron Broches and George D. Woods on the occasion of their signing of the ICSID Convention on behalf of the World Bank, March 18, 1965. With them is Cyril H. Davies of the Secretary's Office of the World Bank.

World Bank Group Archives

claim to the Centre. If, however, the State's unilateral offer had been accepted before the denunciation, then disputes arising between the parties after the date of the denunciation would remain within the jurisdiction of the Centre.[199]

Among the other final provisions discussed by the Executive Directors were those designating the World Bank as the depositary of the Convention and setting out duties that it would perform in that capacity, such as registering the Convention with the U.N. Secretariat and notifying signatory States of each signature and ratification of the Convention.[200] In the Revised Draft, the provisions referred to these depository duties as being performed by "the Bank." On the proposal of one Executive Director,[201] it was agreed to refer instead in these provisions to "the depositary," although not without a caution against "obscuring the role of the Bank upon which the Centre would depend to a great extent at any rate in the early years of its existence."[202]

In the very last meetings of the Committee of the Whole, the Executive Directors considered their Draft Report on the Convention. They agreed that the Report should refer to the Bank as sponsoring "the establishment" of the Centre, rather than the Centre itself, and that it should mention the desirability of electing the Secretary-General initially for a short period, so that countries ratifying the Convention later

199 *See* ibid. 200 *See* Revised Draft (n. 71) Arts. 68, 74 and 75.

201 Gutierrez Cano.

202 MMCW, February 25, 1965 (afternoon) (n. 193) 6. The cautionary words were those of Ralph Hirschtritt, Temporary Alternate Executive Director for the United States in 1964, who was then Special Assistant to the Assistant Secretary of the U.S. Treasury.

could participate in the selection of a Secretary-General for a longer period.[203] Other agreed changes included casting in impersonal terms sentences that, in the Draft Report, specifically attributed certain features of the text to the judgment of the Executive Directors, such as the absence of a definition of "investment."[204]

B. Approval of the final text

The text of the Convention and the accompanying Report of the Executive Directors were finalized to incorporate the changes made by the Committee of the Whole. Reconvened in formal session on March 18, 1965, the Executive Directors adopted a resolution approving the final text of the Convention and the Report for submission to member governments of the Bank. The resolution directed the Bank President to transmit the text of the Convention and the accompanying Report to all members. He and the General Counsel were also authorized by the resolution to sign the Convention on behalf of the Bank, to indicate its acceptance to carry out the depositary duties entrusted to it by the Convention. The copy of the Convention so signed was, the resolution concluded, to remain deposited in the archives of the Bank and to be open for signature on behalf of governments in accordance with its terms.[205]

Woods and Broches duly signed the Convention on behalf of the Bank on March 18, 1965, just after this meeting of the Executive Directors. The following week, on March 23, 1965, Woods transmitted the text of the Convention and the accompanying Report to member governments, "unreservedly recommend[ing] the Convention for [their] early and favorable consideration."[206]

[203] MMCW, March 8, 1965, reprinted in 2 *History of the ICSID Convention* 1024, 1.
[204] MMCW, March 9, 1965, reprinted in 2 *History of the ICSID Convention* 1027, 1.
[205] Executive Directors Resolution No. 65-14, March 18, 1965, reprinted in 2 *History of the ICSID Convention* 1039.
[206] Transmittal letter of Bank President, March 23, 1965, reprinted in 2 *History of the ICSID Convention* 1086.

6

Establishment and Launch of the Centre

After the transmittal of the text of the ICSID Convention to member governments of the World Bank, Aron Broches and other Bank staff continued to promote participation in the Convention by member countries, and to publicize it among other potential users of the facilities to be provided under the Convention.[1] Signatures of the Convention by member countries soon followed. Tunisia and the United Kingdom became the first signatories in May 1965.[2] By the end of August 1965, the Convention had been signed by another eight countries, including the United States.[3] Signings accumulated more quickly in the remaining months of 1965. By the end of the year, there were 30 signatories. Of these, nine were industrial countries.[4] The developing country signatories included just three Asian States[5] and only one Caribbean country.[6] The overwhelming majority, 17 in all, were African States.[7] During 1966, a further 19 States became signatories of the Convention. They included three more Asian countries,[8] another Caribbean State[9] and seven more African States.[10] There were also eight industrial countries among the new signatories.[11]

The first of the signatories to ratify the Convention was Nigeria, which ratified on August 23, 1965. In the course of 1966, another 14 African States ratified the Convention.[12] Any possibility that the Convention might come into force without the ratification of a capital-exporting country was avoided when the largest such country, the United States, ratified on June 10, 1966. During the next three months, the Convention was also ratified by Iceland, Malaysia and Jamaica. Broches's home country, the Netherlands, then became the twentieth country to ratify the Convention. It deposited its instrument of ratification with the World Bank on September 14, 1966. In accordance with its Article 68(2), the Convention came into force 30 days later, on October 14, 1966. On the same day, the World Bank informed all signatories of the Convention of its entry into force. Pursuant to Article 74 of the Convention, the

[1] *See, e.g.*, remarks of Broches at the Annual Meeting of the American Society of International Law in 1965, reprinted in Broches *Selected Essays* 79.

[2] Signing on May 5, 1965, and May 26, 1969, respectively.

[3] The United States signed on August 27, 1965.

[4] The industrial country signatories at the end of 1965 were the United Kingdom, the United States, Japan, Sweden, Luxembourg, Denmark, Italy, Belgium and France. This and the listings in nn. 5, 7, 8 and 10–12 are in the order of signature or ratification.

[5] These were Pakistan, Nepal and Malaysia.

[6] Jamaica.

[7] These were Tunisia, Côte d'Ivoire, Nigeria, Mauritania, Niger, Central African Republic, Liberia, Dahomey (now Benin), Upper Volta (now Burkina Faso), Ethiopia, Gabon, Cameroon, Sierra Leone, Somalia, Morocco, Ghana and Congo-Brazzaville.

[8] Republic of China, Korea and Afghanistan.

[9] Trinidad and Tobago.

[10] Togo, Chad, Kenya, Malagasy Republic (now Madagascar), Uganda, Malawi and Senegal.

[11] These were Germany, Cyprus, Greece, Austria, the Netherlands, Norway, Iceland and Ireland.

[12] Mauritania, Côte d'Ivoire, the Central African Republic, Gabon, Uganda, Tunisia, Congo-Brazzaville, Ghana, Sierra Leone, Malawi, Upper Volta, Chad, Dahomey and the Malagasy Republic.

Tunisia and the United Kingdom were the first signatory States of the ICSID Convention. Pictured above is Ambassador Rachid Driss signing the Convention on behalf of Tunisia on May 5, 1965. The picture below is of Ambassador Patrick H. Dean signing the Convention for the United Kingdom on May 26, 1965. With them both are George D. Woods and Morton M. Mendels, the Secretary of the World Bank.

World Bank Group Archives

Bank then proceeded, on October 17, 1966, to register the Convention with the U.N. Secretariat.[13]

With the entry into force of the ICSID Convention, the Centre had been created, but before it could begin to function, the Administrative Council had to take a number of actions. These included electing a Secretary-General, adopting the regulations and rules of the Centre and approving its administrative arrangements with the World Bank. An inaugural meeting of the Administrative Council was convened for the purpose in February 1967. The work was continued at the first annual meeting of the Council, held in September 1967. These initial meetings of the Administrative Council are discussed below. Also discussed are the resolutions, regulations, rules and arrangements approved at the meetings, which established enduring basic features of the institution.

I. The inaugural meeting of the Administrative Council

On December 15, 1966, the World Bank's President George Woods, acting in his capacity as Chairman of the Administrative Council of ICSID, formally convened the inaugural meeting of the Council to meet on February 2, 1967 at the headquarters of the Bank in Washington, D.C.[14] The meeting, scheduled after consultation with States through the Executive Directors of the Bank, was thus to take place some three and half months after the Convention came into force. This was partly to allow for preparation of the necessary papers and for their study by Contracting States. The delay also permitted more States to complete their ratification procedures in time to participate fully in the meeting. By February 2, 1967, there were 28 Contracting States and 21 other signatories of the Convention. All 28 Contracting States were represented at the meeting.[15] Also present were observers from 13 of the other signatory States[16] and from three non-signatory members of the World Bank.[17] Items on the agenda for the meeting included the election of the Secretary-General, the adoption of provisional versions of ICSID's regulations and rules, the approval of administrative arrangements

[13] The Convention received registration number 8359. The regulations adopted by the U.N. General Assembly on the registration of treaties with the Secretariat provided that registration was to take place after entry into force of the treaty concerned. *See* Regulations to Give Effect to Article 102 of the Charter of the United Nations, December 14, 1946, 859 UNTS xii, Art. 1(2).

[14] The meeting was called under Art. 7(1) of the ICSID Convention, which gave the Chairman of the Administrative Council a free hand to convene special meetings of the Council. Drafts of the Convention had included an article, based on provisions in the Articles of Agreement of the IFC (May 25, 1955, 264 UNTS 117, Art. IX(3)) and IDA (December 16, 1960, 439 UNTS 249, Art. XI(4)), specifically providing for the President of the Bank to convene the inaugural meeting of the Administrative Council after entry into force of the Convention. *See, e.g.*, Revised Draft of the Convention, December 11, 1964, reprinted in 2 *History of the ICSID Convention* 911, Art. 73. In the final meetings of their Committee of the Whole on the Settlement of Investment Disputes, the Executive Directors of the Bank decided to delete the article as unnecessary, given the general authority that the President would have as Chairman of the Administrative Council to convene meetings of the Council. *See* Memorandum of Meeting of the Committee of the Whole, February 25, 1965 (afternoon), reprinted in 2 *History of the ICSID Convention* 1003, 9.

[15] They were Cameroon, the Central African Republic, Chad, Congo-Brazzaville, Cyprus, Dahomey, Gabon, Ghana, Iceland, Ivory Coast, Jamaica, Kenya, Malagasy Republic, Malawi, Malaysia, Mauritania, the Netherlands, Niger, Nigeria, Pakistan, Sierra Leone, Sweden, Trinidad and Tobago, Tunisia, Uganda, the United Kingdom, the United States and Upper Volta.

[16] Austria, Belgium, China, Denmark, France, Germany, Greece, Italy, Japan, Korea, Luxembourg, Norway and Senegal.

[17] Congo-Kinshasa, Sudan and Tanzania.

with the World Bank, the adoption of an initial budget for the Centre, and the invitation to Switzerland to sign the ICSID Convention.

A. Election of the first Secretary-General of ICSID

Under Article 10(1) of the ICSID Convention, the Secretary-General of the Centre was to be elected by the Administrative Council on the nomination of its Chairman for a term of up to six years. Pursuant to Article 10(1), the Chairman would propose one or more candidates for the office after consulting the members of the Administrative Council. In accordance with Article 10(2) of the Convention, the Secretary-General could hold other employment or engage in another occupation only with the approval of the Council.

Referring to these provisions, Woods began his consultations early, in September 1966, even before the entry into force of the Convention.[18] Through the Executive Directors of the Bank, he informed the States that had ratified the Convention of his intention to propose that Broches be elected the first Secretary-General of the Centre. In doing so, Woods reminded States of the consensus of the Executive Directors, recorded in their Report accompanying the Convention, "that the initial election, which will take place shortly after the Convention will have come into force, should be for a short term so as not to deprive the States which ratify the Convention after its entry into force of the possibility of participating in the selection of the high officials of the Centre."[19] Woods foresaw that during the early years, the Secretary-General's activities would probably constitute a part-time, largely educational occupation, explaining the Convention and its purposes to governments and the investing community. There was thus a need for a person of sufficient stature, able to take on for a short period this part-time activity requiring familiarity with the background of the Convention and with the governments and other parties involved. Finding such a person outside the Bank would have been difficult, to say the least; Broches had the necessary qualifications for the role, which he could combine with his functions as General Counsel of the Bank.

For its inaugural meeting, the Administrative Council received a report from Woods on the subject. In it, Woods noted that the reactions of States to his suggestion had been uniformly favorable; he therefore nominated Broches for election as the first Secretary-General of the Centre.[20] The report recommended to the Council that Broches be elected for a term extending until September 30, 1968, and that a new election for Secretary-General be held at the second annual meeting of the Council in September 1968.[21] According to the report, there was no incompatibility between the General Counsel and Secretary-General offices and Broches would serve the Centre without compensation. It therefore also recommended that the Administrative Council, in electing Broches Secretary-General, approve his continued employment by the Bank and determine that he serve without remuneration from ICSID.[22] The report recommended deferring a decision on the election of a Deputy Secretary-General as there was, at this initial stage, "no demonstrable need for more than one high official of the Centre."[23]

[18] Woods chose this time to start the process because the members-to-be of the Administrative Council, the Governors of the Bank for the countries concerned, were then assembling in Washington for the annual meeting of the Board of Governors.

[19] Report of the Executive Directors on the Convention, para. 18.

[20] Doc. AC/67/1, Election of the Secretary-General, Report and Recommendations of the Chairman, January 6, 1967, paras. 2 and 3.

[21] Ibid. para. 5. [22] Ibid. paras. 6 and 7. [23] Ibid. para. 8.

At the inaugural meeting, one participant cautioned that while he had no objection to Broches's qualifications, the election of a person who was to continue as a high functionary of the World Bank should not be allowed to become a precedent as the Bank's financing of many projects might often lead to its involvement in investment disputes.[24] Other delegates disagreed, seeing no incompatibility in Broches's proposed dual functions. The Bank could never be a party to proceedings under the ICSID Convention; nor would the Secretary-General, an administrative officer, have responsibility for the settlement of disputes. Moreover, the arrangement was to be temporary, and the work and resources of the Centre were limited. The Council, one of these other delegates suggested, should record its appreciation of the Bank's offer to make available the services of Broches free of charge, since he was ideally suited for the assignment.[25] The Council proceeded unanimously to adopt the resolution electing Broches for the term and on the conditions recommended in Woods's report.[26] Chairing the meeting, Woods then "reaffirmed his hope and intention that the Centre would finally emerge as a wholly independent entity, with a completely independent staff under the leadership of a full-time Secretary-General" and that "in due time it should also become completely self-supporting."[27]

B. Adoption of the Provisional Regulations and Rules

In accordance with Article 6(1) of the Convention, the Administrative Council was to adopt four sets of regulations and rules of ICSID: Administrative and Financial Regulations; Rules of Procedure for the Institution of Conciliation and Arbitration Proceedings (Institution Rules); Rules of Procedure for Conciliation Proceedings (Conciliation Rules); and Rules of Procedure for Arbitration Proceedings (Arbitration Rules). With the assistance of an outside consultant,[28] Broches and his World Bank Legal Department colleagues began preparing drafts of these regulations and rules in early 1966. They made slow progress, partly because of the absence of precedents for some of the envisaged provisions and partly because the provisions were to be accompanied by detailed explanatory notes.[29] Initial annotated drafts of the Institution, Conciliation and Arbitration Rules were completed by November 1966. Paul C. Szasz then joined the staff of the Bank Legal Department and took up the work on the regulations and rules of the Centre.[30] Within six weeks, he had produced a draft of

[24] Doc. AC/67/7, Administrative Council Proceedings, Inaugural Meeting, February 2, 1967, para. 11 (intervention of Ambassador Daddah (Mauritania)).

[25] Ibid. para. 13 (intervention of Mr. Ayub (Pakistan). *See also* ibid. paras. 12, 14–17 (interventions of Ambassador Gondwe (Malawi), Mr. Woods (Chairman), Mr. Stevens (United Kingdom), Ambassador Gallin-Douathe (Cental African Republic), Mr. Jinadu (Nigeria) and Mr. Ghachem (Tunisia)).

[26] *See* Administrative Council Resolution AC(IM) RES/1, Election of the Secretary-General, February 2, 1967, reprinted in ICSID First Ann. Rep. 1966/1967, 15.

[27] Administrative Council Proceedings, Inaugural Meeting (n. 24) para. 19.

[28] This was Alexander Elkin, who had served as Legal Adviser at the OEEC.

[29] Apart from their other duties, Broches and his colleagues were also engaged during 1966 in the preparation of draft articles of agreement of the International Investment Insurance Agency, completing and distributing the draft to governments for comments in November 1966. *See* I.F.I. Shihata, *MIGA and Foreign Investment* 36 (1988). As explained in Ch. 2, section II(A), this early effort to establish a multilateral investment insurance scheme was eventually discontinued in 1973.

[30] Before joining the Bank, Szasz had been a legal officer with the International Atomic Energy Agency. He left the Bank in 1971 for the Office of Legal Affairs of the United Nations, becoming deputy to the Legal Counsel. Szasz helped with the establishment of the International Fund for Agricultural Development and the United Nations Industrial Organization and (after retiring from

the Administrative and Financial Regulations and revised drafts of the Institution, Conciliation and Arbitration Rules. These were circulated to the members of the Administrative Council in the second half of December 1966 without, however, the explanatory notes.

The Chairman's report on the subject for the inaugural meeting of the Administrative Council noted that it had not been possible to submit the drafts to Council members sufficiently in advance to permit an exhaustive review by their governments. But the Centre was now in existence and could be asked at any time to provide the services for which it had been established; provision also had to be made for its internal administration. It had at least to have interim regulations and rules.[31] The report therefore recommended that the Council adopt the draft regulations and rules as "provisional" instruments and instruct the Secretary-General to undertake a review of them with Contracting States and submit revised texts to the Council at its first annual meeting in September 1967.[32] This recommendation was accepted by the Council.[33] The Provisional Regulations and Rules as thus adopted are discussed later in this chapter, in section II.

C. Approval of administrative and budgetary arrangements

Article 6(1)(d) of the ICSID Convention required the Administrative Council to approve arrangements with the World Bank for the use by the Centre of administrative facilities and services of the Bank. Before the inaugural meeting of the Council, the Executive Directors of the Bank had approved a Memorandum of Administrative Arrangements with the Centre. It was intended to implement Article 2 of the Convention, under which the seat of the Centre was to be at the principal office of the Bank, and the decision of the Executive Directors, recorded in their report accompanying the Convention, that "the Bank should be prepared to provide the Centre with office accommodation free of charge as long as the Centre has its seat at the Bank's headquarters and to underwrite, within reasonable limits, the basic overhead expenditure of the Centre for a period of years to be determined after the Centre is established."[34] At its inaugural meeting, the Administrative Council likewise approved the Memorandum and authorized the Secretary-General to sign it on behalf of the Centre.[35] The memorandum is described later in this chapter, in section III.

In accordance with Article 6(1)(f) of the Convention, the Administrative Council was also to approve "the annual budget of revenues and expenditures of the Centre." The Council was asked to approve, at its inaugural meeting, an initial budget for ICSID's first, partial fiscal year, extending from the entry into force of the Convention

regular U.N. service) with the drafting of the constitutions of Namibia and Bosnia and Herzegovina. Broches hardly exaggerated in once calling Szasz "the greatest international proceduralist known to man or God." World Bank Oral History Program, Transcript of Interview of Aron Broches, May 23, 1984, 54.

[31] Doc. AC/67/2, The Regulations and Rules of the Centre, Report and Recommendations of the Chairman, January 6, 1967, para. 2.

[32] Ibid. para. 3.

[33] *See* Administrative Council Resolution AC(IM)/RES/2, Adoption of the Provisional Regulations and Rules, February 2, 1967, reprinted in ICSID First Ann. Rep. 1966/1967, 15.

[34] Report of the Executive Directors on the Convention, para. 17.

[35] *See* Administrative Council Resolution AC(IM)/RES/3, Approval of Administrative Arrangements with the International Bank for Reconstruction and Development, February 2, 1967, reprinted in ICSID First Ann. Rep. 1966/1967, 15.

The inaugural meeting of the Administrative Council of ICSID, held in Washington, D.C., on February 2, 1967.
World Bank Group Archives

on October 14, 1966 to June 30, 1967. Given the Centre's likely limited functions in this initial period, the budget foresaw expenditures totaling just US$30,000,[36] mostly for staff services. In implementation of its anticipated arrangements with ICSID, the Bank had already agreed to make available for the period services and facilities in the mentioned amount. At the inaugural meeting of the Council, one participant wondered if a larger allocation of funds might be needed in the view of the extensive efforts the Secretariat would have to undertake to promote the institution; he expressed the hope that the Bank would be prepared to provide additional financial support if necessary.[37] Woods explained in reply that he and Broches were confident that the proposed budget was adequate. He also "gave assurance that the Bank took great pride in the new organization and would take whatever steps reasonably necessary to bring it into being."[38] The Council proceeded unanimously to approve the initial budget.[39]

The last item on the agenda of the inaugural meeting of the Administrative Council was for the Council to invite Switzerland to sign the ICSID Convention. Eligibility to participate in the Convention could, under its Article 67, be extended by such an invitation to countries which, like Switzerland, did not belong to the World Bank but were parties to the ICJ Statute. Switzerland having informed the Bank that it would

[36] Equivalent to US$213,000 in 2015.
[37] *See* Administrative Council Proceedings, Inaugural Meeting (n. 24) para. 41 (intervention of Ambassador Daddah (Mauritania)).
[38] Ibid. para. 42.
[39] *See* Administrative Council Resolution AC(IM)RES/4, Adoption of Budget for October 14, 1966 to June 30, 1967, February 2, 1967, reprinted in ICSID First Ann. Rep. 1966/1967, 16.

welcome the invitation, the Administrative Council voted unanimously to invite the country to sign the Convention.[40]

II. The Provisional Regulations and Rules of the Centre

The Provisional Regulations and Rules, comprising Provisional Administrative and Financial Regulations and Provisional Institution, Conciliation and Arbitration Rules, were published by ICSID immediately after the inaugural meeting of the Administrative Council.[41] In accordance with their terms, the Provisional Regulations and Rules were to remain in effect only until the end of 1967.[42] They were issued in English and French language versions, the Provisional Administrative and Financial Regulations designating those the official languages of the Centre, with Spanish to be added as a third official language as soon as a Spanish-speaking country became a party to the ICSID Convention.[43] The main provisions of each of those sets of Provisional Regulations and Rules are discussed in the following subsections. As will be seen, the subsequent definitive Regulations and Rules did not differ greatly from these "provisional" ones.

A. The Provisional Administrative and Financial Regulations

The Provisional Administrative and Financial Regulations provided procedures of the Administrative Council, details on the Secretariat and its functions, provisions on the financing of the Centre and of individual proceedings, and regulations regarding immunities and privileges granted by the ICSID Convention. The procedures of the Council, addressing such matters as the notice and agenda of meetings, were largely adapted from the By-Laws of the World Bank.[44] As envisaged during the preparation of the Convention, there was a regulation providing for the annual meetings of the Council to be held in conjunction with those of the Board of Governors of the Bank.[45] Another regulation established the procedure permitted by Article 7(4) of the Convention for the Chairman of the Council to ask it to vote on a matter without convening a meeting of the Council.[46]

In regard to the Secretariat, the Provisional Administrative and Financial Regulations provided, inter alia, for the eventuality not foreseen by the Convention that a person might have to be designated to act for the Secretary-General at a time when there

[40] *See* Administrative Council Resolution AC(IM)/RES/5, Invitation to Switzerland to Sign the Convention, February 2, 1967, reprinted in ICSID First Ann. Rep. 1966/1967, 16. The Convention was signed by Switzerland on September 22, 1967 and ratified on May 15, 1968.

[41] Doc. ICSID/1, Provisional Regulations and Rules (Provisional Administrative and Financial Regulations, Provisional Rules of Procedure for the Institution of Conciliation and Arbitration Proceedings (Institution Rules), Provisional Conciliation Rules and Provisional Arbitration Rules), February 2, 1967, reprinted in 6 ILM 225 (1967).

[42] *See* Provisional Administrative and Financial Regulations (n. 41) reg. 2.1(c); Provisional Institution Rules (n. 41) Art. 13(2): Provisional Conciliation Rules (n. 41) Art. 30(2); Provisional Arbitration Rules (n. 41) Art. 55(2).

[43] *See* Provisional Administrative and Financial Regulations (n. 41) reg. 10; Provisional Institution Rules (n. 41) Art. 14; Provisional Conciliation Rules (n. 41) Art. 31; Provisional Arbitration Rules (n. 41) Art. 56.

[44] *See* By-Laws of the IBRD, secs. 3 and 5.

[45] Provisional Administrative and Financial Regulations (n. 41) reg. 3.1(a).

[46] *See* ibid. reg. 3.6(c).

was no Deputy Secretary-General.[47] The Provisional Administrative and Financial Regulations also set out the rules, referred to in Article 11 of the Convention, for the appointment of staff by the Secretary-General, and made it clear that any Deputy Secretary-General and the staff, whether on direct appointment or seconded from the Bank, should act solely under the direction of the Secretary-General.[48] It was in addition made clear in the Provisional Administrative and Financial Regulations that no member of the Secretariat could serve on the Panel of Conciliators or of Arbitrators or on any conciliation commission or arbitral tribunal.[49]

Among the functions given the Secretary-General by the Provisional Administrative and Financial Regulations was the maintenance of the listings of Contracting States and measures taken by them for the purpose of the Convention.[50] Details were also provided in the Provisional Administrative and Financial Regulations for the maintenance of the Panels of Conciliators and of Arbitrators; these included a provision according to which the Secretary-General was to seek, from designees to the panels, acceptance of their designations at the outset of their term and, each year thereafter, confirmation of their continued willingness to serve on the relevant panel.[51]

Appropriately for a public institution, the Secretary-General was to publish information not only about the operation of the Centre in general but also on the institution of each proceeding and method of its eventual conclusion.[52] There were to be separate registers for conciliation requests and arbitration requests into which the Secretary-General was to enter "all significant data concerning the institution, conduct and disposition of each proceeding."[53] The Provisional Administrative and Financial Regulations declared that the registers were to be "open for inspection by any person."[54] Beyond that, Article 48(5) of the Convention prohibited the Centre from publishing arbitral awards without the consent of the parties. In order to further "the development of international law in relation to investments," the Secretary-General was to endeavor to obtain the consent of the parties to the publication of such awards; a reference was added in this context to seeking the consent of the parties for the publication of reports of conciliation commissions and minutes and other records of hearings, as they also would otherwise have to be kept confidential by the Centre.[55]

It was not expected that the Centre would receive numerous cases.[56] The provisional Administrative and Financial Regulations could thus provide for each to receive from the Secretariat the extensive administrative support that complex public international law proceedings typically demanded. In particular, the Secretary-General was to appoint a secretary for each conciliation commission, arbitral tribunal and ad hoc committee.[57] If not drawn from the Secretariat, the secretary would, while serving in

[47] *See* ibid. reg. 4.2(b) (providing for the Secretary-General to designate a member of the staff to act during the Secretary-General's absence or inability to act if all Deputy Secretaries-General should also be absent or unable to act or if the office of Deputy should be vacant). Retained in subsequent editions of the regulations, this provision was frequently used as the position of Deputy remained vacant until 1999.

[48] *See* ibid. regs. 4.3–4.5. The latter clarification, regarding the authority of the Secretary-General, was useful inasmuch as all Secretariat personnel came to be seconded from the Bank.

[49] *See* ibid. reg. 4.6. [50] *See* ibid. reg. 6.1.

[51] *See* ibid. reg. 6.2(c). The provision was meant to implement Art. 12 of the ICSID Convention *in fine*, according to which the panels were to consist of qualified persons "willing to serve thereon."

[52] *See* Provisional Administrative and Financial Regulations (n. 41) reg. 6.3(a).

[53] Ibid. reg. 7.1(a). [54] Ibid. reg. 7.1(b). [55] *See* ibid. reg. 6.3(b).

[56] *See* Ch. 7, n. 102.

[57] Provisional Administrative and Financial Regulations (n. 41) reg. 7.3.

that capacity, be considered a member of its staff.[58] The secretary would represent the Secretary-General and perform functions assigned to the latter by the Regulations and Rules with regard to individual proceedings.[59] Tasks of the secretary would include serving as the official channel of communications between the parties and the commission tribunal or committee; making arrangements for hearings; and attending all the hearings and keeping and signing the minutes.[60]

Financial provisions of the Provisional Administrative and Financial Regulations set the fiscal year of ICSID to be the same as that of the World Bank;[61] provided for the preparation by the Secretary-General of the annual budget of the Centre;[62] laid down procedures for the assessment on Contracting States of any excess of expected expenditures over expected revenues;[63] and required the Secretary-General to have the accounts of the Centre audited each year.[64] The provisions also addressed the financing of the direct costs of individual proceedings—the fees and expenses of the conciliators, arbitrators or ad hoc committee members, and of witnesses or experts summoned by them and the costs incurred for the proceeding by the Secretariat of the Centre. For obvious reasons, all of the related payments were to be made by the Centre and not by or through either party to the proceeding.[65] ICSID would make the payments from funds that it would ask the parties each quarter to advance to it to meet expenses estimated to be incurred for the proceeding in the following quarter.[66] Each party would in principle pay half of each advance requested by the Centre subject, in the case of an arbitration proceeding, to the ultimate apportionment of costs by the tribunal under Article 61(2) of the ICSID Convention.[67] If either party defaulted in making a required payment, the Secretary-General was to give the other party an opportunity to make the payment instead; continued non-payment could lead to the suspension and ultimately termination of the proceeding by the commission, tribunal or committee at the request of the Secretary-General.[68]

In accordance with Article 60(1) of the ICSID Convention, each conciliation commission, arbitral tribunal and ad hoc committee was, unless otherwise agreed with the parties to the proceeding, to determine the fees and expenses of its members within limits established by the Administrative Council. Those limits were set forth in the Provisional Administrative and Financial Regulations. Service on the commissions, tribunals and committees "was from the very beginning seen by the Centre as a public service."[69] Reflecting this, the Provisional Administrative and Financial Regulations provided for conciliators, arbitrators and ad hoc committee members to receive a fee

[58] *See* ibid. Assimilating such a "non-Secretariat" secretary to the staff would, among other things, assure that while serving in the capacity, the secretary would have the immunities and privileges of staff under the Convention.

[59] *See* ibid. reg. 7.3(i).

[60] *See* ibid. regs. 7.2(a), 7.3(iii) and 7.4.

[61] *See* ibid. reg. 5.4(a). The fiscal year would thus run from July 1 of each year to June 30 of the following year. Matching ICSID's fiscal year to that of the Bank was not only convenient but almost essential given that the Bank was to be the principal source of funds for the Centre. *See* section III of this chapter.

[62] *See* Provisional Administrative and Financial Regulations (n. 41) reg. 5.4(b).

[63] *See* ibid. regs. 5.4(c)–5.4(e).

[64] *See* ibid. reg. 5.5.

[65] *See* ibid. reg. 5.1(b).

[66] *See* ibid. reg. 5.1(c). The system of advances, intended to preclude any possibility of the Centre not being reimbursed for its expenditures for a proceeding, was necessary to ensure that such expenditures would not end up being assessed on Contracting States pursuant to Art. 17 of the ICSID Convention.

[67] *See* Provisional Administrative and Financial Regulations (n. 41) reg. 5.1(e).

[68] *See* ibid.

[69] A. Broches, The Experience of the International Centre for Settlement of Investment Disputes, International Disputes: Avoidance and Settlement, reprinted in Broches *Selected Essays* 264, 280.

not exceeding US$250 for each day of participation in meetings of the commission, tribunal or committee and a fee not exceeding US $100 for each day of other work performed in connection with the proceeding.[70] They were also to be reimbursed for any direct expenses reasonably incurred except that their subsistence expenses when traveling would be covered by a per diem allowance of up to US$40.[71]

In addition to the fees and expenses of conciliators, arbitrators and ad hoc committee members, the Provisional Administrative and Financial Regulations addressed certain of the "charges payable by the parties for the use of the facilities of the Centre" referred to in Article 59 of the Convention. Thus, the Secretary-General was to promulgate a schedule of fees setting out the charges to be paid by parties, from amounts deposited with ICSID in advance, for such special services as the provision of translations.[72] The Provisional Administrative and Financial Regulations also required a party making a request to institute a conciliation or arbitration proceeding under Article 28 or 36 of the Convention to pay the Secretary-General a fee of US$100.[73] A fee of half that amount, US$50, would be due from a party requesting the institution of any of the post-award proceedings under Articles 49 to 52 of the Convention (for the rectification, supplementation, interpretation, revision or annulment of an award).[74] As charges levied for the use of the facilities of the Centre in the context of the request procedures, these fees were non-reimbursable even if the requests were withdrawn or denied registration.[75] Hence they were referred to as fees for lodging requests, not registration fees.

There were two respects in which the Provisional Administrative and Financial Regulations supplemented the immunities and privileges provisions of the Convention. The first was to authorize the Secretary-General to issue "certificates of official travel" to, among other specified participants in proceedings, conciliators, arbitrators, ad hoc committee members, staff of the Secretariat, parties and their counsel, indicating that they were traveling in connection with a proceeding under the Convention.[76] The purpose was to help ensure recognition in Contracting States of the immunities and privileges accorded to the persons concerned by Articles 21 and 22 of the Convention. The Provisional Administrative and Financial Regulations also specified the organs of the Centre that would exercise the authority to waive immunity from legal process under Articles 20 and 21(a) of the Convention. Under the regulations, the Secretary-General could waive the immunity of the Centre or of its staff members; the Chairman of the Administrative Council could waive the immunity of the Secretary-General and of conciliators, arbitrators and ad hoc committee members; and the Council could waive the immunity of its Chairman and members.[77] The immunity of parties, their counsel, witnesses and experts appearing in a proceeding could be waived by the Chairman of the Council on the recommendation of the commission, tribunal or ad hoc committee concerned or it could be waived by the Council even without such a recommendation.[78]

70 *See* Provisional Administrative and Financial Regulations (n. 41) reg. 5.1(a)(i). The mentioned amounts were equivalent to approximately US$1,700 and US$700 in 2015.

71 *See* ibid. reg. 5.1(a)(ii). In terms of 2015 dollars, the maximum per diem allowance equaled roughly US$280.

72 *See* ibid. reg. 5.2.

73 *See* ibid. reg. 5.3(a).

74 *See* ibid. reg. 5.3(b).

75 *See* ibid. reg. 5.3(a) *in fine*.

76 *See* ibid. reg. 9.1.

77 *See* ibid. regs. 9.2(a), 9.2(b)(i) and (ii) and 9.1(c)(i).

78 *See* ibid. regs. 9.1(b)(iii) and 9.1(c)(ii). The Council could also decide on all other waivers that the Secretary-General and Council Chairman were authorized to make. *See* ibid. reg. 9.1(c)(iii).

B. The Provisional Institution Rules

The Provisional Institution Rules elaborated on the procedure, outlined in Articles 28 and 36 of the ICSID Convention, for the filing with, and registration by, the Secretary-General of requests to institute conciliation and arbitration proceedings under the Convention. As envisaged by Articles 28 and 36 of the Convention, the request would have to furnish information concerning all of the elements of the jurisdiction of the Centre. The Provisional Institution Rules provided details in this respect, requiring, for example, that the request state the nationality of the non-State party on the pertinent date or dates.[79] In view of the importance of the element of the consent of the parties, the Provisional Institution Rules stipulated that, on this score, the request should supply not only information but also supporting documentation.[80]

The Secretary-General was to acknowledge receipt of the request and, so long as the prescribed lodging fee had been paid, immediately send a copy of the request to the other party and decide on its registration as soon as possible.[81] The Provisional Institution Rules made it clear that registration would be effected by registering the request in the conciliation register or the arbitration register that the Secretary-General was to maintain under the Administrative and Financial Regulations.[82] Registration was, in accordance with Articles 28(3) and 36(3) of the Convention, to be refused if the Secretary-General determined, on the basis of the information contained in the request, that the dispute was manifestly outside the jurisdiction of the Centre.[83] Also in accordance with Articles 28(3) and 36(3) of the Convention, the Secretary-General was to notify the parties forthwith of the registration or refusal of registration of a request.[84] The Provisional Institution Rules added to this basic requirement by providing that the notice of registration should, in particular, also invite the parties to proceed as soon as possible to constitute their conciliation commission or arbitral tribunal.[85] In regard to a notice of refusal of registration, the Provisional Institution Rules specified that it should provide the reasons for the refusal.[86] A further provision permitted a requesting party to withdraw its request at any time before the constitution of the conciliation commission or arbitral tribunal.[87]

C. The Provisional Conciliation Rules and Provisional Arbitration Rules

The Provisional Conciliation Rules and Provisional Arbitration Rules set forth procedures for proceedings following the dispatch of the notice of registration of the request for conciliation or arbitration. They dealt, inter alia, with the establishment of the conciliation commission or arbitral tribunal, its sessions and deliberations, procedural orders and languages, written and oral procedures and the preparation of the report or award of the commission or tribunal. Post-award proceedings, for the supplementation or rectification, interpretation, revision or annulment of an award, were also addressed by the Provisional Arbitration Rules. Instruments that had been drawn upon in the preparation of the Convention inspired parts of the Provisional Conciliation Rules and Arbitration Rules. As noted below, some of the provisions of these rules were, in

[79] *See* Provisional Institution Rules (n. 41) Art. 3(2)(a). [80] *See* ibid. Art. 3(3)(b).
[81] *See* ibid. Arts. 7, 8 and 9. [82] *See* ibid. Art. 9(1)(a) and text accompanying n. 53.
[83] *See* Provisional Institution Rules (n. 41) Art. 9(1)(b).
[84] *See* ibid. Art. 9(1)(a) and 9(1)(b). [85] *See* ibid. Art. 10(b).
[86] *See* ibid. Art. 9(1)(b). [87] *See* ibid. Art. 11.

particular, influenced by provisions of the ICJ Statute[88] and of the ILC Model Rules on Arbitral Procedure.[89]

Among the many details that the Provisional Conciliation Rules and Arbitration Rules added to the basic framework of the Convention were time limits intended to help expedite the process. These included time limits for the appointment of conciliators and arbitrators by the Chairman of the Administrative Council,[90] for the holding of the first sessions of conciliation commissions and arbitral tribunals[91] and for the drawing up of their reports and awards.[92] The rules also specified when certain key points in a proceeding would be reached, such as when a party could invoke the default provisions of Article 29(2)(b) or 37(2)(b) of the Convention on the number of conciliators or arbitrators and the method of their appointment,[93] when a commission or tribunal would be deemed officially to be constituted[94] and when (and how) it should close the proceeding.[95]

In regard to the appointment of arbitrators, the Provisional Arbitration Rules solved a problem posed by Article 39 of the Convention. According to Article 39, unless each and every member of an arbitral tribunal were appointed by agreement of the parties, the majority of the arbitrators would have to be nationals of States other than the State party to the dispute and the home State of the other party to the dispute. It had escaped the attention of the drafters of the Convention that Article 39 could operate unfairly, allowing one but not both parties freely to appoint such a co-national to a three-member tribunal. The Provisional Arbitration Rules closed the loophole by providing that, unless all members of a tribunal were to be appointed by agreement of the parties, a party could appoint a co-national only if a similar appointment by the other party would not result in a majority of co-nationals on the tribunal.[96] The intended result, of course, was practically to rule out the appointment by parties of national arbitrators in the typical case of a tribunal comprising three members—a result close to the exclusion of national arbitrators under the Preliminary and First Drafts of the Convention.[97]

[88] Reprinted in A. Zimmermann and others, *The Statute of the International Court of Justice* 1491 (2006) (ICJ Statute).

[89] International Law Commission, Model Rules on Arbitral Procedure, reprinted in 1958 (II) YBILC 82 (ILC Model Rules).

[90] *See* Provisional Conciliation Rules (n. 41) Art. 7(2) and Provisional Arbitration Rules (n. 41) Art. 7(2) (requiring the Chairman, when exercising his appointing authority functions under Arts. 30 and 38 of the Convention, to make the appointments within 30 days of being asked to do so by a party).

[91] *See* Provisional Conciliation Rules (n. 41) Art. 12(1) and Provisional Arbitration Rules (n. 41) Art. 12(1) (requiring conciliation commissions and arbitral tribunals to hold their first sessions within 60 days after their constitution or such other period as the parties might agree).

[92] *See* Provisional Conciliation Rules (n. 41) Art. 28(5) and Provisional Arbitration Rules (n. 41) Art. 46 (establishing basic time limits for the drawing up of a commission's report and tribunal's award of 30 and 60 days respectively from the closure of the proceedings).

[93] *See* Provisional Conciliation Rules (n. 41) Art. 7(1) and Provisional Arbitration Rules (n. 41) Art. 7(1) (providing that, unless the parties otherwise agreed, either could invoke the provisions if the commission or tribunal had not been constituted within 90 days after registration of the request).

[94] *See* Provisional Conciliation Rules (n. 41) Art. 8(1) and Provisional Arbitration Rules (n. 41) Art. 8(1) (providing for the date of constitution to be that of the Secretary-General's receipt of notification that the last remaining appointee to the commission or tribunal had accepted the appointment).

[95] *See* Provisional Conciliation Rules (n. 41) Art. 28(1)–28(3) (providing alternative procedures for closing the proceeding depending on its success or failure) and Provisional Arbitration Rules (n. 41) Art. 38(1) (providing for the proceeding to be formally declared closed on the completion of the presentation of the case by the parties).

[96] *See* Provisional Arbitration Rules (n. 41) Art. 3(2).

[97] *See* Ch. 4, nn. 32 and 33 and accompanying text; Ch. 5, n. 40 and accompanying text.

Following the examples of the ICJ Statute and the ILC Model Rules, the Provisional Arbitration Rules provided that proceedings would comprise both written and oral phases.[98] In the written phase, the claimant would file a memorial with the tribunal and the respondent a counter-memorial; these pleadings would, if necessary, be followed by a reply and rejoinder from the respective parties.[99] The oral phase of a proceeding would consist of the hearing by the tribunal of the parties, counsel, witnesses and experts.[100] The Provisional Conciliation Rules similarly provided for the commission to receive written statements from the parties and envisaged that it might also hold hearings.[101] Both the Provisional Conciliation Rules and Arbitration Rules addressed objections to jurisdiction. They provided that on the making of such an objection, the proceeding on the merits would automatically be suspended until the commission or tribunal could reach its decision on whether to deal with the objection as a preliminary question or join it to the merits.[102] The Provisional Conciliation Rules and Arbitration Rules also made it clear that, in addition to objections raised by parties, a commission or tribunal could on its own initiative consider possible objections to jurisdiction.[103] Procedures regarding requests for the recommendation by a tribunal of provisional measures were set out in the Provisional Arbitration Rules; they required a tribunal to give priority to the consideration of such a request but to recommend provisional measures only after giving both parties the opportunity of presenting their observations.[104] Other particular procedures provided by the Provisional Arbitration Rules included procedures for the discontinuance of proceedings where the parties had reached a settlement or otherwise decided to bring a halt to the arbitration. If the parties had reached a settlement, they could under the rules ask the tribunal to embody it in an award.[105]

Throughout, the Provisional Conciliation Rules and Arbitration Rules emphasized cooperation between the parties and the commission or tribunal on procedural matters. Thus, under the Provisional Arbitration Rules, the tribunal was to make the orders required for the conduct of the proceeding, but was also to take into account, as far as possible, any agreement between the parties on procedural matters.[106] A conciliation commission was placed under a similar duty to respect such agreements of the parties.[107] As early as possible after the constitution of a commission or tribunal, its president was therefore to ascertain the views of the parties on questions of procedure, such as which language or languages would be used in the proceeding.[108] This preliminary inquiry might be held with the agents, counsel or advocates that each party would be free to have represent it in the proceeding.[109]

[98] *See* Provisional Arbitration Rules (n. 41) Art. 24. *Cf.* ICJ Statute (n. 88) Art. 43; ILC Model Rules (n. 89) Art. 15(1).

[99] *See* Provisional Arbitration Rules (n. 41) Art. 25. *Cf.* ICJ Statute (n. 88) Art. 43(2); ILC Model Rules (n. 89) Art. 15(2).

[100] *See* Provisional Arbitration Rules (n. 41) Art. 31(1). *Cf.* ILC Model Rules (n. 89) Art. 15(4).

[101] *See* Provisional Arbitration Rules (n. 41) Arts. 22, 24 and 26.

[102] *See* Provisional Conciliation Rules (n. 41) Art. 21(2); Provisional Arbitration Rules (n. 41) Art. 39(2) and 39(5).

[103] *See* Provisional Conciliation Rules (n. 41) Art. 21(3); Provisional Arbitration Rules (n. 41) Art. 39(6).

[104] *See* Provisional Arbitration Rules (n. 41) Arts. 23(2) and 23(4).

[105] *See* ibid. Art. 43(2).

[106] *See* ibid. Arts. 18 and 17(1).

[107] *See* Provisional Conciliation Rules (n. 41) Art. 17(1).

[108] *See* ibid. Art. 17(2) and 17(3); Provisional Arbitration Rules (n. 41) Art. 17(2) and 17(3).

[109] *See* Provisional Conciliation Rules (n. 41) Art. 16; Provisional Arbitration Rules (n. 41) Art. 16.

Like the ICJ Statute and ILC Model Rules, the Provisional Conciliation Rules and Arbitration Rules specified that the deliberations of commissions and tribunals would take place in private and remain secret.[110] Consistent with the confidential nature of conciliation, the Provisional Conciliation Rules provided that hearings of a commission would likewise take place in private and, except as the parties might otherwise agree, remain secret. The Provisional Arbitration Rules lacked such an extensive claim for the privacy and permanent secrecy of hearings. On the other hand, they made it clear that members of the public could attend hearings only if the tribunal so decided with the consent of both parties.[111] In this respect, the Provisional Arbitration Rules were similar to the ILC Model Rules.[112]

As mentioned earlier, the Provisional Administrative and Financial Regulations provided that the secretary of the commission or tribunal would attend all hearings and keep minutes of them. The Provisional Conciliation Rules and Arbitration Rules outlined the contents of such minutes; they were to include the place and date of the hearing, the names of those present, a summary record of the proceedings and any recommendations of the conciliators or orders of the arbitrators made or announced during the hearing.[113] The minutes were not to be published without the consent of the parties.[114] They were to be the basic means of recording hearings, though an arbitral tribunal could order that they be more fully recorded (by, for example, verbatim transcripts).[115]

The Provisional Arbitration Rules also provided a checklist for the contents of an arbitral award. It incorporated the requirement of Article 48(3) of the Convention, that the award deal with every question submitted to the tribunal and state the reasons on which it was based.[116] The Provisional Arbitration Rules added, in the same spirit, that the award should contain the full names of the arbitrators and parties, their agents, counsel and advocates; a summary of the proceedings; a statement of the facts; and the submissions of the parties.[117] The award was furthermore to contain any decision of the tribunal on the allocation of the cost of the proceeding under Article 61(2) of the Convention.[118]

On its signature by the arbitrators, the Secretary-General was to authenticate the original text of the award, deposit it in the archives of ICSID and dispatch a certified copy of the award to each party.[119] Repeating the second sentence of Article 49(1) of the Convention, the Provisional Arbitration Rules provided that the award would be deemed to have been rendered on the date of dispatch of the certified copies. Reflecting its importance as the starting point of time limits for seeking the rectification, supplementation, interpretation, revision or annulment of the award under Articles 49 to 52

[110] *See* Provisional Conciliation Rules (n. 41) Art. 14; Provisional Arbitration Rules (n. 41) Art. 14. *Cf.* ICJ Statute (n. 88) Art. 54(3); ILC Model Rules (n. 89) Art. 26.

[111] *See* Provisional Arbitration Rules (n. 41) Art. 31(2). *Cf.* Provisional Conciliation Rules (n. 41) Art. 26.

[112] *See* ILC Model Rules (n. 89) Art. 16(1).

[113] *See* Provisional Conciliation Rules (n. 41) Art. 27(1); Provisional Arbitration Rules (n. 41) Art. 37. The Provisional Conciliation Rules, however, highlighted (Art. 27(2)) the possibility of the commission and parties agreeing that the minutes should omit any record of the proceedings or recommendations made or announced during the hearing.

[114] *See* Provisional Conciliation Rules (n. 41) Art. 27(3); Provisional Arbitration Rules (n. 41) Art. 37(2).

[115] *See* Provisional Arbitration Rules (n. 41) Art. 37(3).

[116] *See* ibid. Art. 47(1)(g).

[117] *See* ibid. Art. 47(1)(a)–47(1)(f).

[118] *See* ibid. Art. 47(1)(h).

[119] *See* ibid. Art. 48(1) and 48(2).

of the Convention, the Provisional Arbitration Rules required the Secretary-General to indicate that date on the original text and all certified copies of the award.[120]

Procedures for the submission to, and registration by, the Secretary-General of requests for the rectification, supplementation, interpretation, revision and annulment of awards were briefly set out in four articles of the Provisional Arbitration Rules. These required the Secretary-General to register such requests "forthwith" upon their receipt, on the assumption of course that they were submitted within any applicable time limit prescribed by the Convention.[121] Also concisely laid down in the Provisional Arbitration Rules were the steps that the Secretary-General would take, immediately after registration, to have the request considered by the appropriate body. The Secretary-General would thus reconvene the original tribunal, if possible, to deal with a request for rectification, supplementation, interpretation or revision; and ask the Chairman of the Administrative Council to appoint the ad hoc committee that would decide on a request for annulment.[122]

III. The Memorandum of Administrative Arrangements

The Memorandum of Administrative Arrangements with the World Bank was concluded in the approved form soon after the inaugural meeting of the Administrative Council, on February 13, 1967. As authorized by the Council, Broches signed the Memorandum on behalf of the Centre. The Memorandum was signed for the Bank by the most senior of its vice presidents, J. Burke Knapp.[123]

Formalizing the earlier decision of the Executive Directors of the Bank regarding the assistance it would give ICSID,[124] the Memorandum specified that the Bank would supply ICSID with the services of Bank staff members and consultants and other administrative services and facilities, including office accommodation, furniture and equipment.[125] Such services and facilities would be provided to ICSID within reasonable limits from annual budgetary allocations approved by the Bank after receiving ICSID's estimate of its needs for the year.[126] In accordance with the Memorandum, ICSID would have to reimburse the Bank for the assistance only to the extent that any expenditures were attributable to proceedings for which the Centre itself was to be reimbursed by parties pursuant to the Administrative and Financial Regulations.[127] Examples of such expenditures mentioned in the Provisional Administrative and Financial Regulations included payments to interpreters, translators, reporters or secretaries especially engaged by ICSID for a particular proceeding.[128] The Memorandum emphasized the fact that the Bank would not be required to pay or contribute to the

[120] *See* ibid. Art. 48(2)(b).

[121] *See* ibid. Arts. 49(3), 51(1) and 52(1) (a request for interpretation being the only one not subject to a time limit under the Convention).

[122] *See* ibid. Arts. 49(3)(b), 51(1)(b), 51(2) and 52(1)(b).

[123] Knapp was one of just three vice presidents of the Bank at the time (he was Chairman of the Bank's Loan Committee). Under its President, the Bank now has 29 principal officers, including two managing directors and 25 vice presidents. *See* IBRD, Information Statement 62 (September 2015).

[124] *See* n. 34 and accompanying text.

[125] *See* Memorandum of Administrative Arrangements Agreed between the International Bank for Reconstruction and Development and the International Centre for Settlement of Investment Disputes, February 13, 1967, reprinted in ICSID First Ann. Rep. 1966/1967, 15, para. 1(a) and 1(b) (Memorandum of Administrative Arrangements).

[126] *See* ibid. para. 2(a). [127] *See* ibid. para. 3.

[128] Provisional Administrative and Financial Regulations (n. 41) para. 5.1(b)(iv).

fees and expenses of conciliators, arbitrators and ad hoc committee members, which similarly were to be met from funds advanced to ICSID by the parties.[129]

Though signed on February 13, 1967, the Memorandum was made effective retroactively as of October 14, 1966.[130] The Memorandum provided that it would remain in force until the end of ICSID's first full fiscal year on June 30, 1968 and that it would "thereafter be renewed automatically from year to year unless either party denounces it not less than six months prior to the end of any annual period of extension."[131] Under this provision, the Memorandum was to remain in force and continue to be applied for many years. It has never been formally denounced.

IV. The first annual meeting of the Administrative Council

Since the inception of the World Bank and International Monetary Fund, the annual meetings of their Boards of Governors had been held as joint meetings. In accordance with the Articles of Agreement of the IFC and IDA, the annual meetings of the IFC and IDA Boards of Governors were conducted together with the annual meetings of the Bank Board of Governors—the Governors of the Bank for IFC and IDA members being ex officio the countries' IFC and IDA Governors.[132] As mentioned earlier, the Provisional Administrative and Financial Regulations of the Centre provided that the annual meetings of the Administrative Council would likewise be held in conjunction with the annual meetings of the Bank's Board of Governors,[133] given that under Article 4(2) of the ICSID Convention each Governor of the Bank appointed by a Contracting State would, in the absence of a contrary designation, be ex officio its Representative on the Administrative Council.

In 1967, the annual meetings took place on September 25 in Rio de Janeiro.[134] Though held there in conjunction with the annual meetings of the Boards of Governors of the other institutions, the first annual meeting of the Administrative Council of ICSID was convened as a separate gathering later in the day, after the joint sessions of the IMF, IBRD, IFC and IDA Governors. The annual meetings of the Administrative Council were to be held this way for the next 20 years.[135]

Most of the by then 36 Contracting States were represented at the first annual meeting of the Administrative Council.[136] Woods opened the meeting as Council Chairman, expressing satisfaction that the Centre was now available to governments and foreign investors as "an assured forum" to which they could consent to submit their disputes.[137] He urged countries that had not yet decided to join the Centre to

[129] *See* Memorandum of Administrative Arrangements (n. 125) para. 5.

[130] *See* ibid. para. 6. The Memorandum thus applied to the initial budget covering the balance of the fiscal year from the entry into force of the ICSID Convention on October 14, 1966. *See* text accompanying n. 31.

[131] Memorandum of Administrative Arrangements (n. 125) para. 6.

[132] *See* Articles of Agreement of the IFC, May 25, 1955, 264 UNTS 117, Art. IV(2)(b) and IV(2)(e); Articles of Agreement of IDA, January 26, 1960, 439 UNTS 249, Art. VI(2)(b) and VI(2)(e).

[133] *See* n. 45 and accompanying text.

[134] The annual meetings were held outside Washington, D.C. every third year.

[135] On the abandonment of practice in 1988, see Ch. 7, section I(B).

[136] The eight countries that had become Contracting States since the inaugural meeting of the Council were France, Japan, Korea, Norway, Senegal, Sweden, Togo and Yugoslavia.

[137] Doc. AC/67/18, Administrative Council Proceedings, First Annual Meeting, September 25, 1967, para. 3 (First Annual Meeting Proceedings).

consider the possibility carefully in view of the role that the Centre could play in helping them to attract urgently needed private foreign investment on equitable terms.[138]

Taking the floor, Broches said that, since the inaugural meeting of the Council, substantial progress had been made with respect to the implementation of the Convention. Almost 50 persons had been designated to the Panels of Conciliators and of Arbitrators. Raising an issue that he and his successors would return to often in later years, Broches pointed out, however, that only about a third of the Contracting States had made use of their right to make designations to the Panels; he hoped that many others would do so promptly.[139] Broches also appealed to Contracting States to supplement the efforts that he and his staff had been making, through speeches and articles, to create awareness of the availability of the Convention and Centre.[140] Already some investment contracts provided for the resolution of related disputes under the auspices of ICSID. As the Convention became more widely known, such provisions would become more common.[141]

In his remarks, Broches noted that several Contracting States had enacted legislation for the promotion of foreign investments. Renewing the suggestion contained in the Report of the Bank's Executive Directors on the Convention, Broches said that these States might wish to establish a link between that legislation and the Convention.[142] Another idea that Broches put forward in these introductory remarks related to "Bilateral treaties dealing with the status of investments made by the citizens of one party in the territories of the other."[143] These, he observed, "frequently provide for the settlement of disputes through intergovernmental arbitration" but "[n]ow that the facilities provided by the Convention were available it might be advisable to substitute these procedures, at least on an optional basis, for those provided in these treaties."[144]

Following Broches's remarks, the Council turned to the business at hand and approved, pursuant to Article 6(1)(g) of the Convention, the first annual report of the Centre, covering the period from the establishment of ICSID until the end of its first fiscal year.[145] As mentioned in the annual report, much work had been done during the year to compile for publication the *travaux préparatoires* of the Convention, including its successive drafts, staff memoranda and the record of the consideration of the Convention by Executive Directors of the Bank and by regional Consultative Meetings of Experts and the Legal Committee on the Settlement of Investment Disputes.[146] This explained the comparatively large allocation for printing costs included in the budget for ICSID's second fiscal year, which was also approved by the Council at the meeting.[147] The remaining actions taken by the Administrative Council at its first annual meeting were to adopt the definitive Regulations and Rules of the Centre and

138 *See* ibid. para. 4. 139 *See* ibid. para. 8. 140 *See* ibid. para. 10.

141 *See* ibid. para. 11.

142 *See* ibid. *See also* Report of the Executive Directors, para. 24 (suggesting that "a host State might in its investment promotion legislation offer to submit disputes arising out of certain classes of investments to the jurisdiction of the Centre").

143 First Annual Meeting Proceedings (n. 137) para. 11. 144 Ibid.

145 *See* Administrative Council Resolution AC(1)/RES/6, Approval of the Annual Report, September 25, 1967, reprinted in ICSID Second Ann. Rep. 1967/1968, 16.

146 *See* ICSID First Ann. Rep. 1966/1967, 4. The Executive Directors approved the publication of these documents on June 30, 1967. *See* Excerpt from the Minutes of Joint Meeting of the Executive Directors of the IBRD and IDA, July 11, 1967, reprinted in 2 *History of the ICSID Convention* 1088. The *travaux préparatoires* were published in 1968 as the just-cited history, in English, French and Spanish editions. The compilation was done by Paul Szasz.

147 *See* Administrative Council Resolution AC(1)/RES/8, Adoption of Budget for Fiscal Year 1968, September 25, 1967, reprinted in ICSID Second Ann. Rep. 1967/1968, 16. The budget totaled US $84,000, equivalent in 2015 to US$596,000.

to approve its general arrangements with the Permanent Court of Arbitration.[148] These are discussed in the following subsections.

A. The definitive Regulations and Rules

As explained earlier, the Provisional Regulations and Rules, adopted by the Administrative Council at its inaugural meeting in February 1967, provided that they would remain in effect only until the end of that year. Immediately after the inaugural meeting, Szasz set to work preparing drafts of the definitive texts of the Regulations and Rules that the Council would adopt at its first annual meeting in September. These were dispatched to Contracting States for review as they were produced, in English and French, between March and May 1967. The draft definitive Regulations and Rules were more polished and better organized than the provisional ones. Sections defining such terms as "Centre" or "Convention" had been dropped as unnecessary.[149] There had been some rearranging of provisions; the substance of one, for example, requiring conciliators, arbitrators and ad hoc committee members when appointed to sign declarations attesting to their independence, had been transferred from the Administrative and Financial Regulations to the Conciliation Rules and Arbitration Rules.[150] Relatively small adjustments had been made to other provisions; in the provisions of the Conciliation Rules and Arbitration Rules specifying when a commission or tribunal would be deemed to be constituted, for example, the date of the Secretary-General's announcement to the parties that all members had accepted their appointment was substituted for the date of the Secretary-General's receipt of the last acceptance.[151] Over all, however, the draft definitive Regulations and Rules were very similar to the Provisional Regulations and Rules. A noticeable difference was that the draft definitive Regulations and Rules were accompanied by the detailed explanatory notes that had been omitted from the provisional versions. Some of the provisions, such as those relating to the nationality of arbitrators or post-award procedures, were difficult to understand without explanations of the related provisions of the Convention. The notes were useful especially for such explanations.[152]

Hardly any changes to the draft definitive Regulations and Rules were suggested by Contracting States. Broches invited them to send delegates to an informal meeting in Rio de Janeiro on Saturday, September 23, 1967 to discuss the drafts in advance of the first annual meeting of the Administrative Council the following Monday. A few modifications were proposed and agreed upon at this informal meeting. These included

[148] *See* Administrative Council Resolutions AC(1)/RES/7, Adoption of the Definitive Regulations and Rules, and AC(1)/RES/9, Arrangements with the Permanent Court of Arbitration, September 25, 1967, reprinted in ICSID Second Ann. Rep. 1967/1968, 16.

[149] *Cf.* Provisional Administrative and Financial Regulations (n. 41) reg. 1; Provisional Institution Rules (n. 41) Art. 1(1); Provisional Conciliation Rules (n. 41) Art. 1(1); Provisional Arbitration Rules (n. 41) Art. 1(1).

[150] *See* Doc. AC/67/11, Draft Conciliation Rules, May 10, 1967, Rule 6(2) (Draft Definitive Conciliation Rules); Doc. AC/67/10, Draft Arbitration Rules, April 7, 1967, Rule 6(2) (Draft Definitive Arbitration Rules). *Cf.* Provisional Administrative and Financial Regulations (n. 41) reg. 8.2.

[151] *See* Draft Definitive Conciliation Rules (n. 150) Rule 6(1); Draft Definitive Arbitration Rules (n. 150) Rule 6(1). *Cf.* n. 94. Another example was to specify that a request for conciliation or arbitration could be withdrawn before it was registered (rather than before the commission or tribunal was constituted). *See* Doc. AC/67/9, Draft Definitive Institution Rules, March 20, 1967, Rule 8. *Cf.* n. 87 and accompanying text.

[152] *See, e.g.*, Draft Definitive Arbitration Rules (n. 153) Rules 1 (note G), 49 (note E), 50 (note C) and 51 (note A).

two changes for the Administrative and Financial Regulations. The first concerned a provision of the draft definitive Administrative and Financial Regulations under which the Secretary-General would each year request any person designated to the Panel of Conciliators or the Panel of Arbitrators to confirm that the person continued to be willing to serve on the Panel.[153] At the informal meeting, it was agreed that the provision should require the Secretary-General instead to direct the request to the authority (Contracting State or Administrative Council Chairman) that designated the Panel member.[154] The second agreed change was of the provision according to which the Secretary-General would "endeavor to obtain the consent of the parties" to the publication of reports of conciliation commissions, arbitral awards and the minutes and other records of proceedings.[155] The change was to weaken the provision so that it would authorize the Secretary-General to arrange any publication consented to by the parties but not explicitly direct the Secretary-General to seek the consent.[156]

The definitive Regulations and Rules were adopted at the first annual meeting of the Administrative Council with the modifications agreed upon at the earlier informal meeting.[157] They took effect on January 1, 1968, superseding the Provisional Regulations and Rules from that date. The definitive Regulations and Rules were published by ICSID, in their English and French versions, with the explanatory notes to the Institution, Conciliation and Arbitration Rules.[158] At its first annual meeting, the Administrative Council had decided that this should be done as the notes "might be useful to parties to proceedings."[159]

B. The arrangements with the Permanent Court of Arbitration

These arrangements were set out in a Memorandum of General Arrangements between ICSID and the PCA.[160] The text of the Memorandum was drawn up by Broches in consultation with the then Secretary-General of the PCA, J.P.A. François. It was meant to implement the provision of Article 63(a) of the Convention, foreseeing that ICSID could make arrangements with the PCA, as well as with other appropriate public or private institutions, to enable conciliation and arbitration proceedings to be held at the seat of such institutions if so agreed by the parties to the proceedings.

[153] *See* Doc. AC/67/8, Draft Administrative and Financial Regulations, March 10, 1967, reg. 20(3) (Draft Definitive Administrative and Financial Regulations). The provision was meant to implement the provision Art. 12 of the Convention, according to which the Panels consist of qualified persons "willing to serve thereon."

[154] *See* Doc. AC/67/17, The Regulations and Rules of the Centre, Changes Proposed in the Draft Texts, September 25, 1967 (Proposed Changes). The change was proposed because it seemed inappropriate for the Secretary-General to question a commitment that a designee had initially given to a State. As explained in Ch. 8, the provision as thus changed created another problem and was eventually dropped altogether from the Administrative and Financial Regulations.

[155] *See* Draft Definitive Administrative and Financial Regulations (n. 153) reg. 21.

[156] *See* Proposed Changes (n. 154). The change was aimed, of course, at the possibility of the Secretary-General pressuring parties to grant the necessary consent to publication.

[157] *See* Administrative Council Resolution AC(1)/RES/7, Adoption of the Definitive Regulations and Rules, September 25, 1967, reprinted in ICSID Second Ann. Rep. 1967/1968, 16.

[158] The definitive Regulations and Rules with these notes were published as Doc. ICSID/4, ICSID Regulations and Rules.

[159] ICSID Second Ann. Rep. 1967/1968, 4. *See also* First Annual Meeting Proceedings (n. 137) para. 55.

[160] The Memorandum is reprinted in ICSID Second Ann. Rep. 1967/1968, 19.

The Memorandum recognized, however, that such arrangements should be reciprocal in nature. It thus provided that either institution might host proceedings conducted under the auspices of the other if the parties concerned so desired and the host could make the necessary facilities and services available on the dates in question.[161] The Memorandum set out simple procedures for the institutions to conclude specific arrangements for such cases after consulting with each other and with the parties and members of the commission or tribunal involved.[162] The Memorandum made it clear that the host institution would be reimbursed by the other institution for any expenditures incurred by the former under such arrangements.[163]

After their approval by the Administrative Council of ICSID at its first annual meeting, these arrangements were similarly approved by the Administrative Council of the PCA.[164] The Memorandum was then concluded, becoming effective once it had been signed by both Broches and François on May 1, 1968. The Memorandum has remained in force, unchanged, ever since.

[161] *See* ibid. paras. 1 and 2. [162] *See* ibid. paras. 1–3. [163] *See* ibid. para. 4.
[164] *See* ICSID Second Ann. Rep. 1967/1968, 6.

7

ICSID's First Two Decades

As was seen in Chapter 6, much of 1967 was spent by ICSID laying foundations for its future operation. The present chapter examines the activities of the Centre in the next 20 years, from 1968 to 1988. It is worth remembering some of the broad political and economic developments of the period.

Many of them having just gained political independence, developing countries began more vigorously to pursue economic self-sufficiency.[1] Anti-foreign investment sentiment became widespread among them. There were sharp increases in the number of expropriations of investments from abroad.[2] The quest for economic independence was reflected in the Declaratory Statement of Petroleum Policy adopted in 1968 by the Conference of the Organization of the Petroleum Exporting Countries (OPEC). It recommended that member governments seek to develop their hydrocarbon resources directly or, if that were not possible, to conclude contracts with outside operators under which the governments would retain maximum participation in, and control over, operations.[3] Disputes between governments and operators would in principle be decided by national courts.[4] In 1973, in the wake of the Yom Kippur War and ensuing Arab oil embargos, OPEC countries imposed a fourfold increase in the price of crude oil.[5] The success of the oil exporters in boosting the price of oil encouraged the producers of other primary commodities in the Third World to demand improved terms of trade, as well as greater financial assistance and respect for their sovereignty over their natural resources. These demands were embodied in the Declaration on the Establishment of a New International Economic Order (NIEO) adopted by the United Nations General Assembly on May Day of 1974 and in the Charter of the Economic Rights and Duties of States adopted by the General Assembly later that same year.[6] Prominently featured in the latter were the asserted rights of States to regulate and exercise authority over foreign investments and the activities of transnational corporations (TNCs) in their territories, to expropriate foreign property against payment of "appropriate" compensation and to have any resulting disputes settled in accordance with their domestic laws by their own tribunals.[7] Also in 1974, prompted in part

[1] On some of the intellectual underpinnings of this movement, *see* I. Taylor and K. Smith, *United Nations Conference on Trade and Development (UNCTAD)* 56–59 (2007).

[2] *See* J.E. Spero and J.A. Hart, *The Politics of International Economic Relations* 315 (7th ed. 2010) (citing increases in the number of expropriatory acts, from around ten in 1968 to more than 80 in 1975).

[3] Declaratory Statement of Petroleum Policy in Member Countries, OPEC Conference Resolution XVI 90, June 25, 1968, reprinted in OPEC Official Resolutions and Press Releases 1960–1980, 80, first operative section (1980). For an account of the preparation of the Declaratory Statement by its main author, *see* Francisco Parra's *Oil Politics: A Modern History of Petroleum* 110–112 (2004).

[4] Declaratory Statement (n. 3) ninth operative section.

[5] *See* OPEC Press Release No. 18-78, December 24, 1973, reprinted in OPEC Official Resolutions and Press Releases (n. 2) 143.

[6] G.A. Resolution 3201 (S-VI), Declaration on the Establishment of a New International Economic Order, May 1, 1974; G.A. Resolution 3281 (XXIX), Charter of Economic Rights and Duties of States, December 12, 1974.

[7] Charter of Economic Rights and Duties of States (n. 6) Art. 2(2).

by recent revelations of malfeasance by TNCs,[8] the United Nations Economic and Social Council decided to establish the United Nations Commission on Transnational Corporations charged with developing a code of conduct for TNCs.[9]

In response, the OECD created, at the beginning of 1975, a Committee on International Investment and Multinational Enterprises. Its work resulted in the adoption in 1976 of the OECD Declaration on International Investment and Multinational Enterprises, which included annexed Guidelines for Multinational Enterprises.[10] As has been pointed out, the OECD Guidelines accepted the controlling role of international minimum standards over the extent of the power of countries to regulate the operations of TNCs in their territories.[11] BITs incorporating such standards were also concluded in greater numbers by OECD members with developing countries during the 1970s.[12] The origins of these bilateral treaties are briefly discussed in Chapter 2.[13] They typically set forth broad undertakings of each State party to give nationals and companies of the other party fair and equitable treatment, protection and security, freedom from currency transfer restrictions and prompt, adequate and effective compensation in the event of expropriation. The United States started a program of such BITs in 1977, in part to counter claims that the standard of prompt, adequate and effective compensation for expropriation was being displaced by the evidently weaker standard of "appropriate" compensation.[14] In the meantime, representatives of OPEC members, non-oil developing countries and industrial States had been meeting in Paris at a Conference on International Economic Cooperation to consider energy questions and broad items on the NIEO agenda. This "North-South dialogue," commenced in 1975, came to an unhappy end in mid-1977 with no consensus among participants on the major issues before them.[15]

Inflows of deposits from oil exporters facilitated massively increased lending by commercial banks to developing countries in the 1970s. But by the early 1980s, plunging commodity prices and rapidly rising interest rates resulted in debt service difficulties, leading in turn to drastically curtailed commercial lending to developing countries.[16] Responses to the ensuing debt crisis included enlarged structural adjustment programs

[8] Perhaps the best known of these were revelations of interference by ITT Corporation in Chilean presidential politics. *See* T. Sagafi-Nejad, *The UN and Transnational Corporations: From Code of Conduct to Global Compact* 45 (2008).

[9] *See* U.N. ECOSOC Resolution 1913 (LVII), The Impact of Transnational Corporations on the Development Process and on International Relations, December 5, 1974.

[10] The Declaration and Guidelines are reprinted in OECD, *OECD Guidelines for Multinational Enterprises* (2008).

[11] P.T. Muchlinski, *Multinational Enterprises and the Law* 660 (2d ed. 2007) (citing sec. I, para. 7 of the OECD Guidelines).

[12] A total of 85 BITs were signed in the 1970s, as compared to 63 during the previous decade. *See* Doc. ICSID/17, Bilateral Investment Treaties 1959–1966: Chronological and Country Data, Bibliography, 1–6 (1997) (Bilateral Investment Treaties).

[13] *See* Ch. 2, section II(B).

[14] *See* K.J. Vandevelde, *U.S. International Investment Agreements* 26 (2009). The standard of prompt, adequate and effective compensation was generally associated with the name of Cordell Hull, U.S. Secretary of State from 1933 to 1944, who in an exchange with the Mexican government in 1938 declared that no government was entitled to expropriate private property "without provision for prompt, adequate and effective payment therefor." Hackworth, 3 Digest of International Law 655 (1942) as quoted in I.F.I. Shihata, *Legal Treatment of Foreign Investment: The World Bank Guidelines* 87, note 50 (1993).

[15] For details, *see* J. Amuzegar, A Requiem for the North–South Conference, 56 Foreign Affairs 136 (1977–1978).

[16] *See* Spero and Hart (n. 2) 200–202; I.F.I. Shihata, The World Bank Facing the 21st Century—Developments in the 1980s and Prospects for the 1990s, in I.F.I. Shihata, *The World Bank in a Changing World: Selected Essays* 7, 17 (1991).

of the IMF and World Bank supporting market-oriented economic reforms in debtor countries.[17] They were encouraged to become more open to foreign investment which, as a source of external flows, was not constrained by government aid budgets or the negative experience of commercial creditors.[18] The Bank launched the initiative for the establishment of MIGA, which was to help improve the investment climate in developing countries by providing foreign investors with insurance against non-commercial risks in those countries.[19] As the 1980s progressed, developing countries increasingly enacted new laws to promote foreign investment and concluded BITs with capital-exporting countries for that purpose.[20] Coming full circle, many developing countries also initiated privatization programs often involving foreign investors as purchasers of previously State-owned enterprises.[21]

The economic nationalism, and antipathy to international methods of settling investment disputes, professed by many developing countries in the 1970s contributed to ICSID's "slow start."[22] By the end of the 1970s, just nine proceedings had been instituted under the Convention. Modest increases in the caseload coincided with, and may be partly explained by, the greater receptivity of developing countries to foreign investment in the 1980s. Nevertheless, at the end of 1988, the total number of cases registered stood at only 25. Naturally, the size of the caseload was reflected in the organization and staffing of the Secretariat. These and other institutional developments are examined in the next section of this chapter. The chapter then provides an overview of the cases registered during the period. Experiences in the cases were reflected in some of several amendments of the ICSID Regulations and Rules adopted in 1984, which are also examined in this chapter. The light caseload permitted ICSID to develop additional activities. The remaining sections of this chapter look at the beginnings of those activities: providing facilities for conciliation, arbitration and fact-finding under Additional Facility Rules, undertaking to act as the appointing authority of ad hoc arbitrators and disseminating information on foreign investment law.

I. Institutional developments

A. Ratifications of the Convention

Between 1967 and 1971, the number of Contracting States of the ICSID Convention jumped from 36 to 62. Signatures and ratifications of the Convention thereafter came slowly until the late 1970s, when the pace again picked up. Eight ratifications between 1977 and 1979 brought the number of Contracting States to 75. A further 14 countries became Contracting States between 1980 and 1988. The 62 Contracting States in 1971 comprised 32 African countries, 17 in Europe, ten States in the Asia and Pacific region, and three Western Hemisphere countries. In 1988, the Contracting States included 38 in Africa and 21 in Europe. Most of the growth therefore had come from outside those regions: the number of Asia and Pacific Contracting States had

[17] *See* Spero and Hart (n. 2) 214. [18] Ibid. 286; Shihata (n. 16) 19.

[19] *See* Commentary on the Convention Establishing the Multilateral Investment Guarantee Agency, October 11, 1985, reprinted in 1 ICSID Rev.—FILJ 193, introduction (1986).

[20] Ibid. During the 1980s, the total number of BITs worldwide leapt from 150 to over 360. *See* Bilateral Investment Treaties (n. 12) 6–11.

[21] *See* P. Guislain, *The Privatization Challenge* 1–6 (1997).

[22] The phrase used in R. Dolzer and C. Schreuer, *Principles of International Investment Law* 239 (2d. ed. 2012) to describe ICSID's low intake of cases during its early years.

grown to 21 and six more from the Western Hemisphere had become Contracting States.

The newer Contracting States included two prominent OPEC members: Kuwait, which ratified the ICSID Convention in 1979, and Saudi Arabia, which ratified the following year. An important break with the past was that three Latin American countries had become Contracting States: Paraguay in 1983, El Salvador in 1984 and Ecuador in 1986.[23] Another harbinger of changes that would occur in the following decade was that in 1987 Hungary became the second Soviet bloc country to ratify the Convention, after Romania, which had ratified in 1975. On the other hand, following the ratification of the ICSID Convention by the Taiwan government in 1968, China had been listed as a Contracting State. In 1980, after the People's Republic of China assumed the representation of China in the World Bank and its financial affiliates, China was, at the PRC's request, removed from the list of Contracting States and ceased to be considered a party to the Convention.[24]

B. The Administrative Council

To repeat the explanation provided in Chapter 1, the Administrative Council of ICSID consists of one Representative of each Contracting State. The Representatives of the Contracting States are normally their Governors of the World Bank, who also serve ex officio as Governors of the IFC and IDA (and generally are appointed their States' Governors of MIGA as well). The Governors, in turn, are usually the ministers of finance or economy of the countries concerned. As indicated in Chapter 6, the annual meetings of the Governors of the IMF and World Bank have always been held jointly. Since the establishment of the Bank's above-mentioned financial affiliates, the annual meetings of their Governors have been included in these joint sessions. From 1967 to 1987, however, the annual meetings of the Administrative Council of ICSID were held at the same venue and on one of the same days but separately from the joint sessions of the other institutions.

The meetings of the Administrative Council were generally brief; in most years, the only items on the agenda were the approval of the annual report and of the small administrative budget of the Centre. With the growth in the number of Contracting States, however, these separate meetings became increasingly cumbersome. Alternate or Temporary Alternate Representatives commonly took the places of their busy principals at the meetings. Attendance levels were nevertheless insufficiently high to ensure that there would each year be the two-thirds majority of Council members required by the Convention for such decisions as the adoption of the budget of the Centre.[25] To deal with the problem, the Administrative and Financial Regulations of the Centre were amended in 1970 to provide for the required additional votes of absent members to be taken by correspondence after a meeting.[26]

[23] In anticipation of the first of these countries to ratify the Convention, Spanish joined English and French as an official language of the Centre. *See* ICSID Sixteenth Ann. Rep. 1981/1982, 3.

[24] This was done with the approval of the Administrative Council of ICSID at its 1980 Annual Meeting. *See* Doc. AC/80/5, Communication Received from the Government of the People's Republic of China: Report and Recommendation of the Chairman, September 24, 1980; Doc. AC/80/6, Fourteenth Annual Meeting Summary Proceedings, October 30, 1980.

[25] *See* ICSID Convention, Art. 6(1) *in fine*.

[26] *See* Administrative and Financial Regulations, as amended, 1975, reg. 6(4), reprinted in Doc. ICSID/4/Rev. 1, ICSID Regulations and Rules (May 1975).

In 1968, Robert S. McNamara succeeded George Woods as President of the World Bank, and hence as Chairman of the Administrative Council of ICSID.[27] On taking over the presidency of the Bank, McNamara ushered in an enormous expansion of the operations of the Bank.[28] It was presumably at his request that another amendment of the Administrative and Financial Regulations was made in 1970 "to allow flexibility"[29] in respect of the President's attendance, during the annual gatherings of the IMF and World Bank Group Governors, at the meetings of the Administrative Council of ICSID. There being no requirement in the ICSID Convention that the President, as Chairman of the Administrative Council, preside over its meetings, the amendment stipulated that a member of the Council act as Temporary Presiding Officer in the Chairman's absence. To avoid the inconvenience of any election procedure, the amendment provided that the role of Temporary Presiding Officer would rotate automatically among the members of the Council according to the order in which their States had ratified the Convention.[30] Under this arrangement, there was a Temporary Presiding Officer for each annual meeting of the Council from 1971 to 1987.[31] The President of the Bank would generally attend to open the meeting and then turn it over to the Temporary Presiding Officer.

The amendments of 1970 seemed to testify to the relative unimportance of the meetings, which became increasingly perfunctory. As already mentioned, the business transacted at them was in most years confined to the approval of the annual report and budget of the Centre. In addition, by amendment of the Administrative and Financial Regulations approved by it in 1975, the Administrative Council in effect delegated to the Secretary-General its function, under Article 60(1) of the ICSID Convention, of setting the maximum amounts of the fees payable to conciliators, arbitrators and ad hoc committee members in the absence of agreement on the matter between them and the parties.[32] A further function effectively shed by the Council concerned the

[27] McNamara was to remain President of the Bank until 1981. He had previously served as Secretary of Defense of the United States (from 1961 to 1968) and before that was President of Ford Motor Company (in 1960).

[28] From 1969 to 1973, IBRD and IDA lending commitments jumped 130% and the Bank's professional staff increased by a similar proportion. By the end of McNamara's tenure at the Bank, annual lending was more than three times higher in real terms than it had been before he assumed the presidency, and professional staff had risen fourfold. *See* D. Kapur and others, 1 *The World Bank: Its First Half Century* 16, 216 (1997); J. Kraske and others, *Bankers with a Mission: The Presidents of the World Bank, 1946–91* at 175 (1996).

[29] ICSID Fourth Ann. Rep. 1969/1970, 3.

[30] *See* Administrative and Financial Regulations (n. 26) reg. 3*bis*.

[31] The Temporary Presiding Officer was the representative of Nigeria in 1971 and of Jamaica in 1987.

[32] The amendment, to what was then Administrative and Financial Regulation 13(1), gave the Secretary-General the authority to increase (or decrease) the specified maximum amounts each year with the approval of the Chairman of the Administrative Council. *See* Administrative Council Resolution AC (C)/RES/29, Amendment to the Administrative and Financial Regulations of the Centre, February 28, 1975, reprinted in ICSID Ninth Ann. Rep. 1974/1975, 29. The specified maximum amounts of the fees, previously US$250 for each day of participation in meetings and US$100 for each day of other work, were increased by the amendment to US$350 per day for both meetings and other work, and the per diem subsistence allowance, previously US$40, was related instead to the allowance paid to Executive Directors of the World Bank. The Secretary-General's authority under the amendment was first exercised in 1979, when Broches increased the amount of the daily fee from US$350 to SDR 350. The SDR (Special Drawing Right), which was created in 1969 by the IMF and served as its unit of account, was based on a basket of major currencies. Fees continued to be payable in U.S. dollars, with the dollar equivalent of amounts in SDRs due in respect of any calendar quarter being determined as of the first day of the quarter as published by the IMF. Denominating the fees in SDRs helped to insulate them from fluctuations in the relative value of individual currencies. The

agreements that ICSID could conclude pursuant to Article 63 with other appropriate institutions for the holding of proceedings at the seat of such institutions if the parties so agreed. In 1979, the Council approved an agreement of this kind with the Regional Centre for Commercial Arbitration at Kuala Lumpur, established under the auspices of the Asian-African Legal Consultative Committee (now the Asian-African Legal Consultative Organization), similar to the agreement that ICSID had previously concluded for the same purpose with the PCA.[33] Also in 1979, the Council authorized the Secretary-General to sign future agreements of this kind substantially along the lines of the two previous ones approved by the Council.[34]

Finally, after the 1987 annual meeting, the then Secretary-General, Ibrahim F.I. Shihata, announced that future annual meetings of the Council should, in the interests of economy and efficiency, generally be held entirely together with the joint sessions of the Governors of the other World Bank Group institutions and of the IMF. This arrangement was followed for the next 22 annual meetings.[35] Under the arrangement, the ICSID segment of the joint sessions simply consisted of the President of the Bank, in his capacity as Chairman of the Administrative Council, moving that, in the absence of any objection, the previously circulated draft resolutions of the Council be deemed approved. The resolutions were invariably quickly passed in this way without discussion. A benefit of the arrangement, apart from the efficiency gain, was to make ICSID more visible among the institutions. However, it also served to diminish further the practical role of the Administrative Council.

C. The Secretariat

It will be remembered from Chapter 6 that, at the inaugural meeting of the Administrative Council of ICSID in February 1967, Broches was elected Secretary-General of the Centre for a term extending only until the second annual meeting of the Council in September 1968. This was in keeping with the understanding reached during the preparation of the Convention that the initial election, taking place soon after entry into force of the Convention, should be for a short term so that States ratifying the Convention later could participate in the selection of the Secretary-General.[36]

In June 1968, soon after he became President of the World Bank, McNamara informed the members of the Administrative Council of his intention to propose the re-election of Broches as Secretary-General of ICSID. In subsequently nominating Broches, McNamara explained that the business of the Centre still did not require

daily fee was increased to SDR600 in 1983. As explained in Ch. 10, section I(B), it remained at that level until 2000.

33 For the text of the Kuala Lumpur Centre agreement, *see* ICSID Thirteenth Ann. Rep. 1978/1979, 34. On the agreement with the PCA, *see* Ch. 6, section IV(B).

34 *See* Administrative Council Resolution AC(13)/RES/44, Adoption of the Resolution on Administrative Arrangements Relating to the Place of Proceedings (Art. 63 of the Convention), reprinted in ICSID Fourteenth Ann. Rep. 19779/1980, 35. In 1980, Broches exercised this authority to sign a third such agreement, with the Regional Commercial Arbitration Centre at Cairo, also established under the auspices of the Asian-African Legal Consultative Committee. For the text of this third agreement, *see* ICSID Fourteenth Ann. Rep. 1979/1980, 36.

35 In introducing the arrangement, Shihata made it clear to the Administrative Council in 1988 that a separate meeting might again be held when this was warranted by items on the agenda. *See* Report of the Secretary-General to the Administrative Council at its Twenty-Second Annual Meeting, September 27–29, 1988, 2. It was not until 2010 that there was placed on the agenda an item necessitating a separate session of the Administrative Council. *See* Ch. 11, section I(B).

36 *See* Ch. 6, n. 19 and accompanying text.

a full-time Secretary-General and probably would not do so in the near future. The Bank, McNamara continued, wished to retain Broches as its General Counsel and there appeared to be no incompatibility between the two offices. On that basis, Broches would continue to serve the Centre without compensation. Since over 40 countries had become Contracting States, the initial reason for an abbreviated term no longer applied. McNamara suggested that the new election be for a full term of six years, to expire in September 1974. He added that he would not, however, be nominating any Deputy Secretary-General since, at this early stage in the life of ICSID, there was no demonstrable need for more than one high official of the Centre.[37]

At the second annual meeting, the Council accepted McNamara's proposal and by unanimous consent re-elected Broches for a full term of six years.[38] In 1974, Broches was again re-elected for a full term of six years, giving him a term that extended one year beyond his retirement in 1979 from the Bank post, which was by then that of Vice President and General Counsel.[39] His successor as Vice President and General Counsel, Heribert Golsong,[40] was elected Secretary-General for a full term in 1980.[41] In 1982, however, Golsong resigned from his Bank position. The following year, he relinquished the ICSID position in favor of his successor as Vice President and General Counsel, Ibrahim F.I. Shihata.[42] Shihata was duly elected Secretary-General of ICSID for a full term in 1983.[43]

The resolutions of the Administrative Council for the elections of 1968, 1974, 1980 and 1983 all approved that the incumbent combine the position of Secretary-General with his Bank position and thus receive no remuneration from the Centre.[44] McNamara's reason for proposing, in 1974 and 1980, that the General Counsel of the Bank again be elected to serve concurrently as Secretary-General was the same as in 1968: ICSID did not have enough business to justify a full-time Secretary-General and was unlikely to get much more business in the near future.[45] Another six cases had been registered by 1983. In that year, Alden W. Clausen, the Bank's new President,[46]

[37] *See* Doc. AC/68/4, Election of the Secretary-General and determination on the Conditions of his Service, Nomination and Recommendations of the Chairman, August 15, 1968.

[38] *See* Administrative Council Resolution AC(2)/RES/11, Election of the Secretary-General, September 30, 1968, reprinted in ICSID Fourth Ann. Rep. 1968/1969, 17.

[39] *See* Administrative Council Resolution AC(8)/RES/26, Election of the Secretary-General, October 3, 1974, reprinted in ICSID Ninth Ann. Rep. 1974/1975, 29.

[40] Golsong had previously served for a year as Associate General Counsel of the Bank. Before joining the Bank, he had been Director of Legal Affairs and Human Rights at the Council of Europe and had also served as Registrar of the European Court of Human Rights.

[41] *See* Administrative Council Resolution AC(14)/RES/46, Election of the Secretary-General, October 2, 1980, reprinted in ICSID Fifteenth Ann. Rep. 1980/1981, 29.

[42] Prior to joining the Bank, Shihata had been Director-General of the OPEC Fund for International Development and Executive Director of the International Fund for Agricultural Development. He had also been (and continued to serve as) Chairman of the Board of the International Development Law Institute, which later became the International Development Law Organization. Additional details on Shihata's career are in Ch. 2, n. 65.

[43] *See* Administrative Council Resolution AC(17)/RES/55, Election of the Secretary-General, September 29, 1983, reprinted in ICSID 1984 Ann. Rep. 20.

[44] Starting with the resolution for the 1974 election, it was made clear that the incumbent would not be remunerated by ICSID "while … employed" by the Bank. The refinement made it possible for Broches to be compensated for his service as Secretary-General during the year following his retirement from his Bank position in 1979. *See* text accompanying n. 39.

[45] *See* Doc. AC/74/4, Election of the Secretary-General and Determination of the Conditions of His Service, Nomination and Recommendations of the Chairman, September 16, 1974; Doc. AC/80/3, Election of the Secretary-General and Determination of the Conditions of His Service, Nomination and Recommendations of the Chairman, September 4, 1980.

[46] Clausen served as President of the World Bank from 1981 to 1986. He had previously been President of BankAmerica, a position to which he returned after leaving the World Bank.

gave a different, twofold rationale for continuing the practice: first, there was a close relationship between the objectives of ICSID and those of the Bank; and second, common administrative control of the Centre and the Bank's Legal Department permitted the assignment, as necessary, of legal staff to the Centre.[47] As mentioned below, occasional use was made of that possibility, of assigning Legal Department personnel to the ICSID Secretariat.

For most of the Centre's first 20 years, the Secretariat had five staff members: two lawyers, two secretarial or administrative assistants and a research assistant. From 1981 to 1986, and then again starting in 1988, one of the lawyer positions was filled by a Legal Adviser[48] responsible for managing the Secretariat under the Secretary-General. However, there were periods in which one or the other of the lawyer positions was vacant. At such times, and when the need otherwise arose, Legal Department lawyers were asked to work temporarily on ICSID matters.[49]

Between 1972, when the first case was registered, and 1988, the number of proceedings pending before the Centre each year averaged about six and never exceeded ten. However, the proceedings generally received a high degree of administrative support from the Secretariat which, in accordance with the Administrative and Financial Regulations, managed the finances of the proceedings, served as a channel of communications between the conciliators or arbitrators and the parties and provided each commission and tribunal with a secretary who generally attended and kept minutes of all hearings.[50] The involvement of the Secretariat with individual proceedings was especially extensive at the outset, during Broches's tenure as Secretary-General. In addition to performing the functions just mentioned, the Secretariat drafted the formal parts of awards and decisions as well as recitals of procedural developments and of the facts of the case.[51] In the earliest cases, moreover, Broches himself went with the secretary of the tribunal to its sessions.[52] Later, in the first half of the 1980s, the Secretariat experimented with reduced administrative support for proceedings, allowing tribunals in suitable cases to appoint an assistant to carry out tasks, such as keeping minutes or drafting parts of awards or decisions, that might otherwise be done by the secretary.[53] The practice was soon stopped, however, once staff vacancies underlying it had been filled.[54]

[47] *See* Doc. AC/83/4, Resignation of the Secretary-General and Election of His Successor, Together with Determination of the Conditions of His Service, August 2, 1983.

[48] This title was used in the Legal Department of the World Bank for specialized senior staff heading smaller units, the managers of larger units being called Chief Counsel. The first to serve at ICSID, Georges R. Delaume, was a Senior Legal Adviser. He joined the IMF in 1950, transferred to the Bank Legal Department three years later and worked there in successively more senior positions until moving to ICSID in 1981. The author of several books (including, for instance, his 1967 treatise *Legal Aspects of International Lending and Economic Development*), Delaume retired in 1986.

[49] Thus, tribunal secretaries were drawn from the Legal Department in two proceedings in the 1970s, and the responsibilities of the ICSID Legal Adviser were shared among three Legal Department lawyers when that position was vacant from 1986 to 1988.

[50] *See* Ch. 6, nn. 56–60 and accompanying text.

[51] A. Broches, The Experience of the International Centre for Settlement of Investment Disputes, reprinted in Broches *Selected Essays* 264, 276 note 40.

[52] *See, e.g., AGIP v. Congo*, Award, November 30, 1979, 1 ICSID Rep. 306, para. 1.12 (recording meetings of the tribunal in Paris "in the presence of the Secretary-General of the Centre and the Secretary of the Tribunal").

[53] The appointment of such an assistant (typically a young associate in the law firm of the tribunal president) also required the agreement of the parties, from whose advances the assistant would be paid.

[54] In more recent years, with ICSID's greatly increased caseload, tribunals began again to appoint assistants to serve them alongside the secretaries provided by the Secretariat.

After the institution of the first arbitration proceedings and the start of the investment law information activities in the first half of the 1970s, the budget of ICSID was increased substantially to around US$730,000 in today's dollars, mainly to allow for the appointment of additional staff. Thereafter, for the rest of the 1970s and during the 1980s, ICSID's budget expenditures seldom exceeded and frequently fell short of this level in real terms. In accordance with the Memorandum of Administrative Arrangements between ICSID and the World Bank, the expenditures were all covered by annual contributions of the Bank.[55] Those contributions were amalgamated with the Bank's overall budgetary allocations for its Legal Department up until the mid-1980s. From then on, the Bank's support for ICSID was budgeted separately; in addition to loosening ICSID's connection with the Legal Department, this facilitated planning and an eventual expansion of the budget and staff of the Centre.[56]

D. Designations to the Panels of Conciliators and of Arbitrators

Ensuring that there were enough qualified designees to these Panels proved to be a persistent problem during ICSID's first 20 years. By 1971, despite the appeals of the Secretariat for each Contracting State to avail itself of its right to designate four persons to each Panel, only 33 of the then 62 Contracting States had made designations to the Panels.[57] The proportion of Contracting States contributing designations remained disappointing in later years. Well over a third of the 71 Contracting States in 1978 had not made any designations to the Panels. In addition, several of the other States had failed to make new designations following the expiry of the six-year terms of their initial designees. ICSID's annual report for fiscal year 1978 called attention to this "not ... altogether satisfactory" situation.[58] The report emphasized the need for States to make designations—particularly as the Chairman of the Administrative Council, when appointing conciliators and arbitrators under Articles 30 and 38 of the ICSID Convention, was restricted in his choice to members of the respective panels.[59] The report also emphasized the importance of designating highly qualified individuals who were able and willing to serve on commissions and arbitral tribunals. States had too often chosen as their designees government officials or other persons unable in practice to act as conciliators or arbitrators.[60]

In 1967, after only a handful of Contracting States had made designations to the panels, it was decided that the Chairman of the Administrative Council should delay exercising his own right to make designations to the panels until more had been received from States.[61] As good designations by States remained insufficient, the Chairman continued to refrain from making designations. This reserved the possibility of the Chairman supplementing the panels as might be necessary to enable him adequately

[55] On the Memorandum of Administrative Arrangements, *see* Ch. 6, section III. Revenues from the sale of ICSID publications and fees for lodging requests for conciliation and arbitration were credited to the World Bank, but did not lower the amount of its contribution to ICSID (except in net terms, by a tiny amount, as publications revenues were small, the lodging fee was modest and there were few requests).

[56] The arrangements for holding advances to the Centre by parties to proceedings were also changed at around the same time. The advances had previously been held at a commercial bank in accounts that did not bear interest. In the mid-1980s, it was decided that the advances should instead be held as World Bank trust funds, with investment income accruing on the funds pending their disbursement being credited to the parties' advances.

[57] *See* ICSID Fifth Ann. Rep. 1970/1971, 3.

[58] ICSID Twelfth Ann. Rep. 1977/1978, 4. [59] *See* ibid. [60] *See* ibid.

[61] *See* ICSID First Ann. Rep. 1966/1967, 5.

to discharge his appointing authority function in particular proceedings.[62] In 1974, the Chairman made use of this possibility in complying with requests to complete the constitution of the tribunal in three inter-related proceedings involving Jamaica.[63] The tribunals in those proceedings, constituted in December 1974, each included an arbitrator appointed by the Chairman immediately after designating the individual concerned to the Panel of Arbitrators.[64] The designee's term expired in 1980, just as Broches's last term as Secretary-General of ICSID came to an end. The Chairman then was still McNamara. Expressing his appreciation to Broches "as the architect of the Convention and as Secretary-General of the Centre during its 14-year existence," McNamara designated Broches to the Panel of Arbitrators.[65] Two years later, in 1982, six more designations were made to the Panel of Arbitrators by McNamara's successor, Clausen, on the recommendation of Golsong as the new Secretary-General.[66] When Shihata succeeded Golsong as Secretary-General in 1983, the latter was added by the Chairman to the Panel of Arbitrators along with one other person.[67] This brought the total to nine designees.[68] Three years later, Broches's designation to the Panel was renewed; a combination of further renewals and fresh designations in 1988 resulted again in a nine-person list of designees of the Chairman.[69] There was thus left, as before, one place that the Chairman could in theory fill if necessary for an appointment in a particular proceeding. In practice, no further use was made of this possibility; it nevertheless seemed prudent to allow for it, as the proportion of Contracting States making panel designations continued to show little improvement.

E. Other measures by Contracting States pursuant to the Convention

By the end of ICSID's 2015 fiscal year, just 13 Contracting States had availed themselves of the possibility, afforded them by Article 25(1) of the Convention, to designate subdivisions and agencies as competent to become parties to disputes submitted to

[62] *See* ICSID Twelfth Ann. Rep. 1977/1978, 4.

[63] On these proceedings, *see* section I(E) of this chapter.

[64] This first member of the Panel of Arbitrators was Fuad Rouhani of Iran, on whom *see* Ch. 5, n. 62.

[65] *See* Doc. AC/80/6, Summary Proceedings, Fourteenth Annual Meeting of the Administrative Council, October 2, 1980.

[66] The additional designees who, in accordance with Art. 13(2) of the ICSID Convention each had a different nationality, were Andrés A. Aramburu Menchaca (Peruvian), Bernardo M. Cremades (Spanish), Eduardo Jiménez de Aréchaga (Uruguyan), Berthold Goldman (French), Monroe Leigh (American) and F.A. Mann (British). *See* ICSID Sixteenth Ann. Rep. 1981/1982, 8. It will be noticed that half of the new designees were Spanish-speaking. The hope was that this would encourage Latin American countries to sign and ratify the ICSID Convention.

[67] The other designee was Ignaz Seidl-Hohenveldern (Austrian). *See* ICSID 1984 Ann. Rep. 12.

[68] Golsong was German, so the nine, all men, comprised six Europeans, an American and two Latin Americans. As it ended up, the composition of the list, built up by designations of two Chairmen working with three different Secretaries-General in four years, was not easy to reconcile with the admonition in Art. 14(2) of the ICSID Convention that the designations of the Chairman should be made with due regard to the importance of assuring representation on the panels of the principal legal systems of the world and of the main forms of economic activity.

[69] The new list of nine comprised M.Y. Abdel-Aal (Sudanese), Aron Broches (Dutch), Ian Brownlie (British), Berthold Goldman (French), Heribert Golsong (German), Monroe Leigh (American), Kéba Mbaye (Senegalese), Ignaz Seidl-Hohenveldern (Austrian) and Sompong Sucharitkul (Thai). The designees, again all men, thus comprised five Europeans, an American, two Africans and an Asian. *Cf.* n. 68. From 1988, the designations of the Chairman were to the Panel of Conciliators as well as the Panel of Arbitrators. *See* New Additions to the Panels of Conciliators and of Arbitrators, 5(2) News from ICSID 4 (1988).

the Centre. Most of these designations were made during ICSID's first 20 years.[70] Soon after it became a Contracting State in 1967, the United Kingdom made such designations in respect of Hong Kong and several other of its colonies and dependencies. Between then and 1988, six developing Contracting States[71] designated State oil companies or other State-owned enterprises (SOEs) as agencies under Article 25(1) of the Convention. These designations seem mostly to have been linked to the conclusion by the designated SOEs of particular agreements containing consents to the jurisdiction of ICSID.[72]

Similarly, scant use was made of the mechanism of Article 25(4) of the Convention, whereby Contracting States could notify ICSID of the class or classes of disputes that they would or would not consider submitting to ICSID—oddly, perhaps, after the attention lavished on the mechanism in the preparation of the Convention.[73] In all, just five Contracting States sent notifications of this kind to the Centre between its inception and 1988. The first notification of this kind was given by Jamaica in 1974. It stated that any "[l]egal dispute arising directly out of an investment relating to minerals or other natural resources" would "not be subject to the jurisdiction of the Centre." Guyana made a closely similar notification later that same year.[74] The rather Delphic notification of Papua New Guinea, that it would only consider submitting "disputes ... which are fundamental to the investment itself," was issued in 1978. The two remaining notifications were by Saudi Arabia and Israel, in 1980 and 1983 respectively. The former "reserve[d] the right of not submitting all questions pertaining to oil and ... acts of sovereignty," while the latter stated that it would only consider submitting "disputes related to an approved investment under one of the Israeli Laws for the Encouragement of Capital Investments."[75]

The first of these notifications, that of Jamaica, was made a month before it enacted legislation imposing a production levy on bauxite extracted in the country. The levy was said by U.S. companies that operated bauxite mines in Jamaica—Alcoa, Kaiser and Reynolds—to be contrary to undertakings of Jamaica in earlier agreements with the companies on their revenue obligations. The agreements each had clauses providing for disputes between the parties to be settled by arbitration under the ICSID Convention. Relying on the clauses in their respective agreements, the companies each instituted an arbitration proceeding against Jamaica within weeks of its enactment of

[70] The designations were all listed in Doc. ICSID/8, Contracting States and Measures Taken by Them for the Purpose of the Convention. This list was maintained by the Centre in accordance with its Administrative and Financial Regulations, reprinted in Doc. ICSID/15, ICSID Convention, Regulations and Rules (April 2006), reg. 20.

[71] Ecuador, Guinea, Kenya, Madagascar, Nigeria and Sudan.

[72] Further designations of SOEs were occasionally made explicitly for the purpose of particular agreements (and not listed in the ICSID document mentioned in n. 70). Even if these are also counted, however, there were few designations of SOEs and other State agencies, especially after 1988, translating, of course, into a continued rarity of consents to ICSID jurisdiction by such entities. There are various possible reasons for this. One may be that there simply were fewer SOEs in later years, owing to widespread privatizations. Another may be discouragement at the complexity of the ICSID option in comparison to simpler alternatives that had become available, notably arbitration under the Arbitration Rules of United Nations Commission on International Trade Law (UNCITRAL), U.N. Doc. A/31/17 (1976) (UNCITRAL Arbitration Rules). For SOEs to consent validly to the jurisdiction of ICSID in place of their State, they had not only to be designated by the State under Art. 25(1) of the Convention, but also have their consents approved by the State under Art. 25(3) or have the State notify ICSID that no such approval was required.

[73] *See* Ch. 5, nn. 34 and 109 and accompanying text. These notifications are also set out in Doc. ICSID/8 (n. 70).

[74] However, Guyana withdrew that notification in 1987.

[75] Like Guyana, Israel subsequently withdrew its notification (in 1991).

the production levy legislation. Identically composed tribunals were constituted in each proceeding.[76] On their own initiative (Jamaica did not participate in the proceedings), the tribunals considered whether the State's notification under Article 25(4) of the Convention could defeat their jurisdiction.

In its decision on jurisdiction, the *Kaiser* Tribunal recalled that the parties had, in the arbitration clauses of their agreements, consented to the jurisdiction of ICSID. Alluding to the second sentence of Article 25(1) of the Convention, the Tribunal succinctly noted that "[t]his consent having been given could not be withdrawn."[77] On the specific point regarding the notification, the Tribunal explained that it operated "for the future by way of information to the Centre and potential future investors in undertakings concerning minerals and other resources in Jamaica."[78] The Tribunal referred in this respect to the statement of the World Bank's Executive Directors, in their Report on the Convention, clarifying that a notification under Article 25(4) "would serve for purposes of information only and would not constitute the consent required to give the Centre jurisdiction ... [or] a reservation to the Convention."[79] The Tribunal concluded therefore that Jamaica "could not withdraw, and did not by its notification ... validly withdraw" its consent to arbitration; any other interpretation, the Tribunal added pointedly, "would very largely, if not wholly, deprive the Convention of any practical value for Contracting States and investors and this cannot have been intended."[80] Jurisdictional decisions to the same effect were simultaneously rendered in the *Alcoa* and *Reynolds* proceedings.[81]

From the beginning, there was only patchy compliance by Contracting States with the requirement of Article 54(2) of the Convention that they notify the Secretary-General of the Centre of their designations of courts or other authorities competent to enforce Convention awards. At the end of ICSID's first full fiscal year, fewer than half of the Contracting States had made their notifications under Article 54(2).[82] Nine years later, a quarter of the Contracting States had yet to provide their notifications. They were chided by the Centre's Annual Report to "notify the Centre of [their] designations as soon as possible" since "[t]he requirements concerning the enforceability of arbitral awards rendered pursuant to the Convention are among the key provisions of that instrument."[83] Despite this and similar reminders by the Secretariat in succeeding years, many Contracting States still failed to supply their notifications to the Secretary-General.[84]

II. Promoting consents to the jurisdiction of ICSID

In ICSID's initial years, Broches and his staff were preoccupied with the "urgent task"[85] of disseminating knowledge about the Centre to potential parties to

[76] For further details, *see* Ch. 8, section II.

[77] *Kaiser v. Jamaica*, Decision on Jurisdiction, July 6, 1975, ICSID Rep. 298, 304 (1993).

[78] Ibid.

[79] Ibid. (quoting para. 31 of the Report of the Executive Directors on the Convention).

[80] Ibid.

[81] *Alcoa v. Jamaica*, Decision on Jurisdiction, July 6, 1975, 4 YBCA 206 (1979); *Reynolds v. Jamaica*, Decision on Jurisdiction, 6, 1975 (unpublished).

[82] *See* ICSID Second Ann. Rep. 1967/1968, 5.

[83] ICSID Eleventh Ann. Rep. 1976/1977, 3–4.

[84] This and the similar problem with designations to the Panels of Conciliators and of Arbitrators are returned to in Ch. 10, section I(C).

[85] The phrase used in ICSID's first annual report to describe the work of spreading information on ICSID to possible users of its facilities. ICSID First Ann. Rep. 1966/1967, 4.

proceedings.[86] Efforts focused on promoting the conclusion of the consents to the jurisdiction of ICSID needed for recourse to its dispute settlement facilities. The Secretariat of the Centre soon saw these efforts rewarded with the signing of investment contracts containing clauses providing for the submission of any future disputes to the jurisdiction of the Centre.[87] Guidance for the drafters of such contractual clauses was provided by a set of 32 annotated model clauses published by ICSID in 1968.[88] By the mid-1970s, "[t]he inclusion of ICSID arbitration clauses (and in some cases conciliation clauses) in agreements between host countries and foreign investors ha[d] become a common feature of the foreign investment scene."[89]

Countries also began to enact investment promotion laws with references to the ICSID Convention. By the mid-1970s, there were almost a dozen such laws. Some, such as a 1967 investment law of Afghanistan, authorized the giving of consents to arbitration under the ICSID Convention on a case-by-case basis.[90] Others, following the suggestion of the World Bank Executive Directors in their Report on the ICSID Convention,[91] set out in the law an advance general consent to such arbitration on the part of the State concerned. One such law was Egypt's investment law of 1974.[92] Several of the investment promotion laws promulgated by other developing countries during the 1980s contained similar advance consents.[93]

Reference was made in Chapter 6 to the proposal, advanced by Broches in his remarks at the first annual meeting of the Administrative Council in September 1967, that States provide, in their future BITs, for the settlement of investor–State disputes by arbitration under the ICSID Convention, in addition to or instead of providing for the ad hoc arbitration of disputes between the States parties to the treaties.[94] In 1969, to assist with the negotiation of such treaty provisions, the Centre published a set of model clauses referring to the ICSID Convention that could be inserted into BITs.[95] That same year, Italy signed, with Chad and Côte d'Ivoire, the first BITs with clauses setting forth consents to the jurisdiction of ICSID in respect of disputes with covered investors.[96] Belgium and the United Kingdom began making BITs with similar clauses

[86] Between 1966 and 1969, Broches and his colleagues gave over a dozen speeches and published some 15 articles on the Centre. *See* ibid. 4 and 19; ICSID Second Ann. Rep. 1967/1968, 4 and 18; ICSID Third Ann. Rep. 1968/1969, 3 and 19–20.

[87] *See* ICSID Second Ann. Rep. 1967/1968, 5.

[88] *See* Doc. ICSID/5, Model Clauses Recording Consent to the Jurisdiction of the International Centre for Settlement of Investment Disputes (1968). The drafter of these model clauses was Paul Szasz (on whom, *see* Ch. 6, n. 30 and accompanying text).

[89] ICSID Tenth Ann. Rep. 1975/1976, 3.

[90] *See* Foreign and Domestic Private Investment Law, Official Gazette (Afghanistan), February 20, 1967, No. 72, Art. 19.

[91] *See* Report of the Executive Directors on the Convention, para. 24.

[92] Law No. 43 of 1974 concerning the Investment of Arab and Foreign Funds and the Free Zones, Official Gazette (Egypt), June 27, 1974, No. 26, Art. 8. Jurisdiction was to be founded on the investment dispute settlement provision of this law in two arbitration proceedings instituted under the ICSID Convention, *SPP v. Egypt* and *MHT v. Egypt*.

[93] *See, e.g.*, République Démocratique de Madagascar, Loi No. 85-001 relative au code des investissements, June 18, 1985, reprinted in 1 ICSID Rev.—FILJ 396 (1986), Art. 30; Loi No. 88.004 Portant Code des investissements en République Centrafricaine, May 8, 1988, reprinted in 4 ICSID Rev.—FILJ 167 (1989).

[94] *See* Ch. 6, text accompanying nn. 143 and 144.

[95] *See* Doc. ICSID/16, Model Clauses Relating to the Convention on the Settlement of Investment Disputes Designed for Bilateral Investment Treaties. These model clauses were also prepared by Szasz (*see* n. 88).

[96] *See* Accord en vue de protéger et favoriser les investissements de capitaux, Chad–Italy, June 11, 1969, reprinted in ICSID, Investment Treaties, Release 92-4 (March 1993), Art. VII; Accord pour protéger et favoriser les investissements de capitaux, Côte d'Ivoire–Italy, July 23, 1969, reprinted in ICSID, Investment Treaties, Release 92-4 (March 1993), Art. 7. A year earlier, the Netherlands had

in the first half of the 1970s.[97] The example was thereafter followed in French BITs.[98] The United States included consents to arbitration under the ICSID Convention in the BITs that it started to propose and sign with other parties to the Convention in the early 1980s.[99] Other countries joined the trend in the 1980s, notably Germany and Switzerland.[100] By the middle of the decade, BIT provisions with advance consents to ICSID arbitral jurisdiction were no longer unusual.[101]

signed an economic cooperation treaty with Indonesia with a provision that the State party hosting an investment of a national of the other State party "shall assent to any demand on the part of such national" to submit to the jurisdiction of ICSID a dispute arising in connection with the investment. *See* Agreement on Economic Cooperation, Indonesia-Netherlands, July 7, 1968, reprinted in ICSID Investment Treaties, Release 92-4 (March 1993), Art. 11. Broches took the view, rightly in the present author's opinion, that this and similar provisions of some other early BITs of the Netherlands did not represent consents to the jurisdiction of the Centre but rather undertakings to give such consent when requested by the investor. *See* A. Broches, Bilateral Investment Protection Treaties and Arbitration of Investment Disputes, reprinted in Broches *Selected Essays* 447, 449–450. For a recent arbitral decision supporting this analysis of a similar provision in a much later treaty, *see Planet Mining v. Indonesia*, Decision on Jurisdiction, February 24, 2014, paras. 146–198.

[97] *See* Agreement on the Encouragement and Reciprocal Protection of Investments, Belgium–Indonesia, January 15, 1970, reprinted in ICSID, Investment Treaties, Release 93-2 (July 1993), Art. 10; Agreement for the Promotion and Protection of Investments, Egypt–United Kingdom, June 11, 1975, reprinted in ICSID, Investment Treaties, Release 93-3 (October 1993), Art. 8. Some other BITs of this period had provisions referring to the ICSID Convention that, not unlike the provision in the 1968 treaty between the Netherlands and Indonesia (n. 96), required the host State to give its consent to the jurisdiction of the Centre in agreements with individual investors, rather than setting out the consent for all covered investors in the BIT itself. *See, e.g.*, Convention sur la Protection des investissements, France–Mauritius, March 22, 1973, reprinted in ICSID, Investment Treaties, Release 93-2 (July 1993), Art. 9.

[98] *See, e.g.*, Convention sur l'encouragement et la protection réciproques des investissements, Jordan–France, February 23, 1978, reprinted in ICSID, Investment Treaties, Release 93-3 (October 1993), Art. 8.

[99] The first of these BITs was concluded with Egypt in 1982. *See* Treaty concerning the Reciprocal Encouragement and Protection of Investments, Egypt–United States, September 29, 1982, reprinted in 1 ICSID Rev.—FILJ 432 (1985), Art. VII. The U.S. had long championed ICSID's dispute settlement facilities. Ten years earlier, in his January 19, 1972 Statement Announcing United States Policy on Economic Assistance and Investment Security in Developing Nations, President Richard M. Nixon declared his "support [for] the International Center for the Settlement of Investment Disputes within the World Bank Group," given the positive role that agreed dispute settlement procedures could play in addressing expropriation disputes in particular. The Statement is available from J. Woolley and G. Peters, The American Presidency Project, <http://www.presidency.uscb.edu>. In his address to the Seventh Special Session of the U.N. General Assembly three years later, Secretary of State Henry A. Kissinger urged that "[t]he World Bank's International Center for the Settlement of Investment Disputes ... should be employed to settle the important disputes which inevitably arise" between transnational enterprises and their host countries. Global Consensus and Economic Development: Address by Secretary Kissinger Prepared for Delivery at the Seventh Special Session of the U.N. General Assembly [on September 1, 1975], 73 The Department of State Bulletin, No. 1891, September 22, 1975, 425, 433. Also worth noting is the enactment by the U.S. Congress in 1972 of legislation (known as the González Amendment after its sponsor, Representative Henry B. González) requiring the U.S. to oppose loans from multilateral development banks to countries that had expropriated U.S. nationals unless, among other possible specified steps, "the parties have submitted the dispute to arbitration under the rules of the Convention for the Settlement of Investment Disputes." *See* 22 U.S.C. 285, sec. 285q; 22 U.S.C. 283, sec. 283r; 22 U.S.C. 284, sec. 284j. *Cf.* Vandevelde (n. 14) 18.

[100] *See, e.g.*, Treaty concerning the Encouragement and Reciprocal Protection of Investments, Germany–St. Lucia, March 16, 1985, reprinted in ICSID, Investment Treaties, Release 1985-a (August 1987), Art. 10; Accord concernant la promotion et la protection réciproques des investissements, Switzerland–Turkey, March 3, 1988, reprinted in ICSID, Investment Treaties, Release 99-2 (August 1999), Art. 8.

[101] *See* G.R. Delaume, ICSID and Bilateral Investment Treaties, 2(1) News from ICSID 12 (Winter 1985).

During ICSID's first two decades, therefore, there was an impressively growing network of consents to the jurisdiction of the Centre in investment contracts, laws and treaties. The growth of the network was, however, undoubtedly slowed by anti-foreign investment attitudes among developing countries in the 1970s in particular. As indicated earlier, this helps to explain the modest size of ICSID's caseload in its early years. Broches preferred to see the small number of cases as reflecting the achievement by ICSID of its true purpose, which was to prevent disputes or encourage their amicable settlement.[102] The Centre was in any event fortunate in having few cases at the outset; it allowed for basic provisions of the ICSID Convention to receive their first crucial tests at a deliberate pace—and, not unimportantly, under close supervision by the Secretariat, especially during Broches's time there. An overview of these earlier cases, brought to the Centre between 1972 and 1988, is provided in the next section.

III. An overview of the early cases

As already mentioned, there were 25 of these earlier cases, the first brought to ICSID in 1972,[103] another eight during the 1970s and 16 more from 1981 to 1988. Of the 25 cases, 23 were ICSID Convention arbitrations; just two involved conciliation proceedings under the Convention. The apparent lack of interest in the conciliation option was initially surprising, seeming to contrast with the demand in the past for the assistance of the World Bank in the conciliation of disputes.[104] The pattern nevertheless persisted, parties evidently often preferring simply to stipulate for a binding decision of their dispute by arbitration.[105]

[102] *See, e.g.*, Remarks to the Administrative Council of ICSID (1980 Annual Meeting), reprinted in Broches *Selected Essays* 290, 293. In 1984, Broches had these lively words:

> I never thought that [ICSID] would become an institution that would have an enormous amount of business. I never expected it, and I never said otherwise.... There are large numbers of countries which have made these commitments [to have recourse to ICSID in case of disputes]. If there are no disputes, so much the better. In some cases there are disputes, but they don't come to ICSID, even though there's an agreement to take them to ICSID. Why? Because at the last moment, both sides realize that they may win or may lose, and make a last effort at settlement, which is often successful. Generally, an ironclad commitment to go to a court or to arbitration is a strong incentive to settlement.

World Bank Oral History Program, Transcript of Interview of Aron Broches, May 23, 1984, 42–43.

[103] This was the case of *Holiday Inns v. Morocco. See* P. Lalive, The First "World Bank" Arbitration (*Holiday Inns v. Morocco*)—Some Legal Problems, 51 BYBIL 123 (1980), reprinted in 1 ICSID Rep. 645 (1993).

[104] *See* Ch. 2, section III. Thus, at the 1974 Annual Meeting of the Administrative Council, Broches confessed his astonishment at "the almost total lack of provision for conciliation" in the many investment agreements he had been seeing. Doc. AC/74/6, Administrative Council Proceedings, Eighth Annual Meeting, October 3, 1974, annex A, 2.

[105] The model consent clauses published by ICSID in 1968 (*see* n. 88, cl. I) suggested as one possibility that parties could in their consents to jurisdiction of the Centre combine both mechanisms by agreeing to conciliation followed, if necessary, by arbitration under the Convention. There were consent clauses of this kind underlying both of the two conciliation cases in this period, *SEDITEX v. Madagascar* and *Tesoro v. Trinidad and Tobago. See* L. Nurick and S. Schnably, The First ICSID Conciliation: *Tesoro Petroleum Corporation v. Trinidad and Tobago*, 1 ICSID Rev.—FILJ 340 (1986). But as Broches once observed, many businessmen and lawyers would consider conciliation under such clauses "a waste of time if it is to be followed by arbitration in case of failure of the conciliation effort." Broches (n. 51) 274.

Reflecting their preponderance among the Contracting States in these years, African States were parties to the proceedings in 15 of the 25 cases.[106] Asian countries were the States parties to the proceedings in four of the cases[107] and Anglophone Caribbean countries in another four.[108] In the two remaining cases, the States concerned were Iceland and New Zealand,[109] demonstrating that ICSID's facilities, while created with developing countries in mind, could be used for disputes with developed countries as well.[110] The facilities might also be used for claims of States against investors, as shown by one of the cases involving Gabon.[111] In all of the other cases, however, the proceedings were instituted by investors against their host States. A Saudi individual[112] was the investor in one of these cases. The investors were companies established in or controlled by nationals of European countries in 14 of the cases and by nationals of the United States in the remaining ten. In about half of the cases, the companies were major multinational enterprises and in the others considerably more modest, even obscure, entities. Much of the work of representing parties in these early cases was shared among counsel associated with a small number of international law firms; lawyers from one such firm[113] acted for investors or States in almost half of the cases pending during the 1980s.

Using the World Bank's classification of economic sectors,[114] investments underlying the ICSID cases of this period were concentrated in three sectors: industry and trade;[115] energy and mining;[116] and agriculture, fishing and forestry.[117] Investments in other sectors, such as health, transportation or water and sanitation, were then more exclusively local and public and hence rarely involved in the cases.[118] It appears that

[106] In chronological order, these were *Holiday Inns v. Morocco, Gardella v. Côte d'Ivoire, Gabon v. Serete, AGIP v. Congo, Benvenuti & Bonfant v. Congo, Guadalupe v. Nigeria, Klöckner v. Cameroon, SEDITEX v. Madagascar, SOABI v. Senegal, LETCO v. Liberia, Atlantic Triton v. Guinea, SPP v. Egypt, MINE v. Guinea, Pharaon v. Tunisia* and *SETIMEG v. Gabon.*

[107] In *Amco v. Indonesia, Colt v. Korea, AAPL v. Sri Lanka* and *Occidental v. Pakistan.*

[108] In *Alcoa v. Jamaica, Kaiser v. Jamaica, Reynolds v. Jamaica* and in the conciliation proceeding between Tesoro and Trinidad and Tobago.

[109] *ALUSUISSE v. Iceland* and *Mobil v. New Zealand.*

[110] The attitude nevertheless persisted in some quarters that it would be beneath the dignity of an industrial country to submit to the jurisdiction of ICSID. In the mid-1980s, the Walt Disney Company proposed that France agree to the ICSID arbitral settlement of disputes that might arise between them in relation to the construction of what became Disneyland Paris. A French official was reported to have snapped: "Disney's request for ICSID was shocking and a bit dumb. France is not a banana republic." A. Krause, Dispute Threatens Plan for French Disney Park, *International Herald Tribune,* March 15–16, 1986, 1.

[111] *Gabon v. Serete.*

[112] Ghaith R. Pharaon, later in the news in connection with the closure of the Bank of Credit and Commerce International. *See* his January 20, 1997 letter to the *New York Times,* Not a Fugitive Financier, January 24, 1997, A30.

[113] The now defunct New York firm of Coudert Brothers.

[114] There are ten sectors in this classification. In alphabetical order, they are: agriculture, fishing and forestry; education; energy and mining; finance; health and other social services; industry and trade; information and communications; public administration, law and justice; transportation; and water, sanitation and flood protection. The classification is used by the Bank to classify its projects. *See, e.g.,* World Bank 2015 Ann. Rep. 31.

[115] As in, e.g., *Benvenuti & Bonfant v. Congo,* which concerned a venture for manufacturing plastic bottles and producing mineral water, and *Klöckner v. Cameroon,* which involved agreements for the construction and operation of a fertilizer factory.

[116] For example, investments in petroleum distribution in *AGIP v. Congo*; bauxite mining in the *Alcoa, Kaiser* and *Reynolds* cases; and synthetic gasoline production in *Mobil v. New Zealand.*

[117] Examples include the forestry concession at issue in *LETCO v. Liberia* and the agreement for the conversion, equipping and operation of fishing vessels in *Atlantic Triton v. Guinea.*

[118] One of the exceptions was the investment underlying the arbitration proceeding in *Gabon v. Serete,* which was in the construction of a hospital maternity ward and could hence be regarded as having been in the health sector.

in each of the cases under consideration, the investments were to be made under concession, joint venture or other agreements concluded with the host State or agencies or enterprises of the State. Most of the cases involved asserted breaches of obligations assumed under such agreements.[119] Jurisdiction in all but three of the cases was based on consent clauses in the agreements.[120]

Respondents failed to participate in the proceedings in just a handful of the cases.[121] Objections to jurisdiction or counter-claims were raised by respondents in about a third of the cases.[122] The average duration of individual proceedings in the cases of this period, from the constitution of the conciliation commission or arbitral tribunal to the conclusion of the proceeding, was about two years and nine months.

Over half of the cases concluded with an amicable settlement by the parties of their dispute. Both of the conciliation cases ended in this way, one before the constitution of a conciliation commission and the other in light of the recommendations of the conciliator.[123] The parties in one of the arbitrations had the tribunal embody their settlement agreement in an award.[124] Following settlements agreed by the parties, the proceedings in 11 of the other arbitrations were discontinued prior to the rendition of any award.[125] In four of the remaining arbitration cases that led to awards,[126] there were proceedings for the annulment of the awards under Article 52 of the Convention; the first three of those proceedings are discussed in Chapter 8.

The award in one of the seven remaining cases dismissed the claim on the merits.[127] Claims for damages were upheld, though mostly only partially, by the awards rendered in the six other cases.[128] One of these awards also granted the claimant declaratory

[119] *Cf.* Broches (n. 51) 86.

[120] The exceptions were *Amco v. Indonesia*, *SPP v. Egypt* and *AAPL v. Sri Lanka*, brought to ICSID on the basis of a consent clause in, respectively, an approved investment application, an investment law and a BIT. For details, *see* Ch. 8, section III.

[121] Notably in *LETCO v. Liberia* and in the *Alcoa*, *Kaiser* and *Reynolds* cases.

[122] For examples of objections to jurisdiction made in the cases, *see* Ch. 8, section III.

[123] These were respectively the conciliation proceedings in *SEDITEX v. Madagascar* and *Tesoro v. Trinidad and Tobago*. Although the second was the later case, it is sometimes described as the "first" ICSID conciliation as no commission was constituted in the earlier case. In the *Tesoro* case, the proceeding was conducted before a sole conciliator and was notably cost-effective, with the fees and expenses of the conciliator and charges of the Secretariat totaling less than US$11,000. *See* Nurick and Schnably (n. 105) 345.

[124] This was done in *Guadalupe v. Nigeria* in accordance with Rule 43(2) of the Arbitration Rules of the Centre then in force, reprinted in Doc. ICSID/4/Rev. 1, ICSID Regulations and Rules, (May 1975), according to which, "[i]f the parties file with the Secretary-General the full and signed text of their settlement and in writing request the Tribunal to embody such settlement in an award, the Tribunal may record the settlement in an award."

[125] These were the proceedings in *Holiday Inns v. Morocco*; *Gabon v. Serete*; *SETIMEG v. Gabon*; *Pharaon v. Tunisia*; *Colt v. Korea; Occidental v. Pakistan*; the *Alcoa*, *Kaiser* and *Reynolds* cases; *ALUSUISSE v. Iceland*; and *Mobil v. New Zealand*. In these cases, the procedure was for the tribunal, or the Secretary-General where no tribunal had been constituted, to issue an order taking note of the discontinuance of the proceeding at the request of both parties under Rule 43 of the Arbitration Rules or, in one case, at the request of one party acquiesced in by the other under Rule 44 of the Arbitration Rules (n. 124). For the text of such an order, *see* ICSID Fifteenth Ann. Rep. 1980/1981, 36.

[126] *Klöckner v. Cameroon*, *MINE v. Guinea*, *SPP v. Egypt* and *Amco v. Indonesia*.

[127] *See Gardella v. Côte d'Ivoire*, Award, August 29, 1977, ICSID Rep. 287 (1993). This was the first award to be rendered under the ICSID Convention.

[128] The awards in *AGIP v. Congo* (n. 52); *Benvenuti & Bonfant v. Congo*, August 15, 1980, 1 ICSID Rep. 330 (1993); *SOABI v. Senegal*, February 25, 1988, 2 ICSID Rep. 165 (1994); *LETCO v. Liberia*, March 31, 1986, 2 ICSID Rep. 344 (1994); *Atlantic Triton v. Guinea*, April 21, 1986, 3 ICSID Rep. 17 (1995); and *AAPL v. Sri Lanka*, June 27, 1990, 4 ICSID Rep. 246 (1997).

relief.[129] In none of the cases was a counter-claim upheld. The amounts of these six awards, ranging from some US$336,000 to just over US$8 million,[130] averaged about 40 percent of the amounts claimed. Three of the awards ordered the respondents to bear all or a higher share of the direct expenses of the proceeding (that is, the fees and expenses of the arbitrators and the charges of the Secretariat);[131] two of these three awards[132] also requested the respondents to meet all or part of the legal expenses of their opponents. The three remaining awards provided that the parties should share the direct expenses equally and each bear its own legal expenses. In one of the cases, the allocation of costs was dictated by agreement of the parties.[133] In the other cases, where there was no agreement of the parties on the matter, the tribunals had broad discretion under Article 61(2) to decide on the division of the costs. Elements cited in the awards rendered in those cases as guiding the tribunals in the exercise of this discretion included the presence or absence of procedural bad faith of the parties[134] and the degree of their success in pursuing their claims.[135]

IV. The 1984 amendments of the ICSID Regulations and Rules

Shihata was elected for his first term as Secretary-General of the Centre at the Administrative Council's annual meeting in September 1983. The following April, he dispatched to Council members a Note on the Proposed Revision of the ICSID Regulations and Rules.[136] Appended to it were the texts of the proposed revisions or amendments, each accompanied by an explanatory note. Shihata's covering note pointed out that the Regulations and Rules had remained largely unchanged since their adoption in 1967. Modest revisions could now usefully be made, the note went on, "to simplify or clarify some of the relevant provisions and to introduce greater flexibility into the administration of proceedings."[137]

Proposed simplifications included amending the Administrative and Financial Regulations to provide a uniform fee for lodging requests rather than different fees depending on whether the request was one for conciliation or arbitration or one of the post-award remedies.[138] Another proposal for the Administrative and Financial Regulations was prompted by experience in the first annulment proceeding[139] with the payment to ICSID of the advances to meet the direct costs of the proceeding pending their ultimate apportionment by the ad hoc committee. The proposal was to require,

[129] The award in *AGIP v. Congo*, which declared the respondent State obligated to substitute itself for the claimant in relation to future obligations entered into by the nationalized joint venture company with respect to third parties. *AGIP*, Award (n. 52) A(iii) of operative part.

[130] The amounts of the awards in *Atlantic Triton v. Guinea* (n. 128) and *LETCO v. Liberia* (n. 128), respectively.

[131] The awards in *AGIP v. Congo* (n. 52); *LETCO v. Liberia* (n. 128); and *AAPL v. Sri Lanka* (n. 107).

[132] The awards in *LETCO v. Liberia* (n. 128) and *AAPL v. Sri Lanka* (n. 107).

[133] *See Benvenuti & Bonfant*, Award (n. 128) para. 4.124.

[134] *See LETCO*, Award (n. 128) 278; *Atlantic Triton*, Award (n. 128) 42.

[135] *See SOABI*, Award (n. 128) 273–274.

[136] Note from the Secretary-General on the Proposed Revision of the ICSID Regulations and Rules, April 30, 1984, re-circulated as Attachment to Doc. AC/84/4, July 23, 1984.

[137] Ibid. para. 4.

[138] Ibid. proposed revision of Administrative and Financial Regulation 15.

[139] The annulment proceeding in *Klöckner v. Cameroon*, on which *see* Ch. 8, section VI.

in an annulment proceeding, payment of such advances only from the applicant for annulment rather than both parties in equal shares.[140] A proposal explained as being meant "to import flexibility into the administration of proceedings" was to delete from the Administrative and Financial Regulations a provision requiring the secretary of a conciliation commission, arbitral tribunal or ad hoc committee to attend all hearings of the body in question.[141]

Among the other ideas put forward was the introduction, in the Arbitration Rules, of a provision for pre-hearing conferences that could be held to stipulate uncontested facts (with a view, of course, to expediting the proceeding) or to discuss an amicable settlement.[142] Shihata's covering note highlighted the latter aspect as "particularly important to the attainment of the Centre's paramount objective, which is to promote an atmosphere of mutual confidence between Contracting States and investors."[143] Two further important amendments were advanced for the Arbitration Rules. One was to provide explicitly that provisional measures could only be sought from national courts if the parties had so agreed; as explained in Chapter 8, this reflected an interpretation of Article 26 of the Convention that the Secretariat had been advocating with reference to experiences in two cases in particular.[144] The second further amendment was proposed for a provision of the Arbitration Rules that repeated the prohibition, in Article 48(2) of the Convention, of the publication by ICSID of an award without the consent of the parties. The suggestion was to add a proviso to the effect that, while the Centre would need such consent to publish the award, it could "include in its publications excerpts of the legal rules applied by the Tribunal."[145] The rationale given for the suggestion was not so much greater, as more neutral, disclosure. Parties were unilaterally publishing awards or commentary on them. The argument proffered with the suggestion was that, since the ICSID Secretariat was an "impartial observer of developments taking place in the context of investment disputes," it should undertake the identification and disclosure of "the legal rules that have been raised in past proceedings and may shed a new light upon the implementation of the ICSID Convention."[146]

Shihata's covering note invited comments from Contracting States on the proposed amendments. Apparently only one State responded with mostly minor observations. These were taken into account in another version of the proposed amendments circulated to members of the Administrative Council in August 1984.[147] At the Council's annual meeting a month later, the amendments were approved with little discussion.[148]

[140] Note from the Secretary-General (n. 136) proposed revision of Administrative and Financial Regulation 13.

[141] Ibid. proposed revision of Administrative and Financial Regulation 25. A related proposed change was to delete from the Conciliation Rules and from the Arbitration Rules the requirement that the Secretariat keep minutes of all hearings. Ibid. proposed revision of Conciliation Rule 29 and proposed revision of Arbitration Rule 37. As indicated in the text accompanying n. 53, owing to staffing shortages, the Secretariat was then already curtailing such support for proceedings (with the agreement of the parties concerned).

[142] Note from the Secretary-General (n. 136) proposed new Arbitration Rule 21.

[143] Ibid. para. 6(b). It was thus disappointing that after the adoption of the amendments little use was made by parties of the pre-hearing conference mechanism to try to reach an amicable settlement (or for the other purpose of accelerating fact-finding).

[144] The two cases were *MINE v. Guinea* and *Atlantic Triton v. Guinea*. *See* Ch. 8, section IV.

[145] Note from the Secretary-General (n. 136) proposed revision of Arbitration Rule 48(4).

[146] Ibid. explanatory note accompanying proposed revision of Arbitration Rule 48(4).

[147] *See* Doc. AC/84/6, ICSID Regulations and Rules: Note of the Secretary-General, August 24, 1984.

[148] *See* Administrative Council Resolution AC(18)/RES/57, Revision of the Regulations and Rules of the Centre, September 26, 1984, reprinted in ICSID 1985 Ann. Rep. 18.

They came into force immediately.[149] It was not, however, until January 1985 that the amended Regulations and Rules were published by the Centre, in a booklet entitled *ICSID Basic Documents*.[150] The Institution, Conciliation and Arbitration Rules were set out in this publication without the explanatory notes that had accompanied them in the previous edition of the Regulations and Rules.[151] One reason given for dropping the notes (which were never reissued by ICSID) was that parties and arbitrators often regarded them "as having the same authoritative value" as the Rules themselves.[152] In addition to being confusing in this sense, the notes seemed "cumbersome"; eliminating them would make it possible "to reduce the volume of the publication to a size more comparable to that of the Rules of other arbitration institutions."[153] Ironically, given their original explanatory purpose, scrapping the notes thus gave the Rules a relatively streamlined, less forbiddingly complex, air. This fit well with a broader effort by Shihata to market the facilities of ICSID to potential users. Other initiatives included the launch, earlier in 1984, of a semiannual newsletter, *News from ICSID*.[154] Also worth mentioning in this regard is the inauguration in 1983, a month after Shihata took office, of the series of annual colloquia on international arbitration co-sponsored by ICSID with the American Arbitration Association and International Chamber of Commerce Court of Arbitration.[155]

V. The Additional Facility

ICSID's purpose was narrowly defined by Article 1(2) of the Convention as being "to provide facilities for the conciliation and arbitration of investment disputes between Contracting States and nationals of other Contracting States in accordance with the provisions of this Convention." Yet in the 1970s and 1980s, ICSID assumed additional activities: offering to administer further categories of proceedings under Additional Facility Rules, agreeing to act as the appointing authority of ad hoc arbitrators and publishing materials on foreign investment law. Of these, the Additional

[149] In accordance with Art. 44 of the Convention, the amended Arbitration Rules applied in cases where the parties so agreed or where their consent to arbitration was given on or after the effective date of the amendments. The first case in which the amended Rules applied seems to have been *Mobil v. New Zealand*, brought to ICSID in 1987 pursuant to an arbitration clause in which the parties agreed that "any arbitration proceedings shall be conducted in accordance with the Arbitration Rules of the Centre in effect on the date the dispute is submitted to the Centre." *See Attorney-General v. Mobil*, New Zealand High Court, Judgment, July 1, 1987, 4 ICSID Rep. 119, 123 (1997). The amended Arbitration Rules also applied in the very next case brought to ICSID in 1987, *AAPL v. Sri Lanka*. *See AAPL v. Sri Lanka*, Award (n. 128) 252. In this first BIT case, the treaty containing the State's consent was concluded and came into force in 1980, but the investor's consent, as in most subsequent investment treaty arbitrations, was given in submitting the claim to arbitration; and the ICSID Institution Rules made it clear that, when the parties consent on different days, the later was the "date of consent."

[150] Doc. ICSID/15 (January 1985). Also included in the booklet was the text of the Convention.

[151] *Cf.* Ch. 6, text accompanying nn. 158 and 159.

[152] Note from the Secretary-General (n. 136) para. 4. [153] Ibid.

[154] As Shihata explained in the first issue of the newsletter, it was meant to remedy the "lack of information" about the Centre which had "kept resort to ICSID at a modest level despite its wide membership." Editorial, 1(1) News from ICSID 1 (Winter 1984). After being published twice yearly for 25 years, the newsletter was discontinued in 2009, having by then been displaced by the Centre's website as a source of news about ICSID.

[155] *See* World Bank Hosts an ICSID, AAA, ICC Symposium, 1(1) News from ICSID 3 (Winter 1984). The colloquia have since continued to be held, with ICSID hosting the thirty-second in the series in 2015.

Facility activity proved in time to be the most important.[156] This section examines the start of the facility. The beginnings of the appointing authority role and investment law publishing activities are discussed in sections VI and VII. As will be seen, it was judged, after some debate and hesitation in the case of the Additional Facility, that the activities could be undertaken without amending the Convention. An opposite conclusion would almost certainly have ruled out pursuing such activities, given the large number of Contracting States and the need, under Article 66(1) of the Convention, to have each of them ratify any amendment.

A. The initial proposal for an Additional Facility

In his address to the annual meeting of the Administrative Council in October 1976, Broches observed that ICSID had attained substantial recognition among host States and investors.[157] After reminding participants of the limitations, set out in Article 25 of the Convention, on the jurisdiction of the Centre, he suggested that the growing confidence in ICSID might justify permitting it to provide additional useful services. Broches explained that he had in mind authorizing ICSID to act as administering authority for certain types of proceedings that were not within its jurisdiction under the Convention.[158] These might include proceedings between parties that did not meet the nationality requirements of the Convention. They might also include proceedings for the settlement of disputes that did not arise out of investments.[159] In regard to this second possibility raised by Broches, it should be remembered that at the time, contractual arrangements that today would readily be regarded as investments were often thought of as being "commercial" transactions instead; and as private resource flows to developing countries came increasingly to take such contractual forms,[160] the limitation on the jurisdiction of ICSID to investment disputes seemed to assume greater possible significance.

In his address to the 1976 annual meeting of the Administrative Council, Broches suggested that ICSID might additionally be authorized to administer fact-finding proceedings. He highlighted the potential usefulness of such proceedings in connection with the renegotiation by parties of investment agreements.[161] Broches was and would remain ardently in favor of such renegotiation where necessary to restore the economic equilibrium of long-term agreements in light of changed circumstances.[162] At the 1976 annual meeting, he promised to translate this and his other suggestions into a specific proposal, which he would then circulate to Administrative Council members for their comments.[163]

[156] On the first Additional Facility cases, *see* Ch. 9, section IV.

[157] *See* Summary Proceedings: Tenth Annual Meeting, October 7, 1976, Administrative Council Doc. AC/76/40A, Annex, Statement by Mr. A. Broches, 1 (October 1976 Statement).

[158] *See* ibid. 4. [159] *See* ibid.

[160] Examples included participation contracts of the kind alluded to in the text accompanying n. 3 and the types of transactions singled out in the draft quoted in the text accompanying n. 193. Such contractual arrangements were increasingly sought by developing countries during the 1970s, in preference to traditional direct foreign investments, for the reason, elegantly encapsulated by a 1984 study of the OECD Development Centre, that the former implied whole or majority local ownership of the investment project and the latter whole or majority foreign ownership of the project. C. Oman, *New Forms of International Investment in Developing Countries* 20 (1984).

[161] *See* October 1976 Statement (n. 157) 4.

[162] *See, e.g.*, Doc. AC/80/6, Summary Proceedings: Fourteenth Annual Meeting, October 2, 1980, Annex 2, Statement by Aron Broches, 3.

[163] *See* October 1976 Statement (n. 157) 4.

The proposal was set out in a draft that Broches transmitted to Council members in May 1977.[164] The draft envisaged the creation of an Additional Facility under which the Secretariat of the Centre would act as an administering authority for conciliation, arbitration and fact-finding proceedings on the basis of an agreement to that effect of the parties involved. By analogy with the Convention, use of the Additional Facility would be confined to proceedings where one of the parties was a State, or a constituent subdivision or agency of a State, and the other a nongovernmental national of another State.[165] Additional Facility conciliation and arbitration would, according to the draft, be available for cases where one or neither State was a Contracting State or where the dispute concerned "a commercial transaction" rather than an investment.[166] Animated chiefly by Broches's support for facilitating contract renegotiations, the draft suggested that Additional Facility conciliation might be used to resolve not only legal disputes but also divergences based on considerations of fairness or reasonable behavior.[167] As for fact-finding under the Additional Facility, the draft suggested that it should be limited to the ascertainment of facts by committees constituted in each case; it would be left to the parties to decide what effect should be given to the report of such a committee.[168] An objective investigation and report on facts could nevertheless help to avoid disputes or assist in their resolution.[169] The draft contemplated that the Administrative Council would establish rules for proceedings under the Additional Facility.[170] Permitting ICSID to act as an administering body in the manner proposed would, of course, "increase the potential for the Centre's activity."[171] Reassuringly, this could be achieved "without requiring any structural change" and it "would have no significant budgetary implications since the cost of proceedings would be borne by the parties."[172]

Between May and September 1977, comments were received from the governments of 21 of the then 68 Contracting States.[173] The responses were mostly positive. But several governments had doubts. One took the view that giving non-Contracting States and their nationals access to the Centre's facilities could deprive such States of the incentive to become parties to the Convention. Two governments questioned the advisability of extending ICSID's activities to commercial disputes, for which there were other arbitration mechanisms, and of permitting access to Additional Facility conciliation for non-legal disputes, as this would not be desired by investors or could embroil conciliation commissions in political controversies. Two other governments expressed the more fundamental concern that implementing the proposal would appear to require an amendment of the Convention.[174]

[164] Doc. AC/77/1, Administration by the Centre of Proceedings Outside the Scope of Article 25 of the Convention: Draft Report and Recommendations of the Secretary-General, May 13, 1977.

[165] *See* ibid. para. 14. [166] Ibid. para. 25. [167] *See* ibid. para. 26.

[168] *See* ibid. para. 23. [169] *See* ibid. para. 28. [170] *See* ibid. para. 15.

[171] Ibid. para. 11. [172] Ibid.

[173] The following brief summary of the comments is based on the account in Broches's report to the Administrative Council at its 1977 annual meeting: Doc. AC/77/5, Administration of Proceedings Outside the Scope of Article 25 of the Convention by the Secretariat of the Centre: Report and Recommendations of the Secretary-General, September 6, 1977 (September 1977 Report).

[174] These were the governments of Belgium and the Netherlands. *See* Doc. AC/77/7, Summary Proceedings: Eleventh Annual Meeting, September 29, 1977, paras. 17 and 19 (interventions of Mr. Meulemans (Belgium) and Baron van Ittersum (Netherlands)). The U.K. government subsequently joined them in voicing this concern. *See* Doc. AC/78/17, Summary Proceedings: Twelfth Annual Meeting, September 27, 1978, para. 9 (intervention of Mr. Kirbyshire (United Kingdom)). Supporters of the proposal included the governments of Denmark, France, Germany, Italy, Japan and the United States. *See* Summary Proceedings: Eleventh Annual Meeting, at paras. 16 and 18; Summary Proceedings: Twelfth Annual Meeting, paras. 5–7 and 10–12 (interventions of Mr. Voss

In response, Broches accepted that there would be no need to open the Additional Facility to disputes arising out of "routine commercial transactions" between States and foreign non-State parties; in respect of disputes which were "not investment disputes in the strict sense," Broches continued, it would seem advisable "to limit access to the Additional Facility to special cases, such as contracts for civil works or turn key contracts for industrial plants."[175] As for the requirement of a legal dispute, he indicated his hope that keeping it would not prevent parties engaged in a renegotiation from turning to the Additional Facility if they failed to agree on the new terms.[176] On the more fundamental question, as to whether the creation of the Additional Facility would require an amendment of the Convention, Broches drew a subtle distinction between extending the jurisdiction of ICSID and extending the activities of its Secretariat. The proposal, he argued:

> ... envisages that the Additional Facility would be established by decision of the Administrative Council in the exercise of its power to administer the Centre and, in particular, to adopt the administrative and financial regulations of the Centre (Convention, Article 6(1)(a)). This power could admittedly not be used to extend the applicability of the Convention to parties or to disputes not falling within the jurisdiction of the Centre as defined in Article 25 of the Convention. If this were desired, an amendment of the Convention would be required. However, the proposal does not contemplate an extension of the jurisdiction of the Centre, but merely an extension of the activities of its Secretariat and this would appear to be within the powers of the Administrative Council.[177]

Broches added that it was relevant to note in this connection actions taken by the Administrative Council of the PCA to authorize the Bureau of the PCA, the equivalent of the Secretariat of ICSID, to administer two types of proceedings not contemplated by the Peace Conventions of 1899 and 1907 under which the PCA was established. In the 1930s, he pointed out, the Administrative Council of the PCA had approved the use of the Bureau's services for conciliation proceedings and for arbitration proceedings between parties of which only one was a State;[178] and then in 1962 the PCA Council had approved the Court's Rules of Arbitration and Conciliation of International Disputes between Two Parties of Which Only One is a State.[179]

Reporting to the ICSID Administrative Council at its annual meeting in 1977, Broches remarked that, in any event, comments on the proposal had been received from fewer than a third of the Contracting States. It thus seemed advisable to postpone a decision on the establishment of the Additional Facility to the next annual meeting of the Council. On his recommendation, the Council agreed that he should prepare a detailed proposal for submission to the Council at that meeting and, to secure wider acceptance of the proposal, circulate during the year drafts to Council members for the comments of their governments.[180]

(Denmark), Mr. Metz (France), Mr. Hanfland (Germany), Mr. Rota (Italy), Mr. Marayama (Japan) and Mr. Mundheim (United States)).

[175] September 1977 Report (n. 173) para. 5. [176] *See* ibid. [177] Ibid. para. 3.

[178] The approvals were for the use of the Bureau's services for a conciliation between Denmark and Lithuania and for an arbitration between China and Radio Corporation of America. *See* PCA 1934 Ann. Rep. 7; PCA 1937 Ann. Rep. 7.

[179] *See* September 1977 Report (n. 173) para. 3. *See also* Ch. 2, nn. 51 and 52 and accompanying text.

[180] Administrative Council Resolution AC(11)/RES/37, Administration by the Secretariat of the Centre of Proceedings Outside the Scope of Article 25 of the Convention, reprinted in ICSID Twelfth Ann. Rep. 1977/1978, 32.

B. The draft Additional Facility Rules

Between December 1977 and June 1978, the Secretariat of the Centre circulated to Council members drafts of a principal set of Additional Facility Rules[181] and of four attached schedules of subsidiary rules: Administrative and Financial Rules, Conciliation Rules, Arbitration Rules and Fact-Finding Rules.[182] Comments on the drafts were received from 35 of the Contracting States. The comments were taken into account in revised drafts submitted in August 1978 to the Administrative Council for consideration at its annual meeting in September 1978.[183]

As revised, the draft Additional Facility Rules comprised six articles. Of these, the most important were Articles 2, 3 and 4.[184] Article 2 specified the additional categories of proceedings that the Secretariat would be authorized to administer. Reflecting the comments of governments, those were in two respects narrower than in the proposal of the year before. Under Article 2, the conciliation and arbitration proceedings could not involve cases where neither the State party nor the home State of the foreign national concerned was a Contracting State.[185] In addition, Article 2 made it clear that all disputes submitted to conciliation or arbitration would have to qualify as legal, thus abandoning the idea that the conciliation procedure might also be used to resolve non-legal divergencies arising during contract renegotiations in particular.[186] Article 3 was included in the draft Additional Facility Rules at the request of several governments for an explicit reminder that Additional Facility proceedings would not benefit from the provisions of the Convention, in particular those exempting awards from judicial review and assuring their recognition and enforcement. Article 3 warned that, since the proceedings contemplated by Article 2 would be outside the jurisdiction of ICSID, none of the provisions of the Convention would be applicable to them or to recommendations, awards or reports rendered in the proceedings. Lastly, Article 4 of the draft required that any agreement providing for Additional Facility conciliation or arbitration be approved by the Secretary-General of the Centre.[187] According to the draft, parties could apply for such approval at any time prior to the institution of proceedings by submitting to the Secretariat a copy of their concluded or proposed agreement.[188] The Secretary-General would deny approval if the agreement was outside the

[181] These were to be called in full "Rules Governing the Additional Facility for the Administration of Proceedings by the Secretariat of the International Centre for Settlement of Investment Disputes." Included within the lengthy title was a reminder of Broches's distinction between extending the jurisdiction of ICSID and the mere administration by its Secretariat of certain non-Convention proceedings. *Cf.* text accompanying n. 177.

[182] The Additional Facility Rules and their schedules were drafted by Raj Krishna, an attorney in the World Bank Legal Department who became the Bank's Chief Counsel, South Asia Region, and later its Legal Adviser, International Law (Operations).

[183] *See* Doc. AC/78/7, Additional Facility: Report and Recommendations of the Secretary-General, August 15, 1978 (August 1978 Report); Docs. AC/78/8–AC/78/12, Draft Additional Facility Rules and Additional Facility Administrative and Financial Rules, Conciliation Rules, Arbitration Rules and Fact-Finding Rules, August 15, 1978.

[184] Art. 1 merely defined such terms as "Convention" and "Secretariat," while Arts. 5 and 6 provided for the application, as relevant, of the rules in the respective schedules.

[185] More precisely, Art. 2 specified that the Secretariat would be authorized to administer conciliation and arbitration proceedings between States and foreign nationals that fell outside the jurisdiction of ICSID because either the State party or the home State of the other party was not a Contracting State, or because the dispute did not arise out of an investment provided that at least one party was a Contracting State or a national of such a State. *See* Draft Additional Facility Rules (n. 183) Art. 2(a) and 2(b).

[186] *See* ibid. [187] *See* ibid. Art. 4(1). [188] *See* ibid.

scope of the Additional Facility as defined by Article 2.[189] In addition, where access to the Additional Facility was sought because the State party or the home State of the foreign national was not a Contracting State, the Secretary-General would withhold approval unless the parties also consented to the jurisdiction of ICSID (that is, to have recourse instead to Convention conciliation or arbitration) if, by the time proceedings were instituted, the non-Contracting State concerned had become a party to the Convention.[190] If parties wished to use the Additional Facility because they believed that their transaction was not an investment, but the Secretary-General thought otherwise, the approval would be conditioned on consent by the parties to submit any dispute in the first instance to the jurisdiction of ICSID.[191] Apart from avoiding use of the Additional Facility in cases beyond its scope, the procedure envisaged by Article 4 was thus meant to block any unnecessary diversion of cases away from the jurisdiction of the Centre. It was also intended to meet the concern that routine commercial cases should not be brought to the Centre through the Additional Facility. Article 4 directed the Secretary-General to give the necessary approval in a case not involving an investment only if the underlying transaction had features distinguishing it from "an ordinary commercial transaction."[192] This, according to Article 4 of the draft, would be so if the transaction were "a turnkey contract for a large industrial installation, a major public works contract or, more generally, a contract (other than an ordinary sale or purchase contract) extending over a long period of time or of special importance to the economy of the State party."[193]

The draft of the first of the four schedules, the Administrative and Financial Rules, was based on the provisions of the ICSID Administrative and Financial Regulations concerning the financing and administration of Convention proceedings. A notable difference stemmed from the wish of some governments to have more complete recovery of costs from users of the Additional Facility. In this regard, the draft Administrative and Financial Rules provided that parties would be required not only to meet the Secretariat's out-of-pocket expenditures for their proceeding but also to pay a charge for staff services calculated in line with the formula applied by the World Bank for its reimbursable technical assistance activities.[194]

The draft Conciliation and Arbitration Rules were an amalgam of provisions of the Convention and of the ICSID Institution, Conciliation and Arbitration Rules. The draft Fact-Finding Rules were likewise patterned in part after provisions of the ICSID Convention and Rules. Another source for some provisions of the draft Arbitration Rules was the recently promulgated Arbitration Rules of United Nations Commission on International Trade Law (UNCITRAL).[195] Thus, in another acknowledgment that Additional Facility proceedings would not be covered by the Convention, the draft Arbitration Rules, following the UNCITRAL Arbitration Rules, provided that they would govern the proceedings "save that if any of these Rules is in conflict with a provision of law applicable to the arbitration from which the parties cannot derogate, that provision shall prevail."[196] A provision of the draft Arbitration Rules on interim measures was also influenced by the UNCITRAL Arbitration Rules. The provision stated that parties could apply to a competent judicial authority for such measures and, like

[189] *See* ibid. Art. 4(2) and 4(3). The approval procedure was thus to function as the equivalent of the jurisdictional screening by the Secretary-General of requests for conciliation and arbitration under the Convention.

[190] *See* ibid. Art. 4(2). [191] *See* ibid. Art. 4(4). [192] Ibid. Art. 4(3).

[193] Ibid. [194] *See* Draft Administrative and Financial Rules (n. 183) Art. 7.

[195] *See* n. 72.

[196] Draft Arbitration Rules (n. 183) Art. 1. *Cf.* UNCITRAL Arbitration Rules (n. 72) Art. 1(2).

the UNCITRAL Arbitration Rules, made it clear that they would not be deemed to have thereby infringed their agreement to arbitrate.[197] A further noteworthy feature of the draft Arbitration Rules was that they contained a special restriction on the choice (by the arbitral tribunal) of the place of arbitration and of making the award. To help ensure recognition and enforcement of the award, the draft Rules provided that the place could only be in a State party to the New York Convention on the Recognition and Enforcement of Foreign Arbitral Awards.[198]

C. Adoption of the Additional Facility Rules

Also submitted to the members of the Administrative Council in August 1978 was a draft resolution of the Council, proposed for adoption at the annual meeting the following month, approving the draft Additional Facility Rules and their schedules. As some had suggested, the draft resolution provided for the Additional Facility to be introduced on a trial basis and for the Council to consider after five years whether to continue the facility.[199] Despite this, and all the precautions in the draft Rules, several governments remained skeptical, concerned that the proposed extension of the Secretariat's activities could weaken the Centre, duplicate the work of other arbitration institutions and, in any event, be beyond the power of the Administrative Council to authorize. On this last, most important point, Broches stuck to his view that the skeptics were interpreting the Convention in an "unduly restrictive"[200] manner. He saw the creation of the Additional Facility as presenting "a question of policy rather than of law."[201] Nevertheless, to allow for a last "exchange of views and examination of the Additional Facility documents" before action was taken on the proposal at the annual meeting of the Administrative Council, Broches convened "informal working level meetings" of representatives of governments during the weekend preceding the annual meeting.[202] The legal competence of the Administrative Council to establish the Additional Facility was discussed at length at these informal meetings without, however, changing any minds on the question. Agreement was reached at the informal meetings on some "minor technical amendments" of the draft Additional Facility Rules.[203] The most important of these was to delete, from Article 4 of the draft Additional Facility Rules, the description of contracts that would not be viewed as ordinary commercial transactions,[204] which conveyed the impression that such contracts could never qualify as investments either. It was instead proposed to publish the provision with a comment more cautiously stating that:

> Economic transactions which (a) may or may not, depending on their terms, be regarded by the parties as investments for purposes of the Convention, which (b) involve long-term relationships or the commitment of substantial resources on the part of either party, and which (c) are of special importance to the economy of the State party, can be clearly distinguished from ordinary

[197] *See* Draft Arbitration Rules (n. 183) Art. 47(4); UNCITRAL Arbitration Rules (n. 72) Art. 26(3).

[198] *See* Draft Arbitration Rules (n. 183) Arts. 20 and 21; New York Convention, June 18, 1958, 330 UNTS 3, Arts. III–V.

[199] *See* Doc. AC/78/13, Draft Additional Facility Resolution, August 15, 1978.

[200] August 1978 Report (n. 183) para. 6. [201] Ibid.

[202] Broches Cable to Representatives of Contracting States, August 15, 1978.

[203] Doc. AC/78/16, Proposed Amendments to the Additional Facility Rules: Memorandum of the Secretary-General, September 25, 1978.

[204] Quoted in the text accompanying n. 193.

commercial transactions. Examples of such transactions may be found in various forms of industrial cooperation agreements and major civil works contracts.[205]

At the annual meeting, one delegate, seconded by another, requested a postponement of the vote on the resolution approving the amended draft Additional Facility Rules. A postal vote, he said would allow governments more time to examine the documents.[206] Speaking at the invitation of the Temporary Presiding Officer,[207] Broches said that he doubted postponing the vote would help; during the year, he added, mostly favorable comments on the proposal had been received from about half of the Contracting States.[208] Noting that a quorum was present, the Temporary Presiding Officer decided to put the matter to a vote by roll-call.[209] The roll-call resulted in adoption of the resolution but hardly its ringing endorsement, with nearly as many abstentions as votes cast in favor.[210]

D. Continuation of the Additional Facility

In accordance with the resolution, the Administrative Council was to "review the operation of the Additional Facility after five years in order to decide, in the light of the experience gained during that period, whether to continue the Additional Facility or to terminate it for the future."[211] The five-year period expired in 1983, just as Broches's successor, Heribert Golsong, was himself relinquishing the position of Secretary-General. Before his departure, Golsong recommended to the Administrative Council that it decide to terminate the Additional Facility. Golsong set forth the reasons for this recommendation in a note he sent in July 1983 to the members of the Administrative Council for them to consider at their annual meeting later in the year.[212] In the note, Golsong observed that there had been only one instance of parties requesting access to the Additional Facility under Article 4 of the Additional Facility Rules; it was for the settlement of disputes under an agreement for the provision of technical services

[205] Memorandum (n. 203) annex, 3. This comment was published with the Additional Facility Rules after their approval. *See* Doc. ICSID/11, Additional Facility for the Administration of Conciliation, Arbitration and Fact-Finding Proceedings 5–6 (June 1979).

[206] *See* Summary Proceedings: Twelfth Annual Meeting (n. 174) paras. 8 and 9 (intervention of Mr. Meulemans (Belgium), proposing the postponement, and Mr. Kirbyshire (United Kingdom), seconding the proposal).

[207] *See* Administrative and Financial Regulations (n. 26) reg. 3*bis*. At the 1978 annual meeting, the Temporary Presiding Officer was Mustapha Zaanouni, Minister of Planning of Tunisia and its Representative on the Administrative Council.

[208] *See* Summary Proceedings: Twelfth Annual Meeting (n. 174) para. 16 (intervention of Mr. Broches).

[209] *See* ibid. para. 18.

[210] Thus, of the 51 Contracting States represented at the meeting, 25 voted in favor, two against and 24 abstained. The votes in favor were by Afghanistan, Austria, the Central African Empire, Denmark, Fiji, Finland, France, Germany, Greece, Iceland, Italy, Ivory Coast, Japan, Jordan, Luxembourg, Mali, the Netherlands, Nigeria, Norway, Sierra Leone, Sweden, Switzerland, Togo, Tunisia and the United States. The two votes against were by Pakistan and Western Samoa. Abstaining were Belgium, Benin, Burundi, Cameroon, Gambia, Ghana, Kenya, Korea, Lesotho, Liberia, Madagascar, Malawi, Malaysia, Morocco, Romania, Senegal, Sri Lanka, Swaziland, Trinidad and Tobago, Uganda, the United Kingdom, Yugoslavia, Zaire and Zambia (ibid. note 2).

[211] The resolution further stated that any termination of the Additional Facility would, of course, be "without prejudice to approvals theretofore given under Article 4 of the Additional Rules or any agreement theretofore concluded with respect to fact-finding." Administrative Council Resolution AC (12)/RES/38, Creation of an Additional Facility, September 27, 1978, para. 3, reprinted in ICSID Thirteenth Ann. Rep. 1978/1979, 33.

[212] Doc. AC/83/3, Additional Facility: Note of the Secretary-General, July 27, 1983 (July 1983 Note).

by a national of a Contracting State to the agency of a non-Contracting State.[213] The agreement had been fully performed without giving rise to a dispute. There also was one BIT setting forth the consent of the States concerned to submit investment disputes to Additional Facility arbitration; the treaty had, however, yet to be ratified.[214] Golsong's note argued that the evident lack of interest in the Additional Facility was due partly to the growth in the number of Contracting States since 1978 and partly to the emergence of a "modern notion of investment" encompassing many more kinds of transactions than in earlier years.[215] Since both the number of Contracting States and types of transactions regarded as investments were growing, the initial justification for the creation of the Additional Facility had "largely disappeared."[216] The note added that continuing the Additional Facility "might only give an excuse to potential ICSID Contracting States for not joining ICSID."[217]

At the annual meeting of the Administrative Council in September 1983, however, one delegate cautioned against haste: to allow more time for reflection and consultations, he proposed putting off for a year the decision on the future of the Additional Facility.[218] Several other delegates spoke in favor of this proposal, including two whose countries had started to incorporate the Additional Facility into their BITs.[219] The Administrative Council thereupon resolved to make the decision at its 1984 annual meeting in light of a report by the Secretary-General on the results of consultations.[220] In July 1984, the members of the Administrative Council received the report of the new Secretary-General, Ibrahim Shihata.[221] The report, consisting of hardly more than two pages, first pointed out that several BITs[222] referred to the Additional Facility and that "further reference to the Additional Facility is envisaged by some members in

[213] The approval of access was reported in the ICSID Thirteenth Ann. Rep. 1978/1979, 4.

[214] This was the Treaty Concerning the Treatment and Protection of Investment, Panama–United States, October 27, 1982, reprinted in ICSID, Investment Treaties, Release 94-3 (June 1994), Art. VII(3). At the time of the conclusion of this BIT, Panama was not a party to the ICSID Convention. There was one other BIT, concluded earlier in 1982, that contained a reference to Additional Facility arbitration, but merely as one of several different forms of arbitration that the disputing parties might agree upon. This was the Agreement for the Promotion and Protection of Investments, Belize–United Kingdom, April 13, 1982, reprinted in ICSID, Investment Treaties, Release 94-3 (June 1994), Art. 8(2).

[215] July 1983 Note (n. 212) 2–3. The note explained that the Convention had been formulated "at a time when most investments took the form of concessions, joint ventures or loans made by private financial institutions to foreign public entities and to a certain extent, of arrangements concerning industrial property rights." Reflecting the evolution referred to in n. 160, the note went on to explain that these types of investments were "now supplemented, and sometimes superseded, by new forms of association between States and foreign investors, such as profit-sharing, service and management contracts, contracts for the sale and erection of industrial plants, turn-key contracts, international leasing arrangements, agreements for the transfer of know-how and technology, industrial or business concessions." The note added that investments might even and more generally now be said to comprise "claims to money or to any performance under contracts having financial or economic value" (ibid. 2).

[216] Ibid. 4. [217] Ibid.

[218] *See* Doc. AC/83/6, Summary Proceedings: Seventeenth Annual Meeting, September 29, 1983, para. 13 (intervention of Mr. Arlman (Netherlands)).

[219] *See* ibid. paras. 14 and 15 (interventions of Mr. Munk (United States) and Mr. Smith (United Kingdom)).

[220] *See* ibid. para. 15 and Administrative Council Resolution AC(17)/RES/54, Additional Facility, September 29, 1983, reprinted in ICSID 1984 Ann. Rep. 20.

[221] Doc. AC/84/2, Additional Facility: Report of the Secretary-General, Administrative Council, July 23, 1984 (July 1984 Report).

[222] In addition to the two BITs mentioned in n. 214, these were the Agreement on the Promotion and Protection of Investments, St. Lucia–United Kingdom, January 18, 1983, and the Treaty Concerning the Reciprocal Encouragement and Protection of Investment, Senegal–United States, December 6, 1983, both reprinted in ICSID, Investment Treaties, Release 94-3 (June 1994).

future."[223] Drawing from this the conclusion that the Additional Facility might "still fulfill a useful function, not at all inconsistent with, and rather complementary to, that of ICSID," the report recommended retaining the Additional Facility.[224] Any remaining doubts seem to have vanished with this report; at its annual meeting in September 1984, the Administrative Council approved, without discussion, the indefinite continuation of the Additional Facility.[225]

VI. The appointing authority role

A further role acquired in these early years was that of the authority to appoint arbitrators, in defined contingencies, under agreements providing for the settlement of disputes between parties by ad hoc (that is, non-institutional) arbitration. Often, but not always, the parties to such agreements had decided on this ad hoc alternative because they were ineligible to have recourse to arbitration under the Convention or, after its establishment, the Additional Facility (for example, because they were both governmental entities or private parties). Typically, the agreements provided for the appointing authority function to be exercised if, within stated time limits, either party failed to appoint an arbitrator or the parties or party-appointed arbitrators failed to agree on a presiding arbitrator. From the start, the Centre urged that such agreements entrust the function to the Chairman of the Administrative Council or the Secretary-General but never to ICSID itself.

The *Annual Report* of the Centre for fiscal year 1970 cited precedents and outlined a simple procedure for the assumption of this role by officials of the Centre. The main precedent referred to was that of the ICJ, its President having long accepted the responsibility of appointing arbitrators, especially for disputes between States, even though there was no mention of this "extra-judicial activity" in the Statute of the ICJ.[226] The procedure that the *Annual Report* suggested for parties wishing to include in their agreement a designation of the Chairman or Secretary-General as appointing authority of ad hoc arbitrators was to "consult with the Centre before concluding such agreements and submit at least a draft of the disputes settlement procedure to it for comment."[227] The officials of ICSID approached with such requests would, the *Annual Report* continued, "generally consent to perform the functions foreseen for them in a satisfactorily formulated disputes clause, unless it is foreseeable that this might be inconsistent with the interests of the Centre or of the World Bank Group."[228] The blessing of the Administrative Council for all this may be inferred from its approval of the report.[229] No question arose of the activity's consistency with the Convention as it was to be undertaken by the individual officials rather than the Centre as an institution.

[223] July 1984 Report (n. 221) para. 4. [224] Ibid.

[225] *See* Administrative Council Resolution AC(18)/RES/58, Additional Facility, reprinted in 1985 ICSID Ann. Rep. 18.

[226] On this activity at the ICJ, *see* T. Gill, *Rosenne's The World Court: What It Is and How It Works* 15–16 (6th ed. 2003). The predecessor of the ICJ, the Permanent Court of International Justice, first approved the performance of this activity by its President in 1933. *See* PCIJ Ser. E, No. 10, 164 (1933–1934).

[227] ICSID Fourth Ann. Rep. 1969/1970, 5. [228] Ibid.

[229] *See* Administrative Council Resolution AC(4)/RES/16, Approval of the Annual Report, September 23, 1970, reprinted in ICSID Fifth Ann. Rep. 1970/1971, 18.

As between the Chairman and Secretary-General, the Centre generally encouraged parties to choose the latter as appointing authority. Certainly it was the more straightforward choice as the Chairman would normally only perform the function on the advice of the Secretary-General.[230] When given the opportunity to comment on proposed designations of the Secretary-General as appointing authority, the Centre would routinely ask parties to avoid imposing such constraints as strict time limits on the exercise of the function and unambiguously to cover such matters as the number of persons to be appointed and the circumstances under which the appointments were to be made.[231]

Instruments designating the Secretary-General as the appointing authority of arbitrators in ad hoc proceedings included a number of treaties signed in the 1980s. An annex to the High Ross Treaty made by Canada and the United States in 1984, for example, provided for the settlement of disputes by ad hoc arbitration, with the Secretary-General of ICSID to serve as the appointing authority of last resort.[232] In 1987, the United States entered into its first investment incentive agreement containing a similar reference to the Secretary-General of the Centre. Concluded with Bahrain, the agreement provided for the settlement of disputes between the two States by ad hoc arbitration and named the Secretary-General as the authority to appoint arbitrators not appointed in the normal course.[233] Contractual ad hoc arbitration clauses referring to the Secretary-General of ICSID as the appointing authority of arbitrators also became fairly common in the 1980s. These often were clauses providing for arbitration under the then still new UNCITRAL Arbitration Rules, which gave the designated appointing authority the further task of deciding on challenges of arbitrators for lack of impartiality or independence.[234] Towards the end of the 1980s, such UNCITRAL arbitration clauses referring to the ICSID Secretary-General as appointing authority were increasingly seen in, for instance, contracts of Indonesian SOEs with foreign companies.[235] UNCITRAL clauses of this kind began to appear in BITs a few years later.[236]

At the time, the Centre did not levy any charge in respect of the actual performance by the Secretary-General of the appointing authority function under such

230 *See* The ICSID Secretary-General as Appointing Authority in Ad Hoc Proceedings, 6(2) News from ICSID 6 (1989). As explained in Ch. 8, section II, the appointing authority function of the Chairman in Convention cases was likewise generally performed on the recommendation of the Secretary-General.

231 *See* Ad Hoc Proceedings (n. 230).

232 The annex with this dispute settlement arrangement was an agreement between the Province of British Columbia and the City of Seattle concerning the delivery to the city of electric power produced at the Ross Dam. *See* Treaty between Canada and the United States of America Relating to the Skagit River and Ross Lake, and the Seven Mile Reservoir on the Pend d'Oreille River (High Ross Treaty), April 2, 1984, Annex, sec. 10.

233 *See* Investment Incentive Agreement, Bahrain–United States, April 25, 1987, reprinted in 2 ICSID Rev.—FILJ 531 (1987), Art. 6. This and similar investment incentive agreements of the U.S. provided a framework for the operation in the partner country concerned of programs of the U.S. national investment guarantee agency, OPIC, and were hence colloquially known as OPIC agreements.

234 *See* UNCITRAL Arbitration Rules (n. 72) Art. 12.

235 The well known *Karaha Bodas* and *Himpurna* arbitrations were based on such clauses of contracts of Indonesian SOEs. *See Karaha Bodas v. Pertamina and PLN*, Award, December 18, 2000, summarized at <http://www.biicl.org/files/3931_2000_himpurna_and_karaha_bodas_arbitrations.pdf>; *Himpurna v. PLN*, Award, May 4, 1999, 25 YBCA 13 (2000).

236 *See, e.g.*, Agreement for the Promotion and Protection of Investments, Germany–India, July 10, 1995, reprinted in ICSID, Investment Treaties, Release 96-4 (December 1996), Art. 9(2).

arrangements.[237] There was little forgone income as the Secretary-General was seldom called upon to carry out the function in these early years. Only three appointments to ad hoc tribunals seem to have been made by the Secretary-General during ICSID's first two decades.[238]

VII. The investment law publishing activities

The draft budget for ICSID's 1970 fiscal year, submitted by Broches to the Administrative Council for approval at its 1969 annual meeting, included a proposal for a pilot project that would help to avoid "inactivity" pending the submission of disputes to the Centre.[239] The project was for the collection, classification and eventual dissemination of national legislation and international agreements relating to foreign investments. The aim would be to assist States in making useful comparisons among investment promotion instruments in various parts of the world and to introduce potential investors to legal conditions in different developing countries.[240] Inquiries that ICSID had been receiving from representatives of States and investors confirmed the demand for this service.[241] It had also been verified with other international organizations that the effort envisaged for ICSID would not duplicate their work.[242]

In his address at the 1969 annual meeting of the Administrative Council, Broches tackled the question of the power of the Centre to undertake the proposed activity. He acknowledged in this connection that the First Draft of the ICSID Convention had contained a provision on ancillary research and information activities in the field of international investments.[243] It was true, Broches explained, that the Legal Committee had decided to delete the provision.[244] This had, however, been done on the understanding "that the Centre would not thereby be precluded from carrying out useful work related to its principal purpose and approved by the Contracting States."[245] In interesting contrast to the later reactions of some to the idea of the Additional Facility, this expansive approach urged by Broches was accepted without demur by representatives of Contracting States at the 1969 annual meeting; they unanimously approved the draft budget with the proposed project on investment laws and treaties.[246]

As carried out by ICSID during the 1970s, the project was ambitious in scope, covering constitutional, legislative, regulatory and treaty materials relating to foreign investment from almost 60 developing countries. The materials—full texts or extracts,

237 Such a charge was introduced only in 2000. It was then set at US$1,000. Successive increases in 2001, 2002 and 2005 brought the charge to its present level of US$10,000. *See* ICSID Schedule of Fees, January 1, 2013, para. 4.

238 Two of these appointments are referred to in ICSID as Designating Authority for Non-ICSID Arbitration, 1(1) News from ICSID 3, 4 (1984). The third was one of the co-arbitrators in *Biloune v. Ghana*, a proceeding initiated in early 1988 under the UNCITRAL Arbitration Rules. The tribunal, constituted in late 1988, rendered an award on jurisdiction and liability in 1989 (95 ILR 184) and on damages and costs in 1990 (95 ILR 211).

239 *See* Doc. AC/69/4, Third Annual Meeting: Proceedings, September 2, 1969, paras. 9 and 15.

240 *See* ibid. para. 15; ICSID Fourth Ann. Rep. 1969/1970, 5–6.

241 Third Annual Meeting: Proceedings (n. 239) para. 14.

242 Ibid. para. 15.

243 Ibid. para. 14. *Cf.* Ch. 5, text accompanying n. 23.

244 Third Annual Meeting: Proceedings (n. 239) para. 14. *Cf.* Ch. 5, text accompanying nn. 81 and 82.

245 Third Annual Meeting: Proceedings (n. 239) para. 14. *Cf.* Ch. 5, text accompanying n. 83.

246 *See* Third Annual Meeting: Proceedings (n. 239) para. 32; Administrative Council Resolution AC(3)/RES/14, Adoption of Budget for Fiscal Year 1970, September 29, 1969, reprinted in ICSID Fourth Ann. Rep. 1969/1970, 18.

as appropriate—were compiled on a country-by-country basis, with the materials for each country classified according to a number of subject matter headings. They were presented in the form of a loose-leaf service, called *Investment Laws of the World*, that could readily be updated and supplemented as necessary. ICSID arranged for it to be published and sold commercially by a U.S.-based law publisher, Oceana Publications, Inc. The first binders in the service, with materials of some 20 countries, were published in 1973.[247] By 1980, the publications had grown to 11 binders of laws of 59 countries.[248]

After he became Secretary-General, Golsong transformed the treaty coverage of the collection with a separate set of binders entitled *Investment Treaties*. Also published by Oceana, they contained the full texts of BITs. Nearly 200 BITs were reprinted in the first two of these binders issued in 1983.[249] With its cross-sections of materials needing periodic updates in that format, *Investment Laws of the World* had meanwhile become increasingly difficult to maintain. Following Shihata's election as Secretary-General in 1983, it was therefore decided to transform it into a collection of the complete texts of basic investment laws only. The change was effected through new updates for the collection published starting in 1987.[250]

Shihata gave his first address to the Administrative Council at its 1984 annual meeting. He took the occasion to mention that the Secretariat had begun work on a detailed analysis of BITs.[251] At the annual meeting the following year, Shihata informed the Council that the work had progressed and arrangements were being made to publish the results as a handbook on BITs that could be of assistance to Contracting States in considering the negotiation or renegotiation of investment treaties.[252] Also at the 1985 annual meeting, Shihata announced that the Secretariat had decided to launch a new legal periodical entitled *ICSID Review—Foreign Investment Law Journal*, which would contain articles on such topics as investment legislation, the negotiation and performance of investment agreements and the resolution of investment disputes. He emphasized that no other journal covered all of these subjects combined.[253] Shihata later elaborated on the contribution that the journal might make to achieving ICSID's overall objectives. The journal could, he said, "create greater awareness of the role of law as instrument for the encouragement of financial flows for development purposes"; and "[b]y helping to clarify the law applicable to foreign investments and assisting its balanced and progressive development," the periodical could "play an indirect role in the avoidance of investment disputes and in the settlement of these disputes if they arise."[254]

As with Broches's proposal in 1969 for what became *Investment Laws of the World*, the Administrative Council had no difficulty in accepting these further initiatives by Shihata in the same area and approved the modest initial budgetary allocations

[247] *See* ICSID Seventh Ann. Rep. 1972/1973, 5.

[248] *See* ICSID Fourteenth Ann. Rep. 1979/1980, 6.

[249] *See* ICSID Seventeenth Ann. Rep. 1982/1983, 22. From the start, therefore, the publication was quite comprehensive as the number of BITs worldwide then totaled some 230.

[250] *See* Investment Laws of the World, 4(2) News from ICSID 9 (1987). The Investment Laws of the World and Investment Treaties collections are now published by Oxford University Press, which acquired Oceana Publications in 2005.

[251] Doc. AC/84/8, Eighteenth Annual Meeting: Summary Proceedings, September 26, 1984, Annex A, Report of the Secretary-General, 3.

[252] *See* Doc. AC/85/8, Nineteenth Annual Meeting: Summary Proceedings, October 10, 1985, Annex A, Report of the Secretary-General, 3.

[253] *See* ibid. [254] Note from the Editor, 1 ICSID Rev.—FILJ at v (1986).

Ibrahim F.I. Shihata, Vice President and General Counsel of the World Bank from 1983 to 1998 (with the rank of Senior Vice President from 1994) and Secretary-General of ICSID, 1983 to 2000.

World Bank Group Archives

involved.[255] Made available on a subscription basis through Johns Hopkins University Press, the *ICSID Review—Foreign Investment Law Journal* began appearing twice yearly in 1986.[256] Work on the book on BITs had to be postponed. It was, however, resumed and resulted in the 1995 publication by the Dutch firm Martinus Nijhoff Publishers of *Bilateral Investment Treaties*.[257]

Together, the investment law publications of ICSID made it a leading source of information on the subject in these pre-Internet days. Thanks in large part to the financial success of the *Investment Laws of the World* and *Investment Treaties* collections, income from sales of the publications eventually offset ICSID's out-of-pocket expenses for their production. Revenues were not nearly sufficient to recover the cost of staff time spent on the publications. Through their efforts on these investment law publications, however, legal staff of the Centre inevitably acquired greater expertise in the field. This led them eventually to receive the occasional advisory assignments described in Chapter 9.

[255] *See* Administrative Council Resolution AC(18)/RES/59, Adoption of Budget for Fiscal Year 1985, September 26, 1984, reprinted in ICSID 1985 Ann. Rep. 18; Administrative Council Resolution AC(19)/RES/61, Adoption of Budget for Fiscal Year 1986, October 10, 1985, reprinted in ICSID 1986 Ann. Rep. 18.

[256] In 2012, Oxford University Press took over publication of the periodical, which became a triannual publication two years later.

[257] R. Dolzer and M. Stevens, *Bilateral Investment Treaties* (1995).

8

Aspects of the Early Cases

This chapter is on key aspects of the cases brought to ICSID in its first two decades. It will be remembered from Chapter 7 that there were 25 of these cases—two conciliation cases and the rest arbitrations—registered between 1972 and 1988.

Section I of the chapter examines the ways in which successive Secretaries-General handled the registration of requests to institute proceedings and, in particular, their "screening" of such requests. Patterns in the constitution of the conciliation commissions and arbitral tribunals are traced in section II, as are the first experiences of the Centre with the resignation and challenge of arbitrators.

Section III discusses the distinctly pragmatic approaches of arbitral tribunals in this period to jurisdictional issues, especially the requirement of consent. There was controversy in the early 1980s as to the availability, in the context of an ICSID case, of court-ordered provisional measures. The controversy is reviewed in section IV, which also looks at the first instances of arbitral provisional measures under Article 47 of the ICSID Convention. Contrasting with their notably flexible approaches to jurisdictional issues, arbitral tribunals of the period were (or were admonished by ad hoc committees to be) constrained in their determination of the law applicable to the substance of the dispute where, as was often the case, the parties had no agreement on the matter. The underlying interpretations of Article 42(1) of the Convention are examined in section V.

The first two ad hoc committee decisions rendered under Article 52 of the Convention were seen by many as exposing a fatal flaw in the system of the Convention. They were soon followed, however, by the third ad hoc committee decision, which did much to restore faith in the system. These three ad hoc committee decisions are the subject of section VI. A few court proceedings for the enforcement of ICSID awards took place in these early years; the proceedings are reviewed in the concluding section VII. Also discussed in this section are the more numerous cases of awards that were paid voluntarily, though often only in part, and seldom promptly. A recurring theme throughout is the active role played by the Secretary-General and Secretariat of ICSID—not only, of course, in regard to the institution of proceedings, but also in regard to the constitution of arbitral tribunals, in the debates over provisional measures and the annulment of awards, and in the negotiation of post-award settlements.

I. Registration of requests to institute proceedings

The Report of the Executive Directors of the Bank on the ICSID Convention called attention to the power that Articles 28(3) and 36(3) of the Convention granted the Secretary-General to refuse registration of a request for conciliation or arbitration, and thereby prevent the institution of proceedings, if on the basis of information furnished by the requesting party the Secretary-General found that the dispute was manifestly outside the jurisdiction of the Centre. According to the Report:

The Secretary-General is given this limited power to "screen" requests for conciliation or arbitration proceedings with a view to avoiding the embarrassment to a party (particularly a State) which might result from the institution of proceedings against it in a dispute which it had not consented to submit to the Centre, as well as the possibility that the machinery of the Centre would be set in motion in cases which for other reasons were obviously outside the jurisdiction of the Centre, e.g., because either the applicant or the other party was not eligible to be a party in proceedings under the Convention.[1]

The explanatory notes published with the Regulations and Rules of the Centre in late 1967 dwelled on the limited nature of this "screening power" of the Secretary-General. In accordance with Articles 28(3) and 36(3) of the Convention, it was to be exercised "on the basis of the information contained in the request." According to the explanatory notes, it followed from this that registration could not be refused for reasons other than those based on such information (or contained in the request's supporting documentation) and that the Secretary-General could not, apart from specified supporting documentation, require more than "information."[2] Under Articles 28(3) and 36(3) of the Convention, the Secretary-General had to refuse to register a request when it showed that the dispute was "manifestly outside the jurisdiction of the Centre." The explanatory notes took this as meaning that registration would be denied only where it was "beyond reasonable doubt whatever evidence or argument might be produced subsequently" that the Centre lacked jurisdiction.[3]

This narrow conception of the screening power of the Secretary-General was particularly evident during the tenures of Aron Broches and Heribert Golsong. Then, as in later years, informal consultations with the Secretariat helped to save parties from submitting requests for conciliation or arbitration that would have stood no chance of registration. Nevertheless, the fact remains that in these earlier years there was never a formal refusal of registration of a request for conciliation or arbitration. Partly, of course, because there were so few of them, the requests were registered promptly. In one instance, the request for arbitration was registered on the same day as its receipt by the Secretary-General.[4] Overall, the period between receipt and registration of these first requests for conciliation and arbitration averaged about 12 days.

There was a noticeable shift in approach after Ibrahim Shihata became Secretary-General in 1983. He saw Articles 28(3) and 36(3) of the Convention as providing the Secretary-General with a wider margin of appreciation in deciding on the registration

[1] Report of the Executive Directors on the Convention, para. 20. It will be recalled that the idea of giving this power to the Secretary-General originated with concerns, expressed at the regional consultative meetings of legal experts, to ensure that proceedings were not instituted without at least some prima facie indication that there was mutual consent of the parties to the jurisdiction of ICSID. *See* Ch. 4, text accompanying nn. 136–138.

[2] Doc. ICSID/4/Rev. 1, ICSID Regulations and Rules (reprinted May 1975), Institution Rules, at note B to Rule 6. Except where indicated otherwise, references in this chapter to the Institution and Arbitration Rules of the Centre are to the Rules reprinted in that publication, in effect throughout most of the period covered by the chapter.

[3] Institution Rules (n. 2) note C to Rule 6.

[4] As recorded in *Benvenuti & Bonfant v. Congo*, Award, August 15, 1980, 1 ICSID Rep. 330, 336–337 (1993), the request in that case was both lodged with and registered by the Secretary-General on December 15, 1977. Such speed in registering the request seems, however, to have been questionable as transmission of the request to the opposing party, under Art. 36(1) of the Convention, was envisaged in the preparation of the Convention as a separate step preceding registration under Art. 36(3), to provide a last opportunity for settlement of the dispute before the proceeding was instituted. *See* Ch. 5, n. 133 and accompanying text.

of conciliation and arbitration requests than that described in the explanatory notes of 1967. Partly because the requests were more closely scrutinized (but also partly because there were more of them), the average time between the receipt and registration of a request rose to 25 days in the period 1984 to 1988. The assumption of greater responsibility by the Secretary-General suggested a need to anticipate criticism of decisions to register requests for arbitration and, in particular, to explain that they would not preclude objections to jurisdiction. The Secretariat began to include, in the Secretary-General's correspondence accompanying the notice of registration, a statement to the effect that the registration was "without prejudice" to such objections, which could in due course be raised with the arbitral tribunal.

This was first done in connection with the registration of the request for arbitration in *SPP v. Egypt* in 1984.[5] The following year, a request for arbitration was, for the first time, formally refused registration. The request had been submitted by a Singaporean company called Asian Express International in respect of a dispute with the Greater Colombo Economic Commission, a Sri Lankan government agency. Refusing registration of the request was clearly difficult for the Secretariat, which took five months to issue the refusal.[6] Indeed, the registration process as a whole was becoming more complex in the period 1984 to 1988, independently of any changes of approach within the Secretariat. A main reason for this was that the Secretary-General was beginning to receive requests made, not on the basis of straightforward arbitration clauses in investment contracts, but instead relying on consents said to be embodied in investment laws or treaties of the host State. The requests of SPP and Asian Express International were both of this kind.

It will be remembered from Chapter 6 that the Arbitration Rules of the Centre introduced separate procedures for the registration by the Secretary-General of requests for the rectification, supplementation, interpretation, revision and annulment of awards. From their adoption in 1967, the Rules provided for the Secretary-General to refuse registration of a request for rectification, supplementation, revision or annulment if made beyond the applicable time limit prescribed by the Convention.[7] The gloss in the explanatory notes of 1967 was that the Secretary-General's authority to refuse to register such a request was "restricted to the contingency" that it was not made within the relevant time limit.[8] In 1978, however, Broches had the occasion to refuse to register a request for annulment, not because it was untimely but because it did not relate to an award. The request, made by the claimants in *Holiday Inns v. Morocco*, was for the annulment of a "Decision and Procedural Order" of the tribunal whereby it decided to continue the hitherto suspended proceeding and determined the further steps to be taken by the parties.[9] Broches took the position that the ICSID Convention and Rules reserved the term "award" only for what in other contexts might be called a final award—a decision

[5] As recorded in the first Decision on Jurisdiction rendered by the tribunal in that case (November 27, 1985, 3 ICSID Rep. 112 (1995)), the statement of the Secretary-General on that occasion identified a specific jurisdictional issue. A similar statement concerning a specific jurisdictional issue was made by the Secretary-General on registering the request for arbitration in *MINE v. Guinea* the next month. *See* 2(1) News from ICSID 3 (1985). It was, however, eventually realized that such specificity could be (and was) viewed as inappropriate. The statement was made only in the most general terms in regard to later registrations.

[6] *See* 2(1) News from ICSID 3 (1985) and 2(2) News from ICSID 3 (1985) (respectively reporting receipt of the request on November 6, 1984, and refusal of registration on April 9, 1985).

[7] *See* Arbitration Rules (n. 2) Rules 49(2) and 50(2). The respective time limits were set out in Arts. 49(2), 51(2) and 52(2) of the Convention. It will be recollected that there was no time limit for requests for the interpretation of an award.

[8] Arbitration Rules (n. 2) note C to Rule 49 and note C to Rule 50.

[9] A. Broches, Observations on the Finality of ICSID Awards, reprinted in Broches *Selected Essays* 295, 302, note 25; ICSID Twelfth Ann. Rep. 1977/1978, 5.

by which an arbitral tribunal intended to make a final disposition of the case—and that no decision short of that was covered by the provisions of the Convention and Rules dealing with the annulment of awards. The "Decision and Procedural Order" in the *Holiday Inns* case obviously not being an award in this sense, the Secretary-General could not register a request for its annulment under those provisions.

The same position was taken at ICSID when, in 1988, a request for the annulment of a preliminary decision upholding jurisdiction was refused registration in the *SPP* case.[10] The refusals of registration notified to the parties in the *Holiday Inns* and *SPP* cases both emphasized the Secretary-General's lack of any power to register a request for the annulment of a decision manifestly not qualifying as an award for the purposes of the ICSID Convention and Rules. They both also emphasized that the non-registration of the requests did not in any way prejudice the respective parties' rights to seek annulment of the eventual award which, in accordance with Article 48(3) of the Convention, would have to deal with every question submitted to the tribunal at any stage of the proceedings, even if the tribunal had already addressed some of those questions in interim decisions.[11] In an article written long after his retirement, Broches referred to the request for annulment in the *Holiday Inns* case as having had an "abusive nature."[12] While that may well have been so, the position taken by Broches in that case and followed in the *SPP* case (and in several unpublished instances since) promoted the orderly operation of the relevant provisions of the ICSID Convention and Rules, with an arbitration proceeding, an annulment proceeding and possibly a new arbitration proceeding held sequentially, whereas the registration of requests for the annulment of interim decisions would have raised the specter of original arbitration proceedings continuing alongside annulment proceedings and possibly thereafter simultaneously with new arbitration proceedings.

II. The constitution of commissions and tribunals

As indicated in Chapter 7, a conciliation commission was constituted in only one of the two conciliation proceedings instituted during ICSID's first two decades. It consisted of a sole conciliator, a British Law Lord, appointed by agreement of the parties.[13]

With a single exception,[14] tribunals were constituted in all of the arbitration cases begun during the period; in two of the cases,[15] second tribunals were established

[10] *See* ICSID 1989 Ann. Rep. 7. In this instance, the refusal of registration was by Hugh N. Scott, then Associate General Counsel of the World Bank, who had been designated Acting Secretary-General of ICSID, for the purpose of deciding on the registrability of the request by Shihata in view of the fact that the latter was a national of Egypt, the applicant for the annulment, and had in the early 1970s participated in the preparation of the investment law of Egypt relied upon for its consent to arbitration in the case. The request for annulment related to the second preliminary decision on jurisdiction in the *SPP* case, on which *see* nn. 55–60 and accompanying text. If it had instead been a decision declining jurisdiction over the dispute, in accordance with the Arbitration Rules of the Centre, it would have been an award intended to dispose of the entire dispute, and a request for its annulment could have been registered. *See* Arbitration Rules (n. 2) Rules 41(4) and 41(5), providing respectively for the continuation of the proceeding in the event of a rejection of an objection to jurisdiction and, in the event of a decision upholding an objection to jurisdiction over the dispute, the rendition of "an award to that effect."

[11] *Cf.* ICSID 1989 Ann. Rep. 7.

[12] Broches (n. 9) 302, note 25.

[13] This was Richard Wilberforce, appointed as sole conciliator in *Tesoro v. Trinidad and Tobago*. He served as a Law Lord from 1964 to 1982, having previously been an English High Court Judge.

[14] *ALUSUISSE v. Iceland*, which was settled by the parties before the constitution of any tribunal.

[15] *Klöckner v. Cameroon* and *Amco v. Indonesia*.

following annulments of the original awards. The tribunals were all composed of a president and two other arbitrators. In almost all of the cases, the method for constituting the tribunal agreed by the parties, or applicable in default of such agreement under Article 37(2)(b) of the Convention, was that each party would appoint an arbitrator and agree on the appointment of the president of the tribunal. The parties failed, however, to agree on the appointment of a president in 12 of the 22 arbitration cases in which tribunals were established; in four of these cases, the respondent also failed to make its appointment of one of the other two arbitrators. In these cases, it fell to the Chairman of the Administrative Council to make the missing appointments from the Panel of Arbitrators pursuant to Articles 38 and 40 of the Convention.

From the beginning, this appointing authority function was in practice performed by the Chairman on the recommendation of the Secretary-General. Especially at the outset, appointments of the Chairman were made with an eye to promoting consistency among the cases. This notably was done in the *Alcoa v. Jamaica*, *Kaiser v. Jamaica* and *Reynolds v. Jamaica*. Separate proceedings in these cases were instituted simultaneously in 1974 in consequence of the same legislative measure of Jamaica.[16] It declined to participate in the proceedings. As a result, the Chairman was called upon in each case to appoint both a president and an arbitrator for Jamaica. The appointees of the Chairman were the same persons in all three cases.[17] The claimants likewise appointed the same individual to the respective tribunals.[18] Tribunals with identical compositions were thus established, avoiding duplication and the possibility of divergent decisions in these substantially similar cases. Uniformity of approach was fostered further by the Chairman's appointment, a few years later, of the President in the cases involving Jamaica to preside over the tribunals in *AGIP v. Congo* and *Benvenuti & Bonfant v. Congo*, as well.[19]

A total of 57 different individuals were appointed to tribunals in these first arbitrations under the ICSID Convention. Only a handful were non-lawyers. Most were either law professors or serving or retired judges in national or international courts. A few had backgrounds as government lawyers or other public officials. Just a dozen were primarily private legal practitioners. The majority were Western European; the largest groups among these were nationals of Britain, France and Switzerland. The arbitrators also included nationals of Australia, Canada, New Zealand and the United States. A small minority—only ten—were from developing countries.[20] Parties seldom

[16] For further details, *see* Ch. 7, section I(D).

[17] The appointee as President was Jørgen Trolle, who was shortly to retire after 21 years of service as a Member of the Supreme Court of Denmark, the last four years of which were as President of the Supreme Court. Fuad Rouhani was the Chairman's appointee as co-arbitrator. As explained in Ch. 7, n. 64 and accompanying text, the Chairman had immediately before designated Rouhani to the Panel of Arbitrators to make him eligible for appointment in these cases. Biographical information on Rouhani is provided in Ch. 5, n. 62.

[18] This was Elihu Lauterpacht, then Lecturer in Law (later Reader and eventually Honorary Professor) at the University of Cambridge. In 1975, Lauterpacht was appointed legal adviser to the Australian Department of Foreign Affairs and resigned from the tribunals in these cases. The claimants appointed as his successor Michael Kerr, an English High Court Judge.

[19] In the *AGIP* case, the Chairman also appointed Rouhani to the Tribunal.

[20] In the order of their first appointments as arbitrators, the ten were Fuad Rouhani (*see* Ch. 5, n. 62); Edilbert Razafindralambo, President of the Supreme Court of Madagascar; Eduardo Jiménez de Aréchaga, the Uruguayan former President of the ICJ; Kéba Mbaye, a past President of the Supreme Court of Senegal and Vice President of the ICJ; Mohamed Amin Elabassy El Mahdi, a member of the Supreme Administrative Court of Egypt; Kenneth O. Rattray, the longtime Solicitor General of Jamaica; Jorge Castañeda, a former Foreign Minister of Mexico; Marie-Madeleine Mborantsuo, a member of Gabon's Constitutional Court; Ahmed S. El-Kosheri, founding General Counsel of the

agreed to allow the appointment of "national arbitrators" to the tribunals.[21] None of the arbitrators in this period were appointed from among counsel to parties in ICSID Convention proceedings.[22] With three exceptions, the 57 individuals appointed as arbitrators were all men.[23]

During the 1970s and 1980s, three persons died while serving as ICSID arbitrators, and seven resigned, most of them because of ill health. Successor arbitrators were soon appointed, generally by the same method as their predecessors. In each instance, the proceeding then resumed from the point it had reached at the time of the death or resignation.[24] The resignations of party-appointed arbitrators were consented to by the other arbitrators as a matter of course in every case but the first, *Holiday Inns*. In that case, the Secretary-General notified the parties in July 1976 that the President of the Tribunal had learned from the arbitrator appointed by the claimants, John G. Foster, that he had been appointed a director of one of the claimants, Occidental Petroleum.[25] There were consultations by the President with both co-arbitrators and the Secretary-General, "leading to the conclusion that acceptance by an arbitrator of a post as a director of one of the parties that had designated him was wholly inconsistent with the letter and spirit of the Convention and could not be countenanced."[26] Foster submitted his resignation subject to the condition that the claimants appoint his successor.[27] The two other arbitrators decided in September 1976 that this condition "was not a proper one and should be disregarded." They further decided to withhold the consent required by Article 56 of the ICSID Convention.[28] In accordance with Article 56, the successor

Arab Fund for Economic and Social Development and previously with the Law Faculty at Ain Shams University; and Samuel K.B. Asante, a former Attorney General of Ghana.

[21] With the agreement of the parties under Art. 39 of the ICSID Convention, the Tribunal in *SETIMEG v. Gabon* and the initial Tribunal in *SOABI v. Senegal* each included as co-arbitrators a compatriot of the investor and a national of the host State. The claimant in the *SPP* case agreed to the appointment by the respondent State of a national as arbitrator (thus in effect waiving the provision of then Rule 1(3) of the Arbitration Rules, which would otherwise have precluded such an appointment). Unusually, in *Mobil v. New Zealand*, the parties agreed to the appointment of a national of the host State as President of the Tribunal. This was Graham Speight, a New Zealand High Court Judge.

[22] However, in *Klöckner v. Cameroon*, the arbitrator appointed by the claimants in the first arbitration proceeding, Dominique Schmidt, a Professor at Robert Schuman University, served as one of their counsel in the second arbitration proceeding.

[23] The exceptions were Maureen Brunt, Professor of Economics at Monash University, Rosalyn Higgins, Professor of International Law at the London School of Economics and later a member of the ICJ, and Marie-Madeleine Mborantsuo (*see* n. 20).

[24] Thus, in the few cases where the oral procedure had already commenced, the successor arbitrator did not insist on its recommencement under Arbitration Rule 12.

[25] ICSID Eleventh Ann. Rep. 1976/1977, 34. A barrister, Foster had also been a Member of Parliament in the U.K. since 1945.

[26] The quote is from Broches's report on the matter to the Administrative Council at its annual meeting shortly thereafter. Doc. AC/76/4, Tenth Annual Meeting: Summary Proceedings, October 7, 1976, Annex A, 3.

[27] ICSID Eleventh Ann. Rep. 1976/1977, 34. The journalist Edward Jay Epstein described Foster as advising the Chairman and Chief Executive Officer of Occidental Petroleum, Armand Hammer, before Foster became a director of the company. *See* E. Epstein, *Dossier: The Secret History of Armand Hammer* 251 (1996) (referring to "Sir John Foster … one of England's shrewdest queen's counsels … who advised Hammer on his Middle East ventures … and subsequently served on the board of directors of Occidental"). If Epstein was correct, such advisory activities of Foster could in themselves have thrown doubt on the propriety of his appointment as arbitrator.

[28] ICSID Eleventh Ann. Rep. 1976/1977, 34. The two other arbitrators were Sture Petrén and Paul Reuter. The President of the Tribunal, Petrén was a member of the ICJ and a former President of the Svea Court of Appeal. He died soon after the decisions described in the text and was replaced as President of the Tribunal by Gunnar Lagergren, President of the Court of Appeal for Western Sweden. Reuter, a Professor of the University of Law, Economics and Social Sciences of Paris, had been a member of the ILC since 1964.

arbitrator was therefore appointed not by the claimants but by the Chairman of the Administrative Council, in October 1976.[29] In his remarks at the annual meeting of the Administrative Council that same month, Broches observed that "all Contracting States have a vital interest in the maintenance of the integrity of arbitral proceedings under the Convention, and I trust that they will agree that the actions of the Tribunal and the Centre have served that end."[30]

Also of obvious importance for the maintenance of the integrity of proceedings under the ICSID Convention were the provisions of Articles 57 and 58 of the Convention on the possible disqualification of conciliators and arbitrators. These provisions were first applied in June 1982 in *Amco v. Indonesia*. The request for arbitration in that case was registered in February 1981. The three arbitrators were appointed over a year later, in March 1982. Edward C. Rubin, a Hong Kong-based Canadian lawyer, was the arbitrator appointed by the claimants.[31] In his statement of independence made pursuant to ICSID Arbitration Rule 6 in April 1982, Rubin disclosed that he had provided some advice on Canadian tax matters to T.K. Tan, who was an officer and shareholder of the claimant companies. Rubin also disclosed in his statement of independence that his law firm had had a joint office and profit-sharing arrangement in the period 1972 to 1975 with the law firm representing the claimants in the arbitration. At the first session of the Tribunal in June 1982, the respondent invoked these facts to propose, pursuant to Article 57 of the ICSID Convention, the disqualification of Rubin as manifestly lacking the reliability for independent judgment required by Article 14(1) of the Convention.

Two days later, the Tribunal heard oral arguments of the parties on the disqualification proposal and, as provided for in Arbitration Rule 9, received explanations from Rubin. The tax advice, he explained, had been on a minor question, needing only a 15-minute consultation and a follow-up letter of not more than two pages. The advice had been sought and provided for modest fees in June or July 1981—that is, after registration of the request for arbitration—but Rubin was then completely unaware of the case. Neither he nor his firm had since rendered any counsel or advice to Tan or any of his companies. As for the profit-sharing arrangement with the law firm of counsel for the claimants, this had ended in late 1975; all subsequent dealings between the two firms had been on a purely arm's-length basis.

The decision on the proposal, taken by the two other arbitrators[32] under Article 58 of the Convention, was issued the following day. It set forth several important general observations. The first was that the Convention demanded "absolute impartiality" of all arbitrators; there was no lower standard for party-appointed arbitrators.[33] Another general observation was that, in insisting that the arbitrator be a person "who may be relied upon to exercise independent judgment," the Convention was not laying down an abstract standard so much as aiming "to exclude a person whose particular

[29] The appointee was Jan C. Schultsz, Professor at Erasmus University.

[30] Tenth Annual Meeting: Summary Proceedings (n. 26) Annex A, 3.

[31] Many years later, Rubin served as Vice Chairman and Board Member of the Hong Kong International Arbitration Centre. The following account of the proposal for his disqualification in the *Amco* case is taken from the decision on the proposal of the two other arbitrators. *See Amco v. Indonesia*, Decision on Proposal to Disqualify an Arbitrator, June 24, 1982, reprinted in M.W. Reisman and others, *International Commercial Arbitration* 624 (1997).

[32] These were Berthold Goldman, the President of the Tribunal, and Isi Foighel. Goldman was Professor at the University of Law, Economics and Social Sciences of Paris. Foighel, a Professor of Jurisprudence at the University of Copenhagen, became Minister of Taxation of Denmark soon after his appointment to the *Amco* Tribunal.

[33] *Amco v. Indonesia*, Decision on the Proposal to Disqualify an Arbitrator (n. 31) sec. III, para. 2.

situation in a given case could create a risk of lack of absolute impartiality."[34] This did not, however, preclude "the appointment as an arbitrator of a person who had, before his appointment, some relationship with a party. Such relations would be a reason of non-appointment ... [or] disqualification ... only where they appear as creating a risk of inability to exercise independent judgment."[35]

While interpreting the Convention to require utter impartiality of all arbitrators, the decision saw the Convention as paradoxically stringent in regard to proposals to disqualify them. Thus, the decision pointed out that under Article 57 a disqualification proposal had to be based on a "fact" indicating a "manifest" lack of reliability for independent judgment. According to the decision, this meant, on the one hand, that "the mere feeling of 'non-reliability' does not suffice" and, on the other hand, that the facts had "to indicate not a possible lack of the quality, but a quasicertain, or to go as far as possible, a highly probable one."[36]

In light of these considerations, the decision proceeded to deny the disqualification proposal. The "legal advice on a minor question which could not have been anything but minor, as the fees received show," had "no bear[ing] on the 'reliability' of the adviser to be an arbitrator appointed by the client to whom he had given this advice" as it did not create "the situation of a *regular* counsel of the appointing party."[37] Nor could such significance be given to "relationships between the law firm of the appointed arbitrator and the counsel for said party, that ceased around six years before the appointment was made."[38] In short, the "facts [did] not indicate a manifest lack of reliability" on Rubin's part or even, the decision added, "a reasonable feeling of non-reliability."[39]

III. Approaches to jurisdiction

Arbitral tribunals of the period were notably pragmatic in addressing jurisdictional issues, taking broad, even generous, approaches to the basic requirement of consent in particular. This was so from the very first ICSID Convention arbitration proceeding, *Holiday Inns v. Morocco.* It was instituted on behalf of eight claimants: the American companies Holiday Inns and Occidental Petroleum; a Swiss subsidiary of Holiday Inns and a U.S. subsidiary of Occidental Petroleum; and four Moroccan subsidiaries of Holiday Inns. They invoked in their request for arbitration the consent to the jurisdiction of the Centre recorded in the arbitration clause of a so-called basic agreement for the construction and operation of Holiday Inns hotels in Casablanca, Fez, Marrakech and Tangier. The signatories of the basic agreement were Morocco, represented for the purpose by its Minister of Finance, on the one hand, and on the other, the Swiss subsidiary of Holiday Inns and what became the U.S. subsidiary of Occidental Petroleum. The basic agreement was signed in December 1966. At the same time, the parent companies, Holiday Inns and Occidental Petroleum, provided a letter of guarantee to Morocco warranting the execution of the basic agreement and further agreements of their subsidiaries for the hotels project.

Nevertheless, in the arbitration, Morocco objected that, as the parent companies were not named as parties to the basic agreement they were not entitled to rely on its arbitration clause. The Tribunal disagreed, holding that the consent did extend to the parent companies, given their guarantee of performance of the basic agreement

[34] Ibid. sec. III, para. 3(a). [35] Ibid. sec. III, para. 3(b). [36] Ibid. sec. III, para. 4.
[37] Ibid. sec. III, para. 5 (emphasis in original). [38] Ibid.
[39] Ibid. sec. III, para. 6.

and further agreements and the fact that they had themselves participated in meeting obligations under the basic agreement. For the Tribunal, this was "perfectly in keeping with the spirit of the Basic Agreement which obviously wanted to give the contracting companies a great amount of flexibility in the designation of the companies which would assume responsibility."[40]

Jurisdiction in respect of a parent company was upheld in similar fashion in the first arbitration proceeding in *Amco v. Indonesia*. The claimants in that case included Amco Asia, an American company, which in April 1968 entered into an agreement with PT Wisma, an Indonesian company owned by a cooperative established for the welfare of Indonesian army personnel, for the development of a hotel and office block on land of PT Wisma in Jakarta. The following month, Amco Asia applied to Indonesia for permission to establish an Indonesian company, PT Amco, to implement the investment project. The application, approved by Indonesia in July 1968, contained an arbitration clause providing for the submission to ICSID of any dispute between Indonesia and PT Amco. The latter was established at the beginning of 1969. A decade later, disagreements arose between PT Wisma and PT Amco over their respective shares in profits from the operation. With the assistance of Indonesian army and police personnel, PT Wisma took over the hotel after sums claimed by it were not paid in full. It also reported to the responsible Indonesian authorities alleged failures by PT Amco to meet its investment obligations. The result was the revocation of PT Amco's investment authorization. PT Amco then joined the parent company, Amco Asia, in instituting the arbitration proceeding on the strength of the clause in the 1968 application.

In the proceeding, Indonesia objected that, as the clause did not name Amco Asia as a party, it could not be interpreted as consent to the jurisdiction of the Centre over any claim of the parent company against Indonesia. The latter urged in this respect that the consent given by a State to an arbitration agreement amounting to a limitation of its sovereignty was to be construed restrictively.[41] The Tribunal dismissed the objection. It read the clause as extending necessarily to the benefit of the parent company: "the goal of the clause was to protect the investor," Amco Asia, PT Amco being "but an instrumentality" through which it would realize the investment.[42] The Tribunal observed in this connection, in words that would often be quoted in later cases, that an arbitration agreement:

> ... is not to be construed *restrictively*, nor as a matter of fact, *broadly* or *liberally*. It is to be construed in a way which leads to find out and to respect the common will of the parties: such a method of interpretation is but the application of the fundamental principle *pacta sunt servanda*, a principle common, indeed, to all systems of internal law and to international law.[43]

The Tribunal added that:

> While a consent in writing to ICSID arbitration is indispensable, since it is required by Article 25(1) of the Convention, such consent in writing is not to be expressed in a solemn, ritual and unique formulation. The investment agreement being in writing, it suffices to establish that its interpretation in good faith shows that the parties agreed to ICSID arbitration, in order for the ICSID Tribunal to have jurisdiction over them.[44]

[40] *Holiday Inns v. Morocco*, Decision on Jurisdiction, July 1, 1973, quoted in P. Lalive, The First "World Bank" Arbitration (*Holiday Inns v. Morocco*)—Some Legal Problems, reprinted in 1 ICSID Rep. 645, 672 (1993).

[41] *Amco v. Indonesia*, Decision on Jurisdiction, September 25, 1983, 1 ICSID Rep. 389, 393.

[42] Ibid. 400. [43] Ibid. 394 (emphasis in original). [44] Ibid. 400.

The first *Amco* Tribunal also showed little patience for formalism in dealing with a further argument of Indonesia against participation in the proceeding by PT Amco. The argument was that, although it was foreign-controlled, there was no express agreement between the parties to treat the local company as a national of another Contracting State.[45] Noting that the application to establish PT Amco referred to it as a "foreign business" with "foreign capital," the Tribunal trenchantly concluded that:

> … when agreeing to the Application, the Indonesian Government knew perfectly that PT Amco would be under foreign control. Knowing this expressly stated fact, the Government has agreed to the Application *and* to the arbitration clause in it: therefore, it is crystal clear that it agreed to treat PT Amco as a national of another Contracting State, for the purpose of the Convention … this agreement is … clearly expressed, no formal or ritual clause being provided for in the Convention, nor needed in order for such an agreement to be binding on the parties.[46]

Three years later, the Tribunal in *LETCO v. Liberia* answered essentially the same question in similar terms. The claimant in that case was incorporated in Liberia and hence had its nationality. It was, however, wholly owned and effectively controlled by foreign (French) nationals. The Tribunal noted that, to exercise jurisdiction, it had to determine that, in accordance with Article 25(2)(b) of the Convention, Liberia had agreed because of this control to treat LETCO as a national of another Contracting State—France in this instance. The ICSID clause in the underlying forestry concession agreement between the parties was silent on the matter. After satisfying itself that an agreement to treat LETCO as a foreign national could only have resulted from the fact that it was under French control, the Tribunal observed in its award that:

> … it could be argued with some force that the mere fact that Liberia and LETCO included an ICSID arbitration clause in the Concession Agreement constitutes an agreement to treat LETCO as a "national of another Contracting State." To conclude otherwise would be tantamount to stating that Liberia never intended to honour this part of the Concession Agreement; that Liberia by agreeing to the ICSID clause, acted in bad faith and contrary to the tenor and purpose of the ICSID Convention.
>
> When a Contracting State signs an investment agreement, containing an ICSID arbitration clause, with a foreign controlled juridical person with the same nationality as the Contracting State and it does so with the knowledge that it will only be subject to ICSID jurisdiction if it has agreed to treat that company as a juridical person of another Contracting State, the Contracting State could be deemed to have agreed to such treatment by having agreed to the ICSID arbitration clause.[47]

Further examples of this flexible approach to jurisdictional issues may be drawn from the *Holiday Inns* case. As already mentioned, one of the claimants there was the Swiss subsidiary of Holiday Inns that had, in December 1966, signed the basic agreement containing the consent clause. In the arbitration, Morocco objected that the subsidiary had not been, as required by Article 25(2)(b) of the Convention, "a national of another Contracting State" on the date of the consent. It was then only in the process of being formed; moreover, Switzerland was not then a Contracting State, and nor indeed was Morocco. The *Holiday Inns* Tribunal rejected the objection, taking the view that the Convention allowed parties to subordinate the entry into force of a consent

[45] On this point, Indonesia cited the ruling of the *Holiday Inns* Tribunal a decade earlier that an agreement to treat a locally incorporated company as a national of another Contracting State under Art. 25(2)(b) of the ICSID Convention should normally be express. *See* Lalive (n. 40) 663.

[46] *Amco*, Decision on Jurisdiction (n. 41) 395 (emphasis in original).

[47] *LETCO v. Liberia*, Award, March 31, 1986, 2 ICSID Rep. 346, 352.

agreement to the subsequent fulfillment of certain conditions, such as the adherence of the States concerned to the Convention, or the incorporation of a company covered by the agreement. The Swiss subsidiary of Holiday Inns was constituted in 1967 and Switzerland became a Contracting State the following year, by which time Morocco too was a Contracting State. It was on the date of the fulfillment of the last of those conditions, when Switzerland became a Contracting State, that the parties had "consented to submit [the] dispute to … arbitration" within the meaning of Article 25(2)(b).[48]

The Tribunal in *Holiday Inns* also propounded what has come to be called "the doctrine of the general unity of the investment operation."[49] Under the Basic Agreement in that case, Morocco had to provide financing for the construction of the hotels. This was done by loan contracts with the local subsidiaries of Holiday Inns. In the arbitration, Morocco argued that the Tribunal could not entertain claims relating to those contracts as they had forum selection clauses in favor of Moroccan courts. The Tribunal held otherwise. Invoking the "general unity of the investment operation" as one of several "general principles which have inspired the [ICSID] Convention," the Tribunal said:

> … investment is accomplished by a number of juridical acts of all sorts. It would not be consonant either with economic reality or with the intention of the parties to consider each of these acts in complete isolation from the others. It is particularly important to ascertain which is the act which is the basis of the investment and which entails as measures of execution the other acts which have been concluded in order to carry it out.[50]

The act which was "the basis of the investment" was, of course, the basic agreement containing the consent to the jurisdiction of the Centre.

As mentioned earlier, in *Amco v. Indonesia*, the consent of the parties to the jurisdiction of the Centre was recorded in Amco Asia's application for the establishment for PT Amco and the approval of the application by Indonesia. In all but two of the other 24 cases initiated through the end of 1988, claimants invoked consents set forth in dispute settlement clauses of the underlying investment agreements of the parties. The two exceptions were *SPP v. Egypt* and *AAPL v. Sri Lanka*, the first cases in which ICSID jurisdiction was upheld on the basis of an advance general consent in an investment law or treaty of the State concerned.[51]

The *SPP* case concerned an agreement that SPP, a Hong Kong company, concluded in 1974 with the Egyptian General Organization for Tourism and Hotels (EGOTH) for the development of tourist complexes at the Pyramids Oasis site near Cairo and at Ras El Hakma on the Mediterranean coast. By its terms, the agreement was made in accordance with the 1974 investment law of Egypt mentioned in Chapter 7.[52] The agreement contained an arbitration clause providing for the settlement of related disputes by International Chamber of Commerce (ICC) arbitration. In addition to being signed by representatives of EGOTH and SPP, the agreement was signed by the Minister of Tourism of Egypt next to the words "approved, agreed and ratified." After

[48] *See* Lalive (n. 40) 667–668.
[49] C.H. Schreuer and others, *The ICSID Convention: A Commentary* 111 (2d ed. 2009).
[50] *Holiday Inns v. Morocco*, Decision, May 12, 1974, quoted in Lalive (n. 40) 680.
[51] In a third case of the period, *Pharaon v. Tunisia*, the claimant relied for the State's consent both on a contractual arbitration clause and on a provision of an investment law. The case was, however, settled before the Tribunal could rule on its jurisdiction. *Cf.* J. Paulsson, Arbitration without Privity, 10 ICSID Rev.—FILJ 232, 235 (1995).
[52] *See* Ch. 7, n. 92 and accompanying text.

construction began at the Pyramids site in 1977, the project was called into question in the Egyptian People's Assembly as posing a threat to undiscovered antiquities. Approvals necessary for the implementation of the project were withdrawn by Egypt the following year. SPP and the Hong Kong subsidiary it had created for the project then instituted an ICC arbitration proceeding against Egypt and EGOTH, claiming damages for breach of the 1974 agreement.

The ICC proceeding resulted in 1983 in an award rendered in France in favor of the claimants. The award was, however, set aside by the Court of Appeal of Paris on the ground that Egypt was not bound by the arbitration clause in the 1974 agreement, its signature by the Minister of Tourism merely signifying his approval as supervisory authority of EGOTH.[53] Relying on Article 8 of the 1974 investment law, SPP promptly instituted an arbitration proceeding against Egypt under the ICSID Convention. According to the English translation used in that proceeding, Article 8 of the 1974 law stipulated that:

> Investment disputes in respect of the implementation of the provisions of this Law shall be settled in a manner to be agreed upon with the investor, or within the framework of the agreements in force between the Arab Republic of Egypt and the investor's home country, or within the framework of the Convention for the Settlement of Investment Disputes between the State and the nationals of other countries to which Egypt has adhered by virtue of Law No. 90 of 1971, where such Convention applies.[54]

In the ICSID arbitration, Egypt objected that, as it entailed a waiver of sovereign immunity, consent to ICSID jurisdiction had to be clear and unequivocal. Article 8 of the law contained no language expressly consenting to such jurisdiction and instead simply listed possible methods of dispute settlement that could be negotiated with the investor on a case-by-case basis. Egypt argued in this respect that, in the original Arabic of Article 8 of the law, the words translated as "shall be settled" were less imperative and that, by restricting the availability of ICSID Convention procedures to cases "where such Convention applies," Article 8 implicitly required a further expression of consent to establish the Centre's jurisdiction.

The ICSID Tribunal constituted in the case[55] addressed the arguments in careful detail but found them unconvincing. It explained that:

> ... there is no presumption of jurisdiction—particularly where a sovereign State is involved—and the Tribunal must examine Egypt's objections to the jurisdiction of the Centre with meticulous care, bearing in mind that jurisdiction in the present case exists only insofar as consent thereto has been given by the Parties. This is not to say, however, that there is a presumption against the conferment of jurisdiction with respect to a sovereign State or that instruments

[53] *Egypt v. SPP*, Court of Appeal of Paris, Decision of July 12, 1984, 3 ICSID Rep. 81, 88 (1995). This decision was confirmed by the Court of Cassation, Decision of January 6, 1987, 3 ICSID Rep. 96 (1995).

[54] Translation quoted in *SPP v. Egypt*, Decision on Jurisdiction (n. 5) 126.

[55] The members of the Tribunal were Eduardo Jiménez de Aréchaga, appointed President by agreement of the parties; Mohamed El Mahdi, the arbitrator appointed by Egypt; and Robert F. Pietrowski, the arbitrator appointed by the claimants. On Jiménez de Aréchaga and El Mahdi, *see* n. 20. An American, Pietrowski was a partner with the St. Louis law firm Bryan Cave. In the *SPP* case, the claimants waived their right to object to the appointment of El Mahdi on the ground of his Egyptian nationality. *See SPP v. Egypt*, Award, May 20, 1992, 3 ICSID Rep. 189, 190 (1995). Nor was any issue raised over El Mahdi's employment relationship with Egypt (as a member of its Supreme Administrative Court). In the arbitration, El Mahdi appended dissenting opinions to the 1988 jurisdictional decision (n. 56) and the 1992 award.

purporting to confer jurisdiction should be interpreted restrictively. Judicial and arbitral bodies have repeatedly pronounced in favour of their own competence where the force of the arguments militating in favor of jurisdiction is preponderant.[56]

Echoing the earlier decision of the first *Amco* Tribunal, the *SPP* Tribunal added that jurisdictional instruments were therefore "to be interpreted neither restrictively nor expansively, but rather objectively and in good faith, and jurisdiction will be found to exist if—but only if—the force of the arguments militating in favor of it is preponderant."[57] The *SPP* Tribunal proceeded to hold that Article 8 of the law "establishes mandatory and hierarchic sequence of dispute settlement procedures, and constitutes an express 'consent in writing' to the Centre's jurisdiction within the meaning of Article 25(1)" of the ICSID Convention.[58] The Tribunal pointed out in this respect that the verb in Article 8 of the law that had been translated as "shall be settled" could only be understood as having mandatory effect if, as suggested by Egypt, it would more accurately be rendered in English as "are to be settled." As to the "hierarchic sequence" of procedures in Article 8, the Tribunal noted that the first two options were unavailable in the instant case: the parties had not agreed on a means of dispute settlement and there was then no applicable bilateral treaty.[59] Egypt's argument regarding the words "where it applies" would result in subsuming the third, ICSID Convention, option in the first option of a specifically agreed means of dispute settlement. "No valid method of legal interpretation," the Tribunal said with more than a hint of exasperation, "would warrant the conclusion that the express reference to the Convention in Article 8 is meaningless or pleonastic."[60]

AAPL v. Sri Lanka was, as the Tribunal in that case remarked, the first instance in which ICSID was "seized by an arbitration request exclusively based on a treaty provision and not in implementation of a freely negotiated arbitration agreement directly concluded between the Parties."[61] The investor in that case, AAPL, was the principal foreign shareholder in a joint venture, Serendib Seafoods, approved by the Sri Lankan Ministry of Finance in 1983 to cultivate and export shrimps. Local participants in the venture included the National Development Bank and the Export Development Board of Sri Lanka. Serendib's main production facility was its shrimp farm near Batticaloa in eastern Sri Lanka. Toward the end of 1986, the area came under the control of Tamil Tiger rebels. Government security forces carried out a counter-insurgency operation there in early 1987. It resulted in the destruction of the farm and the death of more than 20 of its staff. AAPL claimed compensation from Sri Lanka; when this was not forthcoming, the company submitted to ICSID its request for arbitration under the Convention.

As a company incorporated in Hong Kong, AAPL qualified as a U.K. national under Article 70 of the ICSID Convention. AAPL was also covered, as "a company of a Contracting Party," by the 1980 BIT between Sri Lanka and the United Kingdom,

56 *SPP v. Egypt*, Decision on Jurisdiction, April 14, 1988, 3 ICSID Rep. 131, 143 (1999).

57 Ibid. 144. 58 Ibid. 161.

59 There was a 1974 Egypt–U.K. BIT, which contained an ICSID clause, but it had not been extended to SPP's place of incorporation, the then U.K. colony of Hong Kong.

60 *SPP v. Egypt*, Decision on Jurisdiction (n. 56) 153.

61 *AAPL v. Sri Lanka*, Award, June 27, 1990, 4 ICSID Rep. 250, 256 (1997). The Tribunal comprised Ahmed S. El-Kosheri, appointed President by the Chairman of the Administrative Council; Berthold Goldman, the arbitrator appointed by AAPL; and Samuel K.B. Asante, the arbitrator appointed by Sri Lanka. On El-Kosheri and Asante, *see* n. 20; on Goldman, *see* n. 32.

The Tribunal in *SPP v. Egypt*, the first "arbitration without privity." Seated are the President of the Tribunal, Eduardo Jiménez de Aréchaga (right) and Robert F. Pietrowski. Standing are Mohamed El Mahdi (left) and the Secretary of the Tribunal, Nassib G. Ziadé.
Courtesy of Nassib G. Ziadé

the BIT having been extended to Hong Kong in 1981. As such, AAPL invoked in its request the consent to the jurisdiction of the Centre in the BIT:

Each Contracting party hereby consents to submit to the International Centre for the Settlement of Investment Disputes (hereinafter referred to as "the Centre") for settlement by conciliation or arbitration under the Convention on the Settlement of Investment Disputes between States and Nationals of Other States opened for signature at Washington on 18 March 1965 any legal disputes arising between that Contracting Party and a national or company of the other Contracting Party concerning an investment of the latter in the territory of the former.[62]

The clarity of the consent helps to explain the speed with which the request was registered (hardly more than ten days after its receipt) and the absence, during the proceeding, of objections to jurisdiction. The proceeding ended in 1990 with an award modestly in favor of the claimant.[63] Sooner than most, the President of the Tribunal in this very first BIT arbitration, Ahmed S. El-Kosheri, saw the potential that such treaties held for ICSID. He addressed the subject in a paper presented at a conference in 1991, a year after the conclusion of the *AAPL* case. In it, El-Kosheri predicted that:

… [in view of the many other BITs with] references to the ICSID system, it seems that recourse to BIT provisions might in the future become the main channel through which ICSID could

[62] Agreement for the Promotion and Protection of Investments, Sri Lanka–United Kingdom, February 13, 1980, reprinted in ICSID, Investment Treaties, Release 94-2 (May 1994), Art. 8(1) (Sri Lanka–U.K. BIT).

[63] *See AAPL v. Sri Lanka*, Award (n. 61) 295 (awarding the claimant compensation of less than US$0.5 million for loss of the investment enterprise's net tangible assets, goodwill and future earnings having been excluded from the calculation of damages as they could not be established with sufficient certainty).

be seized. This in turn might lead to rapid growth in the number of cases submitted to arbitral tribunals established under the system.[64]

IV. Provisional measures

In the first half of the 1980s, opinion (including judicial opinion) was divided on the question whether parties in ICSID Convention arbitrations could seek, from courts in Contracting States, provisional measures such as prejudgment attachments. This section examines the controversy, which was led on one side by the ICSID Secretariat. Also discussed in this section are the first instances of arbitral tribunals issuing provisional or interim measures under Article 47 of the Convention.

The controversy stemmed in part from national court proceedings in the case of *MINE v. Guinea*, even though those proceedings were not aimed at obtaining provisional measures. In 1971, the Swiss Inter Maritime Bank,[65] acting on behalf of MINE, a Liechtenstein company, concluded an agreement with Guinea to form a venture for the shipment of bauxite mined in that country. However, disputes soon arose between the parties concerning the alleged failure by Guinea to take measures required to make the venture viable and Guinea's conclusion of a bauxite shipping agreement with a competing company. In 1975, the parties signed a supplemental agreement consenting to submit these disputes to arbitration under the ICSID Convention. Claiming that the supplemental agreement was nevertheless insufficient to enable it to institute an ICSID Convention proceeding—apparently in part because Liechtenstein was not a Contracting State—MINE petitioned the U.S. District Court for the District of Columbia in 1978 to compel arbitration in accordance with the Federal Arbitration Act. The court granted the petition and ordered arbitration under the auspices of the American Arbitration Association (AAA).[66]

The ensuing AAA arbitration, in which Guinea declined to participate, resulted in an award in favor of MINE. The latter then obtained an order from the District Court confirming the award. Guinea appealed from the order to the Court of Appeals for the District of Columbia. The Court of Appeals was urged, in a brief submitted by the U.S. State Department, to reverse the confirmation order in view of the provision of Article 26 of the ICSID Convention, according to which consent to arbitration under the Convention was, unless otherwise stated, deemed consent to such arbitration to the exclusion of any other remedy. This was said to obligate courts in Contracting States, in the presence of a consent agreement such as had been concluded between MINE and Guinea, to refrain from involvement in a case until called upon to recognize and enforce the eventual ICSID award.[67] The Court of Appeals decided in 1982 to reverse the District Court order but on the different ground that, under the Foreign Sovereign

[64] A. El-Kosheri, ICSID Arbitration and Developing Countries, a paper presented at the Joint Colloquium on International Arbitration, Washington, D.C., November 11, 1991, reprinted in 8 ICSID Rev.—FILJ 104, 107 (1993).

[65] Inter Maritime Bank was partly owned by Bruce Rappaport, who emigrated to Switzerland from Haifa in the 1950s. His far-flung interests, in oil as well as shipping and banking, apparently included ownership of MINE as well. A brief profile is provided in S. Greenhouse, A Secret Emperor of Oil and Shipping, *New York Times*, February 4, 1988, A-6.

[66] *See MINE v. Guinea*, U.S. District Court, District of Columbia, Judgment, January 12, 1981, 4 ICSID Rep. 4 (1997) (extracts).

[67] *See MINE v. Guinea*, U.S. Court of Appeals, D.C. Circuit, Judgment, November 12, 1982, 4 ICSID Rep. 9, 19 (1997).

Immunities Act, the District Court lacked jurisdiction to confirm the AAA award.[68] Two years later, MINE submitted its claim to ICSID Convention arbitration.[69]

In the meantime, the ICSID Secretariat had taken up the call for courts in Contracting States to observe the "rule of judicial abstention" said to be implicit in Article 26 of the ICSID Convention. This was done to great effect in articles by the Centre's Senior Legal Adviser, Georges R. Delaume, commenting on the U.S. court litigation in the *MINE* case. In them, he argued, with his usual eloquence, that the courts had to respect the exclusive nature of the ICSID arbitral remedy; it was, he pointed out, an important part of the "careful balance between the interests of investors and Contracting States" drawn by the ICSID Convention that its Article 26 in effect protected the States "from other forms of foreign or international litigation."[70] The argument was specifically extended to court-ordered provisional measures. A brochure on ICSID published by the Secretariat in 1982 explained that, "[u]nless the parties otherwise agree, consent to submit disputes to ICSID arbitration is exclusive of any other remedy. The parties, therefore, cannot ask local legal or judicial authorities to take provisional measures."[71] This statement in the brochure was cited by the Court of Appeal of Rennes in its 1984 decision vacating conservatory attachments obtained by the claimant in *Atlantic Triton v. Guinea.*

That case arose from a management agreement concluded in 1981 by Atlantic Triton, a Norwegian company, with Guinea for the conversion, equipping and operation of three fishing vessels. The agreement, made in the context of a project to develop and exploit fishery resources in Guinean waters, provided for the settlement of disputes between the parties by arbitration under the ICSID Convention. The conversion work went over budget, however; and after their delivery at the end of 1981, the vessels turned out to need a general overhaul to operate successfully in the region. Guinea refused fully to repay Atlantic Triton for the cost overrun on the conversion work, and the parties failed to agree on steps to correct the vessels' shortcomings. Finally, in April 1983, Atlantic Triton rescinded the management agreement and demanded payment for the balance of the cost overrun and administrative expenses. At the beginning of the following year, Atlantic Triton submitted its claim to ICSID.

In the meantime, the company had obtained, from the President of the Commercial Court of Quimper, an order for the conservatory attachment of the three vessels, by then undergoing repairs at a shipyard in nearby Concarneau. The attachments were effected, Guinea applied unsuccessfully to the Commercial Court to have them vacated and then appealed to the Court of Appeal at Rennes. In its decision of October 1984, the Court of Appeal quoted Article 26 of the ICSID Convention as well as the provision of Article 47 according to which an arbitral tribunal might recommend

[68] *See* ibid. 31.

[69] The Secretary-General of ICSID registered MINE's request for arbitration "without prejudice to the question whether the condition of nationality is satisfied." *See* 2(1) News from ICSID 3 (1985). *See also* n. 5. The issue of the nationality of MINE seems to have been resolved at the outset of the arbitration proceeding in favor of jurisdiction based on the Swiss nationality of MINE's controlling shareholder. *See MINE v. Guinea,* ad hoc Committee Decision, December 22, 1989, 4 ICSID Rep. 79, 80, note 1 (1997).

[70] G.R. Delaume, ICSID and the Courts, 1(1) News from ICSID 6, 7 (1984). *See also* G.R. Delaume, ICSID Arbitration and the Courts, 77 AJIL 784 (1983).

[71] Doc. ICSID/12, ICSID: An International Institution Dealing Exclusively with the Settlement of Investment Disputes between States and Foreign Investors 11. *Cf.* G.R. Delaume, ICSID and the Courts, 2(2) News from ICSID 6 (1985) (stating that "the exclusive character of consent to ICSID arbitration implies that the parties waive their right to seek provisional measures in any forum other than an ICSID forum").

provisional measures.[72] It then referred to the above-mentioned statement in "[t]he guide to the activities of ICSID, drawn up by that body."[73] The Court of Appeal concluded that it was the "clear purpose and spirit of the Convention ... that the arbitral tribunal has the general and exclusive power to rule not only on the merits of the dispute but also on all provisional measures."[74] The appeal was therefore allowed and the attachments vacated.

The decision of the Court of Appeal of Rennes was hailed in *News from ICSID* as "a clear application of the rule of abstention" implied by Article 26 of the Convention.[75] Some, however, criticized the decision as reading too much into Article 26, which it was argued was not meant to preclude the possibility of conservatory measures to guarantee performance of the eventual arbitral award.[76] The Court of Cassation of France agreed, in a 1986 decision setting aside the ruling of the Court of Appeal. In its decision, the Court of Cassation found that:

> ... the Court of Appeal misapplied Article 26 of the Convention because the power of the national judge to order conservatory measures is not excluded by the Convention of Washington and can only be excluded by the express agreement of the parties or by a tacit agreement arising from the adoption of arbitration rules including such a renunciation.[77]

By the time of the decision of the Court of Cassation, the Arbitration Rules of ICSID had been amended to incorporate just "such a renunciation." Amendments approved by the Administrative Council of the Centre in September 1984 included the addition of a new fifth paragraph to the rule on provisional measures, Arbitration Rule 39, making it clear that, unless the parties had agreed otherwise, they could not seek court-ordered provisional measures prior to or after the institution of the arbitration proceeding.[78] In proposing the new paragraph to the Administrative Council in April 1984, the Secretariat explained it as merely a "precision" reflecting the position that had been advanced by the Secretariat on the exclusivity of the arbitral remedy under Article 26 of the Convention.[79] The approval of the new paragraph could be viewed as

[72] *See Guinea v. Atlantic Triton*, Court of Appeal of Rennes, Judgment, October 26, 1984, 3 ICSID Rep. 4, 8 (1995).

[73] Ibid. [74] Ibid. [75] Delaume (n. 71).

[76] *See* E. Gaillard, Note, 112 Journal du droit international 941 (1985). Aron Broches later also criticized the view of Art. 26 as preempting such measures as being "at variance with the almost universal recognition in the area of commercial arbitration that to seek measures from a court and for a court to grant them is not inconsistent with an arbitration agreement (as most recently and clearly expressed in Article 9 of the 1985 UNCITRAL Model Law on International Commercial Arbitration)." A. Broches, A Guide for Users of the ICSID Convention, 8(1) News from ICSID 5, 9 (1991).

[77] *Guinea v. Atlantic Triton*, Court of Cassation, France, Judgment, November 18, 1986, 3 ICSID Rep. 10, 11 (1995).

[78] *See* ICSID Arbitration Rules, as amended, September 26, 1984, reprinted in Doc. ICSID/15, ICSID Basic Documents (January 1985), Rule 39(5).

[79] The explanation, in full, was that "[p]roposed Rule 39(5) is intended to impart an additional precision into the Rule" and, in a note accompanying the paragraph, that:

> Article 26 of the Convention provides that, unless the parties otherwise agree, consent to arbitration is exclusive of any other remedy. This basic feature of the Convention would prevent the parties from seeking provisional measures other than those referred to in Rule 39 [i.e., other than provisional measures recommended by the arbitral tribunal under Article 47 of the Convention]. In order to retain the option of seeking provisional measures, including attachment, in domestic courts, the parties must do so by way of express provisions to that effect. Provisions of this kind are found in arbitration clauses filed with the Secretariat. It seems, therefore, appropriate to mention this type of situation in Rule 39.

Proposed Revision of ICSID Regulations and Rules, Note from the Secretary-General, April 30, 1984, 2 and Note on Addition to Arbitration Rule 39. The explanation was repeated when the amendments

an endorsement by the Administrative Council of the Secretariat's underlying interpretation of Article 26. But whether the interpretation was correct or not hardly mattered any longer. For cases governed by the amended Arbitration Rules, there could be no doubt that court-ordered provisional measures would be unavailable in the absence of contrary agreement of the parties. In that sense, the rule change put an end to the debate over the question.[80]

Among the cases discussed in this chapter, there were just three published instances of arbitral tribunals issuing provisional measures under Article 47 of the Convention. These were in *Holiday Inns v. Morocco*, *MINE v. Guinea* and *AGIP v. Congo*. The *Holiday Inns* case provided a first illustration of an ICSID tribunal affirming its power to recommend provisional measures before it had definitively ruled on its jurisdiction over the dispute. Because of alleged failures of Morocco to make required payments and meet other contractual obligations to them, the claimants ceased construction on two of the hotels in 1971 and threatened closure of the two other, by then completed, hotels. Following the institution of the arbitration proceeding, Morocco obtained from its courts orders for the completion of works on the first two hotels and the appointment of a judicial administrator for the operation of the two others. The claimants turned to the Tribunal for provisional measures that would, among other things, counter those court orders. Morocco questioned the jurisdiction of the Tribunal to recommend provisional measures and argued that the measures taken by the Moroccan courts already "assured the protection of the interests of both parties *pendente lite*."[81]

The Tribunal issued its decision on the claimants' request in July 1972, a year before it decided on its jurisdiction over the dispute. In the decision, the Tribunal upheld its power to recommend provisional measures, the parties "still having the right to express, in the rest of the procedure, any exception to the jurisdiction of the Tribunal on any other aspect of the dispute."[82] Precedents for the decision included rulings of the ICJ in several cases making clear that it could decide on provisional measures prior to establishing its jurisdiction over the dispute if it appeared that there was, prima facie, a basis for asserting such jurisdiction.[83] The decision also showed that a tribunal might not hesitate to exercise its authority to "recommend measures other than those specified in a request"[84] of a party. Thus, rather than grant the measures requested by the claimants, the *Holiday Inns* Tribunal made the broad admonition to both parties that they should "abstain from any measure incompatible with the upholding of the[ir] Contract and to make sure that the action already taken should not result in consequences in the future which would go against such upholding."[85]

were, in July 1984, formally submitted to the Administrative Council for its approval. *See* Doc. AC/84/3, ICSID Regulation and Rules: Note from the Secretary-General, July 23, 1984, Attachment, 3 and Note on Addition to Arbitration Rule 39.

[80] The change did, however, create an odd divergence between the Arbitration Rules applicable to ICSID Convention proceedings, which henceforth specifically ruled out court-ordered provisional measures unless otherwise agreed by the parties, and the ICSID Additional Facility Arbitration Rules, which specifically preserved the right of the parties to apply to national courts for interim or conservatory measures. *See* Doc. ICSID/11, ICSID Additional Facility for the Administration of Conciliation, Arbitration and Fact-Finding Proceedings (June 1979), Arbitration Rules, Rule 47(4).

[81] As quoted in Lalive (n. 40) 657.

[82] As quoted in ibid. 658.

[83] For a review of these ICJ cases, *see* C.N. Brower and R.E.M. Goodman, Provisional Measures and the Protection of ICSID Jurisdictional Exclusivity Against Municipal Proceedings, 6 ICSID Rev. FILJ 431, 453–458 (1991).

[84] Arbitration Rules (n. 2) Rule 39(3).

[85] As quoted in Lalive (n. 40) 658.

Resort to national courts by a party also elicited the request for provisional measures in *MINE v. Guinea*. In that case, MINE, after instituting the ICSID Convention proceeding, continued to seek enforcement of the AAA award. It commenced attachment proceedings for the purpose in Belgium and Switzerland. These resulted in the attachment of Guinean bank accounts in those countries. The ICSID Tribunal having already been formed,[86] Guinea asked it to direct MINE to cease such "lawless" violations of Article 26 of the Convention and lift the attachments.

In December 1985, the Tribunal issued a strongly worded provisional measure affirming that the efforts to enforce the AAA award "breached MINE's submission of its dispute with Guinea to ICSID for arbitration."[87] The measure accordingly recommended "that MINE immediately withdraw and permanently discontinue all pending litigation in national courts ... dissolve every existing attachment and ... seek no new remedy in any national court."[88] This measure was cited by the Court of First Instance of the Canton of Geneva in a March 1986 decision rejecting a request of MINE for the enforcement of the AAA award supporting the attachments in Switzerland. The Court held that the request was "contrary to the exclusive nature of ICSID arbitration as provided in Article 26 of the Washington Convention."[89] The attachments in Belgium were lifted for the same reason by an earlier, September 1985, decision of the Court of First Instance of Antwerp.[90] MINE thereafter abandoned its efforts to enforce the AAA award.

Finally, in the third case, *AGIP v. Congo*, the claimant and Congo each became, following a 1974 agreement between them, half owners of a Congolese oil distribution company. In 1975, Congo nationalized the company without compensating AGIP for its shareholding. Towards the end of 1977, after failing to reach a settlement of the resulting dispute, AGIP submitted it to ICSID pursuant to the arbitration clause of the 1974 agreement. At its first session, the Tribunal[91] was asked by AGIP to recommend, pursuant to Article 47 of the Convention, that Congo collect all of the nationalized company's corporate documents, notify the Tribunal and AGIP of the documents collected and keep them for eventual production to the Tribunal. After giving Congo the opportunity to make its observations,[92] the Tribunal issued the requested recommendation.[93]

The explanatory notes published with the Regulations and Rules in 1967 pointed out that, while under Article 47 of the ICSID Convention a tribunal "only has the

[86] The Tribunal was composed of Donald Zubrod as President, Jack Berg and David J. Sharpe. Zubrod and Berg were both former Presidents of the Society of Maritime Arbitrators, Inc. Sharpe was a Professor at George Washington University Law School specializing in maritime law. As may be inferred from their appointment of this Tribunal, the parties at the outset of the proceeding perceived it as involving a shipping dispute first and foremost.

[87] This quotation is from the summary of the measure by the Tribunal in its Award in *MINE v. Guinea*, January 6, 1988, 4 ICSID Rep. 61, 69 (1997).

[88] Ibid.

[89] *MINE v. Guinea*, Court of First Instance, Geneva, Judgment, March 13, 1986, 4 ICSID Rep. 41, 44 (1997).

[90] *See Guinea v. MINE*, Court of First Instance, Antwerp, Judgment, September 27, 1985, 4 ICSID Rep. 33 (1997).

[91] The Tribunal consisted of Jørgen Trolle as President, René-Jean Dupuy and Fuad Rouhani. On Trolle and Rouhani, *see* Ch. 5, n. 62. Dupuy was then Secretary General of the Hague Academy of International Law and shortly to be named Professor of International Law at the Collège de France.

[92] In accordance with ICSID Arbitration Rule 39(4).

[93] *See AGIP v. Congo*, Award, November 30, 1978, 1 ICSID Rep. 309, 311 (1993).

power to 'recommend'" provisional measures, "[t]his restriction is not as serious as it appears" since a tribunal "can normally take into account in its award the effects of any non-compliance with its recommendations."[94] This sanction was applied for the first time in *AGIP*. Congo failed there to comply with the Tribunal's recommendation for the preservation of corporate documents. This was noted pointedly in the eventual award. It stated that, in evaluating AGIP's claim, the Tribunal did "not lose sight" of the fact "that the Government did not comply with the decision of the Tribunal ... as to the measures of preservation and as a consequence AGIP was unable to have access to a certain number of documents which could have assisted it in presenting its case."[95]

V. Applicable law

It was pointed out earlier that most of the cases brought to ICSID in its first 20 years involved asserted breaches of investment contracts between the parties. In about half of the arbitration cases, the parties had, in provisions in such contracts, agreed on the law that their tribunal would apply to the substance of the dispute. With few exceptions, the provisions referred to the law of the State party to the dispute. One such provision was contained in the contract involved in *Mobil v. New Zealand*. This was a participation agreement entered into by the parties in 1982 for the erection of a synthetic gasoline manufacturing plant near New Plymouth. Its ICSID arbitration clause stipulated that "[a]n Arbitral Tribunal shall apply the law of New Zealand."[96] In the more typical case where the State party was a developing country, the provision rarely referred to its law in such unadorned terms. To protect the investor against subsequent adverse changes by the State of its law, the reference to it in some such cases was subject to a stabilization or "freezing" clause so that the law would be applied as in force on the date of the contract. For example, the provision in the 1971 agreement of the parties in *MINE v. Guinea* called for the application of "la Loi [*sic*] de la République de Guinée en vigeur à la date de signature."[97] In several of the other cases, the reference was to the law of the State party in combination with international law, so that application of the former might if necessary be complemented or tempered by the latter. Thus, for example, the arbitration clause of the 1974 agreement between the parties in *AGIP v. Congo* provided that "la loi [*sic*] congolaise, complétée le cas échéant par tout principe de droit international sera applicable."[98]

In almost all of the remaining cases, the parties had no agreement on applicable law. As required by the second sentence of Article 42(1) of the Convention, their tribunals were thus also to apply the law of the State party "and such rules of international law as may be applicable." The role of international law under Article 42(1) received much attention in two important decisions rendered in the mid-1980s. These were the decisions of the ad hoc committees formed to consider the earliest requests to annul awards pursuant to Article 52 of the Convention. The cases concerned were *Klöckner v. Cameroon* and *Amco v. Indonesia*.

94 Arbitration Rules (n. 2) note B to Rule 39. As shown in Ch. 5 (at text accompanying n. 150), this possible consequence of non-compliance with arbitral provisional measures was foreseen during the preparation of the Convention.

95 *AGIP v. Congo*, Award (n. 93) 317–318.

96 *See Attorney General of New Zealand v. Mobil Oil New Zealand*, High Court of New Zealand, Judgment, July 1, 1987, 2 ICSID Rev.—FILJ 497, 502 (1987).

97 *See MINE v. Guinea*, ad hoc Committee Decision (n. 69) 94.

98 *See AGIP v. Congo*, Award (n. 93) 323.

The claimant in *Klöckner* was a German corporation engaged in the marketing and sale of turnkey industrial plants. Starting in 1971, it concluded a series of agreements with Cameroon to build and run a fertilizer factory there. These included a protocol of agreement, supply contract and establishment agreement, all containing ICSID arbitration clauses. The factory was completed and began to operate in 1976. It did not do so profitably, however, and was soon closed, at first temporarily and then for good at the end of 1981. Klöckner had meanwhile instituted the arbitration proceeding, claiming the balance of the price of the factory. The Tribunal was constituted in late 1981 and rendered its award two years later.[99] The award acknowledged that the parties had no agreement on applicable law, cited the second sentence of Article 42(1) of the Convention, and held Cameroonian law to be applicable. More specifically, it identified as applicable the Cameroonian law of French origin in force in the eastern part of the State, the former French Cameroons, where the parties had signed their agreements and the factory was located.[100] "We take for granted," the award continued, that:

> ... the principle according to which a person who engages in close contractual relations, based on confidence, must deal with its partner in a frank, loyal and candid manner is a basic principle of French civil law, as is indeed the case under the other national codes which we know of. This is the criterion that applies to relations between partners in simple forms of association anywhere. The rule is particularly appropriate in more complex international ventures, such as the present one.
>
> We have not established that there is a law applicable to such contracts. We do not intend to apply new or exceptional legal principles to turnkey operations only because they concern projects affecting the economic and social development of a given country. But we are convinced that it is particularly important that universal requirements of frankness and loyalty in dealings between partners be applied in cases such as this one, where a multinational company seeks and freely undertakes the obligation to supply an overall package of feasibility, analysis, design, management, bidding, construction and marketing for an industrial plant, and obtains in return the agreement of the Government to pay for the factory, whether or not it is profitable.[101]

Klöckner was found to have violated this duty of frankness and loyalty by withholding from Cameroon information about the project's economic viability. The conclusion in the award was to dismiss Klöckner's claim.[102]

Klöckner then requested annulment of the award. In its 1985 decision upholding the request, the ad hoc Committee rebuked the award for merely asserting or postulating the existence of the principle of frankness and loyalty "which (after postulating its existence) the Tribunal *assumes* or takes for granted that it is 'a basic principle of French civil law.'"[103] The mention in the award of "universal requirements of frankness and

[99] The Tribunal was presided over by Eduardo Jiménez de Aréchaga. The other arbitrators were William D. Rogers and Dominique Schmidt. On Jiménez de Aréchaga and Schmidt, *see* nn. 20 and 22. Rogers was a partner in the Washington, D.C. law firm of Arnold & Porter who had held senior positions in the U.S. Department of State in the administration of President Gerald Ford.

[100] *See Klöckner v. Cameroon*, Award, October 21, 1983, 2 ICSID Rep. 9, 59 (1994).

[101] Ibid. 59–60.

[102] *See* ibid. 61. The arbitrator appointed by Klöckner, Dominique Schmidt, appended a vigorous dissent to the award disagreeing on, among other points, the extent of Klöckner's failures to disclose information to Cameroon. *See* Dissenting Opinion, ibid. 77. This was the first dissenting opinion to be filed by an arbitrator in an ICSID case.

[103] *Klöckner v. Cameroon*, ad hoc Committee Decision, May 3, 1985, 2 ICSID Rep. 95, 121 (1994) (emphasis in original). This ad hoc Committee was composed of Pierre Lalive, Ahmed S. El-Kosheri and Ignaz Seidl-Hohenveldern. Lalive, the President of the Committee, was Professor at the Law Faculty of the University of Geneva and senior partner in the Geneva law firm Lalive & Budin.

loyalty" might have been interpreted as a reference to general principles of law, applicable as international law under Article 42(1) of the Convention. The ad hoc Committee pronounced such an interpretation to be "conjectural" and unacceptable.[104] The ad hoc Committee explained that:

> Article 42 of the Washington Convention certainly provides that "in the absence of agreement between the parties, the Tribunal shall apply the law of the Contracting State party to the dispute ... and *such principles of international law as may be applicable*." This gives these principles (perhaps omitting cases in which it should be ascertained whether the domestic law conforms to international law) a dual role, that is, *complementary* (in the case of a "lacuna" in the law of the State), or *corrective*, should the State's law not conform on all points to the principles of international law. *In both cases*, the arbitrators may have recourse to the "principles of international law" only *after* having inquired into and established the content of the law of the State party to the dispute (which cannot be reduced to *one* principle, even a basic one) and *after* having applied the relevant rules of the State's law.[105]

"Article 42(1)," the ad hoc Committee added for good measure, "therefore clearly does not allow the arbitrator to base his decision *solely* on the 'rules' or 'principles of international law.' "[106] It had to be acknowledged, the ad hoc Committee concluded, "that in its reasoning, limited to postulating and not demonstrating the existence of a principle," the Tribunal had failed to apply "the law of the Contracting State."[107]

In *Amco*, the revocation of PT Amco's investment license had been based partly on a shortfall in the amount of its investment. The award of the first *Amco* Tribunal ruled that the shortfall was not, however, large enough to justify the revocation. After the rendition of the award in 1984, Indonesia requested its annulment. The ad hoc Committee was constituted in 1985 and issued its decision the following year.[108] Among the general questions dealt with at the outset of the decision was the law applicable to the substance of the dispute. Like the Tribunal before it, the ad hoc Committee noted that, "[s]ince the parties had not agreed on some other law governing their relations," this would in accordance with Article 42(1) of the Convention be "the law of Indonesia and such rules of international law as may be applicable."[109] Expounding on this, the ad hoc Committee stated that under Article 42(1), "[t]he law of the host State is, in principle, the law to be applied in resolving the dispute," while a tribunal was authorized "to apply rules of international law only to fill up lacunae in the applicable domestic law and to ensure precedence of international law norms where the rules of the applicable domestic law are in collision with such norms."[110] On

Seidl-Hohenveldern was Professor of Public International Law at the University of Vienna. On El-Kosheri, *see* n. 20.

[104] *Klöckner v. Cameroon*, ad hoc Committee Decision (n. 103) 122.

[105] Ibid. (emphases in original). The official version of the ad hoc Committee decision was in French and relied, of course, on the French text of the ICSID Convention. It referred in Art. 42(1) to "principes de droit international" where the English and Spanish texts referred to "rules of international law" and "reglas de derecho internacional."

[106] Ibid. (emphasis in original). [107] Ibid. 125.

[108] The President of the ad hoc Committee was Ignaz Seidl-Hohenveldern, who had served on the first ad hoc Committee in the *Klöckner* case (*see* n. 103). The other members of this first *Amco* ad hoc Committee were Florentino P. Feliciano and Andrea Giardina. Feliciano was managing partner of the Manila law firm SyCip Salazar Feliciano & Hernandez and shortly to become Associate Justice of the Supreme Court of the Philippines. Giardina was Professor at the University of Rome Faculty of Political Sciences.

[109] *Amco v. Indonesia*, ad hoc Committee Decision, May 16, 1986, 1 ICSID Rep. 509, 514–515 (1993).

[110] Ibid. 515.

the substance of the request for annulment, the Amco ad hoc Committee proceeded to uphold the request's complaint that the Tribunal had failed to apply provisions of Indonesian law, under which only sums duly registered with the central bank could be counted as investments, and as a result significantly underestimated the shortfall of PT Amco's investment.[111]

As remarked by this *Amco* ad hoc Committee, its "view on the supplemental and corrective role of international law in relation to the law of the host State" under Article 42(1) was shared by many at the time—including of course the ad hoc Committee in the earlier *Klöckner* proceeding.[112] Among other contemporaneous decisions taking a similar approach to the question was the 1986 award of the Tribunal in *LETCO v. Liberia*, which described Article 42(1) as envisaging "that, in the absence of any express choice of law by the parties, the Tribunal must apply a system of concurrent law. The law of the Contracting State is recognized as paramount within its own territory, but is nevertheless subjected to control by international law."[113] Express stipulations by parties for the application of such a "system of concurrent law" were also typically seen as giving international law a gap-filling and, or, regulatory role in relation to the specified national law. Thus, in *AGIP v. Congo*, the Tribunal observed that the provision quoted earlier,[114] according to which Congolese law supplemented by international law would be applicable, meant "at the very least, that recourse to principles of international law can be made either to fill a lacuna in Congolese law, or to make any necessary additions to it."[115]

While a "supplemental and corrective role" was widely accepted for international law under the provision of the second sentence of Article 42(1) and similar provisions agreed by the parties, there were, among the cases registered in ICSID's first 20 years, few instances of international law actually being applied to supplement or correct national law pursuant to these provisions. In several cases, tribunals confined themselves to affirming that the applicable national law was not in conflict with international law. For example, the *LETCO* Tribunal, after noting that "[t]he role of international law as a 'regulator' of national systems of law has been much discussed," declared itself "satisfied that the rules and principles of Liberian law which it has taken into account are in conformity with generally accepted principles of public international law governing the validity of contracts and the remedies for their breach."[116]

There was a glaring exception to such restraint in the *SPP* award. It appeared to shift the emphasis from a tribunal's duty to apply the applicable municipal law first and foremost to its supposed obligation under Article 42(1) of the ICSID Convention "to apply directly the relevant principles and rules of international law" whenever a lacuna is identified in the municipal law (as well as inconsistency between it and international law).[117]

[111] *See* ibid. 534–535. For a criticism of this aspect of the Committee's decision, equating a failure to apply some provisions of the law to a non-application of the law, *see* Schreuer and others (n. 49) 964.

[112] *See Amco v. Indonesia*, ad hoc Committee Decision (n. 109) 515. The *Amco* ad hoc Committee also cited the drafting history of the ICSID Convention as supporting this view on the exclusively supplemental and corrective role of international law under Art. 42(1) of the Convention. It is doubtful, however, if so much could be read into the drafting history. For an account of the main discussion during the preparation of the Convention, *see* Ch. 5, section II(C). *See also* E. Gaillard and Y. Banifatemi, The Meaning of "and" in Article 42(1), Second Sentence, of the Washington Convention: The Role of International Law in the ICSID Choice of Law Process, 18 ICSID Rev.—FILJ 375, 382–388 (2003).

[113] *LETCO v. Liberia*, Award (n. 47) 358.

[114] *See* text accompanying n. 98.

[115] *AGIP v. Congo*, Award (n. 93) 323–324.

[116] *LETCO v. Liberia*, Award (n. 47) 358–359.

[117] *SPP v. Egypt*, Award (n. 55) 208.

According to the award, there was no specific provision of Egyptian legislation on the starting point for the computation of "compensatory interest for a yet to be determined amount of compensation arising out of an act of expropriation." Given "this lacuna," the award continued, it was "legitimate" to have recourse to international law rules, under which the starting point was "the date on which the dispossession effectively took place."[118] This aspect of the award was roundly criticized by commentators as finding a gap in the applicable national law where in reality none existed. As two of the commentators said, "[t]o the extent that Egyptian law provides for interest, it necessarily provides for the legal framework enabling Egyptian judges to calculate an interest and, by definition, assess the date from which that calculation is carried out."[119]

Among the cases commenced during the period, *AAPL v. Sri Lanka* stands apart in regard to the law applicable to the merits of the dispute. As pointed out by the Tribunal in this first case brought to ICSID on the basis of a consent to arbitration in a BIT, rather than in an arbitration agreement previously concluded by the parties, they had had "no opportunity to exercise their right to choose in advance the applicable law determining the rules governing the various aspects of their eventual disputes."[120] Nor did the BIT in question specifically address the law to be applied in arbitration proceedings initiated by investors under the treaty.[121] The Tribunal took the view that "[u]nder these special circumstances, the choice-of-law process would normally materialize after the emergence of the dispute, by observing and construing the conduct of the Parties throughout the arbitration proceedings."[122] In its award, the Tribunal stated that it had been able to infer from the submissions of the parties "their mutual agreement to consider the provisions of the [BIT] ... as being the primary source of the applicable legal rules."[123] The BIT was not, however, "a self-contained closed legal system" but had "to be envisaged in a wider juridical context" in which there would be recourse to "certain supplementary rules."[124] In addition to general customary international law rules, these supplementary rules included "domestic legal rules" of the host State.[125] The Tribunal explained that this "extension of the applicable legal system" to embrace the supplementary international and domestic rules followed from provisions of the BIT, the primary source of rules, and was also acknowledged by the submissions of the parties.[126]

In short, the *AAPL* Tribunal found that the parties had a tacit agreement on the applicable legal rules[127] that turned on its head the then usual system of concurrent

[118] Ibid.

[119] Gaillard and Banifatemi (n. 112) 399. The idea of lacunae was difficult to reconcile with modern conceptions of the completeness of legal orders and seemed a throwback to older approaches exemplified by the 1951 ad hoc arbitral award in *Petroleum Development (Trucial Coast) Ltd. v. Sheikh of Abu Dhabi* (1 ICLQ 247 (1952)), that the legal systems of some countries were too "primitive" to answer all of the issues that may arise in international commerce. E. Gaillard and J. Savage (eds.), *Fouchard, Gaillard and Goldman on International Commercial Arbitration* 843–844 (1999).

[120] *AAPL v. Sri Lanka*, Award (n. 61) 256.

[121] This, it will be recalled, was the Sri Lanka–U.K. BIT. *See* n. 62. It was similar to most other BITs in being silent on the subject of applicable law.

[122] *AAPL v. Sri Lanka*, Award (n. 61) 256. [123] Ibid. [124] Ibid. 257.

[125] Ibid.

[126] Ibid. The provisions of the BIT that the Tribunal cited for this extension of the applicable law to encompass also general international law and domestic law rules included the provisions requiring each state to accord national treatment to covered investments and most-favored-nation treatment to covered investors. *See* Ibid. and Sri Lanka–U.K. BIT (n. 62) Art. 3(1) and 3(2).

[127] It was acknowledged in the preparation of the Convention that an agreement on applicable law under what became the first sentence of Art. 42(1) need not be express. *See* Regional Consultative Meetings of Legal Experts on Settlement of Investment Disputes: Chairman's Report, July 9, 1964, reprinted in 2 *History of the ICSID Convention* 557, para. 59.

law. Rather than applying host State law supplemented or corrected as needed by international law, the Tribunal was to apply conventional international law provisions—that is, the provisions of the BIT—supplemented by general international law and host State law rules. Holding the BIT to be the principal source of applicable law was logical in the circumstances. As in most of the many other BIT cases that were to follow, the claim in *AAPL* was based on asserted breaches by the respondent of its obligations under the BIT—notably, in *AAPL*, the obligation to accord covered investments "full protection and security."[128] It would have made little sense to judge such a claim mainly by reference to domestic host State law.

One of the arbitrators in *AAPL* appended to the award a dissenting opinion taking issue with the majority on this point. The dissenting opinion argued that, in the absence of express agreement of the parties to regard the provisions of the BIT as the applicable substantive law, it would have been necessary to demonstrate that the BIT authorized covered investors to invoke the treaty itself as the applicable law.[129] Some U.S. BITs, the dissenting opinion pointed out, did this "by specifying in individual treaties that investment disputes which may be submitted to ICSID shall include an alleged 'breach of any right conferred or created by this treaty with respect to an investment.' "[130] In many other BITs, including the Sri Lanka–U.K. BIT involved in the *AAPL* case, the corresponding provision provided broadly for the submission to arbitration of "any" legal disputes concerning covered investments.[131] The dissenting opinion disparaged as "rather unconvincing" the position of the majority based on the pleadings of the parties.[132] The position was, however, difficult to fault—except that it might have been strengthened by adding that the broad provision of the BIT on the settlement of investment disputes plainly covered, first and foremost, disputes over alleged breaches of the treaty and hence implicitly authorized the invocation of treaty law as the applicable law in essentially the same way as the U.S. BITs.

VI. Annulment decisions of the 1980s

The previous section touched upon the first annulment proceedings under Article 52 of the ICSID Convention, instituted by the claimant in *Klöckner v. Cameroon* in 1984 and by the respondent in *Amco v. Indonesia* a year later. It will be recalled that the proceedings led to ad hoc committee decisions in the respective cases in 1985 and 1986. In their decisions, both ad hoc committees emphasized the limited nature of the annulment remedy provided by Article 52 of the Convention and recognized that it had to be distinguished from an appeal against the award, which was specifically excluded by Article 54 of the Convention.[133] The two ad hoc committees acknowledged that they had, in particular, to separate carefully a failure to apply the applicable law from a mistaken application of that law: the former could be a ground for nullity, as a manifest

[128] Under the Sri Lanka–U.K. BIT (n. 62) Art. 2(2).

[129] *See AAPL v. Sri Lanka*, Dissenting Opinion of Samuel K. B. Asante, June 27, 1990, 4 ICSID Rep. 296, 298 (1997).

[130] Ibid. The dissenting arbitrator was quoting Art. 6(1)(c) of the then (1987) U.S. Model BIT, reprinted in K.J. Vandevelde, *U.S. International Investment Agreements* 796, 799 (2009).

[131] *See* Sri Lanka–U.K. BIT (n. 62) Art. 8(1).

[132] *AAPL v. Sri Lanka*, Dissenting Opinion (n. 129) 298.

[133] *See Klöckner v. Cameroon*, ad hoc Committee Decision (n. 103) 97; *Amco v. Indonesia*, ad hoc Committee Decision (n. 109) 515.

excess of powers within the meaning of Article 52(1)(b) of the Convention, but the latter could only be the subject of an appeal.[134]

On the ground of failure to state reasons within the meaning of Article 52(1)(e) of the Convention, the *Klöckner* ad hoc Committee similarly noted the need for caution if an annulment request was not to serve as a disguised appeal. Turning to the text of the ICSID Convention, the ad hoc Committee pointed out that its Article 52(1)(e) required "a statement" of reasons "on which the award is based." "This," the ad hoc Committee declared, "does not mean just any reasons, purely formal or apparent, but rather reasons having some substance, allowing the reader to follow the arbitral tribunal's reasoning, on facts and on law."[135] There would be a failure to state reasons, the ad hoc Committee concluded, "in the absence of a statement of reasons that are 'sufficiently relevant,' that is, reasonably sustainable and capable of providing a basis for the decision."[136] In its decision, the *Amco* ad hoc Committee found this reading of the earlier ad hoc committee to be "convincing" and agreed "that supporting reasons must be more than a matter of nomenclature and must constitute an appropriate foundation for the conclusions reached through such reasons."[137]

As explained in the previous section, both ad hoc committees found that there had been failures on the part of the respective tribunals to apply the applicable law. For both ad hoc committees, the failures represented manifest excesses of power.[138] In *Klöckner,* the ad hoc Committee held that the Tribunal had also failed to state reasons for important conclusions in the award, notably that Klöckner had in substance assumed an "obligation of result" under its agreements with Cameroon.[139] "Despite many readings of the text" of the award, the *Klöckner* ad hoc Committee found it "impossible to discern how and why the Tribunal could reach its decision on this point."[140] The *Klöckner* ad hoc Committee extended its inquiry to considering whether it had the discretion to abstain from annulling an award tainted on one or the other of the grounds for annulment listed in Article 52(1) of the Convention. On this point, the ad hoc Committee took the view that a finding that there is a ground for annulment should in principle result in total or partial annulment, "without the Committee having any discretion, the parties to the Washington Convention and the parties to an arbitration under the ICSID system having an absolute right to compliance with the Convention's provisions, and in particular with the provisions of Article 52."[141] In the case at hand, the award's dismissal of the claim rested on its holding that Klöckner had violated a duty of frankness and loyalty toward Cameroon. That was the part of the award affected by the manifest excess of power for failure to apply the applicable law. Judging the remainder of the award to lack an independent basis, the ad hoc Committee decided to annul it in its entirety.[142]

In *Amco,* the ad hoc Committee detected a failure to state reasons, as well as a failure to apply the applicable law, in the decision of the Tribunal to credit loan funds to the amount of the qualified investment.[143] The failures led the ad hoc Committee to decide to annul the award "as a whole."[144] The ad hoc Committee made this decision

[134] *See Klöckner v. Cameroon*, ad hoc Committee Decision (n. 103) 119; *Amco v. Indonesia*, ad hoc Committee Decision (n. 109) 515–516.

[135] *Klöckner v. Cameroon*, ad hoc Committee Decision (n. 103) 138.

[136] Ibid. 139.

[137] *Amco v. Indonesia*, ad hoc Committee Decision (n. 109) 520.

[138] *Klöckner v. Cameroon*, ad hoc Committee Decision (n. 103) 125; *Amco v. Indonesia*, ad hoc Committee Decision (n. 109) 535.

[139] *See Klöckner v. Cameroon*, ad hoc Committee Decision (n. 103) 147.

[140] Ibid. 148.

[141] Ibid. 162.

[142] *See* ibid. 125–126.

[143] *See Amco v. Indonesia*, ad hoc Committee Decision (n. 109) 535–536.

[144] Ibid. 542.

subject to the qualification that the annulment did not, however, extend to a finding in the award that Indonesian army and police personnel had acted illegally in helping PT Wisma to take control of the hotel from PT Amco.[145] Though confusingly put, the decision was thus for a partial annulment in that it preserved this finding of the Tribunal.

These two ad hoc Committee decisions caused consternation among arbitration and investment law specialists. Many saw them as having crossed the line between annulment and appeal. The *Amco* ad hoc Committee decision in particular was attacked for having interpreted a possible mistake in the application of Indonesian law as a "failure to apply that law."[146] Moreover, by holding that an award could be annulled if the reasons for it did not appear "sufficiently relevant," both decisions were seen as inviting losing parties "to request annulment in every case where there is any hope of persuading a new panel that the judgment of the tribunal is clearly erroneous."[147] The *Klöckner* ad hoc Committee was also lambasted for its view that annulment should generally follow automatically from a finding of a ground for annulment. This was said to make Article 52 of the Convention a "hair-trigger" mechanism, setting off annulment "at the slightest provocation without regard to the magnitude of the defect established."[148] Unhappiness with the decision of the *Klöckner* ad hoc Committee was increased by the combative style of many of its pronouncements.[149]

Several months after the rendition of the *Amco* ad hoc Committee decision, Shihata reported on the situation to the Administrative Council of the Centre. He noted that, following the earlier annulment decision in *Klöckner*, the dispute in that case had been submitted to a new tribunal in accordance with Article 52(5) of the Convention. While saying he could not comment on the two annulment decisions themselves, Shihata warned of the danger "that if parties, dissatisfied with an award, made it a practice to seek annulment, the effectiveness of the ICSID machinery might become questionable and both investors and Contracting States might be deterred from making use of ICSID arbitration."[150] Shihata pointed out that the drafters of the Convention "intended to: (i) assure the finality of ICSID awards; (ii) distinguish carefully an annulment proceeding from an appeal; and (iii) construe narrowly the ground for annulment, so that this procedure remained exceptional."[151] He declared it "our responsibility to ensure that the original intent of the provisions on the annulment procedure be carried out."[152] Shihata promised that if there were in future "unjustified recourse to the annulment procedure," he would "explore further with the members of the Administrative Council ways by which the relevant provisions of the Convention can be clarified through elaboration of the Arbitration Rules."[153]

Despite this "jawboning"[154] by Shihata, annulment proceedings continued to multiply. An award in favor of the claimant was rendered in early January 1988 in *MINE*

[145] *See* ibid.

[146] *See, e.g.*, M.B. Feldman, The Annulment Proceedings and the Finality of ICSID Arbitral Awards, 2 ICSID Rev.—FILJ 85, 102 (1987); E. Gaillard, CIRDI: Chronique des sentences arbitrales, 114 Journal du droit international 135, 189 (1987).

[147] Feldman (n. 146) 102. *See also* Gaillard (n. 146) 190.

[148] M.W. Reisman, The Breakdown of the Control Mechanism in ICSID Arbitration, 4 Duke L.J. 739, 762 (1989).

[149] *See* Broches (n. 9) 340; J. Paulsson, ICSID's Achievements and Prospects, 6 ICSID Rev.—FILJ 380, 392 (1991).

[150] Doc. AC/86/4, Summary Proceedings: Twentieth Annual Meeting, October 2, 1986, Annex A, Report of the Secretary-General, 2 (1986 Report).

[151] Ibid. 3. [152] Ibid. [153] Ibid.

[154] The expression was used by Reisman (n. 148) 804, in reference to Shihata's similar statement in 1988 (quoted in the text accompanying n. 157).

v. Guinea; and shortly thereafter, the respondent applied for annulment of the award. Toward the end of January 1988, the new Tribunal in *Klöckner* rendered its award, deciding the resubmitted dispute in favor of the claimant; both parties thereafter requested annulment of the second award. With challenges of awards so apparently easy to sustain, this development in *Klöckner* seemed to suggest that an ICSID case could become an endless succession of arbitration and annulment proceedings.[155]

Disquiet was again voiced by Shihata. In his report to the 1988 annual meeting of the Administrative Council, he lamented that "[d]espite efforts on my part to promote settlement," Klöckner and Cameroon had been "unable to agree to seek to reach a settlement as an alternative to renewed annulment proceedings."[156] Repeating his warning of two years earlier, Shihata stated:

> It may be expected that use of the annulment procedure would be a rare event because of the seriousness of the shortcomings against which it is meant to be a safeguard. This still seems to be the case, since the annulment procedure has only been invoked in three disputes before the Centre. However, if parties dissatisfied with awards regularly seek annulment such a practice may put in doubt the features which make ICSID arbitration an attractive means of settling investment disputes—namely its speed, comparatively low cost, and its effectiveness. It is also wrong to confuse the annulment proceeding with an appeals process which is not possible in respect of awards issued by ICSID's tribunals.[157]

It will be recalled from Chapter 7 that, in 1984, after the institution of the first *Klöckner* annulment proceeding, the Administrative and Financial Regulations of the Centre were amended to make the applicant for annulment solely responsible for making the advance payments to ICSID to cover the direct costs of an annulment proceeding.[158] Another way of assuring that requests for annulment were not merely dilatory was introduced in the first *Amco* annulment proceeding: the ad hoc Committee there decided to condition a stay of enforcement of the award for the duration of the proceeding on the provision by Indonesia of a bank guarantee for the amount of the award, to be drawn upon by Amco in the event of a rejection of the request for annulment.[159] In view of these annulment proceedings, consideration began to be given to other ways of curbing recourse to the remedy. One possibility, hinted at by Shihata in his report to the Administrative Council in 1986, would have involved amending the Arbitration Rules to provide the Secretary General with the authority to reject "unjustified" requests for annulment.[160] Another possibility raised by some commentators would have been for parties to supplement their consents to arbitration under the Convention with "exclusion agreements" waiving their right to request annulment of an award.[161]

[155] *Cf.* Reisman (n. 148).

[156] Report of the Secretary-General to the Administrative Council at its Twenty-Second Annual Meeting, September 27–29, 1988, 2–3.

[157] Ibid. 3. The wisdom of this statement was questioned by Reisman as it was made by the person who effectively appointed members of ad hoc committees when two such committees were in operation. *See* Reisman (n. 148) 804.

[158] *See* Ch. 7, text accompanying nn. 139 and 140.

[159] *See Amco v. Indonesia*, ad hoc Committee Decision (n. 109) 513.

[160] *See* 1986 Report (n. 150) 2–3. Trying to give the Secretary-General such a screening power in respect of requests for annulment would, however, have been difficult to reconcile with Art. 52(3) of the Convention, which provides for the appointment "forthwith" of an ad hoc committee "[o]n receipt of the request" for annulment.

[161] *See, e.g.*, G.R. Delaume, How to Draft an ICSID Arbitration Clause, 7 ICSID Rev.—FILJ 168, 190–191 (1952). As Delaume acknowledged in this article, the extent to which parties could validly make such exclusion agreements was open to question, given that the annulment remedy was "intended to provide a minimum of safeguards essential to preservation of the standards set forth in

In the end, however, the fears for the ICSID system aroused by the *Klöckner* and *Amco* annulments were calmed by the ad hoc Committee decision in *MINE*.[162]

Rendered in December 1989, the decision emphasized that "[a]nnulment is not a remedy against an incorrect decision" and that an ad hoc committee therefore could "not in fact reverse an award on the merits under the guise of applying Article 52" of the Convention.[163] The *MINE* ad hoc Committee went on in its decision to underscore the importance of distinguishing disregard of the applicable rules of law, which could result in annulment, from erroneous application of those rules "which, even if manifestly unwarranted, furnishes no ground for annulment."[164] As for the ground of failure to state reasons, the *MINE* ad hoc Committee took the view that "the requirement that an award has to be motivated implies that it must enable the reader to follow the reasoning of the Tribunal on points of fact and law. It implies that, and only that."[165] Disagreeing with the two earlier ad hoc committees, the *MINE* ad hoc Committee insisted that "[t]he adequacy of the reasoning is not an appropriate standard of review" as it could lead to "an examination of the substance of the tribunal's decision, in disregard of the exclusion of the remedy of appeal by Article 53 of the Convention."[166] It noted that the requirement to state reasons would not be satisfied "by either contradictory or frivolous reasons."[167] The MINE ad hoc Committee also accepted that "a tribunal's failure to deal with a question submitted to it could render an award unintelligible and thus subject to annulment for failure to state reasons."[168] Finally, the *MINE* ad hoc Committee flatly rejected the notion advanced by the *Klöckner* ad hoc Committee that the Convention required automatic exercise of the authority to annul whenever a party had established one of the grounds for annulment. An ad hoc committee, it explained:

> ... retains a measure of discretion in ruling on applications for annulment. To be sure, its discretion is not unlimited and should not be exercised to the point of defeating the object and purpose of the remedy of annulment. It may, however, refuse to exercise its authority to annul an award where annulment is clearly not required to remedy procedural injustice and annulment would unjustifiably erode the binding force and finality of ICSID awards.[169]

Examining specific grievances of Guinea against the award, the *MINE* ad hoc Committee disagreed that the Tribunal had "failed to apply any law" in deciding that there had been a breach of contract by Guinea. The *MINE* ad hoc Committee noted that the Tribunal had in reaching this decision invoked the requirement of good faith in carrying out contractual obligations imposed by Article 1134 of what the Tribunal called the "French Civil Code."[170] The Tribunal had admittedly erred in citing the French Civil Code when it should have referred to the Code Civil de l'Union Française in force in Guinea. The relevant article of the latter was, however, also numbered 1134 and had the same contents. The *MINE* ad hoc Committee did not consider that the error warranted annulment.[171]

the Convention and to account for the fact that ICSID awards are not subject to any form of judicial control" (ibid. 191).

162 The ad hoc Committee in *MINE v. Guinea* was composed of Sompong Sucharitkul as President and Aron Broches and Kéba Mbaye as the two other members. A former member of the Thai diplomatic service (with the rank of ambassador), Sucharitkul was then Professor of International Law at Notre Dame Law School. On Mbaye, *see* n. 20.

163 *MINE v. Guinea*, ad hoc Committee Decision (n. 69) 85. 164 Ibid. 87.

165 Ibid. 88. 166 Ibid. 167 Ibid. 168 Ibid. 104. 169 Ibid. 86.

170 *See* ibid. 96. 171 *See* ibid.

The *MINE* ad hoc Committee also disagreed that there had been a failure to state reasons for the portion of the award on breach of contract, observing that it was instead "supported by reasons which can be followed without great difficulty."[172] However, the ad hoc Committee found several failures to state reasons in the portion awarding MINE damages. The award did not deal with submissions of Guinea which, if upheld, would have required substantial reductions of the amounts of damages and interest.[173] Moreover, for its damages calculations, the Tribunal had adopted a damages theory that "disregarded the real situation and relied on hypotheses which the Tribunal had itself rejected as a basis for the calculation of damages."[174] The failures to address issues and contradiction represented failures to state reasons that, for the *MINE* ad hoc Committee, appeared "singly to justify, and collectively to compel," annulment of the damages portion of the award.[175]

The *MINE* ad hoc Committee decision therefore partially annulled the award. It was, however, widely applauded for laying to rest concerns about the annulment process raised by the two earlier decisions, especially as it rejected the "hair-trigger" approach to annulment and the holding that an award could be annulled if the reasons for it were not "sufficiently relevant."[176] Ad hoc committee decisions during the next three years seemed to confirm the belief that the remedy would henceforth be applied with restraint. These were decisions of second ad hoc committees established in the *Klöckner* and *Amco* cases.[177] The decision in *Klöckner*, rendered in 1990, totally rejected the request to annul the second award.[178] In *Amco*, the ad hoc Committee decision, which was issued in 1992, annulled only a decision of the Tribunal rectifying a relatively minor numerical error in the operative part of the second award.[179] Among the cases discussed in this chapter, an annulment proceeding was instituted by Egypt in respect of the award rendered in 1992 in *SPP*. But that proceeding was soon discontinued when Egypt and SPP agreed on a settlement.[180]

VII. Enforcement of awards

Klöckner's investment in Cameroon was said to have been insured by the German overseas investment guarantee program. If so, the second award may have been assigned

[172] Ibid. 98. [173] *See* ibid. 107–108. [174] Ibid. 108. [175] Ibid. 107.

[176] *See, e.g.*, D.D. Caron, Reputation and Reality in the ICSID Annulment Process: Understanding the Distinction between Annulment and Appeal, 7 ICSID Rev.—FILJ 21, 47–48 (1992).

[177] Reflecting a decision by Shihata to promote consistency in the jurisprudence of these ad hoc Committees by recommending overlapping memberships for them, the second ad hoc Committee in *Klöckner v. Cameroon* (n. 103) had two members in common with the earlier ad hoc Committee in *MINE v. Guinea* (n. 69). These were Sompong Sucharitkul, who again was elected President of the Committee, and Kéba Mbaye (*see* n. 20). The third member of the second ad hoc Committee in the *Klöckner* case was Andrea Giardina, who had served on the first ad hoc Committee in the *Amco* case (*see* n. 109). Sucharitkul also served as President of the second ad hoc Committee in the *Amco* case. The two other members of that Committee were Arghyrios A. Fatouros, Professor at Aristoteles University of Thessaloniki and Dietrich Schindler, Professor of International and Constitutional Law at the University of Zurich.

[178] *See Klöckner v. Cameroon*, ad hoc Committee Decision, May 17, 1990, 14 ICSID Rep. 101 (2009).

[179] The rectification decision was annulled for breach of a fundamental rule of procedure because the Tribunal had omitted to seek Indonesia's views on the proposed rectification before proceeding with the decision. *See Amco v. Indonesia*, ad hoc Committee Decision, December 3, 1992, 9 ICSID Rep. 9, 56 (2006).

[180] *See* nn. 182 and 199 and accompanying text.

to Germany as subrogee, after which the matter would have been disposed of at the intergovernmental level. In the second *Amco* annulment proceeding, as in the first, the ad hoc Committee had conditioned a continued stay of enforcement of the award on Indonesia's posting of a bank guarantee for the amount of the award.[181] Payment of the second award (minus the small additional sum that would have been due under the annulled rectification) was effected by release of the guarantee following the ad hoc Committee decision. The parties in *MINE* concluded a settlement agreement after the partial annulment of the award in that case; and as mentioned above, the parties in *SPP* also reached an agreed settlement, in preference to a continued annulment proceeding.[182]

In Chapter 7's overview, it was mentioned that awards upholding claims for damages were made in six more of the cases brought to ICSID between 1972 and 1988.[183] In two of these cases, *Benvenuti & Bonfant v. Congo* and *SOABI v. Senegal*, the successful claimants initially sought enforcement of the awards by proceedings in French courts.

The award in *Benvenuti & Bonfant* was rendered in 1980. It granted the claimant, an Italian company, compensation for violations by Congo of their agreement to establish an enterprise producing plastic bottles and mineral water.[184] The claimant then secured an order of *exequatur* from the Tribunal de Grande Instance of Paris declaring the award enforceable. The Tribunal de Grande Instance, however, made the order subject to the condition that it first authorize any measures of execution against assets in France, to ensure they were not "destined for an activity of sovereignty or public service."[185] At the request of the claimant, the Court of Appeal of Paris struck down this condition. In doing so, the Court of Appeal explained that the provisions of Article 54 of the ICSID Convention "lay down a simplified procedure for obtaining an *exequatur* and restrict the function of the court designated for the purposes of the Convention by each Contracting State to ascertaining the authenticity of the award certified by the Secretary-General of the International Centre for Settlement of Investment Disputes."[186] The Court of Appeal added that an *exequatur* for an arbitral award did not "constitute a measure of execution," which might in keeping with Article 55 of the Convention involve a question of sovereign immunity, but was instead "simply a preliminary measure prior to measures of execution."[187] Acting on a request pursuant to Article 54 of the Convention, the lower court had exceeded its competence by delving into "the second stage, that of execution, to which the question of the immunity from execution of foreign States relates."[188]

SOABI, the claimant in the second case, was a Senegalese company ultimately controlled by Belgians. It had concluded a contract with Senegal for the construction of

[181] *See Amco v. Indonesia*, ad hoc Committee Decision (n. 179) 61.

[182] The settlement in the *SPP* case involved the payment by Egypt of US$17.5 million (as compared with the US$27.6 million amount of the award). Counsel for SPP in that case, W. Laurence Craig, subsequently wrote of discounting ICSID awards for the annulment risk, a risk which, with "the associated time and expense of the conduct of annulment proceedings could only lead to the conclusion that a negotiated settlement would present a preferable alternative if reasonable terms could be achieved." W.L. Craig, The Final Chapter in the Pyramids Case: Discounting an ICSID Award for Annulment Risk, 8 ICSID Rev.—FILJ 264, 290 (1993). The above-mentioned amount of Egypt's payment is published in that article (ibid., 291).

[183] The awards are listed in Ch. 7, n. 128.

[184] *See Benvenuti & Bonfant v. Congo*, Award, August 15, 1980, 1 ICSID Rep. 335 (1993).

[185] *Benvenuti & Bonfant v. Congo*, Tribunal de Grande Instance, Paris, Judgment, January 13, 1981, 1 ICSID Rep. 369 (1993).

[186] *Benvenuti & Bonfant v. Congo*, Court of Appeal, Paris, Judgment, June 26, 1981, 1 ICSID Rep. 369, 371 (1993).

[187] Ibid. [188] Ibid.

low-income housing units. Rendered in 1988, the award granted SOABI compensation for Senegal's wrongful termination of the contract eight years earlier.[189] SOABI proceeded to obtain, from the Tribunal de Grande Instance of Paris, an order granting *exequatur* of the award. Senegal appealed to the Court of Appeal of Paris. It held that, in accordance with the New Code of Civil Procedure, the order should be set aside. This was because SOABI had failed to demonstrate "that the award will be enforced on assets assigned by the State of Senegal to an economic and commercial activity, and that no objection could therefore be made for immunity from enforcement."[190] The decision of the Paris Court of Appeal was, however, overturned by the French Court of Cassation. In terms similar to those employed by the Court of Appeal a decade earlier in the *Benvenuti & Bonfant* case, the Court of Cassation held that the Court of Appeal had inappropriately relied on provisions of the New Code of Civil Procedure that were excluded by the "autonomous and simplified regime for recognition and enforcement" instituted by Articles 53 and 54 of the ICSID Convention.[191]

LETCO v. Liberia was a third case of the period in which there were court proceedings to enforce the award. As explained in section III of this chapter, LETCO was a French-controlled Liberian company. The award, made in 1986, granted it compensation for Liberia's breach of the forestry concession agreement signed by the parties in 1970.[192] On the company's application, the award was granted recognition and enforcement by an order of the U.S. District Court for the Southern District of New York. Executions were then issued on registry fees and taxes due to Liberia from ship owners and agents of Liberia in the United States. On Liberia's motion, the same District Court, having found those assets to be immune from execution under the 1976 U.S. Foreign Sovereign Immunities Act (FSIA), because they were sovereign rather than commercial assets, vacated the executions on those assets.[193] LETCO went on to obtain writs of attachment seizing bank accounts of the Embassy of Liberia in Washington, D.C. The U.S. District Court for the District of Columbia, however, quashed the writs on the grounds that the Embassy's bank accounts were immune from attachment because they enjoyed diplomatic immunity under the Vienna Convention on Diplomatic Relations, which the United States ratified in 1972, and also because the accounts were entitled to sovereign immunity under the FSIA, the funds in the accounts being essentially public in nature.[194]

In an article discussing these court proceedings, Broches noted that it would have been unrealistic to try, during the preparation of the ICSID Convention, to incorporate in the treaty a waiver of sovereign immunity from execution. Moreover, it would, he said, be "wrong to cling to such a waiver on the sole assurance of compliance by a State with a Convention award rendered against it."[195]

[189] *See SOABI v. Senegal*, Award, February 25, 1988, 2 ICSID Rep. 190 (1994).

[190] *Senegal v. SOABI*, Court of Appeal, Paris, Decision, December 5, 1989, 5 ICSID Rev.—FILJ 135, 138 (1990). For commentary on this decision, *see* E. Gaillard, The Enforcement of ICSID Awards in France: The Decision of the Paris Court of Appeal in the SOABI Case, 5 ICSID Rev.—FILJ 69 (1990).

[191] *SOABI v. Senegal*, Court of Cassation, France, Decision, June 11, 1991, 2 ICSID Rep. 341 (1994).

[192] *See LETCO v. Liberia*, Award (n. 47).

[193] *See LETCO v. Liberia*, U.S. District Court, S.D.N.Y., Judgment, December 12, 1986, 2 ICSID Rep. 385 (1994).

[194] *See LETCO v. Liberia*, U.S. District Court, D.C., Judgment, April 16, 1987, 2 ICSID Rep. 391 (1994).

[195] A. Broches, Awards Rendered Pursuant to the ICSID Convention: Binding Force, Finality, Recognition, Enforcement, Execution, 2 ICSID Rev.—FILJ 287, 334 (1987).

The situation was, Broches pointed out, correctly summarized by Andrea Giardina in the following words:

Etant donnée la diversité des droits nationaux en matière d'exécution sur les biens appartenant aux Etats ... il se peut que l'exécution nationale des sentences du C.I.R.D.I. ne donne pas de résultants satisfaisants.

L'origine intergouvernementale du système reprend alors toute son importance. Dans la préambule de la convention il est déclaré que l'accord arbitral impose l'obligation d'exécuter la sentence eventuelle, et l'article 53 de la convention confirme que la sentence est obligatoire pour les parties en cause et qu'elle doit être exécutée dans les délais prescrits. La non-exécution constitue donc une violation de cette obligation spécifique permettant l'utilisation, au niveau interétatique, des mécanismes internationaux traditionels, tels que ceux de la protection diplomatique et de la tutelle juridictionnelle directe devant la Cour internationale de justice.[196]

Against that backdrop, in most of the cases considered in this section, the States ultimately voluntarily discharged their payment obligations under the awards, either in accordance with their terms or pursuant to agreements negotiated with their creditors. Thus, in 1983, Benvenuti & Bonfant informed ICSID that Congo had "fully complied with the ICSID award rendered in the dispute between them."[197] Likewise, after the court proceedings in France for the enforcement of the award in *SOABI v. Senegal*, the parties in that case negotiated a settlement. In several instances, successful claimants enlisted the assistance of the ICSID Secretariat and, through it, the help of the World Bank, in urging the States concerned to satisfy the awards. Typically in such cases, the Secretariat, and the Bank's office in charge of lending to the country concerned, would send reminders to the State emphasizing its obligation under the Convention to pay the award. The Secretariat and Bank sometimes became more actively involved in this area. The settlement discussions between SOABI and Senegal were reportedly facilitated by the Bank's resident representative in Dakar. As Secretary-General of ICSID, Shihata assisted parties in post-award settlement discussions on several occasions. Shihata's efforts in this respect in the *Klöckner* case were mentioned in his 1988 report to the Administrative Council quoted in section VI of this chapter.[198] At the request of SPP and Egypt, he arranged meetings of their representatives at World Bank premises in Washington and Paris. Counsel for SPP later reflected that Shihata's assistance may well have acted as a catalyst in achieving the negotiated settlement that emerged from those meetings.[199]

[196] A. Giardina, L'exécution des sentences du Centre international pour le règlement des differends relatifs aux investissements, 71 Revue critique de droit international privé 273, 291–292 (1983) as quoted in Broches (n. 195) 334.

[197] Disputes before the Centre, 1(1) News from ICSID 2 (1984).

[198] *See* text accompanying n. 157.

[199] *See* Craig (n. 182) 291.

9

ICSID from 1989 to 1999

This chapter deals with the last year of the 1980s and all of the subsequent decade. Though mostly placid for ICSID, the period was one of momentous change elsewhere in the World Bank Group and, of course, in the world at large. In 1989, the Communist regimes of Soviet "satellite" States in Eastern Europe collapsed. The Berlin Wall was opened late in 1989; within a year, Germany was reunited. Soon thereafter, in 1991, the Soviet Union was dissolved. This brought an abrupt end to the Cold War. Democracy and market capitalism spread in its aftermath. By one count, the number of electoral democracies increased from some 70 to 120 during the 1990s.[1] In Latin America above all, countries adopted the "Washington Consensus" development strategy of deregulation, liberalization and privatization identified with the World Bank, IMF and U.S. Treasury.[2] Increased global economic integration—globalization—was cemented by the establishment of the World Trade Organization (WTO) and a profusion of new regional and bilateral trade and investment treaties.[3] In relation to world output, the overall volume of trade grew more than twice as fast and investment flows quintupled between 1990 and 2000.[4]

As countries focused on encouraging foreign investment, interest waned in regulating the conduct of investors. Efforts undertaken since 1974 at the United Nations to develop a code of conduct for TNCs were abandoned in 1992, when Secretary-General Boutros Boutros-Ghali reported to the General Assembly that delegations had decided "no consensus was possible" on such a code in "the changed international economic environment."[5] It had been hoped that the code would, among many other topics, deal with the need for TNCs to refrain from corrupt practices in their dealings with foreign public officials.[6] Five years after the demise of the U.N. code, a negotiating group

[1] Or from about 40% to over 60% of the total number of countries in the world in 1989 and 1999, respectively. *See* Freedom in the World, Comparative and Historical Data, Electoral Democracy Data, available at <http://www.freedomhouse.org>.

[2] *See* J.E. Stiglitz, *Making Globalization Work* 16–17 (2007). The term "Washington Consensus," often used as an emotive label for so-called neoliberal policies, was coined by British economist John Williamson in 1989. He meant it then to refer to a set of reforms that "almost everyone in Washington thought were needed in Latin America as of that date" to escape the debt crisis, including fiscal discipline, reordering public expenditure priorities, tax reforms, liberalization of interest rates and a competitive exchange rate, as well as trade liberalization, liberalization of inward foreign direct investment and privatization. J. Williamson, From Reform to Agenda: A Short History of the Washington Consensus and What to Do Next, Finance & Development, September 2003, 10. But as Williamson ruefully recalled being told in 1993, by a former Finance Minister of Brazil, "just because I invented the term did not give me the right to say what it meant." Outspoken: A Conversation with John Williamson, *The Washington Post*, April 12, 2009, B2.

[3] *See* Agreement Establishing the World Trade Organization, April 15, 1994, 33 ILM 13 (1994) and section II of this chapter.

[4] *See* World Bank, *Economic Growth in the 1990s: Learning From a Decade of Reform* 63, 65 (2005); UNCTAD, Interactive Database on Investment Flows, <http://www.unctad.org>.

[5] Doc. AC/47/446, September 15, 1992, Annex, as quoted in T. Sagafi-Nejad, *The UN and Transnational Corporations: From Code of Conduct to Global Compact* 123 (2008). On the start of the efforts to develop a code of conduct for TNCs, *see* Ch. 7, n. 9 and accompanying text.

[6] *See* S. Asante, The Concept of the Good Corporate Citizen in International Business, 4 ICSID Rev—FILJ 1, 16 (1989).

convened by the OECD adopted a convention to achieve such an "internationalization of the basic idea of the 1977 Foreign Corrupt Practices Act of the U.S."[7] This OECD Convention required the parties to criminalize offering or giving bribes to foreign public officials in the conduct of international business.[8] Other international organizations that started to tackle the problem of corruption at this time included the World Bank. Its Executive Directors endorsed the Bank's first anti-corruption strategy in 1997.[9] The strategy called for corruption concerns to be incorporated more explicitly in the design of lending programs. Corruption being an outcome of poor governance, the strategy led to stepped-up assistance for the strengthening of public sector institutions, including civil service, legal and judicial reforms.[10]

The Bank had long resisted involvement in governance issues because of their domestic political overtones. Article IV(10) of the Bank's Articles of Agreement loomed large in this respect. It precluded the Bank from interfering in the political affairs of members or allowing their political character to influence its decisions; according to Article IV(10), only economic considerations were to be relevant to these decisions. In 1991, however, Ibrahim Shihata, as General Counsel of the Bank, issued a legal opinion providing the institution with an ample framework to tackle governance questions. The opinion interpreted Article IV(10) as allowing the Bank to address issues of governance in the "economic" sense of "the good order required for a positive investment climate and for the efficient use of resources."[11] This opinion came at a time when the end of the Cold War and the trend toward globalization had reduced the sensitivities (regarding foreign intervention) underlying the Bank's earlier more conservative understanding of its mandate in the governance area.[12]

The end of the Cold War and the spread of democracy also created more "political space" for environmental, human rights and other social action groups.[13] Many of these non-governmental organizations (NGOs) sprang up in response to economic inequalities and environmental problems associated with globalization; and their voice, influence and ability to form effective alliances were enormously magnified by

[7] Ibid.

[8] *See* OECD Doc. DAFFE/IME/BR (97)20, OECD Convention on Combating Bribery of Foreign Public Officials in International Business Transactions, November 21, 1997, Art. 1.

[9] The strategy was set out in a paper of the Bank's Poverty Reduction and Economic Management Network entitled Helping Countries Combat Corruption: The Role of the World Bank (September 1997). Elaboration of the strategy followed from the initiative of the Bank's new President, James D. Wolfensohn, to commit the institution to fighting the "cancer of corruption," as he put it in his address to the Bank Group Governors at their annual meetings in 1996. For the text of the address, *see* World Bank, *Voice for the World's Poor: Selected Speeches and Writings of World Bank President James D. Wolfensohn, 1995–2005* at 45 (2005). Wolfensohn served as President of the Bank from 1995 to 2005. Before joining the Bank, he had been President and Chief Executive Officer of James D. Wolfensohn, Inc., his own investment and corporate advisory firm, and Chairman of the Board of Trustees of the John F. Kennedy Center for the Performing Arts.

[10] Within a decade, over 20% of Bank-supported operations had public sector reform components. *See* World Bank, Strengthening World Bank Group Engagement on Governance and Anticorruption, March 21, 2007, Annex A, 43.

[11] Issues of "Governance" in Borrowing Members—The Extent of Their Relevance under the Bank's Articles of Agreement, Legal Memorandum by the General Counsel, IBRD Doc. Sec. M91-0131, February 5, 1991, reprinted in I.F.I. Shihata, *The World Bank Legal Papers* 248, 280 (2000).

[12] *Cf.* C. Weaver, *Hypocrisy Trap: The World Bank and the Poverty of Reform* 100 (2008). *Cf. also* D. Kapur and R. Webb, Governance-related Conditionalities of the International Financial Institutions, G-24 Discussion Paper Series, No. 6, August 2000, 2.

[13] B. Rich, *Mortgaging the Earth: The World Bank, Environmental Impoverishment and the Crisis of Development* 133 (1994).

the new computer and telecommunications technologies that became widely available in the 1990s.[14] NGO lobbying of governments was conspicuously successful in North America—resulting, for example, in the 1993 agreements on environmental and labor cooperation supplementing the North American Free Trade Agreement (NAFTA).[15]

Also in 1993, the World Bank, stung by protests of NGOs, acted to improve the accountability and transparency of its operations by establishing its independent Inspection Panel. Consisting of three members appointed by the Executive Directors on the nomination of the President of the Bank, the Panel was to investigate complaints of groups of individuals affected by failures of the Bank to comply with its operational policies and procedures. A related step taken by the Executive Directors in September 1993 was to revise the Bank's Policy on Disclosure of Information, to make more Bank documents publicly available and to set up a Public Information Center to respond to outside requests for documents and information.[16]

As the decade came to a close, NGOs opposing globalization led demonstrations that upstaged the WTO Ministerial Meeting in Seattle. Efforts by some of the same groups were instrumental in putting an end in 1998 to the negotiation of a Multilateral Agreement on Investment (MAI).

The MAI was to have replicated, in a wider instrument, many provisions of the BITs and other investment treaties that were being made in large numbers during the 1990s. Section I of this chapter describes this growing network of treaties, which was to have such a tremendous impact on ICSID. The MAI episode is also discussed in this section. There were many new signatures and ratifications of the ICSID Convention in the 1990s. They are recounted in section II, which also looks at the working of the ICSID Secretariat during the decade. An overview of the cases submitted to ICSID between 1989 and 2000 is provided in section III. Among them were the first Additional Facility cases. The Additional Facility cases, six of which were brought to the Centre under the investment chapter of the NAFTA, are examined in section IV. The potential of BITs to generate cases for ICSID started to be realized in earnest in this period. Several of the new BIT cases led to decisions that were particularly influential in the development of subsequent jurisprudence. These leading BIT cases are examined in section V.

[14] Ibid. 133; J. Mathews, Power Shift, 76 Foreign Affairs 50, 51 (1997). The number of internationally active NGOs is estimated to have grown from some 6,000 in 1990 to 26,000 in 1999. S. Mallaby, *The World's Banker* 262 (2004).

[15] *See* Mathews (n. 14) 54. The supplemental agreements were the North American Agreement on Environmental Cooperation and the North American Agreement on Labor Cooperation, September 13, 1993, reprinted in CCH Inc., *NAFTA Text including supplemental agreements* 747 and 775 (1994).

[16] The Inspection Panel was established by a September 22, 1993 resolution of the Executive Directors of the Bank. Its creation followed an independent review of the implementation of two major projects supported by the Bank on the Narmada River in India. The projects involved the construction of a dam, a water delivery system and drainage network. Local and international NGOs had criticized the environmental assessment and the resettlement and rehabilitation components of the projects. The independent review, commissioned by then World Bank President Barber B. Conable, was chaired by Bradford Morse, who had previously been Administrator of the United Nations Development Programme and, like Conable, was also a former U.S. Congressman. The report of the review team was released in June 1992. It was highly critical of the Bank for failures to abide by its policies in the areas identified by the NGOs. *See* I.F.I. Shihata, *The World Bank Inspection Panel* 5–13, 28–30 (1994).

I. The growing network of investment treaties

Reference was made in Chapter 2 to the conclusion of the first BITs in the late 1950s and early 1960s.[17] Treaties of this kind accumulated slowly in the subsequent two decades; by 1982, there were still fewer than 200 BITs.[18] The tempo of BIT-making quickened in the second half of the 1980s so that there were almost 370 such treaties in existence by the end of that decade. Most of these initial BITs were concluded between industrial and developing countries on the basis of a model text supplied by the industrial country. The industrial countries involved were principally Western European States, with the United States launching its own BIT program only in 1982. Their developing country treaty partners were mainly African and Asian nations. Mention was made in Chapter 2 of the derivation of BITs from FCNs and the OECD Draft Conventions.[19] As subsequently embellished, they typically set forth undertakings by each State party to extend, in respect of admitted investments of nationals of the other party, fair and equitable treatment; full protection and security; and national and most-favored-nation (MFN) treatment. They generally also committed each State to observe undertakings made with regard to investments of nationals of the other State; to guarantee the unrestricted transfer of their investments and returns; and to refrain from expropriating investments, except against prompt, adequate and effective or just compensation.[20] The expropriation provisions normally covered not only direct or outright takings but also indirect expropriations, that is, measures having effect equivalent to expropriation. BITs concluded by the United States took the path-breaking step of providing for national and MFN treatment in respect of admission also, with sectors exempted from the general admission standards specified in lists annexed to the treaties.[21]

Like most treaties, the BITs provided for the ad hoc arbitral settlement of disputes between the States parties over the interpretation or application of the treaty. As proposed by Aron Broches in his address to the Administrative Council of ICSID in 1967, States commenced at the end of the 1960s to add to BITs provisions setting forth their consents to submit disputes with covered investors to arbitration under the ICSID Convention.[22] During the next two decades, such provisions on the arbitral settlement of investment disputes became *de rigueur* in BITs between parties to the ICSID Convention.[23] In the first half of the 1980s, as the circle of countries entering into BITs grew to include more non-parties to the ICSID Convention, BITs started to appear with provisions on the settlement of investment disputes referring to other

[17] *See* Ch. 2, section II(B).

[18] The quantitative data on BITs in this chapter are compiled from the ICSID Database of Bilateral Investment Treaties, available at <https://icsid.worldbank.org/apps/ICSIDWEB/resources/Pages/default.aspx>.

[19] *See* Ch. 2, text accompanying n. 73.

[20] Though the BITs were cast in reciprocal terms, in the usual case of a BIT between an industrial and a developing country, there would generally be only a one-way flow of investment to benefit from the treaty, from the industrial to the developing country. *See* M. Sornarajah, *The International Law on Foreign Investment* 218 (2d ed. 2004).

[21] *See* Treaty Concerning the Reciprocal Encouragement and Protection of Investments, Egypt–United States, September 29, 1982, reprinted in ICSID, Investment Treaties, Release 94-3 (June 1994), Art. II(1) and II(3) and annex. This was the first modern U.S. BIT.

[22] For details, *see* Ch. 6, text accompanying n. 144, and Ch. 7, text accompanying nn. 95–100.

[23] For examples of BITs from the 1970s and 1980s with provisions of this kind referring to ICSID, *see* Ch. 7, nn. 96–100.

forms of arbitration, mainly arbitration under the ICSID Additional Facility Rules[24] or under the UNCITRAL Arbitration Rules.[25]

With the demise of Communism, BITs began to be made at unprecedented rates. In the period 1989 to 1991, the number of BITs signed annually leapt from 30 to over 80. Following the dissolution of the Soviet Union, BIT signings surged to around 120 annually in 1992 and 1993. BIT-making then intensified further: some 160 to 200 of these treaties were concluded in each of the following five years. The pace slackened in 1999, but well over 100 BITs were entered into during that year as well. In all, more than 1,400 BITs were concluded between 1989 and 2000. The treaties of this period were generally similar in content to the earlier BITs. But, as may be surmised from the enormous number of these new BITs, many more countries—some 170 in total—had come to participate in such treaties. About 640 of the roughly 1,400 new BITs were entered into by former Soviet republics and the Eastern European countries in transition from Communism. Having had hardly any BITs before, Latin American countries entered into some 260 BITs in the 1990s; Argentina led the way with 54 of the treaties, followed by Chile with 48. China increased the number of its BITs more than fivefold, to over 80 during the decade. The extent of the acceptance of these kinds of treaties is underlined by the fact that nearly half of the numerous new BITs had no Western industrial country as a party and were instead concluded among developing and transition countries only. Endorsement by such countries of the substance of BITs was demonstrated by their enactment in the 1990s of investment promotion laws with provisions inspired by those of the treaties.[26]

In keeping with the by-then established practice, virtually all of the BITs made in the period 1989 to 1999 had provisions recording the consent of each party to submit to arbitration disputes with investors from the other party to the treaty. As in the earlier treaties, the overwhelming majority of these provisions on the settlement of investment disputes referred to arbitration under the ICSID Convention.[27] Some of the newer BITs, again especially if they involved a non-party to the ICSID Convention, provided instead for the settlement of investment disputes by arbitration under the Additional Facility or UNCITRAL Rules.[28] The BITs concluded by former Soviet republics and other transition countries commonly referred in this context to arbitration under the auspices of the Arbitration Institute of the Stockholm Chamber of

[24] References to the earliest BITs referring to arbitration under the Additional Facility Rules are provided in Ch. 7, n. 214.

[25] The first BITs providing for the settlement of investor–State disputes by arbitration under the UNCITRAL Arbitration Rules (UNGAOR 31st Sess., Supp. No. 17, Doc. A/31/17 (1976)) included, for example, the Agreement for the Promotion and Protection of Investments, Haiti–United Kingdom, March 18, 1985, reprinted in ICSID, Investment Treaties, Release 1985 (June 1986), Art. 8 (signed at a time when Haiti was not an ICSID Convention Contracting State).

[26] *See, e.g.*, Law of Azerbaijan Republic on Protection of Foreign Investments, Law No. 57, January 15, 1992 as amended by Law No. 97, April 7, 1992, reprinted in ICSID, Investment Laws of the World, Release 2004-1 (March 2004).

[27] *See, e.g.*, Accord sur l'encouragement et la protection réciproque des investissements, France–Mongolia, November 8, 1991, reprinted in ICSID, Investment Treaties, Release 95-2 (April 1995), Art. 8; Agreement for the Promotion and Protection of Investments, Malaysia–United Arab Emirates, October 11, 1991, reprinted in ICSID, Investment Treaties, Release 95-2 (April 1995), Art. 9.

[28] *See, e.g.*, Treaty Concerning the Reciprocal Encouragement and Protection of Investment, Germany–South Africa, September 11, 1995, reprinted in ICSID, Investment Treaties, Release 98-1 (March 1998), Art. 11(2) (providing for Additional Facility arbitration); Agreement for the Promotion and Protection of Investments, Bahrain–United Kingdom, October 13, 1991, reprinted in ICSID, Investment Treaties, Release 92-4 (March 1993), Art. 8 (providing for UNCITRAL Rules arbitration). Of the parties to these BITs, South Africa was not an ICSID Convention Contracting State as of June 30, 2010; nor was Bahrain at the time of the conclusion of its BIT with the U.K.

Commerce (SCC).[29] Increasingly during the 1990s, BIT provisions on the settlement of investment disputes referred to two or more of these forms of arbitration, allowing the investor to choose between them for its particular case. A pattern established for U.S. BITs in the early 1990s, and subsequently widely followed, particularly in BITs of Western Hemisphere countries, was for the treaty to provide for arbitration under either the ICSID Convention or Additional Facility Rules, whichever of the two might be applicable, or under the UNCITRAL Arbitration Rules.[30]

The first half of the 1990s also saw the conclusion of several multilateral treaties containing substantive rules on investment and provisions on the settlement of investment disputes like those of BITs. These multilateral treaties notably included the NAFTA,[31] entered into by Canada, Mexico and the United States to promote and protect investment flows as well as to liberalize trade among them. The new multilateral treaties also included the Energy Charter Treaty (ECT).[32] Addressing trade and transit in energy materials and the promotion and protection of investments in the energy sector, the ECT was signed by States of Western and Eastern Europe and the former Soviet Union, among others, to promote energy security in the aftermath of the Cold War.[33] The investment chapter of the NAFTA, and to a lesser extent the investment parts of the ECT, were influenced by U.S. BIT practice. Repeating the pattern set by those BITs, the provisions of the NAFTA and the ECT on the settlement of investment disputes recorded the consent of each party to submit disputes with investors from any of the other parties to arbitration under the ICSID Convention, the ICSID Additional Facility Rules or the UNCITRAL Arbitration Rules.[34] The ECT added arbitration under the SCC Institute Rules to the list of available forms of arbitration.[35] A large role was envisaged for the Secretary-General of ICSID by the NAFTA, which designated that official as the appointing authority of arbitrators for UNCITRAL Rules as well as ICSID Convention and Additional Facility Rules proceedings under the treaty.[36] Like the 1962 OECD Convention, but much more elaborately, the NAFTA foresaw the need to allow for the consolidation of proceedings.[37] According to the NAFTA consolidation provision, since adapted for other treaties, when two or more claims submitted to arbitration had a question of law or fact in common, the claims could "in the interests of fair and efficient resolution of the claims" be consolidated and determined by an UNCITRAL Rules tribunal appointed by the Secretary-General of ICSID.[38]

[29] *See, e.g.*, Agreement on Promotion and Mutual Protection of Investments, Norway–Russia, October 4, 1995, reprinted in ICSID, Investment Treaties, Release 98-2 (September 1998), Art. 8. Arbitration under the SCC Institute Rules had long been favored by parties engaged in "East–West" trade and investment.

[30] The first U.S. BIT with such a provision was the Treaty concerning Business and Economic Relations, Poland–United States, March 21, 1990, reprinted in ICSID, Investment Treaties, Release 92-3 (October 1992), Art. IX. Similar provisions were included in the BITs and signed by the U.S. in 1991 with Argentina and the Czech Republic and then incorporated in the U.S. model BIT in 1992. *See* K.J. Vandelvede, *U.S. International Investment Agreements* 634–639 (2009).

[31] North American Free Trade Agreement, December 17, 1992, 32 ILM 289 (1993). The principal provisions related to investments were set out in Chapter 11 of the NAFTA.

[32] December 17, 1994, 10 ICSID Rev.—FILJ 258 (1995). The main provisions regarding investments were in Parts III and V of the ECT.

[33] Altogether, the ECT had at the outset 49 signatory States. The European Communities also signed the treaty.

[34] *See* NAFTA (n. 31) Art. 1120(1); ECT (n. 32) Art. 26(4)(a) and 26(24)(b).

[35] *See* ECT (n. 32) Art. 26(4)(c).

[36] *See* NAFTA (n. 31) Art. 1124(1).

[37] In regard to the 1962 Draft OECD Convention provision on consolidation, *see* Ch. 2, n. 43 and accompanying text.

[38] *See* NAFTA (n. 31) Art. 1126.

The burgeoning network of mostly bilateral investment treaties had inconsistencies and gaps in its coverage of investment flows. In 1992, the Development Committee, a joint Ministerial Committee of Boards of Governors of the World Bank and the IMF, issued a set of universal guidelines on the legal treatment of foreign investments by their host states. These were the World Bank Guidelines on the Legal Treatment of Foreign Direct Investment. As indicated by their name, however, they were merely hortatory.[39] A few years later, it was decided at the OECD to seek the binding global treaty, providing "an overall cohesive structure,"[40] that had eluded the organization 30 years earlier. Meeting in May 1995, the OECD Ministerial Council approved the start of negotiations in the OECD aimed at reaching such a treaty, the MAI.[41] The communiqué of the meeting confidently proclaimed that the MAI would "provide a broad multilateral framework for international investment with high standards for the liberalization of investment regimes and investment protection with effective dispute settlement procedures."[42] While it would be negotiated by OECD members only, the plan was that, once finalized, the MAI would be offered to non-members as well.[43]

The negotiations were launched at the OECD in September 1995.[44] A negotiating text for the treaty was put together by various OECD expert groups. It owed much to the NAFTA and U.S. BITs. Thus, for example, in addition to the usual general standards of treatment of admitted investments and protections against currency transfer restrictions and expropriations, it envisaged, as a cornerstone of investment liberalization, the extension of national and MFN treatment obligations to the admission process.[45] For the settlement of investment disputes, it suggested the familiar three alternatives—ICSID Convention, Additional Facility Rules and UNCITRAL Rules arbitration—and added, as a fourth, arbitration under the Rules of the International Chamber of Commerce (ICC).[46]

Despite the optimism surrounding the launch of the negotiations, differences soon emerged among OECD members over a number of basic issues, such as the definition of covered investments and the design of the dispute settlement procedures.[47] Criticism of the initiative was meanwhile mounting outside the OECD. Some questioned the wisdom of attempting to formulate such a treaty without substantial developing country participation.[48] In February 1997, the negotiating text was leaked to citizen groups in Canada. It was immediately spread through a network of NGOs, which quickly organized a massive Internet-based campaign against the MAI.[49] In

[39] Further details on the World Bank Guidelines are provided at section II(B) of this chapter.

[40] W. Witherell, Towards an International Set of Rules for Investment: The OECD Initiative, 12(1) News from ICSID 3, 5 (1995).

[41] *See* OECD, Communiqué of the Meeting of the OECD Council at Ministerial Level, May 23–24, 1995 (May 1995 Communiqué). Within the OECD, the English name of the initiative had originally been the Multilateral Investment Agreement, MIA. The order of the second and third words was rearranged when it was realized that, for Americans, the MIA acronym evoked the politically contentious issue of soldiers classified as missing in action in Southeast Asia. In French, the initiative was throughout called l'Accord multilatéral sur l'investissement or, endearingly, l'AMI.

[42] May 1995 Communiqué (n. 41). [43] *See* ibid.

[44] *See* OECD Press Release, SG/PRESS (95) 6, September 27, 1995.

[45] *Cf.* Multilateral Agreement on Investment, Draft Consolidated Text, OECD Doc. DAFFE/MAI (98)7/REV 1, April 22, 1998, Arts III(1) and III(2).

[46] *Cf.* ibid. Art. V(d)(2). The ICC Rules then in force were the 1988 ICC Rules of Conciliation and Arbitration, reprinted in 13 YBCA 179 (1988).

[47] *See* D. Henderson, *The MAI Affair: A Story and its Lessons* 25 (1999).

[48] *See* M. Sornarajah, *The International Law on Foreign Investment* 295 (2d ed. 2004).

[49] K. Tieleman, The Failure of the Multilateral Agreement on Investment (MAI) and the Absence of a Global Public Policy Network, Case Study for the U.N. Vision Project on Global Public Policy Networks, 11, available at <http://old.gppi.net/fileadmin/gppi/Tieleman_MAI_GPP_Network.pdf>.

addition to Internet postings of the negotiating text and critiques of it, the campaigners published books attacking the MAI, petitioned the OECD and member governments and staged street protests in Europe and the United States.[50] Prominently active in the campaign were Public Citizen, a U.S.-based consumer advocacy organization, and other NGOs that had opposed the NAFTA. They saw the provisions of the MAI as potentially undermining the sovereignty of States and in particular their ability to regulate in the public interest. Singled out for special opprobrium were the provisions on the settlement of investment disputes, which seemed to give private investors ample scope to attack governmental measures for inconsistencies with the MAI's terms.[51] The criticisms of these mostly industrial country NGOs thus resembled the arguments, also rooted in concerns for sovereignty, of earlier developing country proponents of the Calvo Doctrine and NIEO.[52]

Fears of NGOs regarding the MAI provisions on the settlement of investment disputes seemed to be confirmed by *Ethyl v. Canada*. This was the first UNCITRAL Arbitration Rules proceeding under the investment chapter of the NAFTA. It had been initiated just after the leak of the MAI negotiating text. A Virginia corporation with a Canadian subsidiary, Ethyl manufactured MMT, a highly toxic fuel additive. Ethyl commenced the arbitration as a result of the enactment, in the context of efforts to reduce air pollution, of a Canadian statute banning MMT imports. In its notice of arbitration, Ethyl claimed compensation of US$250 million in respect of the ban, which it said violated various provisions of the NAFTA investment chapter, including the guarantee against uncompensated expropriatory measures.[53] NGOs called attention to the supposed lack of transparency and accountability of the arbitral process in such cases[54] and raised the specter "that under the MAI, TNCs in the 29 OECD countries would follow Ethyl's example and use the power of the agreement to challenge environmental and other safeguards in order to sue governments."[55]

Support of OECD governments for the MAI initiative, already weakening, began to fall away under the barrage of criticism. In April 1998, the OECD Ministerial Council decided that there should be "a period of assessment and further consultation between

[50] *See* M. Khor, NGOs Mount Protests Against MAI, April 1998, available at <https://www.globalpolicy.org/component/content/article/209/43217.html>. Books referred to in the text included M. Barlow and T. Clarke, *MAI and the Threat to American Freedom* (1998) and A. Jackson and M. Sanger, *Dismantling Democracy: The Multilateral Agreement on Investment and its Impact* (1998). One of the leaders of the campaign against the MAI, Lori Wallach of Public Citizen, described the effort as applying the "Dracula strategy," meaning that, like fictional vampires, the secretly negotiated MAI could not tolerate exposure to daylight. *See* S. George, *The Lugano Report: On Preserving Capitalism in the Twenty-First Century* at x (2003).

[51] The Alarming Multilateral Agreement on Investment (MAI) Now Being Negotiated at the OECD: Public Citizen's Global Trade Watch Backgrounder, available at <www.citizen.org/Page.aspx?pid=3789>.

[52] For a study drawing a similar parallel, between discontent in industrial countries over investment arbitration and earlier developing country critiques, *see* G. Aguilar-Alvarez and W. Park, The New Face of Investment Arbitration: NAFTA Chapter 11, 28 Yale L.J. 365 (2003).

[53] *See Ethyl v. Canada*, Notice of Arbitration under the Arbitration Rules of the United Nations Commission on International Trade Law and the North American Free Trade Agreement, April 14, 1997, secs. E and F, available at <https://www.uncitral.org/res/transparency-registry/registry/data/can/ethyl-corporation_html/ethyl-02.pdf>.

[54] In that "the proceedings are conducted in secret, the records are not publicly accessible and the decision is legally binding" and not subject to appeal to national courts. M. Sforza and M. Vallianatos, Preamble Center for Public Policy, NAFTA & Environmental Laws: Ethyl Corp. v. Government of Canada, available at <https://www.globalpolicy.org/component/content/article/212/45381.html>.

[55] M. Sforza-Roderick and others, A Concise Guide to the Multilateral Agreement on Investment: Supporters' and Opponents' Views, available at <https://www.globalpolicy.org/component/content/article/209/43215.html>.

the negotiating parties and with interested parts of their societies" before the negotiations would resume in October 1998. The French government then appointed a special commission to inquire into the MAI and make recommendations on the next steps; its interim report was completed in September 1998 after consultations with business, labor, NGOs and other interested groups.[56] Like many of the NGOs, the report took the view that the MAI, as proposed, could erode members' sovereignty. It recommended that France should withdraw from the negotiations unless there were a "fundamental reorientation" of the initiative; changes that the report considered necessary included significantly narrowing substantive guarantees, for example to eliminate coverage of indirect expropriations, and confining dispute settlement procedures to cases between States only.[57] Shortly after publication of the report, Prime Minister Lionel Jospin made a statement on the MAI in France's National Assembly. Agreeing with the report that the MAI presented "fundamental problems with respect to the sovereignty of States," he announced that France would not be taking part in the resumed negotiations at the OECD.[58] When the negotiators reconvened without French participation, they could agree only to consult further on the concerns that had been raised with their governments over such issues as sovereignty, protection of labor rights and the environment.[59] The further consultations resulted in a final abandonment of the negotiations in December 1998.[60] The still-growing network of investment treaties was therefore to remain without the "overall cohesive structure"[61] that it might have been given by an MAI.

II. Institutional developments

A. Ratifications of the Convention

In 1992, all but one of the 15 former Soviet republics joined the World Bank. The fifteenth, Tajikistan, joined the following year, as did constituent republics of the old Czechoslovak and Yugoslav federations. Most of these many new members of the World Bank quickly also joined its financial affiliates—the IFC, IDA and MIGA—and signed and ratified the ICSID Convention.[62] In all, 15 of these republics became Contracting States in the 1990s. During the decade, the same reversal of policies that led Latin American countries to sign many investment treaties resulted in the willingness of most of them, after years of hostility, to participate in the ICSID Convention. Argentina, Bolivia, Colombia, Chile, Venezuela and four of the Central American republics became Contracting States in the 1990s. By the end of the decade, almost all Latin American countries were parties to the ICSID Convention. Major exceptions were Brazil and Mexico. Other large countries, however, became Contracting States between 1989 and 2000, including the biggest of all in terms of population, the People's Republic of China. Australia and Turkey finally also ratified the ICSID Convention.

[56] Henderson (n. 47) 31. The commission was headed by Catherine Lalumière, a Member of the European Parliament and former Minister of Consumption of France. Its Rapport intérimaire sur l'Accord Multilatéral sur l'Investissement (AMI) was thus often called the Lalumière Report.

[57] Henderson (n. 47) 31. [58] Ibid. [59] Ibid. 32.

[60] *See* ibid. 2. An editorial in the *Financial Times* had already pronounced an epitaph for the MAI, stating that "there is one lesson for international negotiations worth drawing from the MAI fiasco: this is how not to do it." A Case of MAI Culpa, *Financial Times*, October 20, 1998, 21.

[61] *See* n. 40 and accompanying text.

[62] A notable exception was Russia which, while it joined the IFC, IDA and MIGA, never ratified the ICSID Convention after signing it in 1992.

In addition, African countries that were introducing market-based reforms—Algeria, Mozambique and Tanzania—joined the list of Contracting States during the 1990s. Overall, 40 countries became Contracting States during the period 1989 to 1999, even more than in the first couple of years of the ICSID Convention, bringing the total to 131 by the end of 1999.

B. The Secretariat

In 1989, and again in 1995, Ibrahim Shihata was re-elected Secretary-General of the Centre.[63] He continued to combine the post with service as General Counsel of the World Bank until 1998.[64] Shihata then stepped down from the General Counsel position but remained Secretary-General for another two years. His staff at the Secretariat steadily grew in number during the period. In 1989, as for most of the preceding years, there were five staff members. By 1993, there were eight, half of them lawyers; and at the end of the decade, the Secretariat had 11 staff, including five lawyers. Additional staff meant increased administrative expenditures which, as before, were met entirely by the World Bank. In current dollars, such expenditures of ICSID equaled about US$1.1 million in 1993, rising to US$1.5 million by 1999. Some of the expenditures in 1999 were for the construction and launch of a website for ICSID. Providing electronic access to the Centre's basic documents and several of its publications, the website facilitated outreach by the Secretariat.[65] Also in 1999, the Administrative Council elected a Deputy Secretary-General for the first time.[66] This was ICSID's then Legal Adviser, the election having been proposed as merely formalizing his responsibility for the day-to-day management of the Secretariat under the Secretary-General.[67]

In the first half of the 1990s, ICSID continued to have between five and ten pending cases each year. New advisory activities in the field of foreign investment law ensured that the staff were fully occupied despite the light caseload. As indicated in Chapter 7, their work on ICSID's publications in this field helped them to develop the expertise necessary for these advisory activities. The staff also benefited from assisting with the preparation of the World Bank Guidelines on the Legal Treatment of Foreign Direct Investment. These World Bank Guidelines were, as already mentioned, issued in 1992 by the World Bank-IMF Development Committee.[68] The Guidelines

[63] *See* Administrative Council Resolution AC(23)/RES/70, Election of the Secretary-General, September 28, 1989, reprinted in ICSID 1990 Ann. Rep. 16; Administrative Council Resolution AC(29)/RES/83, Election of the Secretary-General, October 12, 1995, reprinted in ICSID 1996 Ann. Rep. 17.

[64] Unlike earlier proposals for the election of the General Counsel of the Bank as Secretary-General of ICSID, the re-election proposals in 1989 and 1995 did not address the desirability of combining the roles but merely noted the excellence of Shihata's service to the Centre. *See* Selection of the Secretary-General of the International Centre for Settlement of Investment Disputes, Memorandum of the Chairman of the Administrative Council, April 12, 1989, 2; Selection of the Secretary-General of the International Centre for Settlement of Investment Disputes, Memorandum of the Chairman of the Administrative Council, April 28, 1999, 2. As mentioned in Ch. 10 (text accompanying n. 34), the proposals for the election of each of Shihata's three immediate successors cited tradition as the reason for combining the General Counsel and Secretary-General positions.

[65] *See* ICSID Home Page on the Web, 16(1) News from ICSID 1 (Winter 1999).

[66] *See* Administrative Council Resolution AC(33)/RES/92—Election of a Deputy Secretary-General, September 30, 1999, reprinted in 2000 ICSID Ann. Rep. 26.

[67] Doc. AC/99/4, Election of a Deputy Secretary-General: Nomination and Recommendation of the Chairman, September 10, 1999, attachment (Chairman's letter of July 7, 1999 to Administrative Council Members). In this sense, the election entailed a change only in the title rather than the content of the position.

[68] The formal name of the Development Committee was the Joint Ministerial Committee of the Bank and the Fund on the Transfer of Real Resources to Developing Countries. It was established in

were drawn up, by a working group chaired by Shihata, in his capacity as General Counsel of the Bank,[69] in response to a 1991 request of the Development Committee for a "legal framework" embodying "the essential legal principles" conducive to the promotion of foreign direct investment.[70] The Guidelines suggested standards on the admission of foreign investment, on its treatment after admission, including treatment with respect to currency transfers, and on expropriation and the settlement of investment disputes.[71] It was hoped that the Guidelines would help "in the evolution of generally acceptable standards which complement, but do not substitute for, bilateral investment treaties."[72] By design, the Guidelines reflected then-current trends in laws, treaties and other instruments, with additions, especially regarding the transparency of investment regimes, based on what the World Bank had found to be "best practice" in the area.[73] The trends in laws, treaties and other instruments were identified in surveys carried out for the working group by ICSID Secretariat staff, who also assisted the working group in compiling its reports to the Development Committee.[74] Drawing on the experience, the staff went on to collaborate in World Bank Group advisory operations, reviewing and commenting on draft investment laws of some dozen countries in the second half of the 1990s.[75]

C. The Panels of Conciliators and of Arbitrators

The number of proceedings administered by the Centre had meanwhile begun to rise. The annual intake of new cases jumped from one or two in the period 1991 to 1995 to an average of eight from 1996 to 1999. By the last year of the decade, there were 19 cases pending at ICSID, as compared with just five in 1995. The potential for investment disputes had grown with the vast increases of investment flows in the 1990s; and the scope for the disputes to be brought to the Centre had also expanded with the spread of investment treaties containing ICSID clauses. Thus, more than two-thirds of the new cases in 1996 to 1999 came to ICSID under such treaties. The heavier caseload necessitated the enlargement of the Secretariat noted above. It also added to the practical importance of the Panel of Arbitrators of the Centre, especially in view of the greater numbers of appointments to arbitral tribunals that the Chairman of the Administrative Council was required to make under Article

1974 by parallel resolutions of the Boards of Governors of the World Bank and the IMF. The members were Governors of the World Bank or IMF, ministers or others of comparable rank. Each country or group of countries that appointed or elected an Executive Director of the World Bank or IMF appointed a member of the Committee. The Committee met twice annually. Its wide mandate was "to maintain an overview of the development process and ... advise and report to the Boards of Governors of the Bank and the Fund on all aspects of the broad question of the transfer of real resources to developing countries." IBRD Board of Governors Resolution 294 and IMF Board of Governors Resolution 29-9 (October 2, 1974) para. 4(a).

[69] The working group's two other members were the then General Counsel of the IFC, José E. Camacho, and of MIGA, Luis Dodero.

[70] Communiqué of the 41st Meeting of the Development Committee, April 30, 1991, excerpted in I.F.I. Shihata, *Legal Treatment of Foreign Investment: The World Bank Guidelines* 383 (1993).

[71] The Guidelines are reprinted in 7 ICSID Rev.—FILJ 292 (1992) and in Shihata (n. 70) 155.

[72] Guidelines (n. 71) sixth preambular paragraph.

[73] *Cf.* ibid. fourth preambular paragraph.

[74] The surveys and reports are reprinted in Shihata (n. 70) 193–220, 221–336 and 393–400.

[75] *See* ICSID 1995 Ann. Rep. 9; ICSID 1996 Ann. Rep. 10; ICSID 1997 Ann. Rep. 11; ICSID 1998 Ann. Rep. 13. In the same period, a staff member of the ICSID Secretariat participated as an observer in the work of the OECD expert group charged with the elaboration of the provisions of the MAI on the settlement of disputes. *See* ICSID 1997 Ann. Rep. 5.

38 of the ICSID Convention. Between 1991 and 1994, the then Chairman of the Administrative Council[76] had, on Shihata's recommendation, made two new designations to the Panels of Conciliators and of Arbitrators and renewed several earlier designations, resulting again in a nine-person list of Chairman's designees.[77] Coaxing designations out of Contracting States continued, however, to be a problem. As of late 1996, almost half of the Contracting States had made no designations at all to the Panels. Shihata beseeched them to repair the omission in his report to that year's meeting of the Administrative Council.[78] He repeated the plea in his reports for each of the next three annual meetings.[79] Nor was Shihata reticent about the quality of Contracting States' designations to the Panels. As he remarked on one occasion, the designations were often of public officials who, "regardless of their qualifications, may not always be appropriate candidates [for appointment to arbitral tribunals] and at any rate may not have the time to serve as arbitrators."[80] Shihata urged Contracting States instead "to make designations to the Panels of highly qualified experts in international arbitration and conciliation and thus help us maintain those lists of experts who can be called upon to conduct and preside over proceedings in these fields."[81] Shihata's persistence was rewarded with some improvement in the proportion of Contracting States contributing designations although, by the end of the decade, as many as 40 percent of them had still not done so.[82]

D. Agreements with other arbitration institutions

A final development to be noted here is the conclusion by the Centre of several further agreements with other arbitration institutions under Article 63 of the Convention. Reference was made in Chapter 7 to the first such agreements, with the PCA and the Regional Centres for Commercial Arbitration at Kuala Lumpur and Cairo, pursuant to which they might host Convention proceedings if the parties concerned so desired.[83] In the 1990s, ICSID acceded to requests by four more dispute resolution centers to enter into such agreements with them. The centers were the Australian Commercial Disputes Centre and the Australian Centre for International Commercial Arbitration, both based in Sydney; the Singapore International Arbitration Centre; and the Gulf Cooperation Council Commercial Arbitration Centre in Bahrain.[84] Each of these

[76] This was Lewis T. Preston, President of the World Bank from 1991 to 1995. Before assuming the presidency of the Bank, Preston had been Chairman and Chief Executive Officer of J.P. Morgan.

[77] The nine were Mohamed Bedjaoui (Algerian), Aron Broches (Dutch), Ian Brownlie (British), Heribert Golsong (German), Monroe Leigh (American), Kéba Mbaye (Senegalese), José Maria Ruda (Argentine), Ignaz Seidl-Hohenveldern (Austrian) and Sompong Sucharitkul (Thai). *See* ICSID 1994 Ann. Rep. 7. Ruda died soon after his designation. Francisco Orrego Vicuña (Chilean) was designated to succeed him on the Panels in 1995. *See* ICSID 1995 Ann. Rep. 7. The new list, comprising nationals of five industrial countries and four developing countries, was more balanced geographically than before. *Cf.* Ch. 7, n. 69.

[78] *See* Report of the Secretary-General to the Administrative Council at its Thirtieth Annual Meeting, October 1–3, 1996, 2.

[79] *See* Reports of the Secretary-General to the Administrative Council at its Thirty-First Annual Meeting, September 23–25, 1997, 2; Thirty-Second Annual Meeting, October 6–8, 1998, 4; Thirty-Third Annual Meeting, September 28–30, 1999, 3.

[80] I.F.I. Shihata, Obstacles Facing ICSID's Proceedings and International Arbitration in General, 3(1) News from ICSID 9 (1986).

[81] Report of the Secretary-General to the Administrative Council at its Thirty-Third Annual Meeting, September 28–30, 1999, 3.

[82] *See* ibid.

[83] *See* Ch. 7, text accompanying n. 33.

[84] The agreements with the Australian centers were both signed in 1993; the one with the Singapore center was concluded in 1998; and the agreement with the center in Bahrain was signed in 1999.

centers was recently established; and for them the agreements had some promotional, as well as strictly practical, value. For ICSID, the agreements helped to underline that its proceedings did not have to be held at the seat of the Centre at World Bank headquarters in Washington, D.C. Parties nevertheless still often preferred holding proceedings there, or else at the Bank's office in Paris. To avoid overburdening those facilities, the four new agreements were made non-reciprocal; that is, unlike the earlier agreements with the PCA and the Kuala Lumpur and Cairo Centres, the new agreements did not provide for the possibility of ICSID also hosting the other institutions' proceedings.

III. An overview of cases submitted to ICSID between 1989 and 1999

Only one request for conciliation was registered at ICSID in the period 1989 to 1999. It involved, moreover, the same parties, contract and consent clause as in ICSID's very first conciliation case a dozen years earlier.[85] In the further proceeding, a conciliation commission was constituted;[86] and after it eventually issued its report, the parties reached a settlement.

Between 1989 and 1999, arbitration proceedings were instituted at ICSID in 43 new cases. Seven of these were Additional Facility cases[87] and the rest were initiated under the Convention. The governmental party was the respondent in all but one of the cases.[88] Latin American States, completely absent from the earlier cases, were respondents in the largest number of the new cases, 15 in all.[89] African countries were respondents in almost as many proceedings (13),[90] but in proportional terms far fewer than in the 1970s and 1980s. Claims were made against transition countries in five of the cases.[91] Three of the requests registered at ICSID in the 1990s were for arbitration against Western industrial countries including, startlingly at the time, the United States.[92] Asian countries were respondents in just four of the new cases,[93] a drop proportionately from the number of arbitrations launched against such countries during ICSID's first two decades.

[85] In *SEDITEX v. Madagascar.*

[86] As indicated in Ch. 7, n. 123, in the first proceeding the parties agreed to settle the dispute and close the proceeding before the constitution of a commission.

[87] These included six cases brought under the NAFTA: *Metalclad v. Mexico, Azinian v. Mexico, Waste Management v. Mexico, Loewen v. U.S., Feldman v. Mexico* and *Mondev v. U.S.*

[88] The exception was the arbitration brought by the Tanzanian parastatal Tanesco against IPTL, a joint venture with Malaysian participation.

[89] These were the four cases involving Mexico (*see* n. 87) plus the 11 following: *CDSE v. Costa Rica, Fedax v. Venezuela, Vivendi v. Argentina, Lanco v. Argentina, Houston Industries v. Argentina, Pey Casado v. Chile, Olguín v. Paraguay, CMIO v. Peru, Mobil v. Argentina, ENDESA v. Argentina* and *Astaldi v. Honduras.* There were in addition two arbitrations initiated in this period against Anglophone Caribbean countries: *Cable TV v. St. Kitts and Nevis* and *WRB v. Grenada.*

[90] In chronological order, these were *MHT v. Egypt, Vacuum Salt v. Ghana, AMT v. DRC, Goetz v. Burundi, SIREM v. Burkina Faso, Kufpec v. Congo, CFDT v. Côte d'Ivoire, ITC v. Liberia, Wena v. Egypt, Banro v. DRC, Alimenta v. Gambia, Middle East Cement v. Egypt* and *Mitchell v. DRC.*

[91] In *Tradex Hellas v. Albania, Leaf Tobacco v. Albania, CSOB v. Slovak Republic, Lemire v. Ukraine* and *Genin v. Estonia.*

[92] The three cases were *Maffezini v. Spain, Loewen v. U.S.* and *Mondev v. U.S.*

[93] These were *Scimitar v. Bangladesh, Gruslin v. Malaysia, Misima Mines v. Papua New Guinea* and the second *Gruslin v. Malaysia* case.

More than a quarter of the new cases—12, to be precise—involved natural persons as claimant investors. In five of the cases, the individuals were American,[94] and in one, Canadian.[95] Belgian nationals[96] were claimants in three of the cases, and a Spaniard,[97] Argentine[98] and Peruvian[99] in one each. In the remaining 31 arbitrations initiated from 1989 to 1999, the claimants were exclusively juridical persons, almost all of them companies organized in or controlled by nationals of the United States or Western European countries. A handful of the companies were major TNCs,[100] but the majority were much smaller, closely held enterprises. In many of the cases, the investors, and in some of the cases the States as well, were represented by well-known international law firms. More often than in earlier years, however, investors chose instead to be represented by sole practitioners and States by their own government lawyers.

In about 60 percent of the cases, the underlying investments were in the two broad economic sectors of industry and trade[101] and energy and mining.[102] Hardly more than 5 percent of the new cases, as compared with over 15 percent of the cases commenced before 1989, were in the agriculture, fishing and forestry sector.[103] On the other hand, the investments in a quarter of the new cases were in sectors missing in the earlier proceedings, in particular information and communications,[104] water and sanitation[105] and transportation.[106] Needless to say, the shift reflected the opening of those sectors to private foreign investment from the second half of the 1980s, particularly in Latin America.

As already explained, the surge in the number of cases in the 1990s followed from the spread of investment treaties with ICSID clauses. Three-fifths of the requests for arbitration registered at ICSID between 1989 and 1999 were based on such clauses in investment treaties—chiefly BITs but also the NAFTA. The treaties created opportunities not only for more but also different types of claims to be brought to ICSID. In the course of the 1990s, disputes before ICSID involving alleged expropriations and violations of broad treatment standards in investment treaties came to eclipse claims of failures of contractual performance; indeed, in many of the new cases, unlike all of the

[94] Robert Azinian and others (n. 87); Joseph C. Lemire (n. 91); Alex Genin (n. 91); Marvin Roy Feldman Karpa (n. 87); and Patrick Mitchell (n. 90).

[95] Raymond C. Loewen (n. 87).

[96] Philippe Gruslin (n. 93); Antoine Goetz and others (n. 90).

[97] Victor Pey Casado (n. 89). [98] Emilio Agustín Maffezini (n. 92).

[99] Eudoro A. Olguín (n. 89).

[100] Involved, for example, in cases referred to in n. 89 were Vivendi Universal, S.A.; Houston Industries Energy, Inc.; Waste Management, Inc.; Empresa Nacional de Electricidad, S.A.

[101] As in, for example, *AMT v. DRC*, which concerned an enterprise for the production and sale of batteries and importation and resale of consumer goods and foodstuffs, or *Maffezini v. Spain*, which involved a venture for the production of various chemical products. The sectoral classification employed in this paragraph is the classification used by the World Bank for its projects. *See* Ch. 7, n. 114.

[102] For example, the mining operations in *Misima Mines v. Papua New Guinea* and *SIREM v. Burkina Faso*; the oil exploration and development agreements in *Scimitar v. Bangladesh* and *Kufpec v. Congo*; and the power projects in *WRB v. Grenada* and *Tanesco v. IPTL*.

[103] The new cases involving investments in this sector were *Tradex Hellas v. Albania*, *Leaf Tobacco v. Albania* and *Alimenta v. Gambia*.

[104] For example, in *Cable TV v. St. Kitts and Nevis*, which concerned an agreement for the provision of CTV services, and in *Lemire v. Ukraine*, a case concerning a radio broadcasting enterprise.

[105] For example, *Vivendi v. Argentina*, which concerned a water and sewage system concession agreement, and *Waste Management v. Mexico*, a case involving a waste management concession agreement.

[106] For example, *Lanco v. Argentina*, where the investment was in a port terminal project, and *Astaldi v. Honduras*, which concerned a highway rehabilitation project.

earlier ones, the investments did not involve any contracts at all with public entities of the host State.

Arbitral tribunals were constituted in all but three of the 43 arbitration proceedings commenced at ICSID from 1989 to 1999.[107] In three of the cases,[108] the tribunal consisted of a sole arbitrator; in the remaining 37 arbitrations, there were three-member tribunals. One of the sole arbitrators was appointed by agreement of the parties.[109] In the two other cases with sole arbitrators, the parties were unable to agree on the appointment, which then had to be made by the Chairman of the Administrative Council pursuant to Article 38 of the ICSID Convention, a function that the Chairman performed, as in earlier years, on the recommendation of the Secretary-General. The tribunals in 17 of the 37 other cases were composed without the intervention of the Chairman and Secretary-General. In most of these 17 cases, the tribunals consisted of one arbitrator appointed by each party and a presiding arbitrator appointed by agreement of the parties.[110] In the remaining 20 arbitrations, however, the parties failed to complete the constitution of the tribunal. The president of the tribunal in each of these 20 cases was appointed by the Chairman on the recommendation of the Secretary-General or by the Secretary-General directly;[111] in five of the 20 cases, the Chairman also had to appoint an arbitrator for a defaulting respondent.[112] Several of these were repeat appointments of the same persons.[113] It is worth noting that the Secretary-General began in this period to accumulate more substantial experience as appointing authority in cases conducted under the UNCITRAL Arbitration Rules, making appointments of arbitrators in five such cases during the 1990s.[114]

Altogether, 90 different individuals were appointed to tribunals in the 43 ICSID Convention and Additional Facility arbitration cases commenced in 1989–1999. All apparently had legal qualifications. It will be recalled that few of the appointees to tribunals in earlier decades were primarily private legal practitioners. As the caseload

[107] The three arbitration proceedings that were discontinued before the establishment of a tribunal were *Leaf Tobacco v. Albania*, *Kufpec v. Congo* and *Mobil v. Argentina*.

[108] *Misima Mines v. Papua New Guinea* and the two *Gruslin v. Malaysia* cases.

[109] In *Misima Mines v. Papua New Guinea*.

[110] In four of the 17 cases, the president of the tribunal was instead selected by the party-appointed arbitrators, as agreed by the parties.

[111] In *Lanco v. Argentina*, the parties agreed to substitute the Secretary-General for the Chairman as appointing authority.

[112] The proportion of cases, roughly half, in which this appointing authority function had to be exercised thus remained what it had been in earlier decades, although with many more cases the number of appointments of this kind increased greatly.

[113] Thus, for example, the Chairman of the Administrative Council appointed Francisco Orrego Vicuña as president of the tribunal in *Fedax v. Venezuela* and in *Maffezini v. Spain* and Rodrigo Oreamuno as president of the tribunal in *Olguín v. Paraguay* and in *Endesa v. Argentina*. Orrego Vicuña was Professor of International Law at the University of Chile and a member of the World Bank Administrative Tribunal. A former Vice President of Costa Rica, Oreamuno was a partner in the San José law firm of Facio & Cañas. As may be surmised, these appointments reflected the importance, in the cases concerned, of assuring that the presiding arbitrator had, among other qualities, fluency in Spanish.

[114] These notably included the NAFTA case of *Ethyl v. Canada* (*see* section I of this chapter), in which the Secretary-General appointed the presiding arbitrator after the parties failed to agree on the appointment. The Secretary-General's appointee in that case was Karl-Heinz Böckstiegel. A former President of the Iran–U.S. Claims Tribunal, Böckstiegel was Professor of International Business Law and Director of the Institute of Air and Space Law at Cologne University. Under Art. 12 of the UNCITRAL Arbitration Rules (n. 25), a designated appointing authority had the responsibility of deciding on challenges of arbitrators when it was claimed that there were justifiable doubts as to their impartiality or independence. At the end of the 1990s, the Secretary-General also started to be called on to perform this function of the appointing authority under the UNCITRAL Rules. *See* n. 119.

grew, such persons came increasingly to fill the ranks of ICSID arbitrators. Thus, nearly half of the 90 persons appointed in the newer cases were lawyers whose main activity was private legal practice. The rest were law professors and serving or retired judges or other public officials. Another difference from the group of arbitrators in the earlier cases was that a substantial minority, 34, of the arbitrators selected for cases brought to ICSID from 1989 to 2000 were from developing countries. Most were nationals of States in the Latin American and Caribbean region, appointed as arbitrators in the many new cases in which such States were parties.[115] Among the industrial country nationals chosen to serve on the tribunals, 30 were Western European,[116] 15 American, six Canadian and five Australian. The lack of gender diversity was even more extreme than with the appointees to tribunals in the pre-1989 cases: there were just two women among the above-mentioned 90 individuals.[117]

There was only one challenge of an ICSID arbitrator in the 1990s. The arbitrator, Dale Beck Furnish, had been appointed by the claimant in the case concerned.[118] He was challenged because it transpired that the claimant, in addition to being Peruvian, was American, the same nationality as Furnish. The latter immediately resigned and was quickly replaced by another appointee of the claimant.[119]

Contrasting with the rarity of challenges of arbitrators, objections to jurisdiction were raised by respondents in some two-thirds of the cases brought to the Centre from 1989 to 1999, a much higher proportion than in the earlier cases. As explained below, such objections succeeded in a number of instances. Several cases were in consequence abbreviated, helping to lower the average duration of the proceedings.[120]

Of the 43 arbitration cases submitted to ICSID in this period, 17 were settled amicably by the parties. In five of these cases, the parties took advantage of the possibility of having the tribunal embody their settlement agreement in an award.[121]

[115] However, in only one of those cases, *Astaldi v. Honduras*, did the parties agree to allow the appointment of nationals of the State party to the dispute as arbitrators.

[116] Among the Western Europeans, the largest groups were, as in the previous decades, British, French and Swiss.

[117] These were Maureen Ponsonby, who served on the *ITC v. Liberia* Tribunal, and Gabrielle Kaufmann-Kohler, appointed to the second tribunal in *Vivendi v. Argentina*.

[118] *Olguín v. Paraguay*.

[119] Furnish was Professor of Law at Arizona State University. His successor on the tribunal was Eduardo Mayora Alvarado, Senior Partner in the Guatemalan law firm Mayora & Mayora and Professor of Jurisprudence at Francisco Marroquín University. In addition to the challenge in this ICSID Convention case, an arbitrator was challenged in 1999 in *S.D. Myers v. Canada*, an UNCITRAL Rules proceeding initiated under the NAFTA investment chapter in response to a Canadian ban on the export of PCB wastes to the U.S. (the claimant being an Ohio corporation that processed and disposed of such wastes). The challenge was made by the claimant of the arbitrator appointed by the respondent, Robert Keith Rae, a former Premier of Ontario. The challenge was based on the appearance of lack of independence because of Rae's activities as a registered lobbyist in Canada. In accordance with Art. 12 of the UNCITRAL Rules (n. 25), it fell to the Secretary-General of ICSID, as the designated appointing authority of arbitrators, to decide the challenge. After considering submissions of the parties and the challenged arbitrator, Shihata as Secretary-General informed the arbitral tribunal and parties that he would uphold the challenge if Rae did not discontinue the lobbying activities in question. The next day, Rae resigned from the tribunal; Canada proceeded to appoint as his successor Edward C. Chiasson, a Vancouver-based lawyer with the law firm Borden Ladner Gervais.

[120] The average duration of individual arbitrations, in the cases commenced in 1989–1999, was two years and six months, from the constitution of the tribunal to the conclusion of the proceeding, three months less than the corresponding average for the pre-1989 cases.

[121] These cases were *Goetz v. Burundi*, Award, February 10, 1999, 6 ICSID Rep. 5 (2004); *WRB v. Grenada*, Award, December 21, 1998 (unpublished); *CFDT v. Côte d'Ivoire*, Award, April 4, 2000 (unpublished); *Lemire v. Ukraine*, Award, September 18, 2000, 6 ICSID Rep. 60 (2004); and *Astaldi v. Honduras*, Award, October 19, 2000 (unpublished).

In a sixth case, the parties had the tribunal incorporate in its award their settlement of some of the issues in dispute.[122] Eight of the other cases gave rise to proceedings for awards to be annulled under Article 52 of the ICSID Convention or, where they were Additional Facility awards, proceedings for them to be set aside by national courts.[123]

Of the further 17 cases, six led to awards declining jurisdiction over the dispute.[124] In another four of the cases, there were awards dismissing all claims on the merits.[125] The awards in the remaining seven cases[126] upheld claims for compensation in whole or in part. The amounts of these awards ranged from US$760,000 to an extraordinary US$868 million.[127] Two of the awards were among the first in ICSID to award compound instead of only simple interest.[128] Almost all of the awards in this group of 17 cases provided that the parties should share the direct expenses of the arbitration proceedings equally and bear their own legal expenses. An exception was one of the awards declining jurisdiction over the dispute, which ordered the claimant to reimburse the respondents for their expenses.[129]

IV. The first Additional Facility Proceedings

By Article 2 of the Additional Facility Rules of 1978, the Secretariat of the Centre was authorized to:

> ... administer, subject to and in accordance with these Rules, proceedings between a State (or a constituent subdivision or agency of a State) and a national of another State, falling within the following categories:
> (a) conciliation and arbitration proceedings for the settlement of legal disputes arising directly out of an investment which are not within the jurisdiction of the Centre because either the State party to the dispute or the State whose national is a party to the dispute is not a Contracting State;
> (b) conciliation and arbitration proceedings for the settlement of legal disputes which are not within the jurisdiction of the Centre because they do not arise directly out of an investment,

[122] This was done in *Tanesco v. IPTL*, Award, July 12, 2001, 8 ICSID Rep. 226, 318 (2005).

[123] The cases in which there were ICSID Convention annulment proceedings were *Vivendi v. Argentina, Wena v. Egypt*, the second *Gruslin v. Malaysia* case and *Mitchell v. DRC*. The Additional Facility cases in which the awards were challenged in national courts were *Metalclad v. Mexico, Loewen v. U.S.* and *Feldman v. Mexico*. Several of these annulment and set-aside proceedings are discussed later in this chapter and in Ch. 10.

[124] These were the awards in *Vacuum Salt v. Ghana*, Award, February 16, 1994, 4 ICSID Rep. 329 (1997); *Scimitar v. Bangladesh*, Award, May 4, 1994, 5 ICSID Rep. 4 (2002); *Tradex Hellas v. Albania*, Award, April 29, 1999, 5 ICSID Rep. 70 (2002); *Cable TV v. St. Kitts and Nevis*, Award, January 13, 1997, 5 ICSID Rep. 108 (2002); *Banro v. DRC*, Award, September 1, 2000, 17 ICSID Rev.—FILJ 382 (2002) (excerpts); *Waste Management v. Mexico*, Award, June 2, 2000, 5 ICSID Rep. 443 (2002).

[125] *Azinian v. Mexico*, Award, November 1, 1998, 5 ICSID Rep. 272 (2002); *Genin v. Estonia*, Award, June 25, 2001, 6 ICSID Rep. 241 (2004); *Olguín v. Paraguay*, Award, July 26, 2001, 6 ICSID Rep. 164 (2004); *Mondev v. U.S.*, Award, October 11, 2002, 6 ICSID Rep. 192 (2004).

[126] *AMT v. DRC*, Award, February 21, 1997, 5 ICSID Rep. 14 (2002); *CDSE v. Costa Rica*, Award, February 17, 2000, 5 ICSID Rep. 157 (2002); *Fedax v. Venezuela*, Award, March 9, 1998, 5 ICSID Rep. 200 (2002); *SIREM v. Burkina Faso*, Award, January 19, 2000, excerpts available at <https://icsid.worldbank.org/apps/ICSIDWEB/cases/>; *CSOB v. Slovak Republic*, Award, December 29, 2004, IIC 51 (2004) (published); *Maffezini v. Spain*, Award, November 13, 2000, 5 ICSID Rep. 419 (2002); *Middle East Cement v. Egypt*, Award, April 12, 2002, 7 ICSID Rep. 178 (2005).

[127] The amounts, respectively, of the awards in the *Fedax* and *CSOB* cases (n. 126).

[128] The awards in the *CDSE* and *Middle East Cement* cases (n. 126).

[129] The exception was the award in the *Scimitar v. Bangladesh* Award (n. 124).

provided that either the State party to the dispute or the State whose national is a party to the dispute is a Contracting State; and

(c) fact-finding proceedings.[130]

It will be remembered from Chapter 7 that Article 4 of the Additional Facility Rules made access to the Additional Facility in respect of conciliation and arbitration proceedings subject to the approval of the Secretary-General of ICSID. The approval, expressed by Article 4 to be of the parties' "agreement providing for conciliation or arbitration proceedings under the Additional Facility," could be sought by them at any time before the institution proceedings.[131] Approval of access was to be denied if the agreement was outside the scope of the Additional Facility as defined by Article 2.[132]

The first proceedings for which approval was requested had some basic features in common (which were shared by all later Additional Facility cases). They were all arbitration proceedings under Article 2(a) of the Additional Facility Rules; that is, they were for the settlement of investment disputes that were not within the jurisdiction of ICSID under the Convention because the home or the host State of the investor concerned was not a Contracting State. In each case, approval of access under Article 4 of the Additional Facility Rules was sought by the claimant investor in its notice of arbitration (or immediately before the notice).[133] This was related to their all being cases where the parties' consent agreement comprised a consent of the State party in an investment treaty and its acceptance by the claimant given in (or shortly before) the notice for arbitration. In each case, the consent clause in the investment treaty was of the type allowing for the submission of investment disputes to arbitration under the ICSID Convention, Additional Facility Rules or UNCITRAL Arbitration Rules. Although the procedure of Article 4 of the Additional Facility Rules obviously was designed with traditional compromissory clauses and submission agreements in mind, it was found to fit, albeit with some artificiality, the context provided by the investment treaties. Within the Secretariat, it was also quickly determined that the Secretary-General of ICSID should refuse access to the Additional Facility only if the conditions for such access were manifestly unfulfilled, leaving jurisdictional uncertainties for the arbitral tribunal to resolve.[134] The Secretary-General's power to control access to the Additional Facility was therefore to have the same limited extent as the Secretary-General's power to screen requests to institute proceedings under the Convention.[135]

[130] References in this chapter are to the Additional Facility Rules in force from September 27, 1978, to January 1, 2003. These are reprinted in Doc. ICSID/11, ICSID Additional Facility (June 1979). Also included in this publication are the texts of the Administrative and Financial Rules, Conciliation and Arbitration Rules and Fact-Finding Rules annexed to the Additional Facility Rules.

[131] *See* Additional Facility Rules (n. 130) Art. 2; Additional Facility Arbitration Rules (n. 130) Art. 2.

[132] *See* Additional Facility Rules (n. 130) Art. 4(1) and 4(2). In a case based on Art. 2(b) of the Additional Facility Rules, approval was also to be denied if the underlying transaction lacked features distinguishing it from "an ordinary commercial transaction" (ibid. Art. 4(2)).

[133] Even though they came in practice generally to be included in the same document, the request for approval of access and notice of arbitration remained technically distinct; and, under the Additional Facility Rules in force until January 1, 2003, there were separate fees payable to ICSID in respect of each. *See* Additional Facility Administrative and Financial Rules (n. 130) Arts. 4 and 5.

[134] This was first made clear to parties by the ICSID Secretariat in connection with the initiation of the first Additional Facility proceeding in *Waste Management v. Mexico*, on which *see* nn. 140 and 145.

[135] It was mainly because an approval under Art. 4 of the Additional Facility Rules was regarded as having this limited import that the ICSID Secretariat from the start denoted it approval of "access to the Additional Facility" (a label suggested by the heading of Art. 4) rather than approval of an "agreement" of the parties to have recourse to the Additional Facility (the more precisely correct position under the text of Art. 4), as the latter seemed to prejudge any possible issue as to whether there was a valid consent covering the dispute at hand.

The first seven Additional Facility arbitration proceedings were launched through this procedure in the late 1990s. In one of the cases, the underlying investment treaty was a BIT, and in the six others, the NAFTA. The BIT case was *Lemire v. Ukraine.* The claimant in that case was an American citizen. In 1995, he became a shareholder in Gala Radio, a music radio station in Kiev. His dispute with Ukraine arose the following year. It concerned, among other matters, the number of hours the station was permitted to operate daily and its right to obtain licenses to broadcast in other Ukrainian cities. Lemire brought his claim under the 1994 BIT between the United States and Ukraine,[136] choosing the Additional Facility option because Ukraine was not an ICSID Convention Contracting State.[137] The proceeding was instituted in January 1998. An arbitral tribunal was constituted seven months later. Like the tribunals in the six other Additional Facility proceedings, the *Lemire* Tribunal consisted of one arbitrator appointed by each party and a president appointed by agreement of the parties.[138] Ukraine submitted jurisdictional objections to the Tribunal, which eventually ruled, in September 1999, that they should be joined to the merits of the dispute. Soon after, the parties concluded an agreement for the settlement of the dispute. The agreement aimed at continued broadcasting by Gala from Kiev and provided for it to apply for licenses for radio frequencies in eleven more Ukrainian cities. At the request of the parties, the Tribunal recorded the settlement in the form of an award.[139]

As already noted, the six further Additional Facility cases were all brought to ICSID under the NAFTA. Of the NAFTA parties, only the United States was at that time an ICSID Convention Contracting State. Additional Facility arbitration remained, therefore, the only ICSID option that could be used in the NAFTA context, for the settlement of disputes between U.S. investors and either Canada or Mexico or between the United States itself and investors from either of the two other countries. Of the six Additional Facility cases begun in the 1990s under the NAFTA, four involved claims of U.S. investors against Mexico.[140] The two remaining Additional Facility cases were brought by Canadian investors against the United States.[141] Canada was not spared

[136] Treaty Concerning the Encouragement and Reciprocal Protection of Investment, Ukraine–United States, March 4, 1994, reprinted in ICSID, Investment Treaties, Release 97-2 (August 1997).

[137] Ukraine became a Contracting State a few years later, in 2000.

[138] In the *Lemire* case, the parties chose as President Elihu Lauterpacht (on whom *see* Ch. 8, n. 18). The two other arbitrators were Jan Paulsson, appointed by the claimant, and Juergen Voss, appointed by the respondent. A partner in the law firm Freshfields Bruckhaus Deringer, Paulsson was a member of the World Bank Administrative Tribunal and a Vice President of the London Court of International Arbitration. Voss, a longtime official at the Ministry of Economics of Germany, had also been Deputy General Counsel of MIGA.

[139] Pursuant to the Additional Facility Arbitration Rules (n. 130) Art. 50(2). The award, rendered September 18, 2000, is reprinted in 6 ICSID Rep. 60 (2004).

[140] These four cases were *Metalclad v. Mexico*, *Azinian v. Mexico*, *Waste Management v. Mexico* and *Feldman v. Mexico*. The *Metalclad* case is discussed later in this section. The *Azinian* and *Waste Management* cases involved waste collection and disposal concession contracts with different Mexican municipalities. In the *Azinian* case, the municipality terminated the contract after discovering what it characterized as irregularities in connection with its conclusion and performance. In the *Waste Management* case, the municipality, complaining of failures of contractual performance on the part of the concessionaire, did not pay invoices presented by the latter. The investment in the fourth case, *Feldman v. Mexico*, was a cigarette-exporting enterprise that was denied certain tax rebates for its exports.

[141] These two cases were *Loewen v. U.S.* and *Mondev v. U.S.* The *Loewen* case arose out of litigation in Mississippi between Loewen and a local competitor in the funeral home and funeral insurance business. A jury awarded the local competitor US$100 million in compensatory damages and US$400 million in punitive damages. Seeking to appeal the verdict and judgment, Loewen was required by the trial judge and the Mississippi Supreme Court to post an appellate bond of 125% of the judgment, i.e., US$625 million, within seven days or face immediate execution of the judgment. This, Loewen claimed, forced it to settle the case instead, paying its opponent US$175 million. The

NAFTA investment chapter claims in the 1990s. Three such claims were made against it in the closing years of the decade. In each instance, however, the investor elected to have an UNCITRAL rather than Additional Facility Rules proceeding.[142]

In each of these six Additional Facility NAFTA cases, the claimants invoked Article 1105 of the NAFTA, requiring a State party to give investments of investors of another party "treatment in accordance with international law, including fair and equitable treatment and full protection and security." The claimants in all six cases also asserted violations of Article 1110 of the NAFTA, providing that no State party should "directly or indirectly nationalize or expropriate ... or take a measure tantamount to nationalization or expropriation of such an investment" except for a public purpose, on a non-discriminatory basis, in accordance with due process of law and against payment of compensation.[143] In a re-articulation of the so-called Hull formula,[144] Article 1110 specified that such compensation "shall be equivalent to the fair market value of the expropriated investment immediately before the expropriation took place" and "shall be paid without delay and be fully realizable." The claims based on Articles 1105 and 1110 of the NAFTA succeeded in only one of the arbitrations, *Metalclad v. Mexico*.[145] The remainder of this section examines the *Metalclad* case in greater detail. It well illustrated the functioning of the Additional Facility and the relationship between Additional Facility arbitration and national courts. The case also led to one of the most controversial awards in ICSID's history.

A Delaware company, the claimant in *Metalclad* bought a Mexican company, Confinamiento Técnico de Residuos Industriales, in 1993 to acquire, develop and operate the latter's hazardous waste landfill site in the Municipality of Guadalcazar, in the Mexican state of San Luis Potosí (SLP). Permits for the construction of the landfill had been issued by the federal and SLP governments. According to Metalclad, it was repeatedly assured by those governments that no additional permit was required. Construction began in May 1994. In October, however, the municipality demanded that the project also have a municipal permit. Metalclad applied for the permit after allegedly being told by federal officials that it could not legally be denied and would be issued as a matter of course. Thirteen months later, however, the permit application was rejected by the municipality. In the meantime, Metalclad had completed construction of the landfill only to see its opening blocked by demonstrators. Following its

second case involving the U.S., *Mondev v. U.S.*, also related to litigation in state courts, in this instance those of Massachusetts. Lafayette Place Associates (LPA), a Massachusetts limited liability partnership owned by Mondev, had filed suit in the Massachusetts Superior Court against the City of Boston and the Boston Redevelopment Authority (BRA) for breach of a commercial real estate development contract among the three parties. A jury rendered a verdict in favor of LPA. The trial judge upheld the verdict against the City but decided that BRA was immunized from liability by a Massachusetts statute. Both the City and LPA appealed to the Supreme Judicial Court of Massachusetts, which affirmed the trial judge's decision in respect of BRA and allowed the City's appeal in respect of the contract claim.

[142] The three UNCITRAL Rules proceedings were in the *Ethyl v. Canada* and *S.D. Myers v. Canada* cases referred to earlier (nn. 53 and 119) and *Pope & Talbot v. Canada*. The latter case concerned the application of softwood lumber export quotas to the Canadian subsidiary of the claimant company.

[143] In three of the cases (the *Feldman*, *Loewen* and *Mondev* cases), there were also claims based on Art. 1102 of the NAFTA, requiring each State party to accord national treatment to the other parties' investors and their investments.

[144] *See* Ch. 7, n. 14.

[145] All claims were dismissed on the merits in the *Azinian* and *Mondev* cases and on jurisdictional grounds in the *Waste Management* and *Loewen* cases. *See* the awards in the *Azinian* and *Mondev* cases (n. 125), in the *Waste Management* case (n. 124) and in *Loewen v. U.S.*, June 26, 2003, 7 ICSID Rep. 442 (2009). In the *Feldman* case, only a claim based on Art. 1102 of the NAFTA succeeded. *See* n. 143 and *Feldman v. Mexico*, Award, December 16, 2002, 7 ICSID Rep. 341, 396 (2009).

rejection of the permit application, the municipality filed an administrative complaint with the responsible federal authorities challenging their agreement to allow operation of the landfill. When that challenge was dismissed, the municipality obtained an injunction from Mexican courts temporarily barring Metalclad from operating the landfill. During the second half of 1996, Metalclad and SLP attempted to resolve the issues surrounding operation of the landfill. These efforts having failed, Metalclad initiated its Additional Facility proceeding in January 1997. The outgoing Governor of SLP proceeded, in September 1997, to issue an Ecological Decree declaring a natural area for the protection of rare cactus. The decree permanently precluded operation of the landfill, coming as it did within the natural area.

The Tribunal in *Metalclad* was constituted in May 1997.[146] It held its first procedural session with parties in July 1997. During the session, it was observed that minutes of hearings would be kept in accordance with Article 44 of the Additional Facility Arbitration Rules. Article 44 reproduced a provision of the ICSID Arbitration Rules that had been deleted from the latter Rules when they were amended in 1984.[147] The provision outlined what minutes should contain and stated that "[t]hey shall not be published without the consent of the parties." After the first session of the Tribunal, the CEO of Metalclad held a conference call in which he discussed the case and made public some of the initial procedural steps. Citing the discussion at the first session of Article 44 of the Additional Facility Arbitration Rules, including its requirement that minutes not be published without the consent of the parties, Mexico applied to the Tribunal for a provisional measure declaring the proceeding confidential and permitting Mexico to request the Tribunal to enforce sanctions for any breach of the order. In its October 1997 decision on Mexico's application, the Tribunal declined to read into Article 44 of the Additional Facility Rules a prohibition broader than one on the publication of the contents of a particular minute. The freedom of the parties to speak publicly of the arbitration, the Tribunal affirmed, was not otherwise limited by the NAFTA or Additional Facility Rules. Indeed, as a company traded on a public stock exchange in the United States, the claimant was required by U.S. securities laws to provide shareholders with information regarding its involvement in a process such as the present arbitration. The Tribunal explained that an applicant for provisional measures had to show that the measures were urgently required to protect its rights from an injury that could not be repaired by the subsequent payment of compensation. Mexico had failed to meet this burden or even to show that its rights had suffered prejudice. The Tribunal nevertheless concluded with the important directive that:

> ... it would be of advantage to the orderly unfolding of the arbitral process and conducive to the maintenance of working relations between the Parties if during the proceedings they were

[146] The tribunal comprised Elihu Lauterpacht (*see* Ch. 8, n. 18) as President, Benjamin R. Civiletti, Attorney General of the United States in the administration of President Jimmy Carter, and José Luis Siqueiros, past Professor of Private International Law at the Universidad Nacional Autónoma de México. Article 7 of the Additional Facility Arbitration Rules, following Art. 39 of the ICSID Convention and ICSID Arbitration Rule 1(3), effectively prevented parties from appointing "national arbitrators" to a three-member tribunal unless all arbitrators were to be appointed by agreement of the parties. Article 1125 of the NAFTA overcame this restriction by providing the advance agreement of the disputing State to the appointment of each arbitrator and requiring the disputing investor to give its agreement to submitting the claim to arbitration. This allowed for the appointment of national arbitrators not only in the *Metalclad* case but also in the five other Additional Facility/NAFTA proceedings mentioned in this chapter.

[147] The provision deleted in 1984 was Rule 37 of the ICSID Arbitration Rules of 1967. *See* Ch. 7, n. 141.

both to limit public discussion of the case to a minimum, subject only to any externally imposed obligation of disclosure by which either of them may be legally bound.[148]

Almost three years later, the Tribunal rendered its award. The award found that acts of Guadalcazar and SLP—for which Mexico was internationally responsible— had denied Metalclad the fair and equitable treatment required by Article 1105 of the NAFTA. The acts of Guadalcazar and SLP, and therefore the acts of Mexico, were also held to have indirectly expropriated Metalclad's investment without compensation, in violation of Article 1110 of the NAFTA. Central to the first finding was the *Metalclad* Tribunal's view of the obligation of a NAFTA party to accord investments fair and equitable treatment as requiring transparency, that is, "that all relevant legal requirements for the purposes of initiating, completing and successfully operating investments made, or intended to be made, under the [NAFTA] Agreement should be capable of being readily known to all affected investors of another Party."[149] The Tribunal inferred this from the reference to transparency in Article 102(1) of the NAFTA, stating the objectives of the treaty. According to the Tribunal, the authorities of the host State had the heavy responsibility, once they became aware of "any scope for misunderstanding or confusion" on this score, "to ensure that the correct position is promptly determined and clearly stated so that investors can proceed with all appropriate expedition in the confident belief that they are acting in accordance with all relevant laws."[150] In the case at hand, there was no "clear rule as to the requirement or not of a municipal construction permit ... [or] any established practice or procedure as to the manner of handling applications" for such a permit.[151] Even Guadalcazar, the Tribunal observed, "lacked confidence in its right to deny permission for the landfill,"[152] considering it necessary to file the administrative complaint with the federal authorities after rejecting the construction permit application. The Tribunal concluded that:

... Mexico failed to ensure a transparent and predictable framework for Metalclad's business planning and investment. The totality of these circumstances demonstrates a lack of orderly process and timely disposition in relation to an investor of a Party acting in the expectation that it would be treated fairly and justly in accordance with the NAFTA.[153]

Turning to the expropriation claim, the *Metalclad* Tribunal first quoted Article 1110 of the NAFTA, emphasizing that its protection extended to indirect as well as direct expropriations and measures tantamount to expropriation. The Tribunal then explained that:

... expropriation under NAFTA includes not only open, deliberate and acknowledged takings of property, such as outright seizure or formal or obligatory transfer of title in favor of the host State, but also covert or incidental interference with the use of property which has the effect of depriving the owner, in whole or in significant part, of the use or reasonably-to-be-expected economic benefit of property even if not necessarily to the obvious benefit of the host State.[154]

The Tribunal added that:

By permitting or tolerating the conduct of Guadalcazar in relation to Metalclad which the Tribunal has already held amounts to unfair and inequitable treatment breaching Article 1105 and by thus participating or acquiescing in the denial to Metalclad of the right to operate the

[148] *Metalclad v. Mexico*, Decision on a Request by the Respondent for an Order Prohibiting the Claimant from Revealing Information, October 27, 1997, para. 12.
[149] *Metalclad v. Mexico*, Award, August 30, 2000, 5 ICSID Rep. 212, 226 (2002).
[150] Ibid. 227. [151] Ibid. 228. [152] Ibid. 229. [153] Ibid.
[154] Ibid. 230.

The Tribunal in *Metalclad v. Mexico*, the first Additional Facility Rules arbitration under the NAFTA. From left are Benjamin R. Civiletti, Elihu Lauterpacht, the President of the Tribunal, José Luis Siqueiros and Alejandro A. Escobar, the Secretary of the Tribunal.
International Centre for Settlement of Investment Disputes

landfill, notwithstanding the fact that the project was fully approved and endorsed by the federal government, Mexico must be held to have taken a measure tantamount to expropriation in violation of NAFTA Article 1110(1).[155]

Although not considering it necessary for its finding of a violation of Article 1110 of the NAFTA, the *Metalclad* Tribunal identified, as a further ground for this finding, the Ecological Decree issued by the Governor of SLP in September 1997. The Tribunal characterized the decree as "barring forever the operation of the landfill" and implementation of the decree as constituting "in and of itself… an act tantamount to expropriation."[156] In reaching this conclusion, the Tribunal remarked that it did not need to "decide or consider the motivation or intent at the adoption of the Ecological Decree."[157]

As to compensation, the *Metalclad* Tribunal observed that the damages arising under Article 1105 of the NAFTA and compensation due under Article 1110 "would be the same since both situations involve the complete frustration of the operation of the landfill and negate the possibility of any meaningful return on Metalclad's investment."[158] As already mentioned, Article 1110 of the NAFTA required that, in case of expropriation, compensation be equivalent to the fair market value of the expropriated investment. The Tribunal considered whether that value should be established by using a discounted cash flow analysis of future profits. It pointed out that this method would be appropriate to value a historically profitable going concern. But in the case of an enterprise such as Metalclad's landfill, that had never operated and hence had no performance record, "any award based on future profits would be purely

[155] Ibid. [156] Ibid. 231 [157] Ibid. [158] Ibid.

speculative."[159] The Tribunal decided therefore that the fair market value would best be arrived at by reference to Metalclad's actual investment.[160] Deductions by the Tribunal from the amount invested included an amount for remediation of the landfill site, which would have to be relinquished on payment of the award. The compensation would, the Tribunal ruled, include compound interest running from the date, in November 1995, that Guadalcazar rejected the construction permit application. This yielded an award in Metalclad's favor of US$16.685 million.

Since Additional Facility arbitration proceedings were outside the jurisdiction of ICSID, none of the provisions of the ICSID Convention were applicable to them.[161] The proceedings were thus subject to the law and the control of the courts at the place of arbitration. To help ensure, on the other hand, wide recognition and enforcement of the awards, the Additional Facility Arbitration Rules required that the place of arbitration always be in a State party to the New York Convention on the Recognition and Enforcement of Foreign Arbitral Awards.[162] In the case of an Additional Facility NAFTA proceeding, the choice (by the arbitral tribunal) of the place of arbitration was further restricted to the territory of a NAFTA party (all three of which were parties to the New York Convention).[163]

In *Metalclad*, the Tribunal determined that the place of arbitration would be Vancouver, British Columbia.[164] It was because of this that Mexico sought to have the award set aside there. The matter was submitted to the Supreme Court of British Columbia.[165] It had the authority, under the province's International Commercial Arbitration Act—a statute based on the UNCITRAL Model Law on International Commercial Arbitration—to set aside an award "contain[ing] decisions on matters beyond the scope of the submission to arbitration."[166] In its decision on Mexico's challenge of the award, the Court called attention to "the structure of arbitration"[167] under the investment chapter of the NAFTA. It gave investors of a NAFTA party the right to submit to arbitration claims against other NAFTA parties. But the NAFTA limited that right to alleged breaches of the substantive treatment obligations in Section A of the investment chapter (Articles 1101–1114 of the NAFTA) and two Articles (Articles 1502(3)(a) and 1503(2)) in the chapter of the NAFTA on competition policy, monopolies and State enterprises.[168] It did not, the Court pointed out, enable investors to arbitrate claims in respect of alleged breaches of other provisions of the NAFTA. Such other provisions of the NAFTA included the provisions of the treaty's chapter on

[159] *Metalclad v. Mexico*, Award (n. 149).

[160] The Tribunal cited in this connection the similar conservative conclusion on damages of the Tribunal in *AAPL v. Sri Lanka. See* Ch. 8, n. 63.

[161] The Additional Facility Rules (n. 130) Art. 3 included an explicit reminder to this effect. On the background of this article, *see* Ch. 7, section V(B).

[162] June 10, 1958, 330 UNTS 3. The limitation mentioned in the text on the place of arbitration was in the Additional Facility Arbitration Rules (n. 130) Art. 20.

[163] *See* NAFTA (n. 31) Art. 1130(a). [164] *See Metalclad v. Mexico*, Award (n. 149) 215.

[165] The first level of superior court in British Columbia, below the Court of Appeal for British Columbia. P. Foy and R. Deane, Foreign Investment Protection under Investment Treaties: Recent Developments under Chapter 11 of the North American Free Trade Agreement, 16 ICSID Rev.—FILJ 299, 325, note 78 (2001).

[166] International Commercial Arbitration, RSCBC 1996, C. 233, sec. 34(2)(a)(iv). *Cf.* U.N. Doc. A/40/17 (1985), UNCITRAL Model Law on International Commercial Arbitration, Art. 34(2)(a)(iii).

[167] *Mexico v. Metalclad*, Supreme Court of British Columbia, Judgment, May 2, 2001, 5 ICSID Rep. 238, 250 (2002).

[168] The limitation of investment chapter arbitration to such cases was set out in the NAFTA (n. 31) Arts. 1116 and 1117.

the publication, notification and administration of laws (Articles 1801–1806 of the NAFTA). Those provisions, rather than any in the investment chapter, implemented the principle of transparency mentioned in Article 102(1) of the NAFTA.

The *Metalclad* Tribunal had based its finding of a breach of Article 1105 of the NAFTA on transparency, that is on a perceived failure by Mexico to ensure a transparent, predictable framework for Metalclad's business planning and investment. This, the Court ruled, was "a matter beyond the scope of the submission to arbitration because there are no transparency obligations contained in" the investment chapter of the NAFTA.[169] In regard to the Tribunal's rulings on expropriation under Article 1110 of the NAFTA, the Court recalled the first of these was that Mexico had taken a measure tantamount to expropriation in permitting or tolerating Guadalcazar's conduct breaching Article 1105. The Tribunal's analysis of Article 1105 had thus "infected its analysis of Article 1110."[170] Effectively, it had at least partly relied on the concept of transparency to conclude that there had been an expropriation within the meaning of Article 1110. In so doing, the Court held, the Tribunal had "also decided a matter beyond the scope of the submission to arbitration."[171]

The Court noted that the Tribunal had, however, concluded that implementation of the September 1997 Ecological Decree also amounted to an expropriation of the landfill. This conclusion stood on its own and was not based on a lack of transparency or on the finding of a breach of Article 1105. The Court therefore saw no basis for finding that this conclusion of the Tribunal involved a decision on a matter beyond the scope of the submission to arbitration. Nor had the Tribunal committed "a patently unreasonable error" with respect to the Ecological Decree. The Court clearly was troubled by the Tribunal's definition of expropriation as including any "covert or incidental interference with the use of property which has the effect of depriving the owner, in whole or significant part, of the use or reasonably-to-be-expected economic benefit of property."[172] This definition, the Court remarked, was "sufficiently broad to include a legitimate re-zoning of property by a municipality or other zoning authority."[173] The Court recognized, however, that the definition of expropriation was a question of law with which it was not entitled to interfere under the International Commercial Arbitration Act.

The Court therefore found no ground to set aside the award as it related to the conclusion of the Tribunal that implementation of the Ecological Decree amounted to an expropriation of the landfill without compensation. The Court confined itself to setting aside the award as it related to the first two of the Tribunal's findings of breaches of Articles 1105 and 1110 of the NAFTA, which Mexico had succeeded in showing went beyond the scope of the submission to arbitration. In consequence, the Court disallowed the award by the Tribunal of interest prior to the September 1997 date of the Ecological Decree, the remaining basis for a finding of expropriation.[174]

Under Article 2001 of the NAFTA, the three parties had established a Free Trade Commission, consisting of their respective ministers for trade and having, among

[169] *Mexico v. Metalclad*, Supreme Court of British Columbia, Judgment (n. 167) 254.

[170] Ibid. 255. [171] Ibid. [172] *See* text accompanying n. 154.

[173] *Mexico v. Metalclad*, Supreme Court of British Columbia, Judgment (n. 167) 259.

[174] Of the three Additional Facility cases referred to in n. 123 where awards were challenged in national courts, this was the only one in which the challenge succeeded, albeit partially, the challenges in the two others having been entirely dismissed. *See Mexico v. Feldman*, Ontario Superior Court of Justice, Judgment, December 3, 2003, 5 ICSID Rep. 501 (2005) and Ontario Court of Appeal, Judgment, January 11, 2005, 9 ICSID Rep. 509 (2006); *Loewen v. U.S.*, U.S. District Court, District of Columbia, Judgment, October 31, 2005, 10 ICSID Rep. 448 (2006).

other functions, broad authority to resolve disputes regarding the interpretation or application of the treaty.[175] Article 1131 of the NAFTA made it clear that an interpretation by the Commission of a provision of the NAFTA would bind tribunals established under the investment chapter. Shortly after the decision of the Supreme Court of British Columbia, the Commission issued an interpretation meant in part as a further rejection of the approach of the *Metalclad* Tribunal to Article 1105 of the NAFTA. Thus, the interpretation declared that a determination that there had been a breach of another provision of the NAFTA would not establish that there had been a breach of Article 1105.[176]

In the meantime, there had been outcries against the *Metalclad* award in the press and among NGOs. For many, it seemed to confirm the fears, raised a few years before in connection with the MAI and the *Ethyl* case, that arbitral mechanisms such as that of the NAFTA threatened countries' sovereignty and their ability to regulate in the public interest. Particular concern was aroused by the award's definition of expropriation which, as seen earlier, had also troubled the Supreme Court of British Columbia. Critics saw it as suggesting that almost any environmental measure might qualify as expropriatory.[177] A leading Canadian newspaper warned that the ruling in the *Metalclad* case "could have serious implications for Canada's ability to pass environmental regulations."[178] Referring to *Metalclad* and other NAFTA investment chapter arbitrations, the head of a prominent U.S. NGO reportedly accused claimants of using the treaty "not to defend trade [*sic*] but to challenge the functioning of government."[179] Criticism was hardly quietened by the partial annulment of the award in British Columbia and its rebuke by the Free Trade Commission. Years later, the *Metalclad* case was still being cited as showing that "badly designed international trade agreements may compromise countries' ability to protect the environment."[180]

V. Some leading BIT cases of the 1990s

Up until the 1990s, only one case, *AAPL v. Sri Lanka*, had been submitted to ICSID Convention arbitration under a BIT. A host of fundamental issues that such cases would raise therefore remained largely unexplored. These included jurisdictional and choice of law questions arising out of the tangle of disparate relevant provisions in the ICSID Convention, the BIT and any investment contract. Almost inevitably, how problems of these kinds were solved in the earlier BIT cases had a large impact in the many later BIT cases. Four of the BIT cases begun in the 1990s stand out for having played this precedent-setting role. In the order in which the proceedings were first instituted, these were *Fedax v. Venezuela*, *Vivendi v. Argentina*, *Maffezini v. Spain* and *Wena v. Egypt*. The claimant in *Fedax* resorted to ICSID Convention arbitration on the basis of the provision on the settlement of investment disputes in the 1991

[175] *See* NAFTA (n. 31) Art. 2001(2)(c).

[176] *See* Free Trade Commission, Notes of Interpretation on Access to Documents and Minimum Standard of Treatment in Accordance With International Law, July 31, 2001, 6 ICSID Rep. 567, 568 (2004).

[177] This was especially so in view of the award's apparent disregard for the "motivation or intent" of such measures. *See* text accompanying n. 157.

[178] NAFTA Ruling Raises Environmental Questions, *Toronto Globe & Mail*, September 1, 2000, B5.

[179] NAFTA's Powerful Little Secret: Obscure Tribunals Settle Disputes, but Go Too Far, Critics Say, *New York Times*, March 11, 2001, sec. 3, 1 (quoting Joan Claybrook, President of Public Citizen).

[180] Stiglitz (n. 2) 130.

BIT between the Netherlands and Venezuela. It set forth the consent of each State to submit to such arbitration any dispute with a national of the other State concerning an obligation under the BIT of the disputing State.[181] In commencing their ICSID Convention arbitration proceedings, the claimants in the *Vivendi*, *Maffezini* and *Wena* cases relied on the provisions on the settlement of investment disputes of, respectively, the BIT of 1991 between Argentina and France, the 1991 BIT of Argentina with Spain, and the BIT that Egypt and the United Kingdom signed in 1975. Like the corresponding provisions of many other BITs, the provisions in these three treaties were extremely broad in scope, allowing a national of either State to have recourse to ICSID Convention arbitration in respect of any investment-related dispute with the other State.[182] The scope of these provisions was not, in other words, expressly limited to disputes over compliance with the treaty as in the provision on the settlement of investment disputes of the Netherlands–Venezuela BIT and of some other investment treaties. Nevertheless, in their requests for arbitration, the claimants in all four cases alleged violations of the substantive provisions of the BIT by the host State, or entities for which it was responsible. This section considers the principal contributions of these cases to the development of BIT jurisprudence at ICSID.

A. *Fedax v. Venezuela*

This was the first of many BIT cases in which there was an objection to jurisdiction on the ground that the underlying transactions did not qualify as investments for the purpose of the ICSID Convention. The claimant was a company established in the Netherlands Antilles. It acquired by way of endorsement six promissory notes, each for US$99,825, issued by Venezuela pursuant to a contract with a Venezuelan company, Industrias Metalurgicas Van Dam. Venezuela, however, failed to make payments of principal and interest under the notes. Resorting to arbitration under the BIT, Fedax argued that this amounted to a breach by Venezuela of its investment protection undertakings in the treaty. The argument depended on the promissory notes qualifying as investments under the BIT and the ICSID Convention. As far as the BIT was concerned, it, like many other such treaties, defined a protected investment as encompassing "every kind of asset."[183] The promissory notes clearly fit within that exceedingly wide definition. Venezuela objected that the Centre nevertheless lacked jurisdiction because the scope of the ICSID Convention was confined to disputes concerning direct investments.

In its decision rejecting the objection, the *Fedax* Tribunal[184] recalled that, while Article 25(1) of the Convention restricted the jurisdiction of the Centre to investment disputes, it did not define the term "investment." Citing the Report of the World Bank Executive Directors on the Convention and writings of Aron Broches and other

[181] Agreement on Encouragement and Reciprocal Protection of Investments, Netherlands–Venezuela, October 22, 1991, reprinted in ICSID, Investment Treaties, Release 92-4 (March 1993), Art. 9 (Netherlands–Venezuela BIT).

[182] *See* Acuerdo para la Promoción y la Protección Reciproca de las Inversiones, Argentina–France, July 3, 1991, reprinted in ICSID, Investment Treaties, Release 92-4 (March 1993), Art. 8(1) (Argentina–France BIT); Acuerdo para la Promoción y la Protección Reciproca de inversions, Argentina–Spain, October 3, 1991, reprinted in ICSID, Investment Treaties, Release 97-2 (August 1997), Art. X(1) (Argentina–Spain BIT); Agreement for the Promotion and Protection of Investments, Egypt–United Kingdom, June 11, 1975, reprinted in ICSID, Investment Treaties, Release 93-3 (October 1993), Art. 8(1) (Egypt–U.K. BIT).

[183] Netherlands–Venezuela BIT (n. 181) Art. 1(a).

[184] Consisting of Francisco Orrego Vicuña as President, Meir Heth and Roberts B. Owen. On Orrego Vicuña, *see* n. 113. Heth, a Professor at the Law School of the College of Management in

former ICSID officials, the Tribunal noted that the drafters of the Convention had decided instead "to leave any definition of the 'investment' to the consent of the parties."[185] As applied to a BIT case such as *Fedax*, this meant that the definition of "investment" set forth in the treaty was "the one that governs the jurisdiction of ICSID."[186] The Tribunal did not mean by this that the ICSID Convention left the matter wholly to the discretion of the parties but rather that it provided a "broad framework for the definition of investment"[187] through the exercise of that discretion. The Convention clearly was not limited in scope to disputes involving direct investments.[188] Its drafting history showed that the "very broad meaning"[189] contemplated for the term "investment" extended, in particular, to credit transactions such as the promissory notes in the present case. The notes were specifically intended for international circulation; and, when endorsed to a foreign holder as in this case, constituted "a foreign investment ... encompassed by the terms of the Convention and the [BIT] Agreement."[190] The Tribunal added that the "basic features of an investment have been described as involving a certain duration, a certain regularity of profit and return, assumption of risk, a substantial commitment and a significance for the host State's development."[191] These "basic features of an investment" were, the Tribunal explained, all met in this case.[192]

Having determined that the purchase by Fedax of the promissory notes qualified as an investment for the purpose of both the ICSID Convention and the BIT, the Tribunal found in its award that Venezuela was "under the obligation to honor precisely the terms and conditions governing such investment ... as well as to honor the specific payments established in the promissory notes."[193] The Tribunal explained that this obligation of Venezuela was "laid down mainly in Article 3" of the BIT. Article 3 contained a number of provisions regarding the treatment by each State of investments of nationals of the other State. These included provisions requiring that the investments be assured fair and equitable treatment and not be impaired by arbitrary or discriminatory measures.[194] In another clause of Article 3, each State pledged to observe any obligation it may have entered into with regard to the treatment of such investments.[195] The award in *Fedax* is often cited as being the first to apply an observance of undertakings clause such as the one in Article 3.[196] It is doubtful, however, if so much should be read into the award. It instead referred to Article 3 generally, rather than just to its observance of undertakings clause, and indicated that other parts of the BIT were also relevant, thus suggesting that the outcome was dictated by the treatment

Israel, had been Chairman of the Tel Aviv Stock Exchange. Owen was Legal Adviser at the U.S. Department of State in the administration of President Jimmy Carter.

185 *Fedax v. Venezuela*, Decision on Objections to Jurisdiction, July 11, 1997, 5 ICSID Rep. 186, 190 (2002).

186 Ibid. 194. 187 Ibid. 191.

188 Addressing an apparent misreading by Venezuela of Art. 25(1) of the Convention, the Tribunal explained that the term "directly" in the provision referred not to the "investment" but rather to the relationship between it and the dispute. It followed "that jurisdiction can exist even in respect of investments that are not direct, so long as the dispute arises directly from such transaction." Ibid. 192.

189 Ibid. 195. 190 Ibid. 198.

191 Ibid. 199. The Tribunal cited in this connection C.H. Schreuer, Commentary on the ICSID Convention, 11 ICSID Rev.—FILJ 316, 372 (1996).

192 *Fedax v. Venezuela*, Decision on Objections to Jurisdiction (n. 185) 199.

193 *Fedax v. Venezuela*, Award, March 9, 1998, 5 ICSID Rep. 200, 206 (2002).

194 *See* Netherlands–Venezuela BIT (n. 181) Art. 3(1). 195 *See* ibid. Art. 3(4).

196 *See, e.g.*, K. Yannaca-Small, What About This "Umbrella Clause"?, in K. Yannaca-Small (ed.), *Arbitration Under International Investment Agreements: A Guide to the Key Issues* 479, 480 (2010); K.J. Vandevelde, *Bilateral Investment Treaties: History, Policy, and Interpretation* 263 (2010).

provisions of the BIT as a whole.[197] The lack of elaboration in the award may be explained by the fact that it was, for most intents and purposes, a consent award: by the time it was being drawn up, Venezuela had already agreed to make the necessary payments to Fedax under the promissory notes.[198]

B. *Vivendi v. Argentina*

This second case concerned a 1995 concession agreement privatizing the water and sewage services of the Argentine Province of Tucumán. The parties to the agreement included the French TNC Vivendi Universal (then called the Compagnie Générale des Eaux) and its Argentine affiliate, the Compañía de Aguas del Aconquija (referred to here, together with the parent company, as Vivendi), as well as the Province. The agreement provided for disputes concerning its interpretation and application to be submitted to the exclusive jurisdiction of the administrative courts of Tucumán. From an early point in Vivendi's performance of the concession agreement, disputes arose between Vivendi and the Tucumán authorities over such matters as the level of tariffs to customers and the quality of the water delivered. There were attempts to renegotiate the concession agreement. After these failed, Vivendi, alleging default on the part of Tucumán, notified the latter that it was rescinding the agreement. Tucumán rejected the notice of rescission and terminated the agreement, alleging default in performance by Vivendi.

Turning to ICSID, Vivendi contended that Tucumán's alleged breaches of the concession agreement had brought Argentina into breach of the fair and equitable treatment and expropriation provisions of the Argentina–France BIT.[199] The concession agreement provided for the resolution of disputes regarding its interpretation or application to be submitted to the exclusive jurisdiction of the administrative courts of Tucumán. In the first ICSID Convention arbitration in the case, Argentina objected that this provision of the concession agreement deprived the Centre of jurisdiction over the claims. The Tribunal[200] disagreed, ruling in its award that the provision, concerning claims based on the concession agreement, "cannot be deemed to prevent the investor from proceeding under the ICSID Convention against the Argentine Republic on a claim charging the Argentine Republic with a violation of the Argentine-French BIT."[201] On the merits, however, the Tribunal held that, because of the "crucial connection"[202] between the terms of the concession agreement and the alleged violations of the BIT, Argentina could not be held liable unless and until Vivendi had asserted its rights before the administrative courts of Tucumán, as required by the concession

[197] Other possibly relevant parts of the BIT (n. 181) might have included its currency transfer and expropriation provisions (Arts. 5 and 6). The typical observance of undertakings clause applies to any obligations assumed with regard to covered investments. *See* Yannaca-Small (n. 196) 484. In the Netherlands–Venezuela BIT, the wording of the clause was unusual insofar as it applied to obligations regarding the "treatment" of covered investments. This might have been read as referring to general treatment commitments as opposed to specific contractual obligations.

[198] *See Fedax v. Venezuela*, Award (n. 193) 204–205.

[199] In Art. 5(1) and 5(2) of the Argentina–France BIT (n. 182).

[200] Consisting of Francisco Rezek as President, Thomas Buergenthal and Peter Trooboff. A former Foreign Minister of Brazil, Rezek was a member of the ICJ. Buergenthal had recently been elected a member of the ICJ, having previously been Lobinger Professor of Comparative Law and Jurisprudence at George Washington University Law School. Trooboff, a past President of the American Society of International Law, was a partner at the Washington, D.C. law firm of Covington & Burling.

[201] *Vivendi v. Argentina*, Award, November 21, 2000, 5 ICSID Rep. 299, 315–316 (2002).

[202] Ibid. 321.

agreement. Vivendi having failed to seek relief from those courts, the Tribunal concluded that it could only dismiss the claims against Argentina.

Vivendi applied for annulment of the award under Article 52 of the ICSID Convention. The ad hoc Committee that was constituted to consider the application[203] annulled the ruling on the merits. In the view of the Committee, the Tribunal had manifestly exceeded its powers in upholding jurisdiction over a BIT claim and then declining to decide that claim. The Committee noted in its decision that the provision of the BIT on the settlement of investment disputes did not use "a narrower formulation, requiring that the investor's claim allege a breach of the BIT itself,"[204] and so might in principle also accommodate a breach of contract claim. Vivendi had in any event invoked the substantive provisions of the BIT. The Committee addressed the distinction between breaches of contract and breaches of a treaty in terms relied on in many subsequent cases. A State, the Committee explained:

> ... may breach a treaty without breaching a contract, and *vice versa* . . . whether there has been a breach of the BIT and whether there has been a breach of contract are different questions. Each of these claims will be determined by reference to its own proper or applicable law—in the case of the BIT, by international law, in the case of the [concession agreement or contract], by the proper law of the contract, in other words, the law of Tucumán.[205]

Although it acknowledged that the investment disputes provision of the BIT might extend to contract claims, the Committee considered that, where the contract contained a choice of forum clause conferring jurisdiction on local courts, the investor should be held to the choice for such claims. Thus, the Committee posited that, "[i]n a case where the essential basis of a claim brought before an international tribunal is a breach of contract, the tribunal will give effect to any valid choice of forum clause in the contract."[206] The Committee did not explain why this would always be so; and indeed some BITs made it clear that, in the event of an investment dispute, defined to include a dispute concerning the interpretation or application of an investment agreement between a covered investor and the host State, the investor could submit the dispute to arbitration under the BIT instead of seeking to have it resolved by "any applicable previously agreed dispute settlement procedures."[207] Coming, in any event, to its main point, the *Vivendi* Committee stated that where "the fundamental basis of the claim" was instead:

> ... a treaty laying down an independent standard by which the conduct of the parties is to be judged, the existence of an exclusive jurisdiction clause in a contract between the claimant and the respondent state or one of its subdivisions cannot operate as a bar to the application of the treaty standard.[208]

[203] The President of the Committee was L. Yves Fortier. The two other members of the Committee were James R. Crawford and José Carlos Fernández Rozas. Fortier, a former Ambassador of Canada to the U.N., was Chairman of the Montreal law firm Ogilvy Renault. Crawford, a member of the ILC, was Whewell Professor of International Law at the University of Cambridge. Fernández Rozas, Professor of Private International Law at the Complutense University of Madrid, had been representative of Spain at the Hague Conference on Private International Law.

[204] *Vivendi v. Argentina*, ad hoc Committee Decision, July 3, 2002, 6 ICSID Rep. 340, 356 (2004).

[205] Ibid. 365. [206] Ibid. 366.

[207] *See* K.J. Vandevelde, *U.S. International Investment Agreements* 580 (2009).

[208] *Vivendi v. Argentina*, ad hoc Committee Decision (n. 204) 367. Following the annulment decision described in the text, Vivendi resubmitted the dispute to arbitration pursuant to Art. 52(5) of the ICSID Convention. The second arbitration proceeding resulted in an award in Vivendi's favor. An application of Argentina to have the award annulled was rejected in 2010.

C. *Maffezini v. Spain*

Maffezini was the first case to raise the question whether MFN treatment under a BIT extended to the provisions on the settlement of investment disputes. The claimant was an Argentine businessman. He established the eponymous Spanish company Emilio A. Maffezini S.A. (EAMSA) to make various chemical products in Spain's Galicia region. Maffezini subscribed to 70 percent of the capital of EAMSA. The remaining 30 percent was subscribed to by the Sociedad para el Desarollo Industrial de Galicia (SODIGA), a Spanish State agency created to promote investment in Galicia, which also extended a loan to EAMSA at a preferential interest rate. Soon after the commencement of construction of its plant, EAMSA began to experience financial difficulties. Steps taken to address these included a transfer of 30 million pesetas from a personal account of Maffezini by a SODIGA official. The difficulties nevertheless persisted and Maffezini ordered a halt to the construction and the dismissal of EAMSA employees. He then brought to ICSID a claim against Spain under its BIT with his home country.

That BIT provided for investment disputes to be submitted to courts of the respondent State and allowed the investor to have recourse to ICSID Convention arbitration if the courts had not rendered a decision on the merits of the dispute within 18 months.[209] Objecting to the jurisdiction of the Centre, Spain pointed out that Maffezini had not submitted the dispute to Spanish courts before referring it to arbitration. Maffezini argued that the MFN clause of the Argentina–Spain BIT gave him this option. It obliged each State to give covered investments, "[i]n all matters subject to this Agreement," treatment not less favorable than that extended by the State to investments of investors of any third State.[210] According to Maffezini, he could through this clause rely on the investment dispute settlement provisions of the Chile–Spain BIT, which did not condition recourse to ICSID Convention arbitration on a prior referral of the dispute to local courts.[211]

In its decision on jurisdiction, the *Maffezini* Tribunal found that, while the MFN clause did not expressly refer to dispute settlement arrangements, it should be understood as covering them as they were "inextricably related to the protection of foreign investors" under the BIT.[212] The Tribunal observed that the MFN clause could not be used to bypass conditions that the States concerned may have considered to be fundamental to their acceptance of the BIT. These, the Tribunal said, might include requirements to exhaust, or avoid, local remedies before resorting to arbitration; nor could the MFN clause be invoked to replace a designated form of arbitration with another or to alter the operation of "a highly institutionalized system of arbitration that incorporates precise rules of procedure" such as that of the NAFTA.[213] For the Tribunal, the requirement for prior resort to local courts was not a fundamental condition of this kind.[214] It therefore concluded that the claimant "had the right to submit the instant dispute to arbitration without first accessing the Spanish courts."[215]

[209] *See* Argentina–Spain BIT (n. 182) Art. X(2) and X(3)(a).

[210] Ibid. Art. IV(2).

[211] Acuerdo para la Protección y Fomento Reciprocos de Inversiones, Chile–Spain, October 2, 1991, reprinted in ICSID, Investment Treaties, Release 93-2 (July 1993), Art. 10.

[212] *Maffezini v. Spain*, Decision on Objections to Jurisdiction, January 25, 2000, 5 ICSID Rep. 396, 407 (2002).

[213] Ibid. 410.

[214] In particular, it was not a requirement for the exhaustion of local remedies, if only because it referred only to a decision on the merits, which did "not even have to be a final or non-appealable decision under Spanish law" (ibid. 401).

[215] Ibid. 411.

Also to be relied on in later cases was a decision of the *Maffezini* Tribunal on an application for provisional measures filed by Spain at any early stage of the proceeding. Spain argued in its application that, the claim being "worthless," Maffezini would inevitably lose and have to reimburse Spain for its costs in defending the action. He should therefore be required by the Tribunal to post a guarantee in the estimated amount of those costs. The Tribunal decided the application by a procedural order, which one observer has called dramatic for its holding that provisional measures granted under the ICSID Convention were mandatory.[216] Referring to the authority of arbitrators, under Article 47 of the ICSID Convention and ICSID Arbitration Rule 39, to "recommend" provisional measures, the order stated that:

> While there is a semantic difference between the word "recommend" as used in Rule 39 and the word "order" as used elsewhere in the Rules to describe the Tribunal's ability to require a party to take a certain action, the difference is more apparent than real. It should be noted that the Spanish text of that Rule uses also the word "dictación." The Tribunal does not believe that the parties to the Convention meant to create a substantial difference in the effect of these two words. The Tribunal's authority to rule on provisional measures is no less binding than that of a final award. Accordingly, for the purposes of this Order, the Tribunal deems the word "recommend" to be of equivalent value as the word "order."[217]

This interpretation of Article 47 was clearly at odds with the drafting history of the provision. Moreover, while the Spanish text of Arbitration Rule 39 used (once) the word "dictación" in connection with provisional measures, the Arbitration Rules were subordinate to the Convention, which in the Spanish version of its Article 47 referred only to the "recomendación" of provisional measures. On the other hand, the decision of the drafters of the ICSID Convention to give arbitrators only the authority to recommend provisional measures, rather than to "prescribe" such measures, was tempered by their acceptance that arbitrators operating under the ICSID Convention could take into account in the final award the effect of any non-compliance with their provisional measures.[218]

On the substance, the procedural order of the *Maffezini* Tribunal not only denied Spain's application, but also seemed virtually to exclude requiring security for costs by provisional measures under the ICSID Convention. In this respect, the Tribunal pointed out that ICSID Arbitration Rule 39 specified that a party might request "provisional measures for the preservation of its rights." The Tribunal took the view that this text implied "that such rights must exist at the time of the request, must not be hypothetical, nor are ones to be created in the future."[219] Spain's application did not refer to any "present rights," the expectation in the case being merely a conjecture.[220] Clearly, however, of more basic importance to the Tribunal was the consideration that:

> A determination at this time which may cast a shadow on either party's ability to present its case is not acceptable. It would be improper for the Tribunal to pre-judge the Claimant's case by recommending provisional measures of this nature.[221]

[216] C. Brown, *A Common Law of International Adjudication* 149 (2007).
[217] *Maffezini v. Spain*, Procedural Order No. 2, October 28, 1999, 5 ICSID Rep. 393, 394 (2002).
[218] *See* Ch. 5, text accompanying nn. 147–150.
[219] *Maffezini v. Spain*, Procedural Order No. 2 (n. 217) 394. [220] Ibid. 394–395.
[221] Ibid. 395. The Tribunal also pointed out that it could only grant provisional measures related to the subject matter of the dispute while Spain's application was "unrelated to the facts of the dispute" (ibid.). The later award of the Tribunal upheld Maffezini's claim relating to the SODIGA official's unauthorized bank transfer, holding that it violated Spain's BIT obligations to protect the investment and accord it fair and equitable treatment, and granting Maffezini compensation in the amount of the transfer plus interest. *See Maffezini v. Spain*, Award (n. 126) 435–436 and 438–439.

D. *Wena v. Egypt*

Wena, finally, launched a new approach to choice of law under Article 42(1) of the ICSID Convention. The dispute in that case arose out of lease and development agreements concluded between Wena, a company incorporated in the United Kingdom, and the Egyptian Hotels Company (EHC), an Egyptian SOE. In accordance with the agreements, Wena was to operate and manage two hotels, one in Luxor and the other in Cairo. Shortly after the conclusion of the agreements, disputes arose between Wena and EHC. Wena asserted that the condition of the hotels was below that stipulated in the lease and EHC claimed that Wena failed to pay rent. There was an arbitration proceeding in Egypt concerning one of the hotels. It resulted in an award directing EHC to repair the hotel and Wena to pay the rent due. Wena applied to the Egyptian courts to have the award set aside. EHC subsequently took possession of both hotels. Wena soon resumed control over them but then lost its operating license for the Cairo hotel, was denied a permanent operating license for the Luxor hotel, and finally was evicted from the hotels.

Like most BITs, the Egypt–U.K. treaty involved in the ensuing ICSID Convention arbitration did not expressly address the law that the arbitrators should apply to the substance of the dispute. The stance of the *Wena* Tribunal[222] on the issue was somewhat similar to that of the *AAPL* Tribunal nine years earlier. Thus, the *Wena* Tribunal, like the *AAPL* Tribunal, found that the parties, in their written and oral submissions in the proceedings, had agreed in considering the BIT to be "the primary source of applicable law for this arbitration"[223] which, after all, turned on alleged violations of the treaty by Egypt. But the BIT, the *Wena* Tribunal observed, was a "fairly terse agreement"[224] and did not contain all the rules of law applicable to the dispute. Again like the *AAPL* Tribunal, the *Wena* Tribunal found the BIT to be supplemented in this respect by rules of host State law and international law. In *AAPL*, however, the Tribunal inferred an agreement of the parties on these supplementary rules of law from their submissions in the proceeding, just as the Tribunal had seen in the submission a tacit agreement to regard the BIT as "the primary source of applicable legal rules."[225] The *Wena* Tribunal was unable to detect a similar agreement on applicable supplementary rules of law. It therefore turned for those rules to the second sentence of Article 42(1) of the ICSID Convention, holding that, aside from the provisions of the BIT, it would apply "the law of the Contracting State party to the dispute ... and such rules of international law as may be applicable."[226]

The *Wena* Tribunal proceeded to award the claimant compensation for what it determined to have been violations by Egypt of the fair and equitable treatment, full protection and security and expropriation provisions of the BIT. Egypt applied for the annulment of the award under Article 52 of the ICSID Convention. The Tribunal, Egypt argued, had manifestly exceeded its powers by applying the provisions of the BIT as the primary source of rules when it should have applied Egyptian law, the

[222] Consisting of Monroe Leigh, Ibrahim Fadlallah and Don Wallace. Leigh, the President of the Tribunal, had been Legal Adviser at the U.S. Department of State and President of the American Society of International Law. Fadlallah, a Professor of Law at the University of Paris X, had been a member of the ICC International Court of Arbitration. Wallace, Professor of Law at Georgetown University Law Center, was Chairman of the International Law Institute.

[223] *Wena v. Egypt*, Award, December 8, 2000, 6 ICSID Rep. 89, 111 (2004). On the similar finding in the *AAPL* case, *see* Ch. 8, text accompanying n. 123.

[224] *Wena v. Egypt*, Award (n. 223) 111.

[225] *See* Ch. 8, text accompanying nn. 123–126.

[226] *See Wena v. Egypt*, Award (n. 223) 112.

proper law of the underlying lease agreements. The ad hoc Committee[227] dismissed the annulment application. In doing so, it emphasized that the subject matter of the lease agreement governed by Egyptian law was different from the subject matter brought before ICSID under the BIT. As to the latter, the Committee disregarded the finding of the Tribunal that the parties had implicitly agreed to consider the BIT as "the primary source of applicable law."[228] According to the Committee, "it cannot be held that the Parties to the instant case have made a choice of law under the first sentence of Article 42(1) of the ICSID Convention."[229] The Committee found that reliance on the BIT as the primary source of law was nevertheless consistent with the provision of the second sentence of Article 42(1). Some, the Committee noted in its decision, had argued for a broad role of international law under this provision. The Committee acknowledged that the first annulment decision in *Klöckner*, and decisions in several later ICSID Convention cases, had instead seen international law as having a narrower, complementary and corrective, role under the provision of the second sentence of Article 42(1).[230] In a sharp break from the previous decisions, the *Wena* Committee concluded that:

> There seems not to be a single answer as to which of these approaches is the correct one. The circumstances of each case may justify one or another solution.... [T]he use of the word "may" in the second sentence of this provision [of Article 42(1)] indicates that the Convention does not draw a sharp line for the distinction of the respective scope of international and of domestic law and, correspondingly, that this has the effect to confer on to the Tribunal a certain margin and power for interpretation.
>
> What is clear is that the sense and meaning of the negotiations leading to the second sentence of Article 42(1) allowed for both legal orders to have a role. The law of the host State can indeed be applied in conjunction with international law if this is justified. So too international law can be applied by itself if the appropriate rule is found in this other ambit.[231]

This much freer approach to choice of law under the second sentence of Article 42(1) was to find favor in a number of cases initiated at ICSID after the turn of the century.

[227] Composed of Konstantinos D. Kerameus as President and Andreas Bucher and Francisco Orrego Vicuña as members. Kerameus was Professor of Civil Procedure at the University of Athens and Bucher Professor of Private International Law at the University of Geneva. On Orrego Vicuña, *see* n. 113.

[228] *See* n. 223 and accompanying text.

[229] *See Wena v. Egypt*, ad hoc Committee Decision, February 5, 2002, 6 ICSID Rep. 129, 137 (2004).

[230] On these decisions, *see* Ch. 8, section V.

[231] *Wena v. Egypt*, ad hoc Committee Decision (n. 229) 138.

10

ICSID from 2000 to 2010

This chapter examines activities of the Centre in the first decade of the twenty-first century. The decade saw explosive growth of the institution's caseload. Between January 1, 2000 and December 31, 2010, proceedings were instituted under the ICSID Convention or Additional Facility Rules in a total of 262 new cases—nearly four times as many cases as were brought to ICSID during the previous 30 years.[1] Setting the stage for this growth were the massive increases, beginning in the 1990s and continuing into the twenty-first century, in the volume of international investment and the number of investment promotion and protection treaties. World flows of FDI averaged US$1.1 trillion annually in 2000 to 2008, having climbed fivefold to that level in the 1990s.[2] The total number of BITs, having similarly quintupled in the 1990s, reached some 2,600 in 2008.[3] As many as 179 countries had by then become parties to such treaties.[4] Bilateral free trade agreements (FTAs) with provisions on investment inspired by those of BITs also came to be made in larger numbers during the first decade of the century. The United States entered into 11 bilateral FTAs in this period.[5] It also concluded a free trade agreement containing investment provisions with five Central American countries and the Dominican Republic (the CAFTA-DR).[6] Like the NAFTA, the ECT and earlier BITs discussed in Chapter 9, the CAFTA-DR and almost all of the new FTAs and BITs had clauses entitling covered investors to submit disputes with their host States to arbitration under the ICSID Convention or Additional Facility Rules.[7]

[1] *See* ICSID, The ICSID Caseload—Statistics (Issue 2015-2), chart 2.

[2] These data are from UNCTAD's Interactive Database on FDI Flows, <http://unctad.org/en/Pages/DIAE/FDI%20Statistics/Interactive-database.aspx>.

[3] *See* Doc. UNCTAD/ITE/11A/2, Bilateral Investment Treaties: 1959–1999, iii (2000); Doc. UNCTAD/WEB/DIAE/IA/2009/8, Recent Developments in International Investment Agreements (2008–June 2009), 2 (2009).

[4] *See* K.J. Vandevelde, *Bilateral Investment Treaties: History, Policy and Interpretation* 74 (2010). BITs had generally continued, however, to be made with or between developing or transition countries. There remained virtually no BITs exclusively between capital-exporting countries. For further discussion of this point, see n. 137 and accompanying text.

[5] With Australia, Bahrain, Chile, Colombia, Jordan, Korea, Morocco, Oman, Panama, Peru and Singapore.

[6] The Central American countries joining the United States and the Dominican Republic in this treaty were Costa Rica, El Salvador, Guatemala, Honduras and Nicaragua.

[7] *See* Dominican Republic–Central America–United States Free Trade Agreement (CAFTA-DR), August 5, 2004, Art. 10.16(3)(a) and 10.16(3)(b), available at <https://ustr.gov/trade-agreements/free-trade-agreements/cafta-dr-dominican-republic-central-america-fta>. *See also, e.g.*, Singapore–United States Free Trade Agreement, May 26, 2003, Art. 15.15(a) and 15.15(b), available at <https://ustr.gov/trade-agreements/free-trade-agreements/singapore-fta>; Chile–United States Free Trade Agreement, June 6, 2003, Art. 10.15(5)(a) and 10.15(5)(b), available at <https://ustr.gov/trade-agreements/free-trade-agreements/chile-fta>; Agreement on Encouragement and Reciprocal Protection of Investments, Malawi–Netherlands, December 11, 2003, reprinted in ICSID, Investment Treaties, Release 2008-1 (May 2008), Art. 9. As had become increasingly common among investment treaties in the 1990s, many of the newer treaties additionally gave covered investors the option of resorting to arbitration under the UNCITRAL Arbitration Rules for the resolution of disputes with their host States. *See, e.g.*, CAFTA-DR, Art. 10.16(3)(c); Chile–U.S. FTA, Art. 10.15(5)(c); Agreement on the Promotion and Reciprocal Protection of Investments,

Jurisdiction was sought to be based on such clauses of investment treaties in some 200 of the over 260 new cases. In most instances, the treaties concerned were concluded during the 1990s. As the first decade of the twenty-first century drew to a close, however, a growing share of the cases involved treaties made in that decade.

A very high proportion—about 40 percent—of the new cases were brought against Latin American countries. OPEC's Latin American members, Ecuador and Venezuela, together accounted for 30 of the cases; many of them concerned measures implementing nationalistic policies of those countries' recently elected left-of-center governments. Disaffection with globalization and the Washington Consensus strategies, above all privatization, had spread throughout the region. The "Water Revolt" of Cochabamba, Bolivia's third-largest city, became emblematic in this connection. The city's water supply system was privatized under a concession agreement entered into by the government in 1999 with Aguas del Tunari, a company indirectly owned in part by the engineering and construction TNC Bechtel. Rate increases imposed by the concessionaire sparked major protests in early 2000 in which soldiers killed a teenage demonstrator. After declaring a state of emergency and seeing personnel of Aguas del Tunari flee, Bolivia revoked the concession agreement in April 2000.[8] Claiming compensation for the revocation, the company initiated an ICSID Convention arbitration against Bolivia two years later. Steps taken by Bolivia toward the re-nationalization of another privatized utility, the telecommunications company Intel, gave rise to another ICSID Convention proceeding against the country. The proceeding was instituted in 2007 by ETI, an affiliate of Telecom Italia, which in 1995 had acquired half ownership and management control of Intel.

Many more of the cases, however, involved Argentina. It was named as respondent in 44 of the ICSID Convention arbitrations commenced in the period 2000 to 2010. Almost all of them were precipitated by measures of Argentina to address its financial crisis of the early twenty-first century. The claimants included such large TNCs as Mobil, Suez and Endesa. In the majority of the cases, they were investors in Argentine water, electricity, gas and communications utilities that had been privatized in the 1990s. Under the privatization program, the utilities were to have a U.S. dollar-based tariff regime; the crisis measures of Argentina abrogated the regime, effectively devaluing the tariffs.

The onslaught of cases was greeted with an expression of resurgent Calvoist sentiment in late April 2007 at the fifth summit meeting of the Bolivarian Alliance for the Americas (known as ALBA, the acronym formed from its name in Spanish). At the meeting, ALBA members Bolivia, Nicaragua and Venezuela condemned the "pressure from certain multinational companies, which … resist the application of sovereign decisions … commencing international arbitration proceedings against the states before institutions such as ICSID."[9] They announced that they would withdraw from participation in the ICSID Convention "in order to guarantee the sovereign right of the countries to regulate foreign investment on their national territories."[10] In early May 2007, Bolivia made good on this plan and became the first Contracting State to

Romania–Sweden, May 29, 2002, reprinted in ICSID, Investment Treaties, Release 2007-2 (July 2007), Art. 10(2)(ii).

[8] On the "Water Revolt" of Cochabamba, *see* J. Shultz and M.C. Draper (eds.), *Dignity and Defiance: Stories from Bolivia's Challenge to Globalization* ch. 1 (2008). *See also* M. Reid, *Forgotten Continent: The Battle for Latin America's Soul* 141–142 (2007).

[9] This ALBA statement is more fully quoted at <globalarbitrationreview.com/insight/the_arbitration_review_of_the_americas_2008/1036510/Venezuela>.

[10] Ibid.

denounce the ICSID Convention, by written notice to the World Bank as depositary of the Convention. In accordance with Article 71 of the Convention, the denunciation was effective six months later, in early November 2007. The following month, as oil companies prepared to activate consents to the jurisdiction of ICSID in its BITs, Ecuador made a notification under Article 25(4) of the Convention purporting to withdraw such consents in respect of disputes related to the exploitation of natural resources.[11] In June 2009, Ecuador joined ALBA; the next month it took the further step of denouncing the ICSID Convention. Ecuador's denunciation became effective in January 2010.[12]

As was seen in Chapter 9, in the second half of the 1990s opposition arose among some NGOs to arbitration under investment treaties. They too saw it as potentially undermining the sovereignty and regulatory power of States. A point increasingly highlighted by NGO activists in the period 2000 to 2010 was the extent to which recourse to arbitration might counter efforts of governments to uphold such human rights as the right to water, a prime example for the activists being the *Aguas del Tunari* case. As to the arbitral process itself, its privacy and confidentiality came under sustained fire from NGOs, notably Canada's International Institute for Sustainable Development (IISD) and the U.S.-based Center for International Environmental Law (CIEL).[13] They argued that the process should be more fully transparent and open to participation by concerned citizens, given the public importance of the issues at stake in many of the cases.

[11] The notification specified that "[a]ny instrument containing the Republic of Ecuador's previously expressed will to submit [disputes related to the exploitation of natural resources] ... to the jurisdiction of the Centre, which has not been perfected by the express and explicit consent of the other party prior to the date of the submission of the present notification, is hereby withdrawn by the Republic of Ecuador with immediate effect as of this date." Doc. ICSID/8-D, Contracting States and Measures Taken by Them for the Purpose of the Convention, D2 (April 2008). In the ICSID Convention arbitration *Burlington Resources v. Ecuador,* the claimant instituted the proceeding in 2008, in respect of a dispute arising out of oil production-sharing contracts, relying on Ecuador's consent to the jurisdiction of ICSID in its BIT with the U.S. In the proceeding, Ecuador objected to jurisdiction in respect of several of the claims on the basis of its 2007 notification under Art. 25(4). The Tribunal, however, found it unnecessary to address the objection as it dismissed those particular claims on other grounds. *See Burlington Resources v. Ecuador*, Decision on Jurisdiction, June 2, 2010, available at <http://www.italaw.com/cases/documents/183>. The notification of Ecuador was of doubtful efficacy in withdrawing the consents in BITs, which were protected by the law of treaties. *See* C.H. Schreuer and others, *The ICSID Convention: A Commentary* 347 (2d ed. 2009). The Tribunal in the *Burlington Resources* case was composed of Gabrielle Kaufmann-Kohler as President, Francisco Orrego Vicuña and Brigitte Stern. Kaufmann-Kohler was Professor of Private International Law at the University of Geneva and Honorary President of the Swiss Arbitration Association. Stern was retired Professor at the University of Paris I and a member of the U.N. Administrative Tribunal. On Orrego Vicuña, *see* Ch. 9, n. 113.

[12] In addition, in the course of 2008, Ecuador had denounced nine of its BITs, namely those with Cuba, Dominican Republic, El Salvador, Guatemala, Honduras, Nicaragua, Paraguay, Romania and Uruguay. The following year, the President of Ecuador requested a ruling from the country's Constitutional Court on the constitutionality of Ecuador's BITs with Argentina, Canada, Chile, China, Finland, France, Germany, the Netherlands, Sweden, Switzerland, the United Kingdom and the United States. The Constitutional Court made pronouncements on at least four of these BITs, recommending, in each instance, their denunciation on the ground that certain provisions, especially those on the settlement of investment disputes, were not compatible with the Constitution of Ecuador. I am grateful to Alejandro A. Escobar for this information.

[13] *See, e.g.*, Investment and Sustainable Development: A Guide to the Use and Potential of International Investment Agreements, prepared for the International Institute for Sustainable Development by A. Cosbey and others, sec. 2.1.1 (2004); International Legal Framework on Foreign Investment, prepared for the Center for International Environmental Law by N. Bernasconi-Osterwalder, 7 (2003).

Although arbitration under the auspices of ICSID was more open than the other forms of investment treaty arbitration, ICSID bore the brunt of the criticism, partly because most of the cases were being conducted under its auspices and partly because the other main form of arbitration made available in investment treaties, ad hoc arbitration under the UNCITRAL Arbitration Rules, lacked an administering institution to receive complaints. ICSID also was taken to task for its relationship with the World Bank. This was done in letters sent to the Bank and ICSID in connection with the *Aguas del Tunari* and *ETI* cases. Signed on behalf of hundreds of NGOs, the letters portrayed the relationship with the Bank as creating a conflict of interest for ICSID in handling such cases related to the very sort of privatization that the Bank had been promoting among its borrowers.[14] The first of these letters, the one regarding the *Aguas del Tunari* case, was presented to the Bank and ICSID in 2002. It set forth the demand of the signatories that the Arbitral Tribunal adopt procedures allowing affected individuals and organizations to participate in the case as well as disclosing all documents filed with the Tribunal and making its hearings open to the public. As will be seen in this chapter, there were similar requests by NGOs in connection with water privatization cases later in the decade.

Other influential voices were raised to argue that investment treaties and arbitration could unduly constrain governments from introducing much needed reforms, including those concerning human rights. Among those warning of this danger was the Special Representative of the U.N. Secretary-General (SRSG) on Business and Human Rights.[15] The SRSG was appointed in 2005 at the request of the then-U.N. Human Rights Commission. His mandate included identifying and clarifying standards of corporate responsibility and accountability with regard to human rights.[16] Subsequent reports of the SRSG to the U.N. Human Rights Council (the successor to the Commission) lambasted BITs for giving investors overly expansive protections, making it "difficult [for host States] to strengthen domestic social and environmental standards, including those related to human rights, without fear of investor challenge."[17] The SRSG similarly faulted so-called stabilization clauses of investment

[14] The text of the letter relating to the *Aguas del Tunari* case, dated August 29, 2002, is available at <http://www.ciel.org/wp-content/uploads/2015/05/CITIZENS_Aug02l.pdf>. On the letter referring to the *ETI* case, dated January 15, 2008, see <https://www.tni.org/es/art%C3%ADculo/campana-global-contra-las-reglas-antidemocraticas-en-materia-de-inversiones?content_language=en>.

[15] This was John G. Ruggie, Berthold Beitz Professor of International Affairs at Harvard University's John F. Kennedy School of Government. As Assistant Secretary-General and senior advisor for strategic planning at the U.N. from 1997 to 2001, Ruggie had been one of the main architects of the U.N. Global Compact. Launched in 2001, the Compact quickly became the world's largest corporate social responsibility initiative, with over 5,300 corporate participants by the end of June 2009. They were asked by the Compact to align their business operations and strategies with ten basic principles in the areas of human rights, labor standards, the environment and anti-corruption. For further details, *see* U.N. Global Compact: Corporate Citizenship in the World Economy (January 2014), available at <https://www.unglobalcompact.org/docs/news_events/8.1/GC_brochure_FINAL.pdf>; D. Vogel, *The Market for Virtue: The Potential and Limits of Corporate Social Responsibility* 156–158 (2005).

[16] *See* J. Ruggie, Business and Human Rights: The Evolving International Agenda, Corporate Social Responsibility Initiative, Working Paper No. 31, John F. Kennedy School of Government, Harvard University, 4 (citing U.N. Human Rights Commission Resolution 2005/69, April 15, 2005).

[17] U.N. Doc. A/HRC/8/5, April 7, 2008, Protect, Respect and Remedy: a Framework for Business and Human Rights, Report of the Special Representative of the Secretary-General on the issue of human rights and transnational corporations and other business enterprises, John Ruggie, 11 (April 2008 SRSG Report). *See also* U.N. Doc. A/HRC/14/27, Business and Human Rights: Further Steps Toward the Operationalization of the "Protect, Respect and Remedy" Framework, Report of the Special Representative of the Secretary-General on the issue of human rights and transnational corporations and other business enterprises, John Ruggie, April 9, 2010, 6 (April 2010 SRSG Report). The April 2008 SRSG Report set forth a conceptual and policy framework, which was approved by the Human Rights Council, comprising three core principles: the State duty to protect against human

contracts for potentially depriving host States of "the required policy space ... to pursue bona fide human rights obligations."[18] Like many others, the SRSG also condemned the confidentiality and privacy of investor–State arbitration generally, urging that, "[w]here human rights and other public interests are concerned, transparency should be a governing principle."[19]

Although investment treaties and arbitrations continued to proliferate, there was some accommodation of the concerns expressed by NGOs and others, especially as regards transparency of and public participation in the arbitral process. In 2001, in two UNCITRAL Rules cases arising under the NAFTA investment chapter, the tribunals ruled that they could accept and consider written submissions from interested third parties, which included environmental NGOs in the first case and labor unions in the second.[20] The example thus set was eventually followed at ICSID.[21] Within the NAFTA context, the Free Trade Commission confirmed, in 2003, that tribunals had the discretion to accept such *amicus curiae* submissions.[22]

In the meantime, the U.S. Congress had passed the Trade Act of 2002. It set numerous negotiating objectives for U.S. trade agreements. Among the objectives concerning foreign investment was to seek improvements of investor–State dispute settlement mechanisms. The projected improvements included procedures to "eliminate frivolous claims" and "ensure the efficient selection of arbitrators and the expeditious disposition of claims."[23] They also included providing for an appellate body or similar mechanism for investor–State arbitrations arising under the agreements. According to the Trade Act, the purpose of such a mechanism would be "to provide coherence in the interpretations of investment provisions in trade agreements."[24] Another of the investment-related negotiating objectives set

rights abuses by third parties, including business; the corporate responsibility to respect human rights; and the need for more effective access to remedies in cases of abuse. April 2008 SRSG Report, at 4–5.

[18] April 2010 SRSG Report (n. 17) 6. The April 2010 SRSG Report referred to such clauses as provisions "that can either insulate investors from new environmental or social laws or entitle them to seek compensation for compliance." A study prepared for the SRSG and IFC in 2008 pointed out that such clauses were most likely to be found in contracts concluded by developing countries. *See* Stabilization Clauses and Human Rights, March 11, 2008, available at <https://business-humanrights.org/sites/default/files/reports-and-materials/Stabilization-Clauses-and-Human-Rights-11-Mar-2008.pdf>. This was lamented by the SRSG as "it is precisely in developing countries that regulatory development may be most needed." April 2008 SRSG Report (n. 17) 12. These conclusions put in uncomfortable perspective ICSID's longstanding promotion of such clauses and its administration of proceedings pursuant to contracts with stabilization clauses. *See* Doc. ICSID/5/Rev. 1, ICSID Model Clauses (1983), cl. XIV; Doc. ICSID/5/Rev. 2, ICSID Model Clauses (1993), cl. 10, and, for examples of cases involving contracts with such clauses, Ch. 8, text accompanying nn. 97 and 98.

[19] April 2008 SRSG Report (n. 17) 12.

[20] *See Methanex v. U.S.*, Decision of the Tribunal on Petitions from Third Persons to Intervene as "Amici Curiae," January 15, 2001, available at <http://www.italaw.com/cases/683>; *UPS v. Canada*, Decision of the Tribunal on Petitions for Intervention and Participation as Amici Curiae, October 17, 2001, available at <http://www.italaw.com/cases/1138>.

[21] For details, *see* section III of this chapter.

[22] *See* Statement of the Free Trade Commission on Non-Disputing Party Participation, October 7, 2003. The Free Trade Commission, it will be recalled, consisted of the trade ministers of the three NAFTA parties.

[23] *See* Trade Act of 2002, Pub. L. 107-210, 116 Stat. 933, secs. 2102(b)(3)(G)(i) and 2102(b)(3)(G)(ii).

[24] Ibid. sec. 2102(b)(3)(G)(iv). The idea of such an appellate mechanism was not new. At the intergovernmental level, it had been discussed in the late 1990s in the abortive MAI negotiations as a means of fostering the development of a coherent jurisprudence under the treaty. *See* Improving the System of Investor–State Dispute Settlement: An Overview, OECD background paper for Symposium on Making the Most of International Investment Agreement: A Common Agenda, December 12, 2005, 8 and note 18.

by the Trade Act was maximizing the transparency of the dispute settlement mechanisms by ensuring that all filings and rulings were promptly made public, that all hearings were open to the public and that there was a procedure for accepting *amicus curiae* submissions from businesses, unions and NGOs.[25] Provisions aimed at meeting the objectives regarding investor–State dispute settlement mechanisms were incorporated into subsequent FTAs of the United States. They also featured in extensive revisions made by U.S. BIT negotiators in 2004 to their model negotiating text[26] and influenced changes made to the ICSID Arbitration Rules and Additional Facility Rules in 2006.[27]

Despite all the criticisms, and the denunciations of the ICSID Convention by Bolivia and Ecuador, there was a net increase in the number of Contracting States between 2000 and 2010. In another positive development during the period, it was finally decided that ICSID should have a full-time Secretary-General. As explained in the next section of this chapter, the decision was prompted in part by the dramatic growth of the caseload. The deluge of new cases colored other institutional developments dealt with in the next section, notably those related to the finances of ICSID. Two sets of amendments of the Regulations and Rules of the Centre were passed during the decade to meet changing demands on ICSID. These amendments are examined in sections II and III. The cases themselves are discussed in section IV.

I. Institutional developments

This section begins by reviewing ratifications of the ICSID Convention in the period 2000 to 2010. The section then turns to the management, staffing and finances of the Secretariat during the period. Additions to the Panels of Conciliators and of Arbitrators are also considered.

A. Ratifications of the Convention

During the period 2000 to 2010, 17 countries ratified the Convention to join the ranks of the Contracting States. The 17 were regionally diverse. They included two Latin American States, Guatemala and Uruguay.[28] Three Arab countries, Lebanon, Qatar and Yemen, also ratified the ICSID Convention in this period, as did two future EU members, Bulgaria and Malta, and two former Soviet republics, Kazakhstan and Ukraine.[29] In addition, two ASEAN members, Brunei and Cambodia, ratified during the decade. In all, the ratifications of 2000 to 2010 brought the number of Contracting States to 146.

[25] *See* Trade Act of 2002 (n. 23) sec. 2102(b)(3)(H).

[26] The resulting U.S. Model BIT of 2004 is reprinted in K.J. Vandevelde, *U.S. International Investment Agreements* 825 (2009).

[27] On these changes, *see* section III of this chapter.

[28] At the end of the decade, there were therefore as many Latin American Contracting States as at the beginning, the denunciations of Bolivia and Ecuador notwithstanding. Two other Western Hemisphere countries ratified the Convention during the decade: Haiti and St. Vincent and the Grenadines.

[29] Another of the new Contracting States was Serbia.

B. The Secretariat

As mentioned in Chapter 9, Ibrahim Shihata relinquished his position as Senior Vice President and General Counsel of the World Bank in 1998 but remained Secretary-General of ICSID until 2000.[30] His successor as General Counsel, Ko-Yung Tung,[31] held the post from 2000 to 2003. The next two General Counsel were Roberto E. Dañino,[32] who occupied the office between 2003 and 2006, and Ana Palacio,[33] General Counsel from 2006 to 2008. Tung, Dañino and Palacio combined their tenures as General Counsel with service as Secretary-General of ICSID. In proposing them for election as Secretary-General, the Chairman of the Administrative Council in each case simply explained that the General Counsel was traditionally chosen for the ICSID post.[34] The Deputy Secretary-General position also passed from one person to another in this period. On the expiry of his six-year term, the first incumbent (the present author) retired from the staff of the World Bank in 2005. After a two-year gap, a new Chief Counsel was appointed for ICSID and then duly elected Deputy Secretary-General.[35]

Robert B. Zoellick became President of the World Bank and hence Chairman of the Administrative Council of ICSID in July 2007.[36] Toward the end of the following year, he wrote to the members of the Council to propose a new candidate for election as Secretary-General of the Centre. In his letter, Zoellick reminded Council members that, in the past, the General Counsel of the Bank had also served as Secretary-General of ICSID. "Given the increased demands for both positions," Zoellick continued:

> I believe the posts of General Counsel and Secretary-General of ICSID should be held by two individuals. This step will help ensure ICSID receives the full-time attention it warrants. Given both the caseload and the many policy issues related to ICSID, it needs a full-time leader and executive.[37]

Zoellick went on to explain that after a careful and extensive search,[38] he had selected Meg Kinnear as an outstanding candidate for the position.[39] The following month,

[30] When he reached the mandatory retirement age for staff of the World Bank, Shihata had stepped down from the General Counsel position earlier due to ill health.

[31] Tung had previously been chairman of the global practice group at the Los Angeles law firm of O'Melveny & Meyers and Chair of the Board of Governors of the East–West Center in Honolulu.

[32] Dañino had served as Prime Minister of Peru and then as its Ambassador to the U.S. He had previously been chairman of the Latin American practice group at the Washington, D.C. law firm of Wilmer Cutler & Pickering and was the first General Counsel of the Inter-American Investment Corporation.

[33] Palacio, the first woman General Counsel of the Bank, had been a Member of the European Parliament and, before that, Foreign Minister of Spain and a Member of the Spanish Parliament.

[34] *See* letters of the Chairman of the Members of the Administrative Council of April 3, 2000, July 21, 2003 and August 16, 2006. On the elections of Tung, Dañino and Palacio as Secretary-General, *see* 17(2) News from ICSID 1 (2000); 20(2) News from ICSID 1 (2003); and 23(1) News from ICSID (2007), respectively.

[35] This was Nassib G. Ziadé, who had been a Counsel at ICSID before serving for a decade as Executive Secretary of the World Bank Administrative Tribunal. On his election as Deputy Secretary-General, *see* 24(2) News from ICSID 1 (2007).

[36] Zoellick came to the World Bank from the Goldman Sachs Group, where he was Vice Chairman, International. He was previously Deputy Secretary of the U.S. Department of State and, before that, the U.S. Trade Representative.

[37] Letter of the Chairman to the Representatives on the Administrative Council, December 12, 2008.

[38] This involved the establishment earlier in 2008 of a search committee to find suitable candidates for the Secretary-General position. The committee was chaired by the Vice President, Human Resources, of the World Bank and included as members the General Counsel of the IFC, a former Deputy General Counsel of the Bank, the Executive Secretary of the Bank's Administrative Tribunal and ICSID's first Deputy Secretary-General.

[39] Kinnear was Senior General Counsel and Director General of the Trade Law Bureau of Canada, a joint legal unit of the Department of Justice and of Foreign Affairs & International Trade Canada.

Zoellick formally nominated Kinnear for election as Secretary-General. With her election in February 2009, the Secretariat of the Centre at last had its full-time head.[40]

All of these changes at the top came at an exceptionally busy time for the Secretariat. The number of new ICSID Convention and Additional Facility cases registered annually averaged about 25 in the period 2000 to 2010. With each case generally remaining before ICSID for several years, the number of pending Convention and Additional Facility proceedings went from around 40 in 2000 to over 100 at mid-decade and surpassed 150 by 2010. Throughout the second half of the decade, around 45 percent of the pending proceedings were being conducted in two of the Centre's official languages (most often in English and Spanish).

In addition, the Secretariat had begun to receive and accede to requests, from the parties and tribunals in proceedings conducted under non-ICSID rules, for the Centre to administer the proceedings—in other words, to provide them with administrative support services similar to those given to ICSID Convention and Additional Facility proceedings. This was done in 2000 for the arbitral proceeding in the *Southern Bluefin Tuna* case brought by Australia and New Zealand against Japan under Annex VII of the 1982 U.N. Convention on the Law of the Sea.[41] Another inter-State proceeding administered by ICSID, and also involving a natural resource, was the expert determination proceeding conducted in 2005 to 2007 under Annexure F of the 1960 Indus Waters Treaty between Pakistan and India.[42] However, the majority of the approximately 20 non-ICSID proceedings administered by the Centre after 2000 were in cases submitted to UNCITRAL Rules arbitration pursuant to the investor–State dispute settlement provisions of the NAFTA investment chapter (or, in a few instances, of BITs). As mentioned in Chapter 9, in the NAFTA investment chapter (as in some BITs), those provisions entrusted the Secretary-General of ICSID with the role of the appointing authority of arbitrators for the cases.[43] Having ICSID administer the subsequent proceedings was for the parties and arbitrators an attractive extension of this role.

In parallel with the rising caseload, the number of staff of the Secretariat grew rapidly in 2000 to 2010. At the beginning of the decade, there were 11 staff. By 2005, the number had more than doubled. Further increases brought the total at the end of fiscal

In that position, she was responsible for the conduct of all international investment and trade litigation involving Canada.

[40] *See* Meg Kinnear Elected ICSID Secretary-General, ICSID News Release, February 23, 2009.

[41] Annex VII of the U.N. Convention on the Law of the Sea (UNCLOS), December 10, 1982, 1833 UNTS 397, set forth an ad hoc arbitral procedure for the settlement of disputes arising out of the interpretation or application of the UNCLOS. The procedure was invoked in the absence of a declaration by the parties under Art. 287 of the UNCLOS choosing a means of settlement offered by that article (which also included the International Tribunal for the Law of the Sea, the ICJ and, for certain specified categories of disputes, a special arbitral tribunal constituted under Annex VIII of the UNCLOS). The dispute in the *Southern Bluefin Tuna* case was over the legality of a unilateral experimental fishing program undertaken by Japan. The Arbitral Tribunal, the first to be constituted under Art. VII of the UNCLOS, declined jurisdiction over the dispute on the ground that the (non-compulsory) dispute settlement procedures of a separate treaty to which Australia, New Zealand and Japan were parties, the 1993 Convention for the Conservation of Southern Bluefin Tuna, excluded the procedures of the UNCLOS. For further details, *see* T. Stevens, *International Courts and Environmental Protection* 220–228 (2009).

[42] The proceeding concerned a difference between Pakistan and India regarding the Baglihar hydropower plant that India was building on the Chenab River. For details, *see* S. Salman and E. Obadia, The Indus Water Treaty, the Baghlihar Difference and ICSID Administration of the Proceedings, 23(2) News from ICSID 1 (2006). On the World Bank's involvement in the mediation of the original dispute between the parties over the Indus Basin, *see* Ch. 2, n. 89.

[43] *See* Ch. 9, text accompanying n. 36.

year 2010 to just over 30, of whom 20 were lawyers and paralegals. The enlargement of the staff required a fourfold expansion of the administrative budget of the Centre in the course of the decade. Thus, the budget of ICSID was US$1.3 million for fiscal year 2000; it was well over twice that for fiscal year 2005; and it exceeded US$5.1 million for fiscal year 2010.

It will be remembered from Chapter 6 that, in the Memorandum of Administrative Arrangements ICSID concluded with the World Bank in 1967, the Bank undertook to meet the Centre's annual budgetary needs within reasonable limits and against reimbursement only to the extent of expenditures attributable to individual proceedings for which ICSID itself was to be reimbursed by parties. After it started getting cases and launched its publishing activities, ICSID generated income from fees for lodging conciliation and arbitration requests and from the sale of publications. From the beginning, the income was credited to the Bank. But for most of ICSID's history, the amounts involved were negligible. They were therefore disregarded in drawing up the budget which, pursuant to the 1967 Memorandum of Administrative Arrangements, the Bank supported in full for nearly 40 years. This total subvention became more and more difficult to sustain as ICSID's budgetary requirements escalated in the period 2000 to 2010. Yet it would not have been a realistic alternative to ask the Contracting States to cover any funding shortfalls for the Centre pursuant to Article 17 of the Convention.[44] ICSID and the Bank therefore decided, shortly before the beginning of the Centre's 2006 fiscal year in July 2005, that increased fee income should be sought to contain if not reduce the level of budgetary support from the Bank in future.

Substantial hikes in the fees charged in each case were required to meet this goal. Thus, shortly after the start of the fiscal year in July 2005, the fee for lodging conciliation and arbitration requests was raised from US$7,000 to US$25,000.[45] There was also a major increase of the flat administrative charge that ICSID had begun to levy on the parties in each case. In July 2005, this went from a one-time charge of US$3,000 to an annual charge of US$10,000.[46] At the same time, ICSID raised to US$10,000 the fee it had since 2000 levied on parties requesting the Secretary-General to appoint an arbitrator in an UNCITRAL Rules or other non-ICSID proceeding.[47] To achieve the desired result of making ICSID more self-reliant, the flat,

[44] As applied to the US$2.8 million that ICSID required for fiscal year 2005, over and above its fee income and other receipts, the formula in Art. 17 would have entailed annual contributions of less than US$5,000 from most Contracting States (and less than US$1,500 from many of them). The administrative effort involved in trying each year to collect such small amounts from so many different sources would have been disproportionately burdensome.

[45] *See* ICSID, Schedule of Fees, July 6, 2005, para. 1. The lodging fee had been raised three times earlier in the decade: from US$1,000 to US$2,000 in April 2000; to US$5,000 in January 2001; and to US$7,000 in July 2002. *See* ICSID, Schedule of Fees, April 5, 2000, para. 1; ICSID, Schedule of Fees, January 1, 2001, para. 1; ICSID, Schedule of Fees, July 1, 2002, para. 1.

[46] *See* ICSID, Schedule of Fees, July 6, 2005, para. 4. The flat administrative charge (additional to the reimbursement that ICSID continued to claim for its out-of-pocket expenses for the proceeding concerned) was introduced as a one-time charge of US$2,000 in 2001, and increased to US$3,000 the following year. *See* ICSID, Schedule of Fees, January 1, 2001, para. 3; ICSID, Schedule of Fees, July 1, 2002, para. 3.

[47] *See* ICSID, Schedule of Fees, July 6, 2005, para. 7. This fee was introduced at US$1,000. *See* ICSID, Schedule of Fees, April 5, 2000, para. 7. It was raised to US$2,500 in 2001 and US$3,500 the following year. *See* ICSID, Schedule of Fees, January 1, 2001, para. 7; ICSID Schedule of Fees, July 1, 2002, para. 7. In cases where the Secretary-General as the designated appointing authority had the function of deciding on the challenge of an arbitrator (as under the UNCITRAL Arbitration Rules), the fee applied to requests for challenge decisions as well.

now annual, administrative charge had to be doubled to US$20,000 in 2008.[48] The doubling of the charge to US$20,000 was accompanied by the reintroduction of the fee that ICSID had charged parties before 1985 for legal staff to attend hearings outside Washington, D.C. The fee was reintroduced at US$1,500 per day of hearings.[49] As these various increases took hold, the Bank's contribution to ICSID's budgetary requirements fell from some 80 percent of total expenditures in 2005, to under 50 percent of spending in 2007 and 20 percent in 2010.[50] It should, however, be emphasized that the Bank was by no means abandoning ICSID; though proportionately reduced, the financial support of the Bank was, at some US$1.5 million, higher for 2010 than it had been for 2000.

Mention may also be made here of the fee specified for conciliators, arbitrators and ad hoc committee members in the Schedule of Fees of the Centre. In 1983, the fee had been set at 600 Special Drawing Rights (SDRs) for each day of participation in meetings and for each day of other work.[51] It remained at that level for 17 years.[52] By the late 1990s, when SDR 600 was worth roughly US$800, there was growing dissatisfaction among arbitrators with the fee, which was much lower than the remuneration many of them could expect to receive in a commercial arbitration. Tribunals began more often to take the initiative of asking the parties, at the outset of the proceeding, to agree on higher fees for the arbitrators.[53] Finally, in April 2000, the default fee provided for in the Schedule of Fees was raised to US$1,100 daily.[54] Upward revisions of the fee in 2001, 2002 and 2005 brought it to the higher (and many would say, more realistic) level of US$3,000 per day, where it stayed for the rest of the decade.[55]

C. The Panels of Conciliators and of Arbitrators

During the period 2000 to 2010, as in previous years, many Contracting States failed to make or to maintain their designations to the Panels of Conciliators and of Arbitrators. More prompting by the Secretariat brought a further modest improvement in the proportion of designating States, to some 70 percent by 2010. Half of them, however, had allowed the terms of their designees to expire without naming

[48] *See* ICSID, Schedule of Fees, January 1, 2008, para. 4. For proceedings instituted before the date of this increase to US$20,000, however, the previous charge of US$10,000 was maintained for another year.

[49] *See* ibid. para. 5.

[50] The restructuring of the budget, tying it much more closely to revenues from the cases, inevitably gave rise to some uncertainty at the outset. Reflecting this, most of the legal staff recruited between 2005 and 2009 received short-term or temporary appointments; as the budgetary situation stabilized, they were increasingly converted to longer-term appointments.

[51] On the background, including earlier levels of the fee, *see* Ch. 7, n. 32.

[52] The fees of conciliators, arbitrators and ad hoc committee members were of course paid from party advances of parties to the Centre rather than from its administrative budget. The Secretariat was long reluctant to raise the fee in part because an increase would nevertheless have had an impact on the World Bank's administrative expenditures, by encouraging a similar increase in the fees of members of the World Bank Administrative Tribunal paid from the Bank's budget (the amounts of the fees of the Administrative Tribunal were then based on the fees set for ICSID conciliators, arbitrators and ad hoc committee members).

[53] This was done in ten of the ICSID Convention and Additional Facility proceedings instituted in 1997–1999. The higher fees agreed in those cases ranged from SDR 900 per day to US$1,956 per day.

[54] *See* ICSID, Schedule of Fees, April 5, 2000, para. 2. The fees were thenceforth denominated in dollars as the system of calculating them first in SDRs and then converting them to dollars for payment had proven to be too administratively burdensome.

[55] *See* ICSID, Schedule of Fees, January 1, 2001, para. 2; ICSID, Schedule of Fees, July 1, 2002, para. 2; ICSID, Schedule of Fees, July 6, 2005, para. 3.

successors.[56] Some Contracting States, moreover, appeared to have paid scant heed to the reminder, in Article 14(1) of the ICSID Convention, of the importance of competence in the field of law for members of the Panel of Arbitrators.[57]

While the Panel of Arbitrators had suffered from such weaknesses since ICSID's early days, the shortcomings were felt acutely after the turn of the century, when the mushrooming caseload brought increasing calls on the Chairman of the Administrative Council to appoint Panel members to arbitral tribunals and ad hoc committees under Articles 38 and 52(3) of the ICSID Convention. The problem was made somewhat more manageable by the Chairman's designation, in 2000, of his full complement of ten persons to the Panels. The designees—five developing country nationals and five industrial country nationals—included the first woman named to the Panels by the Chairman.[58] In addition, on a number of occasions, the shortage of Panel members that the Chairman could appoint as arbitrators was addressed by the parties agreeing, on the proposal of the Secretariat, to an appointment from outside the Panel.[59]

Contracting States, it may be mentioned here, also continued to be remiss about their designations of courts or other authorities competent to enforce Convention awards. As of the end of 2010, half of the by then 146 Contracting States had failed to make these designations as required by Article 54(2) of the Convention.

II. The 2003 amendments of the Regulations and Rules

In 1999, Shihata's last full year as Secretary-General of ICSID, he agreed that the Secretariat should review the Regulations and Rules of the Centre to identify any needed improvements in light of the rapidly expanding caseload. His successor, Ko-Yung Tung, informed the Administrative Council that the review was under way in September 2000.[60] By early 2002, the initial work was completed. It was presented in a March 2002 report to the members of the Administrative Council setting forth proposed amendments of the ICSID Regulations and Rules and Additional Facility Rules.[61]

[56] In accordance with Art. 15(3) of the ICSID Convention, the incumbents remained Panel members. Yet many of the designations had become stale, having expired five or more years earlier, putting into doubt the continued availability of the individuals concerned.

[57] The designations of around 20 Contracting States to the Panel of Arbitrators included persons apparently lacking legal qualifications.

[58] The ten designees were James R. Crawford (Australian), Robert M. Dossou (Beninese), L. Yves Fortier (Canadian), Michael Hwang (Singaporean), Gabrielle Kaufmann-Kohler (Swiss), Fali S. Nariman (Indian), Francisco Orrego Vicuña (Chilean), Stephen M. Schwebel (American), Ibrahim F.I. Shihata (Egyptian) and Prosper Weil (French). Tragically, Shihata passed away some six months after his designation. He was replaced on the Panels by Ahmed S. El-Kosheri (also Egyptian).

[59] In these cases, the parties were using their freedom, under Art. 37(2)(a) of the ICSID Convention, to decide on a method of constituting their tribunal that did not bring into play the restriction to Panel members in Art. 40(1) of the Convention, which applied only to appointments by the Chairman as default appointing authority under Art. 38. This was primarily done in cases involving Argentina. The large number of these cases quickly depleted the supply of available qualified Panel members (repeat appointments of Panel members were often difficult to make in the cases because one or other party would object to the appointment).

[60] *See* Report of the Secretary-General to the Administrative Council at its Thirty-Fourth Annual Meeting, September 26–28, 2000, 3–4.

[61] Proposed Amendments of the ICSID Regulations and Rules and the Additional Facility Rules: A Report of the Secretariat to the Members of the Administrative Council, March 29, 2002 (March 2002 Report).

The proposed amendments included several intended to clarify provisions that had proved to be confusing or unclear to parties. Thus, for example, a re-draft was suggested for ICSID Arbitration Rule 1(3), regarding the nationality of arbitrators, which parties often found opaque, particularly without the explanatory notes that had been dropped in 1984.[62] The proposed re-draft made it clear that, in the typical case of a three-member tribunal, a party could appoint a co-national as an arbitrator only with the agreement of the other party.[63] A few of the proposals were to reflect in the Regulations and Rules practices that had developed since the provisions were written. Two such proposals were made for the Institution Rules. The first was to codify, in Institution Rule 2, the practice of the Secretariat of requiring corporate claimants to submit, with their requests for conciliation or arbitration, evidence that they had taken any necessary internal steps to authorize the request.[64] Two cases registered in 1992 had underscored the need for this practice.[65] The second proposal for codifying in the Institution Rules a previous practice of the Secretariat was to require that notices of registration of requests for conciliation or arbitration remind the parties that registration of the request was without prejudice to the powers and functions of the conciliators or arbitrators in regard to jurisdiction or the merits.[66]

Another proposal was directed at provisions in the Arbitration Rules imposing absolute 30-day time limits on the appointment and disqualification of arbitrators by the Chairman of the Administrative Council. In view of the growing volume of cases, it was considered prudent to make compliance with these time limits a best efforts obligation of the Chairman.[67] A further proposal concerned the time limit in Arbitration Rule 46 for the preparation by a tribunal of its award. The time limit was 60 days from the tribunal's closure of the proceeding; it could under Rule 46 be extended only once, for a further 30 days, if necessary. The ad hoc Committee in the first annulment proceeding in *Klöckner v. Cameroon* had criticized this time limit as possibly leading to an overly hasty elaboration of the award concerned.[68] The time limit certainly was unrealistically short for many cases, particularly bilingual ones, in which awards had to be drawn up in two languages. The limit could be, and regularly was, sidestepped by the simple expedient of declaring the proceeding closed only after the preparation of the

[62] Rule 1(3) read:

> Except if each member of the Tribunal is appointed by agreement of the parties, nationals of the State party to the dispute or of the State whose national is a party to the dispute may be appointed by a party only if appointment by the other party to the dispute of the same number of arbitrators of either of these nationalities would not result in a majority of arbitrators of these nationalities.

On the origins of this provision, *see* Ch. 6, text accompanying nn. 96 and 97. On the dropping of the explanatory notes that at first accompanied the ICSID Rules, *see* Ch. 7, text accompanying nn. 150–153.

[63] *See* March 2002 Report (n. 61) proposed amendment of ICSID Arbitration Rule 1(3).

[64] *See* ibid. proposed amendment to ICSID Institution Rule 2(1).

[65] The cases were *Vacuum Salt v. Ghana* and *Scimitar v. Bangladesh*.

[66] *See* March 2002 Report (n. 61) proposed amendment of ICSID Institution Rule 7. On the beginnings of this practice, *see* Ch. 8, section I.

[67] *See* March 2002 Report (n. 61) proposed amendments of ICSID Arbitration Rules 4 and 9. The proposal was inspired by the then provision of the Additional Facility Arbitration Rules on the appointment of arbitrators by the Chairman of the Administrative Council, which required no more than that the Chairman use his best efforts to meet the stipulated deadline for such an appointment. *See* Doc. ICSID/11, ICSID Additional Facility (June 1979), Additional Facility Arbitration Rules, Art. 11(2).

[68] *See Klöckner v. Cameroon*, ad hoc Committee Decision, May 3, 1985, 2 ICSID Rep. 95, 136 (1994).

award was well advanced. This, however, was obviously contrary to the spirit of Rule 46. The Secretariat's report to the Administrative Council therefore proposed that the time limit be scrapped and Rule 46 content itself with exhorting arbitrators to finalize their award as soon as possible after the closure of the proceeding.[69]

The majority of the amendments proposed in the March 2002 report of the Secretariat were, however, aimed at the Additional Facility Rules. They had not benefited from the amendments adopted in 1984 for the ICSID Regulations and Rules.[70] Partly because of this, there were many differences of detail between the Additional Facility Rules on the one hand and the ICSID Regulations and Rules on the other hand. Most of those differences were unnecessary and needlessly complicated the task of the Secretariat in simultaneously administering proceedings under the Additional Facility Rules and the ICSID Regulations and Rules. Many of the proposed amendments were to eliminate such unnecessary differences. Simplifications made to the ICSID Regulations and Rules would thus also be made to the Additional Facility Rules.[71] It was also proposed to do away entirely with the Additional Facility Administrative and Financial Rules and instead apply to Additional Facility proceedings the relevant provisions of the ICSID Administrative and Financial Regulations.[72] This was intended to give Additional Facility proceedings a more complete administrative and financial framework than the abbreviated one provided by the Additional Facility Administrative and Financial Rules. By more fully integrating Additional Facility cases into ICSID's regular administrative structure, the suggested change was in keeping with the indefinite continuation of the Additional Facility approved in 1984.[73] It also allowed for significant further streamlining of the Additional Facility Conciliation and Arbitration Rules by permitting the deletion from them of provisions that merely reproduced parts of the ICSID Administrative and Financial Regulations.[74]

The March 2002 report of the Secretariat requested any comments that members of the Administrative Council might have on the proposed amendments by the end of June 2002. All of the comments received were favorable.[75] Several representatives on the Council suggested that a specific period for the preparation of an award nevertheless be retained in ICSID Arbitration Rule 46, even if the period were to be made

[69] The report drew support for this proposal from the fact that there was no similar time limit in the Additional Facility Arbitration Rules for the drawing up of an award, it being understood that an Additional Facility award should be made as soon as feasible after the parties had finished presenting the case.

[70] At the time those amendments were first proposed (April 1984), the Administrative Council had yet to approve the continuation of the Additional Facility (in September 1984). *See* Ch. 7, text accompanying n. 225.

[71] For example, the provision on procedural languages in the Additional Facility Arbitration Rules (Art. 30) was to be simplified in the way that the corresponding provision of the ICSID Arbitration Rules (Rule 22) was simplified in 1984. Another proposal was to delete from the Additional Facility Arbitration Rules the provision on the keeping of minutes of hearings (Art. 44) that reproduced a provision (Rule 37) dropped from the ICSID Arbitration Rules in 1984. Gone with this provision would be its clause forbidding publication of the minutes without the consent of the parties that had been discussed in *Metalclad v. Mexico*. *See* Ch. 9, text accompanying nn. 147 and 148.

[72] *See* March 2002 Report (n. 61) proposed amendment of Additional Facility Rules, Art. 5.

[73] *See* n. 70.

[74] It was, for example, possible to delete from the Additional Facility Conciliation Rules and Additional Facility Arbitration Rules provisions on supporting documentation and the computation of time limits that were based on provisions of the Administrative and Financial Regulations. *See* March 2002 Report (n. 61) proposed amendments of Additional Facility Conciliation Rules, Arts. 31 and 32, and proposed amendments of Additional Facility Arbitration Rules, Arts. 32 and 33.

[75] Doc. AC/02/4, Proposed Amendments of the ICSID Regulations and Rules and Additional Facility Rules: Note of the Secretary-General, July 15, 2002, para. 2.

considerably longer. The proposal was thus changed to require that an award be drawn up and signed within 120 days after closure of the proceeding, subject to a possible extension of the period by a further 60 days.[76] With this change, the proposed amendments were approved by the Administrative Council at its Annual Meeting in September 2002.[77] In accordance with the relevant resolution of the Council, the amendments took effect on January 1, 2003.[78]

III. The 2006 amendments of the Regulations and Rules

After he assumed the position of Secretary-General of ICSID late in 2003, Roberto Dañino launched a further review of the Regulations and Rules to see if additional improvements to them were needed. Though coming hard on the heels of the last set of amendments, the time seemed right for such a further review. The United States had begun to sign its first FTAs following the enactment of the Trade Act of 2002. As envisaged by the Trade Act, the sections of the FTAs on the arbitration of investor–State disputes had provisions meant to facilitate the early dismissal of baseless claims and the expeditious constitution of arbitral tribunals, as well as provisions stipulating that filings and decisions be published, that the tribunals conduct hearings open to the public and that they have the authority to accept and consider *amicus curiae* submissions.[79] Similar provisions were, as indicated earlier, inserted into the new U.S. model BIT of 2004.[80] As to the appellate mechanism foreseen by the Trade Act, the new FTAs and model BIT referred to the possibility of the eventual conclusion of separate treaty arrangements under which such a mechanism might be established.[81] In 2004, it seemed that an appellate mechanism could soon be created pursuant to one of the FTAs. Pressure from the U.S. Congress for progress in this direction led to the inclusion in the CAFTA-DR, signed in August 2004, of a commitment to form a negotiating group, within three months of entry into force of the treaty, charged with developing an appellate mechanism to review awards rendered in investor–State cases arising under the CAFTA-DR.[82]

These developments had a large impact on the near-contemporaneous search by the ICSID Secretariat for further improvements of the Centre's own framework for the settlement of investment disputes. In October 2004, the Secretariat issued a discussion paper on the subject.[83] The paper suggested adding a new procedure to the ICSID Arbitration Rules under which an arbitral tribunal might, at an early stage of a proceeding, be asked on an expedited basis to dismiss a baseless claim.[84] Inspired by

[76] *See* ibid. proposed amendment of ICSID Arbitration Rule 46.

[77] *See* Administrative Council Resolution AC(36)/RES/99, Approval of Amendments of the ICSID Regulations and Rules and Additional Facility Rules, September 29, 2002, reprinted in ICSID 2003 Ann. Rep. 36.

[78] The amended Regulations and Rules were then published in Doc. ICSID/15/Rev. 1, ICSID Convention, Regulations and Rules (January 2003) and Doc. ICSID/11/Rev. 1, ICSID Additional Facility Rules (January 2003).

[79] *See, e.g.*, Singapore–U.S. FTA (n. 7) Arts. 15.15(8)(a), 15.18(3), 15.19(3)–15.19(5) and 15.20; Chile–U.S. FTA (n. 7) Arts. 10.15(8)(a), 10.18(3), 10.19(3)–10.19(5) and 10.20.

[80] *See* 2004 Model BIT (n. 26) Arts. 24(6)(a), 27(3), 28(3)–28(5) and 29.

[81] *See, e.g.*, Singapore–U.S. FTA (n. 7) Art. 15.19(10); Chile–U.S. FTA (n. 7) Art. 10.19(10); 2004 Model BIT (n. 26) Art. 28(10).

[82] *See* CAFTA-DR (n. 7) Annex 10-F. As mentioned later in this section, the arrangement ended up not being implemented after entry into force of the CAFTA-DR.

[83] Possible Improvements of the Framework for ICSID Arbitration: ICSID Secretariat Discussion Paper, October 22, 2004 (October 2004 Discussion Paper).

[84] *See* ibid. para. 10.

the new U.S. treaty provisions aimed at frivolous claims, the procedure would fit well with ICSID's need to address the complaint that the power of the Secretary-General to screen arbitration requests was too limited.[85] Another new procedure suggested in the October 2004 discussion paper concerned provisional measures. As amended in 1984, the ICSID Arbitration Rules made it clear that parties to ICSID Convention arbitration proceedings could seek such measures from national courts only if this were provided for in the consent to arbitration of the parties.[86] The October 2004 discussion paper pointed out that investment treaties rarely took advantage of this possibility to permit recourse to national courts for provisional measures.[87] Parties seeking provisional measures therefore normally had to await the constitution of the tribunal, even if the measures were urgently required. Moreover, when eventually constituted, the tribunal could only recommend provisional measures after each party had had the opportunity to present its observations.[88] The discussion paper proposed that the ICSID Arbitration Rules address the problem by allowing for the early filing of a request for provisional measures and of all of the parties' observations on it, so that the tribunal could consider and decide on the request promptly on its constitution.[89]

Another set of suggestions in the discussion paper were for making the ICSID arbitral process more open or transparent. One of these suggestions was to specify in the ICSID Arbitration Rules, as had been done in the new U.S. treaties, that arbitral tribunals had the authority to accept and consider *amicus curiae* submissions.[90] A more substantial change proposed in the paper was to eliminate the Arbitration Rules' requirement of the consent of both parties for a decision by the tribunal to allow third parties or members of the public at large to attend hearings.[91] The discussion paper also proposed making mandatory the publication by the Secretariat of the Centre of excerpts of the legal reasoning in awards rendered by ICSID tribunals.[92] It will be remembered from Chapter 7 that the authority to publish such excerpts was introduced by one of the amendments of 1984.[93] The October 2004 discussion paper furthermore suggested expanding the disclosure requirements for ICSID arbitrators. The suggestion was to amend the ICSID Arbitration Rules to require arbitrators to disclose, not only any past or present relationship with the parties, but more generally any circumstances likely to give rise to justifiable doubts as to the arbitrator's reliability for independent judgment.[94] This suggestion was prompted by the growing scope for issue conflicts among arbitrators.[95] The suggested amendment was also to make it clear that the expanded disclosure requirement would apply throughout the entire proceeding and not just at its commencement.[96]

The amendments of the ICSID Arbitration Rules suggested in the October 2004 discussion paper were also made with respect to all of the corresponding provisions of the Additional Facility Arbitration Rules, except for the provision on provisional measures. The exception was due to the difference between the ICSID Arbitration Rules

[85] *See further* section IV(A) of this chapter.

[86] On this amendment in 1984 (of ICSID Arbitration Rule 39), *see* Ch. 8, nn. 79 and 80 and accompanying text.

[87] *See* October 2004 Discussion Paper (n. 83) para. 8.

[88] In accordance with Rule 39(4) of the ICSID Arbitration Rules.

[89] *See* October 2004 Discussion Paper (n. 83) para. 8.

[90] *See* ibid. para. 13.

[91] *See* ibid. para. 15.

[92] *See* ibid. para. 12.

[93] On this amendment (of what became ICSID Arbitration Rule 48), *see* Ch. 7, text accompanying nn. 145 and 146.

[94] *See* October 2004 Discussion Paper (n. 83) para. 17.

[95] *See further* section IV(B) of this chapter.

[96] *See* October 2004 Discussion Paper (n. 83) para. 17.

and the Additional Facility Arbitration Rules in regard to court-ordered provisional measures. Under the Additional Facility Arbitration Rules, in contrast to the position under the ICSID Arbitration Rules since their amendment in 1984, it was not deemed inconsistent with the arbitration agreement for a party to seek such measures.[97]

In addition to putting forward these possible amendments of the ICSID Arbitration Rules and Additional Facility Arbitration Rules, the October 2004 discussion paper briefly advanced the ideas that the Centre might sponsor the establishment of a mediation service, as an alternative to its comparatively formal conciliation procedures, and intensify ICSID's training activities.[98] A more far-reaching issue raised by the paper was whether ICSID should create a mechanism for the appeal of awards rendered in investment treaty arbitrations. With the establishment of appellate mechanisms seemingly soon to begin under the CAFTA-DR, the discussion paper argued that economy and efficiency, as well as coherence and consistency, might best be served by ICSID offering a single appellate mechanism as an alternative to multiple mechanisms set up under individual investment treaties.[99]

The discussion paper outlined the features of such an ICSID mechanism, which it named the ICSID Appeals Facility.[100] It would, the discussion paper imagined, be established and operate under a set of ICSID Appeals Facility Rules (on the model, obviously, of the Additional Facility Rules) adopted by the Administrative Council of the Centre. An investment treaty could then provide that awards, made in cases covered by the treaty, would be subject to review in accordance with those rules. The Facility, it was realized, should be designed for use in conjunction with both forms of ICSID arbitration, UNCITRAL Rules arbitration and other forms of arbitration provided for in the investor–State dispute settlement provisions of investment treaties. To address the difficulty that Article 53(1) of the ICSID Convention exempted Convention awards from any appeal, the discussion paper suggested that the investment treaty incorporating the Appeals Facility Rules by reference might also effect a modification of the Convention, to the extent required, as between the parties to the treaty.[101] The Appeals Facility Rules would, the discussion paper foresaw, provide for the establishment of an Appeals Panel composed of 15 persons of different nationalities elected by the Administrative Council of the Centre on the nomination of the Secretary-General. An appeal tribunal would be constituted to decide each challenge of an award; it would consist of three members of the Appeals Panel appointed by the Secretary-General of the Centre. The ensuing proceeding would be administered by the ICSID Secretariat. An award could, the discussion paper continued, be challenged pursuant to the Appeals Facility Rules for a clear error of law or on any of the five grounds for annulment of an award set out in Article 52 of the ICSID Convention.[102]

[97] *See* Ch. 8, n. 80. An alternative to the amendment of the ICSID Arbitration Rules suggested in the October 2004 discussion paper might have been to bring them into line in this respect with the Additional Facility Arbitration Rules. The alternative was not, however, pursued as the 1984 amendment had been presented to and approved by the Administrative Council as following from Art. 26 of the Convention, on the exclusivity of the ICSID arbitral remedy. *See* Ch. 8, n. 79 and accompanying text.

[98] *See* October 2004 Discussion Paper (n. 83) paras. 18 and 19.

[99] *See* ibid. paras. 18, 19 and 23.

[100] *See* ibid. Annex (the paper's eight-page outline of the suggested mechanism's main features, briefly summarized in this paragraph of the text).

[101] Such an *inter se* modification of the ICSID Convention would have been done in accordance with the treaty law rule on the subject reflected in Art. 41 of the Vienna Convention on the Law of Treaties, May 23, 1969, 1155 UNTS 331.

[102] The paper added that a further ground for challenging an award might consist in serious errors of fact. *See* October 2004 Discussion Paper (n. 83) Annex, para. 7.

The appeal tribunal might uphold, modify or reverse the challenged award, or annul it in whole or in part on any of the grounds borrowed from Article 52 of the ICSID Convention.[103] To help avoid abuse of the appeal mechanism, the discussion paper proposed that parties requesting review of an award ordinarily be required to provide a bank guarantee, approved by the appeal tribunal, for the amount of the award.[104] An important final feature of the scheme envisaged by the discussion paper was that the Appeals Facility Rules would make it clear that recourse to the Facility would supersede other rights to appeal or seek annulment of the award, whether before national courts or under the ICSID Convention.[105]

The discussion paper was sent by the Secretariat to the members of the Administrative Council for their comments. The Secretariat simultaneously made the paper publicly available and invited comments on it from all interested parties. This was done through a posting on the ICSID website.[106] The Secretariat also organized meetings to discuss the paper with representatives of NGOs and business groups as well as with arbitration experts. Among NGOs, the IISD issued comments praising the process of consultation initiated by ICSID as "a welcome departure from the historic secrecy surrounding the development of all aspects of the international investment law regime."[107] Though broadly supportive of the substance of the suggestions in the discussion paper, the IISD argued that even more extensive changes were needed, in particular a separation of ICSID from the World Bank.[108]

Others who commented on the discussion paper had generally favorable reactions to the suggestions regarding mediation and training and on the proposed amendments of the Rules. A few expressed the concern that *amicus curiae* submissions and public hearings might unduly burden parties to proceedings. The possibility of creating an appellate mechanism within ICSID caught much more of the attention. Many doubted the wisdom of the suggestion; most considered it premature at best. By 2005, interest had waned in establishing an appellate mechanism under the CAFTA-DR.[109]

[103] Elaborating further, the discussion paper explained that the award as upheld, modified or reversed by the appeal tribunal would in principle be the final award binding on the parties. If, however, an appeal tribunal annulled an award or decided on a modification or reversal resulting in an award that did not dispose of the dispute, either party could submit the dispute to a new tribunal though the Rules might allow appeal tribunals in some such cases to order that the matter be returned to the original tribunal. *See* ibid. Annex, para. 9.

[104] The discussion paper cited in this connection the practice of applicants for annulment of an award in ICSID Convention cases being asked to furnish guarantees as a condition of the continued stay of enforcement of the award. *See* ibid. Annex, para. 10 and Ch. 8, text accompanying n. 181. As explained in section IV(G) of this chapter, ad hoc committees in a number of later cases declined to follow this practice.

[105] The paper added that such post-award remedies as rectification, supplementation and interpretation of the award would, at least in cases governed by the ICSID, Additional Facility and UNCITRAL Rules, remain to be sought from the original tribunal in accordance with those Rules. *See* October 2004 Discussion Paper (n. 83) Annex, para. 13.

[106] *See* Possible Improvements of the Framework for ICSID Arbitration, ICSID News Release, October 26, 2004, <https://icsid.worldbank.org/apps/ICSIDWEB/resources/Pages/Background-Papers.aspx>.

[107] IISD, Comments on ICSID Discussion Paper, Possible Improvements of the Framework for ICSID Arbitration (December 2004), <http://www.iisd.org/pdf/2004/investment_icsid_response.pdf>.

[108] *See* ibid. 12–13. The argument was that ICSID was "financially and structurally dependent upon the Bank," which routinely expressed positions regarding investment treaties and the investor–State process, with the result that ICSID was "from a conflict of interest perspective, undeniably compromised" (ibid. 13).

[109] This may in part have been due to a belated realization that, as pointed out in the ICSID Secretariat's discussion paper, the projected appellate mechanism would presumably have entailed a further internationalization of the investor–State dispute settlement process, an unwelcome outcome

This loss of interest, underscored when there was no action on pursuing the idea after entry into force of the CAFTA-DR, further deflated any plan for ICSID's involvement in this area.

In May 2005, the Secretariat of the Centre sent a follow-up working paper to the members of the Administrative Council. It explained that, in light of the consultations on the discussion paper, the Centre would not attempt to establish an appellate mechanism for the time being.[110] Also postponed were efforts on the suggested mediation and training activities.[111] Budgetary uncertainty would doubtless have made undertaking these additional activities difficult at that juncture. The working paper concentrated instead on the amendments of the Rules sketched in the discussion paper. Drafts of the amendments were provided in the working paper.

The procedure for eliminating frivolous claims was elaborated in a draft amendment of ICSID Arbitration Rule 41. According to the draft, a party could, within 30 days after the constitution of the tribunal, file an objection that the claim was "manifestly without merit"; and the tribunal would, after giving the parties an opportunity to present their observations, decide on the objection at its first session or promptly thereafter.[112] The proposed new procedure regarding provisional measures was set forth in a draft addition to Arbitration Rule 39. The draft specified that a request for provisional measures could be made before the constitution of the tribunal and gave the Secretary-General the role of fixing time limits for the presentation by the parties of their observations in the meantime.[113] *Amicus curiae* submissions were dealt with in a draft amendment of Rule 37. It provided that a tribunal could allow a "non-disputing party" to file a written submission with the tribunal; the draft directed the tribunal, before allowing such a filing, to consult with the parties as far as possible and to consider such factors as the extent to which the filing would assist it in determining a factual or legal issue related to the proceeding.[114] Under a draft modification of Rule 32, the tribunal could, again after consulting the parties as far as possible but without necessarily having their affirmative consent, allow third parties to attend or observe all or part of the hearings.[115] The drafts for Rules 37 and 32 required the tribunal to ensure that the third party participation did not, in the case of attendance at hearings, compromise proprietary information or, in the case of the written submissions, unduly burden or unfairly prejudice either party.[116] A draft adjustment of Arbitration Rule 48 specified that the Centre "shall ... promptly," rather than merely "may" publish excerpts of the legal conclusions in awards.[117] The disclosure requirements for arbitrators were expanded under a draft change of the disclosure form set out in Arbitration Rule 6.[118] The May 2005 working paper recalled that these various changes to the ICSID Arbitration Rules would, where applicable, also be made to the Additional Facility Arbitration Rules.[119] Finally, the working paper presented a suggested change of the ICSID Administrative and Financial Regulations that had not been broached

for some original backers of the appellate mechanism (the further internationalization would have resulted from effectively extending to UNCITRAL Rules, Additional Facility Rules and other non-ICSID Convention awards the exemption of the Convention from review by national courts).

[110] *See* Suggested Changes to the ICSID Rules and Regulations, Working Paper of the ICSID Secretariat, May 12, 2005, 4 (May 2005 Working Paper).

[111] *See* ibid. [112] *See* ibid. 7. [113] *See* ibid. 6.

[114] *See* ibid. 11. Rule 37 was on site visits by a tribunal. It was chosen, *faute de mieux*, as a place to add the provision on amicus curiae submissions without having to re-number all of the subsequent rules.

[115] *See* ibid. 10. [116] *See* ibid. 10 and 11. [117] *See* ibid. 9.

[118] *See* ibid. 12. [119] *See* ibid. 5.

in the October 2004 discussion paper. This was to emphasize, in Regulation 14, that conciliators, arbitrators and ad hoc committee members should only exceptionally seek fees higher than those specified in the Centre's Schedule of Fees and that any request for higher fees should, in any event, be made through the Secretary-General and not directly to the parties involved (as arbitrators had done in several instances).[120]

In addition to seeking reactions of Administrative Council members to the proposed amendments, the Secretariat made the May 2005 working paper available for public comment through the website of the Centre.[121] Most of the responses at this stage, however, came from Council members. The responses included the request that the amendment of ICSID Arbitration Rule 41 clarify that it referred to claims lacking "legal" merit and that the new procedure would not apply where the parties had agreed on another expedited procedure for making preliminary objections (as under the recent FTAs of the United States). Another change that was asked for was to widen, in the amendment of Arbitration Rule 37, the category of possible *amici curiae* to encompass any "entity" (unincorporated associations were not covered by the initial draft). The proposed amendment of Arbitration Rule 37 otherwise found easy acceptance among Council members. In *Aguas del Tunari v. Bolivia*, the Tribunal had ruled in 2003 that it lacked the power to admit *amicus curiae* submissions in the absence of consent of the parties.[122] But in May 2005, fortuitously just one week after the issuance of the Secretariat's working paper, the Tribunal in another ICSID Convention case involving a water privatization, *Suez, AGBAR and Vivendi v. Argentina*, found that it could accept and consider such submissions. In so doing, the Tribunal convincingly explained, it would be exercising its power under Article 44 of the Convention to decide procedural questions not treated in the Convention or Rules.[123] The proposed amendment of Arbitration Rule 37 henceforth could be (and was) regarded as merely codifying the outcome in that case. By this time, ICSID also had a record of successfully organizing and hosting public hearings agreed to by the parties concerned—in the *Southern Bluefin Tuna* case and in two UNCITRAL Arbitration Rules proceedings under the NAFTA.[124] The suggested amendment of Rule 32, however, aroused strong opposition at this stage from some members of the Administrative Council who could not accept a general transfer to arbitrators of the right to decide whether hearings should remain private.

[120] *See* ibid. 13.

[121] *See* Suggested Changes to the ICSID Rules and Regulations, ICSID News Release, June 2005, <https://icsid.worldbank.org/apps/ICSIDWEB/Pages/AllNewsItems.aspx>.

[122] *See Aguas del Tunari v. Bolivia*, Letter from President of Tribunal Responding to Petition, January 29, 2003, available at <http://www.italaw.com/cases/57>.

[123] *See Suez, AGBAR and Vivendi v. Argentina*, Order in Response to a Petition for Transparency and Participation as Amicus Curiae, May 19, 2005, 21 ICSID Rev.—FILJ 342, 346 (2006). This decision was similar to the rulings in 2001 of the UNCITRAL Rules Tribunals in *Methanex v. U.S.* and *UPS v. Canada* (n. 20), which based their authority to admit amicus curiae submissions on their general power, under Art. 15 of the UNCITRAL Rules, to conduct the arbitrations in such manner as they considered appropriate. The Tribunal in the *Suez* case consisted of Jeswald W. Salacuse as President, Gabrielle Kaufmann-Kohler and Pedro Nikken. Salacuse was Henry J. Braker Professor of Law at the Fletcher School of Law and Diplomacy of Tufts University and past Dean of the Fletcher School. Nikken was a former President of the Inter-American Court of Human Rights and past Dean of the Law School of the Central University of Venezuela. On Kaufmann-Kohler, *see* n. 11.

[124] These NAFTA/UNCITRAL Rules cases were *UPS v. Canada* and *Canfor v. U.S.* Later in the decade, as part of its administration of the cases concerned, ICSID organized and hosted public hearings in three further NAFTA/UNCITRAL Rules proceedings (*Glamis Gold v. U.S.*, *Merrill & Ring v. Canada* and *Grand River Enterprises v. U.S.*) and in the CAFTA/ICSID Convention case *Pacific Rim v. El Salvador*.

In November 2005, the proposed amendments of the ICSID Arbitration Rules and of the corresponding provisions of the Additional Facility Arbitration Rules (except their provision on provisional measures) and of Administration and Financial Regulation 14 were re-submitted to the members of the Administrative Council. As re-submitted, the amendments of Arbitration Rules 37 and 41 and their Additional Facility counterparts incorporated the changes described above. A revised amendment of Arbitration Rule 32 and its Additional Facility counterpart provided that a tribunal might permit non-disputing parties to attend or observe hearings only if a disputing party did not object.[125] Members of the Council were invited to vote on the re-submitted amendments by correspondence.[126] The necessary majority was obtained by April 5, 2006; the amended Regulations and Rules came into effect the following week.[127]

IV. Aspects of cases submitted to ICSID from 2000 to 2010

In the middle of the decade, the Secretariat of the Centre made a fresh attempt to promote greater use of conciliation under the ICSID Convention and Additional Facility Rules. In acknowledging receipt of new requests for arbitration, the Secretariat would call the attention of both parties to the conciliation alternative.[128] The practice, followed from 2004 to 2006, had disappointing results: of the 262 Convention and Additional Facility cases initiated during the decade, only three involved conciliation. As with the few conciliation cases registered in earlier decades, these three were all brought to the Centre under contractual dispute resolution clauses requiring recourse to conciliation before any submission of the dispute to arbitration. In one of the cases, the parties settled their dispute before the constitution of a conciliation commission;[129] and while commissions were established in the two other cases, the parties there failed to agree on a settlement.[130]

In proportional terms, fewer Additional Facility proceedings were launched in the period 2000 to 2010 than in the preceding decade: just 22 of the new arbitrations were governed by the Additional Facility Rules. Most of these were cases arising under the NAFTA or BITs of either Canada or Mexico, which were still non-parties to the ICSID Convention. The number of ICSID Convention arbitrations commenced from the beginning of 2000 to the end of 2010 thus totaled 237. The overwhelming majority (about three-quarters) of these were submitted to the Centre pursuant to the dispute settlement provisions of BITs.

[125] This nevertheless was an advance over the existing provision as the affirmative consent of both parties would no longer be required to allow non-disputing parties to attend or observe hearings.

[126] Letter of the Chairman of the Administrative Council to its Members, November 17, 2005.

[127] *See* Amendments of the ICSID Regulations and Rules and Additional Facility Rules, Administrative Council Resolution AC/C/RES/2006; Amendments to the ICSID Rules and Regulations, ICSID News Release, April 5, 2006. The amended Regulations and Rules were published in Doc. ICSID/15, ICSID Convention Regulations and Rules (April 2006) and Doc. ICSID/11, ICSID Additional Facility Rules (April 2006).

[128] *See* ICSID 2004 Ann. Rep. 3; ICSID 2005 Ann. Rep. 4.

[129] *TGW v. Niger.*

[130] *Togo Electricité v. Togo* and *SESAM v. CAR.* The case involving Togo was subsequently referred to arbitration.

Among the ICSID Convention and Additional Facility arbitration cases, the governmental party was the claimant in only one instance.[131] Respondents were virtually all developing and transition States; hardly any were Western industrial countries.[132] This reflected the continued near-total absence of submissions to ICSID Convention or Additional Facility arbitration on the part of the industrial States except in the context of treaties with developing or transition States.[133] On the other hand, the claimant investors were, as in previous years, overwhelmingly (in over 90 percent of the cases) from OECD countries. American investors were the claimants in some 80 of the new cases. About 60 of the cases were brought, in roughly equal shares, by British, Dutch and Italian investors. The next largest groups of investors were French and German, together accounting for around 30 of the cases. The claimants included natural persons in 24 of the proceedings started in the period 2000 to 2010.[134] In much greater numbers than in previous years, companies appearing as claimants in the proceedings included major TNCs; some 90 of the cases involved such enterprises as claimants.[135]

The underlying investments, and the amounts at stake in the cases, were correspondingly large. At the end of 2005, the Secretariat of the Centre estimated, cases pending before ICSID represented over US$30 billion in claims.[136] A far higher total would have been indicated by a similar calculation in 2010: US$30 billion was said to be the amount in dispute in just one (albeit the biggest) of the later cases.[137] However, the sectoral distribution of the investments concerned remained roughly what it had been among the cases of the previous decade: around two-thirds of the investments were in the energy and mining and industrial and trade sectors and most of the rest

[131] *East Kalimantan v. PT Kaltim*, a case ultimately dismissed on jurisdictional grounds.

[132] The sole ICSID Convention proceeding instituted in the period 2000–2010 against a Western industrial State was *Vattenfall v. Germany*, an ECT case. There were two Additional Facility proceedings begun in the period against industrial States, both of them NAFTA cases: *ADF v. U.S.* and *Mobil v. Canada*. Overall, the geographic distribution of the States parties to the 259 ICSID Convention and Additional Facility arbitration cases commenced in the first decade of the 21st century was as follows: Latin American and Caribbean States in 117 cases; former Soviet Union and Eastern European countries in 69 cases; Asian States in 35; African States in 35; and Western industrial countries in 3.

[133] Underlining the point was the 2004 U.S.–Australia FTA. The only FTA made by the U.S. in the period 2000–2010 with another industrial country, it was also the only one of the new U.S. FTAs to lack consents of the parties to the arbitral settlement of investment disputes. A summary of this FTA by the Office of the U.S. Trade Representative candidly explained that this was due to "the unique circumstances of this Agreement—including, for example, the longstanding economic ties between the U.S. and Australia, their shared legal traditions, and the confidence of their investors in operating in each others' markets." USTR, United States–Australia FTA Summary of the Agreement, February 2004, available at <https://ustr.gov/trade-agreements/free-trade-agreements/australian-fta>.

[134] Notable among these were three arbitration proceedings instituted against Argentina by numerous Italian holders of its bonds: *Abaclat v. Argentina*, *Alemanni v. Argentina* and *Ambiente v. Argentina*. The bondholders had refused to participate in the restructuring of bond debt that Argentina defaulted on in 2001.

[135] More than 40 of the companies involved appeared on the 2010 Forbes Global 2000 list of the world's largest public corporations (available at <http://www.forbes.com>).

[136] *See* R. Dañino, Opening Remarks, Making the Most of International Investment Agreements: A Common Agenda, Symposium Co-Organized by ICSID, OECD and UNCTAD, December 12, 2005.

[137] *ConocoPhillips v. Venezuela*, according to L. Peterson, Arbitration Scorecard: Treaties, American Lawyer.com, July 1, 2009, available at <http://www.americanlawyer.com>.

were in the transportation, information and communications and water and sanitation sectors.

Of the 259 arbitration cases launched under the ICSID Convention or Additional Facility Rules in 2000 to 2010, tribunals had been constituted in all but 11 cases by the end of the period. Sole arbitrators were appointed in six of the cases; in the rest, the tribunals had three members.

As in the previous decade, respondents raised objections to jurisdiction in the overwhelming majority of the cases. Sixty-two of them, however, were settled or otherwise discontinued before the rendition of an award; in ten more, there were awards embodying settlement agreements of the parties. One hundred fifty-four of the other arbitration cases gave rise to awards. The awards included the largest in ICSID's history, an award for over US$1.7 billion.[138] In this case, however, and in 62 of the others, the award was challenged in annulment proceedings under Article 52 of the ICSID Convention.

Of the further 91 cases in which there were awards, they dismissed all claims on jurisdictional grounds or on the merits in 58 cases, and upheld claims in whole or in part in 33. In the majority of these cases, the tribunals followed the traditional approach in regard to costs by ruling that the parties should share the direct expenses of the proceeding equally and bear their own legal expenses. As the decade progressed, however, it became increasingly common for the tribunals to provide in their awards that the unsuccessful party should pay a larger share, or all, of the direct expenses and at least partly reimburse the other party for its legal expenses. Tribunals took this approach in around a third of the cases. Sometimes, they did so in consequence of a finding of procedural misconduct by the unsuccessful party.[139] Several of the tribunals, however, emphasized that in any event, and as a general rule, "loser pays" or "costs follow event."[140] As for the average duration of the arbitration cases begun and concluded during the decade, it remained two and a half years, the same as for the cases commenced the previous decade.[141]

Sections IV(A)–(G) look more closely at cases brought to ICSID in 2000 to 2010. Specifically, these parts discuss, in relation to selected 2000–2010 cases, the aspects that Chapter 8 examined of cases submitted to the Centre in its first two decades: the registration by the Secretary-General of requests to institute proceedings; the constitution of conciliation commissions and arbitral tribunals; approaches of arbitral tribunals to jurisdictional issues; provisional measures; the determination by arbitrators of the law applicable to the substance of the dispute; the working of the remedy of annulment afforded by Article 52 of the ICSID Convention; and the enforcement of awards. The picture that emerges is one of rapid development and the emergence of notable discordances on some key issues arising under the Convention and from the investment treaties involved in most of the cases.

A. Registration of requests to institute proceedings

In ICSID's early days, the registration process was not especially burdensome for the Secretariat of the Centre. There were few requests for arbitration and even fewer

[138] *Occidental v. Ecuador*, Award, October 5, 2012, IIC 561 (2012).

[139] *See, e.g.*, *Phoenix Action v. Czech Republic*, Award, April 15, 2009, para. 151, available at <http://www.italaw.com/cases/850>.

[140] *See, e.g.*, *ADC v. Hungary*, Award, October 2, 2006, para. 533, available at <http://www.italaw.com/cases/41>.

[141] This was the average period from the constitution of the tribunal to the conclusion of the proceeding (by award or discontinuance). Cases in which there were annulment or revision proceedings are excluded from the calculation.

requests for conciliation. Such requests as there were generally concerned disputes over the performance of investment contracts containing the needed consent of the parties to the jurisdiction of the Centre. Scrutinizing and registering requests for "arbitration without privity,"[142] based on far-reaching consent clauses in investment laws and treaties, was a riskier and more uncertain exercise for the Secretariat. It was seen in Chapter 8 that, after the first requests of this kind came to ICSID in the 1980s, the Secretariat sought, on the registration of a request for arbitration by the Secretary-General, to forestall criticism by emphasizing that the Secretary-General's power in this respect was limited and, in particular, that registration of the request did not prejudge the eventual tribunal's definitive ruling on jurisdiction.[143] Overwhelmingly, of course, the numerous requests for arbitration lodged with ICSID in the period 2000 to 2010 were based on consents recorded in a BIT or other investment treaty of the host State. In several instances, Latin American Contracting States vigorously protested the registration of requests for arbitration against them, despite the assurance that it did not rule out later objections to jurisdiction.

Metalpar v. Argentina provided a vivid example. In that case, two Chilean companies, Metalpar and Buen Aire, had invested in an Argentine company that manufactured bus bodies. The Argentine company, re-named Metalpar Argentina, extended credits, denominated in U.S. dollars, to customers for their purchase of the bus bodies. Metalpar and Buen Aire filed their request for arbitration in February 2003. It contended that measures of Argentina in 2001 and 2002, restricting currency transfers and "pesifying" the credits and other dollar-denominated obligations, violated the claimants' rights under the 1991 BIT between their home country and Argentina.[144] As required by the Institution Rules,[145] the Secretariat promptly acknowledged receipt of the request and transmitted a copy of it to Argentina. ICSID's then Acting Secretary-General proceeded to register the request in April 2003. In accordance with Institution Rule 7 as amended a few months earlier, the notice of registration reminded the parties that the registration was without prejudice to the powers and functions of the eventual arbitral tribunal in regard to jurisdiction or the merits.[146] Argentina nevertheless condemned the registration as invalid, arguing that the case involved only the rights of Metalpar Argentina against the recipients of its credits. The Tribunal was constituted in September 2003 and held its first session two months later.[147] At the start of the session, one

[142] The phrase coined by Jan Paulsson to refer to investor–State cases submitted to arbitration on the strength of consents recorded in an investment law or treaty of the State. *See* J. Paulsson, Arbitration Without Privity, 10 ICSID Rev.—FILJ 232 (1995).

[143] This was the practice codified in the amendment in 2003 of ICSID Institution Rule 7. *Cf.* n. 66 and accompanying text.

[144] This was the Tratado Sobre Promoción y Protección Reciproca de Inversiones, Argentina–Chile, August 2, 1991, reprinted in ICSID, Investment Treaties, Release 93-2 (July 1993).

[145] The reference is to the Institution Rules as amended in 2003, reprinted in Doc. ICSID/15, ICSID Convention, Regulations and Rules (January 2003).

[146] *See* n. 2.

[147] The Tribunal was composed of Rodrigo Oreamuno, Duncan H. Cameron and Jean Paul Chabaneix. On Oreamuno, who was President of the Tribunal, *see* Ch. 9, n. 113. Cameron was a founding partner of the Washington, D.C. law firm Cameron & Hornbostel. Chabaneix was a partner at Rodrigo, Elías & Medrano, a Lima law firm.

of Argentina's representatives demanded that the Tribunal rule immediately on the validity of the registration of the request for arbitration. The Tribunal replied that this "was not procedurally possible,"[148] whereupon the Argentine delegation left the session.[149] This episode helped to persuade the Secretariat, in working on what became the 2006 amendments of the Regulations and Rules, that it would be desirable to add to the Rules the expedited procedure for dismissing baseless claims.[150]

The Secretariat occasionally found itself embroiled in controversy over the registration of requests even after the introduction of that procedure in 2006. This happened in the case between ETI and Bolivia mentioned in the introductory part of this chapter. ETI's request for arbitration in that case was lodged in October 2007. It invoked the broad consent to the jurisdiction of the Centre contained in Bolivia's BIT with the Netherlands (the country of ETI's incorporation).[151] Bolivia objected that this was precluded by its earlier denunciation of the ICSID Convention. Experts on ICSID were divided over the question. The debate centered on the provision of Article 72 of the Convention specifying that a denunciation notice would not affect the denouncing State's rights or obligations under the Convention arising out of consent to the jurisdiction of the Centre given before receipt of the notice by the IBRD. Some saw this as preserving the consent given in an earlier instrument, such as the BIT in the *ETI* case.[152] Others argued that Article 72 referred to a "perfected" consent, that is one accepted by both parties, and that an unperfected consent in a BIT or similar instrument could not validly be accepted after receipt of the denunciation notice.[153] Eliciting protests not only from Bolivia, but also from many NGOs on its behalf,[154] the then Secretary-General of ICSID registered the request within a month of its receipt.[155]

Registration of a request was often a more protracted process in the period 2000–2010. There were several reasons for this. One was the sheer volume of requests in the period and the limited number of staff to deal with them. In addition, scrutinizing

[148] *See Metalpar v. Argentina*, Award, June 6, 2008, IIC 326 (2008), para. 11.

[149] Argentina nonetheless participated fully in the remaining phases of the proceeding, which culminated in an award dismissing the claim on the merits because, inter alia, the claimants failed to satisfy the Tribunal that their investment had been adversely affected by Argentina's alleged intervention in the credits of Metalpar Argentina. *See* ibid. para. 173.

[150] In view of the gap-filling authority of arbitrators under Art. 44 of the ICSID Convention; however, the *Metalpar* Tribunal exaggerated in suggesting that a summary dismissal of a claim was procedurally impossible in the absence of an explicit provision such as the one added in 2006.

[151] *See* Agreement on Reciprocal Encouragement and Reciprocal Protection of Investments, Bolivia–Netherlands, March 10, 1992, reprinted in ICSID, Investment Treaties, Release 93-2 (July 1993), Art. 9(6).

[152] *See, e.g.*, E. Gaillard, The Denunciation of the ICSID Convention, 237(122) New York L.J. 8 (2007).

[153] *See especially* C.H. Schreuer and others, *The ICSID Convention: A Commentary* 1280–1281 (2d ed. 2009).

[154] *See* M. Khor, 863 NGOs Petition World Bank Chief Against Investment Tribunal, Third World Network, January 16, 2008, <http://www.twnside.org>.

[155] The controversy would presumably have then been resolved by the ICSID Tribunal established in the case. After the constitution of the Tribunal, however, the ICSID Convention proceeding was, by agreement of the parties, abandoned for a proceeding before the same arbitrators under the UNCITRAL Arbitration Rules (the arbitrators being Bruno Simma, a member of the ICJ, as the presiding arbitrator; Francisco Orrego Vicuña—on whom *see* Ch. 9, n. 113; and Philippe Sands, Professor of Law at University College London and a barrister at Matrix Chambers in London).

the many requests based on investment treaties was more time consuming, requiring the Secretariat in every instance to ascertain that the dispute was not manifestly outside the scope of two international instruments: the ICSID Convention or Additional Facility Rules and the investment treaty containing the consent to arbitration. Greater jurisdictional complexity also added to the burden for requesting parties; their requests more commonly omitted to address or document an essential point, which they would then have to cover in a supplementary filing before the request could be registered.[156] Finally, it became increasingly common for prospective respondents to submit replies to requests for arbitration questioning their registrability before it had been decided upon by the Secretariat.[157] The Secretariat would try to integrate the replies into the process, asking the requesting party to comment on the reply.[158] These factors contributed to extending the time typically taken to register a request to some three months by the middle of the decade.[159] With increased staff, however, the average period between receipt and registration of a request was reduced by 50 percent in the second half of the decade.[160]

Although the review of arbitration requests was frequently long drawn out, refusals to register them remained rare. Only about 3 percent of the requests for arbitration received between January 1, 2000 and December 31, 2010 had to be refused registration. In several instances, there were refusals of registration followed by a successful re-filing of the request for arbitration once the requesting party had satisfactorily addressed the obstacle to registration.[161]

As already mentioned, the procedure for the early elimination of baseless claims, introduced in 2006 by amendment of Arbitration Rule 41, was intended to address the complaint that the power of Secretary General to screen arbitration requests was too limited.[162] Whereas that power was confined to requests disclosing a manifest lack of jurisdiction, the new procedure would, the 2005 working paper of the ICSID Secretariat envisaged, be available to filter out claims that were manifestly without merit as to their substance.[163] But, following its introduction, the new procedure, principally embodied in Rule 41(5) of the amended Arbitration Rules, was seen by arbitral tribunals as covering cases that were manifestly unworthy, either on jurisdiction or the merits.[164] Indeed, the very first decision of an arbitral tribunal dismissing claims in their entirety under Rule 41(5) did so on jurisdictional grounds. This

[156] E.g. requests of claimants who were natural persons commonly omitted to affirm, in accordance with Institution Rule 2(1)(d)(ii)(B), that the individual did not, in addition to his foreign nationality, also have the nationality of the host State.

[157] It will be recalled that, pursuant to Art. 36(1) of the ICSID Convention and Institution Rule 5(2), the prospective respondent would ordinarily have received from the Secretariat a copy of the request prior to its registration.

[158] This approach was considered necessary because Art. 36(3) of the ICSID Convention had been construed as requiring the decision on registration to be based exclusively on submissions by the requesting party.

[159] As pointed out by Anthony Sinclair, the delay was in some cases much greater (over two years in one instance). *See* A. Sinclair, ICSID Arbitration: How Long Does it Take?, Global Arbitration Review Briefing, October 26, 2009.

[160] *See* ICSID 2008 Ann. Rep. 3.

[161] E.g. in one case early in the decade, registration was refused for acknowledged non-compliance with a condition for resorting to arbitration under the BIT concerned (the condition was that the investor could submit the dispute to arbitration only if it could not be settled amicably "within six months from the date of a written request for settlement").

[162] *See* May 2005 Working Paper (n. 110) 7. [163] *See* ibid.

[164] On this point, *see* A. Diop, Objection under Rule 41(5) of the ICSID Arbitration Rules, 25 ICSID Rev.—FILJ 311, 321–324 (2010).

tribunal was the one formed in *Globex v. Ukraine.*[165] The claims in that case were for payment of amounts due under poultry purchase and sales contracts. As the Tribunal explained, these were "pure commercial transactions that [could not] on any interpretation be considered to constitute 'investments' within the meaning of Article 25 of the ICSID Convention."[166] The Tribunal accordingly struck out the claims.[167] This effectively reversed the finding implicit in the (then Acting) Secretary-General's registration of the request for arbitration in the case, that jurisdiction was not manifestly lacking.

B. The constitution of commissions and tribunals

It was noted earlier that two of the three conciliation proceedings instituted in the period January 1, 2000, to December 31, 2010, led to the constitution of conciliation commissions.[168] Both consisted of one conciliator appointed by each party and a presiding conciliator named by agreement of the parties. All of the appointees were lawyers; most had extensive experience in the field of arbitration.[169]

Of the 248 cases of the period in which tribunals were established, six consisted of a sole arbitrator and the rest had three members. The sole arbitrators were appointed by agreement of the parties in three cases;[170] for the three other proceedings before sole arbitrators,[171] the parties entrusted the appointment of the arbitrator to the Secretary-General of ICSID. In almost all of the 242 cases with three-member tribunals, each party appointed an arbitrator.[172] The third arbitrator, the president of the tribunal, was in about half of these cases appointed by agreement of the parties, or of the first two arbitrators where the parties had provided for that method of selecting the president. But in the over 120 remaining cases, the parties did not agree on the appointment of the presiding arbitrator; and so that appointment was done by the Chairman of the Administrative Council, acting as always on the recommendation of

[165] Consisting of Franklin D. Berman as President, Emmanuel Gaillard and J. Christopher Thomas. Berman was a barrister at Essex Court Chambers in London and a former Legal Adviser of the U.K. Foreign & Commonwealth Office. The head of Shearman & Sterling's international arbitration practice group, Gaillard was Professor of Law at the University of Paris XII. Thomas was a consultant with Borden Ladner Gervais and former Senior Policy Adviser at Canada's Ministry of International Trade.

[166] *Globex v. Ukraine*, Award, December 1, 2010, III, 466 (2010), para. 57.

[167] *See* ibid. para. 158. The only other case in which Rule 41(5) objections were upheld to dismiss claims in their entirety was *Grynberg v. Grenada*, where the claims were of violations of a BIT stemming from the alleged breach by Grenada of a petroleum agreement with one of the claimants. Grenada, however, had been absolved of such a breach by the tribunal in an earlier ICSID Convention arbitration between the parties. The second tribunal considered the case before it to be no more than an attempt, under the guise of treaty claims, to overturn the prior tribunal's contractual findings. Upholding Grenada's objection made pursuant to Rule 41(5), the second tribunal dismissed as manifestly without legal merit all of the claims put forward in this "improper attempt to circumvent" the exemption of Convention awards from appeal. *Grynberg v. Grenada*, Award, December 10, 2010, paras. 7.3.2, 7.3.6 and 7.3.7. The Tribunal in *Grynberg v. Grenada* consisted of J. William Rowley as President, Edward W. Nottingham and Pierre Tercier. Rowley was Chairman Emeritus of the Canadian law firm McMillan. Nottingham was a former United States federal judge in the U.S. District Court for the District of Colorado. Tercier was Professor of Law at the University of Fribourg and Past Chairman of the ICC International Court of Arbitration.

[168] *See* n. 130 and accompanying text.

[169] None, on the other hand, had experience primarily as a conciliator or mediator.

[170] *Booker v. Guyana*, *Astaldi v. Honduras* and *Elsamex v. Honduras*.

[171] *CDC v. Seychelles*, *MHS v. Malaysia* and *Pantechniki v. Albania*.

[172] In some (11) of these cases, however, the respondent failed to appoint "its" party-appointed arbitrator, leaving that arbitrator to be appointed instead by the Chairman of the Administrative Council or the Secretary-General of the Centre.

the Secretary-General, or directly by the Secretary-General where the latter official was the designated appointing authority.

A total of 218 different persons were appointed to serve on tribunals in the ICSID Convention and Additional Facility Rules arbitrations initiated between January 1, 2000 and June 30, 2010. Almost all of them were lawyers. As in the 1990s, about half of the appointees to tribunals were private legal practitioners and the rest individuals with backgrounds as law professors or judges and other public officials. A significant minority—almost 30—of the arbitrators also served as counsel for parties in cases of the period. The mix of nationalities of the arbitrators remained very much as it had been in the 1990s: about 30 percent were from developing, mostly Latin American, countries; and practically all of the others from Western industrial countries, with the largest groups being American, British, French and Swiss.[173] The lack of gender diversity was less extreme than it had been in the 1990s, although at 5 percent the proportion of women among the arbitrators remained remarkably low.

Obviously, with 218 different persons having been appointed to fill 735 arbitrator positions,[174] many of them served on more than one of the tribunals. Just over 100 of the individuals concerned received repeat appointments as arbitrators. Some were in very high demand. Two of them, both as it happened women,[175] were appointed to serve on over 20 of the tribunals. Another 18 of the individuals[176] each garnered ten to 20 appointments.

These overall patterns were mirrored in the appointments of mostly presiding arbitrators by the Chairman of the Administrative Council and Secretary-General of the Centre. Thus, about 65 percent of their appointees were industrial country nationals; some 35 percent were from developing or transition countries; and 8 percent were women. Seventy-three individuals received such appointments from the Chairman or Secretary-General; and 40 percent of them were appointed more than once by the Chairman or Secretary-General. Five[177] had four or more of these appointments.

In addition, during the decade, the Secretary-General had ten occasions to appoint arbitrators as the appointing authority in proceedings governed by the UNCITRAL Arbitration Rules. Most of these were NAFTA investment chapter proceedings. In four of them,[178] the Secretary-General was called upon to select the presiding arbitrator after the parties had failed to agree on the appointment. The Secretary-General was also asked twice to exercise the appointing authority role to establish two UNCITRAL Rules tribunals under Article 1126 of the NAFTA to consider applications to consolidate cases submitted to NAFTA investment chapter arbitration.[179] All of the

[173] Despite the growing number of cases involving transition countries in the period 2000–2010, just a handful (six) of the appointees to tribunals during the decade were nationals of such countries.

[174] That is, the slots on 243 three-member tribunals plus six sole arbitrator positions (in one of the cases with three-member tribunals a second such tribunal was constituted following annulment of the first tribunal's award).

[175] Gabrielle Kaufmann-Kohler and Brigitte Stern.

[176] These were Henri Alvarez, Albert Jan van den Berg, Franklin D. Berman, Piero Bernardini, Karl-Heinz Böckstiegel, Charles N. Brower, Bernardo M. Cremades, Juan Fernandez-Armesto, L. Yves Fortier, Marc Lalonde, Vaughan Lowe, Rodrigo Oreamuno, Francisco Orrego Vicuña, Jan Paulsson, J. Christopher Thomas, Pierre Tercier, V.V. Veeder and David A.R. Williams.

[177] Juan Fernandez-Armesto, Gilbert Guillaume, Fali Nariman, Rodrigo Oreamuno and Francisco Orrego Vicuña.

[178] *UPS v. Canada*, *Thunderbird v. Mexico*, *Merrill & Ring v. Canada* and *Vito Gallo v. Canada*.

[179] The first of the resulting consolidation tribunals was established to decide on Mexico's application to consolidate two cases initiated against it in connection with a tax that it had imposed on beverages made with high fructose corn syrup. In May 2005, the consolidation tribunal rejected the application. The second consolidation tribunal was formed to rule on the application of the U.S. to consolidate three cases brought against it over certain duties levied on imports of softwood lumber.

appointees of the Secretary-General in these various UNCITRAL Rules cases also served as arbitrators in ICSID Convention or Additional Facility Rules cases in the period 2000 to 2010.[180]

Contrasting with their rarity in the 1990s, proposals of parties to disqualify arbitrators (or ad hoc committee members) became common in the following decade. Between January 1, 2000 and December 31, 2010, parties made such proposals, or challenges, in over 30 ICSID Convention proceedings. Based on what is known publicly about these cases,[181] the proposals in most of them were of one party to disqualify the arbitrator appointed by the opposing party—the challenged arbitrator being claimed to lack the reliability for independent judgment required by Article 14(1) of the Convention owing to a connection with the appointing party or with another ICSID proceeding involving the challenging party. In around a third of the cases, the disqualification proposals were met by resignations of the arbitrators concerned. Most of the remaining challenges, relating to just one of a three-member tribunal (or ad hoc committee), were decided by the other members in accordance with the procedure of Article 58 of the Convention. Pursuant to Article 58, the Chairman of the Administrative Council ruled on the challenge in the few cases where the unchallenged arbitrators were divided on the proposal or it related to a sole arbitrator or the majority of the arbitrators. One of the decisions taken by the Chairman, on a proposal to disqualify the majority of the arbitrators in the case involved, sustained the proposal in respect of one of the arbitrators.[182] Otherwise, all of the above-mentioned decisions on proposals to disqualify a tribunal or ad hoc committee member, whether taken by the two other members or by the Chairman of the Administrative Council, were to reject the proposal.

During the period 2000 to 2010, there were also eight investment treaty proceedings under the UNCITRAL Arbitration Rules in which the Secretary-General of ICSID was called upon, as the designated appointing authority of arbitrators, to perform the task assigned to the appointing authority by the UNCITRAL Rules of deciding on challenges of arbitrators for lack of impartiality or independence.[183] Successful challenges were about as scarce in this context as in the ICSID Convention cases. None, in fact, of the challenges in these UNCITRAL Rules proceedings was finally upheld, though in some of them the arbitrator concerned resigned to avoid that outcome.[184]

This second consolidation tribunal granted the application in September 2005. *See Corn Products v. Mexico* and *ADM v. Mexico*, Consolidation Order, May 20, 2005; *Canfor v. U.S.*, *Tembec et al. v. U.S.* and *Tembec Forest Products Ltd. v. U.S.*, Consolidation Tribunal, Order, September 7, 2005, available at <http://www.italaw.com/cases/200>.

[180] The appointees were Albert Jan van den Berg (twice), Bernardo M. Cremades, Donald Donovan, Juan Fernandez-Armesto, Kenneth Keith, Rolf Knieper, Armand L.C. de Mestral, Francisco Orrego Vicuña, Davis R. Robinson, Arthur W. Rovine and Eduardo Siqueiros.

[181] Principally from the decisions on the proposals published on the ICSID website, <https://icsid.worldbank.org>.

[182] This was in *Pey Casado v. Chile*. The decision was made by the Chairman on the recommendation of the Secretary-General of the PCA. The ICSID Secretariat sought the recommendation of the Secretary-General of the PCA for challenge decisions by the Chairman in cases where the Chairman or ICSID might be thought to have a conflict. This was first done in 2001 in *Generation Ukraine v. Ukraine*, where the Chairman had to decide on a proposal to disqualify an arbitrator who was a former Deputy General Counsel of MIGA (the Chairman had been involved because the other arbitrators failed to agree on the disqualification proposal).

[183] These were mostly NAFTA investment chapter cases.

[184] Or resigned in preference to giving up an activity that the Secretariat had concluded created a conflict for the arbitrator. *See Vito G. Gallo v. Canada*, Decision on the Challenge to an Arbitrator, October 14, 2009, IIC 404 (2009).

The UNCITRAL Arbitration Rules provided for such challenges where there were circumstances giving rise to "justifiable doubts as to the arbitrator's impartiality or independence."[185] There were similar provisions in other major sets of rules for international commercial arbitration.[186] The UNCITRAL Model Law on International Commercial Arbitration likewise allowed for the challenge of an arbitrator in the event of "justifiable doubts as to his impartiality and independence."[187] Many of the decisions on disqualification proposals made in the period 2000 to 2010 under Article 57 of the ICSID Convention stressed that an arbitrator could be disqualified for lack of impartiality, as well as a failure of independence. This was so even though there was no mention of impartiality in the English version of Article 14(1) of the Convention setting forth the qualities to be possessed by arbitrators. Some of the decisions saw the reference to independence in Article 14(1) as encompassing both qualities.[188] Others pointed out that, where the English version of the Convention referred to independence, the equally authentic Spanish text spoke of *imparcialidad*, so that the two concepts were applicable.[189]

Most of the decisions did not, however, interpret Article 57 of the Convention as providing a "justifiable doubts" or similar standard for disqualification. Following the 1982 ruling in *Amco v. Indonesia*, most of the decisions construed Article 57, because of its requirement that a party base its disqualification proposal on a fact indicating a "manifest" lack of the necessary quality, as meaning that the fact had to indicate "not a possible lack of the quality, but a quasi-certain, or to go as far as possible, a highly probable one."[190] The dominant view was encapsulated in the observation, in the decision on a second disqualification proposal in the cases involving Suez and Argentina, that "the language of Article 57 places a heavy burden of proof" on the party challenging an arbitrator "to establish facts that make it obvious and highly probable, *not just possible*," that the arbitrator "is a person who may not be relied upon to exercise independent and impartial judgment."[191] This implied a less strict standard for disqualification under the ICSID Convention than the "justifiable doubts" standard of the commercial arbitration instruments—a conclusion hardly consistent with "the vital interest" that Aron Broches, addressing the ICSID Administrative Council in 1976, saw all Contracting States as having "in the maintenance of the integrity of arbitral proceedings under the Convention."[192]

[185] UNCITRAL Arbitration Rules (as revised in 2010), Art. 12(1) available at <http://www.uncitral.org>.

[186] *See, e.g.*, LCIA Arbitration Rules, January 1, 1998, Art. 10.3, available at <http://www.lcia.org>; SCC Arbitration Institute Arbitration Rules, January 1, 2007, Arts. 14 and 15, available at <http://www.sccinstitute.se>.

[187] U.N. Doc. A/40/17 (1985), UNCITRAL Model Law on International Commercial Arbitration, Art. 12(2).

[188] *See, e.g., Vivendi v. Argentina*, Decision on the Challenge to the President of the Committee October 3, 2001, 6 ICSID Rep. 330 (2004), para. 18.

[189] *See Suez, AGBAR and Interaguas v. Argentina* and *Suez, AGBAR and Vivendi v. Argentina*, Decision on a Second Proposal for the Disqualification of a Member of the Arbitral, May 12, 2008, IIC 342 (2008), para. 27.

[190] *Amco v. Indonesia*, Decision on the Proposal to Disqualify an Arbitrator, June 24, 1984, reprinted in M.W. Reisman and others, *International Commercial Arbitration* 624 (1997), sec. III, para. 4.

[191] *Suez, AGBAR and Interaguas v. Argentina* and *Suez, AGBAR and Vivendi v. Argentina*, Decision on a Second Proposal for the Disqualification of a Member of the Arbitral Tribunal (n. 189) para. 29 (emphasis in the original). The decision here echoed a passage in the first edition of Christoph Schreuer's commentary on the ICSID Convention to the effect that the word "manifest" in Art. 57 imposes "a relatively heavy burden of proof on the party making the proposal" to disqualify an arbitrator. C.H. Schreuer, *The ICSID Convention: A Commentary* 1200 (2001).

[192] *See* Ch. 8, n. 30 and accompanying text for reference and full quotation.

The decision on the disqualification proposal in the *Vivendi v. Argentina* case, however, interpreted Article 57 of the Convention as setting a standard close to that of the UNCITRAL Rules. Recoiling from the possibility that an ICSID arbitrator "might be heard to say that, while he was biased, he was not *manifestly* biased and that he could therefore continue to sit,"[193] the decision took the approach that the term "manifest" in Article 57 of the Convention "must exclude reliance on speculative assumptions or arguments."[194] But if the facts or "circumstances actually established (and not merely suggested or inferred)" raised "some reasonable doubt as to the impartiality of the arbitrator," then "a challenge by either party would have to be upheld."[195] The authors of the decision in the *Vivendi* case described this interpretation as conforming to the object and purpose of the ICSID Convention,[196] presumably because it advanced the interest that Broches had referred to in 1976.[197] It could have been followed, in at least some of the other cases, without changing the outcomes—the decisions in several of them made it clear that there could be no doubts at all as to the independence or impartiality of the arbitrator concerned.[198]

C. Approaches to jurisdiction

Chapter 9 examined contributions to the development of BIT jurisprudence at ICSID of four ICSID Convention arbitrations commenced in the 1990s. Three of these cases were notable for their treatment of jurisdictional issues that recurred in many of the enormous number of cases submitted to ICSID Convention arbitration during the next decade. These cases were *Fedax v. Venezuela*, *Vivendi v. Argentina* and *Maffezini v. Spain*.[199] The *Fedax* case came to ICSID in 1996 and the two others in 1997. In *Fedax*, the Tribunal considered the meaning of "investment" under Article 25(1) of the Convention and the degree to which it might, in the context of a particular BIT case, be determined by the BIT's definition of the term. The first ad hoc Committee in *Vivendi* differentiated between claims for breach of a BIT and claims for breach of contract and examined the extent to which arbitrators might, in a case brought to ICSID under a BIT, have jurisdiction over both types of claims. And in *Maffezini*, the Tribunal dealt with the role of the MFN clause of the underlying BIT in establishing jurisdiction.

This part looks at several decisions by tribunals on these issues—the meaning of "investment," jurisdiction as between treaty and contract claims and the jurisdictional role of MFN clauses—in BIT cases submitted to ICSID Convention arbitration in 2000 to 2010.

The *Fedax* Tribunal noted in its 1997 decision on jurisdiction that the ICSID Convention purposely did not define the term "investment," giving the parties much freedom to determine for themselves whether their transaction was suitable for submission to the jurisdiction of the Centre. In a BIT case, this meant that the definition

[193] *Vivendi v. Argentina*, Decision on the Challenge to the President of the Committee (n. 188) 336.
[194] Ibid. 338. [195] Ibid. [196] *See* ibid. 336.
[197] *See* text accompanying n. 192.
[198] *See, e.g., Suez, AGBAR and Interaguas v. Argentina* and *Suez, AGBAR and Vivendi v. Argentina*, Decision on a Second Proposal for the Disqualification of a Member of the Arbitral Tribunal (n. 189) para. 40.
[199] The influence of the findings of the ad hoc committee in the fourth case, *Wena v. Egypt*, on approaches to applicable law is discussed at section IV(E) of this chapter.

of the term in the BIT would normally be "the one that governs the jurisdiction of ICSID."[200]

Post-2000 cases in which the same approach was taken included *Enron v. Argentina*, the Tribunal there remarking that, "[a]s the ICSID Convention did not attempt to define 'investment,' this task was left largely to the parties to bilateral investment treaties or other expressions of consent."[201] This conformed with the drafting history of the Convention, reflected in the statement, in the Report of the Executive Directors of the World Bank, that "[n]o attempt was made to define 'investment' given the essential requirement of consent by the parties."[202] In referring, however, to the Convention as providing a "framework" for the definition of investment, the *Fedax* Tribunal recognized that the parties' discretion in this area was not unlimited.[203] The *Enron* Tribunal more fully explained that there was "a limit to this discretion of the parties because they could not validly define as investment in connection with the Convention something absurd or entirely incompatible with its object and purpose."[204] Essentially, the same observation had been made by Aron Broches some 30 years before, when he said that the discretion of the parties in this respect "is not unlimited and cannot be exercised to the point of being clearly inconsistent with the purposes of the Convention."[205] The BIT cases increased the need for clarity as to where the limit lay. This was because of the potential for overstepping any such limit under the BITs, given their typically all-encompassing definitions of covered investments.[206]

In its official publications, ICSID never ventured beyond the proposition that, for the purpose of the Convention, the notion of investment "[c]learly excluded ... ordinary commercial transactions, such as the sale of goods."[207] Academic writings published over the years suggested various positive criteria for determining whether a transaction constituted an investment under the Convention. As seen in Chapter 9, the *Fedax* Tribunal, in its 1997 decision on jurisdiction, drew from one such publication five "basic features of an investment," namely "a certain duration, a certain regularity of profit and return, assumption of risk, a substantial commitment and a significance for the host State's development."[208] Based on the same publication and

[200] *Fedax v. Venezuela*, Decision on Objections to Jurisdiction, July 11, 1997, 5 ICSID Rep. 186, 194 (2002).

[201] *Enron v. Argentina*, Decision on Jurisdiction, January 14, 2004, 11 ICSID Rep. 273, 281 (2007). As in the *Fedax* case, the presiding arbitrator in the *Enron* case was Francisco Orrego Vicuña, on whom *see* Ch. 9, n. 113. The two other members of the *Enron* Tribunal were Hector Gros Espiell and Pierre-Yves Tschanz. Gros Espiell was a former Minister of Foreign Affairs of Uruguay and former President of the Inter-American Court of Human Rights. Tschanz, a member of the Executive Board of the Swiss Arbitration Association, was a partner in the Geneva law firm Tavernier Tschanz.

[202] Report of the Executive Directors on the Convention on the Settlement of Investment Disputes between States and Nationals of Other States, March 18, 1965, reprinted at App. IV of this book, para. 27.

[203] *Fedax v. Venezuela*, Decision on Objections to Jurisdiction (n. 200) 191.

[204] *Enron v. Argentina*, Decision on Jurisdiction (n. 201) 281.

[205] The quotation is from Broches's 1972 lectures on the ICSID Convention at The Hague Academy of International Law, reprinted in Broches *Selected Essays* 188, 208.

[206] Standard definitions of covered investments in BITs defined them as comprising "every kind of asset" or "all assets," including all property rights and claims to money or to any performance. *See* R. Dolzer and M. Stevens, *Bilateral Investment Treaties* 26–27 (1995).

[207] Doc. ICSID/12, The International Centre for Settlement of Investment Disputes 16. This statement was repeated in Doc. ICSID/5/Rev. 1, ICSID Model Clauses 7 (July 1981).

[208] *Fedax v. Venezuela*, Decision on Objections to Jurisdiction (n. 200) 199. The publication was C.H. Schreuer, Commentary on the ICSID Convention: Article 25, 11 ICSID Rev.—FILJ 318 (1996), a pre-publication of the relevant portion of the first edition of his magisterial commentary, in which he identified these as features typical of operations involved in ICSID cases. Schreuer warned against the very tendency that eventually developed in the cases to elevate the features to jurisdictional requirements. As he said, "[t]hese features should not necessarily be understood as jurisdictional

other writings, a four-pronged test for investment was adopted in the 2001 decision on jurisdiction in *Salini v. Morocco*.

Joined by another Italian construction company, Salini successfully bid to construct a portion of a motorway linking Rabat to Fez. They concluded their contract for the project with the State-owned National Motorway Company of Morocco (ADM) in 1995. The Italian companies failed to complete the works on time. ADM served a termination notice on them in 1999 and did not accept memoranda that they subsequently submitted justifying the delay. The following year, the companies instituted an ICSID Convention arbitration proceeding against Morocco. They founded the jurisdiction of the Centre on the ICSID arbitration clause in a 1990 BIT between Italy and Morocco.[209] Shortly after the commencement of the proceeding, Morocco raised objections to jurisdiction. Among these was the objection that the companies' construction contract with ADM did not qualify as an investment under the BIT or the ICSID Convention.

In its 2001 decision dealing with the objections, the *Salini* Tribunal[210] quickly found that the contract fit within the BIT's broad definition of covered investments. As to whether there had been an investment within the meaning of the ICSID Convention, the Tribunal emphasized that this was "an objective condition for the Centre's jurisdiction to be activated."[211] While acknowledging the decision in *Fedax*, the *Salini* Tribunal observed that the question had hardly been discussed in other cases. It therefore turned to the academic writings, from which it gleaned that "an investment suggests payments, a certain period of execution of the deal and participation in the risks of the transaction."[212] As to the period of execution, the Tribunal noted that "the minimum period required by the academic writings" was two to five years.[213] To the elements of payment or commitment of resources, duration and assumption of risk, the Tribunal added, as the fourth criterion, "contribution to economic development of the State receiving the investment," which it indicated could be inferred from the preamble of the Convention.[214] Considering the construction contract against these four criteria, the Tribunal pronounced itself satisfied that the contract constituted an investment in the sense not only of the BIT but also of the ICSID Convention.

The *Salini* test, as it was quickly dubbed, was applied in a number of subsequent cases, with some varying it, notably to require that the contribution to the development of the host State be "significant."[215] The criterion of a contribution to development was

requirements but merely as typical characteristics of investments under the Convention." Schreuer, at 373.

209 *See* Accordo sulla Promozione e Protezione degli Investmenti, Italy–Morocco, July 18, 1990, reprinted in ICSID, Investment Treaties, Release 92-10 (1992) Art. 8 (Italy–Morocco BIT).

210 Consisting of Robert Briner, Bernardo M. Cremades and Ibrahim Fadlallah. Briner, the President of the Tribunal, was Chairman of the ICC International Court of Arbitration and a former President of the Iran–U.S. Claims Tribunal. Cremades was senior partner in the Madrid law firm B. Cremades y Asociados and Professor of International Business Law at the University of Madrid. On Fadlallah, *see* Ch. 9, n. 222.

211 *Salini v. Morocco*, Decision on Jurisdiction, July 23, 2001, 6 ICSID Rep. 400, 413 (2004).

212 Ibid. 213 Ibid. 414.

214 Ibid. 413. The reference to the preamble was to its first paragraph, recalling the "need for international cooperation for economic development, and the role of private international investment therein."

215 *See* especially *Joy Mining v. Egypt*, Award on Jurisdiction, August 6, 2004, 13 ICSID Rep. 123, 133 (2008). The Tribunal in this case consisted of Francisco Orrego Vicuña as President, W. Laurence Craig and Christopher G. Weeramantry. On Orrego Vicuña, *see* Ch. 9, n. 113. As a partner at Coudert Brothers in Paris, Craig had been counsel for the claimant in *SPP v. Egypt*, the first "arbitration without privity" (*see* Ch. 8, section III). Weeramantry had been a Justice of the Supreme Court of Sri Lanka and later a member and Vice President of the ICJ. Other cases of the period applying the *Salini*

brought to the fore in *MHS v. Malaysia*. The background to that ICSID Convention arbitration was that a British ship carrying a large cargo of antique Chinese porcelain sank in the Straits of Malacca in the early nineteenth century. MHS, a marine salvage company majority-owned by a U.K. national, signed a contract with the Malaysian government in 1991 to find the wreck and salvage the cargo for the government. After an extended search and salvage operation, the company found the wreck and recovered from it some 24,000 pieces of porcelain. The Government retained some of the pieces, placing several in the Malaysian National Museum. The rest were auctioned at Christie's in Amsterdam. MHS received only 40 percent of the amount realized from the auction. Claiming that it was contractually entitled to 70 percent, and to its share of the best attainable value of the items retained by the government, the company commenced the arbitration in 2005, invoking for the purpose the consent to the jurisdiction of the Centre in the 1981 Malaysia–U.K. BIT.[216] The case was entrusted to a Sole Arbitrator,[217] who rendered his award in 2007.

In the award, the Sole Arbitrator ruled that the contract was not an investment within the meaning of the Convention and therefore dismissed the claim for lack of jurisdiction. He reached the conclusion after examining the contract against the criteria accepted in *Salini* and similar cases. The company made contributions but their size was "in no way comparable to those found in"[218] the earlier cases. The elements of duration and risk similarly appeared "to be only superficially satisfied."[219] The Sole Arbitrator had indicated, however, that not every criterion had to be satisfied for a transaction to qualify as an investment. Thus, the analysis of the remaining element "assume[d] considerable importance."[220] In light of the earlier cases, the Sole Arbitrator determined this to require that "to constitute an 'investment' under the ICSID Convention, the Contract must have made a significant contribution to the economic development of the Respondent."[221] The Sole Arbitrator concluded that the contract of MHS had not provided Malaysia with "substantial" and "lasting" benefits in this sense; the benefits flowing from it were instead "no different from the benefits flowing to the place of performance of any normal service contract."[222]

MHS applied for the annulment of the award in September 2007. The ad hoc Committee was established the following month.[223] Rendered in April 2009, the ad

test included *Helnan v. Egypt*, Decision on Objection to Jurisdiction, October 17, 2006, IIC 130 (2006); *Bayindir v. Pakistan* (*see* Decision on Jurisdiction, November 14, 2005, IIC 27 (2005), para. 137); *Jan de Nul v. Egypt* (*see* Decision on Jurisdiction, June 16, 2006, IIC 144 (2006), para. 91); and *Mitchell v. DRC* (*see* Decision on the Application for Annulment of the Award, November 1, 2006, IIC 172 (2006), paras. 33 and 39). The last-mentioned decision annulled the award rendered in the case in part because of its perceived failure to give any indication as to how the operation concerned, a legal consulting firm, contributed to the development of the host State and thus, in light of the finding in the *Salini* case, qualified as an investment under the Convention. On this much-criticized decision, *see* K. Yannaca-Small, Definition of "Investment": An Open-ended Search for a Balanced Approach, in K. Yannaca-Small (ed.), *Arbitration under International Investment Agreements: A Guide to the Key Issues* 243, 259–260 (2010).

[216] *See* Agreement for the Promotion and Protection of Investments, Malaysia–U.K., May 21, 1981, reprinted in ICSID, Investment Treaties, Release 94-2 (May 1994), Art. 7.

[217] Michael Hwang, a former head of the litigation department of Allen & Gledhill in Singapore and former Judicial Commissioner of the Supreme Court of Singapore.

[218] *MHS v. Malaysia*, Award on Jurisdiction, May 17, 2007, IIC 289 (2007), para. 109.

[219] Ibid. para. 124. [220] Ibid. [221] Ibid. [222] Ibid. paras. 143 and 144.

[223] Stephen M. Schwebel was the President of the ad hoc Committee. Its two other members were Mohamed Shahabudeen and Peter Tomka. Schwebel was a former President of the ICJ. Shahabudeen was a member of the International Criminal Court and former member of the ICJ. Tomka was a serving member of the ICJ.

hoc Committee's strongly worded decision annulled the award as a whole.[224] Casting aside the *Salini* line of cases, the ad hoc Committee returned to the interpretation of the Convention in accordance with international law.[225] The ordinary meaning of the term "investment"—a commitment of money or other assets for the purpose of providing a return—could be regarded as ambiguous. This justified resort to the preparatory works of the Convention. Also to be considered was the Report of the Executive Directors of the World Bank on the Convention.[226]

Summarizing its consideration of the *travaux préparatoires*, the Committee noted that the drafters of the Convention had decided "to reject a monetary floor in the amount of an investment, to reject specification of its duration, to leave 'investment' undefined, and to accord great weight to the definition of investment in the instrument providing for recourse to ICSID."[227] While acknowledging that there were, in the phrase once used by Aron Broches, "outer limits" beyond which the facilities of the Centre could not be used even with the consent of the parties, the Committee emphasized that the *travaux préparatoires* of the Convention:

> … do not support the imposition of "outer limits" such as those imposed by the Sole Arbitrator in this case. Little more about the nature of outer limits is indicated in the *travaux* than is contained in Article 25(1), namely that, "[t]he jurisdiction of the Centre shall extend to any legal dispute arising directly out of an investment…." It appears to have been assumed by the Convention's drafters that use of the term "investment" excluded a simple sale and like transient commercial transactions from the jurisdiction of the Centre. Judicial or arbitral construction going further in interpretation of the meaning of "investment" by the establishment of criteria or hallmarks may or may not be regarded as plausible, but the intentions of the draftsmen of the ICSID Convention, as the *travaux* show them to have been, lend those criteria (and still less, conditions) scant support.[228]

Referring to the Report of the Executive Directors of the World Bank as "similarly illuminating," the ad hoc Committee cited from it the passage quoted earlier, on the drafters' decision not to define "investment" in the Convention, "given the essential requirement of the consent of the parties."[229] In light of this history of the preparation of the text of the Convention and the Report of the Executive Directors, the ad hoc Committee found "the failure of the Sole Arbitrator even to consider, let alone apply, the definition of investment as it is contained in the Agreement to be a gross error that gave rise to a manifest failure to exercise jurisdiction."[230]

Buttressing the conclusions of the *MHS* ad hoc Committee were a number of recent arbitral awards and decisions consistent, in the Committee's words, "with its approach, which it considers consonant with the intentions of the Parties to the ICSID

[224] Over the dissent, however, of one of the Committee members (Shahabudeen).

[225] As reflected in the Vienna Convention (n. 101) Arts. 31 and 32.

[226] Although the ad hoc Committee did not make the point explicitly, the Report of the Executive Directors could be regarded as comparable to a final act in forming part of the context of the Convention, and hence always to be considered in its interpretation. *Cf.* Vienna Convention (n. 101) Art. 31(2) and R. Gardiner, *Treaty Interpretation* 79 (2008).

[227] *MHS v. Malaysia*, ad hoc Committee Decision on the Application for Annulment, April 16, 2009, IIC 372 (2009), para. 80. On those aspects of the drafting history, *see* Ch. 3, n. 55 and Ch. 5, section II(B).

[228] *MHS v. Malaysia*, ad hoc Committee Annulment Decision (n. 227) para. 69. Broches used the phrase quoted in the text in his July 9, 1964 Chairman's Report on the Regional Consultative Meetings of Legal Experts, reprinted in ICSID, 2 *History of the ICSID Convention* 557, 566.

[229] *See MHS v. Malaysia*, ad hoc Committee Annulment Decision (n. 227) para. 70. *See also* n. 202 and accompanying text.

[230] *MHS v. Malaysia*, ad hoc Committee Annulment Decision (n. 227) para. 74.

Convention."[231] The Committee quoted at length from one of these, the 2008 award in *Biwater v. Tanzania*. A "rote, or overly strict, application" of the criteria from the *Salini* and similar cases was rejected in the *Biwater* award in favor of "a more flexible and pragmatic approach" that also took into account "all the circumstances of the case, including the nature of the instrument containing the relevant consent to ICSID."[232] However, the approach taken in *Biwater* risked excessive deference to the parties' characterization of the transaction and rendering superfluous the requirement of "investment" under the Convention.[233]

A middle way was struck in another of the more recent decisions, the award rendered in *LESI v. Algeria*. This case concerned a contract that LESI and a second Italian construction company were awarded by Algeria's National Dam Agency (ANB) in 1993 for the construction of a dam in the Bouira province to supply Algiers with drinking water. Security problems in the region hindered implementation of the project from the start. Work on it was suspended for several years. In 2001, ANB terminated the contract, re-bidding for it having been made a condition of needed financing for the project from the African Development Bank. After they were unable to agree with ANB on compensation, the companies initiated the ICSID Convention arbitration proceeding on the basis of the consent clause in the 1991 BIT between Algeria and Italy.[234] Objections to jurisdiction made by Algeria in the proceeding included the objection that there was no investment in the sense of the ICSID Convention. The Tribunal[235] dismissed the objection. It did so after finding that the contract met each of the conditions that the Tribunal accepted an investment must meet under the Convention. These corresponded to the first three of the criteria identified in the *Salini* case—that, in the case of a contract, the contractor should make a contribution or outlay for a certain duration and in doing so assume a certain risk. The Tribunal did not consider it necessary to specify economic development as a fourth condition, given that it was difficult to establish and implicitly covered by the first three conditions.[236] Another ruling that may be mentioned here, even though the case was commenced before 2000, was the 2008 award in the protracted *Pey Casado v. Chile* arbitration, which concerned an expropriated newspaper business. In the award, the *Pey Casado* Tribunal explained that the preamble of the ICSID Convention presented a contribution to the economic development of the host State:

> as a consequence, not as a condition of the investment: in protecting the investments, the Convention promotes the development of the host State. This does not mean that the development of the host State is a constitutive element of the notion of investment. This is the reason

[231] Ibid. para. 78.

[232] *Biwater v. Tanzania*, Award, July 24, 2008, IIC 330 (2008), paras. 312 and 316. The Tribunal in this case consisted of Bernard Hanotiau, Gary B. Born and Toby T. Landau. Hanotiau, the President of the Tribunal, was a founding partner of the Brussels law firm Hanotiau & van den Berg and Professor of International Dispute Resolution at the University of Louvain. Born was chair of the international arbitration practice group of the Washington, D.C., law firm WilmerHale. Landau was a barrister at Essex Court Chambers, London, and a member of the Board of Directors of the LCIA.

[233] This argument was made in E. Gaillard, "Biwater," Classic Investment Bases: Input, Risk, Duration, New York L.J., December 31, 2008.

[234] *See* Accord sur la promotion et la protection réciproque des investissements, Algeria–Italy, May 18, 1991, reprinted in ICSID, Investment Treaties, Release 92-94 (March 1993), Art. 8.

[235] The Tribunal consisted of Pierre Tercier, André Faurès and Emmanuel Gaillard. Tercier, the President of the Tribunal, was Professor of Law at the University of Fribourg and Chairman of the ICC International Court of Arbitration. Faurès was a Brussels-based member of the Coudert Brothers law firm. On Gaillard, *see* n. 165.

[236] *See LESI v. Algeria*, Award, December 27, 2004, IIC 145 (2005), sec. 2.2, para. 13.

why, as noted by some arbitral tribunals, this fourth condition is in fact encompassed by the three others.[237]

These words found an echo in the 2010 holding of the Tribunal in *Fakes v. Turkey* that "the economic development of a host State is one of the proclaimed objectives of the ICSID Convention… [but] not in and of itself an independent criterion for the definition of an investment."[238] The trend of arbitral decisions to this effect allowed the *Deutsche Bank v. Sri Lanka* Tribunal, which was constituted in 2009 to decide a dispute arising out of an oil hedging agreement, to dismiss the criterion of contribution to economic development as now "discredited and … generally considered … unworkable owing to its subjective nature."[239]

The distinction between contract claims and treaty claims, first articulated in *Vivendi v. Argentina*,[240] was important in many of the BIT cases brought to ICSID after 2000. Examined in these cases were such fundamental issues as the extent of the jurisdiction of the arbitrators over contract, as well as treaty claims, and the related question of the scope and effect of an observance of undertakings provision in the BIT concerned.[241] The cases famously included two launched by the Société Générale de Surveillance (SGS), a Swiss provider of inspection, verification, testing and certification services. Pakistan was the respondent in the first case and the Philippines in the other.

The dispute in the first case concerned a contract, signed by the parties in 1994, under which SGS was to inspect goods for export from certain countries to Pakistan. The objective was to ensure that the goods were properly classified for duty purposes and to enable Pakistan to increase the efficiency of its customs revenues collection. This pre-shipment inspection (PSI) Agreement, as it was called, provided for the settlement of related disputes by arbitration in Pakistan under its arbitration law. The PSI Agreement came into force at the beginning of 1995, was subsequently performed by the parties but terminated by Pakistan at the end of 1996. Alleging unlawful termination, SGS initiated a claim against Pakistan in the courts of Switzerland. Decisions of lower courts rejecting the claim were upheld, on the ground of sovereign immunity, by the Swiss Federal Tribunal late in 2000.

[237] *Pey Casado v. Chile*, Award, May 8, 2008, IIC 324 (2008), para. 232 (as translated in *MHS v. Malaysia*, ad hoc Committee Annulment Decision (n. 227) Dissenting Opinion, para. 27). The Tribunal in the *Pey Casado* case was reconstituted several times in the course of a very long arbitration proceeding. At the time of the rendition of the award in 2008, it was composed of Pierre Lalive, Mohammed Chemloul and Emmanuel Gaillard. On Lalive, the President of the Tribunal, *see* Ch. 8, n. 103, and on Gaillard, *see* n. 165. A member of the Chemloul & Associés law firm in Algiers, Chemloul was a former Secretary General of the Algerian State oil company Sonatrach.

[238] *Fakes v. Turkey*, Award, July 2010, IIC 439 (2010), para. 111. The Tribunal in this case was composed of Hans van Houtte as President, Laurent Lévy and Emmanuel Gaillard. Van Houtte was Professor of Law at the University of Leuven. Lévy was a founding partner of Lévy Kaufmann-Kohler in Geneva. On Gaillard, *see* n. 165.

[239] *Deutsche Bank v. Sri Lanka*, Award, October 31, 2012, HC 578 (2012), para. 306. The *Deutsche Bank v. Sri Lanka* Tribunal comprised Bernard Hanotiau as President, Makhdoom Ali Khan and David A.R. Williams. On Hanotiau, *see* n. 232. Khan was a former Attorney-General of Pakistan. Williams was a former Justice of the High Court of New Zealand.

[240] *See Vivendi v. Argentina*, ad hoc Committee Decision, July 3, 2002, 6 ICSID Rep. 340, 365–367 (2002) and Ch. 9, section V(B).

[241] It will be recalled that observance of undertaking provisions, long standard in BITs, were provisions by which each party to the treaty pledged to observe any undertakings it had assumed with respect to investments of investors of the other party. The provisions were commonly called "umbrella clauses." This was because, according to the view long propounded by specialists, the provisions extended the protective cover of the BIT to contractual commitments, transforming them into treaty obligations. *See especially* P. Weil, Problèmes relatifs aux contrats passés entre un État et un particulier, 128 Recueil des Cours 95, 130 (1969).

Pakistan had meanwhile invoked the dispute settlement clause of the PSI Agreement and applied for an order from the courts of Pakistan to compel arbitration there in accordance with the clause. SGS responded with jurisdictional objections and a counterclaim for alleged breaches of the PSI Agreement. Six months later, in October 2001, SGS filed with ICSID its request for arbitration against Pakistan on the basis of the consent clause in the 1995 BIT between Pakistan and Switzerland.[242] The request claimed for violations of the PSI Agreement, most or all of which the request argued also qualified as violations of the substantive provisions of the BIT. The request was soon registered but the litigation in Pakistan continued, culminating in a Supreme Court decision granting Pakistan's request to proceed with the PSI Agreement arbitration and enjoining SGS from pursuing or participating in the ICSID arbitration. Shortly after its constitution, the ICSID Tribunal[243] issued an order on provisional measures recommending that Pakistan take no steps to initiate a contempt complaint against SGS and that the PSI Agreement arbitration be stayed until the ICSID Tribunal ruled on objections to its jurisdiction by Pakistan.[244]

These included the objection that, irrespective of how SGS chose to label them, its claims were entirely contractual in nature and therefore subject to the arbitration clause of the PSI Agreement. Ruling that, in the jurisdictional phase, it was for the claimant to characterize the claims, the *SGS v. Pakistan* Tribunal proceeded, in its August 2003 decision on jurisdiction, to consider whether it had jurisdiction:

> ... to pass on and determine SGS's claims which are grounded on alleged violations by Pakistan of certain provisions on the BIT ("the Claimant's BIT claims"), or its claims grounded on alleged breaches of certain provisions of the PSI Agreement ("the Claimant's contract claims"), or both such types of claims.[245]

The Tribunal found that it had jurisdiction to decide the BIT claims but not the contract claims. Relying heavily on the analysis of the first ad hoc Committee in the *Vivendi* case, the *SGS v. Pakistan* Tribunal explained that "the same set of facts can give rise to different claims grounded on differing legal orders,"[246] with the respective claims to be determined by reference to the applicable law of each, which would be international law for a BIT claim and the proper law of the contract for a contract claim. The consent clause in the Pakistan–Switzerland BIT was cast in broad terms, covering without other qualification "disputes with respect to investments between a Contracting Party and an investor of the other Contracting Party."[247] If, the *SGS v. Pakistan* Tribunal said, the clause

> ... relates to any dispute at all between an investor and a Contracting Party, it must comprehend disputes constituted by claimed violations of BIT provisions establishing substantive standards of treatment by one Contracting Party of investors of the other Contracting Party. Any other view would tend to erode significantly those substantive treaty standards of treatment.[248]

[242] *See* Agreement on the Promotion and Reciprocal Protection of Investments, Pakistan–Switzerland, July 11, 1995, reprinted in ICSID, Investment Treaties, Release 97-3 (September 1997), Art. 9 (Pakistan–Switzerland BIT).

[243] The Tribunal consisted of Florentino P. Feliciano, President, André Faurès and J. Christopher Thomas. On Feliciano, *see* Ch. 8, n. 108. *See* n. 235 regarding Faurès. Thomas was then Managing Partner of Thomas & Partners, a Vancouver law firm. He had previously been Senior Policy Adviser at Canada's Ministry of International Trade.

[244] *See SGS v. Pakistan*, Procedural Order No. 2, October 16, 2002, 8 ICSID Rep. 388, 397 (2005).

[245] *SGS v. Pakistan*, Decision on Objections to Jurisdiction, August 6, 2003, 8 ICSID Rep. 406, 436 (2005).

[246] Ibid. *Cf. Vivendi v. Argentina*, ad hoc Committee Decision (n. 240) 367.

[247] Pakistan–Switzerland BIT (n. 242) Art. 9(1).

[248] *SGS v. Pakistan*, Decision on Objections to Jurisdiction (n. 245) 438.

Also broadly formulated, the arbitration clause of the PSI Agreement related to "[a]ny dispute, controversy or claim arising out of, or relating to this Agreement, or breach, termination or invalidity thereof."[249] At a minimum, the Tribunal observed, this encompassed contractual and other non-treaty related disputes.[250] It rejected the argument of SGS that the clause should nevertheless give way to the ICSID procedure contemplated in the BIT. Viewing the broad reference in the consent clause of the BIT to "disputes with respect to investments" as merely descriptive of the factual matter of the disputes, the Tribunal declared that:

> ... from that description alone, without more, ... no implication necessarily arises that both BIT and purely contract claims are intended to be covered by the Contracting Parties in Article 9 [of the BIT, containing the ICSID consent clause]. Neither, accordingly, does an implication arise that the Article 9 dispute settlement mechanism would supersede and set at naught all otherwise valid non-ICSID forum selection clauses in all earlier agreements between Swiss investors and the Respondent. Thus, we do not see anything in Article 9 or in any other provision of the BIT that can be read as vesting this Tribunal with jurisdiction over claims resting *ex hypothesi* exclusively on contract.[251]

In terms reminiscent of the first ad hoc Committee decision in *Vivendi*, the *SGS v. Pakistan* Tribunal recorded its belief that the arbitration clause of the PSI Agreement "is a valid forum selection clause *so far as concerns the Claimant's contract claims which do not also amount to BIT claims*, and it is a clause that this Tribunal should respect."[252]

In *SGS v. Pakistan*, the claimant also argued that the observance of undertakings provision, in Article 11 of the Pakistan–Switzerland BIT, turned contract claims into BIT claims over which the Tribunal would clearly have jurisdiction. As indicated earlier, the Tribunal gave this argument short shrift. It said that:

> ... we do not find a convincing basis for accepting the Claimant's contention that Article 11 of the BIT has had the effect of entitling a Contracting Party's investor, like SGS, in the face of a valid forum selection contract clause to "elevate" its claims grounded solely in a contract with another Contracting Party like the PSI Agreement, to claims grounded on the BIT, and accordingly to bring such contract claims to this Tribunal for resolution and decision.[253]

The Tribunal insisted on "clear and convincing evidence" that it was the shared intent of Pakistan and Switzerland that Article 11 of the BIT should operate as urged by SGS, given the "far-reaching" and "burdensome" consequences for a BIT party of treating all breaches of its contracts with investors of the other party as breaches of the BIT.[254] "We do not find such evidence in the text itself of Article 11," the Tribunal observed, and "have not been pointed to any other evidence of the putative common intent of the Contracting Parties by the Claimant."[255] This approach of the *SGS v. Pakistan*

[249] Art. 11.1 of the PSI Agreement, as quoted in *SGS v. Pakistan*, Decision on Objections to Jurisdiction (n. 245) 440.

[250] The Tribunal had found that, on signing the PSI Agreement in 1994, the parties could hardly have intended for treaty disputes to be covered by the arbitration clause of the Agreement since the BIT was concluded a year later and lay "still hidden in the future" (*SGS v. Pakistan*, Decision on Objections to Jurisdiction (n. 245) 439).

[251] Ibid. 441.

[252] Ibid. (emphasis in original). *Cf. Vivendi v. Argentina*, ad hoc Committee Decision (n. 240) 366 (stating that "where the essential basis of a claim brought before an international tribunal is a breach of contract, the tribunal will give effect to any valid choice of forum clause in the contract").

[253] *SGS v. Pakistan*, Decision on Objections to Jurisdiction (n. 245) 442.

[254] Ibid. 443.

[255] Ibid. As for the text of Art. 11 of the Pakistan–Switzerland BIT (n. 242), it stated that "[e]ither Contracting Party shall constantly guarantee the observance of the commitments it has entered into with respect to investments of investors of the other Contracting Party."

Tribunal to the "umbrella clause" was criticized by the *SGS v. Philippines* Tribunal in its own decision on jurisdiction issued some six months later.

The dispute in *SGS v. Philippines* concerned an agreement signed by the parties in 1991 for SGS to furnish a comprehensive import supervision service (CISS), including verification of the quality, quantity and price of imported goods prior to shipment to the Philippines. During the period of performance of this CISS Agreement, SGS carried out huge numbers of inspections in many countries. SGS invoiced the Philippines approximately US$680 million for these inspections. Of that amount, some US$540 million was actually paid. The Philippines questioned SGS's claim for the balance and left it unpaid. After settlement discussions failed, SGS commenced the arbitration under the 1997 BIT between the Philippines and Switzerland, which provided for the ICSID arbitral settlement of investment disputes—and for the observance of undertakings—in terms similar to those of Switzerland's BIT with Pakistan.[256] In the arbitration, SGS argued that the nonpayment by the Philippines of the balance claimed infringed various provisions of the BIT, including the one on observance of undertakings. The Philippines objected that the dispute was purely contractual in character and that the issues involved were governed by the dispute resolution provision in the CISS Agreement, which designated Philippines law as the governing law of the contract and required the submission of contractual disputes to the courts of the Philippines.

In its January 2004 decision on the objections, the *SGS v. Philippines* Tribunal[257] declined to follow the *SGS v. Pakistan* Tribunal's restrictive interpretation of the observance of undertakings provision, describing it as "unconvincing" and as having "failed to give any clear meaning to the 'umbrella clause.' "[258] For the *SGS v. Philippines* Tribunal, the provision "means what it says," making it "a breach of the BIT for the host State to fail to observe binding commitments, including contractual commitments, which it has assumed with regard to specific investments."[259] This, the Tribunal hastened to add:

> ... does not convert the issue of the *extent* or *content* of such obligations into an issue of international law. That issue (in the present case, the issue of how much is payable for services provided under the CISS Agreement) is still governed by the investment agreement.[260]

Again parting company from the *SGS v. Pakistan* Tribunal, the *SGS v. Philippines* Tribunal considered that such contractual issues could in principle be decided by arbitrators in a case brought to ICSID pursuant to the consent to the jurisdiction of the Centre in the BIT. The provision concerned, Article VIII of the BIT, was "entirely general ... allowing for submission of all investment disputes by the investor against

[256] *See* Agreement on the Promotion and Reciprocal Protection of Investments, Philippines–Switzerland, March 31, 1997, reprinted in ICSID, Investment Treaties, Release 2000-1 (July 2000), Arts. VIII and X(2) (Philippines–Switzerland BIT).

[257] The President of the Tribunal was Ahmed S. El-Kosheri. Its two other members were James Crawford and Antonio Crivellaro. On El-Kosheri and Crawford, *see* Ch. 8, n. 20 and Ch. 9, n. 203. Crivellaro was Professor of Law at the University of Padua and partner at Bonelli Erede Pappalardo, a Milan law firm.

[258] *SGS v. Philippines*, Decision on Objections to Jurisdiction, January 29, 2004, 8 ICSID Rep. 518, 552 (2005).

[259] Ibid. 551 and 553. The decision here alluded to the wording of the observance of undertakings provision in the Philippines–Switzerland BIT (n. 256) Art. X(2), according to which "[e]ach Contracting Party shall observe any obligation it has assumed with regard to specific investments in its territory by investors of the other Contracting Party."

[260] *SGS v. Philippines*, Decision on Objections to Jurisdiction (n. 258) 553 (emphasis in original).

the host State."[261] The *SGS v. Philippines* Tribunal agreed, however, with "the concern that the general provisions of BITs should not, unless clearly expressed to do so, override specific and exclusive dispute settlement arrangements made in the investment contract itself."[262] Otherwise:

> ... it will have become impossible for investors validly to agree to an exclusive jurisdiction clause in their contracts; they will always have the hidden capacity to bring contractual claims to BIT arbitration, even in breach of the contract, and it is hard to believe that this result was contemplated by States in concluding generic investment protection agreements.[263]

It should not, the Tribunal continued, "be presumed that such a general provision [as Article VIII of the BIT] has the effect of overriding specific provisions of particular contracts, freely negotiated between the parties."[264] The Tribunal went on to conclude that "the BIT did not purport to override the exclusive jurisdiction clause in the CISS Agreement, or to give SGS an alternative route for the resolution of contract claims which it was bound to submit to the Philippine courts under that Agreement."[265]

As illustrated by these cases, ascertaining the reach of extraordinarily wide BIT provisions was a constant challenge for arbitrators during the period 2000 to 2010. Thus, the *SGS v. Pakistan* Tribunal could not accept, in the absence of "clear and convincing evidence"[266] to the contrary, that Switzerland and Pakistan had intended, by the observance of undertakings provision in Article 11 of their BIT, to make a failure to honor a contract a violation of the BIT. The *SGS v. Philippines* Tribunal similarly found it "hard to believe"[267] that, in making generic BITs, States could have meant to allow investors to submit contract claims to arbitration under the BIT instead of contenting themselves with different dispute settlement arrangements provided for in the contract.

After the publication of the decision on jurisdiction in *SGS v. Pakistan*, however, the Federal Department of Economic Affairs of Switzerland sent a note to the ICSID Secretariat reacting "with a great deal of concern" to the decision's ruling on Article 11 of the Pakistan–Switzerland BIT. According to the note, the Swiss authorities were:

> ... alarmed about the very narrow interpretation given to the meaning of Article 11 by the Tribunal, which not only runs counter to the intention of Switzerland when concluding the Treaty but is quite evidently neither supported by the meaning of similar articles in BITs concluded by other countries nor by academic comments on such provisions.[268]

In regard to the above-mentioned finding in *SGS v. Philippines*, it will be recalled that BITs made by the United States specifically envisaged the possibility of investors taking advantage of the consent to arbitration in the BIT in preference to resorting to "any applicable previously agreed dispute settlement procedures."[269] Invoking the Latin maxim *generalia specialibus non derogant*, the *SGS v. Philippines* Tribunal had argued that the broadly worded consent to ICSID jurisdiction in the BIT should not

261 Ibid. 554. 262 Ibid. 556. 263 Ibid. 264 Ibid. 558.

265 Ibid. One of the arbitrators (Crivellaro) disagreed with this conclusion.

266 *See* text accompanying n. 254. 267 *See* text accompanying n. 263.

268 Note on the Interpretation of Art. 11 of the Bilateral Investment Treaty between Switzerland and Pakistan in light of the Decision on Objections to Jurisdiction of ICSID in Case No. ARB/01/13 SGS Société Générale de Surveillance S.A. versus Islamic Republic of Pakistan, attached to letter of Swiss Federal Department of Economic Affairs to ICSID Secretariat, October 1, 2003, as quoted in E. Gaillard, Investment Treaty Arbitration and Jurisdiction Over Contract Claims—the SGS Cases Considered, in T. Weiler (ed.), *International Investment Law and Arbitration: Leading Cases from the ICSID. NAFTA, Bilateral Treaties and Customary International Law* 325, 341 (2005).

269 *See* nn. 168 and 169 and accompanying text.

be regarded as supplanting the contractually stipulated dispute settlement clause.[270] A more apt comparison, however, would have been between the contractually stipulated clause and the arbitration agreement arising from the investor's acceptance of the State's broad consent proffered in the BIT.[271] That agreement would generally be more specific than the contractual clause since the investor's acceptance or consent pursuant to the BIT would normally extend only to its particular claim. Logically, therefore, the agreement formed under the BIT would supersede the contractual clause in respect of that claim. There remained an obvious way in which BIT negotiators could, if they so desired, prevent contractual dispute settlement arrangements from being "overridden" in this manner by adding to the BIT, as they sometimes did, a provision expressly excluding from the scope of an otherwise broad consent clause disputes covered by such contractual arrangements.[272]

Finally, several of the cases submitted to ICSID Convention arbitration in 2000 to 2010 pursuant to BITs gave rise to decisions that, following the landmark ruling in *Maffezini v. Spain*,[273] allowed claimants to overcome obstacles to jurisdiction in the BIT by importing, through its MFN clause, the more favorable dispute settlement provisions of another BIT. These cases notably included *Siemens v. Argentina*.

A wholly owned subsidiary of the claimant in that case concluded a contract with Argentina in 1998 for the establishment of a system of migration control and personal identification. After it came to power at the end of 1999, a new government of Argentina suspended the contract, allegedly because of technical problems. This was followed, in 2001, by Argentina's termination of the contract. Negotiations having failed to resolve the dispute, Siemens commenced the arbitration in 2003. The 1991 BIT of Argentina with the home country of Siemens, Germany, set forth in its Article 10 consent of the States to submit investment disputes to the jurisdiction of ICSID.[274] Article 10 conditioned recourse to the Centre on a prior referral of the dispute to local courts.[275] Citing the decision on jurisdiction in *Maffezini*, Siemens argued that the MFN clause in Article 3 of the 1991 Argentina–Germany BIT entitled it to benefit from the provision on the ICSID arbitral settlement of investment disputes in the 1991 Argentina–Chile BIT, which did not similarly require that the dispute first be submitted to local courts.[276] Argentina objected that Article 3 of the Argentina–Germany BIT applied to the treatment of commercial or economic transactions and

[270] *See SGS v. Philippines*, Decision on Objections to Jurisdiction (n. 258) 558 and, for the Tribunal's further elaboration, text accompanying n. 196. The rule of statutory interpretation reflected in the maxim was that general provisions do not derogate from specific ones.

[271] It is worth remembering in this respect the provisions of many BITs specifying that the State's consent in the BIT and the investor's submission of the dispute to arbitration thereunder together satisfy the requirements "for written consent of the parties" and "for an [arbitration] 'agreement in writing' " in the ICSID and New York Conventions, respectively. *See, e.g.*, Treaty Concerning the Encouragement and Reciprocal Protection of Investment, El Salvador–U.S., March 10, 1999, reprinted in ICSID, Investment Treaties, Release 2001-2 (April 2001), Art. VIII(4)(a) and VIII(4)(b).

[272] An example of such a provision was Art. 9(2) of the Agreement on the Promotion and Protection of Investments, Italy–Jordan, July 21, 1996, reprinted in ICSID, Investment Treaties, Release 2004-2 (June 2004), applied in *Salini v. Jordan*, ICSID Case No. ARB/02/13, Decision on Jurisdiction, November 29, 2004, 14 ICSID Rep. 306 (2009).

[273] On which, *see* Ch. 9, section V(C).

[274] *See* Tratado sobre Promoción y Protección Reciproca de Inversiones, Argentina–Germany, April 9, 1991, reprinted in ICSID, Investment Treaties, Release 92-4 (March 1993), Art. 10(4) (Argentina–Germany BIT).

[275] *See* ibid. Art. 10(2).

[276] *See* Tratado sobre Promoción y Protección Reciproca de Inversiones, Argentina–Chile, August 2, 1991, reprinted in ICSID, Investment Treaties, Release 93-2 (July 1993), Art. 10 (Argentina–Chile BIT).

protected investments, not investors.[277] If Siemens could claim the benefit of the BIT with Chile, Argentina alternatively argued, that treaty would then apply in its entirety. Unlike the Argentina–Germany BIT, the Argentina–Chile treaty had a fork-in-the-road provision that Siemens would have violated by filing administrative appeals in the immediate aftermath of the termination of its contract.[278]

The Tribunal[279] rejected the objections in its August 2004 decision on jurisdiction. A "plain and contextual reading" of Article 3 of the Argentina–Germany BIT did "not limit the treatment to transactions of a commercial and economic nature."[280] Treatment in Article 3 referred instead to treatment generally under the BIT. The Tribunal also found that it was "[m]ore consistent with [the purpose of the BIT] … to consider that, in Article 3, treatment of the investments includes treatment of the investors."[281] Concurring with the findings of the *Maffezini* Tribunal, the Tribunal in *Siemens* declared that the provision of dispute settlement mechanisms was "part of the protection offered" by the BIT and "part of the treatment of foreign investors and investments and of the advantages accessible through an MFN clause."[282] The *Siemens* Tribunal took the view, moreover, that "claiming a benefit by operation of an MFN clause does not carry with it the acceptance of all the terms of the treaty which provides for such benefit."[283] The Tribunal thus found that an investor could, through the MFN clause of a BIT, "cherry pick" a second treaty. Again agreeing with *Maffezini*, the Tribunal in *Siemens* saw the operation of such an MFN clause as being subject to "public policy considerations judged by the parties essential to their agreement."[284] But the Tribunal held such considerations to be inapplicable in the *Siemens* case. BITs made by Argentina at around the same time as the treaty with Germany, including of course the Argentina–Chile BIT, did not require recourse to local courts prior to arbitration. It thus could not well be argued that the institution of court proceedings was a vital issue for Argentina or an essential part of its consent to arbitration.[285]

Among the cases commenced after 2000, there were also several in which tribunals declined to follow *Maffezini* in this respect. The best known of these cases was *Plama v. Bulgaria*. A Cypriot company, Plama purchased a Bulgarian firm that owned an oil refinery in Bulgaria. According to Plama, various measures of Bulgarian authorities after the purchase seriously damaged the operations of the refinery. Its request

[277] In pertinent part, Art. 3 of the Argentina–Germany BIT (n. 274) provided:

(1) None of the Contracting Parties shall accord in its territory to the investments of nationals or companies of the other Contracting Party or to investments in which they hold shares, a less favorable treatment than the treatment granted to the investments of its own nationals or companies or to the investments of nationals or companies of third States.
(2) None of the Contracting Parties shall accord in its territory to nationals or companies of the other Contracting Party a less favorable treatment of activities related to investments than granted to its own nationals and companies or to the nationals and companies of third States.

[278] *See* Argentina–Chile BIT (n. 276) Art. 10(2).

[279] Comprising Andrés Rigo Sureda, Charles N. Brower and Domingo Bello Janeiro. Rigo Sureda, the President of the Tribunal, was a former Assistant General Counsel and Deputy General Counsel of the World Bank. Before joining the Bank, he had been Assistant Professor of Public International Law at the Universidad Autónoma de Madrid. Brower was a member of the Iran–U.S. Claims Tribunal and former President of the American Society of International Law. Bello Janeiro was Professor of Civil Law at the Universidade da Coruña.

[280] *Siemens v. Argentina*, Decision on Jurisdiction, August 3, 2004, 12 ICSID Rep. 174, 193 (2007).

[281] Ibid. 195. [282] Ibid. 197. [283] Ibid. 199. [284] Ibid.

[285] *See* ibid. 198.

for arbitration based the jurisdiction of the Centre on both the ECT and the BIT signed by Bulgaria and Cyprus in 1987. The provision of the latter treaty on the settlement of investment disputes, Article 4, was typical of BITs made by Communist-era Eastern European countries. Its scope was confined to disputes relating to expropriation. Article 4 reserved for local courts differences over "[t]he legality of the expropriation."[286] The investor was given the right to resort to international arbitration only in respect of disputes "with regard to the amount of compensation."[287] The specified form of international arbitration was ad hoc UNCITRAL Rules arbitration.[288] Article 3 of the BIT was a broad MFN clause that obligated each State to apply to investments of investors of the other State treatment not less favorable than that accorded to investments of investors of third States. Plama maintained that, by operation of this clause, the dispute resolution provisions of other Bulgarian BITs, such as the one concluded with Finland in 1997, which provided for the ICSID arbitral settlement of investment disputes,[289] were imported into the Bulgaria–Cyprus BIT. The decision of the *Plama* Tribunal rejecting this argument was rendered in February 2005. Returning to basics, the Tribunal[290] explained that the BIT phenomenon did "not take away the basic prerequisite for arbitration: an agreement of the parties to arbitrate."[291] According to the Tribunal:

> ... such an agreement should be clear and unambiguous. In the framework of a BIT, the agreement to arbitrate is arrived at by the consent to arbitration that a state gives in advance in respect of investment disputes falling under the BIT, and the acceptance thereof by an investor if the latter so desires.
>
> ... Doubts as to the parties' clear and unambiguous intention can arise if the agreement to arbitrate is achieved by incorporation by reference.... A clause reading "a treatment not less favourable than that accorded to investments of investors of third states," as appears in Article 3(1) of the Bulgaria–Cyprus BIT, ... creates doubt whether the reference to the other document (in this case the other BITs concluded by Bulgaria) clearly and unambiguously includes a reference to the dispute settlement provisions contained in those BITs.[292]

The Tribunal urged that a general rule with regard to an MFN provision in a treaty should be that it "does not incorporate by reference dispute settlement provisions in whole or in part set forth in another treaty, unless the MFN provision in the basic treaty leaves no doubt that the Contracting Parties intended to incorporate them."[293]

As the MFN provision of the Bulgaria–Cyprus BIT created doubt on this score, the Tribunal ruled that the claimant could not rely on the provision to import the dispute settlement provisions of other Bulgarian BITs. Commenting mordantly on the *Maffezini* decision, the *Plama* Tribunal added that, while it was "perhaps understandable" to attempt "to neutralize" a provision on prior recourse to local courts that was "nonsensical from a practical point of view ... such exceptional circumstances should

[286] Agreement on Mutual Encouragement and Protection of Investments, Cyprus–Bulgaria, November 12, 1987, Art. 4(4.1), available at <http://www.unctad.org>.

[287] Ibid. [288] *See* ibid. Art. 4(3).

[289] *See* Agreement on the Promotion and Protection of Investments, Bulgaria–Finland, October 3, 1997, Art. 8(2), available at <http://www.unctad.org>.

[290] The Tribunal was composed of Carl F. Salans, Albert Jan van den Berg and V.V. Veeder. Salans, the President of the Tribunal, was founding partner of the Salans law firm in Paris and Vice Chairman of the ICC International Court of Arbitration. Van den Berg was founding partner of Hanotiau & van den Berg in Brussels and Professor of Law at Erasmus University. Veeder was a barrister at Essex Court Chambers in London.

[291] *Plama v. Bulgaria*, Decision on Jurisdiction, February 8, 2005, 13 ICSID Rep. 272, 315 (2008).

[292] Ibid. [293] Ibid. 320.

not be treated as a statement of general principle guiding future tribunals in other cases where exceptional circumstances are not present."[294]

The *Plama* Tribunal's insistence on clarity and lack of ambiguity corresponded to what it obviously saw as exorbitance in the idea put forward by the claimant that, by operation of the MFN clause, BIT arrangements on the settlement of disputes "could be replaced by a totally different dispute resolution mechanism (ICSID arbitration)."[295] Nevertheless, as expressed with such generality by the *Plama* Tribunal, its approach contrasted with the longstanding rejection at ICSID of the notion that arbitration agreements made by States should receive a narrow or restrictive interpretation.[296] Also, although remarkable, the complete replacement of one dispute settlement mechanism with another through the MFN clause certainly seemed possible under the BITs that specifically defined the ambit of the clause to encompass such mechanisms.[297] Treaties which, conversely, specifically excluded dispute settlement from the application of the MFN clause became more common in the period 2005 to 2010. For example, two of the FTAs signed by the United States in 2006 achieved in this straightforward way the exclusion that the *Plama* Tribunal thought should normally obtain.[298]

D. Provisional measures

This was a further area in which the *Maffezini* case cast a long shadow. It will be remembered from Chapter 9 that a procedural order of the Tribunal in that case boldly characterized as mandatory, arbitral provisional measures granted under Article 47 of the ICSID Convention.[299] Two years later, the Tribunal in another ICSID Convention arbitration proceeding commenced in the 1990s, *Pey Casado v. Chile*, took a similar approach in a decision on provisional measures. Referring to case law of the ICJ and Iran–U.S. Claims Tribunals, as well as the *Maffezini* order, the *Pey Casado* Tribunal[300] affirmed in its decision that a party had a legal obligation to abide by provisional measures issued by an ICSID or other international court or tribunal.[301]

Decisions in several of the cases initiated in the period 2000 to 2010 added to this consensus on the binding quality of arbitral provisional measures. The first of these decisions was issued by the Tribunal in *Tokios Tokelés v. Ukraine*, an ICSID Convention arbitration instituted pursuant to Ukraine's 1994 BIT with Lithuania. Alluding to *Maffezini* and *Pey Casado*, the *Tokios Tokelés* Tribunal observed in its decision that:

> ... according to a well-established principle laid down by the jurisprudence of ICSID tribunals, provisional measures "recommended" by an ICSID tribunal are legally compulsory; they are

[294] Ibid. [295] Ibid. 317. [296] *See* Ch. 8, section III.

[297] As noticed in the Decision on Jurisdiction in the *Maffezini* case (ICSID Case No. ARB/97/7, January 25, 2000, 5 ICSID Rep. 396, 407 (2002)), such treaties notably included BITs of the U.K.

[298] *See* United States–Peru Trade Promotion Agreement, April 12, 2006, Art. 10.4(2), note 2, available at <https://ustr.gov/trade-agreements/free-trade-agreements/peru-tpa>; United States–Colombia Trade Promotion Agreement, November 22, 2006, Art. 10.4(2), note 2, available at <https://ustr.gov/trade-agreements/free-trade-agreements/colombia-tpa>.

[299] *See* Ch. 9, text accompanying n. 217.

[300] The *Pey Casado* Tribunal then consisted of Pierre Lalive as President (*see* Ch. 8, n. 103), Mohammed Bedjaoui and Galo Leoro Franco; Bedjaouni was a past President of the ICJ and Leoro Franco a former Foreign Minister of Ecuador.

[301] *See Pey Casado v. Chile*, Decision on the Request for Provisional Measures, September 23, 2001, 6 ICSID Rep. 375, 380–382 (2004).

in effect "ordered" by the tribunal, and the parties are under a legal obligation to comply with them.[302]

This view of the authority of provisional measures under Article 47 of the ICSID Convention was also taken by tribunals in three of the proceedings instituted by foreign oil companies against Ecuador during the second half of the decade: *Occidental v. Ecuador*, *City Oriente v. Ecuador* and *Perenco v. Ecuador*. Citing the ruling in *Tokios Tokelés*, the *Occidental* Tribunal emphasized in its decision on provisional measures "that, although Article 47 of the ICSID Convention uses the word 'recommend,' the Tribunal is, in fact, empowered to *order* provisional measures."[303] In its decision, the *City Oriente* Tribunal, like the *Maffezini* Tribunal eight years earlier, pointed out that, in its Spanish version, ICSID Arbitration Rule 39(1) mentioned the "ordering" (*dictación*) of provisional measures, demonstrating that in this context the word was interchangeable with "recommend."[304] In further support of its "conclusion that the word 'recommend' is equal in value to the word 'order,'" the *City Oriente* Tribunal introduced what it described as a "teleological interpretation" of Article 47 of the ICSID Convention and Arbitration Rule 39. According to this interpretation, the goals of preserving the rights of the parties and guaranteeing the effectiveness of the award "may only be reached if the measures are binding, and they share the exact same binding nature as the final arbitral award."[305] The decision of the *Perenco* Tribunal was similar to the decision in *Pey Casado* in its reliance on the case law of the ICJ and Iran–U.S. Claims Tribunal, as well as ICSID, for the proposition that "provisional measures are tantamount to orders, and are binding on the party to which they are directed."[306] In its decision, the *Perenco* Tribunal offered a consideration resembling the "teleological" one put forward by the *City Oriente* Tribunal but focusing particularly on the situation of the State party to a proceeding. According to the *Perenco* Tribunal:

In becoming a Party to a treaty such as the ICSID Convention (plus, as in this case, a bilateral treaty for the promotion and protection of investment binding the State Parties to ICSID arbitration), a State confers upon an arbitral tribunal jurisdiction over certain claims and assumes an obligation to take whatever steps might be necessary to comply with decisions rendered by the

[302] *Tokios Tokelés v. Ukraine*, Claimant's Request for Provisional Measures (Procedural Order No. 1), July 1, 2003, 11 ICSID Rep. 310, 311–312 (2007). The Tribunal consisted initially of Prosper Weil as President, Piero Bernardini and Daniel M. Price. Weil, who later resigned, was Professor Emeritus of the University of Paris II and a former President of the World Bank Administrative Tribunal. Bernardini was Of Counsel at Ughi e Nunziante in Rome and a former Professor of Arbitration Law at Rome LUISS University. Chair of Sidley Austin's international trade and dispute resolution practice group, Price had been Principal Deputy General Counsel at the Office of the U.S. Trade Representative.

[303] *Occidental v. Ecuador*, Decision on Provisional Measures, August 17, 2007 IIC 305, para. 58 (emphasis in original). The Tribunal consisted of L. Yves Fortier as President, Brigitte Stern and David A.R. Williams. On Fortier and Stern, *see* Ch. 9, n. 203. On Stern and Williams, *see* nn. 11 and 239.

[304] *City Oriente v. Ecuador*, Decision on Provisional Measures, November 19, 2007, IIC 309 (2007), para. 52. For the similar argument of the Tribunal in the *Maffezini* case, and a criticism of the argument, *see* Ch. 9, text accompanying nn. 217 and 218. The Tribunal in the *City Oriente* case consisted of Juan Fernandez-Armesto as President, J. Christopher Thomas and Horacio A. Grigera Naón. Fernandez-Armesto was a former Chairman of the Spanish Securities and Exchange Commission and Professor of Commercial Law at Comillas University. Grigera Naón was Director of the Center on International Commercial Arbitration at American University's Washington College of Law and a former Secretary General of the International Court of Arbitration of the ICC. On Thomas, *see* n. 243.

[305] *City Oriente v. Ecuador*, Decision on Provisional Measures (n. 304) para. 52.

[306] *Perenco v. Ecuador*, Decision on Provisional Measures, May 8, 2009, IIC 375 (2009), para. 74. The President of the *Perenco* Tribunal was then Thomas H. Bingham, who had been Master of the Rolls, Lord Chief Justice and a Law Lord in the U.K. The other members of the *Perenco* Tribunal were Charles N. Brower (*see* n. 279) and J. Christopher Thomas (*see* n. 243).

> tribunal pursuant to the treaty. So long as and to the extent that the arbitration is in progress, both parties are under an international obligation to comply with whatever the tribunal issues as provisional measures for the purpose of protecting its jurisdiction and its ability, should it so decide, to grant the relief requested.[307]

For the *Perenco* Tribunal, "State Parties to the ICSID Convention thus inherently are under an international obligation to comply with provisional measures issued by an ICSID tribunal."[308]

The order in *Maffezini* dealt with a request by the respondent for provisional measures requiring the claimant to furnish security for the respondent's costs in defending the action. As explained in Chapter 9, the order rejected the request, principally because it concerned inexistent or hypothetical rights and prejudged the outcome of the case.[309] In its decision, dealing with a similar request for security for costs, the *Pey Casado* Tribunal considered that, while the absence of a provision on the subject in the ICSID Convention and Rules raised "a certain presumption" against such requests, they might be acceded to in exceptional circumstances.[310] In *Pey Casado*, however, there was no justification for granting the request, as the respondent had not established that there was an evident risk of non-payment or that the requested measures were otherwise necessary. In ten of the proceedings instituted in the period 2000–2010 there were requests for provisional measures directing a party to furnish security for the opposing party's costs. Contrasting with their boldness on the question of the binding quality of provisional measures, tribunals continued to treat such requests for security for costs cautiously; in fact, in these later proceedings, the requests were all denied. The tribunals concerned doubted that they could recommend provisional measures for the protection of such "hypothetical rights" or "mere expectations";[311] or they saw the proposed measures as prejudging the outcome of the case or possibly denying a party access to justice;[312] or they held such measures, in the absence of express authority for them in the Convention or Rules, to be available only in exceptional circumstances not present in their proceeding.[313] Several of the tribunals gave more than one of these reasons for their rejection of the request. Evidence was beginning to accumulate, however, that unsuccessful claimants did not always comply with awards of costs against them. In such cases, the amounts involved might not justify enforcement proceedings in unfamiliar venues even if the debtors and their assets could be located. But it would not be until 2014 that a tribunal would finally accede to a request for security for costs.[314]

E. Applicable law

In the many ICSID Convention cases initiated under BITs between 2000 and 2010, the arbitrators generally held international law, including the provisions of the BIT, to be applicable to the substance of the dispute (with domestic law also found to be relevant in many instances). It could hardly have been otherwise, as the claims invariably

[307] *Perenco v. Ecuador*, Decision on Provisional Measures (n. 306) para. 67. [308] Ibid.

[309] *See* Ch. 9, text accompanying nn. 219–221.

[310] *Pey Casado v. Chile*, Decision on the Request for Provisional Measures (n. 301) 395–397.

[311] *See Anderson v. Costa Rica*, Award, May 19, 2010, IIC 437 (2010), para. 9 (summarizing a November 2008 decision on the request for provisional measures).

[312] *See* ibid.

[313] *See Libananco v. Turkey*, Decision on Preliminary Issues, June 23, 2008, IIC 327 (2008), para. 57.

[314] *See* Ch. 12, section III.

asserted breaches of the BIT. This outcome was reached in different ways, however, within the framework of the choice-of-law provision of the ICSID Convention, Article 42(1).

Reference was made earlier in this section to *Siemens v. Argentina*. In that case, the BIT explicitly addressed applicable law. It directed arbitrators to decide a dispute "on the basis of this Treaty, and as the case may be, on the basis of other treaties in force between the Contracting Parties, the internal law of Contracting Party in whose territory the investment was made, including its rules of private international law, and on the general principles of international law."[315] As the *Siemens* Tribunal explained in its July 2007 award:

> By accepting the offer of Argentina [set forth in the BIT] to arbitrate disputes related to investments, Siemens agreed that this should be the law to be applied by the Tribunal. This constitutes an agreement for the purposes of the law to be applied under [the first sentence of] Article 42(1) of the Convention.[316]

But few BITs, and none of the ones underlying the other cases discussed here, had such provisions expressly designating the law to be applied by the arbitrators. In several of the cases, tribunals nevertheless found implicit agreements of the parties, falling under the first sentence of Article 42(1) of the Convention, for the application of the BIT and of general international law (as the BIT's governing law). The Tribunal in the first BIT case, *AAPL v. Sri Lanka*, discerned a tacit agreement of the parties on applicable law from their filings in the course of the arbitration.[317] Among the post-2000 cases, agreements on applicable law were more cogently inferred from the acceptance by the investor of the consent to arbitration in the BIT covering treaty claims. This was, for example, done in *ADC v. Hungary*. Article 7 of the BIT involved in that case, the treaty that Hungary made with Cyprus in 1989, provided for the arbitration of "[a]ny dispute between a Contracting Party and an investor of another Contracting Party concerning an expropriation of an investment."[318] In its October 2006 award, the *ADC* Tribunal explained that:

> ... by consenting to arbitration under Article 7 of the BIT with respect to [such a dispute] ... the Parties also consented to the applicability of the provisions of the Treaty, and in particular those set forth in Article 4 [on expropriation].... Those provisions are Treaty provisions pertaining to international law. That consent falls under the first sentence of Article 42(1) of the ICSID Convention.... The consent must also be deemed to comprise a choice for general international law, including customary international law, if and to the extent it comes into play for interpreting and applying the Treaty.[319]

The *ADC* Tribunal pointed out that this was subject to one exception, made by the BIT itself, in favor of the application of domestic law. The exception was that compensation

[315] Argentina–Germany BIT (n. 274) Art. 10(5).

[316] *Siemens v. Argentina*, Award, February 6, 2007, 14 ICSID Rep. 518, 531 (2009).

[317] *See* Ch. 8, text accompanying nn. 123 and 127. The Tribunal in the *Wena v. Egypt* case similarly inferred an agreement (albeit partial) on applicable law from the submissions of the parties during the proceeding. *See* Ch. 9, text accompanying nn. 223–226.

[318] Agreement on the Mutual Promotion and Protection of Investments, Cyprus–Hungary, May 24, 1989, reprinted in ICSID, Investment Treaties, Release 93-3 (October 1993), Art. 7(1) (Cyprus–Hungary BIT).

[319] *ADC v. Hungary*, Award, October 2, 2006, IIC 1 (2006), para. 290. The Tribunal in this case consisted of Neil Kaplan, Charles N. Brower and Albert Jan van den Berg. Kaplan, the President of the Tribunal, was a former High Court Judge for Hong Kong and former President of the Chartered Institute of Arbitrators. On Brower and van den Berg, *see* nn. 279 and 290.

for expropriation could be calculated in accordance with the law of the expropriating State.[320]

The consent clause of BITs involved in many of the post-2000 cases were more broadly drawn than the clause of the BIT in *ADC*, and instead covered "any" or all disputes concerning qualified investments. The BIT underlying *SGS v. Pakistan*, it will be recalled, had such broad consent clause; and, as will also be remembered, the Tribunal in that case rightly concluded that if such a clause related "to any dispute at all between and investor and a Contracting Party, it must comprehend disputes constituted by claimed violations of BIT provisions establishing substantive standards of treatment by one Contracting Party of investors of the other Contracting Party."[321] In this connection, the *SGS* Tribunal quoted with approval the observation of the ad hoc Committee in the first annulment proceeding in *Vivendi v. Argentina* to the effect that the applicable law for determining whether there has been a breach of a BIT is international law.[322] Thus, in the typical case where the dispute concerned violations of the substantive provisions of a BIT with this type of consent clause, acceptance to arbitrate under the clause might also represent a choice for the application of the BIT and general international law.

Tribunals declined to infer agreements on applicable law in several of the other cases involving BITs lacking provisions specifically on the subject. In these cases, the tribunals fell back on the second sentence of Article 42(1) of the ICSID Convention calling for the application, in the absence of party agreement on the matter, of the law of the disputing State and such rules of international law as might be applicable. This did not, however, mean following the first ad hoc committees in *Klöckner v. Cameroon* and *Amco v. Indonesia* and applying the law of the host State first and foremost and international law only to supplement or correct the State's law[323]—an approach that would have been incongruous in a case involving treaty claims. The tribunals in these cases, instead, drew inspiration from the much later holding of the *Wena v. Egypt* ad hoc Committee, that the second sentence of Article 42(1) of the Convention "allowed for both legal orders to have a role," for "the law of the host State … [to] be applied in conjunction with international law if this is justified" or for "international law … [to] be applied by itself if the appropriate rule is found in this other ambit."[324]

The post-2000 cases in which this holding was followed notably included *CMS v. Argentina*. In its May 2005 award, the *CMS* Tribunal lauded the "more pragmatic and less doctrinaire approach" introduced by the *Wena* ad hoc Committee, "allowing for the application of both domestic law and international law if the specific facts of the dispute so justify."[325] Noting their "close interaction" and that they were "inseparable," the *CMS* Tribunal ruled that the relevant domestic legal provisions "and international law, as embodied both in the [BIT] Treaty and in customary international law" would all, "to the extent justified, be applied by the Tribunal."[326] A similar view

[320] *See ADC*, Award (n. 319). The reference was to Art. 4(1) of the Cyprus–Hungary BIT (n. 318).

[321] *SGS v. Pakistan*, Decision on Objections to Jurisdiction (n. 245) 438.

[322] *See* ibid. and, for the quoted observation of the *Vivendi v. Argentina* ad hoc Committee, text accompanying Ch. 9, n. 205.

[323] On the approach taken by the first *Klöckner* and *Amco* ad hoc Committees, *see* Ch. 8, section V.

[324] *Wena v. Egypt*, ad hoc Committee Decision, February 5, 2002, 6 ICSID Rep. 129, 138 (2004). *See further* Ch. 9, section V(D).

[325] *CMS v. Argentina*, Award, May 12, 2005, 14 ICSID Rep. 158, 176 (2009). The Tribunal in this case consisted of Francisco Orrego Vicuña (*see* Ch. 9, n. 113) as President, Francisco Rezek (*see* Ch. 9, n. 200) and Marc Lalonde. The latter had held several Cabinet positions in Liberal governments of Canada, including Minister of Finance and Minister of Energy.

[326] *CMS v. Argentina*, Award (n. 325) 176.

was subsequently taken by the tribunals in *Sempra v. Argentina* and *Enron v. Argentina*, these two tribunals concluding, in their awards rendered within a few months of each other in 2007, that under the second sentence of Article 42(1) they should apply both Argentine law and international law to the extent pertinent to the decision of the claims presented.[327]

Several sets of modern commercial arbitration rules gave arbitrators the freedom, in the absence of party stipulation on the matter, to select the applicable law without referring to a choice-of-law rule (the so-called *voie directe*).[328] Following *Wena*, the tribunals in *CMS*, *Sempra* and similar cases seemed to see the second sentence of Article 42(1) of the ICSID Convention as allowing a similar freedom. The interpretation was much as if the sentence provided, as did its precursors in the 1962 Working Paper and 1963 Preliminary Draft of the Convention, that the tribunal was to apply "such rules of law, whether national or international, as it shall determine to be applicable."[329] In the preparation of the Convention, however, that approach was rejected in favor of one calling for national law (specifically, host State law) and international law to be applied cumulatively rather than as alternatives.[330] The interpretation in *Wena*, *CMS* and similar cases was difficult to reconcile with this drafting history and the text of the second sentence of Article 42(1) requiring the application of the national law "and" applicable international law rules. Moreover, the interpretation, developed as a pragmatic solution in the context of modern BIT cases, seemed less self-evidently sensible for the setting of contract claims uppermost in the minds of the drafters in the mid-1960s. All this seemed to testify to the wisdom, in investment treaty cases, of situating applicable law where possible under the first sentence of Article 42(1).

F. Annulment decisions

Awards were rendered in 19 of the Additional Facility cases and 135 of the ICSID Convention cases launched between 2000 and 2010. Annulment of just three of the Additional Facility awards was sought from a court at the place of arbitration.[331] By contrast, annulment proceedings were instituted under Article 52 of the ICSID Convention in 63, nearly half, of the Convention cases. The danger that Ibrahim Shihata warned against in the late 1980s, of "parties dissatisfied with awards regularly seek[ing] annulment"[332] of such awards, seemed to have materialized.

On the other hand, the success rate of applications for annulment was low indeed: only six of the 63 cases had led to total or partial annulments by June 30,

[327] *See Enron v. Argentina*, Award, May 22, 2007, IIC 292 (2007), para. 209; *Sempra v. Argentina*, Award, September 28, 2007, IIC 304 (2007), paras. 236 and 240. Like the *CMS* Tribunal (*see* n. 325), the Tribunal in the *Sempra* case had Francisco Orrego Vicuña as its President and Marc Lalonde as a co-arbitrator. The third arbitrator was Sandra Morelli Rico, who had been General Counsel of the National Federation of Coffee Growers of Colombia. On the composition of the *Enron* Tribunal, which also included Francisco Orrego Vicuña as President, *see* n. 201.

[328] *See* E. Gaillard and J. Savage (eds.), *Fouchard Gaillard Goldman on International Commercial Arbitration* 876 (1999).

[329] *See* Ch. 3, text accompanying n. 80.

[330] *See* Ch. 4, n. 151 and accompanying text; Ch. 5, nn. 141–145 and accompanying text.

[331] The Ontario Superior Court of Justice in *Cargill v. Mexico* and *Mobil Investments v. Canada* and the Paris Court of Appeal in *Gold Reserve v. Venezuela*. Mexico's application to set aside the award in the first case was dismissed by the Ontario court. The set aside proceeding in the second case was still pending at June 30, 2015. In the third case, following Venezuela's application for annulment, Gold Reserve successfully cross-applied to the Paris Court for enforcement of the award. The case was ultimately settled by the parties.

[332] For full quotation and citation, *see* Ch. 8, n. 157 and accompanying text.

2015. The six cases included three involving Argentina—*CMS v. Argentina*, *Sempra v. Argentina* and *Enron v. Argentina*.[333] In another 29 of the 63 cases, the annulment applications had been dismissed in their entirety and in a further 15 the annulment proceedings had been discontinued. (In the remaining 13 cases, the annulment proceedings were still pending at June 30, 2015.)

However, the decisions to annul, especially those in the three cases involving Argentina, were controversial.[334] These were among the many cases brought to ICSID in the wake of the financial crisis of the early years of the twenty-first century. In the context of Argentina's privatization program for the energy sector in the 1990s, the claimants, U.S.-based TNCs, had acquired shareholdings in Argentine gas transportation and distribution companies. Under the privatization program, tariffs of the companies were to be calculated in U.S. dollars and expressed in Argentine pesos at the prevailing exchange rate. The tariffs were also to be adjusted semiannually in accordance with the U.S. Producer Price Index (PPI). In 2001, as its financial crisis took hold, Argentina suspended the right of the companies to adjust their tariffs on the basis of the PPI. The following year, Argentina terminated the PPI adjustment of tariffs as well as their calculation in U.S. dollars. CMS, Sempra and Enron then resorted to ICSID Convention arbitration pursuant to the 1991 BIT between Argentina and the United States, maintaining that the crisis measures of Argentina infringed protections owed to them under various provisions of the BIT, including those on expropriation, fair and equitable treatment and the observance of obligations.[335]

Before similarly composed tribunals,[336] Argentina contended that it should be exempted from liability on the basis of a state of necessity or emergency. In this connection, Article XI of the BIT stipulated that the treaty would not preclude either State from applying measures necessary for the maintenance of public order or the protection of its essential security interests. Customary international law, as reflected in Article 25 of the ILC Articles on State Responsibility,[337] set forth strict requirements for the invocation of a state of necessity, such as that the otherwise wrongful act would have to be "the only way" for the State to safeguard an essential interest against grave and imminent peril.[338] For the tribunals, those requirements defined conditions for the operation of Article XI of the BIT; and since, in the estimation of the tribunals, the

[333] The three other cases with annulments were *MHS v. Malaysia*, *Helnan v. Egypt* and *Fraport v. Philippines*. The annulment decision in *MHS* (n. 227) is discussed in the text accompanying nn. 223–231. In *Helnan*, the decision (ICSID Case No. ARB/05/19, June 14, 2010, IIC 440 (2010)) annulled a finding on liability based on the claimant's failure to pursue local remedies, the ad hoc committee viewing this as an excess of powers. In *Fraport*, the ad hoc Committee decision (ICSID Case No. ARB/11/12, December 10, 2010, IIC 478 (2010)) annulled the award as a whole for breach of a fundamental procedural rule in view of a failure to reopen the proceeding for submissions by the parties on evidence tendered to the tribunal after the closure of the proceeding.

[334] *See, e.g.*, C. Schreuer, From ICSID Annulment to Appeal: Half Way Down to the Slippery Slope, 10 Law and Practice of International Tribunals 211 (2011); J. Crook, Case Summary [on CMS v. Argentina annulment decision], 22 ICSID Rev.—FILJ 455 (2007); P. Nair and C. Ludwig, ICSID Annulment Awards: The Fourth Generation, 5(5) Global Arbitration Review, October 28, 2010; P. Maslo, Are the ICSID Rules Losing Their Appeal? Annulment Committee Decisions Make ICSID Rules a Less Attractive Choice for Resolving Treaty-Based Investor–State Disputes, 54 Va. J. Int'l L. 1 (2014).

[335] *See* Treaty Concerning the Reciprocal Encouragement and Protection of Investment, Argentina–United States, November 14, 1991, reprinted in ICSID, Investment Treaties Release 2006-2 (June 2006), Arts. II(2)(a), II(2)(c) and IV(1).

[336] *See* nn. 325 and 327.

[337] Reprinted in J. Crawford, *The International Law Commission's Articles on State Responsibility: Introduction, Text and Commentaries* 61 (2002) (ILC Articles on State Responsibility).

[338] *See* ibid. Art. 25(1)(a).

requirements were not met, Argentina could not escape liability on the basis of a state of necessity.[339] Finding that Argentina had violated the fair and equitable treatment and observance of obligations provisions of the BIT, the tribunals ordered Argentina in each case to pay compensation of over US$100 million.[340]

In the first of the ensuing annulment proceedings, in *CMS*, the ad hoc Committee[341] decided on only a partial annulment, of the award's observance of obligations finding, allowing the overall award to stand.[342] The *CMS* ad hoc Committee decision was more noteworthy for its harsh strictures against the award's approach to the plea of necessity. For the Committee, the approach of "assimilat[ing] the conditions necessary for the implementation of Article XI of the BIT to those concerning the existence of the state of necessity under customary international laws" entailed more than one "manifest error of law."[343] The Tribunal, said the Committee, applied the law "cryptically and defectively."[344] Having thus rebuked the award, however, the Committee explained that it could do nothing more about these shortcomings, since only failure to apply the law, as distinct from error in its application, could lead to annulment.[345]

In their decisions, the *Sempra* and *Enron* ad hoc committees[346] went further, concluding that on the plea of necessity, the arbitrators had failed to apply the applicable law, necessitating a total annulment of the award in *Sempra* and a near-total annulment in *Enron*.[347] However, the two committees reached these conclusions in different ways. The *Sempra* ad hoc Committee found that the arbitrators had "adopted Article 25 of the ILC Articles as the primary law to be applied, rather than Article XI of the BIT" and that the *Sempra* Tribunal thus had "in respect of Article XI of the BIT ... failed altogether to apply the applicable law and, by failing to do so, ... committed a manifest excess of powers."[348] By contrast, the *Enron* ad hoc Committee found that the arbitrators in that case had failed to apply customary international law as reflected in Article 25 of the ILC Articles, specifically in regard to the requirements of Article 25 for invoking a state of necessity. The ad hoc Committee considered that on this issue the *Enron* Tribunal had "instead applied an expert opinion" submitted by the

339 *See CMS v. Argentina*, Award (n. 325) 212–213; *Sempra v. Argentina*, Award (n. 327) para. 388; *Enron v. Argentina*, Award (n. 327) para. 313.

340 The amounts awarded were US$133.2 million plus interest in *CMS v. Argentina*, US$128.3 million plus interest in *Sempra v. Argentina* and US$106.2 million plus interest in *Enron v. Argentina*.

341 Composed of Gilbert Guillaume as President, James R. Crawford and Nabil Elaraby. Guillaume was a past President of the ICJ. Before becoming a member of the ICJ, he had been Director of Legal Affairs at the French Foreign Ministry. On Crawford, *see* Ch. 9, n. 203. Elaraby was a member of the ICJ and former Permanent Representative of Egypt to the United Nations.

342 *See CMS v. Argentina*, Decision of the ad hoc Committee on the Application for Annulment of the Argentine Republic, September 25, 2007, 14 ICSID Rep. 251, 269 (2009).

343 Ibid. 274–275. 344 Ibid. 276. 345 Ibid. 275–276.

346 The ad hoc Committee in *Sempra* consisted of Christer Söderlund as President, David A.O. Edward and Andreas Jacovides. Söderlund was a lawyer with the Vinge law firm in Stockholm and a member of the Board of Directors of the SCC Arbitration Institute. Edward was a former member of the European Court of Justice. Jacovides was a former Ambassador of Cyprus to the U.S. and a former member of the ILC. The President of the ad hoc Committee in *Enron* was Gavan Griffith. Its other members were Patrick L. Robinson and Per Tresselt. Griffith was a former Solicitor-General of Australia, Robinson was a member of the International Criminal Tribunal for the Former Yugoslavia and Tresselt a member of the Court of Justice of the European Free Trade Association.

347 *See Sempra v. Argentina*, Decision on the Argentine Republic's Application for Annulment of the Award, June 29, 2010, IIC 438 (2010), para. 229; *Enron v. Argentina*, Decision on Application for Annulment, July 30, 2010, IIC 441 (2010), operative part. The latter decision annulled the award's rulings on fair and equitable treatment, observance of obligations and damages.

348 *Sempra v. Argentina*, Decision on the Argentine Republic's Application for Annulment (n. 347) paras. 165 and 208.

claimants, in which an economist had identified alternative ways of dealing with the crisis.[349]

The three ad hoc committee decisions were convincingly criticized for overstepping the bounds of the annulment function under the ICSID Convention. Thus, the *CMS* ad hoc Committee, while concluding that it could not remedy even manifestly wrong applications of the law still found scope to "scold" the arbitrators and "press its understanding" of the principles involved "with the clear intention of influencing other pending cases."[350] The *Sempra* decision suggested that "despite protestations to the contrary, the ad hoc Committee … abandoned the distinction between a failure to apply the proper law and an error in the application of the law,"[351] equating a failure to apply one norm of the law with its non-application as a whole. The ad hoc Committee decision in *Enron* likewise "confirm[ed] the impression that the distinction between non-application and erroneous application of the proper law [was] being eroded,"[352] the Committee having had "no problem with the Tribunal's reliance on Article 25 of the ILC Articles but [taking] issue with the way the Tribunal had interpreted that provision."[353]

G. Enforcement of awards

In the majority of the annulment proceedings referred to in section IV(F), the applicants for annulment sought to have enforcement of the award stayed for the duration of the proceeding under Article 52(5) of the Convention. Their requests to this effect were generally granted by the ad hoc committees though often on the condition that the applicant to provide security in favor of the award creditor, or at least an assurance regarding performance of the award should the application for annulment fail.

Ad hoc committees in some of the cases followed the example set in *Amco v. Indonesia* and conditioned continuation of the stay on the applicant furnishing a bank guarantee for the amounts due under the award if not annulled.[354] Among the cases involving Argentina, it was only in *Sempra* in 2009 that the ad hoc Committee made the provision of financial security—the placing of part of the amount of the award in escrow—a condition for the continuation of the stay of enforcement.[355] There were some cases involving Argentina in which it instead proffered statements confirming its willingness to enforce the award concerned in accordance with Article 54 of the Convention.

One of these was the *CMS* case. In that case, Argentina responded to a request of the ad hoc Committee for a written assurance with a letter stating that:

> … in accordance with its obligations under the ICSID Convention, it will recognize the award rendered by the Arbitral Tribunal as binding and will enforce the pecuniary obligations imposed by that award within its territories, in the event that annulment is not granted.[356]

[349] *Enron v. Argentina*, Decision on the Argentine Republic's Application for Annulment (n. 347) para. 393.

[350] Crook (n. 334) 464. [351] Schreuer (n. 334) 219. [352] Ibid. 219–220.

[353] Ibid. 220.

[354] *See, e.g., CDC v. Seychelles*, Decision on Whether or Not to Continue Stay and Order, July 14, 2004, 11 ICSID Rep. 225, 235 (2007); *Repsol v. Ecuador*, Procedural Order No. 1, December 22, 2005, IIC 119 (2005).

[355] *See Sempra v. Argentina*, Decision on the Argentine Republic's Request for a Continued Stay of Enforcement of the Award, March 5, 2009, IIC 362 (2009); *Sempra v. Argentina*, Decision on Sempra Energy International's Request for the Termination of the Stay of Enforcement of the Award, August 7, 2009, IIC 384 (2009) (lifting the stay after Argentina failed to meet the condition for its continuation).

[356] Letter of June 12, 2006 of Argentina, as quoted in *CMS v. Argentina*, Decision on the Argentine Republic's Request for a Continued Stay of Enforcement of the Award, September 1, 2006, 14 ICSID Rep. 240, 248 (2009). *See* n. 341 for the composition of the ad hoc Committee in this case.

"Having regard to this statement," the ad hoc Committee decided in 2006 to "grant ... a stay without requesting Argentina to provide a bank guarantee."[357]

While referring to its enforcement obligations under Article 54 of the ICSID Convention, Argentina's letter in *CMS* made no mention of the State's duty under Article 53 to abide by and comply with the terms of a Convention award rendered in a dispute between it and a national of another Contracting State. Argentina expressed a view on a relationship between Articles 53 and 54 in a letter filed with the ad hoc Committee in the *Siemens v. Argentina* annulment proceeding. Submitted in the context of a request by Argentina for a continued stay of enforcement of the award in that case, the letter rejected an argument of Siemens that Article 54 "only comes into play once an award debtor has failed to comply with the obligation under Article 53 and is in default" and asserted that "an investor seeking recognition or enforcement of an ICSID award against Argentina has to follow the procedures provided for in the laws concerning the enforcement of judgments in force in Argentina."[358] Although the *Siemens* case arose under the BIT with Germany, Argentina concluded its letter by stating that "[t]he United States Government has not objected to that interpretation of the ICSID Convention." Considering that this "inaccurately characterized" its own position regarding a Contracting State's obligation to abide by and comply with adverse ICSID awards, the United States responded with an *amicus curiae* submission to the ad hoc Committee. The U.S. submission argued that:

> Article 53(1) of the ICSID Convention addresses a Contracting State party's unequivocal and unconditional obligation to "abide by and comply with the terms of the award," subject to a stay of the award pursuant to other relevant provisions of the Convention. Accordingly, Article 53(1) requires a Contracting State party against which an ICSID award has been entered to satisfy the award once it has been rendered by the Tribunal.
>
> Article 54 does not supersede or condition a Contracting State party's obligation under Article 53 in any way. Rather, Article 54 only applies after the losing State fails to pay an award pursuant to Article 53. In other words, Article 54 simply addresses the obligation of Contracting States to enforce an award in their territories—including where the losing Contracting State has not complied with its Article 53 obligations. The procedural requirements outlined in Article 54—including enforcement of an award "as if it were a final judgment of a court in that State" and execution as "governed by the laws concerning the execution of judgments in force in the State"—certainly do not allow a losing State to avoid its obligation under Article 53 to satisfy an ICSID award in full.

The annulment proceeding in *Siemens* was discontinued before the ad hoc Committee could rule on the matter. A few months after the exchanges in *Siemens*, Argentina again advanced the view that compliance with an award was subject to the creditor initiating procedures under Article 54. The view was put forward by Argentina in connection with its stay application in the *Enron v. Argentina* annulment proceeding. As summarized by the *Enron* ad hoc Committee, Argentina's position was that:

> ... Articles 53 and 54 of the ICSID Convention complement each other and have to be read in conjunction. According to Argentina, Article 53 of the ICSID Convention establishes the final and binding nature of ICSID Awards while Article 54 establishes the way in which ICSID Awards have to be complied with. Argentina submits that Article 53 of the ICSID Convention

[357] *CMS v. Argentina*, Decision on the Argentine Republic's Request for a Continued Stay of Enforcement of the Award (n. 356) 249.

[358] These and the other quotations in this paragraph are from the amicus curiae submission filed by the U.S. in the *Siemens v. Argentina* case. Dated May 1, 2008, the submission is available at <http://www.italaw.com/cases/1026>.

"does not establish an obligation of *voluntary* payment by the State." Rather, it is said that under Article 54, Argentina is required to treat an ICSID award as if it were a final judgment of a court in Argentina. This means that to receive payment, an award creditor has to comply with the same formalities applicable to final judgments of local courts.[359]

At variance with the text and drafting history of Articles 53 and 54,[360] Argentina's argument was rejected in a carefully elaborated decision of the ad hoc Committee. There was nothing, the ad hoc Committee noted, in the language of the provisions to suggest that the obligation in Article 53 had to be read as being subject to an award creditor invoking enforcement mechanisms established pursuant to Article 54. The Committee also remarked that:

> ... it would be inconsistent with the purpose of the ICSID Convention if an award creditor had to bring proceedings pursuant to national law enforcement mechanisms established under Article 54(1) as a prerequisite for compliance with the award by the award debtor. The ICSID dispute settlement mechanism was intended to be an international method of settlement, and it would run counter to this intention for compliance with a final award to be subject, ultimately, to the provisions and mechanisms of national law. The Committee considers that it would inherently undermine confidence in the ICSID system if a State against which an award has been given could make its own compliance with the award subject to the award creditor availing itself of the mechanisms under that State's national law for enforcement of final judgments of courts.[361]

Under a good faith interpretation of Article 53, the ad hoc Committee concluded, the provision imposed on Argentina, in the event the award was not annulled, an international law obligation to abide by and comply with the terms of the award, without the need for action on the part of the claims to seek enforcement under Article 54.[362] In light of this conclusion, however, Argentina had to "be given an opportunity to consider its position going forward."[363] The ad hoc Committee therefore allowed Argentina 60 days "to reconsider its position on the extent of its obligations to pay on the final award if annulment is refused." It meanwhile continued "the stay without any condition that Argentina provide security."[364] Apparently, however, Argentina did not avail itself of this opportunity to reconsider its position.

Among cases covered by this chapter, several ad hoc committees, in later decisions, were exacting on assurances required for the continuation of stays. In *Venezuela Holdings v. Venezuela*, the ad hoc Committee made the continuation of the stay of enforcement of the award subject to the receipt from the applicant for annulment, Venezuela, of "an official undertaking in writing ... that, if the Committee decides not to annul the Award, or to annul it only in part, Venezuela will promptly comply with

[359] *Enron v. Argentina*, Decision on the Argentine Republic's Request for a Continued Stay of Enforcement of the Award, October 7, 2008, IIC 348 (2008), para. 56 (emphasis in original of quoted filing of Argentina).

[360] There was no suggestion in the preparation of the Convention that one provision should be subject to the other in this way. To the contrary, the drafters saw them as distinct from each other, with what became Art. 53 being aimed primarily at enforcement of awards against governments, and what became Art. 54 being meant mainly to facilitate enforcement of awards against investors. *See* Ch. 4, text accompanying nn. 160–164; A. Broches, Awards Rendered Pursuant to the ICSID Convention: Binding Force, Finality, Recognition, Enforcement, Execution, 2 ICSID Rev.—FILJ 287, 302 (1987).

[361] *Enron v. Argentina*, Decision on the Argentine Republic's Request for a Confirmed Stay of Enforcement of the Award (n. 359) para. 68.

[362] *See* ibid. para. 69. [363] Ibid. para. 102. [364] Ibid. paras. 102 and 103.

any or all parts of the Award that have not been annulled."[365] More specific undertakings were required four years later in *Rumeli Telekom v. Kazakhstan* and *Duke Energy v. Peru*. The ad hoc committees in those two cases made continuation of the stay of enforcement of the award subject to the provision by the State of a written assurance that, if the award were not annulled, it would be paid within 30 days after rendition of the committee's decision.[366]

[365] *Venezuela Holdings v. Venezuela*, Decision on Stay of Enforcement of the Award, September 17, 2015, para. 1.

[366] *Rumeli Telekom v. Kazakhstan*, Decision of the ad hoc Committee on the Stay of Enforcement of the Award, March 19, 2009, referred to in *Rumeli Telekom v. Kazakhstan*, Decision of the ad hoc Committee on the Stay of Enforcement, March 25, 2010, IIC 420 (2010), para. 18; *Duke Energy v. Peru*, Decision on Peru's Stay of Enforcement of the Award Request, June 23, 2009, referred to in *Duke Energy v. Peru*, ad hoc Committee Decision on Annulment, March 1, 2011, IIC 483 (2011), para. 17.

11

"The Premier International Investment Arbitration Facility in the World"

During the period covered by this chapter—January 1, 2011 to the end of ICSID's 2015 fiscal year on June 30, 2015—almost 50 percent more cases were registered at ICSID than in the previous five years. In all, from the beginning of 2011 to the end of June 2015, 194 cases were launched at the Centre, including 174 ICSID Convention arbitrations and 17 Additional Facility arbitration cases. Cases commenced in the period also included a Convention conciliation and the two first Additional Facility conciliation proceedings. In addition to these ICSID cases, the Centre accepted during the period to administer another seven investor–State proceedings conducted under the UNCITRAL Arbitration Rules.

As in the preceding decade, the great majority of the cases were brought to ICSID on the basis of the dispute settlement provisions of investment treaties, mostly BITs (in over 60 percent of the cases).[1] A significant proportion of the cases (more than 10 percent) came to ICSID under the ECT.[2] Cases submitted to the Centre pursuant to the dispute resolution clauses of investment contracts accounted for a somewhat smaller share of the total. A handful (5 percent) of the cases were initiated under dispute settlement provisions of an investment law of the host State.

Also as with the cases commenced in 2000 to 2010, the cases initiated in the next five years predominantly concerned investments in the energy and mining and industrial and trade sectors. Seventy-five different States were respondents in the 2011 to 2015 cases.[3] They included Spain, which had 17 of the ICSID Convention arbitrations brought against it. Almost all of these involved ECT claims prompted by government cuts of incentives for investments in renewable energy projects. A few further cases against Western industrial countries, among them Belgium, France, Germany, Greece and Italy, raised to some 25 the number of such cases begun between 2011 and 2015. As in earlier years, however, the respondents in the great majority of the cases were developing and transition countries. Developing States in Latin America and the Caribbean, Africa and Asia and the Pacific were respondents in almost 60 percent of the cases initiated from the start of 2011 to mid-2015. Another 30 percent of these cases involved as respondents transition countries of Eastern Europe and Central Asia. Besides Spain, individual countries most frequently named as respondents were

[1] Claimants in some of the cases invoked the dispute settlement provisions not only of BITs but also of other treaties or of investment contracts or laws of the host State. For simplicity, such cases are excluded from the proportions given in this paragraph.

[2] Other multilateral treaties invoked by claimants in the cases included the North American Free Trade Agreement, December 17, 1992, 32 ILM 289 (1993) (NAFTA) (in three cases) and the Dominican Republic–Central America–United States Free Trade Agreement, August 5, 2004 (CAFTA-DR) (in one case).

[3] The governmental party was the claimant in just one of the cases commenced in 2011 to 2015. This was *Peru v. Caraveli*, a Convention arbitration proceeding that was begun in September 2013 and discontinued three months later.

Venezuela, in 22 of the cases, Egypt in 13 and Hungary in seven. Claimant investors continued overwhelmingly to be individuals and companies from Western industrial countries, though at around 20 percent in cases registered from 2011 to 2015, the proportion of claimants from developing and transition countries was about double the proportion in cases registered from 2000 to 2010.

By the close of fiscal year 2015, the sole ICSID Convention conciliation case and one of the two ICSID Additional Facility conciliation proceedings had been concluded.[4] Nineteen of the arbitration cases had been settled by the parties or otherwise discontinued before the rendition of an award. Awards embodying settlement agreements had been issued in another three of the arbitration cases.[5] A further 24 of the arbitration cases had given rise to awards; as will be seen, most of these awards dismissed the claims concerned. At June 30, 2015, annulment proceedings were pending in respect of two of these awards. The remaining cases commenced since the start of 2011 were also still pending at June 30, 2015. They represented more than a fourth of the 525 cases registered by ICSID since its inception. Of these 525 cases, almost three-quarters had arisen under investment treaties.[6] Investment treaty arbitration cases filed with the Centre pursuant to the ICSID Convention or Additional Facility Rules accounted, in turn, for over 60 percent of all investor–State arbitrations initiated under investment treaties.[7] At least as regards this category of case, the Centre could rightly claim to have become "the premier international investment arbitration facility in the world."[8]

The booming caseload was handled by a flourishing ICSID organization. Some of the main changes within it are reviewed in section I of this chapter. Among ICSID Convention and Additional Facility arbitration proceedings launched during 2011–2015, there were notable new trends in the appointment of arbitrators and in dealing with proposals for their disqualification. The trends are examined in section II. As indicated above, claimants did not generally fare well in the first arbitration cases of the period that gave rise to awards. An overview of these awards is provided in section III. World foreign direct investment (FDI) flows averaged US$1.5 trillion annually in 2011 to 2015, reaching, in 2015, their highest level since the financial crisis of 2008 and 2009.[9] During the period, the number of investment treaties continued to rise, amounting to some 3,200 in 2015.[10] Of those treaties, over 2,900 were BITs (as compared with 2,600 in 2008).[11] Massive levels of foreign investment and a still-growing network of treaties typically providing for resolution of investment disputes under ICSID's auspices seemed to assure sustained demand for the services of the Centre as it entered its second half-century. Inevitably, ICSID would face challenges in maintaining its pre-eminence in the field. Several such challenges emerged in the period 2011 to 2015. They are the subject of section IV.

[4] The concluded Convention conciliation case was *RSM v. Cameroon* and the concluded Additional Facility conciliation was *Equatorial Guinea v. CMS*. The Additional Facility conciliation case still pending at June 30, 2015 was *Hess v. Equatorial Guinea*. (Additional Facility conciliation was employed in the second and third cases as Equatorial Guinea was not a party to the ICSID Convention.)

[5] *Türkiye Petrolleri v. Kazakhstan, Isolux v. Peru* and *Slovak Gas v. Slovak Republic*.

[6] *See* ICSID, The ICSID Caseload—Statistics (Issue 2015-2) chart 4.

[7] *See* UNCTAD, IIA Issues Note, No. 2 (June 2016) 4. Most of the rest of the arbitrations were UNCITRAL Arbitration Rules cases and cases before the SCC Arbitration Institute.

[8] ICSID 2015 Ann. Rep. 5. The phrase is also used in M. Kinnear, Preface, in M. Kinnear and others (eds.), *Building International Investment Law: The First 50 Years of ICSID* 8 (2016).

[9] UNCTAD, World Investment Report 2016, at 2 and Annex, table 1.

[10] *See* UNCTAD, IIA Issue Note, No. 1 (March 2016) 4.

[11] *See* ibid.

I. Institutional developments

A. Participation in the Convention

Participation in the ICSID Convention grew briskly in the period from January 1, 2011 to June 30, 2015. Six countries became Contracting States during that period. The new Contracting States included the world's second-largest country, Canada, and one of the smallest, San Marino.[12] Venezuela became the third country (after Bolivia and Ecuador) to withdraw from participation in the Convention.[13] In spite of the withdrawal, the total number of Contracting States came to 150 in 2014 and reached 151 the following year.

B. The Administrative Council

As noted in Chapter 7, the Administrative Council held its annual meetings in one session together with the joint annual meetings of the Governors of the World Bank and IMF from 1988 until the practice was interrupted in 2010.[14] Placed on the agenda for the 2010 Council meeting was an item that necessitated a further, separate session of the Council later in the day. The agenda item, added by Argentina in the wake of the rejection of its application for annulment of an award rendered against it (in the second *Vivendi v. Argentina* arbitration[15]), called for discussion of the procedure followed in that case, the role of the Secretariat in the proceedings and the appointment of arbitrators. Comments made by the Argentine delegate in these respects received scant support in the ensuing brief discussion. The representative of a second Contracting State observed that proposals for reform should not "be used as a means of reopening individual cases or seeking to reverse decisions."[16] The only other delegate to speak affirmed her country's "confidence in ICSID" and observed that "ICSID's existing procedures [were] the only framework within which ICSID decisions and awards should be challenged."[17]

A year later, there again had to be a separate session of the Administrative Council to consider an item placed on the 2011 annual meeting agenda by the Philippines following the annulment of an award rendered in its favor (in *Fraport v. Philippines*[18]). The agenda item envisaged addressing the possible issuance of guidelines on the implementation of the annulment provisions of the ICSID Convention. At the session, a delegate from the Philippines suggested that the Secretary-General of the Centre "conduct a thorough review of all annulment decisions" after which a "task force could propose guidelines, if warranted."[19] There being no other Contracting State

[12] The other new Contracting States were Moldova, Montenegro, Sao Tome and Principe and South Sudan.

[13] Venezuela's withdrawal, notified to the World Bank on January 24, 2012, took effect on July 25, 2012 in accordance with Art. 71 of the ICSID Convention. On the earlier withdrawals, *see* Ch. 10, nn. 9–12 and accompanying text.

[14] *Cf.* Ch. 7, n. 35 and accompanying text.

[15] *See Vivendi v. Argentina*, Decision on Argentina's Request for Annulment of the Award, August 10, 2010, IIC 446 (2010).

[16] Summary Proceedings: Forty-Fourth Annual Meeting of Administrative Council, October 8, 2010, para. 53.

[17] Ibid. paras. 65 and 71.

[18] *See Fraport v. Philippines*, Decision on Application for Annulment, December 23, 2010, IIC 478 (2010).

[19] Summary Proceedings of the Forty-Fifth Annual Meeting of the Administrative Council, September 23, 2011, para. 50.

representatives wishing to speak, the session was closed after the Secretary-General undertook to prepare the requested review and submit it to the Council. The eventual outcome was a background paper on the operation of the annulment remedy over the years. The Secretariat transmitted the paper to the members of the Administrative Council on August 10, 2012 and posted it on the website of the Centre a week later.[20] The carefully neutral but in-depth paper was widely praised for helping to improve understanding of the remedy. It clearly was judged that follow-up guidelines would not be "warranted."

By the time of the issuance of the background paper, Jim Yong Kim had succeeded Robert Zoellick as President of the World Bank and hence as Chairman of the Administrative Council of ICSID.[21] Under Kim's chairmanship, the Administrative Council resumed, for the rest of the period covered by this chapter, having its annual meetings merged entirely with those of the World Bank and IMF Governors.

C. The Secretariat

The number of cases under administration at ICSID during fiscal year 2015 surpassed 240. In more than 80 of these cases, the proceedings were being conducted in two of the Centre's official languages.[22] Sixty in-person sessions and hearings were held in the cases during the fiscal year, most of them at the World Bank's headquarters in Washington, D.C., or at its office in Paris (another approximately 70 sessions and hearings were held by telephone or videoconference).[23]

The demands on the Centre associated with its administration of the unprecedented number of pending cases were met by an enlarged and re-organized Secretariat. Under ICSID's first full-time Secretary-General, Meg Kinnear, the number of staff of the Secretariat rose from 35 in 2010 (the first full year of Kinnear's tenure) to 55 by mid-2015. Two-thirds of these were lawyers and paralegals. The staff were organized into five teams: three case management teams (corresponding to the three official languages of the Centre), an institutional affairs team and a general administration and financial management team. Each team was headed by a senior lawyer, except for the general administration and financial management team led by a senior administrative officer.

Some basic case administration indicators reflected the strengthened staffing and organization of the Centre: by 2014, the time taken to process requests for arbitration had been reduced a further 50 percent, to about 20 days;[24] the Centre was complying with requests that it appoint arbitrators within around 50 days,[25] a longer time frame than the 30 days envisaged by the Arbitration Rules[26] but shorter than at some

20 *See* ICSID News Release, Background Paper on Annulment by the ICSID Secretariat Provided to Contracting States, August 15, 2012.

21 Before joining the Bank, Kim had been President of Dartmouth College in New Hampshire. He was a co-founder of Partners in Health, a non-profit organization delivering health care to poor communities and a former Director of the HIV/AIDS Department of the World Health Organization.

22 *See* ICSID 2015 Ann. Rep. 32. It will be recalled that the Administrative and Financial Regulations of the Centre, reprinted in Doc. ICSID/15, ICSID Convention, Regulations and Rules (April 2006) designated (reg. 34) English, French and Spanish as the official languages of ICSID. Most of the bilingual proceedings referred to in the text involved Spain and Latin American parties and were being conducted in English and Spanish.

23 *Cf.* ICSID 2015 Ann. Rep. 32.

24 *See* ICSID 2014 Ann. Rep. 19.

25 *See* ibid. 20.

26 *See* ICSID Arbitration Rules, as amended, September 26, 1984, reprinted in Doc. ICSID/15, ICSID Basic Documents (January 1985), Rule 4(4).

points in the previous decade; and the average duration of arbitration proceedings commenced and concluded in the 2011 to 2015 period was just under two years, as compared with two and a half years for the 2000 to 2010 cases.[27]

Outreach and training activities of the Secretariat included the continuation of a series of primer courses on ICSID, started in 2010 and taught by staff at developing country venues in particular. A notable new publication activity, also commenced in 2010, was the Secretariat's production of the biannual compilation, *The ICSID Caseload—The Statistics.* From 2011, the *ICSID Review—Foreign Investment Law Journal* was published in print and electronic form by Oxford University Press.[28] The following year, the journal was restructured; and in 2013 it became a triannual publication (having up until then been published semiannually). An important development was the launch, at the end of 2014, of a new website with greater content and enhanced search capabilities.

The expansion of the Secretariat required significant increases of the Centre's administrative budget. It rose from US$5.6 million in 2011 to US$8.5 million in 2015.[29] The World Bank continued throughout to support the budget—but not, of course, to subsidize it entirely as the Bank had done up until 2005.[30] Thus, in 2015, the Bank contributed US$2.9 million or around 35 percent of the budget, the rest coming from lodging fees and annual administrative charges levied in the cases. With a view to reducing further ICSID's dependence on the Bank, the annual administrative charge for pending cases was increased from US$20,000 to US$32,000 at the beginning of 2013.[31] On the other hand, ICSID had a year earlier stopped charging parties a fee, first levied in 1985 and reintroduced in 2005, for legal staff to attend hearings outside Washington, D.C. As reintroduced in 2005, this "attendance fee" was US$1,500 per day of hearings, or half the usual daily fee of arbitrators for their attendance at hearings.[32] With looming staff shortages in 2005, a purpose of the reinstated attendance fee was to facilitate payment for services of temporary tribunal secretaries resident in venues away from headquarters, in particular seconded personnel of cooperating arbitration institutions in such venues.[33] The anticipated understaffing having been averted in the ensuing decade, the fee lost this rationale.

Meg Kinnear was first elected Secretary-General of the Centre in February 2009.[34] In July 2014, when she was nearing completion of her first six years in office, the Chairman of the Administrative Council informed the Council of his plan to nominate her for re-election for another six-year term. Receiving and acting upon the nomination

[27] The figure for 2011 to 2015 cases is calculated in the same way as the average for 2000 to 2010. *See* Ch. 10, n. 141.

[28] The journal had previously been published for ICSID by Johns Hopkins University Press. *See* Ch. 7, text accompanying nn. 253–256.

[29] *See* ICSID 2011 Ann. Rep. 65; ICSID 2015 Ann. Rep. 72.

[30] On the shift toward greater financial self-reliance from 2005, *see* Ch. 10, section I(B).

[31] *See* ICSID Schedule of Fees (January 1, 2013), para. 5.

[32] *See* Ch. 10, text accompanying n. 49.

[33] ICSID Administrative and Financial Regulations (n. 22) Reg. 25 specifically allowed for the appointment of tribunal secretaries from outside the regular staff of the Centre providing that while performing the service they would nevertheless be considered members of the staff (and thus having the immunities of employees under Article 21 of the ICSID Convention). The agreements concluded by ICSID with other institutions to host proceedings under Art. 63(a) of the ICSID Convention foresaw that staff of the hosting institution might be assigned to work temporarily with the Centre. *See, e.g.*, Memorandum of General Arrangements between the Permanent Court of Arbitration and the International Centre for Settlement of Investment Disputes, reprinted in ICSID 1967/1968 Ann. Rep. 19, para. 5.

[34] *See* Ch. 10, text accompanying n. 40.

Meg Kinnear, Secretary-General of ICSID from 2009 to date.
International Centre for Settlement of Investment Disputes

at its annual meeting in October 2014, the Administrative Council re-elected Kinnear Secretary-General for this further term, extending until February 2021.[35]

D. The Panels of Conciliators and of Arbitrators

Between 2011 and 2015, nearly 80 Contracting States made designations to one or both of the Panels. In 2011, moreover, the Chairman of the Administrative Council made full use of his right to make designations, placing ten names on the Panel of Arbitrators and, for the first time at ICSID, adding a different group of ten persons to the Panel of Conciliators.[36] The designees to the Panel of Arbitrators comprised six developing country nationals and four nationals of industrial countries.[37] Three of them were women.[38] For his new designations to the Panel of Conciliators, the Chairman selected four nationals of industrial countries, four nationals of developing countries and two individuals with both industrial country and developing country nationality.[39] Having a separate set of designees to the Panel of Conciliators, who

[35] *See* Administrative Council Resolution AC(48) RES/127—Election of the Secretary-General, reprinted in ICSID 2015 Ann. Rep. 57.

[36] The previous designations of the Chairman, in 2000, were of the same ten persons to both Panels. *See* Ch. 10, n. 58 and accompanying text.

[37] There were five designees from each group of countries in 2000. *See* Ch. 10, n. 58. The designees to the Panel of Arbitrators in 2011 were Teresa Cheng (Chinese), Azzedine Kettani (Moroccan), Makhdoom Ali Khan (Pakistani), Donald M. McCrae (Canadian and New Zealander), Tinuade Oyekunle (Nigerian), Alain Pellet (French), Lucy Reed (American), Pierre Tercier (Swiss), Claus Von Wobeser (Mexican) and Eduardo Zuleta (Colombian).

[38] As compared with one, the Chairman's first woman designee to the Panels (Gabrielle Kaufmann-Kohler), in 2000.

[39] These designees to the Panel of Conciliators were Luiz Olavo Baptista (Brazilian), Lawrence Boo (Singaporean), Laurence Boulle (Australian and South African), David J.A. Cairns (British and New Zealander), Nayla Comair-Obeid (French and Lebanese), Roberto Echandi (Costa Rican), Siegfried H. Elsing (German), Anna Joubin-Bret (French), James Ogoola (Ugandan) and Jeswald W. Salacuse (American).

included persons specifically skilled in mediation, recognized the distinctiveness and potential of the conciliation mechanism which, however, continued to be underutilized at ICSID.

Despite the new designations, the Panels continued to suffer from lack of support or attention by Contracting States as a whole. Thus, of the 151 Contracting States at June 30, 2015, nearly 60 had made no, or only partial, use of their right to designate Panel members. In addition, the terms had by then expired of the designees of about 50 Contracting States. While those designees remained on the Panels pending their replacement or the renewal of their terms,[40] the expiry date of the terms of some was so far back as to call into question their availability to serve in an actual case. Notwithstanding determined efforts by the Secretariat to draw needed designations out of Contracting States, the Panels remained weaker than they should have been.[41] A consequence was that when parties invoked the appointing authority function of the Chairman of the Administrative Council, under Article 38 of the Convention, they increasingly were invited to agree on possible appointees from outside the Panel of Arbitrators, through the "ballot" procedure described in section II of this chapter.

E. Agreements with other arbitration institutions

Among the earliest of these agreements, concluded by ICSID pursuant to Article 63 of the Convention, were agreements with two arbitration centers established under the auspices of the Asian-African Legal Consultative Committee, now the Asian-African Legal Consultative Organization (AALCO). These two centers were the Regional Centres for Commercial Arbitration at Kuala Lumpur and Cairo.[42] Like the very first agreement made under Article 63, the one with the Permanent Court of Arbitration (PCA),[43] the agreements with the Kuala Lumpur and Cairo Centres were reciprocal in that they provided for the possibility of ICSID hosting proceedings of the partner institutions as well as vice versa. Also reciprocal was the agreement entered into by ICSID in 2003 with a third AALCO center, the Regional Centre for International Commercial Arbitration in Lagos, established a decade after the Kuala Lumpur and Cairo Centres.

By the end of 2010, ICSID had concluded agreements under Article 63 of the Convention with another five institutions: the Australian Commercial Disputes Centre; the Australian Centre for International Commercial Arbitration; the German Institution of Arbitration; the Gulf Cooperation Council Commercial Arbitration Centre; and the Singapore International Arbitration Centre. As explained in Chapter 9,[44] these further agreements were made non-reciprocal, providing only for the hosting of ICSID proceedings by the other institution, given the demands that ICSID's growing caseload was making on its facilities at the World Bank.

Between 2011 and 2015, ICSID concluded seven more Article 63 agreements. Two of these, however, were revised versions of the agreements made earlier with the Kuala Lumpur and Lagos AALCO Centres. Like the predecessor agreements,

[40] *See* ICSID Convention, Art. 15(3).

[41] A similar longstanding problem, again in spite of reminders from the Secretariat, was that about half of the Contracting States still had not made their designations, required by Article 54(2) of the ICSID Convention, of courts or other authorities competent to enforce Convention awards. *Cf.* Ch. 10, section I(C), last para.

[42] On the agreements with the Kuala Lumpur and Cairo centers, *see* Ch. 7, nn. 33 and 34 and accompanying text.

[43] On which *see* Ch. 6, section IV(B).

[44] *See* Ch. 9, section II(D).

these were reciprocal.[45] The five other new agreements, all non-reciprocal, were with the Bogotá Chamber of Commerce Centre for Arbitration and Conciliation; the China International Economic and Trade Arbitration Commission; the Hong Kong International Arbitration Centre; Maxwell Chambers (a dispute resolution complex in Singapore); and the Seoul International Dispute Resolution Center.

As mentioned earlier in this chapter, hearings in ICSID cases were most often held at the headquarters of the World Bank in Washington, D.C. or at its Paris office. With the new and the earlier agreements entered into under Article 63 of the Convention, an impressive array of other venues was made available to parties to ICSID proceedings: in Bahrain, Beijing, Bogotá, Cairo, Frankfurt, The Hague, Hong Kong, Kuala Lumpur, Lagos, Seoul, Singapore and Sydney.[46]

II. The appointment and disqualification of arbitrators

A. Trends in appointments

Among the 191 ICSID Convention and Additional Facility arbitrations commenced between January 1, 2011 and June 30, 2015, arbitral tribunals had been constituted in 142 by the end of the period. There was just one case with a sole arbitrator;[47] the tribunals in all of the other cases had three members. A total of 149 different individuals were appointed to serve on the 142 tribunals. As in the arbitrations begun between 2000 and 2010, 70 percent of the appointed arbitrators were nationals of industrial countries and the rest persons with developing or transition country nationality. At 7 percent, the proportion of women appointees was larger than before,[48] though still very small. Without exception, the appointees had legal backgrounds. Some were retired or serving judges or other public officials. Many were law professors. The majority, however, were private legal practitioners. About 15 percent of the arbitrators also served as counsel for parties in cases of the period. There was a similar proportion of such "double-hatting" in cases registered from 2000 to 2010. Though not insignificant in its extent, the practice was not nearly as widespread as suggested by many critics of the investor–State dispute settlement system.[49]

As can readily be inferred from a comparison of the number of tribunals with the number of different arbitrators, many of the arbitrators were appointed to more than

[45] A notable difference between the new agreements with the Kuala Lumpur and Lagos Centres and the predecessor agreements was that the new agreements provided for cooperation in disseminating and sharing information as well as hosting of arbitration proceedings.

[46] In accordance with Article 63 of the Convention, parties also could agree, and occasionally had agreed, to have hearings at non-World Bank facilities not covered by an Article 63 agreement, though under Article 63 the approval of the arbitral tribunal, after consultation with the Secretary-General, was required for the choice of venue in such cases.

[47] *IGB v. Spain*, in which the sole arbitrator appointed by the parties was Rodrigo Oreamuno (on whom *see* Ch. 9, n. 113).

[48] The corresponding figure for the 2000 to 2010 cases was 5 percent.

[49] According to one study, "[i]t appears that over 50% of ISDS [investor–State dispute settlement] arbitrators have acted as counsel for investors in other ISDS cases while it has been estimated that about 10% of ISDS arbitrators have acted as counsel for States in other cases." D. Gaukrodger and K. Gordon, Investor–State Dispute Settlement: A Scoping Paper for the Investment Policy Community, OECD Working Papers on International Investment, 2012/03, 44. On their face, however, these numbers included arbitrators in non-ICSID investor–State cases and, more importantly, arbitrators with any experience as counsel in investor–State cases, irrespective of when it might have taken place.

one of the tribunals constituted in the 2011 to 2015 cases. In all, 69 or just over 45 percent of the 149 different arbitrators received more than one of the appointments. Nationals of developing or transition countries represented 20 percent of these arbitrators with repeat appointments, as compared to 30 percent of the appointed arbitrators overall. Twenty-three of the 149 arbitrators had five or more appointments to tribunals formed in the 2011 to 2015 cases. One was appointed a remarkable 23 times in these cases.[50]

Each party appointed one arbitrator to all but five of the 141 three-member tribunals referred to above.[51] For about 60 percent of the tribunals, the presiding arbitrator was appointed by agreement of the parties or, less often (when the parties had made special provision to this effect), by the two party-appointed arbitrators. The presiding arbitrator for the remaining 40 percent of the tribunals was appointed by the Chairman of the Administrative Council, or by the Secretary-General of ICSID in the relatively small number of instances where the latter was the designated appointing authority. In comparison, the constitution of some 50 percent of the three-member tribunals constituted in the 2000 to 2010 cases required such interventions by the Chairman or Secretary-General.

The decline in the rate at which the Chairman or Secretary-General had to appoint tribunal presidents and a corresponding rise in the rate of their appointment by agreement of the parties was mainly the result of the introduction of the so-called ballot procedure in 2011. For many years before then, ICSID had encouraged parties, in appropriate cases where the assistance of the Administrative Council Chairman was sought under Article 38 of the Convention to appoint a tribunal president, to try (or try again) to agree under Article 37 on a suitable candidate from outside (or not necessarily on) the Panel of Arbitrators. From 2011, this approach was successfully systemized with the above-mentioned procedure, entailing the circulation to parties of ballots listing possible candidates on which the parties could, if so inclined, mark their agreement to a candidate. The greater frequency of appointments by party agreement attests to the success of this procedure.[52]

Where no agreement emerged from the ballot procedure, the needed appointment would, in accordance with Article 38 of the Convention, be made by the Chairman from the Panel of Arbitrators. Of the 149 appointees to the tribunals established in the 2011–2015 cases, 37 received appointments from the Chairman (or Secretary-General). Fourteen of these, or close to 40 percent, had developing or transition country nationality and 11, about 30 percent, more than one such appointment.[53] It will be

[50] This was Brigitte Stern, easily the most sought-after arbitrator in the Centre's history, with a total of 56 appointments to ICSID tribunals constituted in cases registered from the start of 2000 to mid-2015.

[51] In the five exceptions, the Chairman of the Administrative Council or the Secretary-General of ICSID had to step in to appoint an arbitrator for a respondent that failed to do so.

[52] The extent of the success is, however, a bit overstated by the numbers. In earlier days, when the Centre managed to get the parties to agree in this type of situation on the appointment of an arbitrator from outside the Panel of Arbitrators, the appointment was still formally done by the Chairman, albeit under Article 37 of the Convention rather than Article 38. *Cf.* Ch. 10, n. 59 and accompanying text. However, this had the disadvantage, among others, of occasional confusion over which of the two articles of the Convention was being applied, and hence as to the consistency of the appointment with the Convention. *See, e.g.*, G. Van Harten, *Investment Treaty Arbitration and Public Law* 171, note 86 (2007).

[53] Only three arbitrators had as many as three appointments (Yves Derains, Donald M. McRae and Eduardo Zuleta).

recalled that the corresponding percentages for the appointed arbitrators overall were 30 percent and 45 percent, respectively.[54]

B. Disqualification proposals

In the period from 2011 to mid-2015, proposals to disqualify arbitrators continued to be common in ICSID Convention and Additional Facility cases. During this period, there were disqualification proposals in some 25 of the cases, about as many as in the period 2000–2010.[55] Also as in previous years, the proposals were mostly rejected. There nevertheless was a change in the evaluation of disqualification proposals. It will be remembered from Chapter 10 that the approach that long prevailed at ICSID in this respect was that, to be sustained, a disqualification proposal had to establish facts making it "quasi-certain" or "highly probable" that the challenged arbitrator lacked the reliability for independent judgment or other quality required by Article 14(1) of the Convention.[56] The approach, centering on the provision of Article 57 of the Convention that a disqualification proposal be based on fact indicating a "manifest" lack of the required quality, stood in contrast with the more restrictive approach embodied in such other arbitration instruments as the UNCITRAL Arbitration Rules, allowing for the challenge of an arbitrator if there were circumstances giving rise to "justifiable doubts" as to the arbitrator's impartiality or independence.[57] In a series of decisions issued over a span of just five months, there was a shift in the approach at ICSID, seen by many to interpret Article 57 of the Convention as setting a standard closer to that of the UNCITRAL Rules.[58]

The first of the decisions was taken in November 2013 by the Chairman of the Administrative Council on proposals to disqualify a majority of the arbitrators in *Blue Bank v. Venezuela*. It explained that the legal standard to disqualify an arbitrator was an objective one based on a reasonable evaluation of the evidence by a third party; that it was sufficient under Article 57 of the Convention to establish an appearance of dependence or bias; and that "manifest" in Article 57 meant "evident" or "obvious" and related to the ease with which the alleged lack of required qualities could be perceived.[59] These elements were combined in the ruling of the Chairman upholding the proposal to disqualify one of the arbitrators as "a third party would find an evident or obvious appearance of lack of impartiality on a reasonable evaluation of the facts in this case."[60]

[54] Some criticisms of the patterns of these appointments of arbitrators seemed to overlook such contrasts with the patterns of the appointments overall and the fact that parties, because they had to be consulted as far as possible on the appointments, always had at least the opportunity to influence them.

[55] For a detailed account of disqualification proposals at ICSID through August 2014, *see* M. Kinnear and F. Nitschke, Disqualification of Arbitrators under the ICSID Convention and Rules, in C. Giorgetti (ed.), *Challenges and Recusals of Judges and Arbitrators in International Courts and Tribunals* 34 (2015).

[56] *See* Ch. 10, nn. 190 and 191 and accompanying text.

[57] *See* UNCITRAL Arbitration Rules (1976) Art. 10(1) and UNCITRAL Arbitration Rules (2010) Art. 12, both available at <http://www.uncitral.org/uncitral/en/uncitral_texts/arbitration/2010Arbitration_rules.html>.

[58] *See, e.g.*, K. Daele, The Standard for Disqualifying Arbitrators Finally Settled and Lowered, 29 ICSID Rev—FILJ 296 (2014); M. Lalonde, Quo Vadis Disqualification?, in M. Kinnear and others (n. 8) 641.

[59] *Blue Bank v. Venezuela*, Decision on the Parties' Proposals to Disqualify a Majority of the Tribunal, November 12, 2013, IIC 617 (2013), paras. 59–61.

[60] Ibid. para. 69. The decision of the Chairman dismissed the proposal to disqualify the other arbitrators in view of the arbitrator's earlier resignation from the tribunal.

The decision of the Chairman of the Administrative Council in *Blue Bank* was quickly followed, in December 2013 and February 2014, by decisions on three more disqualification proposals referred to the Chairman pursuant to Article 58 of the Convention. Applying the same standard as expounded in *Blue Bank*, the Chairman upheld one of those proposals and dismissed the others.[61] A month after the issuance of the last of these decisions of the Chairman, a challenge of a member of the tribunal in *Caratube v. Kazakhstan* was sustained by the two other arbitrators in a decision agreeing that an arbitrator could be disqualified if it were "demonstrated that a third party would find that there is an evident or obvious appearance of lack of impartiality or independence based on a reasonable evaluation of the facts in the … case."[62]

It must be admitted, however, that this new standard was not completely clear or easy precisely to distinguish from the one that dominated the cases before; two commentators suggested that, on close inspection, it hardly differed at all from the earlier approach.[63] A main problem might, as these commentators argued, have resulted from qualifying "appearance" in the standard by "evident or obvious."[64] But it surely was not the intention that only a blatant appearance of bias would be disqualifying. Assuming that the intention was instead to see "manifest" in Article 57 of the Convention as excluding reliance on speculation, the view taken in the 2001 challenge decision in *Vivendi v. Argentina*,[65] then a clarification to that effect might be made in an eventual re-articulation of the standard.

III. The first awards in the cases registered from 2011 to 2015

By mid-2015, these cases had given rise to 27 awards. As indicated earlier, the awards included three embodying settlement agreements.[66] This section examines the 24 further awards.[67] They comprised two rendered under the Additional Facility Rules and

[61] *See Burlington Resources v. Ecuador*, Decision on the Proposal for Disqualification of a Member of the Tribunal, December 13, 2015, IIC 620 (2013) (the decision upholding the proposal); *Repsol v. Argentina*, Decision Concerning the Proposal for Disqualification of the Majority of the Tribunal, December 13, 2013, IIC 662 (2013); *Abaclat v. Argentina*, Decision on the Proposal to Disqualify a Majority of the Tribunal, February 4, 2014, IIC 629 (2014).

[62] *Caratube v. Kazakhstan*, Decision on the Proposal for Disqualification of a Member of the Tribunal, March 20, 2014, IIC 639 (2014), para. 91.

[63] *See* B. Vasani and S. Palmer, Challenge and Disqualification of Arbitrators at ICSID: A New Dawn?, 30 ICSID Rev—FILJ 194, 202 (2015).

[64] *See* ibid. 215. [65] *See* Ch. 10, text accompanying nn. 193–196.

[66] *See* n. 5 and accompanying text.

[67] In chronological order, these were: *Arif v. Moldova*, Award, April 8, 2013, IIC 585 (2013); *Caravelí v. Peru*, Award, April 15, 2013, <http://www.italaw.com/cases/1846>; *Burimi v. Albania*, Award, May 29, 2013, IIC 593 (2013); *AHS v. Niger*, Award, July 15, 2013 (excerpts available at <icsid.worldbank.org>); *Rizvi v. Indonesia*, Award, July 16, 2013, <http://www.italaw.com/cases/1188>; *Highbury v. Venezuela*, Award, September 26, 2013, <http://www.italaw.com/cases/documents/2251>; *Tulip Real Estate v. Turkey*, Award, March 10, 2014, IIC 641 (2014); *National Gas v. Egypt*, Award, April 3, 2014, <http://www.italaw.com/cases/2494>; *Emmis v. Hungary*, Award, April 16, 2014, IIC 722 (2014); *NSP v. Venezuela*, Award, April 30, 2014, IIC 654 (2014); *SIBG v. Guinea*, Award, May 21, 2014; *Apotex v. U.S.*, Award, August 25, 2014, IIC 661 (2014); *Vigotop v. Hungary*, Award, October 1, 2014, IIC 721 (2014); *Fraport v. Phillipines*, Award, December 10, 2014, IIC 731 (2014); *Levy v. Peru*, Award, January 9, 2015, IIC 671 (2015); *OI v. Venezuela*, Award, March 10, 2015, IIC 678 (2015); *Mamidoil v. Albania*, Award, March 30, 2015, IIC 682 (2015); *Venoklim v. Venezuela*, Award, April 3, 2015, IIC 683 (2015); *Poštová Banka v. Greece*, Award, April 9, 2015, IIC 679 (2015); *Accession Mezzanine v. Hungary*, Award, April 17, 2015, <http://www.italaw.com/cases/1765>; *Ping An v. Belgium*, Award, April 30, 2015, IIC 691 (2015); *PNG Sustainable Development v. Papua New Guinea*, Award, May 5, 2015, IIC 696 (2015); *Pluspetrol v. Perupetro*, Award, May 21, 2015, <http://www.italaw.com/cases/3111>; *Gambrinus v. Venezuela*, Award, June 15, 2015 (unpublished).

22 under the Convention.[68] In two of the cases concerned,[69] jurisdiction was founded on the ICSID arbitration clause of an investment contract. The claimants in four other cases[70] invoked the disputes provision of an investment law of the host State. Jurisdiction was based in a sixth case[71] on the consent to arbitration in the investment chapter of the NAFTA.[72] The remaining 17 cases leading to awards were brought to ICSID under the investor–State dispute settlement provisions of BITs.

A. Awards upholding claims

Three of the 24 awards upheld one or more claims of the claimants. The largest of these awards was the one rendered in March 2015 in *OI v. Venezuela*, a case brought to ICSID under the Netherlands–Venezuela BIT.[73] The dispute related to Venezuela's expropriation of two plants producing glass containers owned by local subsidiaries of the Dutch-incorporated claimant. Finding that Venezuela had thereby violated guarantees of the BIT regarding expropriation and fair and equitable treatment, the award granted the claimant compensation of US$372 million plus interest.[74] The two other awards, representing only partial victories for the claimants concerned, were much smaller: one granted the claimants some US$5 million equivalent in compensation for the termination of an agreement for the operation of airport ground handling services;[75] and the second provided for the investor to receive, in consequence of a failure to accord fair and equitable treatment to one of his investments in duty-free stores, either restitution of the investment or compensation of about US$2.6 million equivalent.[76]

B. Awards dismissing claims

All of the 21 other awards dismissed in their entirety the claims of the claimants. Five of them rejected claims on their merits. These included the award rendered in March

[68] The two Additional Facility awards were made in *NSP v. Venezuela* and *Apotex v. U.S.* (n. 67), both cases initiated by Canadian claimants before Canada became an ICSID Convention Contracting State.

[69] *Caravelí v. Peru* and *Pluspetrol v. Perupetro*.

[70] *SIBG v. Guinea* (the Guinean law concerned having been its Code des Investissements, Ordonnance No. 001/PRG/87, January 3, 1987, Art. 28(2) of which provided for the possible settlement of related disputes with foreign investors by ICSID Convention arbitration); *AHS v. Niger* (in which the law invoked was Niger's Code des Investissements, Ordonnance No. 89-19, December 8, 1989 as amended through July 2, 2001, providing in its Art. 6(2) for possible recourse by foreigners to ICSID); *Venoklim v. Venezuela* (the law having been Venezuela's Law on the Promotion and Protection of Investments, Decree No. 356 of October 3, 1999, mentioning the ICSID Convention in relation to disputes of international investors); and *PNG Sustainable Development v. Papua New Guinea* (where the claimant relied on Article 39 of Papua New Guinea's Investment Promotion Act 1992, Act 1992, Act No. 8 of 1992, referring to the application to foreign investment disputes of the State's ICSID Convention implementing legislation).

[71] *Apotex v. U.S.* [72] *See* n. 2.

[73] Agreement on Encouragement and Reciprocal Protection of Investments, Netherlands–Venezuela, October 22, 1991, reprinted in ICSID, Investment Treaties, Release 92-4 (March 1993).

[74] *See OI v. Venezuela*, Award (n. 67) para. 984. The Tribunal in the case was composed of Juan Fernandez-Armesto as President, Francisco Orrego-Vicuña and Alexis Mourre. On Fernandez-Armesto and Orrego-Vicuña, *see* Ch. 10, n. 304 and Ch. 9, n. 113, respectively. Mourre was Chairman of the International Court of Arbitration of the International Chamber of Commerce.

[75] *AHS v. Niger*, Award (n. 67) para. 167.

[76] *Arif v. Moldova*, Award (n. 67) para. 633. The fair and equitable treatment obligation was contained in Art. 3 of an underlying BIT, the Accord sur l'encouragement et la protection reciproques des investissements, France–Moldova, September 8, 1997, Investment Claims BIT (IC-BIT) 271 (1997).

2014 in *Tulip Real Estate v. Turkey*. In that case, the Dutch claimant had invested in the construction of a mixed-use residential and commercial real estate development project in Istanbul. The related contract was concluded with a majority State-owned real estate development trust. Several years later, after the project had run into difficulties, the trust terminated the contract. The claimant then initiated the ICSID Convention arbitration pursuant to the Netherlands–Turkey BIT,[77] alleging that through the trust Turkey had violated the expropriation provisions of the BIT and its fair and equitable treatment, observance of undertakings and protection and security standards. In its award, the Tribunal ruled, by a majority, that the trust's actions were not attributable to the Turkish State and, unanimously, that the acts of the trust did not in any event violate the BIT.[78] The second and third awards rejected on their merits contract claims in energy sector cases involving Peru.[79] The fourth award dismissed in their entirety on the merits claims that Albania had violated the expropriation and other substantive provisions of a BIT[80] in closing, for the discharging of oil tankers, the port at which the Greek claimant had invested in building and operating an oil container terminal.[81] Lastly, the fifth award rejected on their merits some of the NAFTA investment chapter claims of Canadian pharmaceutical companies against the United States, and others of their claims on jurisdiction.[82]

The rest of the awards, 16 altogether, dismissed all of the claims on jurisdictional grounds. In several of these awards, the tribunals held that the claimants were not eligible to pursue the claims against the host State under the ICSID Convention. An example was provided by the award issued in April 2014 in *National Gas v. Egypt*. The claimant in that case was an Egyptian company mostly owned by a United Arab Emirates (UAE) company which in turn was owned by another UAE firm. National Gas concluded a concession agreement with the Egyptian General Petroleum Corporation in 1999. A dispute between them led to an arbitration before the Cairo Regional Centre for International Commercial Arbitration (CRCICA). Complaining that, "through denial of justice and abuse of process,"[83] the resulting CRCICA award had been expropriated by Egypt, National Gas instituted the ICSID Convention arbitration proceeding under the Egypt–UAE BIT.[84] The Tribunal found, however, that National Gas did not fit within the exception provided by Article 25(2)(b) of the ICSID Convention for foreign-controlled local enterprises. This was because "[i]n commercial reality, as a fact,"[85] National Gas was controlled by an individual of Egyptian (and Canadian) nationality who owned the UAE companies, described as "shell companies" in the award.[86] The award was accordingly

[77] Agreement on the Reciprocal Encouragement and Protection of Investments, Netherlands–Turkey, March 27, 1986, IC-BIT 998 (1986).

[78] *See Tulip Real Estate v. Turkey*, Award (n. 67) pt. X. The Tribunal was presided over by Gavan Griffith, on whom *see* Ch. 10, n. 346. The two other members of the Tribunal were Michael Evan Jaffre, a partner in the Washington, D.C., office of the Pillsbury law firm; and Rolf Knieper, a former professor of law at the University of Bremen.

[79] These were the awards rendered in *Caravelí v. Peru* and *Pluspetrol v. Perupetro* (*see* n. 67), cases respectively concerning the construction and operation of electricity transmission lines and royalties payable on liquefied natural gas shipments.

[80] Agreement for the Encouragement and Reciprocal Protection of Investments, Albania–Greece, August 1, 1991, reprinted in ICSID, Investment Treaties, Release 93-2 (July 1993).

[81] *See Mamidoil v. Albania*, Award (n. 67) secs. 6–8.

[82] *See Apotex v. U.S.*, Award (n. 67) pt. XI.

[83] *National Gas v. Egypt*, Award (n. 67) para. 2

[84] Signed November 11, 1999 and available (Arabic text) at <investmentpolicyhub.unctad.org/Download/TreatyFile/1121>.

[85] *National Gas v. Egypt*, Award (n. 67) para. 144.

[86] *See* ibid. para. 146.

to decline jurisdiction over the dispute.[87] Two other awards involving similarly situated companies incorporated in the host State also dismissed the claims for lack of jurisdiction.[88] A Dutch company indirectly owned by Venezuelans likewise saw its claims against Venezuela dismissed, but in that case because the investment law of the State that the claimant relied upon in bringing the case covered only foreign-controlled investors.[89]

Awards in a roughly equal number of cases declined jurisdiction because the underlying transactions were judged not to qualify for coverage by the relevant investment treaty, or the ICSID Convention, or by either. One of these was the award rendered in *Poštová Banka v. Greece*. The claimants in that case were a Slovak bank that had purchased Greek government bonds and a Cypriot company that held shares in the bank. Having experienced a significant economic downturn, Greece initiated a sovereign debt restructuring in 2012, subjecting outstanding government bonds to a "haircut." Both parties asserting claims based on the bonds, the Slovak bank and its Cypriot shareholder, initiated the ICSID Convention proceeding pursuant to the investor–State dispute settlement provisions of the BITs of their respective home countries with Greece.[90] In its award, the Tribunal[91] emphasized that the Cypriot company's protected investment was its shareholding in the bank, not the bonds belonging to the bank. The Tribunal consequently declared itself without jurisdiction over the company's claims respecting the bonds.[92] The Tribunal also dismissed the claims of the bank for lack of jurisdiction, taking the view that sovereign bonds were not investments covered by the pertinent BIT, a striking conclusion given the BIT's typically very broad definition of such investments. The definition, as in so many other BITs referred to covered investments as comprising "every kind of asset," followed by a list of examples of particular kinds of covered investments.[93] For the Tribunal, taking the introductory words "in a mere literal manner" would mean that "any asset of any nature whatsoever would qualify as an investment" under the BIT and render the list of examples "useless or meaningless."[94] Rather, the definition had to be interpreted in light of the list of particular kinds of investment, even though they themselves were very broad.[95] To

[87] *See* ibid. para. 158. The Tribunal in National Gas consisted of V.V. Veeder (*see* Ch. 10, n. 290) as President, L. Yves Fortier (*see* Ch. 9, n. 203) and Brigitte Stern (*see* Ch. 10, n. 11).

[88] These were the awards in *Burimi v. Albania*, ICSID Case No. ARB/11/18, May 23, 2013, where the company had a lottery business, and *SIBG v. Guinea* (n. 67), which concerned a beverages plant.

[89] *See Venoklim v. Venezuela*, Award (n. 67) sec. IV(e) and Venezuela's Law on the Promotion and Protection of Investments (n. 70) Art. 3(2) and 3(4). The dispute in this case concerned the alleged compulsory taking of petroleum products assets of affiliates of the claimant. An additional case that might be grouped with those in which the arbitrators found the claimants ineligible to proceed at ICSID was *Highbury v. Venezuela*, where the Tribunal was not satisfied that the Dutch and Panamanian claimants owned, through affiliated companies or directly, the gold and diamond mining concessions concerned. *See Highbury v. Venezuela*, Award (n. 67) paras. 234 and 235.

[90] Agreement for the Promotion and Reciprocal Protection of Investments, Czech and Slovak Republic, June 3, 1991, reprinted in ICSID, Investment Treaties, Release 93-2 (July 1993) Art. 10 (Czech and Slovak Republic–Greece BIT); Agreement for the Reciprocal Promotion and Protection of Investments, Cyprus–Greece, March 30, 1992, IC-BIT 1639 (1992) Art. 9.

[91] Consisting of Eduardo Zuleta as President, Brigitte Stern and John M. Townsend. A partner at Gómez-Pinzón Zuleta, a Bogotá law firm, Zuleta was Vice President of the International Chamber of Commerce International Court of Arbitration. Townsend was a partner at the Washington, D.C., office of the Hughes Hubbard law firm and a former Chairman of the Board of Directors of the American Arbitration Association. On Stern, *see* Ch. 10, n. 11.

[92] *See Poštová Banka v. Greece*, Award (n. 67) paras. 246 and 247.

[93] *See* Czech and Slovak Republic–Greece BIT (n. 90) Art. 1.

[94] *Poštová Banka v. Greece*, Award (n. 67) para. 312.

[95] Including, for instance, "movable and immovable property" and "claims to money." Czech and Slovak Republic–Greece BIT (n. 90) Art. 1(a) and 1(c).

be covered, an asset had to fit within one of the specific examples.[96] In the Tribunal's view, sovereign bonds did not correspond to any of the examples mentioned in the definition of the BIT concerned.[97] By a majority, the Tribunal added to its award the further bold observation that the bonds would not have qualified as investments under the ICSID Convention either since, in the opinion of the majority, the bonds did not meet "objective" criteria for investment under the Convention, namely a contribution to an economic operation creating value and the assumption of an operational risk (as opposed to a commercial or sovereign risk).[98]

One other of the awards rejected the claims on the grounds that the underlying transaction, a coal supply contract in that case, did not qualify as a covered investment under the BIT.[99] Many BITs restricted covered investments to those admitted in accordance with the law of the host State. Two further awards declined jurisdiction over disputes arising from investments made in contravention of local legal requirements.[100] Another of the awards dismissed the case in view of an "abusive restructuring" of the investment in order to gain ICSID jurisdiction under a BIT over a clearly foreseeable dispute.[101]

It was explained in Chapter 10 that a case registered in 2003, *ADC v. Hungary*, was brought to the Centre under the Cyprus–Hungary BIT[102] containing a consent to ICSID jurisdiction restricted to disputes "concerning an expropriation of an investment."[103] A case came to ICSID during the 2011 to 2015 period under the same BIT. This was *Vigotop v. Hungary*. The dispute was over the termination of a concession contract to construct and operate a casino. In its carefully reasoned award, the Tribunal held that there were valid contractual grounds for the termination which the claimants had thus failed to show represented an expropriation.[104] In the two other cases registered against Hungary between 2011 and 2015, ICSID jurisdiction was sought to be established under consents to arbitration in Hungarian BITs which also were restricted to expropriation disputes.[105] The awards in both of those cases,

[96] *See Poštová Banka v. Greece*, Award (n. 67) para. 316.

[97] *See* ibid. paras. 331–349. The Tribunal emphasized, however, that the list of examples in some other BITs might accommodate such bonds. *See* ibid. paras. 298–302.

[98] *See* ibid. paras. 360–371.

[99] *See NSP v. Venezuela*, Award (n. 67) paras. 79, 84, 97 and 112. As indicated in n. 68 above, this case was brought under the Additional Facility Rules (Doc. ICSID/11, April 15, 2006). In accordance with Article 2(b) of the Additional Facility Rules, they were available for certain types of cases that did not concern investments, but this was judged not to help NSP as the transaction involved had been held to fall outside the scope of the BIT containing the consent to arbitration.

[100] *See Rizvi v. Indonesia*, Award (n. 67); *Fraport v. Philippines*, Award (n. 67) paras. 467 and 468. The as-yet-unpublished award in *Gambrinus v. Venezuela* (n. 67) might also be included in this category. *See* Arbitrators in Unpublished *Gambrinus v. Venezuela* Award Dismiss Expropriation Claim After Finding that Off-Shoring of a Local Shareholding Interest Breached Local Law, Investment Arbitration Reporter, July 12, 2015.

[101] *See Levy v. Peru*, Award (n. 67) para. 195.

[102] Agreement on the Mutual Promotion and Protection of Investments, Cyprus–Hungary, May 24, 1989, reprinted in ICSID, Investment Treaties, Release 93-3 (October 1993).

[103] Ibid. Art. 7(1). *See also* Ch. 10, text accompanying nn. 318 and 319.

[104] *See Vigotop v. Hungary*, Award (n. 67) paras. 543, 630 and 634. The Tribunal was composed of Klaus Sachs, the presiding arbitrator, R. Doak Bishop and Veijo Heiskanen. Sachs was a partner in the CMS Hasche Sigle law firm in Munich and a member of the Governing Board of the International Council for Commercial Arbitration. Bishop was a partner at the Atlanta-based King & Spalding law firm and Chairman of the Institute of Transnational Arbitration. Heiskanen was a partner with the Lalive law firm in Geneva and a designee of Finland to the ICSID Panel of Arbitrators.

[105] These BITs were the Agreement for the Promotion and Reciprocal Protection of Investments, Hungary–United Kingdom, March 9, 1987, reprinted in ICSID, Investment Treaties, Release 1987-a (September 1988) (Art. 8); Agreement for the Encouragement and Reciprocal Protection of Investments, Hungary–Netherlands, September 2, 1987, IC-BIT 942 (1987) (Art. 10); and

which related to the non-renewal of radio broadcasting licenses, declined jurisdiction as the claimants had failed to show they had property rights capable of being expropriated.[106] A further award declined jurisdiction over a case brought by Chinese insurance companies against Belgium in relation to an investment in a bank on the basis that the consent to ICSID Convention arbitration in the BIT concerned[107] applied to future disputes and not also to those that, as in this case, had arisen prior to the entry into force of the BIT.[108] A final award declining jurisdiction did so because the provision of the investment law relied upon to supply the consent of the State to ICSID jurisdiction was judged by the arbitrators not in fact to embody such a consent.[109]

C. An interim assessment

As already mentioned, annulment proceedings were pending in respect of two of these awards as of June 15, 2015.[110] Proceedings to annul nine more of the Convention awards were still possible at that date insofar as the 120-day time limit for annulment applications had yet to expire in those cases. A few brief general thoughts might be hazarded in regard to the remaining 13 awards.[111]

A first thought is that the overall picture provided by these 13 awards remained bleak for claimants: just two upheld claims, one granting the claimant only about 5 percent of the sum claimed. A second point to highlight is the high proportion of cases in which claims were defeated on jurisdictional grounds. Nine of the 13 awards had this result. By comparison, fewer than a third of ICSID awards issued in the 1990s declined jurisdiction over the dispute.

Some final remarks, not offered as contrasts with the past, are to note the firm refusal of tribunals to countenance what they determined to be abuses of process and violations of local law in regard to the admission of investments and their vigilance and rigor in regard to such key concepts as investment, foreign control and the expropriation of investments.

IV. New challenges

The continued expansion of the network of investment treaties with ICSID clauses was noted at the beginning of this chapter. A number of developments in the period 2011 to 2015 indicated that the expansion would be longlasting and could indeed accelerate. Thus, the United States adopted a new model BIT in 2012, which, like its predecessor model treaties, provided for the arbitral settlement of investment disputes at ICSID.[112] Between 2008 and 2013, moreover, negotiations were launched on a Trans-Pacific

Agreement on Reciprocal Promotion and Protection of Investments, Hungary–Switzerland, October 5, 1988, IC-BIT 1572 (1988) (Art. 10).

[106] *See Emmis v. Hungary*, Award (n. 67) para. 255; *Accession Mezzanine v. Hungary*, Award (n. 67) para. 185.

[107] Agreement on the Reciprocal Promotion and Protection of Investments, BLEU–China, June 6, 2005, Art. 8, available at <investmentpolicyhub.unctad.org/Download/TreatyFile/338>.

[108] *See Ping An v. Belgium*, Award (n. 67) paras. 224–231.

[109] *See PNG Sustainable Development v. Papua New Guinea*, Award (n. 67) paras. 286 and 287.

[110] These were the awards in *Tulip Real Estate v. Turkey* and *Highbury v. Venezuela* (*see* n. 67).

[111] The awards in *Arif v. Moldova, Caravelí v. Peru, Burimi v. Albania, AHS v. Niger, Rizvi v. Indonesia, National Gas v. Egypt, Emmis v. Hungary, NSP v. Venezuela, SIBG v. Guinea, Apotex v. U.S., Vigotop v. Hungary, Fraport v. Philippines* and *Levy v. Peru* (*see* n. 67).

[112] As had been the case of U.S. model BITs since the 1992 model, the 2012 Model BIT also provided for recourse to arbitration under the UNCITRAL Rules as an alternative to ICSID Convention

Partnership (TPP) Agreement among 12 developed and developing Pacific Rim countries, on a Canada–EU Comprehensive Economic and Trade Agreement (CETA) and on an EU–United States Transatlantic Trade and Partnership (TTIP) Agreement, all free trade agreements that would also cover investment. At the start of negotiations, it seemed possible if not indeed likely that the investment provisions of the agreements would include provisions on the arbitral settlement of investment disputes.[113] The projected agreements therefore raised the prospect, not contemplated on such a large scale since the failed multilateral agreement on investment (MAI) negotiations at the OECD almost 20 years before,[114] of investor–State arbitration, and pre-eminently ICSID arbitration, becoming more significantly available for disputes arising out of investment flows between industrial countries. As in the case of the MAI, however, this contributed to intensified public controversy over investor–State arbitration in the context of investment treaties.[115] A growing sense that the system of investor–State dispute settlement suffered from "systemic deficiencies"[116] spurred a search for ways of repairing the system.[117]

An important initiative of the International Bar Association (IBA) was its elaboration of a set of Investor–State Mediation Rules.[118] Adopted by the IBA in 2012, these rules were drawn up with an eye to strengthening investor–State dispute settlement in the context, among others, of investment treaties.[119] With a modern set of mediation rules specific to investor–State disputes, wider and more effective use might be made of the opportunities such treaties afforded for parties to reach an amicable settlement of their dispute instead of referring it to arbitration. The drafters of the IBA rules were, of course, aware of the ICSID conciliation mechanisms, conciliation under the ICSID Convention and Additional Facility Rules, but saw them "as too similar to arbitration in the procedure contemplated."[120]

The transparency or openness of ICSID's operations was enhanced by the 2006 amendments of the Regulations and Rules of the Centre, described in Chapter 10.[121] These notably required ICSID to publish excerpts of the legal reasoning of awards,

or Additional Facility Rules arbitration for the resolution of investment disputes. *See* 2012 U.S. Model Bilateral Investment Treaty, Arts. 24 and 25, available at <https://ustr.gov/sites/default/files/BIT text for ACIEP Meeting.pdf>.

[113] *See, e.g.*, United States–European Union High Level Working Group on Jobs and Growth, Final Report, February 11, 2013, at 3 (referring to the envisaged TTIP as incorporating the "highest standards of protection that both sides have negotiated to date" on investment).

[114] On the MAI negotiations, *see* Ch. 9, text accompanying nn. 40–61.

[115] For example, *see* Senator Elizabeth Warren, Trans-Pacific Partnership Clause Everyone Should Oppose, Op-ed, *Washington Post*, February 25, 2015. *See also* The Arbitration Game: Governments are Souring on Treaties to Protect Foreign Investors, *The Economist*, October 11, 2014.

[116] UNCTAD, Reform of Investor–State Dispute Settlement: In Search of a Roadmap, IIA Issues Note, No. 2 (June 2013) 2.

[117] It must, however, be acknowledged that many critics focused on jettisoning the system altogether, replacing it with recourse to national courts, State-to-State dispute settlement procedures or a permanent international investment dispute court. *See, e.g.*, Alliance for Justice, Leading Scholars, Former Judges Sign Letter Opposing Investor–State Dispute Settlement, May 12, 2015, <www.afj.org>; S. Anderson and others, The New U.S. Model Bilateral Investment Treaty: A Public Interest Critique, May 9, 2012, at 2, as quoted in M. Kantor, Little Has Changed in the New U.S. Model Bilateral Investment Treaty, 27 ICSID Rev.—FILJU 335, 343 (2012), Van Harten (n. 52) 130–184.

[118] The IBA Rules for Investor–State Mediation are reprinted in 29 ICSID Rev.—FILJ (2014).

[119] A. Joubin-Bret and B. Legum, A Set of Rules Dedicated to Investor–State Mediation: The IBA Investor–State Mediation Rules, 29 ICSID Rev.—FILJ 17, 18 (2014).

[120] Ibid. 20. It will be recalled that ICSID made a similar observation with regard to its conciliation procedures in the 2004 discussion paper on possible improvements on the framework for ICSID arbitration. *See* Ch. 10, n. 98 and accompanying text.

[121] Ch. 10, section III.

even without the consent of the parties concerned, and confirmed the authority of arbitral tribunals to accept and consider amicus curiae submissions.[122] A difficulty with the last-mentioned change, that it did not cover access by intending "friends of the court" to documents filed in the proceeding,[123] was overcome, at least in one case, by an arbitral order granting such access to the third parties concerned.[124]

Following the 2006 amendments, ICSID published excerpts of awards rendered in about a dozen cases and redoubled its efforts to obtain needed consents of the parties for the publication of awards and other rulings (in particular in older cases not subject to the amended rules).[125] In addition, up until mid-2015, there were at least a half-dozen successful applications by NGOs and other third parties to file amicus curiae submissions in the cases.

As a standard-setter in this field, ICSID was however overtaken by UNCITRAL. In 2013, UNCITRAL issued its Rules on Transparency in Treaty-based Investor–State Arbitration,[126] which were said by experienced commentators to "represent a paradigm shift in arbitral assumptions, for treaty-based disputes."[127] Applicable principally to UNCITRAL Arbitration Rules proceedings initiated pursuant to investment treaties concluded after April 1, 2014, the UNCITRAL Transparency Rules provided for all of the main documents in the proceedings to be made available to the public (not nearly as extensively possible in ICSID cases without the consent of the parties), for tribunals to accept and consider submissions of third parties (as also possible in ICSID cases) and for hearings to be public (not possible in ICSID cases if objected to by either party).[128]

In March 2015, the U.N. opened for signature in Mauritius a Convention on Transparency in Treaty-based Investor–State Arbitration, its main purpose being to allow the application of the Transparency Rules to arbitration proceedings under the many investment treaties made before April 1, 2014 that provided for recourse to UNCITRAL Rules arbitration for the settlement of investment disputes.[129] The Mauritius Convention also allowed parties to provide for the application of the Transparency Rules to non-UNCITRAL Rules investor–State arbitrations (such as ICSID arbitrations) initiated pursuant to pre-April 1, 2014 investment treaties.[130]

The last, but by no means the least important, development unfolded in the context of the TTIP negotiations. The decision by ICSID to shelve its 2004 proposal to introduce an optional appeals facility[131] did not mark an end to the idea of establishing a mechanism for the appeal of awards in investment treaty cases. Provisions foreseeing the possible creation of such a mechanism went on being incorporated in treaties made

[122] These were the amendments of ICSID Arbitration Rules 48 and 37, respectively (and of the corresponding provisions of the ICSID Additional Facility Arbitration Rules, Arts. 53 and 41).

[123] On this point, *see* N. Bernasconi-Osterwalder, Transparency and Amicus Curiae, in M. Cordonier Segger and others (eds.), *ICSID Arbitrations, in Sustainable Development in World Investment Law* (2011).

[124] *See Foresti v. South Africa*, Letter Regarding Non-Disputing Parties, October 5, 2009, available at <www.italaw.com/cases/446>.

[125] *See* ICSID 2011 Ann. Rep. 42.

[126] Adopted December 16, 2013 and available at <http://www.uncitral.org/uncitral/uncitral_texts/arbitration.html> (UNCITRAL Transparency Rules).

[127] T. Landau and R. Weeramantry, A Case for Transparency in Investment Arbitration, in M. Kinnear and others (eds.), *Building International Law: The First 50 Years of ICSID* 669, 681 (2016).

[128] *See* UNCITRAL Transparency Rules (n. 126) Arts. 2–6.

[129] *See* United Nations Convention on Transparency in Treaty-based Investor–State Arbitration, March 17, 2015, Arts. 2 and 3, available at <http://www.uncitral.org/uncitral/uncitral_texts/arbitration.html> (the Mauritius Convention).

[130] *See* ibid. [131] *See* Ch. 10, section III.

by the United States.[132] Also still mooted from time to time was the idea of creating a permanent international court to decide the cases instead of relying on arbitral tribunals created for each dispute.[133]

Not long after the start of the TTIP negotiations, strong and well-organized public criticism of investment protection in general, and investor–State arbitration in particular,[134] led the European Commission to re-think its approach to the projected agreement. Elements of a "new approach" were outlined in a "concept paper" that the Trade Commissioner sent to the European Parliament in May 2015.[135] In regard to investor–State dispute settlement, these elements included providing in the TTIP (and other future EU trade and investment agreements) for the appeal of awards and for the appointment of all arbitrators from a roster pre-established by the parties to the agreement.[136] Having "a fixed list of arbitrators" would "move [the] procedures closer to a permanent court."[137] "[T]he creation of one permanent court" on a multilateral basis, "either as a self-standing international body or by embedding it into an existing multilateral organization" would be an ultimate objective for the EU.[138]

The further evolution of this approach, and how ICSID might respond to it and the challenges outlined above, are discussed in the next chapter.

[132] *See, e.g.*, Panama–United States Free Trade Agreement, June 30, 2007, Art 11.20, available at <https://ustr.gov/trade-agreements/free-trade-agreements/panama-tpa>; U.S. 2004 Model Bilateral Investment Treaty, reprinted in K. Vandevelde, U.S. International Investment Treaties 825 (2009) Art. 28(10); U.S. 2012 Model Bilateral Investment Treaty (n. 112) Art. 28(10).

[133] *See, e.g.*, Van Harten (n. 52) 180 184.

[134] A. Reinisch, The European Union and Investor–State Dispute Settlement: From Investor–State Arbitration to a Permanent Investment Court, CIGI Investor–State Arbitration Series, Paper No. 2 (March 2016).

[135] *See* C. Malmstróm, Investments in TTIP and beyond—towards an International Investment Court, Blog Post, May 5, 2015, available at <https://ec.europa.eu/commission/2014-2019/malmstrom/blog_en> and Concept Paper, Investment in TTIP and Beyond—The Path for Reform, May 2015, available at <http://trade.ec.europa.eu/doclib/docs/2015/may/tradoc_153408.PDF>.

[136] *See* Concept Paper (n. 135) 7 and 9. [137] Ibid. 11. [138] Ibid. 11–12.

12

Conclusion

This chapter offers some general observations based on the preceding history. Also considered in the chapter is how ICSID might meet the new challenges outlined in Chapter 11 regarding mediation or conciliation,[1] transparency and an appellate mechanism and permanent investment tribunal. A final section of the present chapter suggests possible changes at ICSID of rules and procedures in several other areas.

I. General observations

From its inception to June 30, 2016, ICSID had registered 570 cases, 65 percent of which had been concluded. Of the concluded cases, around a third had been amicably settled or otherwise discontinued by the parties. Among the concluded cases that gave rise to awards, about half of the cases upheld claims while the other half dismissed them.[2] Overwhelmingly, the cases were ICSID Convention arbitration proceedings, the great majority of them initiated after 2000 under the investor–State dispute settlement provisions of BITs and other investment treaties.

Systems of investment treaty arbitration are occasionally criticized for being based on private arbitration models not fashioned with investment treaties in mind. A first set of general observations is prompted by this criticism, insofar as it may be directed at ICSID Convention arbitration, as well as other forms of investment treaty arbitration. As shown in this book, the provisions of the Convention, and of its implementing Regulations and Rules, were largely based, not on private arbitration models, but on provisions of other public international law instruments—the Conventions for the Pacific Settlement of Disputes, the Statute and Rules of the ICJ, the Model Rules on Arbitral Procedure of the ILC, the Articles of Agreement, By-Laws and Loan Regulations of the IBRD and so forth.[3]

Moreover, ICSID's development was from the start connected with that of investment treaties. The Abs–Shawcross Draft Convention on Investments Abroad and the OECD Draft Conventions on the Protection of Foreign Property combined substantive standards of treatment of investment with arbitration procedures for the settlement of investor–State disputes as well as State–State disputes. In sponsoring the creation of ICSID, the World Bank in effect undertook to provide what it judged to be the more feasible, and less controversial, investor–State procedural part of such schemes.[4]

By the time ICSID was established, late in 1966, countries had started to sign BITs with provisions like those of the Abs–Shawcross and OECD Drafts except that these BITs lacked an investor–State arbitration mechanism. Now that the facilities of ICSID

[1] In the field of international commercial and investment disputes, the terms mediation and conciliation are now generally considered to be synonymous. *See* N. Blackaby and others, *Redfern and Hunter on International Arbitration* 4 (5th ed. 2009).

[2] Most of the numbers in this paragraph are from ICSID, The ICSID Caseload (Issue 2016-2) charts 2, 4, 8.

[3] *See* Ch. 4, section II; Ch. 6, section II.

[4] *See* Ch. 2, section II(C).

were available, the Centre's founding Secretary-General Aron Broches explained to delegates at the first annual meeting of the ICSID Administrative Council in 1967, their governments could repair the omission with clauses providing for ICSID arbitration in their future BITs.[5] Countries soon began to follow the suggestion, which had been reinforced with models for such BIT clauses published by the Centre in 1969.[6] Within a decade, ICSID clauses had become a standard feature of the growing network of BITs uniting the substantive and procedural elements envisaged for investment treaties in the late 1950s and early 1960s.[7]

In addition to representing one of several international arbitration initiatives of some 50 years ago, ICSID is among many institutions created in the same period, at the height of the Cold War, to help the newly independent and other developing countries meet their financing and development needs. Examples of the numerous other institutions set up for this purpose during the period are the Inter-American Development Bank, the World Bank's soft-loan affiliate IDA and, among national aid agencies, the United States Agency for International Development and the Swiss Agency for Development and Cooperation.[8] In the case of ICSID, it was foreseen that the developing countries might foster the confidence necessary to attract and retain private foreign investments by consenting to submit related disputes to the jurisdiction of the Centre, as many developing countries subsequently did in their investment contracts, laws and treaties.[9]

An obvious but seldom emphasized result that may be highlighted here is that the Centre's dispute settlement facilities have in fact been used overwhelmingly for cases involving developing countries and, since the end of the Cold War, countries in transition from Communism. The preponderance of developing country parties has not been reflected in the proportion of developing country nationals among members of ICSID arbitral tribunals. Only around a third of the arbitrators appointed in cases registered since 2000 have been from developing countries. Furthermore, very few women have been appointed to the tribunals. In large measure, parties to the proceedings have been responsible for the imbalances as most of the arbitrators have been their appointees. While improving in recent years, the proportion of developing country arbitrators appointed by the Chairman of the Administrative Council and Secretary-General of ICSID has, however, also remained low.[10] A basic problem in this respect has been the longstanding weakness of the ICSID Panel of Arbitrators, from which the Chairman must generally draw his appointees.[11] The updating in 2011 of the Chairman's designations to the Panel of Arbitrators was welcome in this context, as were renewed efforts on the part of the Secretariat to elicit more designations by Contracting States.[12]

Mention may also be made here of the differing approaches over the years of arbitral tribunals to jurisdictional issues. Broad, even generous, approaches were characteristic

[5] *See* Ch. 6, section IV. [6] *See* Ch. 7, section II. [7] *See* ibid.

[8] For further examples, *see* Ch. 2, text accompanying nn. 6–10.

[9] The extent to which this stimulated increased investment flows is probably impossible to quantify, given the multiplicity of factors involved in investment decisions. However, the majority of empirical studies undertaken since the late 1990s on the influence of BITs and other investment treaties on investment flows conclude that the treaties have had a positive impact on foreign direct investment. *See* UNCTAD, IIA Issues Note, The Impact of International Investment Treaties on Foreign Direct Investment: An Overview of Empirical Studies 1998–2014 (September 2014). A part of the impact presumably should be attributed to the ICSID clauses that have been a central feature of most investment treaties.

[10] *See* Ch. 10, section II(A) and Ch. 11, section II.

[11] *Cf.* ICSID Convention, Art. 40(1).

[12] *See* Ch. 11, section I(D) and ICSID 2015 Ann. Rep. 34.

of tribunals in ICSID's first 20 years. Thus, for example, several of them showed themselves willing to see, as proper parties, entities not specifically mentioned in the consent to arbitration but nevertheless covered by its "spirit."[13] Strikingly narrower approaches have been taken, since the late 1990s, by tribunals operating under the consent clauses of investment treaties. Illustrating these approaches are decisions of some of the tribunals distinguishing between treaty and contract claims, on the scope for importing, through the MFN clause of a BIT, all or part of the consent clause of another BIT, on covered investments, and on the eligibility of locally incorporated companies to resort to ICSID Convention arbitration.[14] Given this, it is puzzling that arbitrators in ICSID cases are commonly reproached nowadays for taking "expansive" decisions on jurisdiction.[15]

II. Meeting new challenges

A. Promoting conciliation

In designing the ICSID initiative, the World Bank decided that the Centre should not just be the "arbitration agency" discussed in various international fora at the time, but that it should also provide procedures for the conciliation of investment disputes. The Bank's experience with the resolution of such disputes in the 1950s had "indicated the value of conciliation."[16] In light of this experience, there was surprise at ICSID, after it started to receive its first cases, how little interest there seemed to be in the conciliation option.[17] Over the ensuing many years, there has been no change, with conciliation cases representing hardly more than one percent of the cumulative caseload of the Centre. Several reasons may be advanced for this, ranging from a desire of parties to engage in third-party dispute settlement procedures only if they produce a definitive outcome to "the nature of bureaucracies, governmental and corporate, to prefer to shift [to an arbitral tribunal, responsibility for the terms of settlement] rather than to assume responsibility" themselves, as they would in a conciliation.[18] However, "[t]he potential benefits of mediation and conciliation are well recognized. In many cases, assisting the parties to come to an agreed solution to their dispute may permit an otherwise productive investment relationship to continue and avoid the cost, delay and uncertainty of arbitration."[19]

The fashioning of the 2012 IBA Investor–State Mediation Rules fit well with the renewed interest of governments in providing, in view of such benefits, for the mediation of investor–State disputes arising under their investment treaties, before recourse to arbitration.[20] There already existed sets of ICSID Conciliation Rules specifically

[13] *See* Ch. 8, section III.

[14] *See* Ch. 10, section III(C) and Ch. 11, sections III(B) and III(C).

[15] *See, e.g.*, M. Sornarajah, *Resistance and Change in the International Law on Foreign Investment* 136–139 (2015).

[16] Note by Aron Broches to the Executive Directors on the Settlement of Disputes between Governments and Private Parties, August 28, 1961, at 3, reprinted in 2 *History of the ICSID Convention* 1. *See also* Ch. 2, section IV.

[17] *See* Ch. 7, n. 104 and accompanying text.

[18] S. Schwebel, Is Mediation of Foreign Investment Disputes Plausible?, 22 ICSID Rev. —FILJ 237 (2007).

[19] A. Joubin-Bret and B. Legum, A Set of Rules Dedicated to Investor–State Mediation: The IBA Investor–State Mediation Rules, 29 ICSID Rev.—FILJ 17, 19 (2014).

[20] *See* ibid. 18. The IBA Rules are reprinted in 29 ICSID Rev.—FILJ 1 (2014).

made for investor–State disputes.[21] But the IBA considered them to be "too similar to arbitration in the procedure contemplated."[22] This judgment of the IBA probably was correct, and it seemed to have been shared by ICSID itself.[23]

The question naturally may be posed, if there is growing interest in this type of procedure for the settlement of investor–State disputes, and ICSID has long offered it but in a form now considered to be "too similar to arbitration," why ICSID does not amend its Conciliation Rules to make "the procedure contemplated" correspond better to current circumstances and expectations. With almost no exceptions, the approaches of the IBA Mediation Rules would fit, in amended ICSID Conciliation Rules, within the frameworks provided by the ICSID Convention and Additional Facility Rules.[24] It would be ironic that inadequacy of the rules provided by ICSID for the purpose might otherwise, if only in small part, be responsible for continued substantial non-fulfillment of a plan entertained for ICSID by its founders.

In the meantime, as has been pointed out,[25] the IBA Mediation Rules could by party agreement be coupled with ICSID in a variety of ways, such as by ICSID's administration of procedures under the IBA Rules (just as ICSID administers UNCITRAL Arbitration Rules proceedings) or by the subjection of ICSID conciliation proceedings to the IBA Rules, to the extent consistent with the relevant ICSID framework.

B. Enhancing transparency

As a public institution, the Centre was from the beginning rightly expected to publish information, not only about its operation in general, but also on the institution, conduct and disposition of each ICSID proceeding.[26] Transparency of the proceedings was furthered by successive amendments of the Arbitration Rules first authorizing, and then requiring, the Centre to publish extracts of legal reasoning in awards even in the absence of the consent of the parties concerned.[27] The Centre still, however, may not disclose other materials from the cases without such consent or have hearings open to the public over the objection of a party.[28] In the previous edition of this book, the situation was described as positively anomalous in an institution linked to the World Bank, which had recently issued its policy of allowing access to all information in its possession, other than narrowly defined exceptions.[29] The anomaly has been

[21] The ICSID Convention Conciliation Rules, reprinted in Doc. ICSID/15, ICSID Convention, Regulations and Rules (April 2006) and the ICSID Additional Facility Conciliation, reprinted in ICSID Doc. ICSID/11, Additional Facility Rules (April 2006) (also available for non-investment disputes between States and foreign nationals).

[22] Joubin-Bret and Legum (n. 19) 20.

[23] *See* Ch. 11, n. 120.

[24] The IBA Mediation Rules (n. 20) Art. 6 allows for co-mediation, that is, for mediation by two mediators, whereas the ICSID Convention specifies (in its Art. 29) that a conciliation commission must "consist of a sole conciliator or any uneven number of conciliators." An even number of conciliators might, however, be provided for under amended Additional Facility Conciliation Rules, not subject to the provisions of the Convention.

[25] By Frauke Nitschke in The IBA's Investor–State Mediation Rules and the ICSID Dispute Settlement Framework, 29 ICSID Rev.—FILJ 112 (2014).

[26] The reference is to the provision of the Administrative and Financial Regulations, first adopted in 1967, on the maintenance by the Centre of public case registers setting forth such information on the proceedings. *See* Ch. 6, section II(A).

[27] The amendments mentioned in the text were adopted in 1984 and 2006. *See* Ch. 7, section IV and Ch. 10, section III.

[28] *See* ICSID Administrative and Finance Regulation 22 and ICSID Arbitration Rules 32 and 48, reprinted in Doc. ICSID/15 (n. 21).

[29] *See* World Bank, Policy on Access to Information, July 1, 2010.

made more glaring by the promulgation of the UNCITRAL Rules on Transparency in Treaty-based Investor–State Arbitration and the conclusion of the U.N. Convention on Transparency in Treaty-based Investor–State Arbitration.[30]

As suggested in the previous edition, ICSID could move to reverse its general rules regarding access to documents and attendance at hearings in its arbitration cases. More particularly, ICSID could amend its Regulations and Rules to provide for the publication of the principal documents generated in proceedings, unless or to the extent decided otherwise by the arbitrators, and for tribunals to have full authority to allow third parties to attend or observe hearings (eliminating a party's right to veto such attendance or observance of hearings).[31]

C. Preparing for a possible appellate mechanism and permanent investment tribunal

Early in the discussions at the World Bank on what became the ICSID Convention, the idea of having a "standing tribunal" for the settlement of investment disputes was mentioned but quickly discarded as "clearly impractical" in the context of those discussions.[32] To help foster uniformity of arbitral decisions on questions of interpretation of the ICSID Convention, proposals were made during the drafting of the Convention to allow such questions to be referred to the ICJ in contentious proceedings under what became Article 64 of the Convention, or by ICSID's invoking the advisory jurisdiction of the ICJ if the Centre became a specialized agency of the U.N. eligible to request advisory opinions from the ICJ. Those proposals also were dismissed by the drafters of the Convention (and ICSID never became a specialized agency).[33]

Concerns over the operation of the annulment remedy in the 1980s[34] led to some talk of instituting a system for the scrutiny, within ICSID, of awards before their rendition, on the model of the procedure of the ICC International Court of Arbitration for scrutinizing draft awards.[35] That possibility was not pursued for the Centre either.

Free trade agreements started to be concluded in the early 2000s with provisions referring to the possible creation of mechanisms for the appeal of investor–State awards made pursuant to the agreements.[36] ICSID considered offering a single such mechanism that parties to investment treaties could accept for ICSID and non-ICSID forms of arbitration available under their treaties. An initial suggestion was that, at least for an ICSID Convention award, the mechanism would provide for the award to be transmitted in draft to the parties, who could then, within a specified time limit, refer it to the appeal body for a ruling that would be binding on the tribunal in finalizing the award. The purpose was to avoid any inconsistency with the exemption of ICSID Convention awards from appeal, applicable only to finally rendered awards. A main drawback of the approach was that the final award rendered by the tribunal after

[30] *See* Ch. 11, text accompanying nn. 125–128.

[31] Such amendments would involve renewing the 2004 suggestion of the Secretariat regarding attendance at hearings. *See* Ch. 10, text accompanying n. 91. Any obstacle to the amendments posed by the requirement in Art. 48(5) of the ICSID Convention, for consent of the parties for any publication by ICSID of an award, could be surmounted by the consent being incorporated in amended Arbitration Rules.

[32] *See* Ch. 3, text accompanying n. 130.

[33] *See* Ch. 4, text accompanying nn. 171–173 and Ch. 1, n. 75 and accompanying text.

[34] *See* Ch. 8, section VI.

[35] For a discussion of the ICC procedure, *see* Y. Derains and E. Schwartz, *A Guide to the ICC Rules of Arbitration* 312–316 (2d ed. 2005).

[36] *See* Ch. 10, text accompanying nn. 24 and 81.

resort to the appeal body would then still be subject to annulment and the other post-award remedies of the Convention, implying a possibly long process of arbitration, appeal and annulment or other Convention remedy. Parties to ICSID Convention proceedings likely cannot opt out in advance of the Convention's post-award remedies,[37] so the problem could not have been solved by a provision to that effect in the appeal mechanism rules.

The plan having been that the appeal mechanism would be available for incorporation by interested governments into individual investment treaties, the Secretariat of the Centre decided that it would be better to offer the mechanism on the basis that the treaty incorporating the mechanism would also effect a modification of the ICSID Convention, to the extent required, as between the parties to the treaty.[38] This approach was embodied in the discussion paper issued by the Secretariat of the Centre in 2004.[39] After consultations with governments and others, the Secretariat published a follow-up working paper in 2005. It explained that:

> There was general agreement [in the consultations] that, if international appellate mechanisms were to be introduced for investment treaty arbitrations, then this might best be done through a single ICSID mechanism rather than by different mechanisms under each treaty concerned. Most, however, considered that it would be premature to attempt to establish such an ICSID mechanism, particularly in view of the difficult technical and policy issues involved.[40]

The proposal was therefore shelved at ICSID.

Against this ICSID background, on November 12, 2015, the European Commission formally proposed to the United States the inclusion in the TTIP of investor–State dispute settlement arrangements rather different from those envisaged in the Commission's "Concept Paper" of earlier the same year.[41] The November 2015 proposal[42] was for the establishment by the TTIP of an "investment court system," comprising a first instance tribunal to hear TTIP claims of investors against their host State and an appeal tribunal to hear appeals from awards of the first instance tribunal.[43] The latter would have 15 members and the appeal tribunal six.[44] Each of the tribunals would be equally composed of nationals of EU member States, nationals of the United States and nationals of third countries.[45] The presiding members of the tribunals would be drawn from the third-country nationals.[46] The first instance tribunal would ordinarily hear cases in divisions of three of its members, as would the appeal tribunals.[47]

According to the proposal of the European Commission, claims of investors could be submitted to the first instance tribunal under the ICSID Convention, ICSID Additional Facility Rules or UNCITRAL Arbitration Rules.[48] How the system would work in conjunction with the ICSID Convention in particular was not, however, clear.

[37] *Cf.* C. Schreuer and others, *The ICSID Convention: A Commentary* 918–920 (2d ed. 2009). *Cf.* also Ch. 8, n. 161.

[38] *See* Ch. 10, n. 101 for an explanation of the treaty law rule under which this might have been possible.

[39] Possible Improvements of the Framework for ICSID Arbitration: ICSID Secretariat Discussion Paper, October 22, 2004. A full description of the paper, including its suggestions for what it called an "ICSID Appeals Facility," is provided in Ch. 10, section III.

[40] Suggested Changes to the ICSID Rules and Regulations, Working Paper of the ICSID Secretariat, May 12, 2005, para. 4. For further details on this paper, *see* Ch. 10, section III.

[41] On the "concept paper," *see* Ch. 11, text accompanying nn. 134–137.

[42] *See* EU finalises proposal for investment protection and Court System for TTIP, European Commission Press Release, November 12, 2015 and attached Commission draft TTIP text, available at <http://europa.eu/rapid/press-release_IP-15-6059_en.htm> (EC Draft TTIP text).

[43] *See* EC Draft TTIP text (n. 42) Arts. 9(1) and 10(1).

[44] *See* ibid. Arts. 9(2) and 10(2).

[45] *See* ibid.

[46] *See* ibid. Arts. 9(8) and 10(6).

[47] *See* ibid. Arts. 9(6) and 10(8).

[48] *See* ibid. Art. 6(2).

Article 37(2)(a) of the Convention, regarding agreements on the number of arbitrators and the method of their appointment, is so broad and flexible that it might accommodate the "court system" proposal in these respects. In regard to the appeal mechanism, the proposal of the Commission actually was for the appeal of "provisional awards" to be finalized in light of the outcome of any appeal (or where the appeal mechanism was not activated with a certain period).[49] There might thus be no inconsistency with the ICSID Convention in this respect either, just as there would not have been under the idea, briefly described above, of providing for the review of draft awards.

There still would remain, however, the question of the continued availability of the post-award remedies of the Convention. The proposal of the European Commission was for the TTIP to specify that final awards issued under it would not be subject to any further remedy.[50] But whether, and to what extent, this might work in relation to ICSID Convention remedies in the ICSID Convention cases is highly uncertain, presenting the same difficulty as the earlier idea of having ICSID Convention awards reviewed in draft form prior to their finalization. To function as planned, the "investment court system," whether included in a TTIP or agreed, as it now has already been, for the CETA and EU–Vietnam FTA,[51] may well have to be understood, at least in this respect, as effecting an *inter se* modification of the ICSID Convention.[52]

While helping to harmonize investor–State dispute settlement jurisprudence under the respective agreements providing for it, the proposed "court system" would not have this effect more broadly because it would in each case operate only bilaterally. The proposal of the European Commission provided, however, for the system to be supplanted in relevant part "[u]pon the entry into force between the parties of an international agreement providing for a multilateral investment tribunal and/or a multilateral appellate mechanism applicable to disputes" under the TTIP or other EU trade and investment treaty.[53]

A meticulous "analysis and roadmap" for just such an international agreement was provided in a June 2016 paper written by Gabrielle Kaufmann-Kohler and Michele Potestà.[54] Prepared under the aegis of the Center for International Dispute Settlement or CIDS (a joint research center of Geneva's Graduate Institute of International and Development Studies and the University of Geneva), the paper considered and convincingly explained how the U.N. Convention on Transparency in Treaty-based Investor–State Arbitration could serve as a model for an opt-in multilateral treaty introducing a single permanent investment tribunal or single appeal mechanism (and effecting appropriate modifications to the ICSID Convention as between the parties to the treaty). In the event (unlooked-for because of the superiority of the CIDS plan) that there is not sufficient progress towards such a multilateral treaty and there

[49] *See* ibid. Art. 28(6) and 28(7). [50] *See* ibid. Art. 30(1).

[51] *See* Joint Statement, Canada–EU Comprehensive Economic and Trade Agreement (CETA), February 29, 2016 and CETA agreed text, available at <http://europa.eu/rapid/press-release_STATEMENT-16-446_en.htm>; EU–Vietnam Free Trade Agreement, agreed text as of January 2016, available at <http://trade.ec.europa.eu/doclib/press/index.cfm?id=1437>.

[52] Among its other noteworthy features specifically concerning ICSID, the CETA text designates the ICSID Secretariat as the secretariat of the investor–State dispute settlement tribunal to be established under the agreement. *See* CETA text (n. 51) Art. 8.27(16).

[53] EC Draft TTIP text (n. 42) Art. 12.

[54] G. Kaufmann-Kohler and M. Potestà, Can the Mauritius Convention serve as a model for the reform of investor–State arbitration in connection with the introduction of a permanent investment tribunal or an appeal mechanism? Analysis and roadmap, Geneva Center for International Dispute Settlement, June 3, 2016, available at <www.uncitral.org>.

nevertheless remains interest in the establishment at a multilateral level of an appeal mechanism, ICSID might consider reviving its 2004 proposal for such a mechanism.

III. Possible changes in other areas

This final section sets out changes that ICSID may wish to consider making to its rules and procedures in several other areas. The possible changes are described in no particular order of importance, except that what the author considers to be the most significant is saved for last.

As proposed in 2005, what became ICSID Arbitration Rule 41(5), on the early elimination of baseless claims, was planned to cover only claims that were manifestly frivolous as to the merits;[55] claims for which there was manifestly no jurisdiction were thought to be addressed well enough by the procedure of Article 36(3) of the Convention. As finally adopted in 2006, however, Rule 41(5) has been understood, in the published decisions of tribunals applying it, as covering both objections to jurisdiction and objections regarding the merits of claims.[56] Accommodating objections to jurisdiction under Rule 41(5) has proved to be useful, notably in allowing for the early dismissal of parts of a case, not just an entire case, for which there is manifestly no jurisdiction.[57]

Rule 41, however, still bears traces of the earlier approach of confining Rule 41(5) to objections going to the merits. There is, in particular, the contrast drawn in Rule 41(6) between a decision of the tribunal "that all claims are manifestly without legal merit" and a decision of the tribunal "that the dispute is not within the jurisdiction of the Centre or not within its own competence." Such confusing traces of the earlier approach might be eliminated in a next round of amendments of the ICSID Regulations and Rules.[58]

The overall record of compliance with ICSID arbitral awards has remained good. For a time, concerns in this regard centered on Argentina, but it has been settling its outstanding awards.[59] However, unsuccessful claimants appear to have had a less than perfect record of performing awards of costs against them. In this connection, tribunals have rarely found themselves able to order claimants to provide security for costs.[60] Such an order has been made in only one case, in 2014.[61] Given the uncertainty that tribunals have more often displayed on the point, it would seem desirable to confirm in amended Arbitration Rules that arbitrators have the power to make such orders.

[55] *See* Ch. 10, text accompanying nn. 162 and 163.

[56] *See* Ch. 10, text accompanying nn. 164 and 165.

[57] *See, e.g.*, *Emmis v. Hungary*, Decision on the Respondent's Objection under ICSID Arbitration Rule 41(5), March 11, 2013, IIC 582 (2013).

[58] The point is reinforced by Art. 29(1) of the Arbitration Rules of the Singapore International Arbitration Centre (SIAC) of 2016, available at <www.siac.org.sg>. Article 29(1), clearly influenced by ICSID Arbitration Rule 41(5), appears to reflect an understanding of the Rule 41(5) expression "manifestly without legal merit" as addressing only the substance of claims. According to Art. 29(1) of the SIAC Rules, a party may apply to the tribunal for the early dismissal of a claim on the basis that the claim "is manifestly without legal merit; or ... manifestly outside the jurisdiction of the Tribunal."

[59] *See, e.g.*, Argentina settles five investment treaty awards, Allen & Overy Publications, November 7, 2013, available at <www.allenovery.com>.

[60] *See* Ch. 10, section IV(D).

[61] In *RSM v. St. Lucia*, Decision on St. Lucia's Request for Security for Costs, August 13, 2014, IIC 655 (2014).

Due for replacement is the system of having the Secretary-General approve the consent agreement as a step distinct from the registration of a request to institute an arbitration proceeding under the Additional Facility Rules.[62] Reflecting long-forgotten hesitations about the Additional Facility, the system has come not merely to be confusing but also to obscure the role of the Secretary-General in screening requests to institute Additional Facility proceedings.[63] Similarly in need of updating are the arrangements regarding the acceptance by the Secretary-General of requests to act as the appointing authority of ad hoc arbitrators.[64] Advantage might be taken of that opportunity to codify ICSID's practices regarding its acceptance to administer proceedings in UNCITRAL Rules or other ad hoc proceedings.

A final theme worth revisiting is the relationship between ICSID and the World Bank. In their preparation of the ICSID Convention, the Executive Directors of the Bank realized that the relationship might have to evolve over time, from an initial close relationship allowing ICSID to share in the Bank's prestige and authority, to greater independence for the Centre as it began to receive cases. Most of the provisions of the ICSID Convention on the relationship, such as the provision on the location of the seat of the Centre, were therefore made flexible.[65] In the end, of course, the relationship was exceedingly close for far longer than anticipated at the outset. ICSID was for many years nestled as a small unit in the World Bank's Legal Department.[66] As the Centre's caseload surged, the relationship was appropriately loosened. In 2005, the budgetary arrangements for the Centre were revised, eventually giving ICSID more financial autonomy.[67] And in 2009, the positions of General Counsel of the Bank and Secretary-General of ICSID were finally separated, with ICSID at last getting a full-time Secretary-General.[68]

A further loosening of the relationship might be looked for in respect of the Centre's responsibilities as the appointing authority of ICSID arbitrators.[69] In formal terms, these responsibilities generally have been fulfilled, in Convention and Additional Facility proceedings, by the President of the World Bank in his capacity as Chairman of the ICSID Administrative Council. Even though he has always relied on the recommendation of the Secretary-General in deciding on the appointment and disqualification of arbitrators, the Chairman's involvement may raise conflict of interest concerns in the occasional cases where a World Bank affiliate is helping to finance the underlying project or in cases involving disputes connected with policy reforms and programs urged by the World Bank. The Chairman should, it is suggested, officially delegate to the Secretary-General his responsibilities regarding the appointment and disqualification of arbitrators.[70] Approval of the delegation by the Administrative

[62] *Cf.* Ch. 9, section IV. [63] *See* Ch. 9, n. 134 and accompanying text.

[64] Embodied in the short statement on the subject published over 45 years ago. *See* Ch. 7, nn. 227 and 228.

[65] *See* Ch. 3, section II; Ch. 4, section I(A).

[66] *See* Ch. 7, section I(C); Ch. 9, section II(B). [67] *See* Ch. 10, section I(B).

[68] *See* ibid.

[69] That is, the responsibilities of appointing arbitrators under Art. 38 of the ICSID Convention and Art. 10 of the Additional Facility Arbitration Rules, appointing ad hoc committee members under Art. 52 of the Convention and deciding on proposals to disqualify arbitrators under Art. 58 of the Convention and Art. 15 of the Additional Facility Arbitration Rules.

[70] Consider, for example, the August 2002 letter sent by NGOs to the Bank and ICSID in relation to the *Aguas del Tunari* case (*see* Ch. 10, n. 14 and accompanying text for background and the reference). It described the Bank as having "forced" the water privatization involved in the case. Referring to the appointment of the presiding arbitrator under Art. 38 of the Convention, the letter also accused "World Bank president James Wolfensohn" of having "violated one of the most important principles of objectivity when he directly appointed the President of the arbitration tribunal that will decide the case."

Council, in the exercise of its broad powers under Article 6(3) of the Convention, would put beyond any doubt the consistency of the delegation with the Convention. The terms of the delegation approved by the Council could include regular reporting by the Secretary-General to the Council and Chairman on the exercise of the delegated authority.

APPENDIX I*

Working Paper in the Form of a Draft Convention for the Resolution of Disputes between States and Nationals of Other States

June 5, 1962

Article I
Purpose

The purpose of this Convention is to promote the resolution of disputes arising between Contracting States and nationals of other Contracting States by encouraging and facilitating recourse to international conciliation and arbitration.

Comment
It may be useful to make clear at the outset that the procedures envisaged in the Convention for the settlement of disputes would be available at the instance of States as well as of private parties. The draft covers disputes involving claims *by* as well as *against* States.

Article II
Undertakings to have recourse to conciliation or arbitration

Section 1. The provisions of this Article shall apply to any undertaking in writing to have recourse to conciliation or arbitration pursuant to the provisions of this Convention for the resolution of any existing or future dispute between a Contracting State and a national of another Contracting State.

Comment
Article II deals with the legal effect of undertakings to have recourse to conciliation or arbitration. Section 1 limits the scope of the Article to undertakings which

(a) contemplate conciliation or arbitration pursuant to the Convention;
(b) are expressed in writing;
(c) relate to a dispute between a Contracting State and a national of another Contracting State.

To the extent that the provisions of Article II constitute a development, rather than a mere codification, of existing international law; it is to be expected that States would not wish the provisions to apply automatically to undertakings given in the past, or to all undertakings given in the future. Hence the requirement that the undertaking must contemplate proceedings "pursuant to the provisions of this Convention".

While the undertaking is required to be in writing, there is no requirement that it be executed in any particular form. Furthermore, it may be unilateral, bilateral or multilateral.

The limitation mentioned under (c) above is necessary, *first*, to exclude disputes between States and their own nationals and, *second*, to assure reciprocity.

It will be noted that Section 1 contains no limitations as to the *nature* of the dispute. Although the Convention and the Center would be intended to be used primarily in connection with what are commonly referred to as "investment disputes," there is no need to write a limitation to that effect into the Convention, since it is up to the parties to an undertaking to decide whether they want to bring it within the terms of the Convention. Moreover, it is difficult to define the term "investment dispute"

* Text reproduced with permission of ICSID.

with the precision required to avoid disagreements arising as to the applicability of the Convention to a given undertaking. And uncertainty on this score would tend to undermine the primary objective of Article II, namely to give confidence that undertakings to have recourse to conciliation or arbitration will be carried out.

Section 2. An undertaking to have recourse to conciliation constitutes a legal obligation and must be carried out in good faith.

Section 3. An undertaking to have recourse to arbitration constitutes a legal obligation and must be carried out in good faith. Such an undertaking carries with it the obligation to comply with the arbitral award and carry the same out in good faith.

Comment
Sections 2 and 3 lay down the basic rule that while the Convention imposes no obligation either on States or on parties other than States to undertake to have recourse to conciliation or arbitration (see Article II, Section 6) undertakings once given constitute legal obligations.

The second sentence of Section 3 is an adaptation of a generally accepted principle of international arbitration to the effect that "recourse to arbitration implies an engagement to submit in good faith to the award" (Article 37 of the Hague Convention of 1907).

Section 4. Except as otherwise stated therein, an undertaking to have recourse to arbitration shall be deemed to be an undertaking to have recourse to arbitration in lieu of any other remedy.

Comment
In connection with an agreement to have recourse to arbitration doubt could conceivably arise as to whether the parties intended either (a) to reserve the right to pursue other remedies or (b) to require that other remedies be exhausted prior to recourse to arbitration. Section 4 is intended to remove doubts on both scores by providing that, in the absence of a stipulation to the contrary, arbitration is to be in lieu of any other remedy.

Section 5. No Contracting State shall give diplomatic protection or bring an international claim in respect of a dispute (a) which one of its nationals and another Contracting State shall have undertaken to submit to arbitration, or (b) which one of its nationals shall have submitted to arbitration pursuant to an undertaking of another Contracting State, or (c) which another Contracting State shall have submitted to arbitration pursuant to an undertaking of such national; provided, however, that nothing herein contained shall affect the right of a Contracting state to give diplomatic protection or bring an international claim in respect of an alleged violation by another Contracting State of any of its obligations under this Convention with respect to such dispute.

Comment
The Convention recognizes the right of a private party, within the limits laid down in the Convention, to proceed against a foreign State before an international arbitral tribunal in its own name, rather than seek the diplomatic protection of its national State or have that State bring an international claim. It would seem to be a natural concomitant of the recognition of the private party's right of direct access to an international jurisdiction, to exclude action by its national State in cases in which such access is available under the Convention; and the same would seem to be true in cases in which the private party is a defendant rather than a plaintiff.

Since the exclusion of the national State rests on the premise that the other Contracting State will abide by the provisions of the Convention, the rule of exclusion is subject to an exception in the event that premise falls away; in that event the right to give diplomatic protection and to bring an international claim remains unaffected.

Section 6. Nothing contained in this Convention shall obligate any Contracting State (a) to undertake to have recourse to conciliation or arbitration in any particular case, or (b) to have recourse to conciliation or arbitration in the absence of an undertaking to that effect, or (c) shall limit the freedom of any Contracting State or of any national of any Contracting State to stipulate in any such undertaking that one or more of the provisions of this Convention shall not apply to such undertaking.

Comment
Clauses (a) and (b) of this section state the obvious; they have been inserted to remove any possible doubt as to the optional character of the Convention. Clause (c) underscores this optional character even further by giving parties to a dispute a choice between being governed by the Convention in its entirety and excluding the applicability of certain provisions of the Convention.

Article III
The International Conciliation and Arbitration Center

(a) Establishment and Organization

Section 1. There is hereby established the International Conciliation and Arbitration Center (hereinafter called the Center). The Center shall have full juridical personality.

Section 2. (1) The seat of the Center shall be at the headquarters of the International Bank for Reconstruction and Development (hereinafter called the Bank).

(2) The Center may make arrangements with the Bank for the use of the Bank's offices and other services and facilities.

(3) The Center may also make arrangements with the Administrative Council of the Permanent Court of Arbitration for the use of the organization and facilities of that Court within the scope of the Hague Treaties for the Pacific Settlement of Disputes of 1899 and 1907 and the decisions of the Administrative Council of the Court.

Comment
The assumptions and considerations underlying this section may be briefly set forth as follows:

(a) It has been assumed that the Center would be sponsored by the Bank and would have an administrative link to the Bank.
(b) Since it will be impossible to predict the volume of business that will come to the Center, the "machinery" must be characterized by flexibility and economy. This is sought to be achieved here by opening the possibility of using the Bank's facilities. And see further Sections 4, 7 and 9(2) of this Article.
(c) To the extent practicable, there should be cooperation with the Hague Court. Under Article 47 of the Hague Convention of 1907 and the decisions of the Administrative Council of the Hague Court, the Bureau of that Court is authorized to make its offices and staff available for conciliation or arbitration proceedings between a State and a party other than a State, provided the State concerned is a party to the Convention. Some 25 members of the Bank are not parties to the Convention. See also Section 11(2) of this Article.

Section 3. The Center shall have a President, an Administrative Council, a Secretariat, a Panel of Conciliators and a Panel of Arbitrators (hereinafter sometimes referred to as Panels).

(b) The President

Section 4. The President of the Bank shall be *ex officio* President of the Center. The President shall be Chairman of the Administrative Council but shall have no vote except a deciding vote in case of an equal division.

Section 5. During any absence or inability to act of the President of the Bank, and during any vacancy in the office of President of the Bank, the person who shall be the chief of the operating staff of the Bank shall act as President of the Center.

Section 6. The President shall serve as such without compensation from the Center.

(c) The Administrative Council

Section 7. The Administrative Council shall be composed of one representative and one alternate representative appointed by each Contracting State. No alternate may vote except in the absence of his principal.

Comment
Consideration should be given to the question whether the parties to the Convention should, because of its Bank sponsorship and the administrative link between the Center and the Bank, be limited to members of the Bank. The reasons for making Bank membership a prerequisite of participation in IFC and IDA do not apply to the same extent in this case.

As an alternative Section 7 might provide that each governor and alternate governor appointed by a member of the Bank which is also a Contracting State shall be *ex officio* the representative and alternate representative of the State in question.

Section 8. The Administrative Council shall be the principal organ of the Center and shall, within the limits of the provisions of this Convention, adopt such rules and regulations and exercise such other powers as may be necessary or useful for the operation of the Center and the achievement of the purposes of this Convention. The Administrative Council may delegate any of its powers to the President, except the power to appoint the Secretary-General and Deputy Secretaries-General.

Comment
The principal functions of the Administrative Council might be, in addition to its statutory task in connection with the appointment of the Secretary-General and Deputy Secretaries-General, the adoption from time to time of rules of procedure, the approval of the budget of the Center and the approval of an annual report.

Section 9. (1) The Administrative Council shall hold an annual meeting and such other meetings as may be provided for by the Administrative Council or called by the President. The Administrative Council may by regulation establish a procedure whereby the President may obtain a vote of the Administrative Council on a specific question without calling a meeting of the Administrative Council.

(2) The annual meeting of the Administrative Council shall be held in conjunction with the annual meeting of the Board of Governors of the Bank.

(3) A quorum for any meeting of the Administrative Council shall be a majority of the members.

(4) Each member of the Administrative Council shall cast one vote and all matters before the Council shall be decided by a majority of the votes cast.

(5) Members of the Administrative Council shall serve as such without compensation from the Center.

Comment
The question of voting rights cannot be considered outside the context of the task of the Administrative Council. To the extent that the Council would deal with important substantive or policy matters, it is possible that on certain issues there would be a clear split between the capital exporting and capital importing countries. For instance, if the Administrative Council were to elect the panels, or if the Secretary-General, who is appointed by the Council, were a quasi-judicial,

rather than an administrative official, the question of voting power might well take on considerable importance. If each member had one vote this would, assuming that all members of the Bank became parties to the Convention, give control over these matters to the capital importing countries. On the other hand, if the weighted voting system of the Bank were carried over into the Council, the capital exporting countries would be in control. In order to avoid either alternative one could devise a system under which a majority vote in the Council would require the vote of a majority of the members representing a majority of the voting power of the members determined in accordance with the Bank formula.

Whatever the merits of the double voting test, it does not appear to be appropriate in the present draft, since the panels would be composed of persons designated by the respective Contracting States (and in addition some persons designated by the Chairman) and the Secretary-General would not possess any judicial or quasi-judicial powers. Nor does it appear that there are any other matters within the competence of the Council that could lead to major controversies between the capital exporting and the capital importing countries as groups. The draft has therefore adopted the simple one-member–one-vote formula.

(d) The Secretariat

Section 10. The Secretariat shall consist of a Secretary-General, one or more Deputy Secretaries-General and staff.

Comment
Since the Secretary-General will have certain formal duties to perform in connection with proceedings under the auspices of the Center, it would seem desirable to provide for at least one deputy.

Section 11. (1) The Secretary-General and Deputy Secretaries-General shall be appointed by the Administrative Council upon the nomination of the President.

(2) The office of Secretary-General or Deputy Secretary-General shall be incompatible with the exercise of any political function, and with any employment or occupation other than employment by the Bank or by the Permanent Court of Arbitration, except as the Administrative Council, with the concurrence of the President, may otherwise decide.

Comment
The considerations underlying this section are the following: Even though the Secretary-General's statutory powers would be limited to administration (see Section 12 of this Article), he could in practice perform a valuable task in promoting use of the Center's facilities and by giving informal assistance and advice to the parties in connection with proceedings under the Center's auspices. His effectiveness will depend on his competence as well as on the degree of confidence which he is able to inspire. If it could be expected with a reasonable degree of certainty that activities under the Convention would be such as to provide a full time occupation for a Secretary-General and one deputy, it would be desirable to provide that they, or at least the Secretary-General himself, may not hold any other office or engage in any other occupation or activity. Since no such degree of certainty exists, the draft permits the Administrative Council to make exceptions to the rule and, in addition, specifically excludes from incompatibility employment by the Bank or by the Hague Court. These provisions give the Administrative Council and the President, who is the nominating authority, adequate flexibility.

Section 12. (1) The Secretary-General shall be the principal administrative officer of the Center and shall be responsible for its administration, including the appointment of staff, in accordance with the provisions of this Convention and the rules to be adopted thereunder.

(2) During any absence or inability to act of the Secretary-General, and during any vacancy of the office of Secretary-General, the Deputy Secretary-General shall act as Secretary-General. If there shall be more than one Deputy Secretary-General, the Secretary-General shall determine in what order they shall act as Secretary-General.

(e) The Panels

Comment

Because of the optional and flexible character of the Convention as a whole and of access to the Center in particular, the Panels have limited significance. Parties to proceedings under the auspices of the Center are entirely free to agree to use conciliators or arbitrators who do not form part of the Panels. On the other hand, as will be seen from Articles V and VI of the draft, unless the parties agree otherwise, conciliators and arbitrators will be selected by them from the respective Panels, and the President, when called upon to appoint a conciliator or arbitrator, will likewise make the selection from the Panels.

The composition of the Panels could be determined in a number of different ways. One method would be to have the Contracting States elect a certain number of panel members from among candidates nominated by each Contracting State. While this method would have certain advantages, particularly in encouraging states to nominate candidates of high quality, it has the disadvantage of necessitating a somewhat complicated voting procedure in order to assure a balanced composition of the Panels as between candidates nominated by the capital exporting and capital importing countries respectively. (See the comment on Article III, Section 9).

The method adopted in the draft largely follows the system of the Hague Conventions of 1899 and 1907, in leaving the composition of the Panels primarily to the Contracting States. Under the draft the President would have the right to designate a specified number of panel members in addition to those designated by the Contracting States. He might exercise this right after the States had made their designations to achieve the balanced representation on the Panels not only of different legal systems but also of different forms of economic activity. (It is to be noted that the Panels would not be composed only of legal experts but of experts in other fields as well).

Section 13. (1) The Panel of Conciliators shall consist of qualified persons, designated as hereafter provided, who are willing to serve as members of the Panel.

(2) Each Contracting State shall designate not more than __ persons to serve on the Panel, who may, but need not, be its own nationals.

(3) The President shall have the right to designate up to __ persons to serve on the Panel.

Section 14. (1) The Panel of Arbitrators shall consist of qualified persons, designated as hereafter provided, who are willing to serve as members of the Panel.

(2) Each *Contracting* State shall designate not more than __ persons to serve on the Panel, who may, but need not, be its own nationals.

(3) The President shall have the right to designate up to __ persons to serve on the Panel.

Section 15. (1) Panel members shall serve for four years.

(2) In case of death or resignation of a member of either Panel, the Contracting State or the *President*, as the case may be, which or who had designated the member, shall have the right to designate another person to serve for the balance of that member's term.

Section 16. (1) The same person may be designated to serve on both Panels.

(2) If a *person* is designated to serve on a Panel by more than one Contracting State, or by one or more Contracting States and the President, he shall be deemed to have been designated by the authority which first designated him.

(3) All designations shall be notified to the Secretary-General and any designation shall take effect from the date when the notification is received.

Section 17. (1) The Contracting States shall pay due regard to the importance of Panels composed of persons of high moral character and recognized competence in the fields of law, commerce, industry or finance and, to that end, shall, before designating Panel members, seek such advice as they may deem appropriate from their highest courts of justice, schools of law, bar associations and such commercial, industrial and financial organizations as shall be considered representative of the professions they embrace.

(2) The President shall, in designating members to the Panels, pay due regard to the importance of assuring the representation on the Panels of the principal legal systems of the world and of the main forms of economic activity.

(f) Financing the Cost of the Center

Section 18. To the extent that the cost of the Center cannot be met out of fees and other charges for the use of its facilities, or out of other receipts, it shall be borne by the Contracting States in proportion to their respective subscriptions to the capital stock of the Bank [except that as to Contracting States which are not members of the Bank, the Administrative Council shall determine the basis for their proportionate share].

Comment

The words "or out of other receipts" have been included in order to take account of the possibility that the Bank might finance the cost of the Center. For the bracketed language see comment on Section 7 of this Article.

(g) Privileges and Immunities

Section 19. The Center shall be immune from all legal process.

Section 20. (1) The President, the members of the Administrative Council, and the officers and employees of the Secretariat

(i) shall be immune from legal process with respect to acts performed by them in their official capacity;

(ii) not being local nationals shall be accorded the same immunities from immigration restrictions, alien registration requirements and national service obligations, the same facilities as regards exchange restrictions and the same treatment in respect of travelling facilities as are accorded by Contracting States to the representatives, officials and employees of comparable rank of other Contracting States.

(2) Paragraph (1)(i) of this Section shall also apply to persons acting as conciliators or arbitrators in proceedings pursuant to this Convention, and to persons appearing as parties, representatives of parties, agents, counsel, experts or witnesses in such proceedings, but only in connection with their travel to and from the seat of the Center or other location where the proceedings are held and their stay at such location for the purpose of such proceedings.

Section 21. (1) The archives of the Center shall be inviolable.

(2) The official communications of the Center shall be accorded the same treatment as is accorded to the official communications of other Contracting States.

Section 22. (1) The Center, its assets, property and income, and its operations and transactions authorized by this Convention, shall be immune from all taxation and customs duties. The Center shall also be immune from liability for the collection or payment of any taxes or customs duties.

(2) No tax shall be levied on or in respect of salaries or emoluments paid by the Center to the President, members of the Administrative Council or officials or employees of the Secretariat who are not local citizens, local subjects or other local nationals.

(3) No tax shall be levied on or in respect of honoraria, fees or other income received by persons acting as conciliators or arbitrators in proceedings pursuant to this Convention for their services in such proceedings, if the sole jurisdictional basis for such tax shall be the location of the Center or the place where such proceedings are conducted or the place where such income is paid.

Article IV
Jurisdiction of the Center

Section 1. (1) The jurisdiction of the Center shall be limited to disputes between Contracting States and nationals of other Contracting States and shall be based on consent.

(2) The consent of any party to a dispute to the jurisdiction of the Center may be evidenced by an undertaking of such party within the meaning of Article II, Section 1, of this Convention or by the acceptance by such party of the jurisdiction of the Center in respect of a dispute submitted to it by another party.

(3) Except as otherwise agreed between the parties, the Center shall not exercise jurisdiction in respect of disputes involving claims of less than the equivalent of one hundred thousand United States dollars determined as of the time of submission of the dispute.

Comment

Paragraph (1) states the basic principle that the activities of the Center must be based on consent. Paragraph (2) distinguishes between consent given in advance, evidenced by an undertaking within the meaning of Article II, Section 1, which—it will be recalled—is binding, and *ad hoc* consent evidenced by voluntary acceptance by a party of the jurisdiction of the Center in respect of a particular dispute submitted to it by another party. Paragraph (3) places a monetary limit on claims to be submitted to the Center. Arbitration is not an inexpensive procedure and parties should not be forced to have resort to it if the amount claimed remains below a certain limit which, for purposes of illustration, has been put at the equivalent of U.S. $100,000.

Section 2. If a Contracting State or a national of a Contracting State shall have given an undertaking to have recourse to conciliation and, having been requested by another party to proceed to conciliation, shall deny the existence of a dispute or shall deny that the dispute is within the scope of the undertaking or that the undertaking is valid, whether such disagreement arises before or after the constitution of a Conciliation Commission, either party may submit such disagreement to arbitration in the same manner and with the same effect as if the parties had expressly undertaken to have recourse to arbitration for the resolution of such disagreement pursuant to this Convention.

Comment

The solution here proposed takes cognizance of the difference between the undertaking to have recourse to conciliation, which constitutes a legal obligation, and the conciliation proceedings in which the emphasis is on efforts to achieve an amicable settlement and which may lead at the most to a non-binding recommendation. In these circumstances it would seem preferable that a dispute concerning the obligation to have recourse to conciliation be settled not by the Conciliation Commission but through arbitration.

Section 3. Neither a Contracting State nor a national of a Contracting State may refuse to carry out an undertaking to have recourse to arbitration claiming that there is no existing dispute or that the existing dispute is not within the scope of the undertaking, or that the undertaking is invalid, but the party making such claim shall be entitled to have such claim disposed of by the Arbitral Tribunal as a preliminary question.

Comment

This provision is merely a reflection of the general principle (stated in Section 5 of this Article) that the Arbitral Tribunal is the judge of its own competence.

Section 4. (1) If at any time, whether before or after the constitution of a Conciliation Commission or an Arbitral Tribunal, a Contracting State which is a party to a dispute (in this Section referred to as the State party) shall claim that the Center lacks jurisdiction on the ground that the other party (in this Section referred to as the non-state party) was not a national of another Contracting State on the date when the dispute was submitted to the Center, the State party may serve a notice to that effect on the non-state party and on the Secretary-General of the Center. Receipt of the notice by the Secretary-General shall have the effect of staying any proceedings which may be in progress and of suspending the running of any periods of time applicable to the dispute until such time as the question of jurisdiction shall have been disposed of as hereafter provided.

(2) The Secretary-General shall promptly and by rapid means of communication address a copy of the notice to the Contracting State or States of which the non-state party claims to be a national.

(3) If, upon the expiration of 60 days after dispatch by the Secretary-General of the copy of the notice, neither the Contracting State or States to which it was addressed, nor any other Contracting State shall have claimed that the non-state party is its or their national, the Secretary-General shall declare that the Center is without jurisdiction and shall so inform the parties to the dispute and the Conciliation Commission or the Arbitral Tribunal, as the case may be, if one shall have been constituted.

(4) If, within 60 days after dispatch by the Secretary-General of the copy of the notice, any Contracting State shall have notified the Secretary-General that it regards the non-state party as its national, the Secretary-General shall promptly send a copy of that notice to the State party by rapid means of communication.

(5) If, within 60 days after dispatch by the Secretary-General of the copy of the notice referred to in (4) above, the State party shall have notified the Secretary-General that it maintains its objections to the jurisdiction of the Center, the Secretary-General shall inform all Contracting States that a disagreement has arisen regarding the interpretation and application of this Convention within the meaning of Article IX.

(6) If the State party shall not, within 60 days after dispatch by the Secretary-General of the copy of the notice referred to in (4) above, have notified the Secretary-General that it maintains its objections to the jurisdiction, it shall be deemed to have withdrawn its objections, and the Secretary-General shall so inform the parties to the dispute and the Conciliation Commission or the Arbitral Tribunal, if one shall have been constituted.

Comment

The objection to the jurisdiction dealt with in this section is based not on a dispute as to the agreement of the parties, i.e. the consent of the parties which is an indispensable prerequisite for the jurisdiction of the Center, but as to the applicability of the Convention to the dispute, which is another indispensable element. While the first interests only the parties, the second is of interest to the Contracting States. For that reason Section 4 prescribes a different method for deciding whether the objection is well-founded.

Section 5. Except as herein otherwise provided, or as otherwise agreed between the parties, any Conciliation Commission and any Arbitral Tribunal constituted pursuant to this Convention shall be the judge of its competence.

Article V
Conciliation

Section 1. Any dispute within the jurisdiction of the Center may be the subject of a request for conciliation by a Conciliation Commission.

Section 2. The Conciliation Commission shall consist of a sole conciliator or several conciliators appointed as the parties may have agreed. In the absence of agreement the Conciliation

Commission shall consist of three conciliators, one appointed by each party and the third appointed by agreement of the parties, all appointees to be selected from the Panel of Conciliators.

Section 3. (1) If the Conciliation Commission shall not have been constituted within three months after the request referred to in Section 1, the President shall, at the request of either party, appoint the conciliator or conciliators not appointed pursuant to Section 2. Before making any such appointment, the President shall instruct the Secretary-General to consult with the parties and to report to him any information or views which may assist him in making the appointment.

(2) In making any appointment under this section the President shall select the appointee from the Panel of Conciliators.

Comment

As to the role of the President as appointing authority, see the comment on Section 3 of Article VI below.

Section 4. (1) Except as the parties shall otherwise agree, the Conciliation Commission shall conduct the conciliation proceedings in such manner, in accordance with the Conciliation Rules adopted under this Convention or otherwise, as may appear to the Commission to be most conducive to a resolution of the dispute.

(2) The Conciliation Commission may at any stage of the proceedings recommend terms of settlement to the parties. If the parties shall reach agreement, the Commission shall draw up a report noting the submission of the dispute and recording that the parties have reached agreement. Except as the parties shall otherwise agree, the report shall not contain the terms of settlement accepted by the parties.

Section 5. If at any time it appears to the Conciliation Commission that there is no likelihood of agreement between the parties, the Commission may declare the proceedings closed. The Commission shall in that event draw up a report noting the submission of the dispute and recording the failure of the conciliation effort. Unless the parties otherwise agree, the report shall not contain the terms of settlement, if any, recommended to the parties by the Commission.

Section 6. The parties shall give the Conciliation Commission their full cooperation in order to enable the Commission to carry out its task, and shall give the most serious consideration to the Commission's recommendations.

Section 7. (1) Without prejudice to the provisions of Section 6 of this Article, neither party to a conciliation proceeding shall be under any obligation to accept any recommendation made by the Conciliation Commission.

(2) Neither party to a conciliation proceeding shall be entitled in any later proceeding concerning the same dispute, whether before arbitrators or in a court of law or otherwise, to invoke or rely on any views expressed or statements or admissions or offers of settlement made by the other party in the conciliation proceeding, or the recommendations, if any, made by the Conciliation Commission therein.

Comment

Paragraph (2) of Section 7 is intended to encourage the parties to seek agreement rather than maintain fixed positions out of fear that a conciliatory attitude might prejudice their position in a later proceeding if the conciliation effort failed.

Section 8. Except as the parties otherwise agree, or as the Conciliation Commission otherwise decides, any conciliation proceeding shall be conducted in accordance with the

Conciliation Rules adopted under this Convention and in effect at the time when the consent on which the proceeding is based was given.

Article VI
Arbitration

Section 1. Any dispute within the jurisdiction of the Center may be the subject of a request for arbitration by an Arbitral Tribunal.

Section 2. The Arbitral Tribunal shall consist of a sole arbitrator or several arbitrators appointed as the parties may have agreed. In the absence of agreement the Arbitral Tribunal shall consist of three arbitrators, one appointed by each party and the third appointed by agreement of the parties, all appointees to be selected from the Panel of Arbitrators.

Comment

The second sentence of Section 2 adopts what is probably the most usual method for the constitution of an arbitral tribunal. It can be argued that it is the least desirable method because of the danger that each party will look upon the arbitrator to be appointed by it as an advocate. Under this pessimistic assumption the umpire would be the only true arbitrator. It has been argued for this reason that it would be preferable to have either a sole arbitrator or a tribunal consisting of five members of whom only two would be directly appointed by the parties. The draft has not followed either alternative because it is believed that a sole arbitrator would not be generally acceptable as a matter of principle and because a five member tribunal would add considerably to the cost of the proceedings. The parties would be free, of course, to make any agreement they thought fit as to the manner of constituting the tribunal as well as regarding the number of arbitrators. It will be noted from the following sections of this Article that an attempt has been made to avoid some of the dangers of having "party arbitrators".

Section 3. (1) If the Arbitral Tribunal shall not have been constituted within three months after the request referred to in Section 1, the President shall, at the request of either party, appoint the arbitrator or arbitrators not appointed pursuant to Section (2). Before making any such appointment, the President shall instruct the Secretary-General to consult with the parties and to report to him any information or views which may assist him in making the appointment.

(2) In making any appointment under this section, the President shall select the appointee from the Panel of Arbitrators.

Comment

It is a necessary corollary of the binding character of an undertaking to have recourse to arbitration that the Convention contain provisions designed to prevent frustration of that undertaking by an unwilling party. This is the purpose of the appointment procedure laid down in Section 3. It will be noted that, as in the case of conciliation (Section 3 of Article V), the President has been designated the appointing authority, except, of course, as the parties may otherwise agree. Beyond the requirement that the appointee must be selected from the Panel, the President is left free in his choice. It will be noted that the President would exercise his power of appointment even if he were of the same nationality as one of the parties, and that he would not be required to see to it that the arbitrator appointed by him in lieu of an unwilling party be of that party's nationality or that the umpire be of a nationality other than those of the parties. While none of these points are essential, it can be argued in favor of the solution embodied in the draft that in disputes of the type likely to be submitted to the Center nationality does not have the same importance as in political disputes, that the President would presumably wherever possible appoint a tribunal on which the nationalities of the parties would be represented by two arbitrators with an umpire of a different nationality, and that the flexibility provided by the draft would be of practical importance in the—probably unusual—case in which all members of the Panel of the nationality of one of the parties would be unable or unwilling to act, or would be disqualified. But the basic consideration underlying the draft is that the appointing authority must be a person who, because of his office, may be conclusively presumed to be capable of showing impartiality in the selection of arbitrators under all circumstances. It may be noted that under the Bank's Loan Regulations the President of the International Court of Justice and the Secretary-General of the United Nations have a similar unrestricted power of appointment.

Section 4. Except as the parties otherwise agree, any arbitration proceeding shall be conducted in accordance with the Arbitration Rules adopted under this Convention and in effect at the time when the consent on which the proceeding is based was given. If any question of procedure arises which is not covered by the applicable Arbitration Rules, the Arbitral Tribunal shall decide that question.

Section 5. (1) In the absence of any agreement between the parties concerning the law to be applied, and unless the parties shall have given the Arbitral Tribunal the power to decide *ex aequo et bono*, the Arbitral Tribunal shall decide the dispute submitted to it in accordance with such rules of law, whether national or international, as it shall determine to be applicable.

(2) The Arbitral Tribunal may not bring in a finding of *non liquet* on the ground of the silence or obscurity of the law to be applied.

Comment

In the absence of any basis for determining a generally valid rule concerning the law to be applied by arbitrators, the matter has been left to the parties or, in the absence of agreement between the parties, to the arbitral tribunal. The parties may also give the tribunal the power to decide *ex aequo et bono*, without being bound by rules of law.

Section 6. Except as the parties otherwise agree, the Arbitral Tribunal shall have the power to prescribe, at the request of either party, any provisional measures necessary for the protection of the rights of the parties.

Section 7. Except as the parties otherwise agree, the Arbitral Tribunal shall have the power to hear and determine any counter-claims arising directly out of the subject-matter of the dispute.

Section 8. All questions before the Arbitral Tribunal shall be decided by a majority of the Tribunal.

Section 9. (1) The Arbitral Tribunal shall render its award in writing. An award signed by a majority of the Arbitral Tribunal shall constitute the award of the Tribunal.

(2) The award may be rendered by default.

Comment

The power to render an award by default is also possessed by the arbitral tribunals provided for in the Bank's Loan Regulations. It is a necessary corollary of the binding character of the undertaking to have recourse to arbitration.

Section 10. The award shall be final and binding on the parties. Each party shall abide by and comply with the award immediately, unless the Arbitral Tribunal shall have allowed a time limit for the carrying out of the award or any part thereof.

Section 11. (1) Any dispute between the parties as to the meaning and scope of the award may, at the request of either party made within __ months after the date of the award, be submitted to the Arbitral Tribunal which rendered the award. Such a request shall stay the execution of the award pending the decision of the Tribunal.

(2) If for any reason it is impossible to submit the dispute to the Tribunal which rendered the award, a new Arbitral Tribunal shall be constituted in accordance with the terms of the agreement, if any, between the parties regarding the constitution of the Arbitral Tribunal which rendered the award, and otherwise pursuant to the provisions of this Article.

Section 12. (1) An application for revision of the award may be made by either party on the ground of the discovery of some fact of such a nature as to have a decisive influence on the award, provided that when the award was rendered that fact was unknown to the Arbitral Tribunal and to the party requesting revision and that such ignorance was not due to the negligence of the party requesting revision.

(2) The application for revision must be made within six months of the discovery of the new fact and in any case within ten years of the rendering of the award.

(3) The application shall, if possible, be submitted to the Arbitral Tribunal which rendered the award. If this shall not be possible, a new Arbitral Tribunal shall be constituted in accordance with the terms of the agreement, if any, between the parties regarding the constitution of the Arbitral Tribunal which rendered the award, and otherwise pursuant to the provisions of this Article.

Article VII
Provisions Common to Conciliation and Arbitration

Section 1. Except as otherwise agreed by the parties, each party to a conciliation or arbitration proceeding shall bear its own expenses and the fees and expenses of the Center and of the Conciliation Commission or the Arbitral Tribunal, as the case may be, shall be divided between and borne equally by the parties; provided, however, that if a Commission or Tribunal determines that a party has instituted the proceedings frivolously or in bad faith, it may assess any part or all of such fees and expenses against that party.

Section 2. The fees and expenses of the Center to be charged to the parties shall be fixed by the Secretary-General within the limits approved from time to time by the Administrative Council.

Section 3. The fees and expenses of any Conciliation Commission or Arbitral Tribunal shall, in the absence of agreement with the parties, be fixed by the Commission or Tribunal concerned after consultation with the Secretary General.

Section 4. (1) Conciliation and arbitration proceedings shall be held either at the seat of the Center or, to the extent permitted under any arrangements made pursuant to Article III, Section 2 (3), at the seat of the Permanent Court of Arbitration, as the parties may agree. In the absence of agreement on this point between the parties, the Secretary-General shall determine the place where the proceedings shall be held after consultation with the parties and with the Conciliation Commission or Arbitral Tribunal, as the case may be.

(2) Notwithstanding the provisions of paragraph 1 of this section, proceedings may be held away from the seat of the Center or the seat of the Permanent Court of Arbitration, if the parties so agree and if the Conciliation Commission or Arbitral Tribunal; as the case may be, so approve after consultation with the Secretary-General.

Comment

Paragraph (1) of Section 4 is based on the assumption that the Contracting States would wish a close cooperation between the Center and the Permanent Court of Arbitration. (See in this connection also Article III, Sections 2 and 11).

Section 5. Once a Conciliation Commission or an Arbitral Tribunal shall have been constituted and proceedings shall have begun, its composition shall remain unchanged; provided, however, that if a conciliator or arbitrator shall die or become incapacitated, or shall have resigned, the resulting vacancy shall be filled by the method used for the original appointment, except that if a conciliator or arbitrator appointed by a party shall have resigned without the consent of the Commission or Tribunal of which he was a member, the resulting vacancy shall be filled by the President.

Comment

The principal clause of Section 5 embodies what is called the "principle of immutability" and is intended to preclude the replacement of Panel members by the parties during the proceedings with a view to influencing the outcome of the proceedings as well as the resignation of Panel members under pressure. Under the draft the principle is applied to both conciliation and arbitration proceedings. It is clearly important for the latter; whether it should apply to the former is less clear. As a protection against resignation of a Panel member under pressure of the party which had appointed him, a vacancy created by resignation without the consent of his fellow members will be filled not by the appointing party but by the President. Other vacancies will be filled by the method used for the original appointment.

Section 6. (1) A party may propose the disqualification of a conciliator or arbitrator on the ground that he has an interest in the subject matter of the dispute or that he had, prior to his appointment, dealt with the dispute in any capacity whatever.

(2) The proposal shall be made at the beginning of the conciliation or arbitration proceedings, unless the facts on which the proposed disqualification is based were not then known and knowledge of them could not reasonably be imputed to the party making the proposal.

(3) The decision on the proposed disqualification shall be taken by the other members of the Conciliation Commission or Arbitral Tribunal, as the case may be, or, in the case of a single conciliator or arbitrator, by the President. If the decision is that the proposal is well-founded, the conciliator or arbitrator in question shall resign.

Article VIII
Recognition of Arbitral Awards by Contracting States

[Here will be inserted a provision substantially to the effect that Contracting States will give to awards rendered pursuant to the Convention the most favorable treatment they give to foreign arbitral awards whether under their internal law or pursuant to the Geneva Convention of 1927 on the execution of foreign arbitral awards or the United Nations Convention of 1958 on the recognition and enforcement of foreign arbitral awards.]

Article IX
Interpretation

[Here will be inserted a provision providing for the settlement of disputes among Contracting States regarding the interpretation or application of the Convention. The section might provide for the acceptance of the compulsory jurisdiction of the International Court of Justice.]

Article X
Definitions

[To be supplied. Among the terms to be covered would be "party" and "national."]

Article XI
Final Provisions

[To be supplied. This Article would provide for such matters as Signature, acceptance, accession, entry into force, territorial application, withdrawal, the inauguration of the Center and administrative details such as depositary arrangements and arrangements for registration.]

APPENDIX II*

Preliminary Draft of a Convention on the Settlement of Investment Disputes between States and Nationals of Other States

October 15, 1963

Preamble

The Contracting States

1. CONSIDERING the need for international cooperation for economic development, and the role of international investment therein;
2. BEARING IN MIND the possibility that from time to time disputes may arise in connection with such investment between Contracting States and the nationals of other Contracting States, and the desirability that such disputes be settled in a spirit of mutual confidence, with due respect for the principle of equal rights of States in the exercise of their sovereignty in accordance with international law;
3. RECOGNIZING that while such disputes would usually be subject to national legal processes (without prejudice to the right of any State to espouse a claim of one of its nationals in accordance with international law), international methods of settlement may be appropriate in certain cases;
4. ATTACHING PARTICULAR IMPORTANCE to the establishment of facilities for international conciliation or arbitration to which Contracting States and the nationals of other Contracting States may submit such disputes if they so desire;
5. RECOGNIZING an undertaking to submit such disputes to conciliation or to arbitration through such facilities as a legal obligation to be carried out in good faith, which requires in particular that due consideration be given to any recommendation of conciliators, and that any arbitral award be complied with; and
6. DECLARING that no Contracting State shall by the mere fact of its ratification or acceptance of this Convention be required to have recourse to conciliation or arbitration in any particular case, in the absence of a specific undertaking to that effect,

HAVE AGREED as follows:

Comment

1. The Preamble contains a general statement of the aims and purposes of the Convention, and is, in addition, intended to be declaratory of the fundamental norms upon which the specific rules of the Convention are based. Paragraph 1 places the Convention in the context of the need for promoting economic development while paragraph 2 assures respect for the proper exercise of national sovereignty. The purpose for which conciliation and arbitration machinery is set up is limited in paragraph 2 to the settlement of investment disputes between Contracting States and the nationals of other Contracting States.

2. Paragraph 3 makes it clear that the procedures set forth in the Convention are in no way intended generally to supersede national legal processes or the existing rights of States under international law, but suggests that other methods of settlement of the disputes covered may be appropriate in certain cases. Paragraphs 4 and 6 emphasize that recourse to the Center is purely optional.

3. Finally, paragraph 5 recognizes as binding the obligations deriving from an undertaking to submit investment disputes to conciliation and arbitration under the auspices of the Center and represents an adaptation of a generally accepted principle of international arbitration to the effect that "recourse to arbitration implies an engagement to submit in good faith to the award" (Article 37 of the Hague Convention of 1907).

* Text reproduced with permission of ICSID.

Article I
International Conciliation and Arbitration Center

Establishment and Organization

Section 1. There is hereby established the International Conciliation and Arbitration Center (hereinafter called the Center). The Center shall have full juridical personality.

Section 2. (1) The seat of the Center shall be at the headquarters of the International Bank for Reconstruction and Development (hereinafter called the Bank).

(2) The Center may make arrangements with the Bank for the use of the Bank's offices and administrative services and facilities.

(3) The Center may make similar arrangements with the Permanent Court of Arbitration and with such other public international institutions as the Administrative Council of the Center may from time to time designate by a two-thirds majority of the votes of all members.

Section 3. The Center shall have an Administrative Council, a Secretariat, a Panel of Conciliators and a Panel of Arbitrators (hereinafter sometimes referred to as Panels).

Comment

1. It is envisaged that the Center would be sponsored by the Bank, which might, in addition, provide it with purely administrative or "housekeeping" facilities and staff. By thus linking it to the Bank the Center would be invested with the image of the Bank and its prestige and reputation for impartiality. On the other hand, the Bank would have no role to play, and could not exercise any influence whatever on the proceedings under the auspices of the Center. These proceedings would be the sole responsibility of conciliators and arbitrators appointed by the parties to a particular dispute or by an authority of their choice.

2. Section 2(1) states that the seat of the Center shall be at the headquarters of the Bank. Section 6 (vi) of this article, however, empowers the Administrative Council to move the seat of the Center to some other location should circumstances so demand in the future.

3. As it would, in its initial stages, be impossible to predict the volume of business that would be brought to the Center, its machinery must be characterized by flexibility and economy. This is sought to be achieved in part through provision for use of the Bank's facilities. In this connection reference is also made to Sections 4(2), 5 and 7(2) of this article.

4. To the extent practicable, there would be cooperation with the Permanent Court of Arbitration. Under Article 47 of the Hague Convention of 1907 and decisions of the Administrative Council of the Court, the Bureau of that Court is authorized to make its offices and staff available for conciliation and arbitration proceedings between a State and a party other than a State, provided the State concerned is a party to the Convention. (Not all members of the Bank are parties to that Convention.) The arrangements contemplated by Section 2(3) are of a simple administrative nature, e.g. for the use of the Court's staff, facilities, offices and services such as translation, the keeping of records, as well as channelling of communications in cases where parties found it convenient to meet at The Hague rather than in Washington or elsewhere. (See also Section 9(2) of this article). The section also opens the possibility for similar arrangements with other public international institutions which might in the future establish machinery for the settlement of investment disputes.

5. The structure of the Center is conceived on the simplest lines and consists of a) an Administrative Council (except as provided in Section 4, the members of the Bank's Board of Governors would double in function), b) a small Secretariat (personnel of the Bank's staff doubling in function) headed by a Secretary-General, and c) the Panels.

The Administrative Council

Section 4. (1) The Administrative Council shall be composed of one representative and one alternate representative of each Contracting State. No alternate may vote except in the absence of his principal.

(2) In the absence of a contrary designation, each governor and alternate governor of the Bank appointed by a Contracting State shall be *ex officio* the representative and alternate representative of that State.

Section 5. The President of the Bank shall be *ex officio* Chairman of the Administrative Council (hereinafter called the Chairman) but shall have no vote except a deciding vote in case of an equal division. During the President's absence or inability to act and during any vacancy in the office of President of the Bank, the person who shall be the chief of the operating staff of the Bank shall act as Chairman.

Section 6. In addition to the powers granted to it by other provisions of this Convention, the Administrative Council shall have the following powers:

(i) To adopt such administrative rules and regulations, including financial regulations, as may be necessary or useful for the operation of the Center.
(ii) To approve the terms of service of the Secretary-General and of any Deputy Secretary-General.
(iii) To approve the annual budget of the Center.
(iv) To approve an annual report of the operation of the Center.
(v) To adopt Conciliation Rules and Arbitration Rules not inconsistent with any provision of this Convention by a two-thirds majority of the votes of all members.
(vi) To move the seat of the Center from the headquarters of the Bank by a two-thirds majority of the votes of all members.

Comment

6. The Convention would be open to all States whether or not members of the Bank, each State being represented on the Administrative Council. While Section 4(2) assumes that Contracting States members of the Bank would usually wish to designate their Governors and Alternate Governors to represent them on the Administrative Council, it provides that a member State which might feel it more appropriate to designate another person or persons in that capacity may do so.

7. The Administrative Council, as its name implies, will have purely administrative functions and the only rules which it may adopt with binding effect are those of an administrative nature envisaged in paragraph (i) of Section 6. The Conciliation and Arbitration Rules to be adopted pursuant to paragraph (v) of that section would become binding on the parties to a dispute only with their consent (see Section 4 of Article III and Section 5 of Article IV).

Section 7. (1) The Administrative Council shall hold an annual meeting and such other meetings as may be provided for by the Administrative Council or called by the Chairman. The Administrative Council may by regulation establish a procedure whereby the Chairman may obtain a vote of the Administrative Council on a specific question without calling a meeting of the Administrative Council.

(2) The annual meeting of the Administrative Council shall be held in conjunction with the annual meeting of the Board of Governors of the Bank.

(3) A quorum for any meeting of the Administrative Council shall be a majority of the members.

(4) Each member of the Administrative Council shall cast one vote and, except as otherwise provided, all matters before the Council shall be decided by a majority of the votes cast.

(5) Members of the Administrative Council and the Chairman shall serve as such without compensation from the Center.

Comment

8. The question of voting rights has been considered in the context of the functions of the Administrative Council. If the Council were to have dealt with important substantive or policy matters, it is possible that on certain issues there would have been a division between the capital-exporting and capital-importing countries. Thus, if the Council were to have elected the Panels, or if

the Secretary-General—who is appointed by the Council—were to have been a quasi-judicial rather than an administrative official, the question of voting power might well have been of considerable significance. On that hypothesis, if each member of the council had one vote and if all members of the Bank became parties to the Convention, the capital-importing countries would have had control over those matters. On the other hand, if the weighted voting system of the Bank were applied in the Council, the capital-exporting countries would have gained control. To avoid both consequences, a system might have been devised requiring matters to be decided by the vote of a majority of the members representing a majority of the voting power determined in accordance with the Bank formula.

9. Whatever the merits of that double test, it does not appear to be appropriate in the present context, since the Contracting States (and the Chairman) would designate the members of the Panels, and the Secretary-General would have no judicial or quasi-judicial powers. Nor does it appear that there are any matters within the competence of the Council that could lead to major divisions between the capital-exporting and the capital-importing countries as groups. The text, therefore, proposes in Section 7(4) a simple one-member–one-vote formula.

The Secretariat

Section 8. The Secretariat shall consist of a Secretary-General, one or more Deputy Secretaries-General and staff.

Section 9. (1) The Secretary-General and Deputy Secretaries-General shall be appointed by the Administrative Council upon the nomination of the Chairman.

(2) The office of Secretary-General or Deputy Secretary-General shall be incompatible with the exercise of any political function, and with any employment or occupation other than employment by the Bank or by the Permanent Court of Arbitration, except as the Administrative Council, with the concurrence of the Chairman, may otherwise decide.

Section 10. (1) The Secretary-General shall be the principal officer of the Center and shall be responsible for its administration, including the appointment of staff, in accordance with the provisions of this Convention and the rules and regulations adopted thereunder by the Administrative Council.

(2) During any absence or inability to act of the Secretary-General, and during any vacancy of the office of Secretary-General, the Deputy Secretary-General shall act as Secretary-General. If there shall be more than one Deputy Secretary-General, the Secretary-General shall determine in what order they shall act as Secretary-General.

Comment

10. As indicated in Section 10(1) the Secretary-General would be the principal administrative officer of the Center. While he would have no influence whatever on the outcome of proceedings under the auspices of the Center he could, however, in practice perform a valuable task in promoting use of the Center's facilities and by giving informal assistance and advice to parties in connection with such proceedings. In addition it is contemplated that he would be asked by the Chairman to consult with parties in order to assist the Chairman in choosing conciliators (Art. III, Sec. 3) and arbitrators (Art. IV, Sec. 3). He would fix, within such limits as were set by the Administrative Council, charges payable by the parties for the use of the facilities of the Center (Art. VI, Sec. 2), and might also be consulted regarding the fees and expenses of conciliators and arbitrators (Art. VI, Sec. 3), as well as the location of any proceedings to take place outside Washington or The Hague (Art. VII, Sec. 2). The proper performance of these various functions would seem to require that the office of Secretary-General be one of complete independence—independence of Contracting States as well as of the Administrative Council—hence the general rule in Section 9(2) that that office "shall be incompatible with the exercise of any political function, and with any [other] employment or occupation.... "

11. If it could be expected with reasonable certainty that activities under the Convention would be such as to provide a full-time occupation for a Secretary-General and one Deputy, it would be desirable to provide that they, or at least the Secretary-General himself, should not hold any other office or engage in any other occupation or activity. Since no such certainty exists, the text permits a

degree of flexibility which would allow the Administrative Council and the Chairman, as nominating authority, to make exceptions to the rule and, in addition, specifically excludes from incompatibility concurrent employment by the Bank or by the Permanent Court of Arbitration.

12. As the Secretary-General in addition to his other functions would have to perform certain purely formal functions such as dealing with routine correspondence, dispatching notices, or making a finding that a certain period of time prescribed under the Convention had expired, it seemed desirable to provide for at least one Deputy who could assume those functions when necessary.

The Panels

Section 11. (1) The Panel of Conciliators shall consist of qualified persons, designated as hereafter provided, who are willing to serve as members of the Panel.

(2) Each Contracting State shall designate not more than [six] persons to serve on the Panel, who may, but need not, be its own nationals.

(3) The Chairman shall have the right to designate up to [twelve] persons to serve on the Panel.

Section 12. (1) The Panel of Arbitrators shall consist of qualified persons, designated as hereafter provided, who are willing to serve as members of the Panel.

(2) Each Contracting State shall designate not more than [six] persons to serve on the Panel, who may, but need not, be its own nationals.

(3) The Chairman shall have the right to designate up to [twelve] persons to serve on the Panel.

Section 13. (1) Panel members shall serve for four years.

(2) In case of death or resignation of a member of either Panel, the Contracting State or the Chairman, as the case may be, which or who had designated the member, shall have the right to designate another person to serve for the balance of that member's term.

Section 14. (1) Designation to serve on one Panel shall not preclude designation to serve on the other.

(2) If a person is designated to serve on a Panel by more than one Contracting State, or by one or more Contracting States and the Chairman, he shall be deemed to have been designated by the authority which first designated him.

(3) All designations shall be notified to the Secretary-General and shall take effect from the date on which the notification is received.

Section 15. (1) The Contracting States shall pay due regard to the importance of designating persons of high moral character and recognized competence in the fields of law, commerce, industry or finance. To that end, they shall seek such advice as they may deem appropriate from their highest courts of justice, schools of law, bar associations and such commercial, industrial and financial organizations as shall be considered representative of the professions they embrace.

(2) The Chairman shall, in designating members to the Panels, pay due regard to the importance of assuring representation on the Panels of the principal legal systems of the world and of the main forms of economic activity.

Comment

13. In view of the optional and flexible character of the Convention as a whole, and of access to the Center in particular, the Panels have limited significance. Parties to proceedings under the auspices of the Center are entirely free to agree to use conciliators and arbitrators who have not been designated to the Panels. On the other hand, as will be seen from Articles III and IV of the text, unless the parties otherwise agree, conciliators and arbitrators are to be selected by them, or by the Chairman when called upon to do so, from the respective Panels.

14. The composition of the Panels could be determined in a variety of ways. One method would be to have the Contracting States elect a certain number of Panel members from among candidates nominated by each Contracting State. While this method would have certain advantages, particularly in encouraging States to nominate candidates of high quality, it has the disadvantage of necessitating a somewhat complicated voting procedure in order to assure a balanced composition of the Panels as between candidates nominated by the capital-exporting and capital-importing countries respectively. In this connection reference is made to the comment to Section 7 of this article.

15. The method adopted in the present text largely follows the system of the Hague Conventions of 1899 and 1907, in leaving the composition of the Panels primarily to the Contracting States. The Panels are to consist not only of legal experts, but also of experts in other fields. They would be composed of a certain number of experts designated by each Contracting State while it is provided in addition, that the Chairman would have the right to designate a specified number of panel members in addition to those designated by the Contracting States. It might be desirable for the Chairman to exercise his right of designation after the States had made their designations, and with a view to achieving balanced representation on the Panels not only of different legal systems but also of different forms of economic activity.

16. With regard to cases of multiple designation referred to in Section 14(2), the Administrative Rules of the Center would, in implementation of that provision, indicate how prior designation is to be determined.

Financing the Center

Section 16. To the extent that expenditure of the Center cannot be met out of charges for the use of its facilities, or out of other receipts, it shall be borne by the Contracting States which are members of the Bank in proportion to their respective subscriptions to the capital stock of the Bank, and by Contracting States which are not members of the Bank in accordance with rules adopted by the Administrative Council.

Comment
17. As some Contracting States might not be members of the Bank, it is provided that the Administrative Rules of the Center would specify the contribution of non-member States. The words "or out of other receipts" have been included in order to take account of the possibility that the Bank might finance the cost of the Center. Reference is also made to the comment to Article VI.

Privileges and Immunities

Section 17. The Center shall be immune from all legal process.

Section 18 (1) The Chairman, the members of the Administrative Council, and the officers and employees of the Secretariat

(i) shall be immune from legal process with respect to acts performed by them in their official capacity;
(ii) not being local nationals shall be accorded the same immunities from immigration restrictions, alien registration requirements and national service obligations, the same facilities as regards exchange restrictions and the same treatment in respect of travelling facilities as are accorded by Contracting States to the representatives, officials and employees of comparable rank of other Contracting States.

(2) Paragraph (1) (ii) of this Section shall also apply to persons acting as conciliators or arbitrators in proceedings pursuant to this Convention, and to persons appearing as parties, representatives of parties, agents, counsel, experts or witnesses in such proceedings, but only in connection with their travel to and from the seat of the Center or other location where the proceedings are held and their stay at such location for the purpose of such proceedings.

Section 19. (1) The archives of the Center shall be inviolable.

(2) The official communications of the Center shall be accorded by each Contracting State the same treatment as is accorded to the official communications of other Contracting States.

Section 20. (1) The Center, its assets, property and income, and its operations and transactions authorized by this Convention shall be immune from all taxation and customs duties. The Center shall also be immune from liability for the collection or payment of any taxes or customs duties.

(2) No tax shall be levied on or in respect of salaries or emoluments paid by the Center to the Chairman, members of the Administrative Council or officials or employees of the Secretariat who are not local citizens, local subjects or other local nationals.

(3) No tax shall be levied on or in respect of honoraria, fees or other income received by persons acting as conciliators or arbitrators in proceedings pursuant to this Convention for their services in such proceedings, if the sole jurisdictional basis for such tax shall be the location of the Center or the place where such proceedings are conducted or the place where such income is paid.

Comment

18. These provisions are in general patterned after the privileges and immunities of the Bank, except that the Center has been given full immunity from legal process, whereas the Bank in view of the nature of its dealings with capital markets, enjoys only limited immunity in that respect. Section 18(2) is desirable to ensure the proper functioning of proceedings under the auspices of the Center. It will be noted that Section 20(3) does not confer a tax exemption, but merely seeks to avoid taxation based solely on the location of the Center, the place where proceedings are held, or the place of payment. Similar restrictions on taxation of interest paid on the Bank's bonds are found in Article VII, Section 9(c), of the Bank's Articles of Agreement.

Article II
Jurisdiction of the Center

Section 1. The jurisdiction of the Center shall be limited to proceedings for conciliation and arbitration with respect to any existing or future investment dispute of a legal character between a Contracting State and a national of another Contracting State (or that State when subrogated in the rights of its national) and shall be based on the consent of the parties thereto.

Section 2. Consent to the jurisdiction of the Center by any party to a dispute may be evidenced by

(i) a prior written undertaking by such party to have recourse pursuant to the terms of this Convention, to conciliation or arbitration;
(ii) *ad hoc* submission of a dispute by such party to the Center; or
(iii) acceptance by such party of jurisdiction in respect of a dispute submitted to the Center by another party.

Section 3. (1) Any Conciliation Commission and any Arbitral Tribunal constituted pursuant to this Convention shall be the judge of its own competence.

(2) Any claim of a party to a dispute that the Commission or the Tribunal lacks competence on the ground that

(i) there is no dispute;
(ii) there is no valid consent to jurisdiction;
(iii) the dispute is not within the scope of the consent; or
(iv) a party to the dispute is not a national of a Contracting State,

shall be dealt with by the Commission or Tribunal, as the case may be, as a preliminary question.

(3) In any proceedings in connection with paragraph (2)(iv) of this Section, a written affirmation of nationality signed by or on behalf of the Minister of Foreign Affairs of the State whose nationality is claimed by the party and issued for the purpose of those proceedings shall be conclusive proof of the facts stated therein.

Comment

1. The term "jurisdiction" is used in Section 1 and in the title of Article II in its broadest sense to denote the scope of the facilities made available by the Center. The terminology used follows the precedent of the Hague Convention of 1907 which speaks of the "jurisdiction of the Permanent Court" (see for example Article 47 of the Convention) even though that Court, like the proposed Center does not itself exercise judicial or quasi-judicial functions.

2. Section 1 of this article deals with the scope of the facilities available under the auspices of the Center in relation to (a) the type of proceedings, (b) the category of dispute, (c) the parties to the dispute and (d) the consensual nature of jurisdiction.

Type of Proceedings

3. Proceedings under the auspices of the Center are limited to conciliation and arbitration. Section 1 also permits the parties to a dispute, if they so agree, to have recourse to both procedures consecutively.

Category of Disputes

4. No detailed definition of the category of disputes in respect of which the facilities of the Center would be available has been included in the Convention. Instead, the general understanding reflected in the Preamble, the use of the term "investment dispute," and the requirement that the dispute be of a legal character as distinct from political, economic or purely commercial disputes, were thought adequate to limit the scope of the Convention in this regard. Within those limits Contracting States would be free to determine in each particular case what disputes they would submit to the Center. To include a more precise definition would tend to open the door to frequent disagreements as to the applicability of the Convention to a particular undertaking, thus undermining the primary objective of this article viz., to give confidence that undertakings to have recourse to conciliation or arbitration will be carried out.

5. Consideration was given to fixing a lower limit for the value of the subject-matter of a dispute. It was, however, recognized that the parties would in practice be best qualified to decide whether, having regard to pertinent facts and circumstances including the value of the subject-matter, a dispute is one which ought to be submitted to the Center. The subject-matter of a dispute might be of insignificant pecuniary value, but might involve important questions of principle, thus justifying the bringing of a test case. In other instances the pecuniary value might not be readily ascertainable, as where a host government fails to implement a provision in an investment agreement conferring immunity from immigration restrictions on foreign personnel, or might not be ascertainable at all, as where an investor fails to implement an agreement with a host government to train local personnel.

The Parties to the Dispute

6. Section 1 indicates that the facilities of the Center would be available only in disputes between a Contracting State on the one hand and a national of another Contracting State on the other, with a view to ensuring reciprocal performance of obligations which arise out of the application of the Convention. The facilities would thus not be available in a dispute involving a non-contracting State or a national of such State. Also excluded from jurisdiction are disputes (a) between private individuals, (b) between Governments (except where a Government had satisfied the claim of its national, e.g. under a scheme of investment insurance, and was thereby subrogated in the rights of that national in a dispute before the Center) and (c) between a Contracting State and one of its own nationals (unless that person possessed concurrently the nationality of another State which was a party to the Convention; see Article X, 2).

Consensual Nature of Jurisdiction

7. To the extent that the provisions of Article II constitute a development, rather than a mere codification of existing international law, it is to be expected that States would not wish its provisions to apply automatically to undertakings given in the past, nor to all undertakings to be given in the future. Section 2(i), therefore, limits the application of the Convention to cases where the parties have specifically undertaken to have recourse "pursuant to the terms of this Convention."

8. Section 1 *in fine* declares that the facilities can only be utilized if the parties to the dispute have consented to have recourse to the Center, while Section 2 specifies the manner in which consent may be given, i.e. by a prior undertaking in writing, or by *ad hoc* acceptance of jurisdiction. No particular form is prescribed for the prior written undertaking, which may be unilateral e.g. by enactment of legislation, bilateral or multilateral.

9. When entering into any undertaking pursuant to Section 2 a party would, of course, be free to include such limitations on the scope of the particular undertaking as may seem to it appropriate provided that those limitations were not inconsistent with its obligations deriving from the Convention as a whole.

Determination of Competence

10. The power of an arbitral tribunal to determine its competence is well established in international law. Section 3(1) confers that power alike on conciliation commissions and arbitral tribunals constituted pursuant to the Convention, thus providing a safeguard against frustration of proceedings through unilateral determination of competence by a party.

Preliminary Questions

11. Section 3(2) lists four classes of objection to competence and declares that they shall be dealt with by the commission or tribunal as preliminary questions to be disposed of before entering upon the merits of the case. Thus, objections to conciliation on the grounds enumerated, while they would not prevent constitution of a commission or commencement of conciliation proceedings would be the subject of a preliminary non-binding recommendation to the parties. In the case of arbitration proceedings similar objections would, however, be the subject of a preliminary binding ruling by the tribunal.

Nationality

12. While preliminary questions based on nationality would be subject to the procedure prescribed for dealing with preliminary questions generally, Section 3(3) contains an additional rule relating to determination of nationality in a given case. This rule is based on the view that, in the circumstances envisaged, a question of a claim of nationality by a party ought in the first instance to be determined by the State whose nationality is claimed, the question being dealt with by the commission or tribunal only where that State failed to do so. Accordingly, it is provided that the written affirmation of nationality by a Minister of Foreign Affairs, or official of corresponding rank responsible for the conduct of that State's external affairs, issued for the purpose of the particular proceedings, shall be conclusive proof of the facts stated therein. The affirmation would relate to that party's nationality on the date on which he consented to the jurisdiction of the Center. (In this connection reference is made to the definition of "National of a Contracting State" and of "National of another Contracting State" in Article X.) Where such affirmation is not introduced, other evidence of nationality satisfactory to the commission or tribunal must be produced.

Article III
Conciliation

Request for Conciliation

Section 1. Any dispute within the jurisdiction of the Center may be the subject of a request for conciliation by a Conciliation Commission (hereinafter called the Commission). The request may be made by either party to the dispute, shall be addressed to the Secretary-General in writing, and shall state that the other party has consented to the jurisdiction of the Center.

Constitution of the Commission

Section 2. (1) The Commission shall consist of a sole conciliator or several conciliators appointed as the parties shall agree.

(2) Where the parties have not so agreed, the Commission shall consist of three conciliators, one appointed by each party and the third appointed by agreement of the parties, all appointees to be selected from the Panel of Conciliators.

Section 3. (1) If the Commission shall not have been constituted within three months after the request referred to in Section 1, the Chairman shall, at the request of either party, appoint the conciliator or conciliators not appointed pursuant to Section 2. Before making any such appointment, the Chairman shall instruct the Secretary-General to consult with the parties and to report to him any information or views which might assist him in making the appointment.

(2) In making any appointment under this Section the Chairman shall select the appointee from the Panel of Conciliators.

Comment

1. The composition of the Commission, its precise terms of reference and the procedure applicable in proceedings before it are matters for agreement between the parties concerned. It is only in the absence of such agreement that the provisions of this article thereon would become operative.

2. In recognition of differences between the conciliation and arbitration process, Section 2(2), in contrast to the corresponding provision on appointment of arbitrators (see Section 2(2) of Article IV), does not preclude appointment of a conciliator on the ground that he is a national of a state party to the dispute, or of the State whose national is a party to the dispute.

3. As to the role of the Chairman as appointing authority under Section 3, reference is made to the comment on Sections 2 and 3 of Article IV.

Powers and Functions of the Commission

Section 4. Except as the parties and the Commission shall otherwise agree, the Commission shall conduct the conciliation proceedings in accordance with the Conciliation Rules adopted under this Convention and in effect on the date on which the consent to conciliation became effective.

Section 5. (1) It shall be the duty of the Commission to clarify the points in dispute between the parties and to endeavor to bring about agreement between them upon mutually acceptable terms. To that end, the Commission may at any stage of the proceedings and from time to time recommend terms of settlement to the parties.

(2) If the parties reach agreement, the Commission shall draw up a report noting the submission of the dispute, and recording that the parties have reached agreement. If, at any time, it appears to the Commission that there is no likelihood of agreement between the parties it may declare the proceedings closed, and shall, in that event, draw up a report noting the submission of the dispute and recording the failure of the parties to reach agreement. If one party fails to appear or participate in the proceedings, the Commission shall so state in its report.

(3) Except as the parties shall otherwise agree, the reports referred to in paragraph (2) shall not contain terms of settlement recommended to or accepted by the parties.

Comment

4. Section 5(1) describes the duties of the Commission, and is based upon generally accepted concepts of the conciliation function. (See Article 15(1) of the General Act for the Pacific Settlement of International Disputes, 1928; Article XXII of the American Treaty on Pacific Settlement, 1948.) The Commission is specifically empowered to make recommendations to the parties at any stage of the proceedings. In order to avoid any interpretation to the effect that after a recommendation made in the course of proceedings and before their termination, the Commission was *functus officio*, the words "and from time to time" have been inserted in the second sentence of Section 5(1).

Obligations of the Parties

Section 6. The parties shall give the Commission their full cooperation in order to enable the Commission to carry out its functions and shall give their most serious consideration to its recommendations. Except as the parties to the dispute shall otherwise agree, the recommendations of the Commission shall not be binding upon them.

Section 7. Neither party to a conciliation proceeding shall be entitled in any later proceeding concerning the same dispute, whether before arbitrators or in a court of law or otherwise, to invoke or rely on any views expressed or statements or admissions or offers of settlement made by the other party in the conciliation proceedings, or the recommendations, if any, made by the Commission therein.

Comment

5. Section 6, in accordance with principle, declares that recommendations of the Commission shall not be binding, while leaving it open to the parties to agree to be bound by them. The requirement that the parties cooperate with the Commission and give serious consideration to its recommendations is a corollary of the fundamental principle of good faith.

6. Section 7 is intended to encourage the parties to seek agreement rather than maintain fixed positions out of the fear that a conciliatory attitude might prejudice their position in a possible later proceeding.

Article IV
Arbitration

Request for Arbitration

Section 1. Any dispute within the jurisdiction of the Center may be the subject of a request for arbitration by an Arbitral Tribunal (hereinafter called the Tribunal). The request may be made by either party to the dispute, shall be addressed to the Secretary-General in writing, and shall state that the other party has consented to the jurisdiction of the Center.

Constitution of the Tribunal

Section 2. (1) The Tribunal shall consist of a sole arbitrator or several arbitrators appointed as the parties shall agree. Where the parties have not so agreed, the Tribunal shall consist of three arbitrators, one arbitrator appointed by each party and the third appointed by agreement of the parties.

(2) The arbitrators so appointed shall be selected from the Panel of Arbitrators. None of the arbitrators shall be a national of a State party to the dispute or of a State whose national is a party to the dispute, or shall have acted as a conciliator in the same dispute.

Section 3. If the Tribunal shall not have been constituted within three months after the request referred to in Section 1, the Chairman shall, at the request of either party, appoint the arbitrator or arbitrators not appointed pursuant to Section 2. The provisions of paragraph 2 of Section 2 of this Article shall apply to the appointment of arbitrators by the Chairman. Before making any such appointment, the Chairman shall instruct the Secretary-General to consult with the parties and to report to him any information or views which might assist him in making the appointment.

Comment
1. The composition of the Tribunal, its terms of reference, and the procedure applicable in proceedings before it are, as in the case of conciliation, matters for agreement between the parties concerned, and the provisions of this article thereon would become operative only in the absence of such agreement (Sections 2 and 5). Section 2(1) adopts what is perhaps the most usual method for the constitution of an arbitral tribunal viz., each party appoints an arbitrator, and a third is appointed by agreement of the parties. However, Section 2(2) introduces a significant innovation by specifying that none of the arbitrators shall be nationals of the State party to the dispute, or of the State whose national is a party to the dispute, thus seeking to minimize as far as possible the danger, inherent in conventional systems, of appointment of partisan arbitrators.[1] This new principle applies also to appointments of arbitrators made by the Chairman under Section 3 of this article.

2. It is a necessary concomitant of the binding character of an undertaking to have recourse to arbitration that adequate provision should be made to prevent frustration of that undertaking by an unwilling party. That is the purpose of the appointment procedure laid down in Section 3. As in the case of conciliation (see Section 3 of Article III), the Chairman is appointing authority unless the parties have otherwise agreed. It may be noted that the Chairman would exercise his power of appointment even if he were of the same nationality as one of the parties. The basic consideration underlying these provisions is that the appointing authority is a person who, because of his office, may be conclusively presumed to be capable of acting impartially in the selection of conciliators or arbitrators under all circumstances. It may be noted that under the Bank's Loan Regulations[2] an unrestricted power of appointment is conferred upon the President of the International Court of Justice and the Secretary-General of the United Nations regardless of their nationality.

Powers and Functions of the Tribunal

Section 4. (1) In the absence of agreement between the parties concerning the law to be applied, and unless the parties shall have given the Tribunal the power to decide *ex aequo et bono*, the Tribunal shall decide the dispute submitted to it in accordance with such rules of law, whether national or international, as it shall determine to be applicable.

(2) The Tribunal may not bring in a finding of *non liquet* on the ground of the silence or obscurity of the law to be applied.

Section 5. Except as the parties otherwise agree, any arbitration proceeding shall be conducted in accordance with the Arbitration Rules adopted under this Convention and in effect on the date when the consent to arbitration became effective. If any question of procedure arises which is not covered by the applicable arbitration rules, the Arbitral Tribunal shall decide that question.

[1] One writer has said: "It is a grave mistake to construct a tribunal out of two national members and one neutral member. Few men are capable of holding the balance between two contending national commissioners. If the governments do not object to the possibility of decision by compromise rather than by adjudication, they should provide for two national commissioners with an umpire in case of disagreement. Otherwise they should provide either for one, or better still three, neutral commissioners." A. H. Feller, *The Mexican Claims Commissions, 1923–1934* (New York, 1935) at p. 317.

[2] See Loan Regulations No. 3 and No. 4, dated February 15, 1961 (amended February 9, 1967), respectively Sections 7.03(c) and 7.04(c)

Section 6. All questions before the Tribunal shall be decided by majority vote.

Section 7. (1) An award signed by a majority of the Tribunal shall constitute the award of the Tribunal. The award shall be in writing and shall state the reasons upon which it is based.

(2) The award shall immediately be communicated to the parties.

Section 8. (1) Whenever one of the parties does not appear before the Tribunal, or fails to defend its case, the other party may call upon the Tribunal to decide in favor of its claim.

(2) In such case, the Tribunal may render an award if it is satisfied that it has jurisdiction and that the claim appears to be well-founded in fact and in law.

Section 9. Except as the parties otherwise agree, the Tribunal shall have the power to hear and determine incidental or additional claims or counter-claims arising directly out of the subject-matter of the dispute.

Section 10. Except as the parties otherwise agree, the Tribunal shall have the power to prescribe, at the request of either party, any provisional measures necessary for the protection of the rights of the parties.

Comment

3. Section 4(1) leaves the determination of the law to be applied in a particular case to the parties, and if they cannot agree thereon, to the Tribunal. The parties may also give the Tribunal the power to decide *ex aequo et bono*, that is, in accordance with what is just and equitable in the circumstances, rather than by application of rules of law. Section 4(2) states that the Tribunal will not be excused from rendering an award on the ground that the law is not sufficiently clear.

4. The power conferred on the Tribunal by Section 8 to render an award upon the default of one party is a corollary of the binding character of the undertaking to have recourse to arbitration and is possessed by arbitration tribunals provided for in the Bank's Loan Regulations Nos. 3 and 4, Sections 7.03(h) and 7.04(h), respectively. (See also Article 53 of the Statute of the International Court of Justice.) Before an award can be rendered under this section, however, the Tribunal must be satisfied not only that it has jurisdiction but also that the claim on the merits appears to be well-founded.

5. Unless the parties to a dispute agree to restrict its competence to certain principal claims, the Tribunal will have the power to determine incidental and additional claims as well as counter-claims, provided that they arise directly out of the subject-matter of the dispute. In addition, unless the parties specifically preclude it from doing so, the Tribunal would have the power to prescribe provisional measures designed to preserve the *status quo* between the parties pending its final decision on the merits.

Interpretation, Revision and Annulment of the Award

Section 11. (1) Any dispute between the parties as to the meaning and scope of the award may, at the request of either party made within [three] months after the date of the award, be submitted to the Tribunal which rendered the award. Such a request shall stay the enforcement of the award pending the decision of the Tribunal.

(2) If for any reason it is impossible to submit the dispute to the Tribunal which rendered the award, a new Tribunal shall be constituted in accordance with the terms of the agreement, if any, between the parties regarding the constitution of the Tribunal which rendered the award, and otherwise pursuant to the provisions of this Article.

Section 12. (1) An application for revision of the award may be made by either party on the ground of the discovery of some fact of such a nature as to have a decisive influence on the award, provided that when the award was rendered that fact was unknown to the Tribunal and to the party requesting revision and that such ignorance was not due to the negligence of the party requesting revision.

(2) The application for revision must be made within [six] months of the discovery of the new fact and in any case within [ten] years of the rendering of the award.

(3) The application shall, if possible, be submitted to the Tribunal which rendered the award. If this shall not be possible, a new Tribunal shall be constituted in accordance with the terms of the agreement, if any, between the parties regarding the constitution of the Tribunal which rendered the award, and otherwise pursuant to the provisions of this Article. The Tribunal to which the application is made may stay the enforcement of the award pending its decision.

Section 13. (1) The validity of an award may be challenged by either party on one or more of the following grounds:

(a) that the Tribunal has exceeded its powers;
(b) that there was corruption on the part of a member of the Tribunal; or
(c) that there has been a serious departure from a fundamental rule of procedure, including failure to state the reasons for the award.

(2) An application pursuant to paragraph 1 of this Section shall be made in writing to the Chairman who shall forthwith appoint from the Panel of Arbitrators an *ad hoc* Committee of three persons which shall be competent to declare the nullity of the award or any part thereof on any of the grounds set forth in the preceding paragraph. None of the members of the Committee shall have been a member of the Tribunal which rendered the award, shall be a national of the State party to the dispute or of the State whose national is a party to the dispute, or shall have acted as a conciliator in the same dispute.

(3) The provisions of Sections 5, 6, 7 and 8 of this Article shall apply *mutatis mutandis* to proceedings before the Committee.

(4) In cases covered by sub-paragraphs (a) and (c) of paragraph (1), application must be made within sixty days of the rendering of the award, and in cases covered by sub-paragraph (b) of paragraph (1), within six months.

(5) The Committee shall have the power to stay enforcement of the award pending its decision and to recommend any provisional measures necessary for the protection of the rights of the parties.

(6) If the award is declared invalid the dispute shall, at the request of either party, be submitted to a new tribunal constituted by agreement between the parties or, failing such agreement in the manner specified in Sections 2 and 3 of this Article.

Enforcement of the Award

Section 14. The award shall be final and binding on the parties. Each party shall abide by and comply with the award immediately, unless the Tribunal shall have allowed a time limit for the carrying out of the award or any part thereof, or the enforcement of the award shall have been stayed pursuant to Sections 11, 12 or 13 of this Article.

Section 15. Each Contracting State shall recognize an award of the Tribunal as binding and enforce it within its territories as if it were a final judgment of the courts of that State.

Comment

6. It was recognized in the Preamble as a corollary of the principle that an undertaking must be implemented in good faith, that the award of a Tribunal must be complied with. As a general rule the award of the Tribunal is final, and there is no provision for appeal. Sections 11 and 12, however, provide for interpretation and revision of the award, respectively. In addition, where there has been some violation of the fundamental principles of law governing the Tribunal's proceedings such as are listed in Section 13, the aggrieved party may apply to the Chairman for a declaration that the award is invalid. Under that section the Chairman is required to refer the matter to a Committee of three persons which shall be competent to declare the nullity of the award. It may be noted that this is not a procedure by way

of appeal requiring consideration of the merits of the case, but one that merely calls for an affirmative or negative ruling based upon one or other of the three grounds listed in Section 13(1).

7. The award is binding on the parties to the dispute who are required to implement it forthwith. However, implementation of the award may be delayed in certain prescribed circumstances, viz.,

1) where the Tribunal has, in rendering the award, expressly allowed a time limit for carrying it out (Section 14);
2) upon stay of enforcement by the Tribunal consequent upon
   (a) a request for interpretation of the award (Section 11(1)); or
   (b) an application for revision of the award (Section 12(3)); and
3) upon stay of enforcement by the Committee appointed pursuant to Section 13 pending its decision upon the validity of the award (Section 13(5)).

8. Section 15 requires each Contracting State, whether or not it or its national as a party to the proceedings, to recognize awards of tribunals pursuant to the Convention as binding and to enforce them as though they were final judgments of its own courts, irrespective of the treatment under its law of other arbitral awards.

Relationship of Arbitration to other Remedies

Section 16. Consent to have recourse to arbitration pursuant to this Convention shall, unless otherwise stated, be deemed consent to have recourse to such proceedings in lieu of any other remedy.

Comment

9. Section 16 states a rule of interpretation rather than of substance. The section leaves a party free to stipulate that notwithstanding its undertaking to submit a dispute to arbitration, it reserves the right to have recourse to courts of law. Similarly, Section 16 leaves it open to a State to stipulate that its consent to have recourse to arbitration is subject to the condition that the foreign investor first exhaust his remedies in the State's national courts or administrative agencies. Section 16 merely provides that in the absence of any such stipulations consent to have recourse to arbitration will be regarded as excluding any other remedy.

10. To illustrate the foregoing by an example: An investment agreement between a State and a foreign investor provides without qualification that "any controversy arising between the parties concerning the interpretation or application of this agreement shall be submitted to arbitration in accordance with the provisions of the Convention [etc.]." A dispute arises with respect to the tax exemption provisions of the investment agreement. If either the foreign investor or the State were to bring this dispute before the Tax Court of the State rather than submit it to the Center, the other party could object, in which event the Tax Court would have to dismiss the claim. If the investor were to bring the dispute before the Center, the State could not object on the ground that the investor had not exhausted his remedies in the Tax Court.

11. As stated in paragraph 9 of the Comment to this section, States are free to qualify their consent to have recourse to arbitration, as by inclusion of a stipulation in an undertaking that local remedies must be exhausted. However, if a State were to include an unqualified arbitration clause in an agreement with a foreign investor, it would seem to run counter to normal rules of interpretation to read into that clause a requirement of the prior exhaustion of local remedies. All that Section 16 does is to assure that effect will be given to the expressed intention of the parties

Section 17. (1) No Contracting State shall give diplomatic protection or bring an international claim in respect of a dispute which one of its nationals and another Contracting State shall have consented to submit, or shall have submitted to arbitration pursuant to this Convention, except on the ground that the other Contracting State has failed to perform its obligations under this Convention with respect to that dispute.

(2) Nothing in this Section shall be construed as precluding a Contracting State from founding an international claim against another Contracting State upon the facts of a dispute which one of these Contracting States and a national of the other shall have consented to submit or shall have submitted to arbitration pursuant to this Convention, where

those facts also give rise to a dispute concerning the interpretation or application of an agreement between the States concerned; without prejudice, however, to the finality and binding character of any arbitral award rendered pursuant to this Convention as between the parties to the arbitral proceedings.

Comment

12. Unlike Section 16, which gives merely a rule of interpretation, Section 17 lays down a rule of substantive law. It should be noted that this section constitutes a significant innovation.

13. The proposed Convention would recognize the right of an investor, within specified limits, to proceed in his own name against a foreign State before an arbitral tribunal constituted pursuant to the Convention instead of seeking the diplomatic protection of his State or having that State bring an international claim. It would seem to be a reasonable concomitant of the recognition of the investor's right of direct access to an international jurisdiction, to exclude action by his national State in cases in which such direct access has been availed of by, or is available to, the investor, whether as plaintiff or defendant, under the Convention. Since the exclusion of the national State rests on the premise that the other Contracting State party to the dispute will abide by the provisions of the Convention, the rule of exclusion is subject to an exception in the event that that premise falls away. In such a case rights of providing diplomatic protection and of bringing an international claim remain unaffected.

14. Section 17(2) preserves the right of the national State of the investor to bring an international claim where the same facts give rise not only to a dispute covered by the Convention but also to a breach of some other international agreement between the States concerned. That section does, however, maintain the finality and binding character of an award rendered by a tribunal under the Convention as regards the parties to which it relates. For example, the dispute covered by the Convention may involve a claim for damages for an alleged breach of an investment agreement and the facts alleged may at the same time constitute a breach of a bilateral agreement between the host State and the investor's national State. Whether the investor, in an action before the Center, is successful or unsuccessful, his national State would be free to have recourse to such procedures as may have been provided in the bilateral agreement. The outcome of the proceedings between the two States under the bilateral agreement would not, however, affect the award rendered by the tribunal constituted under the Convention. Thus, if the investor had been unsuccessful before the Center, even though his national State may prevail in the proceedings under the bilateral agreement, the investor could not benefit thereby.

Article V
Replacement and Disqualification of Conciliators and Arbitrators

Section 1. After a Conciliation Commission or an Arbitral Tribunal has been constituted and proceedings have begun, its composition shall remain unchanged; provided, however, that if a conciliator or arbitrator should die, become incapacitated, or resign, the resulting vacancy shall be filled by the method used for the original appointment, except that if a conciliator or arbitrator appointed by a party shall have resigned without the consent of the Commission or Tribunal of which he was a member, or consequent upon a decision to disqualify him pursuant to Section 2 (2) of this Article, the resulting vacancy shall be filled by the Chairman.

Section 2. (1) (a) A party may propose the disqualification of a conciliator or arbitrator appointed pursuant to Article III, Section 2, or Article IV, Section 2, respectively, on account of any fact whether antecedent or subsequent to the constitution of the Commission or Tribunal.

(b) A party may propose the disqualification of a conciliator or arbitrator appointed by the Chairman pursuant to Article III, Section 3, or Article IV, Section 3, on account of any fact arising subsequent to the constitution of the Commission or Tribunal. It may propose disqualification of such conciliator or arbitrator on account of any fact which arose prior to the constitution of the Commission or Tribunal only if it can show that the appointment was made without knowledge of that fact or as a result of fraud.

(2) The decision on any proposed disqualification shall be taken by the other members of the Commission or Tribunal as the case may be, provided that where those members are equally divided, or in the case of a proposed disqualification of a single conciliator or arbitrator, the Chairman shall take that decision. If it is decided that the proposal is well-founded, the conciliator or arbitrator to whom the decision relates shall resign, and the resulting vacancy shall be filled in the manner provided for in Section 1 of this Article.

Comment
1. Section 1 incorporates what has been called the "principle of immutability" and is intended to preclude the replacement of conciliators and arbitrators by the parties during proceedings with a view to influencing the outcome of those proceedings, as well as their resignation under pressure.

2. Section 2 relates to disqualification of a conciliator or an arbitrator. Section 2(1)(a) covers the case of a conciliator or an arbitrator appointed by a party to the dispute, and is to the effect that a party may at any time propose their disqualification. Such proposal may be based upon any fact, such as general unfitness, personal prejudice, misconduct or interest in the subject-matter, and regardless of whether that fact arose before or after constitution of the Commission or Tribunal.

3. While, under Section 2(1)(b), a party may at any time propose the disqualification of a conciliator or arbitrator appointed by the Chairman, as a rule such proposal must be founded upon facts which arose *after* constitution of the Commission or Tribunal as the Chairman must be deemed to have passed conclusively on the qualifications of his nominee. A proposal to disqualify under this section may be founded on a fact which existed prior to the constitution of the Commission or Tribunal only if it can be shown that the Chairman made the appointment in question without knowledge of that fact, or was induced to do so as a result of fraud.

Article VI
Apportionment of Costs of Proceedings

Section 1. Except as the parties shall otherwise agree,

(a) each party to a conciliation or arbitration proceeding shall bear its own expenses in connection therewith, and

(b) charges payable for the use of the facilities of the Center, as well as the fees and expenses of members of the Commission or Tribunal as the case may be, shall be borne equally by the parties;

provided, however, that if a Commission or Tribunal determines that a party has instituted proceedings frivolously or in bad faith, it may assess any part or all of such expenses, fees and charges against that party.

Section 2. The charges payable by the parties for the use of the facilities of the Center shall be fixed by the Secretary-General within the limits approved from time to time by the Administrative Council.

Section 3. The fees and expenses of conciliators and arbitrators shall, in the absence of agreement between them and the parties, be fixed by the Commission or Tribunal concerned after consultation with the Secretary-General.

Comment
This article contemplates that the parties may be called upon to make certain payments to the Center for the use of its services. It is intended that "charges" should cover the out-of-pocket costs or other clearly identifiable costs incurred by the Center in connection with a proceeding, such as hiring of translators and interpreters, engagement of additional secretarial or clerical staff and the like.

Article VII
Place of Proceedings

Section 1. Conciliation and arbitration proceedings shall be held either at the seat of the Center or, pursuant to any arrangements made under Article I, Section 2(3), at the seat of the Permanent Court of Arbitration or other public international institution, as the parties may agree. If the parties do not so agree the Secretary-General shall, after consultation with the parties and with the Conciliation Commission or the Arbitral Tribunal, as the case may be, determine the place of the proceedings.

Section 2. Notwithstanding the provisions of Section 1, proceedings may be held elsewhere, if the parties so agree and if the Conciliation Commission or Arbitral Tribunal, as the case may be, so approves after consultation with the Secretary-General.

Article VIII
Interpretation

Any question or dispute arising between Contracting States concerning the interpretation or application of this Convention which is not settled by negotiation shall be referred to the International Court of Justice, unless the States concerned agree to another mode of settlement.

Comment

The text of this article follows in general the pattern of similar clauses in the constituent instruments of international organizations within the United Nations family. While it leaves the Contracting States free to decide upon the mode of settlement of questions or disputes regarding interpretation of the Convention, it provides for adjudication by the International Court of Justice in the event of their being unable to agree on the mode of settlement.

Article IX
Amendment

Section 1. Any Contracting State may propose amendment of this Convention. The text of such proposed amendment shall be communicated to the Chairman of the Administrative Council not less than [three] months prior to the meeting of the Council at which such amendment is to be considered and shall forthwith be transmitted by him to all Contracting States.

Section 2. Amendments shall be adopted by a majority of [four-fifths] of the members of the Council. [Twelve] months after its adoption each amendment shall become effective for all Contracting States; provided, however, that such amendment shall not affect the rights and obligations of any Contracting State or of any national of a Contracting State under this Convention with respect to or arising out of proceedings for conciliation or arbitration pursuant to consent to the jurisdiction of the Center given prior to the effective date of the amendment.

Comment

In the absence of a provision for amendment, the Convention could only be changed by a new international agreement. In order to avoid this difficulty the text tentatively suggests inclusion of an amendment procedure. The Administrative Council is designated as the authority competent to decide upon proposals for amendment. Such proposals are required to be transmitted to it through the Chairman well in advance of the meeting of the Council at which such amendment is to be considered so as to enable members to consult with the authorities within Contracting States and take their views into account during a discussion of the issues involved. The support of a substantial majority—four-fifths is tentatively suggested—of the members of the Council would be required for adoption of a proposed amendment, which would come into effect for all the members after a period of say 12 months after such adoption. No provision is made regarding States which oppose the amendment after its adoption. It would, however, always be open to a State to declare its withdrawal from the Convention under Section 5 of Article XI. The period specified for effectiveness of the denunciation could be made to conform to the period required for effectiveness of the amendment adopted, thus permitting a State which wished to denounce the treaty to do so immediately following adoption of the amendment and thereby avoid becoming subject to the Convention as amended. The proviso in Section 2 ensures that amendments will not have retroactive effect.

Article X
Definitions

1. "National of a Contracting State" means a person natural or juridical possessing the nationality of any Contracting State on the date on which that person's consent to the jurisdiction of the Center pursuant to Section 2 of Article II became effective, and includes (a) any company which under the domestic law of that State is its national, and (b) any company in which the nationals of that State have a controlling interest. "Company" includes any association of natural or juridical persons, whether or not such association is recognized by the domestic law of the Contracting State concerned as having juridical personality.
2. "National of another Contracting State" means any national of a Contracting State other than the State party to the dispute, notwithstanding that such person may possess concurrently the nationality of a State not party to this Convention or of the State party to the dispute.

[Other definitions may be added if necessary]

Comment
1. The definitions have been broadly drawn. "Nationals" include both natural and juridical persons as well as associations of such persons. It will be noted that the term "national" is not restricted to privately-owned companies, thus permitting a wholly or partially government-owned company to be a party to proceedings brought by or against a foreign State.

2. Under the definition of "National of a Contracting State" a company may be a national of a given State either because it has that nationality under the State's domestic law, or because it is controlled by nationals of that State.

3. The question of dual nationality is dealt with in this sense, that a person is recognized as a "national of another Contracting State," if he has the nationality of that State even though he may at the same time be a national of the State party to the dispute or of a State which is not a party to the Convention.

4. Nationality is determined as of the date when consent to have recourse to conciliation or arbitration became effective.

Article XI
Final Provisions

[Final provisions have been inserted in the present draft tentatively and to provide some indication of formal legal items with which it will be necessary to deal. In general, they follow the pattern set by multilateral agreements in the past.]

Entry into Force

Section 1. This Convention shall be open for signature on behalf of States members of the Bank and all other sovereign States.

Section 2. This Convention shall be subject to ratification or acceptance by the signatory States in accordance with their respective constitutional procedures. The instruments of ratification or acceptance shall be deposited with the Bank and shall declare that the State concerned has taken all steps necessary to enable it to carry out all of its obligations under this Convention.

Section 3. This Convention shall enter into force when it has been ratified or accepted by [. . . . . .] States.

Comment
1. By Section 2 ratification or acceptance (either of which must be preceded by signature) is to be accompanied by a declaration that the "State concerned has taken all steps necessary to enable it to carry out all of its obligations under this Convention," a requirement also found in the Articles of Agreement of the Bank and its affiliates. When a State ratifies, therefore, other States would be entitled to rely on the implicit assurance of that State that adequate facilities exist—whether created by legislative or other means—to give full effect within its territories to the provisions of the Convention. Thus, for instance, it would be assumed that the obligations of private parties deriving from undertakings to have recourse to arbitration pursuant to the Convention would be fully enforceable against them under the local law, and that the award of an arbitral tribunal could be enforced as if it were a final judgment of a local court of competent jurisdiction.

Territorial Application

Section 4. By its signature of this Convention, each State accepts it both on its own behalf and in respect of all territories for whose international relations such State is responsible except those which are excluded by such State by written notice to the Bank.

Comment
2. By this section a signatory State agrees to the application of the Convention in respect of all territories for whose international relations such State is responsible, e.g. dependent or protected States. It would, however, be open to a State to exclude such application, if it so desires, by written notice to the Bank at the time of signature or at any time thereafter. This section is in substance identical with Section 3 of Article XI of the Articles of Agreement of the International Development Association.

Denunciation

Section 5. (1) Any Contracting State may denounce this Convention by written notice to the Bank.

(2) The denunciation shall take effect [twelve] months after receipt by the Bank of such notice; provided that the obligations of the State concerned arising out of undertakings given prior to the date of such notice shall remain in full force and effect.

Comment
3. In keeping with a practice followed in several multilateral agreements, the right of a State under general international law to denounce the Convention is recognized in Section 5. However, Section 5 (2) provides for lapse of a period of time—tentatively fixed at 12 months—before such denunciation could become effective. The general obligations of the denouncing State under the Convention would remain intact during that period, while its obligations arising out of undertakings given prior to the date of such notice are declared to remain in full force and effect regardless of the denunciation. In this connection reference is also made to the comment to Article IX (Amendment).

Inauguration of the Center

Section 6. Promptly upon the entry into force of this Convention, the President of the Bank shall convene the inaugural meeting of the Administrative Council.

Registration

Section 7. The Bank is authorized to register this Convention with the Secretariat of the United Nations in accordance with Article 102 of the Charter of the United Nations and the Regulations thereunder adopted by the General Assembly.

Comment
4. This section which authorizes registration of the Convention by the Bank, as depository, with the United Nations, is in substance identical with Section 5 of Article XI of the Articles of Agreement of the International Development Association.

DONE at ...., in a single copy which shall remain deposited in the archives of the International Bank for Reconstruction and Development, which has indicated by its signature below its agreement to act as depository of this Convention, to register this Convention with the Secretariat of the United Nations and to notify all signatory States of the date on which this Convention shall have entered into force.

Comment
5. The concluding formula adopted is in substance identical with that contained in the Articles of Agreement of the International Development Association.

APPENDIX III*

Draft Convention on the Settlement of Investment Disputes between States and Nationals of Other States (First Draft)

September 11, 1964

Preamble

The Contracting States

1. CONSIDERING the need for international cooperation for economic development, and the role of international investment therein;
2. BEARING IN MIND the possibility that from time to time disputes may arise in connection with such investment between Contracting States and nationals of other Contracting States and bearing in mind the desirability that such disputes be settled in a spirit of mutual confidence, and with due respect for the principle of equal rights of States in the exercise of their sovereignty;
3. RECOGNIZING that while such disputes would usually be subject to national legal processes, international methods of settlement may be appropriate in certain cases;
4. ATTACHING PARTICULAR IMPORTANCE to the availability of facilities for international conciliation or arbitration to which Contracting States and nationals of other Contracting States may submit such disputes if they so desire;
5. DESIRING to establish such facilities under the auspices of the International Bank for Reconstruction and Development;
6. RECOGNIZING that mutual consent by the parties to submit such disputes to conciliation or to arbitration through such facilities constitutes an agreement to be observed in good faith which requires in particular that due consideration be given to any recommendation of conciliation, and that any arbitral award be complied with; and
7. DECLARING that no Contracting State shall by the mere fact of its ratification or acceptance of this Convention be deemed to be under any obligation to submit any particular dispute to conciliation or arbitration in the absence of a specific undertaking to that effect,

HAVE AGREED as follows:

Chapter I
International Center for the Settlement of Investment Disputes

Title 1
Establishment and Organization

Article 1. (1) There is hereby established the International Center for the Settlement of Investment Disputes (hereinafter called the Center).

(2) The purpose of the Center is to provide facilities for conciliation and arbitration of investment disputes in accordance with the provisions of this Convention. The Center may in addition undertake such ancillary activities, including research and the collection and dissemination

* Text reproduced with permission of ICSID.

of information in the field of international investment, as the Administrative Council may, by a majority of not less than two-thirds of the votes of all its members, from time to time authorize.

Comment
Article 1 (1) corresponds to P.D. Art. I, Sec. 1. The title of the Center has been changed and provision reworded. No change of substance. Article 1(2) is new.

Article 2. (1) The seat of the Center shall be established at the headquarters of the International Bank for Reconstruction and Development (hereinafter called the Bank). The Center shall make arrangements with the Bank for the use of the Bank's offices and administrative services and facilities. The seat may be moved to another location by decision of the Administrative Council adopted by a majority of not less than two-thirds of the votes of all its members.

(2) Conciliation and arbitration proceedings pursuant to this Convention shall be held at the seat of the Center or elsewhere as may be determined in accordance with the provisions of Chapter VII. In order to facilitate the conduct of proceedings at places other than the seat of the Center, the Center may make arrangements with the Permanent Court of Arbitration and other public international institutions for the use of their offices and their administrative services and facilities.

Comment
Corresponds to P.D. Art. I, Sec. 2. The provision has been reworded and, in addition, now includes the substance of P.D. Art. I, Sec. 6(vi) concerning removal of the seat. The two-thirds majority required for arrangements with "other public international institutions" has been deleted.

Article 3. The Center shall have an Administrative Council, a Secretariat, a Panel of Conciliators and a Panel of Arbitrators.

Comment
Corresponds to P.D. Art. I, Sec. 3, reworded.

Title 2
The Administrative Council

Article 4. (1) The Administrative Council shall be composed of one representative and one alternate representative of each Contracting State. No alternate may vote or otherwise act as a representative except in case of the absence or inability to act of his principal.

(2) In the absence of a contrary designation, each governor and each alternate governor of the Bank appointed by a Contracting State shall be *ex-officio* the representative and alternate representative of that State on the Administrative Council.

Comment
Corresponds to P.D. Art. I, Sec. 4. In paragraph (1) the words "or otherwise act as a representative" have been added.

Article 5. The President of the Bank shall be *ex officio* Chairman of the Administrative Council (hereinafter called the Chairman) but shall have no vote. During the President's absence or inability to act and during any vacancy in the office of President of the Bank, the person for the time being acting as President shall act as Chairman of the Council.

Comment
Corresponds to P.D. Art. I, Sec. 5. Provision for the casting vote of the Chairman has been deleted and the second sentence reworded.

Article 6. In addition to the powers and functions vested in it by other provisions of this convention, the Administrative Council shall

(i) adopt such administrative rules and regulations, including financial regulations, as may be necessary or useful for the operation of the Center;
(ii) adopt rules governing the procedure for the institution of proceedings pursuant to this Convention;
(iii) adopt procedural rules applicable to conciliation and arbitration proceedings instituted pursuant to this Convention (hereinafter called the Conciliation Rules and the Arbitration Rules, respectively) by a majority of not less than two-thirds of the votes of all its members;
(iv) approve the terms of service of the Secretary-General and of any Deputy Secretary-General;
(v) approve the annual budget of the Center;
(vi) approve the annual report on the operation of the Center; and shall exercise such other powers and perform such other functions as it shall determine to be necessary or useful for the implementation of the provisions of this Convention and for the achievement of its purposes.

Comment
Corresponds to P.D. Art. I, Sec. 6. Clause (ii) is new and a residual clause has been added.

Article 7. (1) The Administrative Council shall hold an annual meeting and such other meetings as may be provided for by the Council, called by the Chairman, or convened by the Secretary-General at the request of not less than one-tenth of the members of the Council. The annual meeting of the Administrative Council shall be held in conjunction with the annual meeting of the Board of Governors of the Bank.

(2) Each member of the Administrative Council shall have one vote and, except as otherwise herein provided, all matters before the Council shall be decided by a majority of the votes cast.

(3) A quorum for any meeting of the Administrative Council shall be a majority of its members.

(4) The Administrative Council may establish a procedure whereby the Chairman may obtain a vote of the Council on a specific question without calling a meeting of the Council; provided, however, that in the case of a vote taken pursuant to such procedure, unless replies are received from a majority of the members of the Council, the motion shall be considered lost.

Comment
Corresponds to P.D. Art. I, Sec. 7. Provision has been made for meetings at the request of members. The previous provision for a vote without meeting has been elaborated.

Article 8. Members of the Administrative Council and the Chairman shall serve as such without remuneration.

Comment
Corresponds to P.D. Art. I, Sec. 7(5) reworded.

Title 3
The Secretariat

Article 9. The Secretariat shall consist of a Secretary-General, one or more Deputy Secretaries-General and staff.

Comment
Corresponds to P.D. Art. I, Sec. 8, unchanged.

Article 10. (1) The Secretary-General and Deputy Secretaries-General shall be elected by the Administrative Council upon the nomination of the Chairman. The Chairman may propose one or more candidates for each such office. A majority of not less than two-thirds of the votes of all members of the Council shall be required for their election.

(2) The offices of Secretary-General and Deputy Secretary-General shall be incompatible with the exercise of any political function. Neither the Secretary-General nor a Deputy Secretary-General may hold any other employment or engage in any other occupation except with the approval of the Administrative Council.

Comment
Corresponds to P.D. Art. I, Sec. 9. Para. (1) now opens the possibility of a list of candidates, and requires a two-thirds majority for election. Para. (2) no longer gives the Administrative Council discretion to permit exercise by the Secretary-General or a Deputy Secretary-General of any political function and now leaves decision on other employment or occupation (including employment by the Bank and the Permanent Court) solely to the discretion of the Council.

Article 11. (1) The Secretary-General shall be the principal officer of the Center and shall be responsible for its administration, including the appointment of staff, in accordance with the provisions of this Convention and the rules adopted thereunder by the Administrative Council. He shall perform the function of registrar and shall have the power to authenticate arbitral awards rendered pursuant to this Convention, and to certify copies thereof.

(2) During any absence or inability to act of the Secretary-General, and during any vacancy of the office of Secretary-General, the Deputy Secretary-General shall act as Secretary-General. If there shall be more than one Deputy Secretary-General, the Administrative Council shall determine in advance the order in which they shall act as Secretary-General.

Comment
Corresponds to P.D. Art. I, Sec. 10, elaborated.

Title 4
The Panels

Article 12. The Panel of Conciliators and the Panel of Arbitrators shall each consist of qualified persons, designated as hereinafter provided, who are willing to serve thereon.

Comment
Corresponds to P.D. Art. I, Secs. 11(1) and 12(1) combined.

Article 13. (1) Each Contracting State may designate to each Panel four persons who may but need not be its nationals.

(2) The Chairman may designate ten persons to each Panel. The persons so designated to a Panel shall each have a different nationality.

Comment
P.D. Art. I, Secs. 11(2) and 12(2) are combined in Article 13(1); P.D. Art. I, Secs. 11(3) and 12(3) are combined in modified form in Article 13(2).

Article 14. (1) Persons designated to serve on the Panels shall be persons of high moral character and recognized competence in the fields of law, commerce, industry or finance, who may be relied upon to exercise independent judgment.

(2) The Chairman, in designating persons to Panels, shall in addition pay due regard to the importance of assuring representation on the Panels of the principal legal systems of the world and of the main forms of economic activity.

Comment
Corresponds to P.D. Art. I, Sec. 15. The second sentence of Sec. 15(1) has been deleted and its provisions reworded and elaborated. Section 15(2) is substantially unchanged.

Article 15. (1) Panel members shall serve for four years.

(2) In case of death or resignation of a member of either Panel, the Contracting State or the Chairman, as the case may be, which or who had designated the member, shall have the right to designate another person to serve for the remainder of that member's term.

Comment
Corresponds to P.D. Art. I, Sec. 13.

Article 16. (1) Designation to serve on one Panel shall not preclude designation to serve on the other.

(2) If a person shall have been designated to serve on a Panel by more than one Contracting State, or by one or more Contracting States and the Chairman, he shall be deemed to have been designated by the authority which first designated him or, if one such authority is the State of which he is a national, by that State.

(3) All designations shall be notified to the Secretary-General and shall take effect from the date on which the notification is received.

Comment
Para. (1) corresponds to P.D. Art. I, Sec. 14(1), unchanged; para. (2) corresponds to Sec. 14(2) modified; para. (3) is new.

Title 5
Financing the Center

Article 17. To the extent that expenditure of the Center cannot be met out of charges for the use of its facilities, or out of other receipts, it shall be borne by the Contracting States which are members of the Bank in proportion to their respective subscriptions to the capital stock of the Bank, and by Contracting States which are not members of the Bank in accordance with rules adopted by the Administrative Council.

Comment
Corresponds to P.D. Art. I, Sec. 16, unchanged.

Title 6 Status, Immunities and Privileges

Article 18. The Center shall have international legal personality. To enable the Center to fulfil its functions, it shall have in the territories of each Contracting State the capacity, immunities and privileges hereinafter set forth.

Comment
This Article and Article 19 are an elaboration of P.D. Art. I, Sec. 1.

Article 19. The Center shall have the capacity

(i) to contract;
(ii) to acquire and dispose of movable and immovable property; and
(iii) to institute legal proceedings.

Article 20. The Center, its property and assets shall enjoy immunity from all legal process.

Comment
Corresponds to P.D. Art. I, Sec. 17, elaborated.

Article 21. The Chairman, the members of the Administrative Council, persons acting as conciliators or arbitrators, and the officers and employees of the Secretariat

(i) shall be immune from legal process with respect to acts performed by them in their official capacity;
(ii) not being local nationals shall be accorded the same immunities from immigration restrictions, alien registration requirements and national service obligations, the same facilities as regards exchange restrictions and the same treatment in respect of travelling facilities as are accorded by Contracting States to the representatives, officials and employees of comparable rank of other Contracting States.

Comment
Corresponds to P.D. Art. I, Sec. 18(1) extended to apply to conciliators and arbitrators.

Article 22. The agents, counsel, advocates, witnesses, experts and other persons participating in proceedings pursuant to this Convention shall be accorded in any Contracting State where their presence is required in connection with such proceedings such immunities and facilities for residence and travel as may be necessary for the independent exercise of their functions.

Comment
Corresponds to P.D. Art. I, Sec. 18(2), redrafted.

Article 23. (1) The archives of the Center shall be inviolable.

(2) The official communications of the Center shall be accorded by each Contracting State the same treatment as is accorded to the official communications of other Contracting States.

Comment
Corresponds to P.D. Art. I, Sec. 19, unchanged.

Article 24. (1) The Center, its assets, property and income, and its operations and transactions authorized by this Convention shall be immune from all taxation and customs duties. The Center shall also be immune from liability for the collection or payment of any taxes or customs duties.

(2) No tax shall be levied on or in respect of expense allowances paid by the Center to the Chairman or members of the Administrative Council, or on or in respect of salaries or emoluments paid by the Center to officials or employees of the Secretariat who are not local nationals.

(3) No tax shall be levied on or in respect of fees or expense allowances received by persons acting as conciliators or arbitrators in proceedings pursuant to this Convention for their services in such proceedings, if the sole jurisdictional basis for such tax shall be the location of the Center or the place where such proceedings are conducted or the place where such fees or allowances are paid.

Comment
Para. (1) corresponds to P.D. Art. I, Sec. 20(1), unchanged; paras. (2) and (3) correspond to Secs. 20 (2) and 20(3), reworded.

Article 25. Each Contracting State shall take such action as may be necessary in its own territories for the purposes of making the provisions of this Title effective in terms of its own law.

Comment
Article 25 is new. It is based on Art. VII, Sec. 10 of the Articles of Agreement of the Bank.

Chapter II
Jurisdiction of the Center

Article 26. (1) The jurisdiction of the Center shall extend to all legal disputes between a Contracting State (or one of its political subdivisions or agencies) and a national of another Contracting State, arising out of or in connection with any investment, which the parties to such disputes have consented to submit to it.

(2) Consent to the submission of any dispute to the Center shall be in writing. It may be given either before or after the dispute has arisen. Consent by a political subdivision or agency of a Contracting State shall require the approval of that State.

Comment
Combines P.D. Art. II, Secs. 1 and 2(i), modified. Secs. 2(ii) and 2(iii) have been deleted. Article 26 permits a political subdivision or agency of a Contracting State, under the conditions stated, to be a party to a dispute before the Center.

Article 27. (1) Consent to have recourse to arbitration pursuant to this Convention shall, unless otherwise stated, be deemed consent to have recourse to such proceedings to the exclusion of any other remedy.

(2) Consent by a Contracting State to the submission of any dispute with a national of another Contracting State to the Center shall, unless otherwise stated, be deemed consent to the substitution of that national in proceedings pursuant to this Convention by its State or by any public international institution if that State or institution, having compensated such national for its claim, has been subrogated to its rights.

Comment
Article 27(1) corresponds to P.D. Art. IV, Sec. 16 reworded. The idea formerly expressed in the parenthetical clause of P.D. Art. II, Sec. 1 is now elaborated in Article 27(2) and extended to cover an international investment guarantee fund.

Article 28. No Contracting State shall give diplomatic protection or bring an international claim in respect of a dispute which one of its nationals and another Contracting State shall have consented to submit or shall have submitted to arbitration pursuant to this Convention, unless such other Contracting State shall have failed to abide by and comply with the award rendered in such dispute.

Comment
Corresponds to P.D. Art. IV, Sec. 17(1), reworded.

Article 29. Any Contracting State may at any time transmit to the Secretary-General for purposes of information a statement indicating in general or specific terms the class or classes of dispute within the jurisdiction of the Center which it would in principle consider submitting to conciliation or arbitration pursuant to this Convention. Such statement shall not constitute, or be deemed to constitute, the consent required by Article 26.

Comment
Article 29 is new.

Article 30. For the purpose of this Chapter

(i) "investment" means any contribution of money or other asset of economic value for an indefinite period or, if the period be defined, for not less than five years;

(ii) "legal dispute" means any dispute concerning a legal right or obligation or concerning a fact relevant to the determination of a legal right or obligation;

(iiii) "national of another Contracting State" means (a) any natural person who possessed the nationality of a Contracting State other than the State party to the dispute on the date on which the parties consented to jurisdiction of the Center in respect of that dispute as well as on the date on which proceedings were instituted pursuant to this Convention; and (b) any juridical person which possessed the nationality of a Contracting State other than the State party to the dispute on the date on which the parties consented to the jurisdiction of the Center in respect of that dispute, and any juridical person which the parties have agreed shall be treated as a "national of another Contracting State".

Comment
Paras. (i) and (ii) of Article 30 are new. Para. (iii) replaces P.D. Art. X.

Chapter III
Conciliation

Title 1
Request for Conciliation

Article 31. (1) Any Contracting state or any national of a Contracting State wishing to institute conciliation proceedings pursuant to this Convention shall address a request to that effect to the Secretary-General in writing.

(2) The request shall contain information concerning the subject-matter of the dispute, the identity of the parties and their consent to conciliation sufficient to establish *prima facie* that the dispute is within the jurisdiction of the Center.

(3) The Secretary-General shall forthwith notify the other party to the dispute of the request, if it is found to conform to the provisions of paragraph (2) of this Article.

Comment
Para. (1) corresponds to P.D. Art. III, Sec. 1. Paras. (2) and (3) are new.

Title 2
Constitution of the Conciliation Commission

Article 32. (1) A Conciliation Commission (hereinafter called the Commission) shall be constituted as soon as possible after the request made pursuant to Article 31.

(2) (a) The Commission shall consist of a sole conciliator or any uneven number of conciliators appointed as the parties shall agree.

(b) Where the parties have not agreed upon the number of conciliators and the mode of their appointment, the Commission shall consist of three conciliators, one conciliator appointed by each party and the third, who shall be the president of the Commission, appointed by agreement of the parties.

Comment
Para. (1) is new. Para. (2) corresponds to P.D. Art. III, Sec. 2, elaborated.

Article 33. If the Commission shall not have been constituted within three months after notice of the request has been dispatched by the Secretary-General pursuant to Article 31(3), or such other period as the parties may agree, the Chairman shall, at the request of either party, and after consultation with both, appoint the conciliator or conciliators not yet appointed.

Comment
Corresponds to P.D. Art. III, Sec. 3(1), modified.

Article 34. (1) Any conciliator appointed pursuant to Article 32(2)(b) or Article 33 shall be selected from the Panel of Conciliators.

(2) Any conciliator appointed from outside the Panel of Conciliators shall possess the qualifications stated in Article 14(1).

Comment

Article 34(1) combines provisions for appointment from the Panel of Conciliators formerly contained in P.D. Art. III, Sec. 2(2) and P.D. Art. III, Sec. 3(2). Article 34(2) is new.

Title 3
Powers and Functions of the Commission

Article 35. (1) The Commission shall be the judge of its own competence.

(2) The Commission shall be constituted notwithstanding any claim of a party to the dispute that that dispute is not one in respect of which conciliation proceedings may be instituted pursuant to this Convention, or is not within the scope of its consent to such proceedings. Such claim shall be submitted to the Commission which shall determine whether to deal with it as a preliminary question or to join it to the merits of the dispute.

Comment

Corresponds to P.D. Art. II, Secs. 3(1) and 3(2), to the extent applicable to conciliation proceedings. The new text leaves it to the discretion of the Commission whether or not to deal with objections to its competence as preliminary questions. P.D. Art. II, Sec. 3(3) has been deleted.

Article 36. Except as the parties shall otherwise agree, any conciliation proceeding shall be conducted in accordance with the Conciliation Rules in effect on the date on which the consent to conciliation was given. If any question of procedure arises which is not covered by the Conciliation Rules or such other rules as may be agreed by the parties, the Commission shall decide that question.

Comment

Corresponds to P.D. Art. III, Sec. 4, modified to conform to the corresponding provisions in Chapter IV.

Article 37. (1) It shall be the duty of the Commission to clarify the issues in dispute between the parties and to endeavor to bring about agreement between them upon mutually acceptable terms. To that end, the Commission may at any stage of the proceedings and from time to time recommend terms of settlement to the parties.

(2) If the parties reach agreement, the Commission shall draw up a report noting the facts in issue and the submission of the dispute, and recording that the parties have reached agreement. If, at any stage of the proceedings, it appears to the Commission that there is no likelihood of agreement between the parties it may declare the proceedings closed, and shall, in that event, draw up a report noting the submission of the dispute and recording the failure of the parties to reach agreement. If one party fails to appear or participate in the proceedings, the Commission shall so state in its report.

Comment

Corresponds to P.D. Art. III, Sec. 5, reworded. P.D. Art. III, Sec. 5(3) has been deleted.

Title 4
Obligations of the Parties

Article 38. The parties shall cooperate in good faith with the Commission in order to enable the Commission to carry out its functions and shall give their most serious consideration to its recommendations. Except as the parties to the dispute shall otherwise agree, the recommendations of the Commission shall not be binding upon them.

Comment
Corresponds to P.D. Art. III, Sec. 6, reworded.

Article 39. Except as the parties to the dispute shall otherwise agree, neither party to a conciliation proceeding shall be entitled in any later proceeding concerning the same dispute, whether before arbitrators or in a court of law or otherwise, to invoke or rely on any views expressed or statements or admissions or offers of settlement made by the other party in the conciliation proceedings, or the recommendations, if any, made by the Commission therein.

Comment
Corresponds to P.D. Art. III, Sec. 7, modified to permit the parties to waive the protection afforded by that section.

Chapter IV
Arbitration

Title 1
Request for Arbitration

Article 40. (1) Any Contracting state or any national of a Contracting State wishing to institute arbitration proceedings pursuant to this Convention shall address a request to that effect to the Secretary-General in writing.

(2) The request shall contain information concerning the subject-matter of the dispute, the identity of the parties and their consent to arbitration sufficient to establish *prima facie* that the dispute is within the jurisdiction of the Center.

(3) The Secretary-General shall forthwith notify the other party to the dispute of the request, if it is found to conform to the provisions of paragraph (2) of this Article.

Comment
Para. (l) corresponds to P.D. Art. IV, Sec. 1. Paras. (2) and (3) are new.

Title 2
Constitution of the Tribunal

Article 41. (1) An Arbitral Tribunal (hereinafter called the Tribunal) shall be constituted as soon as possible after the request made pursuant to Article 40.

(2) (a) The Tribunal shall consist of a sole arbitrator or any uneven number of arbitrators appointed as the parties shall agree.

(b) Where the parties have not agreed upon the number of arbitrators and the mode of their appointment, the Tribunal shall consist of three arbitrators, one arbitrator appointed by each party and the third, who shall be the president of the Tribunal, appointed by agreement of the parties.

Comment
Para. (1) is new. Para. (2) corresponds to P.D. Art. IV, Sec. 2(1) elaborated and reworded.

Article 42. If the Tribunal shall not have been constituted within three months after notice of the request has been dispatched by the Secretary-General pursuant to Article 40(3) or such other period as the parties may agree, the Chairman shall, at the request of either party, appoint the arbitrator or arbitrators not yet appointed.

Comment
Corresponds to P.D. Art. IV, Sec. 3, modified.

Article 43. (1) No arbitrator appointed pursuant to this Convention shall be a national of the State party to the dispute or of a State whose national is a party to the dispute, shall have been designated to the Panel of Arbitrators by either of those States, or shall have acted as a conciliator in the same dispute.

(2) Any arbitrator appointed pursuant to Article 41(2)(b) or Article 42 shall be selected from the Panel of Arbitrators.

(3) Any arbitrator appointed from outside the Panel of Arbitrators shall possess the qualifications stated in Article 14(1).

Comment
Para. (1) which corresponds to the second sentence of P.D. Art. IV, Sec. 2(2), modified, now applies the rules precluding appointment of certain classes of persons from serving as arbitrators to all appointments of arbitrators under the Convention. The provisions of para. (2) correspond to the first sentence of P.D. Art. IV, Sec. 2(2) which was incorporated by reference in the second sentence of P.D. Art. IV, Sec. (3). Para. (3) is new.

Title 3
Powers and Functions of the Tribunal

Article 44. (1) The Tribunal shall be the judge of its own competence.

(2) The Tribunal shall be constituted notwithstanding any claim of a party to the dispute that that dispute is not one in respect of which arbitration proceedings may be instituted pursuant to this Convention, or is not within the scope of its consent to such proceedings. Such claim shall be submitted to the Tribunal which shall determine whether to deal with it as a preliminary question or to join it to the merits of the dispute.

Comment
Corresponds to P.D. Art. II, Secs. 3(1) and 3(2), to the extent applicable to arbitration proceedings. The new text leaves it to the discretion of the Tribunal whether or not to deal with objections to its competence as preliminary questions. P.D. Art. II, Sec. 3 (3) has been deleted.

Article 45. (1) In the absence of agreement between the parties concerning the law to be applied, the Tribunal shall decide the dispute submitted to it in accordance with such rules of national and international law as it shall determine to be applicable. The term "international law" shall be understood in the sense given to it by Article 38 of the Statute of the International Court of Justice.

(2) The Tribunal may not bring in a finding of *non liquet* on the ground of silence or obscurity of the law to be applied.

(3) The provisions of this Article shall not prejudice the power of the Tribunal to decide a dispute *ex aequo et bono* if the parties agree thereto.

Comment
Corresponds to P.D. Art. IV, Sec. 4, elaborated and re-drafted.

Article 46. Except as the parties otherwise agree, the Tribunal may, if it deems it necessary at any stage of the proceedings

(i) call upon the parties to produce documents or other information, and

(ii) visit the scene connected with the dispute before it, and there conduct such enquiries as it may deem appropriate.

Comment
Article 46 is new.

Article 47. Except as the parties otherwise agree, any arbitration proceeding shall be conducted in accordance with the Arbitration Rules in effect on the date on which the consent to arbitration was given. If any question of procedure arises which is not covered by the Arbitration Rules or such other rules as may be agreed upon by the parties, the Tribunal shall decide that question.

Comment
Corresponds to P.D. Art. IV, Sec. 5, reworded.

Article 48. (1) Whenever one of the parties has not appeared before the Tribunal or has failed to present its case, the other party may call upon the Tribunal to accept its submissions and to render an award in its favor. Before doing so, the Tribunal shall satisfy itself that it has jurisdiction and that the submissions are well-founded in fact and in law.

(2) The Tribunal shall grant to the party which has failed to appear a period of grace before rendering the award unless it is satisfied that the party in default does not intend to appear.

Comment
Para. (1) corresponds to P.D. Art. IV, Sec. 8, reworded. Para. (2) is new.

Article 49. Except as the parties otherwise agree, the Tribunal may hear and determine incidental or additional claims or counter-claims arising directly out of the subject-matter of the dispute provided that they are within the jurisdiction of the Center.

Comment
Corresponds to P.D. Art. IV, Sec. 9, elaborated to make clear that Article 49 does not extend the competence of the Tribunal to disputes not already within the jurisdiction of the Center.

Article 50. (1) Except as the parties otherwise agree, the Tribunal may, if it considers that the circumstances so require, prescribe such provisional measures as it deems necessary to prevent or halt any action by either party which might frustrate an eventual award.

(2) The Tribunal may fix a penalty for failure to comply with such provisional measures.

Comment
Para. (1) corresponds to P.D. Art. IV, Sec. 10, reworded. Para. (2) is new.

Title 4
The Award

Article 51. (1) The Tribunal shall decide all questions by a majority of the votes of all its members.

(2) The award of the Tribunal shall be in writing and shall be signed by all the members of the Tribunal. Refusal of a minority to sign shall be mentioned in the award but shall not invalidate it.

(3) Except as the parties otherwise agree:

(a) the award shall state the reasons upon which it is based; and

(b) any arbitrator dissenting from the majority decision may attach his dissenting opinion or a bare statement of his dissent.

Comment
Para. (1) corresponds to P.D. Art. IV, Sec. 6, reworded. Paras. (2) and (3) correspond to P.D. Art. IV, Sec. 7(1), elaborated.

Article 52. (1) The award of the Tribunal shall be delivered by the Tribunal or by the Secretary-General, acting at the request and on behalf of the Tribunal, the parties or their agents or counsel being present or having been duly summoned to appear. The award shall be deemed to have been rendered on the date on which it was so delivered.

(2) The Secretary-General shall promptly transmit certified copies of the award to the parties.

Comment
Article 52 is new and incorporates the provisions of P.D. Art. IV, Sec. 7(2), elaborated.

Title 5
Interpretation, Revision and Annulment of the Award

Article 53. (1) If any dispute shall arise between the parties as to the meaning and scope of the award, either party may request interpretation of the award by an application in writing addressed to the Secretary-General.

(2) The request for interpretation shall, if possible, be submitted to the Tribunal which rendered the award. If this shall not be possible, a new Tribunal shall be constituted in accordance with the terms of the agreement, if any, between the parties regarding the constitution of the Tribunal which rendered the award, and otherwise pursuant to the provisions of this Chapter. The Tribunal may, if it considers that the circumstances so require, stay enforcement of the award pending its decision.

Comment
Corresponds to P.D. Art. IV, Sec. 11, reworded.

Article 54 (1) Either party may request revision of the award by an application in writing addressed to the Secretary-General on the ground of the discovery of some fact of such a nature as decisively to affect the award, provided that when the award was rendered that fact was unknown to the Tribunal and to the applicant and that the applicant's ignorance of that fact was not due to negligence.

(2) The application for revision must be made within three months after the discovery of the new fact and in any case within three years after the date on which the award was rendered.

(3) The request for revision shall, if possible, be submitted to the Tribunal which rendered the award. If this shall not be possible, a new Tribunal shall be constituted in accordance with the terms of the agreement, if any, between the parties regarding the constitution of the Tribunal which rendered the award, and otherwise pursuant to the provisions of this Chapter. The Tribunal may, if it considers that the circumstances so require, stay the enforcement of the award pending its decision.

Comment
Corresponds to P.D. Art. IV, Sec. 12, reworded.

Article 55. (1) Either party may request annulment of the award by an application in writing addressed to the Secretary-General on one or more of the following grounds:

(a) that the Tribunal was not properly constituted;
(b) that the Tribunal has manifestly exceeded its powers;
(c) that there was corruption on the part of a member of the Tribunal;
(d) that there has been a serious departure from a fundamental rule of procedure; or
(e) failure to state the reasons for the award, unless the parties have agreed that reasons need not be stated.

(2) Upon an application pursuant to paragraph (1) of this Article the Chairman shall forthwith appoint from the Panel of Arbitrators an *ad hoc* Committee of three persons which shall be competent to declare the nullity of the award or any part thereof on any of the grounds set forth in the preceding paragraph. None of the members of the Committee shall have been a member of the Tribunal which rendered the award, shall be a national of the State party to the dispute or of the State whose national is a party to the dispute, shall have been designated to the Panel of Arbitrators by either of those States, or shall have acted as a conciliator in the same dispute.

(3) The provisions of Articles 44–48, 51, 52, 56 and 57 shall apply *mutatis mutandis* to proceedings before the Committee.

(4) An application pursuant to this Article must be made within sixty days after the date on which the award was rendered except that when annulment is requested on the ground of corruption such application shall be made within sixty days after discovery of the corruption and in any case within three years after the date on which the award was rendered.

(5) The Committee may, if it considers that the circumstances so require, stay enforcement of the award pending its decision.

(6) If the award is annulled the dispute shall, at the request of either party, be submitted to a new Tribunal constituted in the manner specified in Articles 41–43.

Comment
Corresponds to P.D. Art. IV, Sec. 13, elaborated.

Title 6
Recognition and Enforcement of the Award

Article 56. The award shall be final and without appeal. Each party shall abide by and comply with the award in accordance with its terms.

Comment
Corresponds to P.D. Art. IV, Sec. 14, reworded.

Article 57. (1) Each Contracting State shall recognize an award rendered pursuant to this Convention as binding and enforce it within its territories as if it were a final judgment of the courts of that State.

(2) To obtain recognition and enforcement, the applicant shall furnish to the domestic authority which each Contracting State shall designate for this purpose (the Competent Authority) the duly authenticated original award or a duly certified copy thereof. Each Contracting state shall notify the Secretary-General of the designation of the Competent Authority and of any subsequent change in such designation.

(3) Execution of the award shall be governed by the rules of civil procedure in force in the State in whose territories such execution is sought. The writ of execution shall be issued by the Competent Authority without other review than verification of the authenticity of the award.

(4) Each Contracting State shall take such action as may be necessary to enable it to carry out its obligations under this Article.

Comment
Para. (1) corresponds to P.D. Art. IV, Sec. 15. Paras. (2)–(4) are new.

Article 58. Nothing in Article 57 shall be construed as derogating from the law in force in any Contracting State relating to immunity of that State or of any foreign State from execution.

Comment
Article 58 is new.

Chapter V
Replacement and Disqualification of Conciliators and Arbitrators

Article 59. (1) After a Conciliation Commission or an Arbitral Tribunal has been constituted and proceedings have begun, its composition shall remain unchanged; provided, however, that if a conciliator or an arbitrator should die, become incapacitated, or resign, the resulting vacancy shall be filled by the method prescribed for the original appointment.

(2) If a conciliator or arbitrator appointed by a party shall have resigned without the consent of the Commission or Tribunal of which he was a member, the Chairman shall appoint a person to fill the resulting vacancy.

Comment
Corresponds to P.D. Art. V, Sec. 1, reworded.

Article 60. A party may propose the disqualification of a conciliator or an arbitrator on account of any fact indicating a manifest lack of the qualities required by Article 14(1). A party to arbitration proceedings may, in addition, propose the disqualification of an arbitrator on the ground that he was ineligible for appointment to the Arbitral Tribunal under Article 43(1).

Comment
Corresponds to P.D. Art. V, Sec. 2(1). Sec. 2(1)(b), which contained special rules on disqualification of arbitrators and conciliators appointed by the Chairman, has been deleted.

Article 61. The decision on any proposed disqualification shall be taken by the other members of the Commission or Tribunal as the case may be, provided that where those members are equally divided, or in the case of a proposed disqualification of a sole conciliator or arbitrator, the Chairman shall take that decision. If it is decided that the proposal is well-founded, the conciliator or arbitrator to whom the decision relates shall resign, and the resulting vacancy shall be filled in accordance with the procedure prescribed for the original appointment.

Comment
Corresponds to P.D. Art. V, Sec. 2(2), the last sentence of which has been modified.

Chapter VI
Cost of Proceedings

Article 62. The charges payable for the use of the facilities of the Center, as well as the fees and expenses of members of the Conciliation Commission or Arbitral Tribunal, shall be borne equally by the parties, and each party respectively shall bear such other expenses as it may incur in connection with any conciliation or arbitration proceedings; provided, however, that if in any arbitration proceeding the Tribunal determines that a party has instituted proceedings or has conducted its defense frivolously or in bad faith, it may assess any part or all of such charges, fees and expenses against such party.

Comment
Corresponds to P.D. Art. VI, Sec. 1, reworded.

Article 63. The charges payable by the parties for the use of the facilities of the Center shall be determined by the Secretary-General in accordance with the applicable rules and regulations adopted by the Administrative Council.

Comment
Corresponds to P.D. Art. VI, Sec. 2, reworded.

Article 64. (1) Each Conciliation Commission and each Arbitral Tribunal shall determine the fees and expenses of its members within limits established from time to time by the Administrative Council and after consultation with the Secretary-General.

(2) Nothing in paragraph (1) of this Article shall preclude the parties from agreeing in advance with the Commission or Tribunal concerned upon the fees and expenses of its members.

(3) The fees and expenses of the members of the Arbitral Tribunal may be included in the award.

Comment
Paras. (1) and (2) of Article 64 correspond to P.D. Art. VI, Sec. 3, redrafted. Para. (3) is new.

Chapter VII
Place of Proceedings

Article 65. Conciliation and arbitration proceedings pursuant to this Convention shall be held at the seat of the Center except as hereinafter provided.

Article 66. Conciliation and arbitration proceedings may be held, if the parties so agree,

(i) at the seat of the Permanent Court of Arbitration or of such other public international institution with which the Center has entered into arrangements pursuant to Article 2(2); or
(ii) at any other place approved by the Conciliation Commission or Arbitral Tribunal after consultation with the Secretary-General.

Comment
Chapter VII corresponds to P.D. Art. VII, redrafted.

Chapter VIII
Disputes between Contracting States

Article 67. Any dispute arising between Contracting States concerning the interpretation or application of this Convention which is not settled by negotiation shall be referred to the International Court of Justice by the application of either party to such dispute, unless the States concerned agree to another mode of settlement.

Comment
Corresponds to P.D. Art. VIII, modified to make clear that the provision establishes compulsory jurisdiction of the Court.

Chapter IX
Amendment

Article 68. Any Contracting State may propose amendment of this Convention. The text of a proposed amendment shall be communicated to the Secretary-General not less than three months prior to the meeting of the Administrative Council at which such amendment is to be considered and shall forthwith be transmitted by him to all Contracting States.

Comment
Corresponds to P.D. Art. IX, Sec. 1, modified by substituting the Secretary-General for the Chairman as the channel of communications.

Article 69. (1) Amendments involving new obligations for Contracting States or any fundamental alteration in the nature or scope of this Convention shall require for their adoption approval by all the members of the Council.

(2) All other amendments shall be adopted by a majority of not less than two-thirds of the votes of all the members of the Council.

(3) Each amendment shall become effective for all Contracting States at the end of twelve months following its adoption; provided, however, that such amendment shall not affect the rights and obligations of any Contracting State or of any national of a Contracting State under this Convention with respect to or arising out of proceedings for conciliation or arbitration pursuant to consent to the jurisdiction of the Center given prior to the effective date of the amendment.

Comment
Para. (1) is new. Paras. (2) and (3) correspond to P.D. Art. IX, Sec. 2. The majority required for adoption of amendments has been reduced to two-thirds.

Chapter X
Final Provisions

Title 1
Entry into Force

Article 70. This Convention shall be open for signature on behalf of States members of the Bank, States members of the United Nations or any of its specialized agencies and States parties to the Statute of the International Court of Justice.

Comment
Corresponds to P.D. Art. XI, Sec. 1, modified.

Article 71. This Convention shall be subject to ratification or acceptance by the signatory States in accordance with their respective constitutional procedures. The instruments of ratification or acceptance shall be deposited with the Bank.

Comment
Corresponds to P.D. Art. XI, Sec. 2, modified.

Article 72. At any time after this Convention shall have been ratified or accepted by 12 States, the Executive Directors of the Bank, acting on the recommendation of the President, may declare that this Convention shall enter into force and this Convention shall enter into force 90 days after such declaration. It shall enter into force for each State which subsequently deposits its instrument of ratification or acceptance on the date of such deposit.

Comment
Corresponds to P.D. Art. XI, Sec. 3, modified.

Title 2
Territorial Application

Article 73. This Convention shall apply to all territories for whose international relations a Contracting State is responsible except those which are excluded by such State by written notice to the Bank either at the time of signature or subsequently.

Comment
Corresponds to P.D. Art. XI, Sec. 4, reworded.

Title 3
Denunciation

Article 74. Any Contracting State may denounce this Convention by written notice to the Bank.

Comment
Corresponds to P.D. Art. XI, Sec. 5(1).

Article 75. The denunciation shall take effect six months after receipt by the Bank of such notice; provided, however, that the provisions of this Convention shall continue to apply to the obligations of the State concerned with respect to or arising out of proceedings for conciliation or arbitration pursuant to consent to the jurisdiction of the Center given prior to such notice by that State, by any of its political subdivisions or agencies, or by any of its nationals.

Comment
Corresponds to P.D. Art. XI, Sec. 5(2), modified.

Title 4
Inauguration of the Center

Article 76. Promptly upon the entry into force of this Convention, the President of the Bank shall convene the inaugural meeting of the Administrative Council.

Comment
Corresponds to P.D. Art. XI, Sec. 6.

Title 5
Registration and Notifications

Article 77. The Bank shall register this Convention with the Secretariat of the United Nations in accordance with Article 102 of the Charter of the United Nations and the Regulations thereunder adopted by the General Assembly.

Comment
Corresponds to P.D. Art. XI, Sec. 7, reworded.

Article 78. The Bank shall notify all signatory States of the following:

(i) signatures pursuant to Article 70 of this Convention;
(ii) ratifications and acceptances pursuant to Article 71 of this Convention;
(iii) exclusions from territorial application pursuant to Article 73 of this Convention;
(iv) declarations pursuant to Article 29 of this Convention;
(v) the date upon which this Convention enters into force in accordance with Article 72 hereof;
(vi) denunciations pursuant to Article 74 of this Convention.

Comment
Article 78 is new.

DONE at Washington, D.C. in the English, French and Spanish languages, all three texts being equally authoritative, in a single copy which shall remain deposited in the archives of the International Bank for Reconstruction and Development, which has indicated by its signature below its agreement to fulfil the functions with which it is charged by Articles 76 and 77.

APPENDIX IV

Convention on the Settlement of Investment Disputes between States and Nationals of Other States and Accompanying Report of the Executive Directors

March 18, 1965

Convention on the Settlement of Investment Disputes between States and Nationals of Other States

Preamble

The Contracting States

CONSIDERING the need for international cooperation for economic development, and the role of private international investment therein;
BEARING IN MIND the possibility that from time to time disputes may arise in connection with such investment between Contracting States and nationals of other Contracting States;
RECOGNIZING that while such disputes would usually be subject to national legal processes, international methods of settlement may be appropriate in certain cases;
ATTACHING PARTICULAR IMPORTANCE to the availability of facilities for international conciliation or arbitration to which Contracting States and nationals of other Contracting States may submit such disputes if they so desire;
DESIRING to establish such facilities under the auspices of the International Bank for Reconstruction and Development;
RECOGNIZING that mutual consent by the parties to submit such disputes to conciliation or to arbitration through such facilities constitutes a binding agreement which requires in particular that due consideration be given to any recommendation of conciliators, and that any arbitral award be complied with; and
DECLARING that no Contracting State shall by the mere fact of its ratification, acceptance or approval of this Convention and without its consent be deemed to be under any obligation to submit any particular dispute to conciliation or arbitration,

HAVE AGREED as follows:

Chapter I
International Centre for Settlement of Investment Disputes

Section 1
Establishment and Organization

Article 1. (1) There is hereby established the International Centre for Settlement of Investment Disputes (hereinafter called the Centre).

(2) The purpose of the Centre shall be to provide facilities for conciliation and arbitration of investment disputes between Contracting States and nationals of other Contracting States in accordance with the provisions of this Convention.

Article 2. The seat of the Centre shall be at the principal office of the International Bank for Reconstruction and Development (hereinafter called the Bank). The seat may be moved to another place by decision of the Administrative Council adopted by a majority of two-thirds of its members.

Article 3. The Centre shall have an Administrative Council and a Secretariat and shall maintain a Panel of Conciliators and a Panel of Arbitrators.

Section 2
The Administrative Council

Article 4. (1) The Administrative Council shall be composed of one representative of each Contracting State. An alternate may act as representative in case of his principal's absence from a meeting or inability to act.

(2) In the absence of a contrary designation, each governor and alternate governor of the Bank appointed by a Contracting State shall be *ex officio* its representative and its alternate respectively.

Article 5. The President of the Bank shall be *ex officio* Chairman of the Administrative Council (hereinafter called the Chairman) but shall have no vote. During his absence or inability to act and during any vacancy in the office of President of the Bank, the person for the time being acting as President shall act as Chairman of the Administrative Council.

Article 6. (1) Without prejudice to the powers and functions vested in it by other provisions of this Convention, the Administrative Council shall

(a) adopt the administrative and financial regulations of the Centre;(b) adopt the rules of procedure for the institution of conciliation and arbitration proceedings;

(c) adopt the rules of procedure for conciliation and arbitration proceedings (hereinafter called the Conciliation Rules and the Arbitration Rules);

(d) approve arrangements with the Bank for the use of the Bank's administrative facilities and services;

(e) determine the conditions of service of the Secretary-General and of any Deputy Secretary-General;

(f) adopt the annual budget of revenues and expenditures of the Centre;

(g) approve the annual report on the operation of the Centre.

The decisions referred to in sub-paragraphs (a), (b), (c) and (f) above shall be adopted by a majority of two-thirds of the members of the Administrative Council.

(2) The Administrative Council may appoint such committees as it considers necessary.

(3) The Administrative Council shall also exercise such other powers and perform such other functions as it shall determine to be necessary for the implementation of the provisions of this Convention.

Article 7. (1) The Administrative Council shall hold an annual meeting and such other meetings as may be determined by the Council, or convened by the Chairman, or convened by the Secretary-General at the request of not less than five members of the Council.

(2) Each member of the Administrative Council shall have one vote and, except as otherwise herein provided, all matters before the Council shall be decided by a majority of the votes cast.

(3) A quorum for any meeting of the Administrative Council shall be a majority of its members.

(4) The Administrative Council may establish, by a majority of two-thirds of its members, a procedure whereby the Chairman may seek a vote of the Council without convening a meeting of the Council. The vote shall be considered valid only if the majority of the members of the Council cast their votes within the time limit fixed by the said procedure.

Article 8. Members of the Administrative Council and the Chairman shall serve without remuneration from the Centre.

Section 3
The Secretariat

Article 9. The Secretariat shall consist of a Secretary-General, one or more Deputy Secretaries-General and staff.

Article 10. (1) The Secretary-General and any Deputy Secretary-General shall be elected by the Administrative Council by a majority of two-thirds of its members upon the nomination of the Chairman for a term of service not exceeding six years and shall be eligible for re-election. After consulting the members of the Administrative Council, the Chairman shall propose one or more candidates for each such office.

(2) The offices of Secretary-General and Deputy Secretary-General shall be incompatible with the exercise of any political function. Neither the Secretary-General nor any Deputy Secretary-General may hold any other employment or engage in any other occupation except with the approval of the Administrative Council.

(3) During the Secretary-General's absence or inability to act, and during any vacancy of the office of Secretary-General, the Deputy Secretary-General shall act as Secretary-General. If there shall be more than one Deputy Secretary-General, the Administrative Council shall determine in advance the order in which they shall act as Secretary-General.

Article 11. The Secretary-General shall be the legal representative and the principal officer of the Centre and shall be responsible for its administration, including the appointment of staff, in accordance with the provisions of this Convention and the rules adopted by the Administrative Council. He shall perform the function of registrar and shall have the power to authenticate arbitral awards rendered pursuant to this Convention, and to certify copies thereof.

Section 4
The Panels

Article 12. The Panel of Conciliators and the Panel of Arbitrators shall each consist of qualified persons, designated as hereinafter provided, who are willing to serve thereon.

Article 13. (1) Each Contracting State may designate to each Panel four persons who may but need not be its nationals.

(2) The Chairman may designate ten persons to each Panel. The persons so designated to a Panel shall each have a different nationality.

Article 14. (1) Persons designated to serve on the Panels shall be persons of high moral character and recognized competence in the fields of law, commerce, industry or finance, who may be relied upon to exercise independent judgment. Competence in the field of law shall be of particular importance in the case of persons on the Panel of Arbitrators.

(2) The Chairman, in designating persons to serve on the Panels, shall in addition pay due regard to the importance of assuring representation on the Panels of the principal legal systems of the world and of the main forms of economic activity.

Article 15. (1) Panel members shall serve for renewable periods of six years.

(2) In case of death or resignation of a member of a Panel, the authority which designated the member shall have the right to designate another person to serve for the remainder of that member's term.

(3) Panel members shall continue in office until their successors have been designated.

Article 16. (1) A person may serve on both Panels.

(2) If a person shall have been designated to serve on the same Panel by more than one Contracting State, or by one or more Contracting States and the Chairman, he shall be deemed to have been designated by the authority which first designated him or, if one such authority is the State of which he is a national, by that State.

(3) All designations shall be notified to the Secretary-General and shall take effect from the date on which the notification is received.

Section 5
Financing the Centre

Article 17. If the expenditure of the Centre cannot be met out of charges for the use of its facilities, or out of other receipts, the excess shall be borne by Contracting States which are members of the Bank in proportion to their respective subscriptions to the capital stock of the Bank, and by Contracting States which are not members of the Bank in accordance with rules adopted by the Administrative Council.

Section 6
Status, Immunities and Privileges

Article 18. The Centre shall have full international legal personality. The legal capacity of the Centre shall include the capacity

(a) to contract;
(b) to acquire and dispose of movable and immovable property;
(c) to institute legal proceedings.

Article 19. To enable the Centre to fulfil its functions, it shall enjoy in the territories of each Contracting State the immunities and privileges set forth in this Section.

Article 20. The Centre, its property and assets shall enjoy immunity from all legal process, except when the Centre waives this immunity.

Article 21. The Chairman, the members of the Administrative Council, persons acting as conciliators or arbitrators or members of a Committee appointed pursuant to paragraph (3) of Article 52, and the officers and employees of the Secretariat

(a) shall enjoy immunity from legal process with respect to acts performed by them in the exercise of their functions, except when the Centre waives this immunity;

(b) not being local nationals, shall enjoy the same immunities from immigration restrictions, alien registration requirements and national service obligations, the same facilities as regards exchange restrictions and the same treatment in respect of travelling facilities as are accorded by Contracting States to the representatives, officials and employees of comparable rank of other Contracting States.

Article 22. The provisions of Article 21 shall apply to persons appearing in proceedings under this Convention as parties, agents, counsel, advocates, witnesses or experts; provided, however, that sub-paragraph (b) thereof shall apply only in connection with their travel to and from, and their stay at, the place where the proceedings are held.

Article 23. (1) The archives of the Centre shall be inviolable, wherever they may be.

(2) With regard to its official communications, the Centre shall be accorded by each Contracting State treatment not less favourable than that accorded to other international organizations.

Article 24. (1) The Centre, its assets, property and income, and its operations and transactions authorized by this Convention shall be exempt from all taxation and customs duties. The Centre shall also be exempt from liability for the collection or payment of any taxes or customs duties.

(2) Except in the case of local nationals, no tax shall be levied on or in respect of expense allowances paid by the Centre to the Chairman or members of the Administrative Council, or on or in respect of salaries, expense allowances or other emoluments paid by the Centre to officials or employees of the Secretariat.

(3) No tax shall be levied on or in respect of fees or expense allowances received by persons acting as conciliators, or arbitrators, or members of a Committee appointed pursuant to paragraph (3) of Article 52, in proceedings under this Convention, if the sole jurisdictional basis for such tax is the location of the Centre or the place where such proceedings are conducted or the place where such fees or allowances are paid.

Chapter II
Jurisdiction of the Centre

Article 25. (1) The jurisdiction of the Centre shall extend to any legal dispute arising directly out of an investment, between a Contracting State (or any constituent subdivision or agency of a Contracting State designated to the Centre by that State) and a national of another Contracting State, which the parties to the dispute consent in writing to submit to the Centre. When the parties have given their consent, no party may withdraw its consent unilaterally.

(2) "National of another Contracting State" means:

(a) any natural person who had the nationality of a Contracting State other than the State party to the dispute on the date on which the parties consented to submit such dispute to conciliation or arbitration as well as on the date on which the request was registered pursuant to paragraph (3) of Article 28 or paragraph (3) of Article 36, but does not include any person who on either date also had the nationality of the Contracting State party to the dispute; and

(b) any juridical person which had the nationality of a Contracting State other than the State party to the dispute on the date on which the parties consented to submit such dispute to conciliation or arbitration and any juridical person which had the nationality of the Contracting State party to the dispute on that date and which, because of foreign control, the parties have agreed should be treated as a national of another Contracting State for the purposes of this Convention.

(3) Consent by a constituent subdivision or agency of a Contracting State shall require the approval of that State unless that State notifies the Centre that no such approval is required.

(4) Any Contracting State may, at the time of ratification, acceptance or approval of this Convention or at any time thereafter, notify the Centre of the class or classes of disputes which it would or would not consider submitting to the jurisdiction of the Centre. The Secretary-General shall forthwith transmit such notification to all Contracting States. Such notification shall not constitute the consent required by paragraph (1).

Article 26. Consent of the parties to arbitration under this Convention shall, unless otherwise stated, be deemed consent to such arbitration to the exclusion of any other remedy. A Contracting State may require the exhaustion of local administrative or judicial remedies as a condition of its consent to arbitration under this Convention.

Article 27. (1) No Contracting State shall give diplomatic protection, or bring an international claim, in respect of a dispute which one of its nationals and another Contracting State shall have consented to submit or shall have submitted to arbitration under this Convention, unless such other Contracting State shall have failed to abide by and comply with the award rendered in such dispute.

(2) Diplomatic protection, for the purposes of paragraph (1), shall not include informal diplomatic exchanges for the sole purpose of facilitating a settlement of the dispute.

Chapter III
Conciliation

Section 1
Request for Conciliation

Article 28. (1) Any Contracting State or any national of a Contracting State wishing to institute conciliation proceedings shall address a request to that effect in writing to the Secretary-General who shall send a copy of the request to the other party.

(2) The request shall contain information concerning the issues in dispute, the identity of the parties and their consent to conciliation in accordance with the rules of procedure for the institution of conciliation and arbitration proceedings.

(3) The Secretary-General shall register the request unless he finds, on the basis of the information contained in the request, that the dispute is manifestly outside the jurisdiction of the Centre. He shall forthwith notify the parties of registration or refusal to register.

Section 2
Constitution of the Conciliation Commission

Article 29. (1) The Conciliation Commission (hereinafter called the Commission) shall be constituted as soon as possible after registration of a request pursuant to Article 28.

(2) (a) The Commission shall consist of a sole conciliator or any uneven number of conciliators appointed as the parties shall agree.

(b) Where the parties do not agree upon the number of conciliators and the method of their appointment, the Commission shall consist of three conciliators, one conciliator appointed by each party and the third, who shall be the president of the Commission, appointed by agreement of the parties.

Article 30. If the Commission shall not have been constituted within 90 days after notice of registration of the request has been dispatched by the Secretary-General in accordance with paragraph (3) of Article 28, or such other period as the parties may agree, the Chairman shall, at the request of either party and after consulting both parties as far as possible, appoint the conciliator or conciliators not yet appointed.

Article 31. (1) Conciliators may be appointed from outside the Panel of Conciliators, except in the case of appointments by the Chairman pursuant to Article 30.

(2) Conciliators appointed from outside the Panel of Conciliators shall possess the qualities stated in paragraph (1) of Article 14.

Section 3 Conciliation Proceedings

Article 32. (1) The Commission shall be the judge of its own competence.

(2) Any objection by a party to the dispute that that dispute is not within the jurisdiction of the Centre, or for other reasons is not within the competence of the Commission, shall be considered by the Commission which shall determine whether to deal with it as a preliminary question or to join it to the merits of the dispute.

Article 33. Any conciliation proceeding shall be conducted in accordance with the provisions of this Section and, except as the parties otherwise agree, in accordance with the Conciliation Rules in effect on the date on which the parties consented to conciliation. If any question of procedure arises which is not covered by this Section or the Conciliation Rules or any rules agreed by the parties, the Commission shall decide the question.

Article 34. (1) It shall be the duty of the Commission to clarify the issues in dispute between the parties and to endeavour to bring about agreement between them upon mutually acceptable terms. To that end, the Commission may at any stage of the proceedings and from time to time recommend terms of settlement to the parties. The parties shall cooperate in good faith with the Commission in order to enable the Commission to carry out its functions, and shall give their most serious consideration to its recommendations.

(2) If the parties reach agreement, the Commission shall draw up a report noting the issues in dispute and recording that the parties have reached agreement. If, at any stage of the proceedings, it appears to the Commission that there is no likelihood of agreement between the parties, it shall close the proceedings and shall draw up a report noting the submission of the dispute and recording the failure of the parties to reach agreement. If one party fails to appear or participate in the proceedings, the Commission shall close the proceedings and shall draw up a report noting that party's failure to appear or participate.

Article 35. Except as the parties to the dispute shall otherwise agree, neither party to a conciliation proceeding shall be entitled in any other proceeding, whether before arbitrators or in a court of law or otherwise, to invoke or rely on any views expressed or statements or admissions or offers of settlement made by the other party in the conciliation proceedings, or the report or any recommendations made by the Commission.

Chapter IV
Arbitration

Section 1
Request for Arbitration

Article 36. (1) Any Contracting State or any national of a Contracting State wishing to institute arbitration proceedings shall address a request to that effect in writing to the Secretary-General who shall send a copy of the request to the other party.

(2) The request shall contain information concerning the issues in dispute, the identity of the parties and their consent to arbitration in accordance with the rules of procedure for the institution of conciliation and arbitration proceedings.

(3) The Secretary-General shall register the request unless he finds, on the basis of the information contained in the request, that the dispute is manifestly outside the jurisdiction of the Centre. He shall forthwith notify the parties of registration or refusal to register.

Section 2
Constitution of the Tribunal

Article 37. (1) The Arbitral Tribunal (hereinafter called the Tribunal) shall be constituted as soon as possible after registration of a request pursuant to Article 36.

(2) (a) The Tribunal shall consist of a sole arbitrator or any uneven number of arbitrators appointed as the parties shall agree.

(b) Where the parties do not agree upon the number of arbitrators and the method of their appointment, the Tribunal shall consist of three arbitrators, one arbitrator appointed by each party and the third, who shall be the president of the Tribunal, appointed by agreement of the parties.

Article 38. If the Tribunal shall not have been constituted within 90 days after notice of registration of the request has been dispatched by the Secretary-General in accordance with paragraph (3) of Article 36, or such other period as the parties may agree, the Chairman shall, at the request of either party and after consulting both parties as far as possible, appoint the arbitrator or arbitrators not yet appointed. Arbitrators appointed by the Chairman pursuant to this Article shall not be nationals of the Contracting State party to the dispute or of the Contracting State whose national is a party to the dispute.

Article 39. The majority of the arbitrators shall be nationals of States other than the Contracting State party to the dispute and the Contracting State whose national is a party to the dispute; provided, however, that the foregoing provisions of this Article shall not apply if the sole arbitrator or each individual member of the Tribunal has been appointed by agreement of the parties.

Article 40. (1) Arbitrators may be appointed from outside the Panel of Arbitrators, except in the case of appointments by the Chairman pursuant to Article 38.

(2) Arbitrators appointed from outside the Panel of Arbitrators shall possess the qualities stated in paragraph (1) of Article 14.

Section 3
Powers and Functions of the Tribunal

Article 41. (1) The Tribunal shall be the judge of its own competence.

(2) Any objection by a party to the dispute that that dispute is not within the jurisdiction of the Centre, or for other reasons is not within the competence of the Tribunal, shall be considered by the Tribunal which shall determine whether to deal with it as a preliminary question or to join it to the merits of the dispute.

Article 42. (1) The Tribunal shall decide a dispute in accordance with such rules of law as may be agreed by the parties. In the absence of such agreement, the Tribunal shall apply the law of the Contracting State party to the dispute (including its rules on the conflict of laws) and such rules of international law as may be applicable.

(2) The Tribunal may not bring in a finding of *non liquet* on the ground of silence or obscurity of the law.

(3) The provisions of paragraphs (1) and (2) shall not prejudice the power of the Tribunal to decide a dispute *ex aequo et bono* if the parties so agree.

Article 43. Except as the parties otherwise agree, the Tribunal may, if it deems it necessary at any stage of the proceedings,

(a) call upon the parties to produce documents or other evidence, and
(b) visit the scene connected with the dispute, and conduct such inquiries there as it may deem appropriate.

Article 44. Any arbitration proceeding shall be conducted in accordance with the provisions of this Section and, except as the parties otherwise agree, in accordance with the Arbitration Rules in effect on the date on which the parties consented to arbitration. If any question of procedure arises which is not covered by this Section or the Arbitration Rules or any rules agreed by the parties, the Tribunal shall decide the question.

Article 45. (1) Failure of a party to appear or to present his case shall not be deemed an admission of the other party's assertions.

(2) If a party fails to appear or to present his case at any stage of the proceedings the other party may request the Tribunal to deal with the questions submitted to it and to render an award. Before rendering an award, the Tribunal shall notify, and grant a period of grace to, the party failing to appear or to present its case, unless it is satisfied that that party does not intend to do so.

Article 46. Except as the parties otherwise agree, the Tribunal shall, if requested by a party, determine any incidental or additional claims or counter-claims arising directly out of the subject-matter of the dispute provided that they are within the scope of the consent of the parties and are otherwise within the jurisdiction of the Centre.

Article 47. Except as the parties otherwise agree, the Tribunal may, if it considers that the circumstances so require, recommend any provisional measures which should be taken to preserve the respective rights of either party.

Section 4
The Award

Article 48. (1) The Tribunal shall decide questions by a majority of the votes of all its members.

(2) The award of the Tribunal shall be in writing and shall be signed by the members of the Tribunal who voted for it.

(3) The award shall deal with every question submitted to the Tribunal, and shall state the reasons upon which it is based.

(4) Any member of the Tribunal may attach his individual opinion to the award, whether he dissents from the majority or not, or a statement of his dissent.

(5) The Centre shall not publish the award without the consent of the parties.

Article 49. (1) The Secretary-General shall promptly dispatch certified copies of the award to the parties. The award shall be deemed to have been rendered on the date on which the certified copies were dispatched.

(2) The Tribunal upon the request of a party made within 45 days after the date on which the award was rendered may after notice to the other party decide any question

which it had omitted to decide in the award, and shall rectify any clerical, arithmetical or similar error in the award. Its decision shall become part of the award and shall be notified to the parties in the same manner as the award. The periods or time provided for under paragraph (2) of Article 51 and paragraph (2) of Article 52 shall run from the date on which the decision was rendered.

Section 5
Interpretation, Revision and Annulment of the Award

Article 50. (1) If any dispute shall arise between the parties as to the meaning or scope of an award, either party may request interpretation of the award by an application in writing addressed to the Secretary-General.

(2) The request shall, if possible, be submitted to the Tribunal which rendered the award. If this shall not be possible, a new Tribunal shall be constituted in accordance with Section 2 of this Chapter. The Tribunal may, if it considers that the circumstances so require, stay enforcement of the award pending its decision.

Article 51. (1) Either party may request revision of the award by an application in writing addressed to the Secretary-General on the ground of discovery of some fact of such a nature as decisively to affect the award, provided that when the award was rendered that fact was unknown to the Tribunal and to the applicant and that the applicant's ignorance of that fact was not due to negligence.

(2) The application shall be made within 90 days after the discovery of such fact and in any event within three years after the date on which the award was rendered.

(3) The request shall, if possible, be submitted to the Tribunal which rendered the award. If this shall not be possible, a new Tribunal shall be constituted in accordance with Section 2 of this Chapter.

(4) The Tribunal may, if it considers that the circumstances so require, stay enforcement of the award pending its decision. If the applicant requests a stay of enforcement of the award in his application, enforcement shall be stayed provisionally until the Tribunal rules on such request.

Article 52. (1) Either party may request annulment of the award by an application in writing addressed to the Secretary-General on one or more of the following grounds:

(a) that the Tribunal was not properly constituted;
(b) that the Tribunal has manifestly exceeded its powers;
(c) that there was corruption on the part of a member of the Tribunal;
(d) that there has been a serious departure from a fundamental rule of procedure; or
(e) that the award has failed to state the reasons on which it is based.

(2) The application shall be made within 120 days after the date on which the award was rendered except that when annulment is requested on the ground of corruption such application shall be made within 120 days after discovery of the corruption and in any event within three years after the date on which the award was rendered.

(3) On receipt of the request the Chairman shall forthwith appoint from the Panel of Arbitrators an ad hoc Committee of three persons. None of the members of the Committee shall have been a member of the Tribunal which rendered the award, shall be of the same nationality as any such member, shall be a national of the State party to the dispute or of the State whose national is a party to the dispute, shall have been designated to the Panel of Arbitrators by either of those States, or shall have acted as a conciliator in the same dispute. The Committee shall have the authority to annul the award or any part thereof on any of the grounds set forth in paragraph (1).

(4) The provisions of Articles 41–45, 48, 49, 53 and 54, and of Chapters VI and VII shall apply *mutatis mutandis* to proceedings before the Committee.

(5) The Committee may, if it considers that the circumstances so require, stay enforcement of the award pending its decision. If the applicant requests a stay of enforcement of the award in his application, enforcement shall be stayed provisionally until the Committee rules on such request.

(6) If the award is annulled the dispute shall, at the request of either party, be submitted to a new Tribunal constituted in accordance with Section 2 of this Chapter.

Section 6
Recognition and Enforcement of the Award

Article 53. (1) The award shall be binding on the parties and shall not be subject to any appeal or to any other remedy except those provided for in this Convention. Each party shall abide by and comply with the terms of the award except to the extent that enforcement shall have been stayed pursuant to the relevant provisions of this Convention.

(2) For the purposes of this Section, "award" shall include any decision interpreting, revising or annulling such award pursuant to Articles 50, 51 or 52.

Article 54. (1) Each Contracting State shall recognize an award rendered pursuant to this Convention as binding and enforce the pecuniary obligations imposed by that award within its territories as if it were a final judgment of a court in that State. A Contracting State with a federal constitution may enforce such an award in or through its federal courts and may provide that such courts shall treat the award as if it were a final judgment of the courts of a constituent state.

(2) A party seeking recognition or enforcement in the territories of a Contracting State shall furnish to a competent court or other authority which such State shall have designated for this purpose a copy of the award certified by the Secretary-General. Each Contracting State shall notify the Secretary-General of the designation of the competent court or other authority for this purpose and of any subsequent change in such designation.

(3) Execution of the award shall be governed by the laws concerning the execution of judgments in force in the State in whose territories such execution is sought.

Article 55. Nothing in Article 54 shall be construed as derogating from the law in force in any Contracting State relating to immunity of that State or of any foreign State from execution.

Chapter V
Replacement and Disqualification of Conciliators and Arbitrators

Article 56. (1) After a Commission or a Tribunal has been constituted and proceedings have begun, its composition shall remain unchanged; provided, however, that if a conciliator or an arbitrator should die, become incapacitated, or resign, the resulting vacancy shall he filled in accordance with the provisions of Section 2 of Chapter III or Section 2 of Chapter IV.

(2) A member of a Commission or Tribunal shall continue to serve in that capacity notwithstanding that he shall have ceased to be a member of the Panel.

(3) If a conciliator or arbitrator appointed by a party shall have resigned without the consent of the Commission or Tribunal of which he was a member, the Chairman shall appoint a person from the appropriate Panel to fill the resulting vacancy.

Article 57. A party may propose to a Commission or Tribunal the disqualification of any of its members on account of any fact indicating a manifest lack of the qualities required by paragraph (1) of Article 14. A party to arbitration proceedings may, in addition, propose the disqualification of an arbitrator on the ground that he was ineligible for appointment to the Tribunal under Section 2 of Chapter IV.

Article 58. The decision on any proposal to disqualify a conciliator or arbitrator shall be taken by the other members of the Commission or Tribunal as the case may be, provided that where those members are equally divided, or in the case of a proposal to disqualify a sole conciliator or arbitrator, or a majority of the conciliators or arbitrators, the Chairman shall take that decision. If it is decided that the proposal is well-founded the conciliator or arbitrator to whom the decision relates shall be replaced in accordance with the provisions of Section 2 of Chapter III or Section 2 of Chapter IV.

Chapter VI
Cost of Proceedings

Article 59. The charges payable by the parties for the use of the facilities of the Centre shall be determined by the Secretary-General in accordance with the regulations adopted by the Administrative Council.

Article 60. (1) Each Commission and each Tribunal shall determine the fees and expenses of its members within limits established from time to time by the Administrative Council and after consultation with the Secretary-General.

(2) Nothing in paragraph (1) of this Article shall preclude the parties from agreeing in advance with the Commission or Tribunal concerned upon the fees and expenses of its members.

Article 61. (1) In the case of conciliation proceedings the fees and expenses of members of the Commission as well as the charges for the use of the facilities of the Centre, shall be borne equally by the parties. Each party shall bear any other expenses it incurs in connection with the proceedings.

(2) In the case of arbitration proceedings the Tribunal shall, except as the parties otherwise agree, assess the expenses incurred by the parties in connection with the proceedings, and shall decide how and by whom those expenses, the fees and expenses of the members of the Tribunal and the charges for the use of the facilities of the Centre shall be paid. Such decision shall form part of the award.

Chapter VII
Place of Proceedings

Article 62. Conciliation and arbitration proceedings shall be held at the seat of the Centre except as hereinafter provided.

Article 63. Conciliation and arbitration proceedings may be held, if the parties so agree,

(a) at the seat of the Permanent Court of Arbitration or of any other appropriate institution, whether private or public, with which the Centre may make arrangements for that purpose; or
(b) at any other place approved by the Commission or Tribunal after consultation with the Secretary-General.

Chapter VIII
Disputes between Contracting States

Article 64. Any dispute arising between Contracting States concerning the interpretation or application of this Convention which is not settled by negotiation shall be referred to the International Court of Justice by the application of any party to such dispute, unless the States concerned agree to another method of settlement.

Chapter IX
Amendment

Article 65. Any Contracting State may propose amendment of this Convention. The text of a proposed amendment shall be communicated to the Secretary-General not less than 90 days prior to the meeting of the Administrative Council at which such amendment is to be considered and shall forthwith be transmitted by him to all the members of the Administrative Council.

Article 66. (1) If the Administrative Council shall so decide by a majority of two-thirds of its members, the proposed amendment shall be circulated to all Contracting States for ratification, acceptance or approval. Each amendment shall enter into force 30 days after dispatch by the depositary of this Convention of a notification to Contracting States that all Contracting States have ratified, accepted or approved the amendment.

(2) No amendment shall affect the rights and obligations under this Convention of any Contracting State or of any of its constituent subdivisions or agencies, or of any national of such State arising out of consent to the jurisdiction of the Centre given before the date of entry into force of the amendment.

Chapter X
Final Provisions

Article 67. This Convention shall be open for signature on behalf of States members of the Bank. It shall also be open for signature on behalf of any other State which is a party to the Statute of the International Court of Justice and which the Administrative Council, by a vote of two-thirds of its members, shall have invited to sign the Convention.

Article 68. (1) This Convention shall be subject to ratification, acceptance or approval by the signatory States in accordance with their respective constitutional procedures.

(2) This Convention shall enter into force 30 days after the date of deposit of the twentieth instrument of ratification, acceptance or approval. It shall enter into force for each State which subsequently deposits its instrument of ratification, acceptance or approval 30 days after the date of such deposit.

Article 69. Each Contracting State shall take such legislative or other measures as may be necessary for making the provisions of this Convention effective in its territories.

Article 70. This Convention shall apply to all territories for whose international relations a Contracting State is responsible, except those which are excluded by such State by written notice to the depositary of this Convention either at the time of ratification, acceptance or approval or subsequently.

Article 71. Any Contracting State may denounce this Convention by written notice to the depositary of this Convention. The denunciation shall take effect six months after receipt of such notice.

Article 72. Notice by a Contracting State pursuant to Articles 70 or 71 shall not affect the rights or obligations under this Convention of that State or of any of its constituent subdivisions or agencies or of any national of that State arising out of consent to the jurisdiction of the Centre given by one of them before such notice was received by the depositary.

Article 73. Instruments of ratification, acceptance or approval of this Convention and of amendments thereto shall be deposited with the Bank which shall act as the depositary of this Convention. The depositary shall transmit certified copies of this Convention to States members of the Bank and to any other State invited to sign the Convention.

Article 74. The depositary shall register this Convention with the Secretariat of the United Nations in accordance with Article 102 of the Charter of the United Nations and the Regulations thereunder adopted by the General Assembly.

Article 75. The depositary shall notify all signatory States of the following:

(a) signatures in accordance with Article 67;
(b) deposits of instruments of ratification, acceptance and approval in accordance with Article 73;
(c) the date on which this Convention enters into force in accordance with Article 68;
(d) exclusions from territorial application pursuant to Article 70;
(e) the date on which any amendment of this Convention enters into force in accordance with Article 66; and
(f) denunciations in accordance with Article 71.

DONE at Washington, in the English, French and Spanish languages, all three texts being equally authentic, in a single copy which shall remain deposited in the archives of the International Bank for Reconstruction and Development, which has indicated by its signature below its agreement to fulfil the functions with which it is charged under this Convention.

Report of the Executive Directors on the Convention on the Settlement of Investment Disputes between States and Nationals of Other States

I

1. Resolution No. 214, adopted by the Board of Governors of the International Bank for Reconstruction and Development on 10 September 1964, provides as follows:

"RESOLVED:

(a) The report of the Executive Directors on "Settlement of Investment Disputes," dated 6 August 1964, is hereby approved.

(b) The Executive Directors are requested to formulate a convention establishing facilities and procedures which would be available on a voluntary basis for the settlement of investment disputes between contracting States and Nationals of other contracting States through conciliation and arbitration.

(c) In formulating such a convention, the Executive Directors shall take into account the views of member governments and shall keep in mind the desirability of arriving at a text which could be accepted by the largest possible number of governments.

(d) The Executive Directors shall submit the text of such a convention to member governments with such recommendations as they shall deem appropriate."

2. The Executive Directors of the Bank, acting pursuant to the foregoing Resolution, have formulated a Convention on the Settlement of Investment Disputes between States and Nationals of Other States and, on 18 March 1965, approved the submission of the text of the Convention, as attached hereto, to member governments of the Bank. This action by the Executive Directors does not, of course, imply that the governments represented by the individual Executive Directors are committed to take action on the Convention.

3. The action by the Executive Directors was preceded by extensive preparatory work, details of which are given in paragraphs 6–8 below. The Executive Directors are satisfied that the Convention in the form attached hereto represents a broad consensus of the views of those governments which accept the principle of establishing by intergovernmental agreement facilities and procedures for the settlement of investment disputes which States and foreign investors wish to submit to conciliation or arbitration. They are also satisfied that the Convention constitutes a suitable framework for such facilities and procedures. Accordingly, the text of the Convention is submitted to member governments for consideration with a view to signature and ratification, acceptance or approval.

4. The Executive Directors invite attention to the provisions of Article 68(2) pursuant to which the Convention will enter into force as between the Contracting States 30 days after deposit with the Bank, the depositary of the Convention, of the twentieth instrument of ratification, acceptance or approval.

5. The attached text of the Convention in the English, French and Spanish languages has been deposited in the archives of the Bank, as depositary, and is open for signature.

II

6. The question of the desirability and practicability of establishing institutional facilities, sponsored by the Bank, for the settlement through conciliation and arbitration of investment disputes between States and foreign investors was first placed before the Board of Governors of the Bank at its Seventeenth Annual Meeting, held in Washington, D.C. in September 1962.

At that Meeting the Board of Governors, by Resolution No. 174, adopted on 18 September 1962, requested the Executive Directors to study the question.

7. After a series of informal discussions on the basis of working papers prepared by the staff of the Bank, the Executive Directors decided that the Bank should convene consultative meetings of legal experts designated by member governments to consider the subject in greater detail. The consultative meetings were held on a regional basis in Addis Ababa (16–20 December 1963), Santiago de Chile (3–7 February 1964), Geneva (17–21 February 1964), and Bangkok (27 April–1 May 1964), with the administrative assistance of the United Nations Economic Commissions and the European Office of the United Nations, and took as the basis for discussion a Preliminary Draft of a Convention on Settlement of Investment Disputes between States and Nationals of Other States prepared by the staff of the Bank in the light of the discussions of the Executive Directors and the views of governments. The meetings were attended by legal experts from 86 countries.

8. In the light of the preparatory work and of the views expressed at the consultative meetings, the Executive Directors reported to the Board of Governors at its Nineteenth Annual Meeting in Tokyo, in September 1964, that it would be desirable to establish the institutional facilities envisaged, and to do so within the framework of an intergovernmental agreement. The Board of Governors adopted the Resolution set forth in paragraph 1 of this Report, whereupon the Executive Directors undertook the formulation of the present Convention. With a view to arriving at a text which could be accepted by the largest possible number of governments, the Bank invited its members to designate representatives to a Legal Committee which would assist the Executive Directors in their task. This Committee met in Washington from November 23 through 11 December 1964, and the Executive Directors gratefully acknowledge the valuable advice they received from the representatives of the 61 member countries who served on the Committee.

III

9. In submitting the attached Convention to governments, the Executive Directors are prompted by the desire to strengthen the partnership between countries in the cause of economic development. The creation of an institution designed to facilitate the settlement of disputes between States and foreign investors can be a major step toward promoting an atmosphere of mutual confidence and thus stimulating a larger flow of private international capital into those countries which wish to attract it.

10. The Executive Directors recognize that investment disputes are as a rule settled through administrative, judicial or arbitral procedures available under the laws of the country in which the investment concerned is made. However, experience shows that disputes may arise which the parties wish to settle by other methods; and investment agreements entered into in recent years show that both States and investors frequently consider that it is in their mutual interest to agree to resort to international methods of settlement.

11. The present Convention would offer international methods of settlement designed to take account of the special characteristics of the disputes covered, as well as of the parties to whom it would apply. It would provide facilities for conciliation and arbitration by specially qualified persons of independent judgment carried out according to rules known and accepted in advance by the parties concerned. In particular, it would ensure that once a government or investor had given consent to conciliation or arbitration under the auspices of the Centre, such consent could not be unilaterally withdrawn.

12. The Executive Directors believe that private capital will continue to flow to countries offering a favorable climate for attractive and sound investments, even if such countries did not become parties to the Convention or, having joined, did not make use of the facilities of the Centre. On the other hand, adherence to the Convention by a country would provide additional inducement and stimulate a larger flow of private international investment into its territories, which is the primary purpose of the Convention.

13. While the broad objective of the Convention is to encourage a larger flow of private international investment, the provisions of the Convention maintain a careful balance between the interests of investors and those of host States. Moreover, the Convention permits the institution of proceedings by host States as well as by investors and the Executive Directors have constantly had in mind that the provisions of the Convention should be equally adapted to the requirements of both cases.

14. The provisions of the attached Convention are for the most part self-explanatory. Brief comment on a few principal features may, however, be useful to member governments in their consideration of the Convention.

IV
The International Centre for Settlement of Investment Disputes

General

15. The Convention establishes the International Centre for Settlement of Investment Disputes as an autonomous international institution (Articles 18–24). The purpose of the Centre is "to provide facilities for conciliation and arbitration of investment disputes ***" (Article 1(2)). The Centre will not itself engage in conciliation or arbitration activities. This will be the task of Conciliation Commissions and Arbitral Tribunals constituted in accordance with the provisions of the Convention.

16. As sponsor of the establishment of the institution the Bank will provide the Centre with premises for its seat (Article 2) and, pursuant to arrangements between the two institutions, with other administrative facilities and services (Article 6(d)).

17. With respect to the financing of the Centre (Article 17), the Executive Directors have decided that the Bank should be prepared to provide the Centre with office accommodation free of charge as long as the Centre has its seat at the Bank's headquarters and to underwrite, within reasonable limits, the basic overhead expenditure of the Centre for a period of years to be determined after the Centre is established.

18. Simplicity and economy consistent with the efficient discharge of the functions of the Centre characterize its structure. The organs of the Centre are the Administrative Council (Articles 4–8) and the Secretariat (Articles 9–11). The Administrative Council will be composed of one representative of each Contracting State, serving without remuneration from the Centre. Each member of the Council casts one vote and matters before the Council are decided by a majority of the votes cast unless a different majority is required by the Convention. The President of the Bank will serve *ex officio* as the Council's Chairman but will have no vote. The Secretariat will consist of a Secretary-General, one or more Deputy Secretaries-General and staff. In the interest of flexibility the Convention provides for the possibility of there being more than one Deputy Secretary-General, but the Executive Directors do not now foresee a need for more than one or two full time high officials of the Centre. Article 10, which requires that the Secretary-General and any Deputy Secretary-General be elected by the Administrative Council by a majority of two-thirds of its members, on the nomination of the Chairman, limits their terms of office to a period not exceeding six years and permits their re-election. The Executive Directors believe that the initial election, which will take place shortly after the Convention will have come into force, should be for a short term so as not to deprive the States which ratify the Convention after its entry into force of the possibility of participating in the selection of the high officials of the Centre. Article 10 also limits the extent to which these officials may engage in activities other than their official functions.

Functions of the Administrative Council

19. The principal functions of the Administrative Council are the election of the Secretary-General and any Deputy Secretary-General, the adoption of the budget of the Centre and

the adoption of administrative and financial regulations, rules governing the institution of proceedings and rules of procedure for conciliation and arbitration proceedings. Action on all these matters requires a majority of two-thirds of the members of the Council.

Functions of the Secretary-General

20. The Convention requires the Secretary-General to perform a variety of administrative functions as legal representative, registrar and principal officer of the Centre (Articles 7(1), 11, 16(3), 25(4), 28, 36, 49(1), 50(1), 51(1), 52(1), 54(2), 59, 60(1), 63(b) and 65). In addition, the Secretary-General is given the power to refuse registration of a request for conciliation proceedings or arbitration proceedings, and thereby to prevent the institution of such proceedings, if on the basis of the information furnished by the applicant he finds that the dispute is *manifestly* outside the jurisdiction of the Centre (Articles 28(3) and 36(3)). The Secretary-General is given this limited power to "screen" requests for conciliation or arbitration proceedings with a view to avoiding the embarrassment to a party (particularly a State) which might result from the institution of proceedings against it in a dispute which it had not consented to submit to the Centre, as well as the possibility that the machinery of the Centre would be set in motion in cases which for other reasons were obviously outside the jurisdiction of the Centre e.g., because either the applicant or the other party was not eligible to be a party in proceedings under the Convention.

The Panels

21. Article 3 requires the Centre to maintain a Panel of Conciliators and a Panel of Arbitrators, while Articles 12–16 outline the manner and terms of designation of Panel members. In particular, Article 14(1) seeks to ensure that Panel members will possess a high degree of competence and be capable of exercising independent judgment. In keeping with the essentially flexible character of the proceedings, the Convention permits the parties to appoint conciliators and arbitrators from outside the Panels but requires (Articles 31(2) and 40(2)) that such appointees possess the qualities stated in Article 14(1). The Chairman, when called upon to appoint a conciliator or arbitrator pursuant to Article 30 or 38, is restricted in his choice to Panel members.

V
Jurisdiction of the Centre

22. The term "jurisdiction of the Centre" is used in the Convention as a convenient expression to mean the limits within which the provisions of the Convention will apply and the facilities of the Centre will be available for conciliation and arbitration proceedings. The jurisdiction of the Centre is dealt with in Chapter II of the Convention (Articles 25–27).

Consent

23. Consent of the parties is the cornerstone of the jurisdiction of the Centre. Consent to jurisdiction must be in writing and once given cannot be withdrawn unilaterally (Article 25(1)).

24. Consent of the parties must exist when the Centre is seized (Articles 28(3) and 36(3)) but the Convention does not otherwise specify the time at which consent should be given. Consent may be given, for example, in a clause included in an investment agreement, providing for the submission to the Centre of future disputes arising out of that agreement, or in a *compromis* regarding a dispute which has already arisen. Nor does the Convention require that the consent of both parties be expressed in a single instrument. Thus, a host State might in its investment promotion legislation offer to submit disputes arising out of certain classes of investments to the jurisdiction of the Centre, and the investor might give his consent by accepting the offer in writing.

25. While consent of the parties is an essential prerequisite for the jurisdiction of the Centre, consent alone will not suffice to bring a dispute within its jurisdiction. In keeping with the

purpose of the Convention, the jurisdiction of the Centre is further limited by reference to the nature of the dispute and the parties thereto.

Nature of the dispute

26. Article 25(1) requires that the dispute must be a "legal dispute arising directly out of an investment." The expression "legal dispute" has been used to make clear that while conflicts of rights are within the jurisdiction of the Centre, mere conflicts of interests are not. The dispute must concern the existence or scope of a legal right or obligation, or the nature or extent of the reparation to be made for breach of a legal obligation.

27. No attempt was made to define the term "investment" given the essential requirement of consent by the parties, and the mechanism through which Contracting States can make known in advance, if they so desire, the classes of disputes which they would or would not consider submitting to the Centre (Article 25 (4)).

Parties to the dispute

28. For a dispute to be within the jurisdiction of the Centre one of the parties must be a Contracting State (or a constituent subdivision or agency of a Contracting State) and the other party must be a "national of another Contracting State." The latter term as defined in paragraph (2) of Article 25 covers both natural persons and juridical persons.

29. It should be noted that under clause (a) of Article 25(2) a natural person who was a national of the State party to the dispute would not be eligible to be a party in proceedings under the auspices of the Centre, even if at the same time he had the nationality of another State. This ineligibility is absolute and cannot be cured even if the State party to the dispute had given its consent.

30. Clause (b) of Article 25(2), which deals with juridical persons, is more flexible. A juridical person which had the nationality of the State party to the dispute would be eligible to be a party to proceedings under the auspices of the Centre if that State had agreed to treat it as a national of another Contracting State because of foreign control.

Notifications by Contracting States

31. While no conciliation or arbitration proceedings could be brought against a Contracting State without its consent and while no Contracting State is under any obligation to give its consent to such proceedings, it was nevertheless felt that adherence to the Convention might be interpreted as holding out an expectation that Contracting States would give favorable consideration to requests by investors for the submission of a dispute to the Centre. It was pointed out in that connection that there might be classes of investment disputes which governments would consider unsuitable for submission to the Centre or which, under their own law, they were not permitted to submit to the Centre. In order to avoid any risk of misunderstanding on this score, Article 25(4) expressly permits Contracting States to make known to the Centre in advance, if they so desire, the classes of disputes which they would or would not consider submitting to the Centre. The provision makes clear that a statement by a Contracting State that it would consider submitting a certain class of dispute to the Centre would serve for purposes of information only and would not constitute the consent required to give the Centre jurisdiction. Of course, a statement excluding certain classes of disputes from consideration would not constitute a reservation to the Convention.

Arbitration as exclusive remedy

32. It may be presumed that when a State and an investor agree to have recourse to arbitration, and do not reserve the right to have recourse to other remedies or require the prior exhaustion

of other remedies, the intention of the parties is to have recourse to arbitration to the exclusion of any other remedy. This rule of interpretation is embodied in the first sentence of Article 26. In order to make clear that it was not intended thereby to modify the rules of international law regarding the exhaustion of local remedies, the second sentence explicitly recognizes the right of a State to require the prior exhaustion of local remedies.

Claims by the investor's State

33. When a host State consents to the submission of a dispute with an investor to the Centre, thereby giving the investor direct access to an international jurisdiction, the investor should not he in a position to ask his State to espouse his case and that State should not be permitted to do so. Accordingly, Article 27 expressly prohibits a Contracting State from giving diplomatic protection, or bringing an international claim, in respect of a dispute which one of its nationals and another Contracting State have consented to submit, or have submitted, to arbitration under the Convention, unless the State party to the dispute fails to honor the award rendered in that dispute.

VI
Proceedings under the Convention

Institution of proceedings

34. Proceedings are instituted by means of a request addressed to the Secretary-General (Articles 28 and 36). After registration of the request the Conciliation Commission or Arbitral Tribunal, as the case may be, will be constituted. Reference is made to paragraph 20 above on the power of the Secretary-General to refuse registration.

Constitution of Conciliation Commissions and Arbitral Tribunals

35. Although the Convention leaves the parties a large measure of freedom as regards the constitution of Commissions and Tribunals, it assures that a lack of agreement between the parties on these matters or the unwillingness of a party to cooperate will not frustrate proceedings (Articles 29–30 and 37–38, respectively).

36. Mention has already been made of the fact that the parties are free to appoint conciliators and arbitrators from outside the Panels (see paragraph 21 above). While the Convention does not restrict the appointment of conciliators with reference to nationality, Article 39 lays down the rule that the majority of the members of an Arbitral Tribunal should not be nationals either of the State party to the dispute or of the State whose national is a party to the dispute. This rule is likely to have the effect of excluding persons having these nationalities from serving on a Tribunal composed of not more than three members. However, the rule will not apply where each and every arbitrator on the Tribunal has been appointed by agreement of the parties.

Conciliation proceedings; powers and functions of Arbitral Tribunals

37. In general, the provisions of Articles 32–35 dealing with conciliation proceedings and of Articles 41–49, dealing with the powers and functions of Arbitral Tribunals and awards rendered by such Tribunals, are self-explanatory. The differences between the two sets of provisions reflect the basic distinction between the process of conciliation which seeks to bring the parties to agreement and that of arbitration which aims at a binding determination of the dispute by the Tribunal.

38. Article 41 reiterates the well-established principle that international tribunals are to be the judges of their own competence and Article 32 applies the same principle to Conciliation

Commissions. It is to be noted in this connection that the power of the Secretary-General to refuse registration of a request for conciliation or arbitration (see paragraph 20 above) is so narrowly defined as not to encroach on the prerogative of Commissions and Tribunals to determine their own competence and, on the other hand, that registration of a request by the Secretary-General does not, of course, preclude a Commission or Tribunal from finding that the dispute is outside the jurisdiction of the Centre.

39. In keeping with the consensual character of proceedings under the Convention, the parties to conciliation or arbitration proceedings may agree on the rules of procedure which will apply in those proceedings. However, if or to the extent that they have not so agreed the Conciliation Rules and Arbitration Rules adopted by the Administrative Council will apply (Articles 33 and 44).

40. Under the Convention an Arbitral Tribunal is required to apply the law agreed by the parties. Failing such agreement, the Tribunal must apply the law of the State party to the dispute (unless that law calls for the application of some other law), as well as such rules of international law as may be applicable. The term "international law" as used in this context should be understood in the sense given to it by Article 38(1) of the Statute of the International Court of Justice, allowance being made for the fact that Article 38 was designed to apply to interState disputes.[1]

Recognition and enforcement of arbitral awards

41. Article 53 declares that the parties are bound by the award and that it shall not be subject to appeal or to any other remedy except those provided for in the Convention. The remedies provided for are revision (Article 51) and annulment (Article 52). In addition, a party may ask a Tribunal which had omitted to decide any question submitted to it, to supplement its award (Article 49(2)) and may request interpretation of the award (Article 50).

42. Subject to any stay of enforcement in connection with any of the above proceedings in accordance with the provisions of the Convention, the parties are obliged to abide by and comply with the award and Article 54 requires every Contracting State to recognize the award as binding and to enforce the pecuniary obligations imposed by the award as if it were a final decision of a domestic court. Because of the different legal techniques followed in common law and civil law jurisdictions and the different judicial systems found in unitary and federal or other non-unitary States, Article 54 does not prescribe any particular method to be followed in its domestic implementation, but requires each Contracting State to meet the requirements of the Article in accordance with its own legal system.

43. The doctrine of sovereign immunity may prevent the forced execution in a State of judgments obtained against foreign States or against the State in which execution is sought. Article 54 requires Contracting States to equate an award rendered pursuant to the Convention with a final judgment of its own courts. It does not require them to go beyond that and to undertake forced execution of awards rendered pursuant to the Convention in

[1] Article 38(1) of the Statute of the International Court of Justice reads as follows:

"1. The Court, whose function it is to decide in accordance with international law such disputes as are submitted to it, shall apply:

a. international conventions, whether general or particular, establishing rules expressly recognized by the contesting states;
b. international custom, as evidence of a general practice accepted as law;
c. the general principles of law recognized by civilized nations;
d. subject to the provisions of Article 59, judicial decisions and the teachings of the most highly qualified publicists of the various nations, as subsidiary means for the determination of rules of law."

cases in which final judgments could not be executed. In order to leave no doubt on this point Article 55 provides that nothing in Article 54 shall be construed as derogating from the law in force in any Contracting State relating to immunity of that State or of any foreign State from execution.

VII
Place of Proceedings

44. In dealing with proceedings away from the Centre, Article 63 provides that proceedings may be held, if the parties so agree, at the seat of the Permanent Court of Arbitration or of any other appropriate institution with which the Centre may enter into arrangements for that purpose. These arrangements are likely to vary with the type of institution and to range from merely making premises available for the proceedings to the provision of complete secretariat services.

VIII
Disputes Between Contracting States

45. Article 64 confers on the International Court of Justice jurisdiction over disputes between Contracting States regarding the interpretation or application of the Convention which are not settled by negotiation and which the parties do not agree to settle by other methods. While the provision is couched in general terms, it must be read in the context of the Convention as a whole. Specifically, the provision does not confer jurisdiction on the Court to review the decision of a Conciliation Commission or Arbitral Tribunal as to its competence with respect to any dispute before it. Nor does it empower a State to institute proceedings before the Court in respect of a dispute which one of its nationals and another Contracting State have consented to submit or have submitted to arbitration, since such proceedings would contravene the provisions of Article 27, unless the other Contracting State had failed to abide by and comply with the award rendered in that dispute.

IX
Entry into Force

46. The Convention is open for signature on behalf of States members of the Bank. It will also be open for signature on behalf of any other State which is a party to the Statute of the International Court of Justice and which the Administrative Council, by a vote of two-thirds of its members, shall have invited to sign. No time limit has been prescribed for signature. Signature is required both of States joining before the Convention enters into force and those joining thereafter (Article 67). The Convention is subject to ratification, acceptance or approval by the signatory States in accordance with their constitutional procedures (Article 68). As already stated, the Convention will enter into force upon the deposit of the twentieth instrument of ratification, acceptance or approval.

Select Bibliography

I. ICSID DOCUMENTS AND PUBLICATIONS

List of Contracting States and Other Signatories of the Convention (periodically updated list)

Contracting States and Measures Taken by Them for the Purpose of the Convention (periodically updated list)

Members of the Panels of Conciliators and of Arbitrators (periodically updated list)

ICSID Regulations and Rules (May 1975) (contains the texts of the Centre's Regulations and Rules in effect from January 1, 1968 to September 25, 1984)

ICSID Basic Documents (January 1985) (contains the texts of the Centre's Regulations and Rules in effect from September 26, 1984 to December 31, 2002 and the text of the ICSID Convention)

ICSID Convention, Regulations and Rules (January 2003) (contains the texts of the Centre's Regulations and Rules in effect from January 1, 2003 to April 9, 2006 and the text of the ICSID Convention)

ICSID Convention, Regulations and Rules (April 2006) (contains the texts of the Centre's Regulations and Rules in effect from April 10, 2006 and the text of the ICSID Convention)

ICSID Additional Facility for the Administration of Conciliation, Arbitration and Fact-Finding Proceedings (June 1979) (contains the texts of the Additional Facility Rules in effect from September 27, 1978 until December 31, 2002)

ICSID Additional Facility Rules (January 2003) (contains the texts of the Additional Facility Rules in effect from January 1, 2003 to April 9, 2006)

ICSID Additional Facility Rules (April 2006) (contains the texts of the Additional Facility Rules in effect from April 10, 2006)

ICSID Model Clauses (February 1, 1993)

ICSID Annual Report (1966/1967–)

The ICSID Caseload—Statistics (2010–)

Practice Notes for Respondents in ICSID Arbitration (2015)

Background Papers on Annulment (2012 and 2016)

History of the ICSID Convention: Documents Concerning the Origin and Formulation of the Convention on the Settlement of Investment Disputes between States and Nationals of Other States (1970)

II. BOOKS

Alvarez, J.E., *The Public International Law Regime Governing International Investment* (2011)

Amerasinghe, C.F., *Principles of the Institutional Law of International Organizations* (2d ed. 2005)

Aust, A., *Modern Treaty Law and Practice* (3d ed. 2013).

Babb, S., *Behind the Development Banks: Washington Politics, World Poverty, and the Wealth of Nations* (2009)

Black, E. R., *The Diplomacy of Economic Development* (1960)

Blackaby, N. and Partasides, C. with Redfern, A. and Hunter, M., *Redfern and Hunter on International Arbitration* (6th ed. 2015)

Bonnitcha, J., *Substantive Protection under Investment Treaties: A Legal and Economic Analysis* (2014)

Born, G. B. *International Arbitration: Law and Practice* (2012)

Broches, A., *Selected Essays: World Bank, ICSID, and Other Subjects of Public and Private International Law* (1995)

Brown, C., *A Common Law of International Adjudication* (2007)
Caufield, C., *Masters of Illusion: The World Bank and the Poverty of Nations* (1996)
Chasek, P.S., Downie, D.L. and Brown, J.W., *Global Environmental Politics* (6th ed. 2014)
Collier, J. and Lowe, V., *The Settlement of Disputes in International Law: Institutions and Procedures* (1999)
Cordonier Segger, M.-C., Gehring, M.W. and Newcombe, A. (eds.), *Sustainable Development and World Investment Law* (2011)
Crawford, J., *The International Law Commission's Articles on State Responsibility: Introduction, Text and Commentaries* (2002)
De Brabandere, E., *Investment Treaty Arbitration as Public International Law: Procedural Aspects and Implications* (2014)
Derains, Y. and Schwartz, E.A., *A Guide to the ICC Rules of Arbitration* (2d. ed. 2005)
Dolzer, R. and Schreuer, C., *Principles of International Investment Law* (2d. ed. 2013)
—— and Stevens, M., *Bilateral Investment Treaties* (1995)
Douglas, Z., *The International Law of Investment Claims* (2009)
Dupuy, P.-M., Francioni, F. and Petersmann, E.-U. (eds.), *Human Rights in International Investment Law and Arbitration* (2009)
Elm, M., *Oil, Power and Principle: Iran's Oil Nationalization and its Aftermath* (1992)
Fatouros, A.A., *Government Guarantees to Foreign Investors* (1962)
Gaddis, J.L., *The Cold War: A New History* (2005)
Gaillard, E., *La Jurisprudence du CIRDI* (2004)
—— and Banifatemi, Y. (eds.), *Annulment of ICSID Awards* (2004)
—— and Savage, J. (eds.), *Fouchard, Gaillard Goldman on International Commercial Arbitration* (1999)
Gardiner, R., *Treaty Interpretation* (2d. ed. 2015)
Giorgetti, C. (ed.), *Challenges and Recusals of Judges and Arbitrators in International Courts and Tribunals* (2015)
Gray, C., *Judicial Remedies in International Law* (1990)
Guislain, P., *The Privatization Challenge: A Strategic, Legal, and Institutional Analysis of International Experience* (1997)
Happ, R. and Rubins, N., *Digest of ICSID Awards and Decisions 2003–2007* (2009)
—— and Rubins, N., *Digest of ICSID Awards and Decisions 1974–2002* (2013)
Head, J.W., *Losing the Global Development War: A Contemporary Critique of the IMF, the World Bank, and the WTO* (2008)
Henderson, D., *The MAI Affair: A Story and its Lessons* (1999)
Jennings, R. and Watts, A. (eds.), *Oppenheim's International Law* (9th ed. 1996)
Judt, T., Postwar: *A History of Europe Since 1945* (2005)
Kalicki, J.E. and Joubin-Bret, A. (eds), *Reshaping the Investor–State Dispute Settlement System: Journeys for the 21st Century* (2015)
Kapur, D., Lewis, J.P. and Webb, R., *The World Bank: Its First Half Century* (1997)
Keylor, W.R., *A World of Nations: The International Order Since 1945* (2d ed. 2009)
Kinnear, M.N., Bjorklund, A.K. and Hannaford, J.F.G., *Investment Disputes under NAFTA: An Annotated Guide to NAFTA Chapter 11* (2006)
——, Fischer, G.R., Almeida, J.M., Torres, L.F. and Bidegain, M.U. (eds.), *Building International Investment Law: The First 50 Years of ICSID* (2016)
Kjos, H. E. *Applicable Law in Investor–State Arbitration: The Interplay Between National and international Law* (2013)
Klabbers, J., *An Introduction to International Organizations Law* (3d ed. 2015)
Kraske, J. with Becker, W.H., Diamond, W. and Galambos, L., *Bankers with a Mission: The Presidents of the World Bank, 1946–91* (1996)
Kyle, K., *Suez: Britain's End of Empire in the Middle East* (1991)
Llamzon, A.P., *Corruption in International Investment Arbitration* (2014)

Lauterpacht, E., *Aspects of the Administration of International Justice* (1991)
Lauterpacht, H. (ed.), 1 *Oppenheim's International Law* (8th ed. 1955)
Mallaby, S., *The World's Banker: A Story of Failed States, Financial Crises, and the Wealth and Poverty of Nations* (2004)
Malloch-Brown, M., *The Unfinished Global Revolution: The Pursuit of a New International Politics* (2011)
Mason, E.S. and Asher, R.E., *The World Bank Since Bretton Woods* (1973)
McLachlan, C., Shore, L. and Weiniger, M., *International Investment Arbitration: Substantive Principles* (2007)
Miles, K., *The Origins of International Investment Law: Empire, Environment and the Safeguarding of Capital* (2013)
Morris, J., *The Road to Huddersfield: A Journey to Five Continents* (1963)
Moses, M.L., *The Principles and Practice of International Commercial Arbitration* (2d ed. 2012)
Muchlinski, P.T., *Multinational Enterprises and the Law* (2d ed. 2007)
Newcombe, A. and Paradell, L., *Law and Practice of Investment Treaties: Standards of Treatment* (2009)
Oliver, R.W., *George Woods and the World Bank* (1995)
Orrego Vicuña, F., *International Dispute Settlement in an Evolving Global Society: Constitutionalization, Accessibility, Privatization* (2004)
Paparinskis, M., *The International Minimum Standard and Fair and Equitable Treatment* (2013)
Parra, F., *Oil Politics: A Modern History of Petroleum* (2004)
Paulsson, J., *Denial of Justice in International Law* (2005)
Phillips, D.A., *Reforming the World Bank: Twenty Years of Trial—and Error* (2009)
Pohl, M., *Hermann J. Abs: A Biography in Text and Pictures* (1983)
Poulsen, L.N.S., *Bounded Rationality and Economic Diplomacy: The Politics of Investment Treaties in Developing Countries* (2015)
Reed, L., Paulsson, J. and Blackaby, N., *Guide to ICSID Arbitration* (2d. ed. 2010)
Reid, M., *Forgotten Continent: The Battle for Latin America's Soul* (2007)
Reisman, W.M., *Systems of Control in International Adjudication and Arbitration: Breakdown and Repair* (1992)
Rich, B., *Mortgaging the Earth: The World Bank, Environmental Impoverishment, and the Crisis of Development* (1994)
——, *Foreclosing the Future: The World Bank and the Politics of Environmental Destruction* (2013)
Rigo Sureda, A., *Investment Treaty Arbitration: Judging Under Uncertainty* (2012)
Ripinsky, S. with Williams, K., *Damages in International Investment Law* (2008)
Rodrik, D., *The Globalization Paradox: Democracy and the Future of the World Economy* (2011)
Rogers, C.A., *Ethics in International Arbitration* (2014)
Ruggie, J.G., *Just Business: Multinational Corporations and Human Rights* (2013)
Sagafi-Nejad, T., *The UN and Transnational Corporations: From Code of Conduct to Global Compact* (2008)
Salacuse, J.W., *The Law of Investment Treaties* (2d. ed. 2015)
——, *The Three Laws of International Investment: National, Contractual, and International Frameworks for Foreign Capital* (2013)
Sands, P., *Lawless World: Making and Breaking Global Rules* (2005)
Sarfaty, G.A., *Values in Translation: Human Rights and the Culture of the World Bank* (2012)
Schill, S.W., *International Investment Law and Comparative Public Law* (2010)
Schreuer, C.H., *The ICSID Convention: A Commentary* (2001)
—— with Malintoppi, L., Reinisch, A. and Sinclair, A., *The ICSID Convention: A Commentary* (2d ed. 2009)
Schwarzenberger, G., *Foreign Investments and International Law* (1969)
Schwebel, S.M., *Justice in International Law* (1994)
Shapley, D., *Promise and Power: The Life and Times of Robert McNamara* (1993)

Shawcross, H., *Life Sentence: The Memoirs of Lord Shawcross* (1995)
Shea, D.R., *The Calvo Clause: A Problem of Inter-American International Law and Diplomacy* (1955)
Shihata, I.F.I., *MIGA and Foreign Investment* (1988)
——, *The World Bank in a Changing World: Selected Essays* (1991)
——, *Legal Treatment of Foreign Investment: The World Bank Guidelines* (1993)
——, *The World Bank Legal Papers* (2000)
Sornarajah, M., *The International Law on Foreign Investment* (3d ed. 2010)
——, *Resistance and Change in the International Law on Foreign Investment* (2015)
Spero, J.E. and Hart, J.A., *The Politics of International Economic Relations* (7th ed. 2009)
Stephens, T., *International Courts and Environmental Protection* (2009)
Stiglitz, J.E., *Globalization and its Discontents* (2003)
——, *The Roaring Nineties: A New History of the World's Most Prosperous Decade* (2004)
——, *Making Globalization Work* (2006)
Taylor, I. and Smith, K., *United Nations Conference on Trade and Development (UNCTAD)* (2007)
Toope, S.I., *Mixed International Arbitration: Studies in Arbitration Between States and Private Persons* (1990)
Van Harten, G., *Investment Treaty Arbitration and Public Law* (2007)
——, *Sovereign Choices and Sovereign Constraints: Judicial Restraint in Investment Treaty Arbitration* (2013)
Vandevelde, K.J., *U.S. International Investment Agreements* (2009)
——, *Bilateral Investment Treaties: History, Policy, and Interpretation* (2010)
Viñuales, J.E., *Foreign Investment and the Environment in International Law* (2012)
Waibel, M., *Sovereign Defaults before International Courts and Tribunals* (2011)
Weaver, C., *Hypocrisy Trap: The World Bank and the Poverty of Reform* (2008)
Weiler, T., *The Interpretation of International Investment Law: Equality, Discrimination and Minimum Standards of Treatment in Historical Context* (2013)
Wetter, J.G., *The International Arbitration Process: Public and Private* (1979)
Woods, N., *The Globalizers: The IMF, the World Bank, and Their Borrowers* (2006)
Wright, R., *The Color Curtain: A Report on the Bandung Conference* (1956)
Yannaca-Small, K. (ed.), *Arbitration under International Investment Agreements: A Guide to the Key Issues* (2010)
Zimmerman, A., Tomuschat, C. and Oellers-Frahm, K. (eds.), *The Statute of the International Court of Justice: A Commentary* (2006)

III. ARTICLES, BOOK CHAPTERS AND PAPERS

Aguilar Alvarez, G. and Park, W.W., The New Face of Investment Arbitration, 28 Yale J. Int'l L. 365 (2003)
Alexandrov, S.A., Breaches of Contract and Breaches of Treaty: The Jurisdiction of Treaty-Based Arbitration Tribunals to Decide Breach of Contract Claims in *SGS v. Pakistan* and *SGS v. Philippines*, 5 J. World Investment and Trade 555 (2004)
Amerasinghe, C.F., The Prawn Farm (AAPL) Arbitration, 4 Sri Lanka J. Int'l L. 155 (1992)
Amuzegar, J., A Requiem for the North–South Conference, 56 Foreign Affairs 236 (1977–1978)
Antonietti, A., The 2006 Amendments of the ICSID Rules and Regulations and the Additional Facility Rules, 21 ICSID Rev.—FILJ 427 (2006)
Bishop, D., Investor–State Dispute Settlement under the Transatlantic Trade and Investment Partnership: Have the Negotiations Run Aground?, 30 ICSID Rev.—FILJ 1 (2015)
Bjorklund, A.K., Investment Treaty Arbitral Decisions as *Jurisprudence Constante*, UC Davis Legal Studies Research Paper, No. 158 (2009)

Boisson de Chazournes, L., Transparency and *Amicus Curiae* Briefs, 5 J. World Trade and Investment 333 (2004)
Broches, A., Awards Rendered Pursuant to the ICSID Convention: Binding Force, Finality, Recognition, Enforcement, Execution, 2 ICSID Rev.—FILJ 287 (1987)
——, Observations on the Finality of ICSID Awards, 6 ICSID Rev.—FILJ 321 (1991)
Brower, C.N. and Goodman, R.E.M., Provisional Measures and the Protection of ICSID Jurisdictional Exclusivity Against Municipal Proceedings, 6 ICSID Rev.—FILJ 431 (1991)
Burke-White, W.W. and Staden, A., Investment Protection in Extraordinary Times: The Interpretation and Application of Non-Precluded Measures Provisions in Bilateral Investment Treaties, 48 Va. J. Int'l L. 307 (2008)
Caron, D.D., Reputation and Reality in the ICSID Annulment Process: Understanding the Distinction between Annulment and Appeal, 7 ICSID Rev.—FILJ 21 (1992)
Craig, W.L., The Final Chapter in the Pyramids Case: Discounting an ICSID Award for Annulment Risk, 8 ICSID Rev.—FILJ 264 (1993)
Crawford, J., Treaty and Contract in Investment Arbitration, 24 Arb. Int'l 351 (2008)
——, Ten Investment Arbitration Awards that Shook the World: Introduction and Overview, 4 Dispute Resolution International 71 (2010)
Daele, K., The Standard for Disqualifying Arbitrators Finally Settled and Lowered, 29 ICSID Rev.—FILJ 296 (2014)
Delaume, G.R., ICSID Arbitration and the Courts, 77 AJIL 784 (1983)
——, How to Draft an ICSID Arbitration Clause, 7 ICSID Rev.—FILJ 168 (1992)
——, The Pyramids Stand—The Pharaohs Can Rest in Peace, 8 ICSID Rev.—FILJ 231 (1993)
Dolzer, R. Indirect Expropriation of Alien Property, 1 ICSID Rev.—FILJ 41 (1986)
Douglas, Z., The Hybrid Foundations of Investment Treaty Arbitration, 74 BYBIL 151 (2003)
Feldman, M.B., The Annulment Proceedings and the Finality of ICSID Arbitral Awards, 2 ICSID Rev.—FILJ 85 (1987)
Fernández-Arnesto, J., The Time Has Come—A Plea for Abandoning Secrecy in Arbitration, 3 Les cahiers de l'arbitrage 583 (2012)
Fouret, J., The World Bank and ICSID: Family or Incestuous Ties?, 4 Int'l Organizations L. Rev. 121 (2007)
Franck, S.D., The Legitimacy Crisis in Investment Treaty Arbitration: Privatizing Public International Law Through Inconsistent Decisions, 73 Fordham L. Rev. 1521 (2005)
Friedland, P.D. and Wong, E., Measuring Damages for the Deprivation of Income-Producing Assets: ICSID Case Studies, 6 ICSID Rev.—FILJ 400 (1991)
Gaillard, E., Investment Treaty Arbitration and Jurisdiction over Contractual Claims—The SGS Cases Considered, in T. Weiler (ed.), *International Investment Law and Arbitration: Leading Cases from the ICSID, NAFTA, Bilateral Treaties and Customary International Law* 325 (2005)
——, Identify or Define? Reflections on the Evolution of the Concept of Investment in ICSID Practice, in Binder, C., Kriebaum, U., Renisch, A. and Wittich, S. (eds.), *International Investment Law in the 21st Century,* Liber Amicorum *in Honour of Christoph Schreuer* 403 (2009)
—— and Banifatemi, Y., The Meaning of "and" in Article 42(1), Second Sentence of the Washington Convention: The Role of International Law in the ICSID Choice of Law Process, 18 ICSID Rev.—FILJ 375 (2003)
Gantz, D.A., An Appellate Mechanism for Review of Arbitral Decisions in Investor State Disputes: Prospects and Challenges, 39 Vanderbilt J. Transnat'l L. 29 (2006)
Gaukrodger, D. and Gordon, K., Investor–State Dispute Settlement: A Scoping Paper for the Investment Policy Community, OECD Working Papers on International Investment, 2012/03
Gharavi, H., ICSID and its Monarch, in M. Abdel Raouf and others (eds.), *Festschrift Ahmed Sadek El-Kosheri: From the Arab World to the Globalization of International Law and Arbitration* 325 (2015)

Gotanda, J.Y., Consistently Inconsistent: The Need for Predictability in Awarding Costs and Fees in Investment Treaty Arbitrations, 28 ICSID Rev.—FILJ 420 (2013)

Hoffmann, A.K., Counterclaims in Investment Arbitration, 28 ICSID Rev.—FILJ 438 (2013)

Joubin-Bret, A. and Legum, B., A Set of Rules Dedicated to Investor-State Mediation: The IBA Investor-State Mediation Rules, 29 ICSID Rev.—FILJ 17, 18 (2014)

Kalicki, J. and Medeiros, S., Fair and Equitable and Ambiguous: What Is Fair and Equitable Treatment in International Investment Law?, 22 ICSID Rev.—FILJ 24 (2007)

Kaufmann-Kohler, G., Arbitral Precedent: Dream, Necessity, or Excuse?, 23 Arb. Int'l 357 (2007)

——, Is Consistency a Myth?, in Gaillard, E. and Banifatemi, Y. (eds.), *Precedent in International Arbitration* 137 (2008)

—— and Potestà, M., Can the Mauritius Convention serve as a model for the reform of investor–State arbitration in connection with the introduction of a permanent investment tribunal or an appeal mechanism? Analysis and roadmap, Geneva Center for International Dispute Settlement, June 3, 2016, available at <www.uncitral.org>

Kinnear, M. and Nitschke, F., Disqualification of Arbitrators under the ICSID Convention and Rules, in C. Giorgetti (ed.), *Challenges and Recusals of Judges and Arbitrators in International Courts and Tribunals* 34 (2015).

Kriebaum, U., Human Rights of the Population of the Host State in International Investment Arbitration, 10 J. World Investment and Trade 677 (2009)

Lalive, P., The First "World Bank" Arbitration (*Holiday Inns v. Morocco*)—Some Legal Problems, 51 BYBIL 123 (1980)

——, Some Threats to International Investment Arbitration, 1 ICSID Rev.—FILJ 26 (1986)

Lalonde, M., Quo Vadis Disqualification?, in M. Kinnear and others (eds.), *Building International Investment Law: The First 50 Years of ICSID* 641 (2016)

Lamm, C.B., Jurisdiction of the International Settlement of Investment Disputes, 6 ICSID Rev.—FILJ 462 (1991)

Landau, T. and Weeramantry, R., A Case for Transparency in Investment Arbitration, in M. Kinnear and others (eds.), *Building International Law: The First 50 Years of ICSID* 669 (2016)

Legum, B., Lessons Learned from the NAFTA: The New Generation of U.S. Investment Treaty Arbitration Provisions, 19 ICSID Rev.—FILJ 344 (2004)

Mallaby, S., NGOs: Fighting Poverty, Hurting the Poor, Foreign Policy, September–October 2004, at 50.

Marchais, B.P., Mesures provisoires et autonomie du systeme d'arbitrage C.I.R.D.I., 14 Droit et pratique du commerce international 275 (1988)

Mathews, J.T., Power Shift, 76 Foreign Affairs 50 (1997)

Mortenson, J.D., The Meaning of Investment: ICSID's Travaux and the Domain of International Investment Law, 51 Harvard Int'l L.J. 257 (2010)

Muchlinski, P.T., "Caveat Investor"? The Relevance of the Conduct of the Investor under the Fair and Equitable Treatment Standard, 55 ICLQ 527 (2006)

Nassar, N., Internationalization of State Contracts: ICSID, The Last Citadel, 14 J. Int'l Arb. 183 (1997)

Newcombe, A., The Boundaries of Regulatory Expropriation in International Law, 20 ICSID Rev.—FILJ 1 (2005)

Nitschke, F., The IBA's Investor-State Mediation Rules and the ICSID Dispute Settlement Framework, 29 ICSID Rev.—FILJ 112 (2014)

Nurick, L., Costs in International Arbitrations, 7 ICSID Rev.—FILJ 57 (1992)

—— and Schnably, S.J., The First ICSID Conciliation: *Tesoro Petroleum Corporation v. Trinidad and Tobago*, 1 ICSID Rev.—FILJ 340 (1986)

Paulsson, J., ICSID's Achievements and Prospects, 6 ICSID Rev.—FILJ 380 (1991)

——, Arbitration Without Privity, 10 ICSID Rev.—FILJ 232 (1995)

——, Moral Hazard in International Dispute Resolution, 25 ICSID Rev.—FILJ 339 (2010)
Pauwelyn, J., At the Edge of Chaos? Foreign Investment Law as a Complex Adaptive System, How it Emerged and How it Can Be Reformed, 29 ICSID Rev.—FILJ 372 (2014)
Pogany, S. I., Economic Development Agreements, 7 ICSID Rev.—FILJ 1 (1992)
Polasek, M., The Threshold for Registration of a Request for Arbitration under the ICSID Convention, 5 Dispute Resolution Int'l 177 (2011)
Price, D.M., An Overview of the NAFTA Investment Chapter: Substantive Rules and Investor–State Dispute Settlement, 24 International Lawyer 655 (1990)
Redfern, A., ICSID—Losing its Appeal?, 3 Arb. Int'l 98 (1987)
Reinisch, A., The European Union and Investor–State Dispute Settlement: From Investor-State Arbitration to a Permanent Investment Court, CIGI Investor–State Arbitration Series, Paper No. 2 (March 2016)
Reisman, W.M., The Regime for *Lacunae* in the ICSID Choice of Law Provision and the Question of its Threshold, 15 ICSID Rev.—FILJ 562 (2000)
Rogers, W.D., Of Missionaries, Fanatics, and Lawyers: Some Thoughts on Investment Disputes in the Americas, 22 AJIL 1 (1978)
Rubins, N.D., The Allocation of Costs and Attorney's Fees in Investor–State Arbitration, 18 ICSID Rev.—FILJ 109 (2003)
Salman, S.M.A., Good Offices and Mediation and International Water Disputes, in Permanent Court of Arbitration (ed.), *Resolution of International Water Disputes* 155 (2002)
—— and Obadia, E.M., The Indus Waters Treaty, the Baglihar Difference and ICSID Administration of the Proceedings, 23(2) News from ICSID 1 (2006)
Sampliner, G.H., Arbitration of Expropriation Cases Under U.S. Investment Treaties—A Threat to Democracy or the Dog That Didn't Bark?, 15 ICSID Rev.—FILJ 1 (2003)
Schreuer, C., Failure to Apply the Governing Law in International Investment Arbitration, 7 Austrian Rev. of Int'l and European L. 147 (2002)
——, Travelling the BIT Route: Of Waiting Periods, Umbrella Clauses and Forks in the Road, 5 J. World Investment and Trade 231 (2004)
——, Calvo's Grandchildren: The Return of Local Remedies in Investment Arbitration, 4 Law and Practice of International Courts and Tribunals 1 (2005)
——, Fair and Equitable Treatment in Arbitral Practice, 6 J. World Investment and Trade 359 (2005)
Schwebel, S.M., The United States 2004 Model Bilateral Investment Treaty: An Exercise in the Regressive Development of International Law, in International Chamber of Commerce (ed.), *Global Reflections on International Law, Commerce and Dispute Resolution,* Liber Amicorum *in Honour of Robert Briner* 815 (2005)
——, Is Mediation of Foreign Investment Disputes Plausible?, 22 ICSID Rev.—FILJ 237 (2007)
——, A BIT About ICSID, 23 ICSID Rev.—FILJ 1 (2008)
Sheppard, A., Arbitrator Independence in ICSID Arbitration, in Binder, C., Kriebaum, U., Renisch, A. and Wittich, S. (eds.), *Investment Law in the 21st Century,* Liber Amicorum *in Honour of Christoph Schreuer* 131 (2009)
Shihata, I.F.I., Towards a Greater Depoliticization of Investment Disputes: The Roles of ICSID and MIGA, 1 ICSID Rev.—FILJ 1 (1986)
Sinclair, A., The Origins of the Umbrella Clause in the International Law of Investment Protection, 4 Arb. Int'l 411 (2004)
——, ICSID's Nationality Requirements, 23 ICSID Rev.—FILJ 57 (2008)
Stern, B., Civil Society's Voice in the Settlement of International Economic Disputes, 22 ICSID Rev.—FILJ 280 (2007)
Szasz, P.C., Arbitration Under the Auspices of the World Bank, 3 Int'l L. 312 (1969)
——, The Investment Disputes Convention—Opportunities and Pitfalls (How to Submit Disputes to ICSID), 5 J. L. and Economic Development 23 (1970)

Thomas J.C., Reflections on Article 1105 of NAFTA: History, State Practice and the Influence of Commentators, 17 ICSID Rev.—FILJ 21 (2002)
Tupman, W.M., Challenge and Disqualification of Arbitrators in International Commercial Arbitration, 38 ICLQ 26 (1989)
Van den Berg, A.J., Dissenting Opinions by Party-Appointed Arbitrators in Investment Arbitration, in M. Arsanjani and others (eds.), *The Practice of Arbitration: Essays in International Law in Honor of W. Michael Reisman* 821 (2010)
Vandevelde, K. The Political Economy of a Bilateral Investment Treaty, 92 AJIL 621 (1998)
Vasani, B. and Palmer, S., Challenge and Disqualification of Arbitrators at ICSID: A New Dawn?, 30 ICSID Rev—FILJ 194 (2015)
Voss, J., The Protection and Promotion of Foreign Direct Investment in Developing Countries: Interests, Interdependencies, Intricacies, 31 ICLQ 686 (1982)
Vuylsteke, C., Foreign Investment Protection and ICSID Arbitration, 4 Georgia J. Int'l and Comparative L. 343 (1974)
Waelde, T.W., Procedural Challenges in Investment Arbitration under the Shadow of the Dual Role of the State: Asymmetrics and Tribunals' Duty to Ensure, Proactively the Equality of Arms, 26 Arb. Int'l 3 (2010)
Waibel, M., Opening Pandora's Box: Sovereign Bonds in International Arbitration, 101 AJIL 711 (2007)
Warren, E., Trans-Pacific Partnership Clause Everyone Should Oppose, Op-ed, Washington Post, February 25, 2015
Weil, P., The State, the Foreign Investor and International Law: The No Longer Stormy Relationship of a *Ménage à Trois*, 15 ICSID Rev.—FILJ 401 (2000)
Weiler, T., *Metalclad v. Mexico*—A Play in Three Parts, 2 J. World Investment 685 (2001)
Ziade, N., How Should Arbitral Institutions Address Issues of Conflicts of Interest?, in M. Abdel Raouf and others (eds.), *Festschrift Ahmed Sadek El-Kosheri: From the Arab World to the Globalization of International Law and Arbitration* 211 (2015)
———, Is ICSID Heading in the Wrong Direction?, Global Arbitration Review, February 24, 2015

Index

During the negotiation of the ICSID Convention the spelling of *Center* was changed to *Centre*. The appropriate spellings are used throughout the book but for indexing purposes *Centre* has been exclusively used.

AAPL v. Sri Lanka
applicable law
BIT silent with regard to 166–7
jurisdiction
consent to 153, 155–6
Abs, H.J. 13, 14
Abdel-Aal, M.Y. 119
Abs–Shawcross Draft Convention 14–15, 17, 19, 287
Additional Facility
continuation 135–7
establishment 7
initial proposal 129–31
proceedings
categories applicable to 128–9
characteristics common to 194–6
instances of 193–202, 268
number of proceedings related to (2000 to 2010) 231
Additional Facility Rules
adoption 134–5
amendments
(2003) 223–4
(2006) 226–7
draft rules 132–4
proceedings applicable to 7, 193–4
sources 133–4
Administrative Council *see* **International Centre for Settlement of Investment Disputes**
Administrative and Financial Regulations *see also* **arbitration proceedings**
adoption of 105–6
amendments 126–8
definitive texts, adoption of 105–6
provisional regulations
Administrative Council procedures 94
administrative support to parties 95–6
budgetary provisions 96
fees and expenses 96–7
fiscal year 96
immunities and privileges 97
information, publication of 95
Secretariat 94–5
Secretary-General
appointment 94
functions 95
staff, appointment 95
Afghanistan
investment promotion law 121
African Development Bank
establishment 11
ALBA *see* **Bolivarian Alliance**
alternates
executive director appointments
immunities 4
Alvarez, H.C. 237
***amicus curiae* submissions**
proposals for 225, 227–8
Amco v. Indonesia
annulment decision
commentary 167–9, 170–2
applicable law
agreement, absent 162, 164
annulment
cases
(1980s) 167–72
(2000 to 2010) 259–62
(2011 to 2015) 282
costs of proceedings 126, 170
failure to state reasons 168–9, 172
financial crisis 260
first annulment proceedings 163–4
non-application and erroneous application of applicable law 167–8, 262
"remedy against an incorrect decision" distinguished 171
success rate 259–6
appeals
appellate mechanism
standing tribunal 291–4
proposal for 226–7, 228, 284–5
applicable law
agreement, on 162
BITs, cases initiated under 166–7, 256–9
cases
(1980s) 162–7
(2000 to 2010) 256–9
consent 258
domestic law
interaction with international law 257–8
inference of agreement, on 258–9
international law
interaction with domestic law 257–8
"supplemental and corrective role" 165
Aramburu Menchaca, A.A. 119
arbitral awards
annulment 43–4, 47, 145–6, 167–75, 259–62
appeals, proposal for 226–7, 228, 284–5
awards dismissing claims 278–82
awards upholding claims 278
authentication 101
checklist of contents 101
compliance 294
date 101

arbitral awards (*cont.*)
enforcement 66, 172–5, 262–65
finality of 66
publication 78, 95, 106, 127, 225, 284
reasons, requirement for statement of 43, 66, 101, 168, 169
recognition 44, 78
rectification 101, 145–6
signature 101
stay of enforcement 259–62
time limits 101
arbitral tribunals
administrative support 95–6
appointment
Chairman of Administrative Council, by 147–8
constitution 65, 146–50
ex aequo et bono decision-making power 33
fees and expenses 96, 97, 220–1
annulment proceedings 126, 170
uniformity of 126
powers and functions 43, 54
arbitration proceedings
ad hoc arbitration proceedings 137–8
annulment decisions
(1980s) 168–75
(2000 to 2010) 259–62
applicable law 76–7, 162–7, 209–10, 256–9
failure to apply 168–9
arbitrators *see* **arbitrators**
awards *see* **arbitral awards**
default procedure 54, 77, 99
integrity of proceedings 149–50
international commercial institutions 16
international investment disputes
arbitral body to resolve 15–17
minutes 95
oral phases 100
parties
identification of 64
place of proceedings 85, 114
pre-hearing conferences 127
precedent setting cases under BITs 202–10
privacy and secrecy
deliberations of 101
procedural cooperation 100
provisional regulations
filing of requests 98
registration of requests 98
rules *see* **Arbitration Rules** *and specific regulations e.g.* Administrative and Financial Regulations
time limits 99
amendment (2003) 222–3
tribunals and commissions *see* **arbitral tribunals; conciliation commissions**
written phases 100
Arbitration Rules
adoption of 105–6
amendments
(1984) 126–8
(2003) 221–4
(2006) 224–30
definitive texts, adoption of 105–6
provisional rules 98–102
time limits 222–3
arbitrators
appointing authority 137–9, 147–8
appointment
Chairman of the Administrative Council, by 147, 237, 275
exclusion of national arbitrators 75
freedom, of 42
individuals appointed 147–8
trends 268, 274–6
death 148–9
disqualification 42, 65, 150, 238–40, 276–7
criteria 238–40, 276
legal standard, applied 276, 277
publication of decisions 229–30
fees and expenses 65, 96, 114
gender 148
impartiality 150, 239, 240, 277
investment treaty proceedings 238
nationality 109, 147, 222, 237, 275
patterns in 237
qualifications 147
resignations 148, 238
Asante, S.K.B. 148, 155
Asian Development Bank
establishment 11
Asian-African Legal Consultative Organization 114, 273
Association for the Promotion and Protection of Private Foreign Investment 13, 14
Atlantic Triton v. Guinea
provisional measures, court ordered
commentary 158–9
Australian Centre for International Commercial Arbitration 188, 273
Australian Commercial Dispute Centre 188, 273

Bandung Conference (1955) 11
Baptista, L.O. 272
decolonization
Suez Crisis, effect of 11
Bedjaoui, M. 188
Bello Janeiro, D. 252
Benvenuti & Bonfant v. Congo
arbitral awards, enforcement
commentary 173–4
Berg, J. 161
van den Berg, A.J. 238, 253, 257
Berman, F. 236, 237
Bernardini, P. 237, 255
Bertram, W. 79
bilateral investment treaties (BITs)
cases
(1990s) 202–10

(2000 to 2010) 256–9
clauses providing for arbitration under ICSID 121–3, 181–2
development 180–5
Germany
development of 20
free trade agreements 211–12
most favored nation (MFN)
role of MFN clause establishing jurisdiction 207–8, 259–64
treatment, of 180
purpose 20–1
rate of growth 181, 211
transnational corporations
incorporation of minimum standards of regulation 110
Bingham, T.H. 255
Bishop, R.D. 281
BITs *see* **bilateral investment treaties**
Black, E.R. 20, 22 fig., 24
Black's Bank *see* **International Bank for Reconstruction and Development**
Böckstiegel, K.-H. 191, 237, 291
Bogotá Chamber of Commerce Centre for Arbitration and Conciliation 274
Bolivarian Alliance (ALBA) 212–13
Boo, L. 272
Born, G.B. 245
Boulle, L. 272
Boutros Boutros-Ghali 177
Bretton Woods Conference 2, 23, 34
Briner, R. 277
Broches, A. 10, 17–19, 25, 44, 50 fig., 84 fig., 114, 116, 118, 171, 188
Additional Facility
proposals for 129–31
dispute settlement approach
early pursuit of 23–4
Legal Committee
first meeting of 68
regional consultative meetings
chairman of 54
rationale for holding 39
registration of request to institute proceedings 144
Secretary-General of ICSID
election as 90–1
re-election as 114–15
submission of draft budget 139
support for availability of court-ordered provisional measures 159
working paper on draft ICSID Convention 25–34
conciliation and arbitration provisions 32–4
establishment and organization of centre 28–31
jurisdictional matters 31–2
Brower, C.N. 237, 252, 257
Brownlie, I. 119, 188
Brun, A.A. 37
Brunt, M. 148
Bucher, A. 210
Buergenthal, T. 205
Bullitt J.C. 35
Burrows, F. 69, 71, 72

Cairns, D.J.A. 272
Calvo Doctrine 49, 56, 61, 184, 212–13
Camacho, J.E. 187
Cameron, D.H. 233
van Campenhout, A. 36–7
Canada
aid agency, establishment of 11
Cancio, L. 39
Castañeda, J. 147
Center for International Environmental Law (CIEL) 213
Chabaneix, J.P. 234
Charter of the Economic Rights and Duties of States (1974) 109
Chemloul, M. 246
Cheng, T. 272
Chiasson, E.C. 192
China International Economic and Trade Arbitration Commission 274
Civiletti, B.R. 197, 199 fig.
claims
contract claims vs treaty claims 246–54
frivolous claims 225, 228, 294
Clausen, A.W. 15, 115
code of conduct
foreign investments, treatment of
Abs–Shawcross Draft Convention 14–15
German Society for the Protection of Foreign Investments 13
IBRD refusal to be involved in project 18
OECD Draft Convention on the Protection of Foreign Property (1962) 15, 18
OECD Draft Convention on the Protection of Foreign Property (1967) 18–20
Cold War 11, 177–8
Comair-Obeid, N. 272
Committee of the Whole on the Settlement of Investment Disputes
establishment 27, 34
meetings
final 81–5
initial (1962 to mid-1963) 27, 34–8
July 1964 60
Conable, B.B. 179
conciliation commissions
administrative support 95–6
constitution 65, 146–50, 236
fees and expenses 96–7, 220–1
immunities and privileges 97
minutes 101
oral phases 100
parties
cooperation between 100
identification of 64
place of proceedings 76, 101, 114
powers and functions 43

conciliation commissions (*cont.*)
privacy and secrecy
deliberations of 101
hearings of 101
procedural cooperation 100
provisional regulations
filing of requests 98
registration of requests 95, 98
rules
adoption of 105–6
definitive texts, adoption of 105–6
provisional rules 98–101
time limits 99
written phases 100
conciliation proceedings
encouragement of as alternative to arbitration 230, 289–90
Conciliation Rules
adoption of 105–6
definitive text, adoption of 105–6
provisional rules 98–101
conciliators
appointment, freedom of 42
disqualification 42, 65, 150
fees and expenses 65, 96–7, 113
patterns in 264
Conference on International Economic Cooperation 110
Convention on the Settlement of Investment Disputes between States and Nationals of Other States *see also* **First Draft**
amendments 45, 56–7
applicable law 54–5, 76–7
Broches Working Paper *see* Working Paper (1962)
Draft Convention for the Resolution of Disputes between States and Nationals of Other States *see* Working Paper (1962)
Draft Report 80–1
entry into force 1, 7, 83
First Preliminary Draft (August 9, 1963) 39
final text, approval of 85
finalization of text 59–85
formulation of
Executive Directors of IBRD, role in 25–27
Legal Committee on the Settlement of Investment Disputes
Administrative Council, powers 70
ancillary activities of the Centre 69
applicable law 76–7
arbitration proceedings 75–9
arbitrators, appointment 75–6
consensus 68
conciliation proceedings 75–9
default procedure 77
establishment of the Centre 69–71
host institutions 76
ICJ, reference to 79–80
inter-State disputes 73–4
jurisdiction 71–5
meetings 67–9
nationals, definition 73
office holders 71
organization of the Centre 69–71
place of proceedings 76
registration of proceedings 75
remedies 74, 78
rules of procedure 67–9
objections to 35–6, 59
origins
introduction 11–12
participation 269
Preliminary Draft (October 15, 1963)
Administrative Council
powers 41
role 41
amendment of the Convention 45
arbitral awards 43, 44
arbitral tribunals, powers and functions 43
arbitrators
appointment 42–3
disqualification 42–3
arrangement of provisions 40
conciliation commissions, powers and functions 43
conciliators
appointment 42–3
disqualification 42–3
denunciation of the Convention 45
disqualification 47–8
enforcement 44
entry into force of the Convention 45
establishment of the Centre 40–1
inauguration of ICSID 45
interpretation and application disputes 44–5
inter-State proceedings 44
jurisdiction 41–2
nationals, definition 42
organization of the Centre 40–1
President of IBRD, role of 40–1
recognition 44
regional consultative meetings 39
remedies 43–4
sources 45–8
territorial application of the Convention 45
Working Paper, provisions compared 40–8
ratifications 1, 87, 111–12, 216
regional consultative meetings 39
Administrative Council, powers 50–1
arbitral awards 56
arbitral tribunals, powers and functions 54
arbitrators
appointment 53
disqualification 53
attendance 48
Broches, A., role of 48
chairman 48

conciliation commissions, powers and functions 53–4
conciliators
appointment 53
disqualification 53
enforcement 55–6
establishment of 39
establishment of the Centre 49–51
IBRD, links with 50
inter-State proceedings 56
interpretation and application disputes 55–6
jurisdiction 51–3
nationals, definition 52
opposition 49
organization of the Centre 49–51
Panels of Conciliators and Arbitrators, structure 51
participants 48
recognition 55
remedies 54–5
Revised Draft 81
signatories 82, 87
standing tribunal 291
text, approval of 1
Working Paper (1962)
Administrative Council, powers 28–9
arbitral awards 33
arbitral tribunals
constitution 32
decisions 33
arbitrators, appointment 32
conciliation commissions
constitution 32
recommendations 33
conciliators, appointment 32
establishment of the Centre 28–31
good faith, requirement of 31
IBRD, links with 30
jurisdiction 31–2
objections to 33
offices
organization of the Centre 28–31
Panels of Conciliators and Arbitrators, structure 29–31
Preliminary Draft (October 15, 1963), compared 40–8
President of IBRD, role of 28, 30
proceedings
initiation of 32
rules 32
privileges and immunities 30–1
purpose 28
remedies 34
Secretariat, structure 29
corporations
local companies
treatment as national of another Contracting State 152–3
parent companies not signatories to arbitration clause
jurisdiction of arbitral tribunal 151–2
transnational corporations
rights of states to regulate 109–110
UN code of conduct
abandoned 177–8
corruption
World Bank strategy to overcome 178
Council of Europe
Consultative Assembly
multilateral investment guarantee scheme proposal 13
Craig, W.L. 173, 278
Crawford, J.R. 206, 221, 249, 261
Cremades, B.M. 118, 237–8, 242
Crivellaro, A. 249, 250
Cuban missile crisis 11

D'Andelot Belin, G. 60
Dañino, R.E. 217
Davies, C.H. 84 fig.
Dean, P.H. 88 fig.
debt crisis (1980s)
IMF response to 111
World Bank response to 111
Declaration on the Establishment of a New International Economic Order (NIEO) (1974) 109
Declaratory Statement of Petroleum Policy 109
Delaume, G.R. 116, 158
Derains, Y. 275
developing countries
anti-foreign investment sentiment 109
economic independence, and 109
ICSID
importance of institution to 288
investment
attraction of 12
promotion of 111
privatization programs 111
Third World
designation of poor countries as 11
diplomatic protection *see also* **Calvo Doctrine**
arbitral awards, enforcement 37, 55
exercise of 15–16, 46, 75
prohibition 32, 44, 56, 75
disputes
notification of classes for submission to ICSID 119–20
Dodero, L. 187
Donner, O. 36, 60
Donovan, D. 238
Dossou, R.M. 221
Draft Convention on Investments Abroad (1959) *see* **Abs–Shawcross Draft Convention**
Draft Convention on the Protection of Foreign Property (1962) 15, 18
Draft Convention on the Protection of Foreign Property (1967) 18–20

Draft Convention on the Settlement of Investment Disputes between States and Nationals of Other States (First Draft)
amendments to the Convention 67
arbitration proceedings 64–6
conciliation proceedings 64–6
establishment of the Centre 62–3
ICJ, reference to 67
jurisdiction 63–4
nationals, definition 64
organization of the Centre 62–3
provisions 61–2
Driss, R. 88 fig.
Dulles, J.F. 11
Dupuy, R.-J. 161

Echandi, R. 272
Edward, D.A.O. 261
Egypt
Aswan High Dam project finance
IBRD role in settlement of dispute with Britain and France 21–2
investment promotion law 121
Elaraby, N. 261
Elias, T.O. 48
Elkin, A. 91
El-Kosheri, A.S. 147, 155, 163, 221
El Mahdi, M.A.E. 147, 154, 156 fig.
El No de Tokio 61
Elsing, S.H. 272
Escobar, A.A. 199 fig., 213
Ethyl v. Canada
NGO concerns regarding the arbitral process 184
Europe
bilateral organizations
development of 11
European Community
Treaty Establishing
influence on ICSID Convention 47
European Investment Bank
establishment 11
European Investment Fund
establishment 11

Fadlallah, I. 209, 242
Fatouros, A.A. 172
Faurès, A. 245, 247
FCNs *see* **friendship, commerce and navigation treaties**
Fedax v. Venezuela
commentary 203–5, 240–1
Federal Republic of Germany *see also* **Germany**
investment insurance 12–13
Feliciano, F.P. 164, 247
Fernandez-Armesto, J. 237–8, 278
Fernández Rozas, J.C. 206, 268
First Draft *see* **Draft Convention on the Settlement of Investment Disputes between States and Nationals of Other States**
Foighel, I. 149
foreign investment
dispute settlement approach, to 19–20
encouragement of in 1950s 19
private foreign investment
investment insurance 12–13
world flows
(2000 to 2008) 211
(2011 to 2015) 268
Fortier, L.Y. 206, 221, 237
forum prorogatum 31, 53, 64
Foster, J.G. 148
François, J.P.A. 106, 107
free trade agreements (FTAs)
appellate mechanisms 291–2
friendship, commerce and navigation treaties (FCNs)
United States during 1950s 19
FTAs *see* **free trade agreements** 192
Furnish, D.B. 192

Gaillard, E. 236, 145, 246
Garland, J.M. 36
Garner, R. 2
German Institution of Arbitration 273
German Society for the Protection of Foreign Investments
private foreign investment
code of conduct 13
Germany
ICSID proposals at initial meetings of Committee of the Whole 37–8
reunification 177
general unity of the investment operation
doctrine, of 153–4
Giardina, A. 164, 172
globalization
development of 178, 179
disaffection with 212
Goldman, B. 119, 149, 155
Golsong, H. 18, 115, 118, 135, 140, 144, 188
González, H.B. 122
Griffith, G. 261, 279
Grigera Naón, H A. 255
Gros Espiell, H. 241
Guillaume, G. 237, 261
Gulf Cooperation Council Commercial Arbitration Centre 188, 273
Gutierrez Cano, J.G. 82–4
Guyana
notification of disputes subject to jurisdiction of ICSID 119

Hanotiau, B. 245
hearings *see also* **public hearings**
location 270, 274
Heiskanen, V. 281
Heth, M. 203
Higgins, R. 148,
Hirschtritt, R. 84

Holiday Inns v. Morocco (_Holiday Inns_ case)
annulment of decision and procedural order, request for
commentary 145–6
jurisdiction
pragmatic approach to, commentary 150–1, 152–3
provisional measures, court ordered, commentary 160
Hong Kong International Arbitration Centre 274
human rights
reform constraints 214
Hwang, M. 221, 243

ICSID Basic Documents 128
ICSID Review—Foreign Investment Law Journal 140, 141
IIIA *see* **International Investment Insurance Agency**
Ikeda, H. 63 fig.
Illanes, F. 34, 60
Iliff, W.A.B. 21
Institution Rules
adoption of 105–6
amendments 126–8
definitive texts
adoption of 105–6
provisional rules
filing of requests 98
registration of requests 98
insurance
private foreign investment 12–13
Inter-American Development Bank
establishment 12
International Bank for Reconstruction and Development (IBRD) 1
see also **International Development Association; International Finance Corporation; Multilateral Investment Guarantee Agency; World Bank Group**
Articles of Agreement 2, 3
Committee of the Whole on the Settlement of Investment Disputes 27, 34–8, 60, 81–5
Black's Bank 20–4
Board of Governors 3
capital 3
corruption, strategy to overcome 178
debt crisis (1980s)
response to 110–111
depositary duties 84
dispute resolution
development of role (1950s and 1960s) 20–4
dispute settlement approach 20–3
Executive Directors
appointment 3–4
dual character 3–4
function 3
role in formulation of ICSID Convention 25–7
voting 27
ICSID, relationship with 7, 62, 295–6
immunities 4
Inspection Panel 179
membership 2–3
increase
(1957 to 1963) 11
(1965) 25
multilateral character, of 20
NGO lobbying, effect of 179
objectives 5–6
offices 4, 6
powers 26
President 4
Black, E.R. 20, 22 fig.
function 4
McNamara, R.S. 113
role in the ICSID, proposals 28, 40
term 4
Woods, G.D. 25, 26 fig., 88 fig.
Zoellick, R.B. 217
project lending on infrastructure projects 20
purposes 2
staff 4
structure 3
subscriptions 3
International Bar Association
arbitral body for investment disputes 16
International Centre for Settlement of Investment Disputes (ICSID) (Centre) *see also* **Additional Facility;** *individual aspects e.g.* **Administrative and Financial Regulations; Institution Rules; Panels of Conciliators and Arbitrators; Secretariat of ICSID; Secretary General of ICSID**
appellate mechanisms 291–4
Administrative Council
administrative arrangements 92–4
annual meetings 114, 269–70
budgetary arrangements 92–4
composition 112–13
first annual meeting (1967) 103–5
First Draft 62
functions 113–14
inaugural meeting 89–90
Legal Committee 70–1
meetings 112, 113
Preliminary Draft (October 15, 1963) 40–1
procedural rules 91–2, 94–102
regional consultative meetings 45
Temporary Presiding Officer 113
Working Paper (1962) 28–9
agreements with other institutions 114, 188–9, 273–4
arbitration proceedings
applicable law 76–7
First Draft 64–6
Institution Rules, provisional 98
Legal Committee 75–9
Preliminary Draft (October 15, 1963) provisions 42–4

International Centre for Settlement of Investment Disputes (*cont.*)
regional consultative meetings 53–6
Working Paper 27–33
caseload
analysis of participants and economic sectors
(1972 to 1988) 123–6
(1989 to 1999) 190–3
(2000 to 2010) 211–16, 231–3
(2011 to 2015) 267–8
development
(1970s and 1980s) 111
(1990s) 186–7
(2000 to 2010) 230–1
(2011 to 2015) 268
numerical analysis
(1972 to 1988) 116
(1989 to 1999) 189
(2000 to 2010) 230–1
(2011 to 2015) 267
conciliation proceedings
First Draft 64–6
Institution Rules, provisional 97–8
Legal Committee 75–9
Preliminary Draft (October 15, 1963) provisions 42–4
regional consultative meetings 53–6
Working Paper 27–33
conclusion 287–96
creation 89
disputes
notification of nature of 119–20
types of 7, 8
enforcement of awards
designation of courts and authorities 120
establishment
First Draft 62–3
introduction to 1, 7
Legal Committee 71–5
Preliminary Draft (October 15, 1963) provisions 40–1
regional consultative meetings 49–51
Working Paper 27–33, 35–6
expansion 282
expenditure
annual 117, 219
fiscal regulations
budgets 92–3, 219–20
fiscal year 92–3
general observations 287–9
IBRD
"affiliated" with 8
links with 9, 62
immunities and privileges 8, 94, 96–7
inter-State proceedings
Preliminary Draft (October 15, 1963) provisions 44–5
regional consultative meetings 56–7
investment law publishing activities 139–41
jurisdiction
First Draft 63–4
Legal Committee 79–83
Preliminary Draft (October 15, 1963) provisions 41–2
regional consultative meetings 51–3
Working Paper 31–3
legal personality 8
name
reflective of role 62
spelling 69
organization
First Draft 62–3
Legal Committee 71–5
Preliminary Draft (October 15, 1963) provisions 40–1
regional consultative meetings 49–51
Working Paper 28–31
parties
designation of 119
procedural rules
adoption of 105–6
provisional rules 98–102
proceedings
types of disputes applicable to 7
public registers 95
staff 8, 95, 220
structure 8–9
transparency of proceedings 179, 184, 187, 282–3, 284
enhancement 290–1
International Chamber of Commerce
Court of Arbitration 16
International Court of Justice
Statute
influence on ICSID Convention and Rules 44–5, 47, 99
reference, to 14, 45
International Development Association (IDA)
Articles of Agreement 8
establishment 5, 12
funding 5
IBRD
"affiliate" of 2, 5
connection with 6–7
immunities 6
membership 6
structure 6–7
International Finance Corporation (IFC)
Articles of Agreement 26
capital 5
establishment 5, 12
IBRD
"affiliate" of 5
connection with 6–7
immunities 6
membership 5–6
structure 6–7
International Institute for Sustainable Development (IISD) 213, 227
International Investment Insurance Agency (IIIA) 17–18
International Law Association
arbitral body for investment disputes 16
International Law Commission
Model Rules on Arbitral Procedure
adoption by ILC 16

influence on ICSID Convention and Rules 46, 99
International Monetary Fund
membership of IBRD 3
inter-State proceedings
ICJ, reference to 45
interpretation or application of a treaty
Preliminary Draft 44–5
regional consultative meetings 56–7
investment *see also* **foreign investment**
abusive restructuring **281**
meaning of 240–6
qualifying investments 203, 281
standard definitions 241
Investment Laws of the World 140–1
investor–State dispute resolution
harmonization of jurisprudence 293–4
Iran
nationalization of oil industry
IBRD efforts to foster settlement of dispute with Britain 21
Israel
notification of disputes subject to jurisdiction of ICSID 119

Jacovides, A.J. 261
Jaffre, M.E. 279
Jamaica
notification of disputes subject to jurisdiction of ICSID 119–20
Japan
investment insurance 12–13
Tokyo city bonds
IBRD role in settlement of dispute with French nationals 22–3
Jiménez de Aréchaga, E. 119, 147, 154, 156 fig., 163
Jospin, L. 185
Joubin-Bret, A. 272
judicial abstention
rule of 158, 159
jurisdiction
approaches to 150–7, 240–54, 279–81
consent
advance general consent in investment law 153–5
bilateral investment treaty provisions 281–2
evidence of 34
First Draft 64
Legal Committee 72–3
pragmatic approach to 150–6
Preliminary Draft 42
pressures on 64
promotion of 120–3
regional consultative meetings 52, 54
scope of 74–5
treaty provision, based on 155
withdrawal 74, 131–2
Working Paper 42
contract claims vs treaty claims 240, 246–52
contractual choice of forum clause
effect of 205–6
forum prorogatum 31, 53, 64
general unity of the investment operation
doctrine of 153–4
good faith
requirement of 31
"investment" jurisdiction 240–6
MFN clause
role establishing jurisdiction 252–4
nature of the dispute
definitions 51–2, 63–4, 71–2, 240–6
limitations, and 31
objections to 43, 54, 65, 100, 203–5

Kaplan, N. 257
Kaufmann-Kohler, G. 192, 213, 221, 229, 237, 272, 293
Keith, K. 238
Kennedy, President John F. 12
Kerameus, K.D. 210
Kerr, M. 147
Kettani, A. 272
Khan, M.A. 272
Kim, J.Y.
Administrative Council
chairman of 270
World Bank
President of 270
Kinnear, M. 217, 218, 271, 272 fig.
Secretary-General
election to full-time appointment 270
re-election 271–2
Kissinger, H.A. 122
Klöckner v. Cameroon
annulment decision
commentary 167–8, 172
applicable law unstated in agreement
commentary 163–4
Krishna, R. 132
Knapp, J.B. 102
Kneiper, R. 238, 279

Lagergren, G. 148
Lalive, J.-F. 30
Lalive, P. 163, 246, 254
Lalonde, M. 237, 258–9
Lalumière, C. 185
Landau, T.T. 245
Latin America
ICSID cases, involving (2000 to 2010) 212–13
ratifications 216
"Washington Consensus" 177, 212
Lauterpacht, E. 147, 195, 197, 199 fig.
Lauterpacht, H. 14, 15
Legal Committee on the Settlement of Investment Disputes (Legal Committee) *see also* **Convention on the Settlement of Investment Disputes between States and Nationals of Other States**
decision by consensus 68
meetings (November 23 to December 11, 1964) 67
membership 67
Rules of Procedure 67–8

legal publishing
ICSID publications on investment law 139–41
Leigh, M. 119, 188
Lemire v. Ukraine
Additional Facility case (BIT)
commentary 195
Leoro Franco, G. 254
LETCO v. Liberia
applicable law
commentary 165
arbitral awards, enforcement
commentary 174–5
Lieftinck P. 35–6, 60
Lowe, V. 237

Machado, L. 34, 60, 81
Maffezini, E.A. 190
Maffezini v. Spain
commentary 207–8, 240, 254, 256
MAI *see* **Multilateral Agreement on Investment**
Mann, F.A. 119
Maxwell Chambers 274
Mayora Alvarado, E. 192
Mbaye, K. 119, 147, 171, 188
Mborantsuo, M.-M. 147–8
McCloy, J.J. 20
McCrae, D.M. 272
McNamara, R.S. 113, 115, 118–9
mediation
proposal for establishment of ICSID service 226–8
rules, adoption by IBA 283
Mejia-Palacio, J. 35, 60
Memorandum of Administrative Arrangements
approval, of 102–3
Permanent Court of Arbitration
arrangements, with 106–7
Mendels, M.M. 88 fig.
de Mestral, A. 238
Metalclad v. Mexico
Additional Facility arbitration (NAFTA)
commentary 197–202
***MINE v.* Guinea**
annulment decision
commentary 169–70, 171–2
applicable law
commentary 162
provisional measures, court-ordered
commentary 157, 161
Mitchell, P. 190
Model Rules on Arbitral Procedure
adoption 16
influence on ICSID Convention and Rules 52
Moorthi, C.S.K. 35, 37
Morelli Rico, S. 259
Morris, J. 22
Morse, B. 179
Mourre, A. 278
Multilateral Agreement on Investment (MAI)
negotiation of 179, 183
Multilateral Investment Guarantee Agency (MIGA)
capital 5
Convention text
finalization of 26
establishment 5, 111
IBRD
"affiliate" of 5
connection with 6–7
immunities 6
membership 6
structure 6–7
multilateral investment guarantee schemes *see also* **code of conduct; friendship, commerce and navigation treaties (FCNs)**
Association for the Promotion and Protection of Private Foreign Investment 12
Council of Europe 12
Inter-Parliamentary Union 12
World Bank, consideration of 17–18
multilateral investment treaties
conclusion of (1990s) 182

Nariman, F.S. 221, 237
News from ICSID 128
Nikken, P. 229
Nixon, President Richard M. 122
non-governmental organizations
opposition to investment treaty arbitration 212–13
opposition to MAI 184–5
role
(1990s) 178–9
(2000 to 2010) 212–13
"North-South" dialogue 110
Nottingham, E.W. 236

OECD *see* **Organisation for European Economic Co-operation and Development**
Ogoola, J. 272
OPEC *see* **Organization of the Petroleum Exporting Countries**
Oreamuno, R. 191, 233, 237, 274
Organisation for European Economic Co-operation (OEEC)
Abs–Shawcross Draft Convention
introduction to 14–15
Organisation for Economic Co-operation and Development (OECD)
Abs–Shawcross Draft Convention
introduction to 14–15
Declaration on International Investment and Multinational Enterprises (1976) 110
Development Assistance Committee (DAC) 12
consideration of multilateral investment guarantee by World Bank 17–18

Draft Convention on the Protection of Foreign Property (1962) 15, 18
Draft Convention on the Protection of Foreign Property (1967) 18–20
establishment 11–12
MAI
support for 182–4
Organization of the Petroleum Exporting Countries (OPEC)
economic independence and 109
Orrego Vicuña, F. 188, 191, 203, 210, 213, 221, 234, 237, 238, 241, 258, 259, 278
Owen, R.B. 203
Oyekunle, T. 272

Palacio, A. 217
Panels of Conciliators and Arbitrators
Chairman of Administrative Council
role 117–18
designations, to 117–18, 187–8, 220–1, 272–3
membership
qualities required, for 62
structure 29–30
Papua New Guinea
notification of disputes subject to jurisdiction of ICSID 119
Parra, F. 109
parties
designation 118–19
Paulsson, J. 195, 233, 237
Pellet, A. 272
Permanent Court of Arbitration (PCA)
establishment 16
ICSID
arrangements with 106–7, 114, 188
influence on creation, of 46
relationship with 36
International Bureau, of 16
Rules of Arbitration and Conciliation for Settlement of Investment Disputes Between Two Parties of Which Only One is a State 16
Petrén, S. 148
Pinto C.W. 39, 52, 68
Pietrowski, R.F. 154, 156 fig.
Potestà, M. 293
Preston, L.T. 188
Price, D.M. 298
private foreign investment *see* **foreign investment**
provisional measures
court ordered provisional measures
availability of without prior agreement 157–62
instances when granted 160–2
judicial abstention
rule of 158, 159
mandatory nature of 254–6
prejudgment attachments 157
security for costs 256
provisional rules and regulations *see also specific measures e.g.* **Administrative and Financial Regulations**
adoption 91–2
languages 94
Provisional Administrative and Financial Regulations 94–7
Provisional Arbitration Rules 98–102
Provisional Conciliation Rules 98–102
Provisional Institution Rules 98
publication 94
public hearings
non-disputing parties
attendance and observation by 230
proposals for 225, 227, 229

Rae, R.K. 192
Rahman, Tunku Abdul 13
Rattray, K.O. 147
Razafindralambo, E. 147
Reed, L. 272
Regional Centres for Commercial Arbitration
Cairo 188–9, 273
Kuala Lumpur 188–9, 273
registration of requests to institute proceedings
"arbitration without privity" 233
duration of process 234–5
frivolous claims
dismissal of 234–5, 294
provisional rules 102
Secretary-General of ICSID
screening power 143–6, 233, 295
refusal 143–4, 235
time between receipt and registration 145
"without prejudice" correspondence 145
Reisman, M. 169, 170
Reuter, P. 148
Rezek, F. 205, 258
Rigo Sureda, A. 252
Robinson, D.R. 238
Robinson, P.L. 261
Rogers, W.D. 163
Roll, E. 59
Rouhani, F. 119, 147, 161
Rovine, A.W. 238
Rowley, J.W. 236
Rubin, E.C. 149, 150
Ruda, J.M. 188
Ruggie, J.G. 214
Ruiz, F. 61

Sachs, K. 281
Salacuse, J.W. 229, 272
Salans, C.F. 253
Sands, P. 234
Saudi Arabia
notification of disputes subject to jurisdiction of ICSID 119
Schindler, D. 172
Schmidt, D. 148, 163
Schreuer, C. 277, 279
Schultsz, J. 163
Schwarzenberger, G. 15, 18, 21
Schwebel, S.M. 221, 243

Secretariat of ICSID
administrative support to proceedings 116
budget 271
development
(1970s to 1980s) 114–17
(1990s) 186–7
(2000 to 2010) 217–20
(2011 to 2015) 270–2
enlargement 270
outreach activities 271
proceedings
involvement, with 116
reorganization 270
staff 116, 270
legal to support staff ratio 270
team structure 270
training activities 271
Secretary-General of ICSID
appointing authority as 138–9
election
combination of position with World Bank 91, 115
Broches, A., role of 90–1, 114–15
Kinnear, M. 270–1
Shihata, I. 115, 126, 186
full-time appointment 270
functions 95
registration of requests to institute proceedings
screening power 143–6
term 114–15
Seidl-Hohenveldern, I. 119, 163–4, 188
Sella, P. 39, 68
Seoul International Dispute Resolution Centre 274
SGS v. Pakistan
contract and treaty claims
commentary 248–50
Shahabudeen, M. 282
Sharpe, D.J. 161
Shawcross, H. 13–14
Shihata, I. 18, 26, 91, 115, 127, 141 fig., 192, 217, 221
Administrative Council
report to 136, 140
approach to screening power 144–5
Bank's work on an IIIA 17–18
designations by Contracting States 188
absence of 188
governance
framework for 178
General Counsel of the Bank
appointment 186
Inter-Arab Investment Guarantee Corporation 18
creation of 18
joint sessions, proposal for 115
MIGA Convention, work on 26
promotion of consistency in jurisprudence 172
registration of requests 144–5
Secretary-General of ICSID
election as 115, 118, 126
re-election as 186
Senior Vice-President of Bank
resignation, as 217
warnings of annulment applications 169, 170, 259
Silva Romero, E. 316
Simma, B. 234
Sinclair, A. 235
Singapore International Arbitration Centre 188
Siquieros, E. 238
Siqueiros, J.L. 197, 199 fig.
SOABI v. Senegal
arbitral awards, enforcement
commentary 173, 175
Söderlund, C. 261
Sucharitkul, S. 118, 171–2, 188
Soviet Union
dissolution 177
effect on growth in number of BITs 181
SPP v. Egypt
applicable law
balance between application of local and international law 165–6
jurisdiction, consent to
commentary 153–5
registration of arbitration request
commentary 144
SRSG *see* **United Nations**
Stern, B. 213, 237, 255, 275, 280
Suez Canal Company *see* **Egypt**
Suez Crisis
decolonization, effect on 11
Suzuki, G. 37
Switzerland
membership of ICSID 90, 93–4
Szasz, P.C. 91, 104–5, 121

Tercier, P. 236–7, 245, 272
Third World
developing countries
described as 11
Thomas, J.C. 236–7, 247, 255
TNCs *see* **corporations**
Tomka, P. 243
Townsend, J.M. 280
training
activities 271
ICSID proposal for intensification of 226–8
transnational corporations *see* **corporations**
Tresselt, P. 261
Trolle, J. 147, 161
Trooboff, P. 205
Tschanz, P.-Y. 241
Tung, K.-Y. 217

United Nations
arbitration
promoted as means of international dispute resolution 16
Development Decade (1960s) 12
Inter-Parliamentary Union
multilateral investment guarantee scheme proposal 12

membership increase (1957 to 1962) 11
Special Representative of the UN Secretary General (SRSG) on Business and Human Rights 214–15
critic of BITs as 214–15
transnational corporations
code of conduct abandoned 177–8
United Nations Commission on Transnational Corporations
establishment 110
United Nations Monetary and Financial Conference (July 1944) 2
United States
assistance program to developing countries 11
BITs
programme begun in 1977 110
provisions on *amicus curiae* submissions 225
FTAs 211–212, 224–225
negotiating objectives 215–16
investment insurance 12

Veeder, V.V. 237, 253
Vivendi v. Argentina
commentary 205–6, 240, 246–8
Voss, J. 195

"Washington Consensus" 177
"Water revolt" of Cochabamba 212
Weeramantry, C.G. 242
Weil, P. 221, 255
Wena v. Egypt
commentary 209–10
Wilberforce, R. 146
Williams, D.A.R. 237, 246, 255
Williamson, J. 177
Wobeser, C. Von 272
Wolfensohn, J.D. 178
Woods, G.D. 26 fig., 84 fig., 88 fig.
administrative and budgetary arrangements
approval of 92
Administrative Council
first annual meeting 103
inaugural meeting 89, 93
Black's representative 21
Convention text
approval of final text 85
final process 59, 60
Legal Committee, first meeting of 68
President, appointment of 25
ratification requirements 92
recommendations for follow-up steps 59
Secretary-General
consultation for election of the first 90
successor 113
World Bank *see* **International Bank for Reconstruction and Development; International Development Association**
World Bank Group 9
World Bank Guidelines on the Legal Treatment of Foreign Direct Investment 183, 186
World Trade Organization (WTO)
establishment 177
Working Paper *see* **Convention on the Settlement of Investment Disputes between States and Nationals of Other States**
Wright, R. 11

Yom Kippur War 109

Ziadé, N.G. 156 fig., 217
Zoellick, R.B.
Administrative Council, chairman of 217
World Bank, President of 217
Zubrod, D. 161
Zuleta, E. 272, 280

The manufacturer's authorised representative in the EU for product safety is Oxford University Press España S.A. of El Parque Empresarial San Fernando de Henares, Avenida de Castilla, 2 - 28830 Madrid (www.oup.es/en or product.safety@oup.com). OUP España S.A. also acts as importer into Spain of products made by the manufacturer.
Printed and bound by CPI Group (UK) Ltd, Croydon, CR0 4YY
14/09/2026
02216288-0007